Quotations on
the Vietnam War

ALSO BY GREGORY R. CLARK

Words of the Vietnam War:
The Slang, Jargon, Abbreviations, Acronyms,
Nomenclature, Nicknames, Pseudonyms, Slogans,
Specs, Euphemisms, Double-talk, Chants,
and Names and Places of the Era
of United States Involvement in Vietnam
(McFarland, 1990)

Quotations on the Vietnam War

Compiled and Edited by
GREGORY R. CLARK

with a foreword by
DANIEL McDOWELL, Lt. Col., USAF

McFarland & Company, Inc., Publishers
Jefferson, North Carolina, and London

Acknowledgment: This book bears witness to the indispensable support and assistance provided by my wife, Ginny. It would not have been possible without her help and attention to detail.

Library of Congress Cataloguing-in-Publication Data

Quotations on the Vietnam War / compiled and edited by Gregory R. Clark.
p. cm.
Includes bibliographical references and index.
ISBN 0-7864-0945-2 (illustrated case binding : 50# alkaline paper)
1. Vietnamese Conflict, 1961–1975 — United States. 2. Vietnamese Conflict, 1961–1975 — Quotations, maxims, etc. — Dictionaries. 3. Vietnam — Politics and government — 1945–1975. I. Clark, Gregory R., 1948–

DS558 .Q67 2001
959.704'3373 — dc21 00-49640

British Library cataloguing data are available

Manufactured in the United States of America

Cover image: December 28, 1967, in the Mekong Delta, a member of Co. A, Fourth Battalion, 47th Infantry, crouches in a vast plain of elephant grass. *©2001 Bettman/Corbis*

McFarland & Company, Inc., Publishers
Box 611, Jefferson, North Carolina 28640
www.mcfarlandpub.com

Contents

Foreword

More than 58,000 Americans were killed and over 248,000 wounded during the thirty-year course of the Vietnam conflict. The chaos and upheaval of the war touched nearly all of us. Many of us could say we had a relative or friend who died there.

This was the first war (undeclared) to be brought to our homes via television to a stunned and disrupted nation. Daily, on nearly every television station, the media showed us fierce gun battles and the suffering of wounded and dying soldiers. The brutal reality of combat was shown for the most part, as it actually was, and it turned the stomach of an entire nation. It is a fact that the media played a major role in turning people's support away from the war, and sadly, away from the men and women who served in Southeast Asia.

During this period there was a growing vocal minority who shouted slogans such as "end the war in Vietnam," "free love," and "give peace a chance." Some of those discordant voices have also found their way into the pages of this book.

Now, through the culmination of years of extensive research and in-depth compilation, author Gregory R. Clark — himself an Army veteran of the Vietnam conflict — has brought together the words and thoughts of many political leaders and veterans who fought valiantly in combat, and on the home front.

Through these words, you will experience not only the bravado and concerns of the young warriors, but also the ideals, thoughts and tribulations of the leaders and losers of the free world's greatest nation.

This book, *Quotations on the Vietnam War*, is one of the best history books written about the American involvement in Vietnam. It is a stunning work that when read page by page paints a clearer picture of the war that has until now been clouded in conjecture and half-truths. It is an honest and truthful record of the Vietnam conflict as seen not just from an American point of view but also from the views of our allies and opposition from around the globe.

Reading this book opens a small window onto an understanding of the conflict that forever changed our nation.

Through more than 3,300 quotes, Clark captures the emotions, trials of life and death, sadness and sarcasm, of those who participated in those turbulent times.

Clark has provided an amazing amount of supporting information and has made it easy to understand the quotes presented. This volume leads the way as a model for future historians compiling the facts of history. It will be done not through editorial comment or personal bias, not by guesswork and poetic license, but rather with the truth and words of those who made that history. This book does not glorify war, not does it take a "Hollywood" approach to history. These words, though sometimes harsh and painful, have not been changed to make them more palatable.

Quotations on the Vietnam War will help to bring knowledge and understanding to some, while bringing final understanding and closure to others.

This work presents an opportunity to correct those grievous errors in the education of our youths about a turbulent time in the history of this great nation. This book provides an easily read, clearly written account of the changes — and changers — of an entire nation. It gives clear glimpses into the period, and humanizes the war by presenting the actual thoughts and words spoken by those who led the countries and those who led the men and women who fought the war. It takes you from the days of the French occupation and brings you into the twenty-first century.

I was a Weapons Systems Officer in the U.S. Air Force flying the F-4 Phantom II aircraft in Vietnam. I flew many missions into Route Pack 6 and saw enough flak and SAMs to stop and restart my heart a thousand times. Now the thing that stops my heart is the continuing lack of truth about the Vietnam conflict presented in history books in our schools.

Quotations on the Vietnam War should be required reading for every new and current military member, whether officer or enlisted, in all the services, in all the academies, and in every ROTC unit in the nation. It should be required reading in every high school and college, and for anyone who plans to go into politics.

Gregory R. Clark's superb work gives the world an outstanding opportunity to look back in time. Now, many veterans and non-veterans alike can understand with more clarity the truth that has been clouded for so long. Perhaps old wounds can finally heal.

Lt. Col. Daniel McDowell, USAF, ACAP
Commander, 1st Flight Launch Action Group
December 2000
Hudson, Wisconsin

Introduction

The old clichés hold true; the Vietnam War is America's longest and least understood. The length of the war is reflected in the millions of words that have been written or spoken about it—and the words will continue to flow for many decades to come. This quotations dictionary is a distillation of the words so far.

The book consists of 17 chronologically arranged sections covering the involvement of the United States in Vietnam from 1944 into the year 2000, followed by an overview covering the entire 56-year period. At the back of the book are specific notes on the source of a quote, a summary list of all references used, and an index.

Each entry has the following: an entry number (for use by the index), the quotation itself, the person or organization that wrote or uttered the quotation and the date, and frequently some background information clarifying the quotation. All entries end with a superscript number referring to the printed source or sources.

Whenever possible I have used the language of the quotation in its original form, which sometimes included spelling and grammatical errors. I have used brackets to clarify or otherwise make distinctions within a quote.

In the course of compiling this dictionary I have discovered cases in which sources do not agree on the exact wording of a particular quotation. While I have attempted to locate and identify the best source in every case, there inevitably may be slight variances in a given quotation between this reference work and another.

I have attempted to be as objective as possible in the comments and background information associated with a given quotation. I apologize in advance for those few instances when my objectivity may have been clouded by my past experiences as a veteran of this war.

Gregory R. Clark, winter 2000

Abbreviations Used

The following abbreviations are used throughout this book.

ACLU	American Civil Liberties Union
AFVN	Armed Forces Radio Vietnam
AHC	Assault Helicopter Company
AID	U.S. Agency for International Development
ALC	Air Liaison Controller (Officer)
APC	Armored Personnel Carrier
ARVN	Army Republic of Vietnam
ASU	American Serviceman's Union
AWOL	Absent Without Leave
BEQ	Bachelor Enlisted Men's Quarters
BOQ	Bachelor Officer Quarters
C & C	Command and Control
CAP	Combined Action Company (Civic Action Program)
CCTS	Combat Crew Training Squadron
CDC	California Democratic Party
Chicom	Chinese Communists
CINCPAC	Commander-in-Chief, Pacific Command
CMRI	Children's Medical Relief International
ComUSMACV	Commander U.S. Military Assistance Command Vietnam
CORDS	Civil Operations and Revolutionary Development
CORE	Congress of Racial Equality
COSVN	Central Office South Vietnam
Cpl.	Corporal
DCI	Director Central Intelligence
DDI	Director Defense Intelligence Agency
DIA	Defense Intelligence Agency
DMZ	Demilitarized Zone
DoD	Department of Defense
DRV	Democratic Republic of Vietnam
FAC	Forward Air Controller
FBI	Federal Bureau of Investigation
FSO	Foreign Service Officer
FWF	Free World Forces
GI	American servicemen
GVN	Government of Vietnam
H and I	Harassment and Interdiction
ICC	International Control Commission
ICCS	International Commission for Control and Supervision
ICEX	Intelligence Coordination and Exploitation Team
IDA	Institute for Defense Analysis
JCS	Joint Chiefs of Staff
JGS	Joint General Staff
KIA	Killed in Action
KKK	Ku Klux Klan
LOC	Lines of Communication
LSD	Lysergic acid diethylamide — hallucinogen also called "acid"
Lt. Col.	Lieutenant Colonel
LZ	Landing Zone
MAAGI	Military Assistance Advisory Group, Indochina
MAAGV	Military Assistance Advisory Group Vietnam

MACV	Military Assistance Command Vietnam
MAG	Marine Air Group
MIA	Missing in Action
NCO	Non-Commissioned Officer
NIE	National Intelligence Estimate
NLF	National Liberation Front
NSA	National Security Agency
NSC	National Security Council
NVA	North Vietnamese Army
NVN	North Vietnam
O/B (OB)	Order of Battle
ONE	Office of National Estimates
OPLAN	Operation Plan
OSS	Office of Strategic Services
PAVN	People's Army of Vietnam
PBR	Patrol Boat, River
PF	Popular Forces
PFC	Private First Class
PLAF	People's Liberation Armed Forces
POL	Petroleum, Oil, and Lubricants
POW	Prisoner of War (U.S.)
PRC	People's Republic of China
PRG	Provisional Revolutionary Government
PSA	Province Senior Adviser
PSDF	People's Self-Defense Force
PTSS	Post Traumatic Stress Syndrome
PW	Prisoner of War (VC/NVA)
RD	Revolutionary Development Program
REMF	Rear Echelon Mother Fucker
RF	Regional Forces
RF/PF	Ruff Puffs (Regional/Popular Forces)
RIO	Radio Intercept Officer
RLG	Royal Lao Government
ROK	Republic of Korea
RPG	Rocket Propelled Grenade
RTAF	Royal Thai Air Force
RVN	Republic of Vietnam
RVNAF	Republic of Vietnam Armed Forces
SAC	Strategic Air Command
SAM	Surface to Air Missile
SAVA	Southeast Asia–Vietnamese Affairs
SCLC	Southern Christian Leadership Council
SDS	Students for a Democratic Society
SEATO	Southeast Asia Treaty Organization
SNCC	Student Non-Violent Coordinating Committee
SNIE	Special National Intelligence Estimate
SP/4	Specialist 4th Class (U.S.A.)
SP/5	Specialist 5th Class (U.S.A.)
SRV	Socialist Republic of Vietnam
SSgt.	Staff Sergeant
SVN	Republic of South Vietnam
TF	Task Force
TFW	Tactical Fighter Wing
U.N.	United Nations
USA	U.S. Army
USACGSC	U.S. Army Command and General Staff College
USAF	U.S. Air Force
USAID	U.S. Agency for International Development
USAWC	U.S. Army War College
USG	United States Government
USMC	U.S. Marine Corps
USN	U.S. Navy
USSF	U.S. Army Special Forces
VC	Viet Cong
VCI	Viet Cong Infrastructure
VD	Venereal Disease
VDC	Vietnam Day Committee
Ville	Village
VNAF	Vietnam Air Force
WHAM	Winning Hearts and Minds
WIA	Wounded in Action
WSO	Weapons System Officer (Operator)

Quotations on
the Vietnam War

1944–1953

Wars teach us not to love our enemies, but to hate our allies.
—W. L. George

1 **There is nothing left but to fight.**—*Ho Chi Minh, Provisional President of Vietnam, 14 September 1946.*[451]

Ho went to France to negotiate with the French for the independence of Vietnam. While he was in France, the French high commissioner in Vietnam sanctioned the establishment of the Republic of Cochinchina. By the time he returned to Vietnam, it was divided roughly in half; both halves were still part of the French Union. He saw that his only recourse for Vietnamese independence was to drive the French from Indochina.

2 **[I] regard the French as poor colonizers who had badly mismanaged Indochina and exploited its people.**—*President Franklin D. Roosevelt, as noted in the diary of Edward R. Stettinius, Jr., 7 March 1944.*[337]

Roosevelt did not like the French and believed, after the war, their colony of Indochina (currently occupied by the Japanese) should be placed in international trusteeship until it was ready for independence.

3 **The United States had no interest in championing schemes of international trusteeship that would weaken and alienate the European states whose help we needed to balance Soviet power in Europe.**—*Harry S Truman's administration's position on Indochina, April 1945.*[342]

Truman adopted a hands-off policy towards European colonies after the war. He was attempting to build a coalition of Western European countries to counter the growing power of the Soviet Union.

4 **A fertile field for American capital and enterprise.**—*Ho Chi Minh, leader of the Vietnamese independence movement in Vietnam, 1947.*[346]

Ho tried on several occasions to gain U.S. support of Vietnam's independence from the French. He also offered them the possibility of a U.S. Navy base at Cam Ranh Bay.

5 **If ever the tiger [Viet Minh] pauses, the elephant [France] will impale him on his mighty tusks. But the tiger will not pause, and the elephant will die of exhaustion and loss of blood.**—*Ho Chi Minh.*[339]

6 **[Should Southeast Asia fall to Communism] ... we shall have suffered a major political rout the repercussions of which will be felt throughout the world.**—*National Security Council paper, December 1949.*[341]

Following the fall of China to the Communist in 1949, the U.S. was very wary of Communist expansion into Southeast Asia.

7 **[Ho Chin Minh's recognition by the Soviets reveal him in his] true colors as the mortal enemy of native independence in Indochina.**—*Dean Acheson, Secretary of State, February 1950.*[347]

Ho was viewed as a nationalist until his loyalties to the Soviet Union surfaced.

8 **We must then follow blindly down a dead-end alley, expending our limited resources ... in a fight that would be hopeless.**—*Charles Reed, U.S. State Department official, in a memorandum to C. Walton Butterworth, 14 April 1949.*[347]

In 1949 the French installed Bao Dai as the head of state of the French Union State of Vietnam. This was a French effort to give the Vietnamese token freedom in an effort to weaken the Vietnamese nationalist movement led by Ho Chi Minh. The Bao Dai government was immediately recognized by the United States.

9 **[The French seemed] paralyzed, in a state of moving neither forward or backward.**—*Dean Acheson, Secretary of State, during an NSC meeting, May 1950.*[311]

The French in 1950 were unable to put down the Viet Minh independence movement. They needed additional military supplies and support. America provided material support, allowing the French to continue the fight against the communist.

10 **[France] ... a poor cousin in Vietnamese eyes.**—*General Jean de Lattre de Tassigny, Commander, French forces, Indochina, public comment, 1951.*[347]

De Lattre complained of the American intrusion into the French war against the Viet Minh. The Americans insisted that since they were supplying material and arms they wanted to oversee the distribution and actions of the French. There were many American "advisors" in Vietnam overseeing the distribution of aid to the French. The Americans, who appeared rich by French and Vietnamese standards, did not play down their wealth.

11 **It would be futile and a mistake to defend Indochina in Indochina. We could not have another Korea, we could not put ground forces into Indochina.**—*Dean Acheson, Secretary of State, memorandum to President Truman, 17 June 1952.*[317]

In 1952 the war in Korea was still in progress and the French were still unable to control the situation in Indochina. The Truman administration faced the possibility of additional support to keep the French from collapsing. At this point the introduction of American troops to assist the French was categorically ruled out. The administration wanted to avoid another Korean War situation in Southeast Asia.

12 **The enemy, once painted as a bomb-throwing terrorist or hill sniper lurking in night ambush has become a modern army, increasingly skillful, armed with artillery, organized into divisional groups.**—*Theodore H. White, correspondent in an article for the New York Times, June 1952.*[251]

During the war with the French, the Viet Minh army lacked only armor and air support.

13 **[The problem in Indochina is a lack of] French will to carry on the ... war.**—*Dean Acheson, Secretary of State, comments to the Eisenhower administration, 1953.*[284]

Acheson's opinion of the French war effort in Vietnam. In late 1952 some French politicians began to publicly discuss the prospect of French withdrawal from Indochina. Such a withdrawal was not supported or encouraged by the United States.

14 **[Impress the French with the importance of appointing a] forceful and inspirational leader ... with the means and authority to win victory [in Indochina]...**—*President Dwight Eisenhower, directing Ambassador Douglas Dillon, 6 May 1953.*[270]

The war was not going well for the French military leadership in Indochina. Eisenhower wanted Dillon, Ambassador to France, to press the French to appoint a commander who could secure a victory over the Viet Minh.

15 **[The new French war strategy would] break the organized body of Communist aggression by the end of the 1955 fighting season.**—*John Foster Dulles, Secretary of State, in a report to NSC, 5 August 1953.*[315]

General Henri Navarre was appointed commander of French forces in Indochina. His plan was to establish a Vietnamese National Army and use it along with French forces to dislodge Viet Minh forces from their base areas in the northern part of Vietnam.

16 **You can kill ten of my men for every one I kill of yours, but even at those odds, you will lose and I will win.**—*Ho Chi Minh, to the French in the late–1940s.*[374]

Pronouncement to the French in the late–1940s, at the beginning of the first Indochina war.

17 **Every minute hundreds of thousands of people die on this earth. The life or death of a hundred, a thousand, tens of thousands of human beings, even our compatriots, means little.**—*General Vo Nguyen Giap, 1945.*[374]

General Giap had little regard for life in winning his cause. He measured success not by his losses but to by his enemy's losses. His casualties were inconsequential, his goal was the independence of Vietnam from the French, and a unified Vietnam under communist control.

18 **[To side with the Japanese against the French is to] drive the tiger out the front door while letting the wolf in through the back.**—*Ho Chi Minh.*[374]

Ho's observation about the changing fortunes of war during W.W.II when the French retreated from Indochina and the Japanese swept in.

19 **If those gooks want a fight, they'll get it.**—*General Etienne Valluy, Commander, French Military Forces, Indochina, December 1946.*[374]

Valluy replaced Leclerc as the French Indochina Military Commander. He was reacting to the murder of three French soldiers in Hanoi by the Viet Minh.

20 **[France has] milked it [Indochina] for one hundred years and left its people worse off than they were at the beginning.**—*President Franklin D. Roosevelt, 1944.*[374]

In 1944 Roosevelt proposed that when W.W.II ended French Indochina be designated an international trusteeship blocking the French from regaining control of Indochina as a colony.

21 **[The Americans] are only interested in replacing the French.... They want to reorganize our economy in order to control it. They are capitalists to the core. All that counts for them is business.**—*Ho Chi Minh, during a conversation with Bao Dai, 1945.*[374]

22 **Cochinchina is burning, the French and British are finished here, and we [the United States] ought to clear out of Southeast Asia.**—*Lt. Col. Peter A. Dewey, OSS Mission Chief, Cochinchina, 1945.*[374]

Dewey commanded the American OSS team in southern Vietnam which worked with the Viet Minh to rescue downed Allied pilots. Dewey was killed in a Viet Minh ambush in September 1945 becoming the first American killed in post–W.W.II Vietnam. Cochinchina was the southern part of

Vietnam, roughly from the southern edge of the Central Highlands south to the Cau Mau peninsula.

23 **We would welcome a million American soldiers ... but no French.**—*Ho Chi Minh, self-proclaimed leader of the DRV, commenting to a U.S. OSS agent, September 1945.*[374]

In 1945 Ho formed the Democratic Republic of Vietnam in the interim between the defeat of the Japanese and the return of the French. Ho sent several letters to President Truman requesting U.S. recognition of the new, independent Vietnam.

24 **[Regard the United States as a] good friend ... it is a democracy without territorial ambitions.**—*Vo Nguyen Giap, military leader of the Viet Minh, from a speech in Hanoi, August 1945.*[374]

During the interim period between the fall of the Japanese and the return of the French at the end of W.W.II, the Viet Minh and the newly declared DRV continually pushed for American recognition of their independence from the French.

25 **I prefer to sniff French shit for five years than eat Chinese shit for the rest of my life.... The last time the Chinese came they stayed for a thousand years.**—*Ho Chi Minh, during a meeting with leaders of the DRV, 1946.*[374]

If Ho had to be burdened with foreigners he preferred the French over the Chinese. The Chinese conquered Vietnam in 111 B.C. and remained until driven out by the Vietnamese in A.D. 939. Prior to the end of W.W.II, the Allied powers decided the British would disarm the Japanese below the 16th Parallel, and the Chinese would secure Vietnam above the 16th Parallel. This plan was supposed to remain in effect until the French returned to reclaim Indochina.

26 **I order all soldiers and militia in the center, south, and north to stand together, go into battle, destroy the invaders, and save the nation.... The resistance will be long and arduous, but our cause is just and we will surely triumph.**—*Vo Nguyen Giap, military leader of the Viet Minh, at the start of the first Indochina war, December 1946.*[374]

Open warfare between the Viet Minh and the French started in Hanoi, December 1946.

27 **The question of whether Ho is as much nationalist as Commie was irrelevant since all Stalinists in colonial areas are nationalists.**—*Dean Acheson, Secretary of State, 1949.*[374]

There was much discussion between 1945 and 1949 as to whether Ho Chi Minh was a communist and part of the "world communist conspiracy" or simply a nationalist. The Truman administration decided Ho was indeed a communist, linking him to the Chinese Communist movement as well.

28 **A year ago none of us could see victory. There wasn't a prayer. Now we can see [success in Vietnam] clearly—like light at the end of a tunnel.**—*General Henri Navarre, Commander, French Forces, Indochina, comments to the press, May 1953.*[108]

Navarre arrived in Indochina in May 1953 with a plan to bait a trap for the Viet Minh. The Navarre plan called for the bait to be placed in the open at Dien Bien Phu. When the enemy massed to attack the French fortifications, French forces would crush the Viet Minh in a set piece battle. Navarre was confident of success. The plan commenced November 1953 and ended with the defeat of the French, May 1954.

29 **The resources of the United States will henceforth be deployed to reserve Indochina and Southeast Asia from further Communist encroachment.**—*Dean Rusk, Under Secretary of State, in a public announcement, 1949.*[374]

With the fall of Nationalist China to the communists, the U.S. decided to back the French in Indochina in an attempt to stop the spread of communism in Southeast Asia.

30 **The Soviet endorsement [of the Democratic Republic of Vietnam] should remove any illusions as to the "nationalist" nature of Ho Chi Minh's aims, and reveals Ho in his true colors as the mortal enemy of native independence in Indochina.** —*Dean Rusk, Under Secretary of State, 1950.*[374]

In late 1949 Ho again declared the independence of Vietnam from France and the establishment of the DRV. The Soviet Union and Red China recognized the DRV in early 1950. The U.S. continued to recognize and support the French.

31 **Whether the French like it or not, independence is coming to Indochina. Why, therefore, do we tie ourselves to the tail of their battered kite?**—*Raymond B. Fosdick, State Department analysts, State Department memorandum, 1950.*[374]

Some in the U.S. State Department believed the French would lose in their attempts to maintain French colonialism over Vietnam, and considered colonialism outdated.

32 **Because Ho Chi Minh is tied in with the [Soviet] Politburo, our policy is to support Bao Dai and the French in Indochina until we have time to help them establish a going concern.**—*Dean Rusk, Assistant Secretary of State for Far Eastern Affairs, in testimony before Senate Foreign Relations Committee, June 1950.*[374]

The U.S. saw the recognition of the DRV by the Soviets and the Communist Chinese as proof of Ho's ties to international communism. Rusk argued for strong support of the new French-created Bao Dai government and the French in their fight against the communist in Vietnam.

33 **She is only plying her trade. I am the real whore.**—*Bao Dai, last emperor of Vietnam, commenting on his services to the French, 1952.*[374]

A member of Bao Dai's entourage commented on one of Bao's many consorts, referring to her as a whore. Bao Dai responded that he was the whore for allowing himself to be used by the French. The French installed Bao Dai as the figurehead leader of the State of Vietnam in 1950. The State was formed from the southern section of Vietnam in the region called Cochinchina, with the capital located at Saigon. The French recognized the Bao Dai government as an independent member of the French Union.

34 **This recognition [of the State of Viet Nam] is consistent with our fundamental policy of giving support to the peaceful and democratic evolution of dependent peoples toward self-government and independence.**—*U.S. State Department, announcement recognizing the State of Viet Nam, 7 February 1950.*[504]

Initial U.S. recognition of the French-selected Bao Dai government. At about the same time Red China and the Soviet Union were recognizing the Democratic Republic of Vietnam under Ho Chi Minh.

35 **[Diem] is a hero ... revered by the Vietnamese because he is honest and independent and stood firm against the**

French influence.—*William O. Douglas, Supreme Court Justice, comments, 1953.*[887]

Diem refused to collaborate with the French when they were trying to establish a puppet government in South Vietnam.

36 **We apparently stand quite alone; we shall have to depend on ourselves.**—*Ho Chi Minh, Leader of the Viet Minh, 1946.*[887]

Ho had tried several times to have his newly announced government recognized by the United States. He asked that America intervene in Vietnam to keep the French from re-establishing colonial control in Vietnam. He also asked that America make Vietnam one of its protectorates. The Truman administration refused to acknowledge Ho's claim of independence from the French, citing Ho's communist background.

37 **France has had the country — thirty million inhabitants for nearly one hundred years, and the people are worse off then they were at the beginning.... The people of Indochina are entitled to something better than that.**—*Cordell Hull, Secretary of State, January 1944.*[887]

38 **We are convinced that the Allied nations, which at Tehran and San Francisco have acknowledged the principles of self-determination and the equality of nations, will not refuse to acknowledge the independence of Vietnam.**—*Ho Chi Minh, self proclaimed leader of the Democratic Republic of Vietnam in a proclamation to the world, 1945.*[629]

Ho thought Vietnam would be allowed its independence with the end of W.W.II.

39 **[I am] encouraged by the prospects of victory in Indochina in the next twelve to fifteen months.**—*General John W. O'Daniel, Chief, U.S. Military Mission, Vietnam, during briefing of the JCS, November 1953.*[205]

O'Daniel commanded the American effort which supported the French during the First Indochina War. He believed the French Navarre Plan would destroy the bulk of the hardcore Viet Minh, reducing the war to the guerrilla level, which he considered more manageable.

40 **The extension of Communist authority in China represents a grievous political defeat for us.... If Southeast Asia is also swept by communism, we shall have suffered a major political rout the repercussions of which will be felt throughout the rest of the world, especially in the Middle East and in a then critically exposed Australia.**—*Excerpt from NSC report, June 1949.*[224]

An early theory of the Truman administration regarding the spread of communism, later defined in the Eisenhower administration as the "Domino Theory."

41 **The colonial-nationalist conflict provides a fertile field for subversive Communist movements, and it is now clear that Southeast Asia is the target for a coordinated offensive directed by the Kremlin.**—*Excerpt from NSC report, June 1949.*[224]

42 **It is recognized that the threat of Communist aggression against Indochina is only one phase of anticipated Communist plans to seize all of Southeast Asia.... The neighboring countries of Thailand and Burma could be expected to fall under Communist domination if Indochina were controlled by a Communist-dominated government.**—*Excerpt from NSC report, 27 February 1950.*[224]

The NSC forecast the spread of communism in Southeast Asia putting the Truman administration on notice that, as they had lost China to the communists, so could they lose the rest of Asia.

43 **[Military assistance for Indochina is essential because] it is generally acknowledged that if Indochina were to fall under control of the Communists, Burma and Thailand would follow suit almost immediately. Thereafter, it would be difficult, if not impossible for Indonesia, India and the others to remain outside the Soviet-dominated Asian Bloc.**—*Dean Rusk, Assistant Secretary of State, 3 January 1951.*[231]

Early Truman administration theory regarding the spread of communism, later defined in the Eisenhower administration as the "Domino Theory." The main threat was perceived as being from the Soviets.

44 **If they [the French] quit and Indochina falls to Commies, it is easily possible that the entire Southeast Asia and Indonesia will go, soon to be followed by India.**—*Dwight Eisenhower, President, Columbia University, diary entry, 17 March 1951.*[228]

45 **Communist domination of Southeast Asia, whether by means of overt invasion, subversion, or accommodation on the part of the indigenous governments, would be critical to United States security interests.**—*Excerpt from National Security Council staff study, 13 February 1952.*[224]

Truman administration's assessment that a communist Southeast Asia was a threat to U.S. national security.

46 **In the long run the loss of Southeast Asia, especially Malaya and Indonesia, could result in such economic and political pressures in Japan as to make it extremely difficult to prevent Japan's political accommodation to the Soviet Bloc.**—*Excerpt from National Security Council staff study, 13 February 1952.*[224]

47 **The object of war is specifically to preserve oneself and destroy the enemy ... or deprive him of the power to resist.**—*Mao Tse-tung, leader of the communist revolution in China, from his writings, May 1938.*[495]

The North Vietnamese followed many of Mao's teachings and strategies as they fought against the French and later the Americans in Vietnam.

48 **Without preparedness superiority is not real superiority and there can be no initiative either.**—*Mao Tse-tung, leader of the communist revolution in China, from his writings, May 1938.*[495]

The North Vietnamese followed many of Mao's teachings and strategies as they fought against the French and later the Americans in Vietnam. The VC/NVA typically prepared for many weeks or months in advance of a major operation or attack.

49 **Anyone looking at a map of Asia where the Communist-occupied territories are marked in red sees a vast red thundercloud from which a few drops of scalding rain are descending. There are drops in India and Pakistan, in Iran, in Burma and Malaya; there are large splashes in the Philippines and in Indochina. A thundercloud cannot be contained. It must pass**

on or be broke up, or it must change into some other kind of cloud altogether.... The thundercloud has been gathering for a long time, and before it is finally dissipated, if it is ever dissipated, we can expect more raindrops to fall...—*Robert Payne, Asian historian and author, writing in 1951.*[879]

50 **Make clear to the American people the importance of Southeast Asia to the security of the United States so that they may be prepared for any of the courses of action proposed herein.**—*An excerpt from policy statement by the National Security Council, 25 June 1952.*[876]

The NSC proposed the U.S. should join with other free nations to warn Communist China against expansion in Asia. The NSC also proposed the use of covert operations to further U.S. goals for Southeast Asia and to assist the countries of Southeast Asia in defense of their territories. The NSC also recognized the importance of having the support of the American people during the process.

51 **The unpleasant fact [is] that Communist Ho Chi Minh is the strongest and perhaps the ablest figure in Indochina and that any suggested solution which excludes him is an expedient of uncertain outcome.**—*Excerpt from State Department document, September 1948.*[903]

During the formulation of American policy towards Southeast Asia, the Truman administration wanted to support nationalism in emerging countries, provided their emergence was not under a communist banner.

52 **[America must aid the French and the Associated States of Indochina] to defend the territorial integrity of IC [Indochina] and prevent the incorporation of the ASSOC[iated] States within the COMMIE-dominated bloc of slave states.**—*Dean Acheson, Secretary of State, in a cable to Saigon, October 1950.*[903]

53 **This war must stop being a French war supported by Vietnam and become a Vietnamese war supported by France.**—*Paul Reynaud, Vice-Premier of France, June 1953.*[109]

A call for Vietnamization, French style.

54 **I will never agree to equipment being given directly to the Viet Namese.... The Viet Namese have no generals, no colonels, no military organization that could effectively utilize the equipment. It would be wasted, and in China the United States has had enough of that.**—*General Marcel Carpentier, French commander in chief in Indo-China, during an interview, 7 March 1950.*[191]

Carpentier's response to the question of an American proposal to provide U.S. military equipment directly to the Vietnamese National Army, currently operating under French leadership. Large quantities of supplies and equipment were given to the Nationalist Chinese in the unsuccessful attempt to stop the Mao Tse-tung led communists revolution in China.

55 **The danger in this region ... is not primarily or principally external. The Chinese Communists have not invaded Southeast Asia.**—*Walter Lippmann, Columnist and author, 28 January 1952.*[190]

The Eisenhower administration predicted the Communist Chinese would eventually take over Southeast Asia unless they were stopped. Their first country was to be Vietnam, with the rest of Indochina and Southeast Asia to follow. Lippmann's voice was one of many who argued that the political instability in Indochina was an internal problem and not a function of Communist Chinese expansion.

56 **I have ... directed acceleration in the furnishing of military assistance to the forces of France and the associated states in Indo-China and the dispatch of a military mission to provide close working relations with those forces.**—*President Harry Truman, 27 July 1950.*[191]

Military Assistance Advisory Group Indochina (MAAGI) was established in August 1950 and it consisted of 65 America advisers whose mission was to observe the use and disposition of American equipment given to the French and Vietnamese. The French were not receptive to MAAGI's participation, but it was a condition for receipt of the aid they needed to fight the Viet Minh.

57 **Saigon is more or less a French-held "island" in a Viet Minh "sea." One does not drive on the roads outside the city or even in the outskirts. At night and even in the daytime vehicles are generally armed or in convoy.**—*Hansom W. Baldwin, correspondent, writing for the New York Times, 22 November 1950.*[191]

French forces numbered about 200,000 in 1952. The bulk of the forces were deployed in central and northern Vietnam.

58 **Approximately 35 percent of France's military budget is expended in Viet Nam ... in a struggle that shows no sign of ending.**—*C. L. Sulzberger, foreign correspondent for the New York Times, 28 January 1950.*[191]

1954–1960

Those who cannot remember the past are condemned to repeat it.
—George Santayana

59 **[I] opposed sending American G.I.s into the mud and muck of Indochina on a bloodletting spree to perpetuate colonialism and [the] white man's exploitation in Asia.**—*Senator Lyndon Johnson of Texas, speaking in response to Vice President Nixon, April 1954.*[255]

Nixon had made an off the record statement that if the U.S. could not band together with other nations to intervene in Indochina, the U.S. might have to act unilaterally.

60 **If in order to avoid further Communist expansion in Asia and particularly in Indochina, if in order to avoid it we must take the risk of now putting American boys in.... I personally would support such a decision.**—*Richard Nixon, Vice President, in a speech in 1954.*[474]

Nixon advocating the use of U.S. combat forces to aid the French in securing Vietnam from communism during the First Indochina War.

61 **[The French fortress at Dien Bien Phu can] withstand any kind of attack the Vietminh are capable of launching.**—*Unidentified American observer, in a report to the Eisenhower administration, 5 February 1954.*[270]

There were 12–13,000 French force troops at Dien Bien Phu; there were over 100,000 Viet Minh forces surrounding them.

62 **No Vietminh cannon will be able to fire three rounds before being destroyed by my artillery.**—*Colonel Charles Piroth, Commanding French artillery forces, Dien Bien Phu, 1954.*[374]

When the French deployed to Dien Bien Phu they did not believe the Viet Minh would be able to move artillery pieces to ring the French position. With French control of the air and their own artillery, they believed they could silence the few guns the enemy might bring to bear. The French had 60 artillery pieces; the Viet Minh, 192 pieces larger than 75mm.

63 **We resolutely chose to strike and advance surely ... strike to win, strike only when success is certain. If it is not, then do not strike.**—*Vo Nguyen Giap, military leader of the Viet Minh, 1954.*[374]

Tactics used by Giap in defeating the French at Dien Bien Phu. After an initial frontal assault failed, Giap chose a slower, careful approach, slowly strangling the French positions. He isolated sections, defeating in detail, cutting the French off from reinforcement, resupply, and retreat.

64 **We have granted Vietnam "full independence" eighteen times since 1949. Isn't it about time we did it just once, but for good?**—*François Mitterrand, a Deputy in the French National Assembly, from a speech, 1954.*[974]

The French government granted Vietnamese independence several times between 1949 and 1954. The grants of independence always had strings attached which did not allow Vietnam to actually be free and independent of France. In 1954, recognition of Vietnam's independence was forced upon the French with their loss of the Indochina War against the Viet Minh. DRV and Republic of South Vietnam (SVN) were declared independent of France. The French maintained ties with South

Vietnam until the end of 1956 when they officially departed Indochina.

65 **One cannot go over Niagara Falls in a barrel only slightly.**—*Unidentified Analyst, Department of Defense, March 1954.*[317]

Many military advisors within the Eisenhower administration argued against direct U.S. intervention in Indochina in support of the French. They did not believe a limited war could be successfully fought in Indochina.

66 **Indochina is devoid of decisive military objectives [and involvement there] would be a serious diversion of limited U.S. capabilities.**—*Joint Chiefs of Staff, March 1954.*[374]

The JCS were considering a plan to provide the French with direct U.S. military support in the form of air strikes against Viet Minh forces surrounding Dien Bien Phu. The JCS advised against deploying U.S. troops in support of the French.

67 **The loss of Southeast Asia to Communism would, through economic and political pressures, drive Japan into an accommodation with the Communist Bloc. The communization of Japan would be the predictable result.** —*Admiral Arthur Radford, Chairman, Joint Chiefs of Staff, in a memorandum to the Secretary of Defense, 12 March 1954.*[224]

Radford was linking a communist Southeast Asia to an indirect threat against Japan.

68 **Should Indochina be lost to the Communists and in the absence of immediate and effective counteraction on the part of the Western Powers which would of necessity be on a much greater scale than that which could be decisive in Indochina, the conquest of the remainder of Southeast Asia would inevitably follow.**—*Admiral Arthur Radford, Chairman, Joint Chiefs of Staff, in a memorandum to the Secretary of Defense, 12 March 1954.*[224]

69 **[If the United States intervened at Dien Bien Phu its prestige would be] engaged to a point where we would want success. We could not afford a defeat that would have world-wide repercussions.**—*John Foster Dulles, Secretary of State, in a conversation with President Eisenhower, 24 March 1954.*[308]

The U.S. did not want to intervene militarily in Indochina unless they knew they could win. They also wanted concessions from France before such a move could be made. The French were not receptive and not eager to relinquish their colonial control.

70 **[I can] conceive of no greater tragedy than for the United States to become involved in an all-out war in Indochina.**—*President Dwight Eisenhower, 1954.*[79]

71 **You have a row of dominoes set up, you knock over the first one, and what will happen to the last one is that it will go over very quickly. So you have the beginning of a disintegration that would have the most profound influences.**—*President Dwight D. Eisenhower, during a press conference, 7 April 1954.*[886]

The press conference was held after the defeat of the French at Dien Bien Phu, March 54.

72 **Should Indochina fall [to the Communist], the rest of Southeast Asia would go over very quickly, like a row of dominoes ... causing much greater losses of raw materials and people, jeopardizing America's strategic position in the Far East, and driving Japan into the Communist camp. So the possible consequences of the loss are just incalculable to the free world.**—*President Dwight Eisenhower, during a news conference 7 April 1954.*[271]

Eisenhower appealed to the public and the world to garner support for free world intervention in Indochina. He stated that Indochina was rich in rubber, tungsten, and tin, and it should not be lost to the communists. Eisenhower needed free world support before Congress would back a plan to send U.S. combat troops to Indochina.

73 **[No amount of military aid could conquer] an enemy of the people which has the support and covert appeal of the people.**—*Senator John F. Kennedy of Massachusetts, speaking in the Senate, April 1954.*[347]

Congress would not approve unilateral U.S. intervention in Indochina on behalf of the French. They insisted intervention could only be jointly accomplished with other nations of the free world as participants.

74 **If France stopped fighting in Indo-China and the situation demanded it the United States would have to send troops to fight the Communists in that area.**—*Unidentified, high administration source, to the press, 16 April 1954.*[503]

The source was not an official Eisenhower administration spokesman, but was involved in the formation of policy.

75 **It would be a tragic error to go in [to Vietnam] alone as a partner of France.**—*President Dwight Eisenhower, speaking to Congressional leaders, 26 April 1954.*[270]

The U.S. was unable to convince Britain to join in a force to intervene in Indochina. Eisenhower lobbied against unilateral military action in Vietnam.

76 **A strictly military solution to the war in Indochina is not possible.**—*General Thomas T. H. Trapnall, Jr., former Chief of Military Assistance Advisory Group Indochina, during briefing, 3 May 1954.*[861]

Trapnall was speaking of the three Associated States that made up Vietnam at the time—Laos, Cambodia and Vietnam.

77 **[The Eisenhower administration had put the United States] in clear danger of being left naked and alone in a hostile world.**—*Senator Lyndon B. Johnson, of Texas, to the press, 6 May 1954.*[505]

Johnson accused the Eisenhower administration of "alienating" America's allies with talk of unilaterally considering sending troops to Vietnam in support of the French.

78 **Present conditions in Indo-China do not provide a suitable basis for armed intervention by the United States, the possibility under other circumstances of serious commitments by the United States nevertheless exists.**—*John Foster Dulles, Secretary of State, to the press, 7 May 1954.*[506]

Dulles was speaking after the fall of Dien Bien Phu, his comments aimed at the Viet Minh.

79 **In making commitments which might involve the use of armed force, the Congress is a full partner. Only the Congress can declare war.**—*John Foster Dulles, Secretary of State, to the press, 7 May 1954.*[506]

80 **An epic battle has ended but great causes have, before now, been won out of lost battles.**—*John Foster Dulles, Secretary of State, to the press, 7 May 1954.*[506]

Dulles commenting on the fall of the French fortress of Dien Bien Phu.

81 **The gallant garrison at Dien Bien Phu ... will forever stand as a symbol of the free world's determination to resist Communist aggression.**—*President Dwight D. Eisenhower, in a message sent to the French and Bao Dai, 8 May 1954.*[656]

Eisenhower, noting the fall of the French position at Dien Bien Phu to the Viet Minh, effectively signaling the end for France as a colonial power in Indochina.

82 **[As a nation without unity] we can lose victory before the final battle is fought. As a nation united, America need fear no foreign foe or agnostic creed.**—*Charles Thomas, Secretary of the Navy, during a Memorial Day speech at Arlington National Cemetery, 1 June 1954.*[655]

83 **People just don't pull up their roots and transplant themselves because of slogans. They honestly feared what might happen to them, and the emotion was strong enough to overcome their attachment to their land, their homes, and their ancestral graves.**—*Colonel Edward Lansdale, commenting on the flight of Catholics from North Vietnam in 1954.*[374]

Just prior to the Viet Minh takeover of Hanoi, nearly a million Catholic Vietnamese left North Vietnam to become refugees in South Vietnam. They feared reprisals from the "godless" communists who won control of North Vietnam through conquest of the French and by judgment of the 1954 Geneva Accords.

84 **[This is] the greatest victory the Communists have won in twenty years.**—*Senator William Knowland of California, speaking against the 1954 Geneva Accords.*[347]

The 1954 Geneva Accords temporarily partitioned Vietnam and set a schedule for a popular vote on reunification of the country under one government. The Accords did not allow the two Vietnams to enter into foreign military alliances or the importation of new military equipment or forces.

85 **We must work with these people, and then they themselves will soon find out that we are their friends and that they can't live without us.**—*President Dwight Eisenhower, July 1954.*[347]

Eisenhower believed the South Vietnamese could become a self-sufficient country with U.S. help and guidance. He wanted South Vietnam to be a friend of America, not a subordinate state.

86 **Our successes have awakened the American imperialists. After the Dien Bien Phu campaign, the latter's intentions and plan for intervention have also undergone changes aimed at protracting and internationalizing the Indochina war, sabotaging the Geneva Conference, and ousting the French by every means, in order to occupy Viet Nam, Cambodia and Laos, enslave the peoples of these countries and create further tension in the world.**—*Ho Chi Minh, President, Democratic Republic of Vietnam, speaking before the Communist Party Central Committee, 15 July 1954.*[864]

Ho lays the foundation for subsequent claims of American imperialism and colonialism in Vietnam.

87 **The US imperialists not only are the enemy of the world's people but are becoming the main and direct enemy of the Vietnamese, Cambodian and Lao peoples.**—*Ho Chi Minh, President, Democratic Republic of Vietnam, speaking before the Communist Party Central Committee, 15 July 1954.*[864]

88 **Peace with Honor...**—*Excerpt from the French statement on the results of peace talks in Geneva, Switzerland, 21 July 1954.*[657]

The French classified their final agreement with the Communist Vietnamese regime as "peace with honor." Terms of the agreement included the withdrawal of French forces from northern Vietnam and the temporary demarcation of Vietnam, pending a unification vote in 1956. The communists won their independence from the French and recognition for their country, the Democratic Republic of Vietnam.

89 **Christ has gone to the south.**—*Anonymous, 1954.*[347]

A reference to the exodus of hundreds of thousands of Catholics who fled North Vietnam after the partition of Vietnam under the 1954 Geneva Accords. Rumors spread through the Northern Catholic communities of future atrocities to be inflicted on them by the new communist regime in Hanoi.

90 **[The United States] must make every possible effort, not openly inconsistent with the U.S. position as to the armistice agreements ... to maintain a friendly non-Communist South Vietnam and to prevent a Communist victory through all-Vietnam elections.**—*National Security Council recommendation, August 1954.*[347]

Though the U.S. did not sign the 1954 Geneva Accords, they agreed not to disturb the terms of the agreement by threat or the use of force. The NSC recommended paramilitary and "black psyche" operations to weaken the Ho Chi Minh regime.

91 **I feel this is war in every sense. Wartime methods, therefore, are in order [in] all fields until emergency passed.**—*General John W. O'Daniel, Chief, U.S. Military Assistance Advisory Group Vietnam, in a cable to Secretary of State, John Foster Dulles, 8 August 1954.*[875]

O'Daniel saw the conflict in Vietnam as a war between the forces of communism and the free world, as defended by the U.S.

92 **Indeed we must be desperate.**—*John Foster Dulles, Secretary of State, comment, December 1954.*[347]

During the interim period after the French defeat and their withdrawal from Indochina they lobbied America to back Bao Dai as the leader of South Vietnam. They complained that Diem, who was supported by America, was not fit to rule the country. Dulles saw a Vietnam under Bao Dai as hopeless; America would, he thought, be desperate to back Bao Dai.

93 **A fair election in a communist country was a contradiction of terms.**—*Attributed to Ngo Dinh Diem by Dave Richard Palmer. Diem as Premier of the State of Vietnam was speaking to the press, 1955.*[713]

The 1954 Geneva Accords on Vietnam called for a temporary partition of Vietnam at the 17th Parallel, with a unification vote to take place in 1956. The vote would determine the leadership of all Vietnam, the unification of the Democratic Republic of Vietnam (North of the 17th Parallel) and the State of Vietnam (South of the 17th Parallel).

94 **Give 'em hell, boys.**—*General John W. O'Daniel, Chief, U.S. Military Mission, Vietnam, shouted at ARVN troops as they drove paramilitary troops of the Binh Xuyen into Cholon, 1955.*[273]

ARVN troops, who had previously been ineffective, successfully drove the Binh Xuyen troops back to their base in Cholon. This strengthened Diem's position of leadership within the country, allowing him to continue to put down other factional sects in South Vietnam.

95 **[Diem] ... did not have the capacity to achieve the necessary unity of purpose and action ... to prevent the country from falling under Communist control.**—*General J. Lawton Collins, U.S. Ambassador to South Vietnam, in a cable to the State Department, 7 April 1955.*[328]

Diem was unable to control, disband or eliminate religious sects that split South Vietnam. Collins did not believe Diem a capable leader and unsuccessfully lobbied with the Eisenhower administration for his removal.

96 **The government of Ngo Dinh Diem in South Vietnam was not equal to the task.**—*Edgar Faure, French Premier, during a press conference, 29 April 1955.*[507]

Faure did not believe Diem could successfully lead the army against the communist insurgents nor gain control over the militant sects and corruption that were strangling Saigon.

97 **The Army will be above all ... a police force capable of spotting guerrillas and communist efforts at infiltration.**—*General John O'Daniel, Commander, U.S. Military Assistance Advisory Group Vietnam, 1955.*[40]

O'Daniel planned to train the Vietnamese military to function as a large police force instead of a counterinsurgency force.

98 **[We reject] an election obviously stacked and subverted in advance, urged upon us by those who have already broken their own pledge under the agreement they now seek to enforce.**—*Senator John F. Kennedy of Massachusetts, as quoted by William P. Bundy, September 1967.*[82]

Kennedy was speaking out in support of Diem's refusal to hold the nationwide reunification election called for in the 1954 Geneva accords. The Accords called for free, internationally supervised elections. At the time it was believed that North Vietnam would not agree to election supervision.

99 **We ... executed too many honest people ... and, seeing enemies everywhere, resorted to terror, which became far too widespread.... Worse still, torture came to be regarded as a normal practice.**—*Vo Nguyen Giap, defense minister, Democratic Republic of Vietnam, from a speech to the Communist Central Committee, 1956.*[887]

Giap was speaking of the land-reform campaign that resulted in the deaths of thousands of North Vietnam land owners and small farmers. After two years of excesses, Ho Chi Minh called an end to the reform campaign.

100 **We were supposed to explain why the communist were bad and why the people must follow the government. But during the Resistance the communists had been the only ones in the village to fight against the French, so when we tried to explain that the communists were evil people, the villagers just didn't listen to us.**—*Unidentified South Vietnamese cadre leader, 1956.*[24]

The Diem government formed cadre units that visited the rural villages attempting to gain peasant support for the Diem regime. Many of those they talked to had suffered under the French and were more likely to favor the communists who had driven the French out of Vietnam. Diem, unknown by rural peasants, for the most part, ignored their needs.

101 **Vietnam represents a proving ground of democracy in Asia ... the alternative to Communist dictatorship.**—*Senator John F. Kennedy of Massachusetts, speaking before the American Friends of Vietnam association, 1 June 1956*[875]

102 **The key position of Vietnam in Southeast Asia ... makes inevitable the involvement of this nation's security in any new outbreak of trouble.**—*Senator John F. Kennedy of Massachusetts, speaking before the American Friends of Vietnam association, 1 June 1956.*[875]

Kennedy was linking U.S. interest with the success and freedom of South Vietnam.

103 **What we must offer [the Vietnamese people] is a revolution — a political, economic and social revolution far superior to anything the Communists can offer — far more peaceful, far more democratic, and far more locally controlled.** —*Senator John Kennedy, June 1956.*[73]

104 **Vietnam represents a test of American responsibility and determination in Asia. If we are not the parents of little Vietnam, then surely we are the godparents.... If it falls victim to any of the perils that threaten its existence ... our prestige in Asia will sink to a new low.**—*Senator John F. Kennedy of Massachusetts, speaking before the American Friends of Vietnam association, 1 June 1956.*[886]

105 **The independence of Free Vietnam is crucial to the free world in fields other than the military. Her economy is essential to the economy of all of Southeast Asia; and her political liberty is an inspiration to those seeking to obtain or maintain their liberty in all parts of Asia — and indeed the world. The fundamental tenets of this nation's foreign policy, in short, depend in considerable measure upon a strong and free Vietnamese nation.**—*Senator John F. Kennedy from Massachusetts, from a speech to the American Friends of Vietnam, 1 June 1956.*[900]

Kennedy stressed the importance of keeping Southeast Asia free of communism, and the special importance of keeping South Vietnam free and independent.

106 **Vietnam represents the cornerstone of the Free World in Southeast Asia, the keystone in the arch, the finger in the dike. Burma, Thailand, India, Japan, the Philippines and, obviously, Laos and Cambodia are among those whose security would be threatened if the red tide of Communism overflowed into Vietnam.**—*Senator John F. Kennedy from Massachusetts, from a speech to the American Friends of Vietnam, 1 June 1956.*[301]

107 **Our policy is to consolidate the North and to keep in mind the South.**—*Ho Chi Minh, President, Democratic Republic of Vietnam, in a public letter to the North Vietnamese people, June 1956.*[887]

Ho tried to explain to a group of southern Vietnamese why they could not return to South Vietnam. The group numbered more than 130,000 cadre, Viet Minh soldiers and their families who had moved to North Vietnam when the country was partitioned in 1954. They were supposed to return to the South after the planned elections to unify the country. There was no reunification election, and South Vietnam declared itself an independent country. Many of the group would eventually infiltrate south to bolster the ranks of the VC.

108 **The militant march of Communism has been halted.** —*Vice President Richard Nixon, speaking during a state visit to South Vietnam, 1956.*[629]

Speaking of the relatively quiet period in South Vietnam immediately following the Geneva Accords that partitioned North and South Vietnam, and the end of the war in Korea. His speech was broadcast over Vietnamese radio.

109 **[Vietnam] ... it is our offspring. We cannot abandon it, we cannot ignore its needs.**—*Senator John F. Kennedy from Massachusetts, from a speech to the American Friends of Vietnam, 1 August 1956.*[301]

110 **... We will be in Saigon tomorrow.**—*Pham Van Dong, North Vietnam's Premier's comments to French Consul Georges-Picot, 12 September 1959.*[899]

Dong was projecting Hanoi's success in using armed force to overthrow the Diem regime and expel American from Vietnam.

111 **[Diem is] a man history may judge as one of the great figures of the twentieth century.**—*Robert Wagner, Mayor of New York City, during welcoming ceremonies for President Diem, 1957.*[629]

Diem was perceived at the time as the man to stem the tide against communism in Vietnam.

112 **The prerequisite of victory in a limited war is to determine under what circumstances one side might be willing to run greater risks for winning than its opponent will accept to avoid losing.**—*Henry Kissinger, Study Director, Nuclear Weapons and Foreign Policy, Harvard University, writing in his book, 1957.*[929]

113 **[Diem] ... must be rated as one of the ablest free Asian leaders. We can take pride in our support.**—*Ernest K. Lindley, Newsweek correspondent, in an article, June 1959.*[274]

Many Americans applauded Diem's efforts and the apparent stabilization he brought to Vietnam. Because of his strict control of the media, many of the troubles within Vietnam were not readily apparent to the American public.

114 **Strategically, South Vietnam's capture by the Communists would bring their power several hundred miles into a hitherto free region. The remaining countries of Southeast Asia would be menaced by a great flanking movement. The loss of South Vietnam would set in motion a crumbling process which could, as it progresses, have grave consequences for the forces of freedom.**—*President Dwight Eisenhower, 1959.*[713]

Eisenhower's theory of the systematic fall of free countries to communism was labeled the "Domino Theory."

115 **Laos might develop into another Korea.**—*President Dwight Eisenhower, comments, September 1959.*[279]

The American-sponsored Laotian government was under heavy pressure from North Vietnamese–backed Communist Pathet Lao insurgents. At the time, the fall of Laos to communism was seen as more dangerous than the situation with Diem and the Viet Cong in South Vietnam.

116 **If a son is mistreated by his father, he may adopt another.**—*Vietnamese farmer's adage, 1959.*[374]

The Vietnamese farmer was speaking of his ability to bend with the direction of the "political wind." The allegiance of many rural Vietnamese was to neither the VC nor the GVN, but grudging support was often given to the faction that harassed them the least; the lesser of the two evils.

117 **[The defeat at Tay Ninh was a] severe blow to the prestige of the Vietnamese Army and an indication of the VC ability to stage large-size well-planned attacks.**—*General Samuel Williams, Commander, U.S. Military Advisory Group Vietnam, 1960.*[34]

The armed struggle of the VC began in 1959. In January 1960 a reinforced VC battalion overran the 32d ARVN Regiment Headquarters (Tay Ninh City), killing 23 ARVN and capturing a large number of weapons.

118 **South Vietnam is the model of the national liberation movement of our time. If the special warfare that the United States imperialists are testing in South Vietnam is overcome, then it can be defeated anywhere in the world.**—*General Vo Nguyen Giap, Defense Minister of North Vietnam, 1960.*[713]

Giap speaking of what Nikita Khrushchev called a war of "national liberation." In such a war communist insurgents would seek to overthrow the ruling democracy or dictatorship, replacing it with a communist regime. Giap viewed the struggle in SVN against the American-backed Diem regime as such a war.

119 **[The GVN] has tended to treat the population with suspicion or coerce it and has been rewarded with an attitude of apathy or resentment.**—*American intelligence report to the Eisenhower administration, March 1960.*[253]

The Diem regime severely repressed opposition to the government, imprisoning tens of thousands of Vietnamese and abolishing the traditional system of village autonomy, replacing it with Diem appointed officials.

120 **There is a little bit of all of us in that faraway country.**—*General John W. O'Daniel, former Chief, U.S. Military Mission, Vietnam, comments, 1960.*[288]

121 **Probably the greatest single problem encountered by the MAAG is the continual task of assuring the Vietnamese that the United States is not a colonial power — an assurance that must be renewed on an individual basis by each new adviser.**—*Unidentified MAAG officer, 1960.*[296]

Military Assistance and Advisory Group Indochina was renamed Military Assistance and Advisory Group Vietnam (MAAGV) in 1956. It took over the role of trainer to the SVN military. MAAGV initially consisted of 342 men.

122 **No one can make good ... commanders by sending uneducated, poorly trained, and poorly equipped and motivated boys to Benning or Knox or Leavenworth or Quantico.**—*Unidentified MAAG officer, commenting of the caliber of ARVN officers, 1960.*[322]

Officers within the Diem army were appointed and promoted based on their loyalty to Diem, not on their abilities or qualifications. Diem loyalists were sent to the American military schools, regardless of their abilities to lead or command.

123 **Ky, the next time you fly me like that so close to the water, let me know beforehand and I'll bring my fishing rod.**—*William E. Colby, CIA officer and later director of the CIA, during a conversation with Nguyen Cao Ky, 1960.*[629]

Ky was demonstrating his low level flying skills for Colby. Colby was directing operations to infiltrate South Vietnamese agents into North Vietnam. Ky and his air unit were responsible for flying them to their drop locations.

124 **If Diem's position in-country continues [to] deteriorate as [a] result [of] failure [to] adopt proper political, psychological, economic and security measures, it may become necessary for US Government to begin consideration alternative courses of action and leaders in order [to] achieve our objective.**—*Eldridge Durbrow, U.S. Ambassador to South Vietnam, in a cable to the State Department, 16 September 1960.*[214]

Diem's policies became increasingly oppressive against the rural population and the Buddhists. Because of his fear of a coup, he kept his military leaders at odds with each other so they could not align themselves into a force for change. The military leadership was unable to effectively lead the war against the communist insurgents.

125 **We will drive the Americans into the sea.**—*Pham Van Dong, Premier of North Vietnam, 1960.*[629]

Nguyen Cao Ky, former Vice President of South Vietnam, claims this to be "one of the most prophetic boasts of the war." To be more accurate it was the South Vietnamese that were driven into the sea, those who became "boat people" fleeing the communist regime. The Americans were successfully expelled from Vietnam through negotiations and a lack of public support.

126 **If ever there was a war where we would have been engaged in a hopeless struggle without allies, for an unpopular colonialist cause, it was the 1954 war in Indochina.**—*Senator John F. Kennedy of Massachusetts, campaign comments to the Democratic National Committee, 12 October 1960.*[194]

127 **The United States may well be forced, in the not too distant future, to undertake the difficult task of identifying and supporting alternate leadership.**—*Eldridge Durbrow, U.S. Ambassador to South Vietnam, during a meeting with President Diem, 4 December 1960.*[36]

Durbrow was attempting to reform Diem's repressive policies and garner more popular support. The Diem regime became increasingly distant from the needs and support of the Vietnamese people. Because Diem was supported by the U.S., many Vietnamese thought of Diem and the Americans as one.

1961

War is like love; it always finds a way.
— Bertolt Brecht

128 **Let every nation know, whether it wishes us well or ill, that we shall pay any price, bear any burden, meet any hardship, support any friend, oppose any foe, in order to assure the survival and the success of liberty.**—*President John F. Kennedy, inaugural address, 20 January 1961.*[375]

129 **The Front for the Liberation of South Vietnam calls on the entire people to unite and heroically rise up and struggle ... to overthrow the disguised colonial regime of the imperialists and dictatorial administration, and to form a national and democratic coalition administration.**—*Hanoi Radio broadcast, 29 January 1961.*

In December 1960, Hanoi announced the formation and recognition of the NLF (National Liberation Front). In January 1961, it publicly recognized the NLF and called upon the SVN people to join the NLF in expelling America from Vietnam. Hanoi also called for the people to form a coalition government to take control of the country.

130 **And so my fellow Americans / Ask not what your country can do for you / Ask what you can do for your country / My fellow citizens of the world — ask not / What America will do for you — but what together / We can do for the freedom of man**—*President John F. Kennedy, inaugural address, 20 January 1961.*[375]

131 **Let us never negotiate out of fear. But let us never fear to negotiate.**—*President John F. Kennedy, inaugural address, 20 January 1961.*[83]

132 **Vietnam has progressed faster in material things than it has spiritually. The people have more possessions but are starting to lose the will to protect their liberty.**—*General Edward Lansdale, in a report to the Secretary of Defense, January 1961.*[875]

Lansdale was sent to South Vietnam in January 1961 on a fact finding visit. His report was not very optimistic. He stressed the need for stability in the Saigon government but made no specific recommendations as to how America could accomplish stability. He felt the sudden influx of U.S. aid had been detrimental to the social progress of the people.

133 **The principal export of this country [South Vietnam] is anti–Communism.**—*Ngo Dinh Diem, President, South Vietnam, comment to the media, 1961.*[887]

Diem often used this phrase as indication of his anti-communist beliefs.

134 **Why take risks over Laos? It will fall into our laps like a ripe apple.**—*Nikita Khrushchev, Soviet Prime Minister, comments to the U.S. Ambassador, March 1961.*[886]

Khrushchev made his comments to Llewellyn Thompson. One of the first confrontations between the U.S. and the Soviets after Kennedy took office was over Laos. Laos wanted neutrality, but communist and pro-western Laotian forces were vying for control. The Soviets backed the communist Pathet Lao, and the U.S. backed the Royal Laotian Government. When the Soviets departed Laos in 1962 support for the Pathet Lao was secretly continued by North Vietnam, while the U.S. secretly continued limited support of the Royal Lao Army and Meo tribesman to counter North Vietnam's involvement.

135 **If Vietnam can be held, Thailand, Laos, and Cambodia could be saved, and we shall have demonstrated that the Communist technique of guerrilla warfare can be dealt with.**—*Walt Rostow, from the State Department, in a memorandum to the President, 29 March 1961.*[299]

Rostow wanted to make a stand against communism in Vietnam. The Administration concluded that Laos was the place to make a stand against communism in Southeast Asia, and opted for negotiations.

136 **The struggle is far from lost in Southeast Asia and it is by no means inevitable that it must be lost.... There is no alternative to United States leadership in Southeast Asia.**—*Vice President Lyndon Johnson, in a message to President Kennedy, May 1961.*[713]

Johnson had recently returned from a fact finding tour of South Vietnam, and gave President Kennedy his evaluation of the situation. He advocated aid to South Vietnam, but not the introduction of U.S. combat units.

137 **The United States stands ready to assist in meeting the grave situation that confronts you. ... There are many things the United States is willing to do.**—*Vice President Lyndon Johnson, speaking to South Vietnam's National Assembly, 12 May 1961.*[508]

Johnson was in South Vietnam to review the situation and demonstrate American support for the Saigon regime.

138 **As a military ally the entire Laos nation is clearly inferior to a battalion of conscientious objectors from World War I.**—*John Kenneth Galbraith, American Ambassador to India, in a letter to President Kennedy, May 1961.*[340]

Many Kennedy advisers saw Laos as the choice for America to make a stand against communism. It was landlocked and had no viable military force capable of sustained combat against the North Vietnam backed communist Pathet Lao forces.

139 **Don't tell me about Diem, he's all we've got out there.**—*Vice President Lyndon Johnson, comment to a reporter, May 61.*[725]

140 **The battle against Communism must be joined in Southeast Asia with strength and determination ... or the United States, inevitably, must surrender the Pacific and take up our defenses on our own shores.**—*Vice President Lyndon Johnson, in a message to President Kennedy, May 1961.*[374]

Johnson had just completed an inspection visit to South Vietnam, during which he met with President Diem.

141 **Communist domination of Laos is a foregone conclusion.**—*Professor Hans Morgenthau, University of Chicago political scientist, in his writings on foreign policy in 1961.*[748]

His prediction of Communist domination later turned out to be true, but in 1965 Laos had a U.N. brokered coalition government, and was not totally communist dominated.

142 **The last great confrontation with Communism.**—*Walt Rostow, State Department Foreign Affairs Adviser, comments, 1961.*[374]

Rostow's view of the struggle against the communists in Vietnam.

143 **What you have chosen to do for your country ... is the greatest contribution that any man can make.**—*President John F. Kennedy, from a speech at the U.S. Naval Academy, June 1961.*[976]

Kennedy, in reference to military service.

144 **[The United States is the] locomotive at the head of mankind, and the rest of the world the caboose.**—*McGeorge Bundy, National Security Adviser to President Kennedy, 1961.*[330]

145 **American combat troop involvement is not only not required, it is not desirable.**—*Vice President Lyndon Johnson, during a White House meeting, 1961.*[223]

Johnson's comments were based on his trip to Saigon in May, 1961, and his long-time opposition to deployment of American troops in Southeast Asia. In 1961 the Joint Chiefs of Staff argued for U.S. forces to go to South Vietnam to stabilize the situation.

146 **[George Ball]—Vietnam may one day demand as many as three hundred thousand U.S. troops.**

[President Kennedy]—Well, George, you're supposed to be one of the smartest guys in town, but you're crazier than hell. That will never happen.—*President John F. Kennedy, in an exchange with George Ball, 1961.*[374]

George Ball was Deputy Under Secretary of State.

147 **[Johnson]—President Diem is the Churchill of the decade ... in the vanguard of those leaders who stand for freedom.**

[Reporter]—Did you really mean it?

[Johnson]—Shit ... Diem's the only boy we got out there.—*An exchange between Vice President Lyndon Johnson and a correspondent, September 1961.*[374]

148 **Now we have a problem in making our power credible, and Vietnam is the place.**—*President John F. Kennedy, comments to The New York Times, 1961.*[374]

Kennedy, commenting on a conference with Soviet Prime Minister Khrushchev, where he appeared to be bullied by the Soviet Premier.

149 **[The strategic hamlet program was designed to reduce the Vietcong to] hungry, marauding bands of outlaws devoting all their energies to remaining alive...**—*Roger Hilsman, Kennedy administration adviser, 1961.*[324]

Peasants were collected from scattered areas and deposited into large fortified (strategic) hamlets in an effort to keep the people away from the VC, thus denying the VC support and recruits.

150 **[The Diem government suffers from a] deep and pervasive crisis of confidence and a serious loss in national morale...**—*General Maxwell Taylor, military adviser to President Kennedy, in a report on South Vietnam, October 1961.*[307]

Taylor recommended an increase in U.S. aid and advisory personnel to South Vietnam.

151 **[Deployment of a task force would be] a visible symbol of the seriousness of American intentions.**—*General Maxwell Taylor, Military adviser to President Kennedy, in a report on South Vietnam, October 1961.*[307]

Taylor and Rostow recommended the deployment of an 8,000-man task force to assist the South Vietnamese with recent Mekong River flood damage, and do a little national building at the same time. The force was billed as a humanitarian effort, negating the 1954 Geneva Accords' restrictions on increases in U.S. military personnel levels in South Vietnam.

152 **[The greatest threat there (Asia) was not the momentary threat of Communism, but the danger of] hunger, ignorance, poverty and disease ... we must keep these enemies at the point of our attack.**—*Lyndon Johnson, Vice President, in a report to President Kennedy, 1961.*[416]

Johnson was sent to Asia on a fact finding tour in 1961.

153 **The troops will march in, the bands will play, the crowds will cheer, and in four days everyone will have forgotten. Then we will be told we have to send in more troops. It's like taking a drink. The effect wears off, and you have to take another.**—*President John F. Kennedy, to Arthur M. Schlesinger, November 1961.*[83]

Kennedy was discussing the implications of sending an 8,000 man task force to Vietnam to assist the recovery of the South Vietnamese after especially heavy seasonal flooding.

154 **We could not sit still and be the puppets of Diem's anti-Buddhist policies.**—*Roger Hilsman, Kennedy administration adviser, 1961.*[345]

Diem had publicly assured U.S. Ambassador Nolting that he would cease attacks and repression of the Buddhist. Within a few days of the promise, Diem's brother Nhu raided several Buddhist pagodas, beating and arresting Buddhist supporters. In response, some members of the Kennedy administration began to consider backing out of Vietnam or the possibility of a Vietnamese military coup against Diem.

155 **The gut issue was not whether Diem was a good ruler but whether the United States could continue to accept the impunity of Communist aggression in South Vietnam.**—*President John Kennedy, during a meeting, 14 November 1961.*[300]

156 **If Vietnam goes, it will be exceedingly difficult if not impossible to hold Southeast Asia whose loss would shatter the faith that the United States has the will and the capacity to deal with the Communist offensive in that area.**—*General Maxwell Taylor, in a report to President Kennedy, November 1961.*[374]

In October 1961 Taylor reviewed the situation in Vietnam. He advised the president that U.S. intervention would be required to stop the deterioration of the Diem government and the military situation against the Viet Cong.

157 **[The] decisive military factor is not manpower or even confidence but bad organization, incompetent use and deployment of forces, inability to protect territory once cleared, and probably poor political base. American forces would not correct this. Their inability to do so would create a worse crisis of confidence as this became evident.**—*John Kenneth Galbraith, U.S. Ambassador to India, in a message to President Kennedy, 20 November 1961.*[875]

Galbraith pointed out the poor military and political situation in South Vietnam. At the time, the ARVN were fighting more amongst themselves and jockeying for favorable positions with Diem, than they were trying to counter the communist insurgency.

158 **There is no solution that will not involve a change of government ... we must look ahead to a new government.**—*John Kenneth Galbraith, U.S. Ambassador to India, in a message to President Kennedy, 20 November 1961.*[875]

Galbraith conducted an inspection tour of South Vietnam in November, 1961, and reported his observations and conclusions to President Kennedy. Galbraith did not believe Diem capable of the political and social reforms that were required to win the support of the people and stabilize the government. And stability was essential if the military was to receive proper direction and support in the war against the communist insurgents.

159 **North Vietnam is extremely vulnerable to conventional bombing.... There is no case for fearing a mass onslaught of Communist manpower into South Vietnam and its neighboring states, particularly if our air power is allowed a free hand against logistical targets.**—*General Maxwell Taylor, in a report to President Kennedy, November 1961.*[374]

In October 1961 Taylor reviewed the situation in Vietnam. He advised the president that U.S. intervention would be required to stop the deterioration of the Diem government and the military situation against the Viet Cong.

160 **There is scarcely the slightest practical chance that the administration and political reforms now being pressed upon Diem will result in real change. They reckon without deeper political realities and insecurities of his position and the nature of politicians of this age. He will promise but he will not perform because it is most unlikely that he can perform.** —*John Kenneth Galbraith, U.S. Ambassador to India, in a message to President Kennedy, 20 November 1961.*[875]

Galbraith conducted an inspection tour of South Vietnam in November 1961.

161 **American aid has built a castle of sand.**—*Milton C. Taylor, writer, 1961.*[310]

American support of South Vietnam amounted to billions of dollars in aid between 1955 and 1960. Without this influx of aid, South Vietnam could not stand on its own. It had no viable exports, relying solely on American imports and aid to sustain the economy.

1962

The essence of war is violence. Moderation in war is imbecility.
Hit first! Hit hard! and hit anywhere!
—Admiral Sir John Fisher

162 **It isn't much of a war, but it's the only war we've got, so enjoy it.**—*General Charles J. Timmes, Military Assistance and Advisory Group Vietnam, speaking to American advisers during a meeting, 1962.*[887]

Military Assistance and Advisory Group Vietnam was the designation for American advisers assisting the South Vietnamese military. MAAGV was renamed Military Assistance Command Vietnam in 1962.

163 **Any war in the Southeast Asia Mainland will be a peninsula and island-type campaign — a mode of warfare in which all elements of the Armed Forces of the United States have gained a wealth of experience and in which we have excelled both in WWII and Korea.**—*Excerpt from memorandum from the Joint Chiefs of Staff to Robert McNamara, 13 January 1962.*[924]

Perceived readiness of U.S. forces for war in Southeast Asia.

164 **You have to land right on top of them or they disappear.**—*Unidentified Army adviser, with the ARVN, 1962.*[333]

Commenting on the difficulty of bringing the VC to combat. The VC often withdrew from an area before they could be pinned down with air strikes or artillery and before large numbers of ARVN troops could be brought in to do battle.

165 **Until surgery invents a technique for operating on Siamese twins, they cannot be separated.**—*Unidentified American diplomat, commenting on the Ngo brothers, February 1962.*[374]

After the aborted attempt on Diem's life in February, 1962, he became totally reclusive, delegating the running of the government to his brother Nhu. Diem could make few decisions without advising his brother or seeking his council.

166 **The solution lies in our winning it. This is what the President intends to do.**—*Robert Kennedy, Attorney General, comments to the press during stopover in Hong Kong, February 1962.*[87]

Robert Kennedy is believed to have accurately reflected President Kennedy's views on the war against the communists in South Vietnam. Saigon was too weak to stand on its own and Kennedy felt America had too much invested in Southeast Asia to abandon Vietnam.

167 **We don't see the end of the tunnel, but I must say I don't think it is darker than it was a year ago, and in some ways [it is] lighter.**—*President John F. Kennedy, comments to the press, 1962.*[374]

168 **We have not sent combat troops there [to Vietnam], though the training missions that we have there have been instructed if they are fired upon to ... fire back to protect themselves.**—*President John F. Kennedy, during a news conference, 14 February 1962.*[658]

American advisers and trainers were authorized to accompany the South Vietnamese on training flights. These flights included actual attack and support missions, although the Pentagon did not acknowledge to the press that Americans were accompanying Vietnamese support missions.

169 **In providing the GVN the tools to do the job, the US must not offer so much that they forget that the job of saving the country is theirs [GVN]—only they can do it.**—*General Lionel McGarr, to President Kennedy, 22 February 1962.*[87]

McGarr was one of several people within the military who lobbied against the introduction of U.S. combat forces to Vietnam. He insisted America should provide the South Vietnamese with the tools and support to defend their freedom, without direct American intervention in the war.

170 **We will win in Vietnam and we shall remain here until we do.**—*Robert Kennedy, Attorney General, comments to the press during a visit to Saigon, February 1962.*[650]

171 **Without security, nothing we do will last.**—*Lt.Col. John Paul Vann, Senior Adviser to the 7th ARVN Infantry Division, 1962.*[887]

Vann emphasized the importance of protecting the villages and their ability to protect themselves.

172 **The people ... have learned from early childhood to view reality through the prism of Viet Cong ideas, beliefs and prejudices. Success in turning these people toward actual allegiance to a nationalist government would thus require extraordinary measures applied over a long period of time.**—*Gerald Hickey, American anthropologist, observations, 1962.*[17]

173 **The war in Vietnam is likely to last a long time.**—*Robert McNamara, Secretary of Defense, during an interview, Honolulu, Hawaii, 21 March 1962.*[659]

174 **To introduce white [sic] forces, US forces, in large numbers there today, while it might have an initial favorable military impact would almost certainly lead to adverse political and in the long run adverse military consequences.**—*Robert McNamara, Secretary of Defense, during Congressional testimony, March 1962.*[223]

McNamara publicly advocated that U.S. ground forces not be used in South Vietnam.

175 **[The United States is becoming entrapped in a] long drawn out indecisive involvement and might bleed as the French did.**—*John Kenneth Galbraith, American Ambassador to India, in a letter to President Kennedy, 4 April 1962.*[298]

176 **The following considerations influence our thinking on Vietnam: 1. We have a growing military commitment. This could expand step by step into a major, long-drawn out indecisive military involvement. 2. We are backing a weak and, on the record, ineffectual government and a leader who as a politician may be beyond the point of no return. 3. There is consequent danger we shall replace the French as the colonial forces in the area and bleed as the French did.**—*John Kenneth Galbraith, U.S. Ambassador to India, in a memorandum to President Kennedy, 7 April 1962.*[223]

177 **Too many amateur counter-insurgency cooks have had their hands at stirring the revolutionary warfare broth.**—*Bernard Fall, historian, 1962.*[713]

Speaking of all the advisers within the Kennedy administration offering comment and advice on policy to be pursued in South Vietnam.

178 **Every quantitative measurement we have shows that we're winning this war.**—*Robert McNamara, Secretary of Defense, during a press conference in Saigon, May 1962.*[887]

Results of McNamara's first fact-finding trip to South Vietnam.

179 **There is a new feeling of confidence that victory is possible.**—*Robert McNamara, Secretary of Defense, comments to the press, 1962.*[374]

McNamara's public declaration that the situation in Vietnam was improving to the point that a victorious end was deemed possible.

180 **Nothing would stop the southward movement of Communism through Indonesia and this would have the effect of cutting the world in half.**—*Dwight D. Eisenhower, former President, to John McCone, 10 May 1962.*[211]

McCone functioned as a liaison between Eisenhower and John F. Kennedy. Eisenhower tried to impress upon the Kennedy administration the importance of not losing South Vietnam to the communists.

181 **The most important causes of dissatisfaction are indiscriminate attacks on villages and being considered and treated as VC.**—*Unidentified former NLF cadre, during interrogation, 1962.*[11]

During the cadre's interrogation he was asked why the people of Hau Nghia province did not actively support the GVN. Besides being forced to relocate to Strategic Hamlets and drafted into working on the hamlet's defenses, the people did not appreciate the treatment they received from the GVN or ARVN officials.

182 **We cannot win the war with the Diem-Nhu methods, and we cannot change those methods no matter how much pressure we put on them.**—*Joseph Mendenhall, former political counselor, U.S. Embassy Vietnam, in a memorandum to Deputy Assistant Secretary of State, 16 May 1962.*[215]

183 **I've seen nothing but progress and hopeful indications of further progress in the future.**—*Robert McNamara, Secretary of Defense, during a press conference in Saigon, May 1962.*[887]

McNamara had been sent to South Vietnam on a fact finding tour by President Kennedy.

184 **If war comes in Southeast Asia the United States will suffer a worse defeat than it did in Korea.**—*Communist Chinese statement, released to the press, 20 May 1962.*[660]

Red China was responding to the deployment of 5,000 Marine, Army, and Air Force troops to Thailand. The U.S. troops were sent to counter a move by Chinese-backed communist Pathet Lao forces across the Laotian border into Thailand.

185 **Americans do not like long, inconclusive wars—and this is going to be a long, inconclusive war. Thus we are sure to win in the end.**—*Pham Van Dong, Prime Minister, Democratic Republic of Vietnam, during an interview, 1962.*[635]

This phrase was also repeated by Ho Chi Minh in 1962. Ho Chi Minh was prepared to fight a war of attrition against the Americans as he had done against the French. Hanoi was willing to spend more lives in the conquest of South Vietnam than they believed America was willing to sacrifice in defense of the South.

186 **[The Strategic Hamlet Program is] an enthusiastic movement of solidarity and self-sufficiency.**—*Ngo Dinh Nhu, political and personal adviser to President Diem, 1962.*[374]

Nhu's description of the Strategic Hamlet Program, a government program that forced peasants and farmers from their ancestral lands to live in fortified government hamlets. The program was designed to separate the people from the VC insurgents. But the program was so hated by the people that it created more recruits and supporters of the VC than it saved from them. Nhu used the program to enhance his power and increase his cash flow.

187 **[A United States] withdrawal in the case of Viet-Nam and in the case of Thailand might mean a collapse in the entire area.**—*President John F. Kennedy, during a press conference, 14 June 1962.*[82]

According to McGeorge Bundy this was proof that Kennedy supported the "Domino Theory."

188 **Time will tell, but looks to me like we're pissing our goodies into a sinkhole ... and there's no bottom.**—*Lieutenant Kenneth Babbs, U.S. Marine Corps pilot, journal entry, 1962.*[887]

Babbs was a member of one of the first Marine helicopter squadrons deployed to South Vietnam in support of ARVN forces. His squadron operated from Soc Trang in the Delta.

189 **The war in Vietnam is as insane as it is hideous.**—*Akihiko Okamura, news photographer, comments after being captured by the Viet Cong, June 1962.*[398]

Okamura was captured by the VC and held for 53 days.

190 **[The] battle can be won only by the will, energy, and political acumen of the resisting governments themselves. US power can supplement and enlarge their power but it cannot be substituted. Even if the US could defeat the Communists militarily by a massive injection of its own forces, the odds are that what it would win would be, not a political victory which created a stable and independent government, but an uneasy and costly colony.**—*Sherman Kent, Director, Office of National Estimates, speaking to the director of the CIA, 18 June 1962.*[195]

Kent, stating the importance of the GVN winning the battle against the communists and gaining the support of the people.

191 **[I was] not optimistic about the success of the whole United States program. ... [I did not think that the various American efforts] would succeed over the long run, pointing out that we were merely chipping away at the toe of the glacier from the North.**—*John McCone, Director, Central Intelligence Agency, in a report to Robert McNamara, 18 June 1962.*[208]

The CIA's information on the situation in South Vietnam indicated the VC were getting stronger, with increased support and direction from North Vietnam.

192 **What we get out of it depends on what we're looking for. For some, air medals, badges of glory, but no gory — please. For others, the warriors, war! A poor war admittedly but the only one we got. For Washington, a testing ground for tactics and weapons. For Saigon, an accumulation of American money and supplies. At a remote outpost, plenty of beer and rice magically dropped from the skies in a magnificent green whirlybird...**—*Lieutenant Kenneth Babbs, U.S. Marine Corps pilot, journal entry, 1962.*[877]

193 **There is no doubt we are on the winning side.**—*General Paul Harkins, Commander, Military Assistance and Advisory Group, Vietnam, during conference in Honolulu, 23 July 1962.*[887]

Harkins made this assessment of the war, even though he had received reports to the contrary from his advisers in the field. American field advisers reported incidents of ARVN abuse, thievery, and coercion against the peasant population they were supposed to be assisting and protecting.

194 **Contact is being made with the VC every day.... The GVN still needs to work on their organization but progress is being made. President Diem has indicated that he plans that his troops will get out into the field more often and stay out longer.**—*General Paul Harkins, Commander, Military Assistance and Advisory Group, Vietnam, during conference in Honolulu, 23 July 1962.*[887]

Harkins's optimistic outlook of the war. A view not shared by all of his field commanders who worked with the ARVN on a daily basis.

195 **Our military assistance to Vietnam is paying off. The Vietnamese are beginning to hit the Viet Cong insurgents where it hurts the most — in winning the people to the side of the government.**—*Robert McNamara, Secretary of Defense, during a strategy conference in Honolulu, Hawaii, 25 July 1962.*[661]

196 **They only want to please the regime. They haven't the faintest idea what makes the peasants tick.... They're city boys who earned promotions by kissing the asses of the bosses, and all they care about is getting back to Saigon to get promoted again.**—*Unidentified American adviser, 1962.*[374]

Speaking of the GVN programs and those running them.

197 **[The] VC are on the move. They pop out of canals and mangrove swamps to hit an outpost, capture guns and radios, disappear into the brush. ARVN plays hide and seek, tries to catch the attack before it happens, like an angry housewife stomping at an erratic cockroach before it makes the refuge between the baseboard and floor.**—*Lieutenant Kenneth Babbs, U.S. Marine Corps pilot, journal entry, 1962.*[877]

198 **[When the] nuclear shit hit the atomic fan ... we're in the safest place. No one's going to nuke Nam.**—*Lieutenant Cochran, U.S. Marine Corps pilot, comments as recorded in Babbs' journal, 1962.*[877]

Based on the strategic unimportance of Vietnam and its geological placement, the Marine doubted it would make the Soviet or American nuclear hit list.

199 **I think our progress in Vietnam is encouraging, and I don't think our efforts there should be criticized.**—*General Maxwell Taylor, Special Military Adviser to the President, during a press conference, Tokyo, Japan, 4 September 1962.*[662]

200 **It is their country, their future is at stake, not ours. To ignore that reality will not only be immensely costly in terms of American lives and resources, but it may also draw us inexorably into some variation of the unenviable position in Vietnam that was formerly occupied by the French...**—*Senator*

Mike Mansfield of Montana, in a recommendation to President Kennedy, 1962.[374]

Mansfield went to South Vietnam on a fact finding mission at President Kennedy's request. He pointed out that U.S. policy was inconsistent and that the Diem regime did not have the backing of the South Vietnamese people.

201 **These people may be the world's greatest lovers, but they're not the world's greatest fighters. But they're good people, and they can win a war if someone shows them how.**—*Colonel John Paul Vann, Senior Adviser to the ARVN 7th Infantry Division, 1962.*[374]

Vietnamese men considered themselves excellent lovers.

202 **When the bullets are flying past his ear, even the tamest dove tends to ruffle his feathers a bit, and this then is what the pro-war or anti-war sentiment always comes down to: you can have any philosophical attitude of war you want, but none of it means diddly until the moment you have to decide whether to pull that trigger or not.... That's the moment every man who's ever been there never forgets.**—*Lieutenant Kenneth Babbs, U.S. Marine Corps pilot, in a letter to John Pratt, 1962.*[886]

203 **In 30 percent of all the combat missions flown in Vietnamese Air Force planes, Americans are at the controls...**—*Noam Chomsky, political dissenter and linguistics professor, attributed to article in the* New York Times, *October 1962.*[88]

American Air Force advisers were sent to Vietnam to train the South Vietnam Air Force. As the military situation in Vietnam began to deteriorate, American pilots accompanied South Vietnam pilots on missions, and in some cases it was the South Vietnam pilot who was along for the ride while the American pilot flew the mission.

204 **I think the Americans greatly underestimate the character of the Vietnamese people. We have always shown great determination when faced with a foreign invader.**—*Ho Chi Minh, President, Democratic Republic of Vietnam, during an interview in Hanoi, 1962.*[949]

205 **The Americans are much stronger than the French, though they know us less well. So it may perhaps take ten years or so to do it, but our heroic compatriots will defeat them in the end.**—*Ho Chi Minh, President, Democratic Republic of Vietnam, during an interview in Hanoi, 1962.*[949]

Ho's goal was to reunite North and South Vietnam under communist rule and force out the Americans. In late-1972, the pending cease-fire and peace agreement spelled a partial failure of North Vietnam to achieve their goal. Under terms of the peace agreement America withdrew from Vietnam, leaving a coalition government in South Vietnam.

206 **Sink or swim with Ngo Dinh Diem.**—*David Halberstam, correspondent, 1962.*[266]

This was a generic press reference to the Kennedy administration's policy of backing Diem, even though his government was perceived by many in the press corps as "corrupt, repressive, and unpopular."

207 **[The VC were not taken seriously because they] operated with a collection of handmade and homemade weapons and arms taken from Government troops.**—*Excerpt from newspaper article, 6 December 1962.*[100]

In 1957 the VC were not seen as a serious threat to the security of South Vietnam. The Diem regime, as supported by America, believed the danger was posed by North Vietnam and Red China. The shooting war started in 1957 when the VC, poorly equipped and small in number, began successfully attacking Government outpost, conducting political kidnappings and murders.

208 **No USAF pilot has ever flown in tactical missions except in the role of tactical instructor.**—*Official U.S. response to press questions about tactical use of American instructors, South Vietnam, December 1962.*[930]

This was the official response to be given to press queries on the operation of the 4400th CCTS. In December, 1962, U.S. Air Force personnel arrived in South Vietnam under the code name Farm Gate, tasked with the training and support of the South Vietnamese Air Force. The actual unit designation was the 4400th Combat Crew Training Squadron. The squadron was equipped with T-28, B-26, and SC-47 aircraft and the crews to operate and maintain them. In actuality, the squadron's prime mission was to support the South Vietnamese military against the communist force. Training of the Vietnamese was secondary.

209 **[Napalm] really puts the fear of God into the Vietcong. And that is what counts.**—*General Paul Harkins, Commander, Military Assistance and Advisory Group, Vietnam, 1962.*[324]

1963

Older men declare war. But it is the youth that must fight and die.
—Herbert Hoover, 1944

210 **Shoot that rotten, cowardly son of a bitch right now and move out.**—*Lt.Col. John Paul Vann, Senior Adviser to the 7th ARVN Infantry Division, speaking to Captain Robert Mays, 2 January 1963.*[887]

During the battle of Ap Bac, an ARVN company was pinned down outside the village. An ARVN APC company involved in the battle, but not engaged, was ordered to go to the assistance of the pinned company. The ARVN APC commander refused to go. Vann was above the battle in a spotter plane attempting to direct the ARVN. Mays, the American adviser to the ARVN APC company, eventually convinced the ARVN commander to move.

211 **We are winning, this we know.... General Harkins tells us so.... In the delta, things are rough.... In the mountains, mighty tough.... But we're winning, this we know.... General Harkins tells us so.... If you doubt that this is true, McNamara says so too.**—*Anonymously written little song, reportedly sung by some skeptical journalists in Saigon, 1963.*[192]

This was sung to the tune of "Twinkle, Twinkle, Little Star," often after the daily 5 P.M. MACV briefing, when the journalists gathered at the bar of the hotel Continental or Caravelle.

212 **A miserable fucking performance, just like it always is.**—*Col. John Paul Vann, Senior Advisor, 7th ARVN Infantry Division, comments to the press, 1963.*[374]

Vann was commenting on the ARVN's terrible combat performance at the battle of Ap Bac, where they out-numbered the VC five to one. Yet even with armor, artillery and American helicopter support, they were not able to crush the VC. The ARVN suffered 172 casualties compared to 18 VC KIA. Five helicopters were shot down and the VC unit was allowed to escape.

213 **They were brave men. They gave a good account of themselves today.**—*Lt.Col. John Paul Vann, Senior Adviser to the 7th ARVN Infantry Division, commenting to correspondents, 2 January 1963.*[887]

Vann was complimenting the VC who fought at the battle of Ap Bac. It was the first battle in which the VC stood their ground against ARVN forces. 2,000 ARVN were engaged and fought to a standstill by 350-400 Main Force VC. The VC held the poorly led, well equipped and supported ARVN at bay for an entire day, then withdrew without incident that night.

214 **They chose to reinforce defeat.**—*Lt.Col. John Paul Vann, Senior Adviser to the 7th ARVN Infantry Division, commenting on the battle of Ap Bac, January 1963.*[887]

Near the village of Ap Bac, the VC were surrounded on three sides by ARVN forces. The Americans advised the 7th ARVN to deploy a battalion of ARVN paratroopers into the battle to close off the VC escape route. The ARVN commander refused. He instead inserted the paratroopers behind the existing ARVN line. This allowed the VC to escape. More than 2,000 ARVN attempted to defeat a VC force numbering between 350 to 400 men. The result was the largest defeat for the ARVN to date. The enemy suffered 18 KIA, the ARVN lost 63 KIA and 109 WIA. American losses were 3 KIA, 8 WIA.

215 **A long road tests a horse's strength, and a long march proves a man's heart.**—*Mao Tse-tung, Chairman, People's Republic of China, directing the Vietnamese, 1963.*[374]

Mao suggested that Hanoi wage a protracted war against South Vietnam and the Americans, wearing them down until they surrendered.

216 **There is no question, that in the military field in the past year we have established what I would call the human and materiel infrastructure which can be the basis for a successful military operation.**—*Excerpted from a secret report by a JCS fact finding team, January 1963.*[887]

The Joint Chiefs of Staff's team consisted of six generals and an admiral and was tasked with the mission of determining whether America was winning or losing in Vietnam. The results of the investigation backed General Harkins's position that "we" were winning in Vietnam. The team did not consider the negative reports on ARVN ineffectiveness and disorganization sufficient to change the official view that the ARVN and the GVN were progressing to a point of self-sufficiency and would be able to overcome the communist threat.

217 **It is better to stand and die than run and be slaughtered.**—*Unidentified Vietcong commander, in his after-action report, January 1963.*[886]

The VC commanded a main force VC battalion that was located at the village of Ap Bac. The ARVNs deployed 2,000 soldiers against the 350-400 man VC force in the ville. After a day's fighting the VC suffered 18 killed, while the ARVN had 172 casualties, and were unable to force the VC from the ville. During the night the VC withdrew from the ville. It was a humiliating defeat for the ARVN, yet Diem, MACV, and Washington proclaimed a SVN victory. The VC, in large numbers, for the first time in the war stood their ground and took on the ARVN who were supported by American helicopters.

218 **If it were not for General Harkins things would not be in the state we found them by any manner or means. It would be pretty deplorable. His own attitude and leadership have permeated the whole command...**—*Excerpted from a secret report by a JCS fact finding team, January 1963.*[887]

The Joint Chiefs of Staff's team consisted of six generals and an admiral and was tasked with the mission of determining whether America was winning or losing in Vietnam. The results of the investigation backed General Harkins's position that "we" were winning in Vietnam. The team did not consider the negative reports on ARVN ineffectiveness and disorganization sufficient to change the official view that the ARVN and the GVN were progressing to a point of self-sufficiency and would be able to overcome the communist threat.

219 **The spear point of aggression has been blunted in South Vietnam.** *President John F. Kennedy, comments on progress in Vietnam, January 1963.*[218]

220 **It is not prudent to corner the rat.**—*General Huynh Van Cao, ARVN IV Corp commander, January 1963.*[713]

Cao's response to questions of his selection of a drop zone during the Battle of Ap Bac. Elements of the 7th ARVN Infantry Division had boxed in a Main Force VC battalion at Ap Bac. The enemy was well dug in and fought back, choosing not to retreat. The ARVNs were in blocking positions on the north, south, and west of Ap Bac. Cao air dropped a battalion of ARVN airborne troops into the battle. The 7th Division's American adviser, Lt.Col. John Paul Vann requested that the airborne battalion be dropped east of Ap Bac to completely surround the enemy force. Cao had the battalion dropped to the west, allowing the enemy to escape. Cao later explained that allowing the enemy to escape reduced ARVN casualties.

221 **The conclusion seems inescapable that the Viet Cong could continue the war effort at the present level, or perhaps increase it, even if the infiltration routes were completely closed.**—*Roger Hilsman, Assistant Secretary of State, in a memorandum to President Kennedy, 25 January 1963.*[87]

Hilsman argued for increased U.S. counterinsurgency efforts against the communists to curtail their growth until they could be conquered by the ARVN.

222 **I consider it a victory. We took the objective [Ap Bac].**—*General Paul Harkins, Commander, Military Assistance and Advisory Group, Vietnam, comments to the press, January 1963.*[887]

During the battle of Ap Bac, 350-400 VC held off 2,000 ARVN troops, pinning them in place around the village of Ap Bac. During the night following the battle the VC withdrew, suffering 18 KIA. The ARVN suffered 63 KIA, 109 WIA, 3 Americans were KIA and 8 WIA. The U.S. employed 15 helicopters to assist the ARVN, of these 5 were destroyed and 9 damaged. John Paul Vann, the American senior adviser to the ARVN, characterized the ARVN conduct as "a miserable damn performance." The ARVN claimed the battle as a victory because they occupied the village after the VC withdrew. Harkins chose to sustain the ARVN version of the battle.

223 **[The United States and Vietnam are] probably winning, but the war will probably last longer than we would like and cost more in terms of both lives and money than we had anticipated.**—*Excerpt from the Hilsman-Forrestal Report, presented to President Kennedy, February 1963.*[324]

Michael Forrestal was a Kennedy adviser. He and Roger Hilsman investigated the situation in Vietnam and reported to the President.

224 **The people think that this [issuing of ID cards] is the finest thing since canned beer because it indicates to them that the government loves them, has an interest in them.... They don't regard this as harassment or as a means of keeping tabs on them, which, of course, it is; but here you are.**—*Unidentified U.S. Army general, during a meeting in Hawaii, January 1963.*[887]

The general was one of six sent to South Vietnam by the Joint Chiefs of Staff to evaluate the war effort. The GVN issued the South Vietnamese ID cards as a means of identifying the people and for screening out the enemy. It was a common practice for enemy agents to have forged cards and was not uncommon for enemy agents to have valid government issued ID cards as well.

225 **The unfortunate aftermath of reports of the fight at Ap Bac on 2 January 1963 is a prime instance of the harm being done to the war effort [by the resident correspondents]. Press members ... insist that the stories were derived from United States sources. The latter is true, but only to the extent that the stories were based on ill-considered statements made at**

a time of high excitement and frustrations by a few American officers.—*Excerpted from a secret report by JCS fact finding team, January 1963.*[887]

The battle of Ap Bac was the largest failure by South Vietnamese forces to date. The American advisers accompanying the ARVN during the battle wrote detailed After Action reports indicating a high degree of ARVN ineffectiveness, disorganization, and cowardice. The Joint Chiefs of Staff's team declined to validate the findings of the After Action reports, instead blaming the Press for exaggerated stories about the battle.

226 **The only thing wrong with what he wrote is that all of it is true.**—*Colonel James Winterbottom, U.S. Air Force, MAAGV intelligence chief, during a meeting with General Harkins, February 1963.*[887]

On 8 February 1963 Lt. Col. John Paul Vann submitted a detail report to his commander and the MAAGV commander, General Harkins. The report indicated 45 locations where the VC were located in significant numbers in the IV Corps area. The report also indicated that the ARVN division commander was aware of the locations and went to great lengths to avoid them. Repeated attempts by the division's American adviser to get the South Vietnamese division commander to attack any of the enemy locations failed. Harkins sent an intelligence team, headed by Winterbottom, to try to invalidate Vann's report. Winterbottom validated the report. Harkins refused to act upon the enemy locations or the ARVN commander.

227 **We must ensure that the assault from the inside, and which is manipulated from the North, is ended.**—*President John F. Kennedy, public position on Vietnam, 1963.*[85]

228 **We believe that Communist progress has been blunted and that the situation is improving.... Improvements which have occurred during the past year now indicate that the Viet Cong can be contained militarily and that further progress can be made in expanding the area of government control and in creating greater security in the countryside.**—*An excerpt from National Intelligence Estimate, 25 February 1963.*[237]

This was the evaluation of the situation in South Vietnam as composed by the U.S. Intelligence Board. This optimistic outlook was instrumental in the Kennedy Administration's formulation of policy in Vietnam.

229 **Barring greatly increased resupply and reinforcement of the Viet Cong by infiltration, the military phase of the war can be virtually won in 1963.**—*An excerpt from a Defense Intelligence Agency summary, 1963.*[223]

230 **In East Asia it was to be expected that the soldier will kick the peasant as he goes by.**—*General Victor Krulak, U.S. Marine Corps, supporting member of the JCS, during a meeting, 8 March 1963.*[197]

Krulak's response was to reported incidents of ARVN's predatory behavior against the rural Vietnamese population. The reports were publicized by the media and found in some of the intelligence reports transmitted to Washington.

231 **Charges of [ARVN] rape, pillage, and outright brutality are made by Radio Hanoi. We should not parlay them.**—*Admiral Harry Felt, U.S. Navy, Commander-in-Chief Pacific, in a cable to DIA, 12 March 1963.*[196]

Admiral Felt took exception to reports critical of ARVN actions, especially those detailing predatory acts against the rural population. Such reports were turning up as raw data in the National Intelligence Estimate drafts and in public press reports.

232 **Get out of my way, I'd rather do it myself!**—*Unidentified American adviser to the South Vietnamese, 1963.*[57]

An attitude held by many American advisers who worked with the Vietnamese. Many were frustrated by the Vietnamese lack of initiative, inability to accomplish task in a timely direct (Western) manner; only to meet delays, procrastination, obfuscation, and the perceived Asian infinite patience.

233 **There is a serious lack of firm and aggressive leadership at all levels of [ARVN] command.**—*General Earle Wheeler, Army Chief of Staff, from memorandum of meeting, 27 March 1963.*[219]

234 **This is a political war and it calls for discrimination in killing. The best weapon for killing would be a knife, but I'm afraid we can't do it that way. The worst is an airplane. The next worst is artillery. Barring a knife, the best is a rifle — you know who you are killing.**—*One of Lt.Col. John Paul Vann's maxims on guerrilla warfare, 1963.*[887]

235 **If I tried to pull out completely now from Vietnam, we would have another Joe McCarthy red scare on our hands.**—*President John Kennedy, speaking to Mike Mansfield, 1963.*[316]

It is speculated that by mid 1963 Kennedy realized America's poor position in South Vietnam. Militarily the South Vietnamese were not able to resist the Viet Cong guerrillas, the Diem regime was unpopular and isolated from the people, and there was no compelling interest to rouse the American people in defense of Vietnam.

236 **The corner has definitely been turned toward victory in South Vietnam and Defense officials are hopeful that the 12,000 man U.S. force in Vietnam could be reduced in one to three years.**—*Unidentified Pentagon spokesman, during a press release, 6 May 1963.*[217]

237 **If Diem does not take prompt and effective steps to reestablish Buddhist confidence in him we will have to reexamine our entire relationship with his regime.**—*Frederick Nolting, U.S. Ambassador to South Vietnam, in a letter to the State Department, 23 May 1963.*[230]

There were student riots and Buddhist demonstrations against the repressive tactics of the Diem regime. The U.S. did not want to be seen as supporting a regime which raided Buddhist pagodas, beat and tortured priests and students, and encouraged its people to acts of self-immolation in protest of government sponsored discrimination and abuse.

238 **If the Buddhists wish to have another barbecue, I will be glad to supply the gasoline and a match.**—*Madame Ngo Dinh Nhu, sister-in-law of President Ngo Dinh Diem, in comments made during a state dinner, Saigon, June 1963.*[887]

Mme. Nhu was referring to the self-immolation of the Buddhist monk, Quang Duc, 11 June 1963. Quang Duc was protesting the discrimination and oppression suffered by the Buddhist under the Diem regime. Several other protest immolations followed.

239 **The Communists will defeat us, not by virtue of their strength, but because of our weakness. They will win by default.**—*Ngo Dinh Nhu, personal and political advisor to President Diem, 1963.*[374]

240 **I shall clap my hands at another [Buddhist] suicide.**—*Madame Ngo Dinh Nhu, sister-in-law of President Ngo Dinh Diem, during a press interview, Saigon, June 1963.*[887]

Mme. Nhu was referring to the self-immolation of Buddhist monks protesting discrimination and oppressive treatment of Buddhists under the Diem regime. Quang Duc was the first of the Buddhist priests and nuns to commit public suicide in protest of Diem.

241 **I am an optimist, and I am not going to allow my staff to be pessimistic.**—*General Paul D. Harkins, former ComUSMACV, comments to the press, 1963.*[949]

In the early sixties Harkins was a strong supporter of the Diem regime and tried to build the South Vietnamese military into a force that could counter the communist insurgency of the Vietcong. Many on his staff believed the ARVN, alone, were not equal to the task of stopping the Vietcong, who were supported and directed by North Vietnam.

242 **Today we are committed to a world-wide struggle to promote and protect the rights of all who wish to be free. And when Americans are sent to Vietnam or West Berlin we do not ask for whites only.**—*President John F. Kennedy, in a speech, 11 June 1963.*[782]

243 **Buddhist barbecues.... Let them burn, and we shall clap our hands.**—*Madame Nhu, President Diem's sister-in-law, during an interview, June 1963.*[374]

Several Buddhist monks immolated themselves in demonstration against the Diem regime's religious persecution. Diem and his security forces used force against several Buddhist demonstrations, claiming the demonstrations were communist-inspired.

244 **I would clap my hands at seeing another monk barbecue show.**—*Tran Le Xuan Nhu, Madame Nhu, wife of Ngo Dinh Nhu, commenting to reporters during Buddhist demonstrations, 1963.*[629]

Madame Nhu, commenting on Buddhist self-immolations in protest of the Diem regime. Buddhist and students demonstrated against Diems' oppressive and abusive policies toward those practicing the Buddhist religion. The population of South Vietnam was more than 90 percent Buddhist.

245 **We had also ... been one of the bright shining lies.**—*Lt.Col. John Paul Vann, U.S. Army, during an interview with an Army historian, July 1963.*[887]

Vann was referring to the support he had initially given to MAAGV's claims of progress in the war against the VC. Vann was the senior adviser to the 7th ARVN Division. Initially he was effective in maneuvering the ARVN division commander to make gains against the VC. But as the ARVN commander became more prominent in Saigon's eyes, he became more reluctant to pursue the enemy. Vann had praised the ARVN commander and backed up MAAGV's claims of progress in the war for so long, that when he finally did speak out against the cowardice, ineffectiveness and poor leadership of the ARVN he had great difficulty in getting the higher echelons of the U.S. government to listen.

246 **[American newsman are] worse than Communists.**—*Madame Ngo Dinh Nhu, Sister-in-law of President Diem, 1963.*[194] Mme. Nhu complained about the rough treatment her husband (Ngo Dinh Nhu) and brother-in-law (Ngo Dinh Diem), were suffering at the hands of the American press. The press pointed out problems with the Diem regime regarding the ARVN's handling of the war against the communists, graft and corruption within the regime, and the hostilities between the GVN and the rural population.

247 **The shooting part of the war is moving to a climax.**—*General Victor Krulak, supporting member of the JCS, in a report to the JCS, July 1963.*[887]

Krulak's report discussed the situation in Vietnam. He had gathered the information while on a fact finding mission to Vietnam in July 1963.

248 **General Harkins considers that a reduction of 1,000 men could be accomplished now, without affecting adversely the conduct of the war.**—*General Victor Krulak, supporting member of the JCS, in a report to the JCS, July 1963.*[887]

Krulak's report discussed the situation in Vietnam. He had gathered the information while on a fact finding mission to Vietnam in July 1963. Harkins overly optimistic appraisal of the situation in Vietnam was passed on to the Joint Chiefs of Staff through Krulak.

249 **I believe we can win in Viet-Nam.**—*Roger Hilsman, Assistant Secretary of State, 1963.*[87]

Hilsman advised Kennedy to increase the U.S. counterinsurgency effort in Vietnam to counter the communists. He advised against the introduction of American combat forces into South Vietnam.

250 **[The U.S. will work with the GVN] to deny this country to Communism and to suppress the externally stimulated and supported insurgency of the Viet Cong as promptly as possible.**—*Excerpt from a White House press release, 1963.*[87]

251 **There is not one chance in a hundred for victory [over the Communists with my daughter and her husband and brother-in-law in power].**—*Tran Van Chuong, South Vietnamese Ambassador to the United States, speaking to the press, August 1963.*[887]

Tran Van Chuong resigned in protest over the brutal attacks by GVN security forces against Buddhists. The Buddhists were protesting the discriminatory and repressive treatment at the hands of the Saigon regime.

252 **Too damn many Americans in this country are sleeping with Vietnamese women. It's bad for our image. The Vietnamese don't like it.**—*Lt.Col. John Paul Vann, commenting to correspondent, 1963.*[887]

Vann was speaking to correspondent David Halberstam. It should be noted that Vann had several Vietnamese mistresses and took a Vietnamese "wife" during his final years in Vietnam.

253 **[The war against the Communist cannot be prosecuted effectively] unless a greater effort is made by the [Diem] government to win popular support.**—*President John F. Kennedy, from a TV interview, August 1963.*[374]

At this point, Kennedy had authorized Ambassador Lodge to press Diem for change and removal of his chief adviser, Nhu. Lodge had the authority to cut off U.S. aid if Diem did not comply. The cutoff of aid would be perceived as a signal of U.S. support to ARVN generals plotting a coup against Diem. Diem's administration had become increasingly totalitarian and he was not effectively prosecuting the war against the communist insurgents.

254 **[American policy] appears [to] be throwing away bird in hand before we have adequately identified birds in bush, or songs they may sing.**—*William Colby, Chief, CIA Far East Division, in a cable to Saigon, 25 August 1963.*[195]

Colby was referring to tentative Administration plans to back a group of Vietnamese generals who advocated a change in the GVN. His comment indicated a lack of knowledge as to exactly what the generals proposed for the country, if they were successful.

255 **The US must give wholehearted support to the prosecution of the war against the Viet Cong terrorists, and continue assistance to any government in South Vietnam which shows itself capable of sustaining this effort.**—*Michael Forrestal, adviser to President Kennedy, in a report to the President, 27 August 1963.*[87]

256 **I don't agree with those who say we should withdraw [from Vietnam]. That would be a great mistake. We must be patient. We must persist.**—*President John F. Kennedy, during a TV interview, August 1963.*[374]

Some in Kennedy's administration argued that Vietnam was of no strategic value to the U.S.

257 **[The question of U.S. withdrawal from SVN] hovered for a moment, then died away, a hopelessly alien thought in a field of unexamined assumptions and entrenched convictions.**—*Arthur Schlesinger, Jr., White House aide and historian, 1963.*[374]

During a White House strategy meeting in late August, 1963, Robert Kennedy posed the question that if there was doubt that any Saigon government could defeat the communist insurgents then perhaps it was a good time to consider withdrawing from Vietnam completely.

258 **The oppressed peoples and nations must not pin their hopes for liberation on the "sensibleness" of imperialism and its lackeys. They will only triumph by strengthening their unity and persevering in their struggle.**—*Mao Tse-tung, Chairman, People's Republic of China, statement, 29 August 1963.*[495]

Mao advocated the defeat of "U.S. aggressors and all their lackeys." Red China backed North Vietnam with arms, materials, advisors and labor assistance.

259 **We are now launched on a course from which there is no respectable turning back: the overthrow of the Diem government.... There is no turning back because there is no possibility ... that the war can be won under a Diem administration.**—*Henry Cabot Lodge, U.S. Ambassador to South Vietnam, in a cable to Washington, 29 August 1963.*[248]

Lodge sent the cable requesting a decision by Kennedy whether the U.S. would or would not back a Vietnamese coup against Diem. Lodge requested that U.S. aid to Diem be suspended as a signal to the generals plotting the coup that their efforts would not be interfered with by the U.S.

260 **We will not pull out ... until the war is won.**—*Dean Rusk, Secretary of State, during a NSA meeting, 31 August 1963.*[374]

There was a suggestion at the meeting that the U.S. might consider pulling out of South Vietnam due to the unstable political and military situation there, and the inability of the U.S. to foster a change in the Diem regime.

261 **There is neither the will nor the organization among the generals to accomplish anything.**—*Henry Cabot Lodge, Ambassador to South Vietnam, in a cable to Washington, 31 August 1963.*[317]

Lodge was referring to a planned coup against Diem by a group of Vietnamese generals. Washington acknowledged the generals, but neither supported nor discouraged their plan — at the time.

262 **We should stop playing cops and robbers [and] go about winning the war.**—*Vice President Lyndon Johnson, during a NSA meeting, 31 August 1963.*[374]

263 **In the final analysis, it is their war. They are the ones who have to win it or lose it. We can help them, we can give them equipment, we can send our men out there as advisers, but they have to win it, the people of Vietnam.**—*President John F. Kennedy, during a news interview with Walter Cronkite, September 1963.*[83]

264 **Victory [in Vietnam] is doubtful if not impossible.**—*John McCone, Director, Central Intelligence, during a meeting with President Kennedy, 10 September 1963.*[212]

In 1962 McCone was pessimistic about reported U.S./GVN progress in Vietnam, but based on the character of those giving optimistic reports of progress, he changed his opinion to be more optimistic. By mid-1963, the pessimism had returned based on fresh field reports from Vietnam indicating the Diem regime was not supported by the people and the SVN military were ineffective and inept at combating the VC.

265 **In some ways I think the Vietnamese people and ourselves agree; we want the war to be won, the Communists contained, and the Americans to go home.**—*President John Kennedy, during a press conference, 12 September 1963.*[876]

266 **From the President on down everybody is determined to support you and the country team in winning the war against the Viet Cong ... there are no quitters here.**—*Averell Harriman, Ambassador at large and adviser to President Kennedy, in a cable to Ambassador Henry Cabot Lodge, 14 September 1963.*[87]

The Kennedy administration believed the war against the communists could not be won as long as the Diem brothers were in power. The Diem regime was not focused on the war against the communists, but on maintaining control over the South Vietnamese populace. Kennedy wanted to win the war against the communists and stop the spread of communism throughout Southeast Asia.

267 **We are not there [in Vietnam] to see a war lost, and we will follow the policy ... of advancing those causes and issues which help win the war.**—*President John Kennedy, during a press conference, 12 September 1963.*[876]

Kennedy's outlined American policy in Vietnam was first and foremost the winning the war against the communists and stopping the spread of communism in Southeast Asia.

268 **Things were going well in Vietnam militarily, but that Ho Chi Minh was fighting the war for peanuts and if we ever expected to win that affair out there, we had to make him bleed a little bit.**—*General Earle Wheeler, Chairman, Joint Chiefs of Staff, in a report to President Kennedy, 1963.*[86]

The reports to Kennedy indicate success by American advisers in preparing the South Vietnamese to overcome the VC, but the outside influence from Hanoi posed a threat to South Vietnam.

269 **China is so large, looms so high just beyond the frontier, that if South Vietnam went, it would not only give them an improved geographic position for a guerrilla assault on Malaya, but would also give the impression that the wave of the future in Southeast Asia was China and the Communists.**—*President John Kennedy, during an interview for NBC, September 1963.*[202]

Kennedy was responding to the question posed by Chet Huntley whether he believed in the domino theory. The components of the domino theory went back to the Truman administration, but it was the Eisenhower administration that gave the theory a name, the "Domino Theory." The theory predicted the fall of Southeast Asian countries to communism, if SVN were allowed to fall to the communists. In some versions of the theory, countries that were subject to fall included Cambodia, Laos, Thailand, Burma, Malaya, and Indonesia. Others threatened would be the Philippines, New Zealand, Australia, Formosa, and finally Japan.

270 **The way to confound the press is to win the war.**—*President John F. Kennedy, to Ambassador Henry Cabot Lodge, 17 September 1963.*[87]

Kennedy's goal in Vietnam was to win the war against the communists in South Vietnam and stop the spread of communism in Southeast Asia. Press reports at the time were indicating the ARVN were not winning the war against the VC and the Diem regime was so oppressive that it did not have the support of the majority of the Vietnamese people.

271 **[The] heart of the Army is not in the war.**—*General Duong Van Minh, military advisor to Ngo Dinh Diem, as quoted in a cable to President Kennedy, 19 September 1963.*[887]

Big Minh, as he was called, was the leader of a military plot to overthrow the Diem government. In a cable to the President, Henry Cabot Lodge explained Minh's views of the deteriorating situation in Vietnam. The South Vietnam Army was unable to focus on the war against the communists because of the internal turmoil within the government.

272 **You two did visit the same country, didn't you?**—*President John F. Kennedy, commenting on conflicting reports from his advisers, September 1963.*[324]

General Victor Krulak and Joseph Mendenhall reported to Kennedy on their fact finding visit to South Vietnam. Krulak was upbeat about progress in the shooting war and backed Diem. Mendenhall believed the country was on the verge of collapse and possible civil war with Diem and Nhu at the heart of the problems.

273 **The constant pressure of the reportorial crusade against the government [of South Vietnam] has also helped mightily to transform Diem from a courageous, quite viable national leader into a man afflicted with a galloping persecution mania, seeing plots around every corner, and therefore misjudging everything.**—*Joseph Alsop, newspaper columnist, writing in his column, 1963.*[887]

Alsop was speaking against the younger reporters who were filing stories out of Saigon that were critical of the Diem regime. At the time, Alsop accepted the reports of progress and brightness detailed by MAAGV.

274 **Viet-Nam is not a thoroughly strong police state ... because, unlike Hitler's Germany, it is not efficient and is thus unable to suppress the large and well-organized underground opponent strongly and ever-freshly motivated by vigorous hatred.**—*Henry Cabot Lodge, U.S. Ambassador to South Vietnam, in a message to President Kennedy, October 1963.*[87]

275 **[The United States does not] wish to stimulate a coup, it would not thwart a change of government or deny economic and military assistance to a new regime if it appeared capable of increasing [the] effectiveness of the military effort, ensuring popular support to win [the] war and improving working relations with the U.S.**—*CIA instructions to Henry Cabot Lodge, October 1963.*[317]

In the interest of secrecy, communications between the U.S. Embassy in South Vietnam and the Administration in Washington regarding the coup against Diem were transmitted through the CIA. Lodge was instructed to inform the coup generals that although the U.S. would not actively support their coup, it also would not interfere.

276 **Coups, like eggs, must be smashed before they are hatched.**—*Ngo Dinh Nhu, Diem's chief political adviser, in comments to General Ton That Dinh, October 1963.*[374]

Nhu told Dinh that he knew of the generals' plan to overthrow Diem and he had a preemptive coup plan of his own which would increase his own power within the Diem regime. Dinh was expected to control local Army forces in Saigon when Nhu activated his preemptive plan.

277 **All planning will be directed towards preparing RVN (Republic of Vietnam) forces for the withdrawal of all U.S. special assistance units and personnel by the end of calendar year 1965.**—*President John Kennedy in a memorandum to the Joint Chiefs of Staff, 4 October 1963.*[5]

Kennedy issued the memo to the JCS in preparation of a possible wind-down of the U.S. commitment in South Vietnam. He also planned to withdraw all U.S. advisory and support personnel by the end of 1965. These historical documents were declassified December 1997.

278 **Execute the plan to withdraw 1,000 U.S. military personnel by the end of 1963.**—*President John Kennedy in a memorandum to the Joint Chiefs of Staff, 4 October 1963.*[5]

Kennedy issued the memo to the JCS in preparation of a possible wind-down of the U.S. commitment in South Vietnam. He also planned to withdraw all U.S. advisory and support personnel by the end of 1965. These historical documents were declassified December 1997.

279 **[Regarding the Vietcong,] the Americans have done everything to push me into their arms.**—*Ngo Dinh Nhu, Diem's chief political adviser, speaking to the press, October 1963.*[374]

Nhu had spread rumors that he was conducting secret talks with the Vietcong, hinting of a coalition between the Saigon government and the VC, which would expel the U.S. from South Vietnam.

280 **[The Saigon regime] has become unwittingly the greatest asset to the Communists.**—*Tran Van Chuong, former South Vietnam Ambassador to the U.S., speaking to the press, October 1963.*[374]

Tran Van Chuong was the father of Madame Nhu.

281 **The restrictive US press policy in Vietnam ... unquestionably contributed to the lack of information about conditions in Vietnam which created an international crisis. Instead of hiding the facts from the American public, the State Department should have done everything possible to expose the true situation to full view.**—*Excerpted from a House Subcommittee report, 10 October 1963.*[202]

From the findings of the House Subcommittee on Foreign Operations and Government Information. According to testimony American journalists in Vietnam were "encouraged" to report stories supporting the Diem regime and the progress of the U.S. effort in South Vietnam. Negative reports, or those critical of Diem, were severely frowned upon and often labeled as irresponsible, speculative, or flatly untrue.

282 **We have not seen a successor government in the wings that we could say positively would be an improvement over Diem ... we must proceed cautiously, otherwise a situation might flare up which might result in something of a civil war, and the Communists would come out the victor merely by sitting on the sidelines.**—*John McCone, Director, Central Intelligence, during Senate testimony, 10 October 1963.*[220]

McCone argued for caution in SVN regarding the replacement of Diem. The CIA believed there were currently no political groups or individuals capable of uniting the country and leading the war against the communists. McCone predicted political turmoil if Diem were deposed without someone waiting in the wings to take firm control of the GVN.

283 **[Buddhist self-immolations] were merely staged murders for the sake of publicity.**—*Madame Ngo Dinh Nhu, sister-in-law of President Ngo Dinh Diem, to the press, 1963.*[388]

Madame Nhu was outspoken against the Buddhists and became increasingly abusive of Americans and American support to South Vietnam.

284 **Rightly or wrongly we have backed Diem for eight long, hard years. To me it seems incongruous now to get him down, kick him around, and get rid of him. The United States has been his mother superior and father confessor since he's been in office and he leaned on us heavily.**—*General Paul Harkins, Commander, Military Assistance Command, Vietnam, in a message to the Pentagon, October 1963.*[374]

Harkins was a supporter of Diem and believed he should get a better deal than the planned Vietnamese military coup. The U.S. reportedly did not actively support nor interfere with the coup. Diem was warned repeatedly by U.S. officials to change his ways and disassociate himself from Nhu.

285 **[Buddhist monks are] hooligans in robes.**—*Madame Nhu, wife of Ngo Dinh Nhu, speaking to the American press, October 1963.*[374]

Madame Nhu's description of dissident Buddhist monks.

286 **My general view is that the United States is trying to bring this medieval country into the twentieth century...**—*Henry Cabot Lodge, U.S. Ambassador to South Vietnam, in a cable to President John Kennedy, October 1963.*[374]

287 **If you should conclude that there is not clearly a high prospect of success, you should communicate this doubt to the generals in a way calculated to persuade them to desist at least until chances are better.... But once a coup under responsible leadership has begun ... it is in the interest of the U.S. government that it should succeed.**—*President John Kennedy's instructions to U.S. Ambassador Henry Cabot Lodge, October 1963.*[374]

Just prior to the coup against Diem the Kennedy administration had doubts about the possibility of the coup's success. Kennedy left it to Lodge to decide the chances of success and whether the U.S. should interfere or remain silent.

288 **Begin a complete and very profound review of how we got into this country, what we thought we were doing, and what we now think we can do ... I even want to think about whether or not we should be there.**—*President John F. Kennedy to Michael Forrestal, November 1963.*[1027]

Kennedy gave Forrestal the task of reviewing the U.S. position and policy in Vietnam following the coup that toppled the Diem government. Kennedy was assassinated before the report was completed.

289 **[Some American officers in Vietnam were acting like] little soldiers of fortune.**—*Madame Ngo Dinh Nhu, sister-in-law of President Ngo Dinh Diem, to the press, 1963.*[388]

When confronted by U.S. Ambassador Henry Cabot Lodge, she claimed she was misquoted by the American press on this one.

290 **It is entirely possible that the Diem government has alienated an important segment in the population; unless the government and population can work together in a unified effort to defeat the Viet Cong, the Communists won't be defeated.**—*Robert McNamara, Secretary of Defense, speaking to reporters, October 1963.*[388]

McNamara had just completed a fact finding tour of South Vietnam and was referring to South Vietnam's predominately Buddhist population.

291 **It seems at least an even bet that the next government would not bungle and fumble as the present one has.**—*Henry Cabot Lodge, in a cable to President John Kennedy, 25 October 1963.*[374]

The Kennedy administration was worried that if the Diem coup failed, the blame for the coup would be laid at the U.S. doorstep, even though the U.S. could plausibly deny having either encouraged or interfered with the coup attempt. Lodge was stating his belief that the coup was worth the risk in an effort to change the GVN to one more responsive to the people of South Vietnam and able to fight the communist insurgents.

292 **MACV has no info from advisory rpt [repeat] advisory personnel which could be interpreted as clear evidence of an impending coup.**—*General Paul Harkins, ComUSMACV, in a cable to Washington, 31 October 63.*[195]

Harkins's cable was sent to Washington, ten hours before the coup against Diem started.

293 **We do not find that the presently revealed plans [to overthrow Diem] give a clear prospect of quick results.**—*McGeorge Bundy, National Security Adviser, in a cable to Ambassador Lodge, 29 October 1963.*[374]

During a NSA meeting the President and several of his advisers began to have second thoughts about the planned coup by Vietnamese generals. In a message to Lodge, President Kennedy sought to have the coup attempt postponed.

294 **Watching a police state in action, particularly an American-financed one, is a sad experience.**—*David Halberstam, correspondent for the Times, in a letter to John Paul Vann, 29 October 1963.*[887]

Halberstam was working in Saigon, reporting on the police and military action against the Buddhists and student protesters. Diem's security police, personal guards, and the general military were all trained, and in the main, financed by the U.S.

295 **No coup can erupt without American incitement and backing.**—*Madame Ngo Dinh Nhu, sister-in-law of the assassinated President of South Vietnam, speaking to the press, 1 November 1963.*[509]

Mme. Nhu blamed the U.S. for the coup and told reporters it was not the first time the U.S. had tried to overthrow the Diem regime.

296 **I cannot stay in a country with people who have stabbed my government ... all the devils of hell are against us ... but we shall triumph.**—*Madame Ngo Dinh Nhu, sister-in-law of the assassinated President of South Vietnam, speaking to the press, 1 November 1963.*[509]

Mme. Nhu was responding to a press question whether she would seek political asylum in the U.S. She was visiting the U.S. and staying in Beverly Hills during the coup which resulted in the assassination of her husband Ngo Dinh Nhu and his brother, the President of South Vietnam, Ngo Dinh Diem.

297 **Whatever happened to my family will be an indelible stigma against the United States.**—*Madame Ngo Dinh Nhu, sister-in-law of the assassinated President of South Vietnam, speaking to the press, 1 November 1963.*[509]

Mme. Nhu was responding to reports of the coup against President Diem and her husband Ngo Dinh Nhu. Initial reports from Saigon indicated Diem and Nhu had committed suicide while in custody of the new government.

298 **I've saved you motherfuckers many times, but not now, you bastards. You shits are finished. It's all over.**—*General Ton That Dinh, Commander, Saigon Regional Forces, responding to a request for help from President Ngo Dinh Diem, 2 November 1963.*[374]

This was Dinh's response to Diem's request for help during the coup. Diem was in hiding and the general had been hand-picked by Diem and Nhu to control ARVN units in Saigon, in support of Diem. The general was actually a co-conspirator in the coup that deposed Diem.

299 **Stay where you are. If there are any suspicious troop movements, the air force will bomb you.**—*Nguyen Cao Ky, South Vietnamese Air Force officer, in a note dropped to General Huyuh Van Cao, during the November 1963 coup.*[629]

Cao was the commander of ARVN troops in the Mekong Delta, and was loyal to the Diem regime. The note was dropped on his headquarters, by plane, cautioning him not to move his troops to Saigon in support of Diem. His troops did not move.

300 **If really my family has been treacherously killed with either the official or unofficial blessing of the American government, I can predict to you all that the story in Vietnam is only at the beginning.**—*Madame Ngo Dinh Nhu, sister-in-law of the assassinated President of South Vietnam, speaking to the press, 2 November 1963.*[509]

Initial reports from the military junta in Saigon indicated President Diem and his brother Ngo Dinh Nhu had committed suicide while in custody. Mme. Nhu rejected this because Diem and Nhu were devout Catholics and suicide was not an option. A later indicator throwing doubt on the suicide theory was the fact that Diem and Nhu had each been shot and stabbed several times.

301 **I can categorically state that the United States government was not in any way involved in this coup attempt.**—*Richard I. Phillips, U.S. State Department press officer, press release, 3 November 1963.*[665]

302 **Any crimes against the Nhu family cannot be hidden under the label of suicide.**—*Madame Ngo Dinh Nhu, sister-in-law of the assassinated President of South Vietnam, speaking to the press, 2 November 1963.*[509]

Initial reports from the military junta in Saigon indicated President Diem and his brother Ngo Dinh Nhu had committed suicide while in custody. Mme. Nhu rejected this because Diem and Nhu were devout Catholics and suicide was not an option. A later indicator throwing doubt on the suicide theory was the fact that Diem and Nhu had each been shot and stabbed several times.

303 **I feel we must bear a good deal of responsibility for it. In my judgment that wire was badly drafted, it should have never been sent on a Saturday. I should have never given my consent to it without roundtable conference.**—*President John Kennedy, conversation in the Oval Office, 4 November 1963.*[184]

Kennedy, second guessing the decision to notify Ambassador Lodge that South Vietnam's President Diem must remove his brother Nhu from the government and if Diem did not do so, the U.S. would not interfere with a planned Vietnamese military coup against Diem. From taped conversation recently released by the Kennedy Museum.

304 **I was shocked by the death of Ngo Dinh Diem. He was an extraordinary character, while he became increasingly difficult in the last few months. He has been able to hold his country together for the last 10 months.**—*President John Kennedy, conversation in the Oval Office, 4 November 1963.*[184]

Diem was assassinated 2 November 1963 during a military coup. It was first announced that Diem and his brother Nhu had committed suicide. It was later revealed that Nhu and Diem died from multiple gun shot and stab wounds, ruling out the suicide explanation released by the new ruling junta.

305 **[It is] a dirty crime and nothing less than murder.**—*Madame Nhu, wife of Ngo Dinh Nhu, to reporters, Los Angeles, California, November 1963.*[666]

Mme. Nhu, sister-in-law to South Vietnam's President Ngo Dinh Diem, was out of the country when the coup against Diem took place. During the coup Diem and his brother Nhu were assassinated while in the custody of the generals who overthrew the regime.

306 **The ground in which the coup seed grew into a robust plant was prepared by us, and that coup would not have happened [as] it did without our preparation.**—*Henry Cabot Lodge, in a cable to President John Kennedy, 6 November 1963.*[374]

Lodge would later claim publicly that the coup against Diem had been entirely a Vietnamese affair with neither U.S. support or interference.

307 **The prospects are now for a shorter war.**—*Henry Cabot Lodge, U.S. Ambassador to South Vietnam, in a cable to President John Kennedy, November 1963.*[374]

Lodge believed that following the coup against Diem, the war against the communist insurgents would improve and end in a South Vietnamese victory.

308 **The Vietnamese armed forces are as professional as you can get...**—*General Charles J. Timmes, Chief, U.S. Military Assistance Advisory Group, Vietnam, during a press interview, 1 November 1963.*[664]

Timmes commanded the U.S. advisers in Vietnam, while over all command of all American forces was under General Paul D. Harkins.

309 **Victory, in the sense it would apply to this kind of war is just months away and reduction of American advisers can begin at that time.**—*General Paul D. Harkins, ComUSMACV, during comments to the press, Saigon, 1 November 1963.*[663]

Harkins made this statement just two days before the Diem government was overthrown and replaced by a military junta.

310 **We must help the coup regime to confront the real problems of winning the contest against the Communists and holding the confidence of its own people.**—*President John F. Kennedy, in a message to Ambassador Henry Cabot Lodge, November 1963.*[87]

Following the successful coup by a group of South Vietnamese generals, Kennedy impressed upon Lodge the importance of pursuing the war against the communist in South Vietnam and the American assistance to that end.

311 **Never do business on the weekend.**—*McGeorge Bundy, National Security Adviser, on the events leading to the Diem coup.*[374]

The Kennedy administration's policy directive (24 August 1963) to Ambassador Lodge, concerning Diem and his brother Nhu, was generated on a weekend. As a result, some of the primary parties that should have been involved in the policy were not readily available. Instead, deputies formulated the policy and received a passing approval from President Kennedy, Dean Rusk, and McNamara's deputy. The policy was construed by the generals involved in the coup against Diem to be Washington's blessing on their plan.

312 **Johnson definitely feels that we place too much emphasis on social reforms; he has very little tolerance with our spending so much time being "do-gooders."**—*John McCone, Director, Central Intelligence, during a meeting with President Johnson, 24 November 1963.*[214]

McCone was speaking of Johnson's first formal meeting dealing with Vietnam following his rise to the presidency.

313 **I thought I was about to become another statistic when the First and Second Companies broke and ran. We beat them back to their positions with rifle butts, but finally, there was no holding them.**—*Captain Ralph Thomas, American advisor to the 14th ARVN Regiment, 1963.*[1021]

This was an early indication of the morale and combat efficiency of the ARVN. Incidents of this type were more the rule than the exception.

314 **It remains the central objective of the United States in South Vietnam to assist the people and government of that country to win their contest against the externally directed and supported communist conspiracy. The test of all U.S. decisions and actions in this area should be the effectiveness of their contribution to this purpose.**—*President Lyndon Johnson, from NSA memorandum 273, 26 November 1963.*[150]

Johnson was stating the proposed American policy for South Vietnam. He had become president just four days prior to the issuance of the memorandum.

315 **They had to be killed. Diem could not be allowed to live because he was too much respected among simple, gullible people in the countryside, especially the Catholics and the refugees. We had to kill Nhu because he was so widely feared — and he had created organizations that were arms of his personal power.**—*General Duong Van "Big" Minh military advisor to Ngo dinh Diem, 1963.*[1027]

Big Minh was one of several South Vietnamese officers who staged the coup that overthrew Diem and his brother Nhu. The brothers were killed shortly after their capture.

316 **Current trends, unless reversed in the next two or three months, will lead to neutralization at best or more likely to a Communist-controlled state.**—*Robert McNamara, Secretary of Defense, in a report to President Johnson, December 1963.*[374]

Publicly McNamara was optimistic about the situation in Vietnam, but privately he informed Johnson that the situation was deteriorating rapidly.

317 **We should watch the situation very carefully, running scared, hoping for the best, but preparing for more forceful moves if the situation does not show early signs of improvement.**—*Robert McNamara, Secretary of Defense, in a report to President Johnson, December 1963.*[374]

McNamara had just returned from an inspection tour of SVN and was very pessimistic about the outcome of the war.

318 **We ought to get in with both feet and get the chore over with, and do things that are necessary to be done.**—*General Curtis LeMay, U.S. Air Force Chief of Staff, 1963.*[926]

LeMay advocated all-out bombing of North Vietnam, early and completely to stop their support and direction of the VC insurgents in South Vietnam.

319 **There are more reasons to doubt the future of the effort ... than there are reasons to be optimistic about the future of**

our cause.—*Robert McNamara, Secretary of Defense, in a report to President Johnson, December 1963.*[374]

McNamara was reporting on his fact finding visit to South Vietnam. His outlook was pessimistic. The government in South Vietnam was unstable and so filled with internal squabbling that they were virtually ignoring the war against the communists.

320 **The possibility that a limited war in South Viet-Nam would turn into a world war is almost nonexistent because the purpose and significance of this war cannot generate conditions leading to a world war.**—*An excerpt from the Resolution of the Ninth Conference of the Lao Dong Party, December 1963.*[882]

The Lao Dong Party, Worker's Party (formerly the Indochinese Communist Party), expressed its readiness to gradually meet any threat America might pose, but did not advocate a general offensive, which would mean all-out war in Vietnam. The conference resolved to maintain support for the insurgency in the South until final victory.

321 **In a real sense, South Vietnam is a country with an army and no government.**—*George Ball, State Department official.*[244]

322 **There is no organized government in South Vietnam at this time.... It is abundantly clear that statistics received over the past year or more from the GVN officials and reported by the US military on which we gauged the trend of the war were grossly in error.**—*John McCone, Director, Central Intelligence, in a memorandum, 21 December 1963.*[195]

Despite McCone's warning of the erroneous information coming from Saigon, the Johnson administration continued to believe the hopeful reports of progress coming out of the U.S. Embassy and MACV.

1964

I hate war. And if the day ever comes when my vote must be cast to send your boy to the trenches, that day Lyndon Johnson will leave his Senate seat to go with him.
—Lyndon Baines Johnson

323 ***Ce pays pourri.***—*Charles de Gaulle, President of France, in a comment to George Ball, 1964.*[374]

"This rotten country," French nickname for Vietnam. De Gaulle cautioned Ball that the U.S. was following a path that would lead them to an end not unlike that which befell France in its fight against the Viet Minh.

324 **We are not about to send American boys nine or ten thousand miles away from home to do what Asian boys ought to be doing for themselves.**—*President Lyndon Johnson, from a speech in Manchester, New Hampshire, 28 September 1964.*[728]

Johnson, on the introduction of American combat troops to Vietnam—just prior to the 1964 presidential election.

325 **[I have] the terrible feeling that something has grabbed me around the ankles and won't let go.**—*President Lyndon Johnson, comments to Bill Moyers, January 1964.*[374]

326 **The drive for independence is a most powerful force. We can honestly align our policy with this force. In the end the Communists cannot, and this is one fundamental reason why the Communist offensive in the underdeveloped areas will fail.**—*Walt Rostow, Special Assistant to the President, from his book, 1964.*[242]

327 **If the war is to be won, then it must be done by the Vietnamese—nothing would be more foolhardy than the employment of U.S. (or any other foreign) troops in quantity. We could pour an entire Army into Vietnam—and accomplish nothing worth while.**—*John Paul Vann, civilian aerospace executive, in a letter, 1964.*[887]

Vann retired from the Army in July 1963 and went to work for an aerospace firm in Denver. He was writing to a close friend who was an assistant to Ambassador Henry Cabot Lodge. Vann believed all along that the introduction of U.S. combat troops would be a mistake for the Vietnamese and the United States.

328 **[American intervention in Vietnam would be limited merely to] logistical and training support ... it is a Vietnamese war ... that can only be won by the Vietnamese themselves.**—*Robert McNamara, Secretary of Defense, during testimony before the House Armed Services Committee, January 1964.*[374]

During testimony, McNamara was publicly hopeful that the U.S. commitment of advisers and support personnel would eventually be withdrawn and South Vietnam would stand on its own.

329 **This administration today, here and now, declares unconditional war on poverty in America. ... It will not be a short or easy struggle, no single weapon or strategy will suffice, but we shall not rest until that war is won.**—*President Lyndon Johnson, State of the Union message, 8 January 1964.*[778]

Johnson's declaration of the war against poverty in America, while at the same time managing the growing war in Vietnam.

330 **Keeping the crutch there too long would weaken the Vietnamese rather than strengthen them.**—*Robert McNamara, Secretary of Defense, during testimony before the House Armed Services Committee, January 1964.*[374]

That "crutch" being U.S. military, economic, and humanitarian aid.

331 **It is the old problem of having people who are responsible for operations also responsible for evaluating the results.**—*Michael Forrestal, NSC officer, in a memorandum to McGeorge Bundy, 8 January 1964.*[230]

Forrestal was commenting on problem reports from MACV, GVN, and the U.S. Embassy regarding details of the war and the political situation in South Vietnam. Much of the information was so skewed to the optimistic, that a flawed picture of the situation was used by the Administration to create Vietnam policy and guidelines.

332 **[John Paul Vann] had ... done what no other American official had done in that land where there was such a disparity between theory and practice: he had thought that the failures and the mendacity were serious enough to merit a resignation, the traditional American protest.**—*David Halberstam, correspondent and author, writing of John Paul Vann, 1964.*[887]

Vann retired from the U.S. Army in July 1963, citing his disagreement with the Administration's handling of the war in Vietnam.

333 **The situation there [Vietnam] remains grave.... I must report that they [the Communists] have made considerable progress since the coup.**—*Robert McNamara, Secretary of Defense, in testimony before the House Armed Services Committee, 29 January 1964.*[667]

McNamara was testifying in support of President Johnson's military budget request. He outlined the need for a strong American military to cope with communist expansion around the world, and specifically the need to back the anti-communist government of South Vietnam.

334 **Most ARVN units suffered defeat because of military incompetence and cowardice, rather than any inferiority in numbers or firepower.**—*Excerpt from the Pentagon Papers, 1971.*[36]

In reference to the deterioration of the ARVN military between 1960 and 1964.

335 **[It is] the worst division in any army in the world.** —*General Cao Van Vien, Chief, Joint General Staff, Saigon, 1964.*[12]

The 25th ARVN deployed from its original home location in Quang Ngai province to Hau Nghia province, III Corps, in April 1964. The Joint General Staff was the ARVN functional equivalent of the U.S. JCS.

336 **Ho Chi Minh has an industrial complex to protect: he is no longer a guerrilla fighter with nothing to lose.**—*Walt Rostow, State Department Foreign Affairs Adviser, in a memorandum to Dean Rusk, February 1964.*[887]

Rostow believed North Vietnam was vulnerable to U.S. bombing and that such a threat could force Hanoi to back down from its support and direction of the communist insurgency in South Vietnam.

337 **I was shocked by the number of our people and of the military, even those whose job is always to say we are winning, who feel that the tide is against us.**—*Lyman Kirkpatrick, CIA officer, following an inspection visit to South Vietnam, February 1964.*[374]

338 **Our strength imposes on us an obligation to assure that this type of aggression does not succeed.**—*President Lyndon Johnson, to Charles Bohlen, February 1964.*[347]

Johnson was speaking of the external aggression posed by North Vietnam and perceived by some in Washington to be encouraged, if not directed, by Peking.

339 **The contest in which South Vietnam is now engaged is first and foremost a contest to be won by the government and the people of that country for themselves. But those engaged in external direction and supply would do well to be reminded and to remember that this type of aggression is a dangerous game.**—*President Lyndon Johnson, from a speech at UCLA, 21 February 1964.*[800]

340 **Unless there is a marked improvement in the effectiveness of the South Vietnamese government and armed forces, the country has only an even chance of withstanding the insurgency menace during the next few weeks or months.**—*Unspecified American official's prognosis for South Vietnam, February 1964.*[374]

The situation continued to deteriorate with the instability of the Khanh government and the political infighting between the military leadership.

341 **It is not likely that North Vietnam would (if it could) call off the war in the South even though U.S. actions would in time have serious economic and political impact. Overt action against North Vietnam would be unlikely to produce reduction in Viet Cong activity sufficiently to make victory on the ground possible in South Vietnam unless accompanied by new U.S. bolstering actions in South Vietnam and considerable improvement in the government there.**—*An excerpt from conclusions of the Sullivan Task Force, 1 March 1964.*[223]

In February 1964 a special task force was created by the State Department to investigate options for the U.S. in Vietnam, including attacks against North Vietnam. The task force was directed by William H. Sullivan. A subcommittee of the task force headed by Robert H. Johnson concluded that attacking North Vietnam would delay VC success in the South, but not completely stop Hanoi's support or direction for the communist war effort in South Vietnam.

342 **[If the bombing of North Vietnam was not successful] the costs of failure might be greater than the cost of failure under a counter-insurgency strategy because of the deeper U.S. commitment and the broader world implications.**—*An excerpt from the conclusions of the Sullivan Task Force subcommittee, headed by Robert Johnson, 2 March 1964.*[223]

Under the Sullivan report, the task force indicated that bombing North Vietnam would have minimal impact on the war in South Vietnam. It would also probably not force Hanoi to stop its support and direction of the insurgency in the South.

343 **We could come out of there ... and as soon as we get out, they could swallow up South Vietnam.... Or we can say this is the Vietnamese war and they've got 200,000 men,**

they're untrained, and we've got to bring their morale up ... and we can train them how to fight ... and the 200,000 ultimately will be able to take care of these 25,000 (Viet Cong) and that after considering all of these ... it seems offers the best alternative to follow.—*President Lyndon Johnson, in conversation with Robert McNamara, 2 March 1964.*[973]

Johnson was outlining to McNamara what he believed the options were in Vietnam.

344 **We have been misinformed about conditions in Vietnam.**—*John McCone, Director, Central Intelligence Agency, in a memorandum, 3 March 1964.*[232]

This was McCone's appraisal of the situation in Vietnam. Reports from the field were intermittent and often inaccurate. According to McCone, bad news was suppressed, and good news overblown, sending a totally inaccurate picture of what the true situation was in South Vietnam. In reality there was no focused GVN effort against the VC, nor creation of programs responsive to the needs of the people. The VC were making territorial gains and continually improving their position within the country.

345 **The president doesn't know the position of the administration, so you can't know it.**—*President Lyndon Johnson, in a phone conversation with Walt Rostow, 4 March 1964.*[973]

Rostow informed Johnson that he had told the press that the Johnson administration's position was to hold Southeast Asia. Johnson curtly reminded him that the new Administration's position on Southeast Asia had not as yet been completely formed.

346 **There is a growing feeling that the VC may be the wave of the future.**—*John McCone, Director, Central Intelligence Agency, in a memorandum, 3 March 1964.*[232]

McCone's appraisal of the situation in Vietnam, based on his field sources, indicated there was no focused GVN effort against the VC, nor creation of programs responsive to the needs of the people. The VC were making territorial gains and continually improving their position within the country.

347 **Bombing the North would not win the war in South Vietnam and would cause the United States such serious problems in every corner of the world that we should not sanction such an effort.**—*John McCone, Director, Central Intelligence Agency, in a memorandum, 3 March 1964.*[232]

348 **We shall stay for as long as it takes to ... win the battle against the Communist insurgents.**—*Robert McNamara, Secretary of Defense, during statements covered by the press, Saigon, 8 March 1964.*[374]

349 **[Press the South Vietnamese toward] increased activity [against North Vietnam while considering] the plausibility of denial; possible North Vietnamese retaliation; (and) other international reaction.**—*President Lyndon Johnson to his military commanders, 1964, as related by Ronald Spector of George Washington University.*[352]

From government documents released in 1997, it appears that the Diem regime may have stifled reports to the Americans that indicated the South Vietnamese war against the communists was going badly. Johnson wanted more action from the ARVN in the effort against the communists. This took place in December 1963, before the Tonkin Incident.

350 **The military tools and concepts of the GVN-US effort are generally sound and adequate.... Substantial reductions in the number of US military training personnel should be possible before the end of 1965.**—*Robert McNamara, Secretary of Defense, in a memorandum to President Johnson, 14 March 1964.*[213]

351 **I don't think any Negro should fight for anything that does not produce for him what it produces for others. Whenever a Negro fights for "democracy," he's fighting for something he has not got, never had, and never will.**—*Malcom X, Muslim Black Nationalist, 1964.*[390]

352 **If [Martin Luther] King and others can tell Negroes to boycott buses or industries or schools, I see no reason why they cannot boycott the Army, Navy, and Air Force.**—*Malcom X, Muslim Black Nationalist, 1964.*[390]

King and the non-violent civil rights movement used the boycott to draw attention to their cause, the search for equality in America. Malcom X advocated segregation and isolation of the races.

353 **We would have to calculate the effect of such military actions [as bombing North Vietnam] against a specified political objective. That objective, while being cast in terms of eliminating North Vietnamese control and direction of the insurgency, would in practical terms be directed toward collapsing the morale and self-assurance of the Viet Cong cadres now operating in South Vietnam and bolstering the morale of the Khanh regime. We could not, of course, be sure that our objective could be achieved by any means within the practical range of our options.**—*Robert McNamara, Secretary of Defense, in a memorandum to the President, 16 March 1964.*[182]

354 **I think the most useful thing I can do is here where Americans are under fire.**—*Henry Cabot Lodge, Jr., American Ambassador to South Vietnam, 1964.*[389]

Lodge volunteered for the appointment of ambassador to South Vietnam. He was asked by the press, why?

355 **The large indigenous support that the Vietcong receives means the solutions must be as political and economic as military.... There can be no such thing as a purely "military" solution to the war in South Vietnam.**—*Robert McNamara, Secretary of Defense, March 1964.*[79]

356 **When the day comes that we can safely withdraw, we expect to leave an independent and stable South Vietnam, rich with resources and bright with prospects for contributing to the peace and prosperity of Southeast Asia and the world.**—*Robert McNamara, Secretary of Defense, from a speech, March 1964.*[169]

357 **That damned little pissant country.**—*President Lyndon Johnson, 1964.*[501]

One of President Johnson's descriptions of Vietnam.

358 **You must have whatever you need to help the Vietnamese do the job, and I assure you that I will act at once to eliminate obstacles or restraints wherever they may appear.**—*President Lyndon Johnson, to Henry Cabot Lodge, 4 April 1964.*[291]

359 **Son, don't ever get yourself bogged down in a land war in Asia.**—*General Douglas MacArthur, 5 April 1964.*[399]

MacArthur reportedly made this statement from his death bed. President Johnson often repeated the quote in reference to Asia and Vietnam.

360 **It is impossible to foresee a stable and effective government under any name in anything like the near future.... We sense the mounting feeling of war weariness and hopelessness that pervades South Vietnam.... There is chronic discouragement.**—*General Maxwell Taylor, Ambassador to South Vietnam, during a White House meeting, late-1964.*[374]

Taylor argued that a solid government in Saigon was essential to the success of U.S. policy in Vietnam.

361 **Somehow we must change the pace at which these people move ... perhaps this can only be done with a pervasive intrusion of Americans into their affairs.**—*Dean Rusk, Secretary of State, in a cable to the U.S. Embassy in Saigon, 1964.*[374]

The pace of change was much too slow for Rusk's liking. The Saigon government was not moving forward and militarily they were losing more and more territory to the VC every day. Rusk wanted Saigon to focus on the war against the communists.

362 **I think a trip, Mr. Prime Minister, on this situation would be very misunderstood and I don't think any good would flow from it. If one of us jumps across the Atlantic every time there is a critical situation, next week I'll be flying over when Sukarno jumps on you and I'll be giving you advice.**—*President Lyndon Johnson, speaking to England's Prime Minister Harold Wilson, 1964.*[479]

Johnson received a call from Wilson shortly after a VC attack on a U.S. service club in Saigon, offering to talk with Johnson about the situation in Vietnam. Wilson was fearful that Johnson might be urged to escalate the war and perhaps even consider nuclear weapons. Johnson was not thrilled with the call. He had earlier asked Wilson for assistance in Vietnam — even token assistance — but Wilson had refused.

363 **As far as my problem in Vietnam, we have asked everyone to share with us. They are willing to share advice but not responsibility.**—*President Lyndon Johnson, speaking to England's Prime Minister Harold Wilson, 1964.*[479]

Johnson attempted to get the non-communist nations of the world to stand with the United States against the communist in Vietnam, but only a handful of countries were willing to provide any military support to the effort.

364 **I won't tell you how to run Malaysia and you don't tell us how to run Vietnam.... If you want to help us some in Vietnam send us some men and send us some folks to deal with these guerrillas. And announce to the press that you are going to help us. Now if you don't feel like doing that, go on with your Malaysian problem...**—*President Lyndon Johnson, speaking to England's Prime Minister Harold Wilson, 1964.*[479]

The British were having trouble with communist insurgents in Malaysia at the time. Johnson was still chaffed at Wilson's earlier refusal to help militarily in Vietnam.

365 **I suffer to see the war go on, develop, intensify, yet our people are determined to struggle.**—*Pham Van Dong, Prime Minister, Democratic Republic of Vietnam, comments to J. Blair Seaborn, 1964.*[374]

Dong was responding to a secret Johnson peace initiative. Seaborn was a Canadian member of the ICC with access to North Vietnamese leaders. Johnson proposed economic aid to Hanoi if they would stop supporting the VC insurgents in South Vietnam. In the event they rejected the proposal Johnson held forth the possibility of direct U.S. military action against North Vietnam. Hanoi rejected Johnson's proposal.

366 **Outmoded concepts, directives and practices, bureaucratic constipation, [and] insufficient on-the-spot resources.** —*William Colby, Chief, Far East Division, CIA, in a memorandum to President Johnson, 11 May 1964.*[291]

Colby explaining some of the difficulties American advisers were experiencing with progress in Vietnam.

367 **There are things you don't have to worry about anymore, like do you have to take the country into war over Vietnam.**—*Nelson Rockefeller, Governor of New York, during his presidential campaign, 1964.*[830]

Rockefeller was commenting on his lost bid to become the Republican Party candidate for president.

368 **Both in Laos and in Vietnam there is a simple prescription for peace — leave your neighbors alone.**—*Dean Rusk, Secretary of State, in a speech before the American Law Institute, 22 May 1964.*[510]

Rusk was referring to communist aggression in both Laos and South Vietnam. In Laos, North Vietnamese–backed communist Pathet Lao forces were pressuring the neutralist government of Premier Souvanna Phouma. In South Vietnam, North Vietnamese–backed Vietcong insurgents were attempting to overthrow the Saigon government and take control of South Vietnam.

369 **[The Government of South Vietnam] would favor any real international control of the border, whether by the United Nations, the International Control Commission or any other international body that could be truly effective.**—*Nguyen Khanh, Premier, South Vietnam, speaking to the press, 22 May 1964.*[511]

Adlai Stevenson, during a U.N. security council meeting, suggested that a U.N. force could monitor the border between South Vietnam and Cambodia in an effort to stop cross border raids by the VC.

370 **[I plan to carry America] ... not only toward the rich society and the powerful society, but upward to the great society.**—*President Johnson, from a speech at the University of Michigan, 22 May 1964.*[804]

This was the birth of Johnson's Great Society. Johnson had high hopes for his Great Society programs, but the funding for many of the programs had to be shared with the war in Vietnam.

371 **If we go into North Vietnam we should go in hard and not limit our action to pinpricks.**—*John McCone, Director, Central Intelligence Agency, during NSC meeting, 24 May 1964.*[231]

McCone argued that if force was to be used against Hanoi, it should be massive. He was not a supporter of the "graduated response" strategy.

372 **We have made it clear that we are not going to abandon people who are trying to preserve their independence and**

freedom.—*Dean Rusk, Secretary of State, in a speech before the American Law Institute, 22 May 1964.*[510]

Rusk indicated that efforts to support South Vietnam could be escalated if the Communist continued their aggression against South Vietnam.

373 **How is it that the government can protect the Vietnamese from the Vietcong and the same government will not accept the moral responsibility of protecting [black] people in Mississippi?**—*Question from a white student, training for the voting rights project in the south, to John Doar, Justice Department's Civil Rights Division, June 1964.*[825]

This followed the slaying of three civil rights workers in Philadelphia, Mississippi in June 1964.

374 **[In Saigon the] atmosphere fairly smelled of discontent, with workers on strike, students demonstrating, the local press pursuing a persistent campaign of criticism of the new government.**—*General William Westmoreland, ComUSMACV, 1976.*[335]

Westmoreland, referring to Saigon under the General Khanh regime.

375 **Screams from the North have a very tonic effect and strengthen morale here; it is also vital to frighten Ho.**—*Henry Cabot Lodge, U.S. Ambassador to South Vietnam, in a cable to Washington, 5 June 1964.*[231]

Lodge recommended that the Johnson administration conduct direct actions (bombing) against North Vietnam. He believed it would be a morale booster for the GVN and the military.

376 **It is likely that no nation in the area would quickly succumb to Communism as a result of the fall of Laos and Vietnam. Furthermore, a continuation of the spread of Communism in the area would not be inexorable, and any spread which did occur would take time — time in which the total situation might change in any number of ways unfavorable to the Communist cause.**—*Excerpt from a CIA memorandum to President Johnson, 9 June 1964.*[225]

Johnson asked the CIA, "Would the rest of Southeast Asia necessarily fall if Laos and South Vietnam came under North Vietnamese control?" The reply was prepared by the CIA's Office of National Estimates. The reply directly challenged the Domino Theory put forth and supported by the Eisenhower and Kennedy administrations. Despite the reply, the Johnson administration used the Domino Theory as a factor for the continued U.S. commitment in Vietnam.

377 **But this is my duty.**—*ARVN soldier, to correspondent, June 1964.*[392]

The soldier was responding to protest from a *Life* photographer to stop the torture of a Vietcong prisoners. The ARVN were interrogating 43 VC guerrillas captured near a ville along the Cambodian border. The ARVN used beatings and water torture to try to extract information from the guerrillas.

378 **Curtis LeMay wants to bomb Hanoi and Hai Phong. You know how he likes to go around bombing.**—*President Lyndon Johnson, comment to his staff, 1964.*[414]

LeMay was an advocate of swift and heavy use of air power against an enemy.

379 **[Vietnam is] obviously the most important problem facing the United States and ... I am at your service.**—*Robert F. Kennedy, in a letter to President Johnson, June 1964.*[414]

Kennedy volunteered to be Ambassador to South Vietnam, following Lodge's resignation to pursue the Republican nomination for President in the upcoming election.

380 **Back in 1776 British "experts" were sure they could beat the ragged colonists. ... The British had the second best army in the world; the colonists only those ridiculous guerrillas. ... The British lost because they didn't understand the power of wars of national liberation.**—*Comments made by Sidney Lens, in Liberation magazine.*[1022]

381 **The overthrow ... of the Diem regime was purely a Vietnamese affair. We never participated in the planning. We never gave advice. We had nothing whatsoever to do with it. We were punctilious in drawing that line.**—*Henry Cabot Lodge, U.S. Ambassador to South Vietnam, during an interview covered by The New York Times, 30 June 1964.*[374]

One of several public statements by the Johnson administration regarding the Vietnamese military coup against Diem. The U.S. in fact knew the coup was planned and decided to let it happen rather than warn Diem or interfere.

382 **The stakes in Europe were enormous but if South Vietnam fell we would not be losing much.**—*Unidentified French diplomat in a conversation with Dean Rusk, 1 July 1964.*[347]

383 **The best thing that can be said about Khanh's government is that it has lasted six months and has a 50-50 chance of lasting a year.**—*General Maxwell Taylor, Ambassador to South Vietnam, July 1964.*[317]

Khanh led a coup in January 1964 against the military junta which had ousted Diem in November 1963.

384 **Every one of these sons of bitches drives by the palace and thinks about how he'd like to shack up in there with his mistress.**—*Lucien Conein, U.S. CIA agent, comments picked up by the press, 1964.*[887]

Conein was speaking of the plague of coup and countercoup plots by the South Vietnamese military, between 1963 and 1965.

385 **I was sure, that once we showed how weak we were [in Vietnam], Moscow and Peking would move in a flash to exploit our weakness. And so would begin World War III.**—*President Lyndon Johnson's comments on holding firm in Vietnam, 1964.*[174]

Johnson, on the importance of standing with Saigon against communist aggression from North Vietnam, which he saw as an agent of Red China and the Soviet Union.

386 **Every military man with whom I talked [during my recent Southeast Asia tour] privately admitted that we are losing the war.**—*Richard Nixon, former Vice President, from an article in Reader's Digest, August 1964.*[227]

Nixon toured South Vietnam in 1964 as a private citizen.

387 **We have got to remember that we are rather heavily committed out there [in Vietnam], and that in view of our involvement such occasions will arise from time to time. We hope they do not, but we should not be surprised if they do.**—*Senator Mike Mansfield of Montana, comments to the press, 2 August 1964.*[512]

Mansfield was responding to a call by Congressional Republicans for a re-evaluation of the Johnson administration's policy in Vietnam. This followed the attack by North Vietnamese torpedo boats on the *USS Maddox* off the coast of North Vietnam.

388 **North Vietnamese PT boats made a deliberate attack today on two United States destroyers patrolling international waters in the Gulf of Tonkin off North Vietnam ... the attack was made by an undetermined number of North Vietnamese PT boats, during darkness from about 65 miles from the nearest land.**—*Defense Department announcement to the press, 4 August 1964.*[513]

This was the second reported attack on U.S. Navy vessels operating in the Gulf of Tonkin. The first attack took place on 2 August against the *USS Maddox*. There is considerable doubt that the second attack actually took place, yet it was still used as justification for the first retaliatory air strikes against North Vietnam.

389 **I am sure every American will subscribe to the action outlined in the President's statement. I believe it is the only thing that he can do under the circumstances. We cannot allow the American flag to be shot at anywhere on earth if we are to retain our respect and prestige.**—*Senator Barry Goldwater, of Arizona, press release, 4 August 1964.*[764]

Goldwater was stating his support for President Johnson's military retaliation against North Vietnam for their attack on the *USS Maddox*.

390 **We Americans know — although others appear to forget — the risk of spreading conflict. We still seek no wider war.**—*President Lyndon Johnson, during a nationwide broadcast, 4 August 1964.*[514]

391 **Grave consequences would inevitably result from any further unprovoked offensive military action against American ships deployed on the high seas off North Vietnam.**—*Excerpt from a diplomatic note sent to Hanoi on President Johnson's approval, August 1964.*[374]

The American response to the attack by North Vietnamese torpedo boats on the *USS Maddox* in international waters off the coast of North Vietnam, 2 August 1964.

392 **Aggression — deliberate, willful and systematic aggression — has unmasked its face to the world. The world remembers — the world must never forget — that aggression unchallenged is aggression unleashed.**—*President Lyndon Johnson, from a speech in Syracuse, New York, 5 August 1964.*[668]

Johnson was referring to the North Vietnamese attacks on U.S. Navy destroyers in the Gulf of Tonkin, August 1964. In retaliation, Johnson ordered air strikes against four North Vietnamese PT boat bases.

393 **This is not just a jungle war, but a struggle for freedom on every front of human activity. Our military and economic assistance to South Vietnam and Laos in particular has the purpose of helping these countries to repel aggression and strengthen their independence.**—*President Lyndon Johnson, in a message to Congress, 5 August 1964.*[368]

Johnson reported to Congress the attacks against U.S. Navy destroyers in the Gulf of Tonkin and the air strikes he ordered in retaliation against North Vietnam.

394 **We cannot sit still as a nation and let them attack us on the high seas and get away with it.**—*Robert McNamara, Secretary of Defense, August 1964.*[289]

McNamara, referring to the attack on the USS *Maddox* on 2 August and later the reported attack on the *C. Turner Joy* and the *Maddox*, on 4 August 1964.

395 **As I have repeatedly made clear, the United States intends no rashness, and seeks no wider war. We must make it clear to all that the United States is united in its determination to bring about the end of Communist subversion and aggression in the area. We seek the full and effective restoration of the international agreements signed in Geneva in 1954, with respect to South Vietnam, and again in Geneva in 1962, with respect to Laos...**—*President Lyndon Johnson, in a message to Congress, 5 August 1964.*[368]

Johnson reported to Congress the attacks against U.S. Navy destroyers in the Gulf of Tonkin and the air strikes he ordered in retaliation against North Vietnam. Congress went on to pass Resolution 1145, The Southeast Asia Resolution, giving the President Congressional backing for what he deemed necessary to achieve the goals of American policy for Southeast Asia.

396 **To any who may be tempted to support or to widen the present aggression, I say this: There is no threat to any peaceful power from the United States of America. But there can be no peace by aggression, and no immunity from reply.**—*President Lyndon Johnson, speaking at Syracuse University, New York, 5 August 1964.*[515]

Johnson was referring to U.S. air strikes against North Vietnam. The strikes were in response to the reported attacks by North Vietnamese PT boats on U.S. Navy destroyers operating in international waters off the coast of North Vietnam.

397 **We are in Southeast Asia to help our friends preserve their own opportunity to be free of imported terror, or alien assassination managed by the North Vietnamese Communist based in Hanoi and backed by the Chinese Communist from Peking.**—*Adlai Stevenson, U.S. delegate to the United Nations, speaking before the Security Council, 5 August 1964.*[516]

Stevenson denounced Hanoi's aggression and explained the U.S. strikes against North Vietnamese PT boat bases in retaliation for North Vietnam's attacks against U.S. destroyers on the high seas.

398 **This is a single action designed to make unmistakably clear that the United States cannot be diverted by military attack from its obligations to help its friends establish and protect their independence.**—*Adlai Stevenson, U.S. delegate to the United Nations, speaking before the Security Council, 5 August 1964.*[516]

Stevenson was referring to the retaliatory strike by U.S. aircraft on North Vietnamese locations. The strike was in response to the reported attacks by North Vietnamese PT boats on U.S. Navy destroyers operating in international waters in the Gulf of Tonkin.

399 **[In the View of the Soviet Union] the United States has committed an act of aggression ... if such actions were repeated the United States will have to bear a heavy responsibility.**—*Platon D. Morozov, Soviet delegate to the United Nations, speaking before the Security Council, 5 August 1964.*[516]

Morozov was referring to U.S. air strike against North Vietnam. The strike was in response to the reported attacks by North Vietnamese PT boats on U.S. Navy destroyers operating in international waters in the Gulf of Tonkin.

400 **Our navy played absolutely no part in, was not associated with, was not aware of, any South Vietnamese actions, if there were any.... I say this flatly. This is a fact.**—*Robert McNamara, Secretary of State, during testimony before Congress, 5 August 1964.*[374]

McNamara was questioned as to whether the actions of the *USS Maddox* had been in conjunction with South Vietnamese raids along the North Vietnamese coast during the same time frame. Contrary to his testimony, the captain of the *Maddox* had been informed of the ongoing South Vietnam actions along the coast of North Vietnam prior to the start of his patrol.

401 **We will live to regret it.**—*Senator Wayne Morse, of Oregon, during debate of the Southeast Asia Resolution, 6 August 1964.*[374]

Morse was one of two Senators that voted against the Southeast Asia Resolution. He was opposed to U.S. military involvement in Vietnam and feared the results of escalation.

402 **Such actions, generating a threat to the security of the people of other countries, can entail dangerous consequences, the scope of which it is now hard to foresee.**—*Andrei A. Gromyko, Foreign Minister, U.S.S.R., to the press, 7 August 1964.*[519]

Soviet Union warning the U.S. against further hostile action against North Vietnam. President Johnson ordered air strikes against North Vietnam facilities in retaliation of attacks on U.S. Navy ships operating off the coast of North Vietnam.

403 **Let no friend needlessly fear, and no foe vainly hope, that this is a nation divided in this election year. Our free elections — our full and free debate — are America's strength, not America's weakness.**—*President Lyndon Johnson, speaking at Syracuse University, New York, 5 August 1964.*[515]

Johnson was dispelling rumors of a split in the nation's unity on the issue of Vietnam. Hawks argued for increased force to stop communist aggression in Southeast Asia, and doves demanded American withdrawal from Vietnam.

404 **This new act of aggression aimed directly at our own forces again brings home to all of us in the United States the importance of the struggle for peace and security in Southeast Asia.**—*President Lyndon Johnson, during a nationwide broadcast, 4 August 1964.*[514]

Johnson was speaking of the North Vietnamese attacks against the *USS Maddox* and *C. Turner Joy* in the Gulf of Tonkin. During the broadcast he announced the retaliatory air strikes against North Vietnam in response to those attacks.

405 **There is no backing out of Vietnam. ... We have drawn the line here, and the America we all know and love best is not one to back away.**—*Captain James Spruill, U.S.A., military advisor to the ARVN, in a letter home, 1964.*[1021]

Spruill was killed in Vietnam, 21 April 1964.

406 **Washington has taken the first step toward extending the war in Indochina ... the Chinese people would not sit idly by.**—*Announcement by the government of Communist China, 6 August 1964.*[517]

Peking was referring to U.S. air strikes against North Vietnam. The strikes were in response to the reported attacks by North Vietnamese PT boats on U.S. Navy destroyers operating in international waters off the coast of North Vietnam.

407 **North Vietnamese vessels downed one American airplane and damaged two others before chasing away the U.S. pirates ... on the sea and in the air.**—*Radio Hanoi, news announcement, August 1964.*[374]

Hanoi's version of the Gulf of Tonkin incident, in which three North Vietnamese torpedo boats attacked the *USS Maddox* in international waters off the coast of North Vietnam. The *Maddox* fired on the boats, damaging two and sinking one. U.S. aircraft from the *USS Ticonderoga* also strafed the enemy boats. There were no U.S. casualties or loss of aircraft in the attack.

408 **The place to settle the controversy is not on the battlefield but around the conference table.**—*Senator Wayne Morse, of Oregon, during debate of the Southeast Asia resolution, 6 August 1964.*[374]

Senators Morse and Gruening were the only two members of Congress to vote against the Gulf of Tonkin Resolution (Southeast Asia Resolution).

409 **Repeated acts of violence against the armed forces of the United States must be met not only with alert defense, but with positive reply. That reply is being given as I speak to you tonight.**—*President Lyndon Johnson, during a televised speech, 4 August 1964.*[374]

Johnson was notifying the nation of retaliatory strikes against North Vietnam for their attacks on U.S. destroyers in the Gulf of Tonkin, 2 & 4 August 1964.

410 **Hell, those dumb stupid sailors were just shooting at flying fish.**—*President Lyndon Johnson, comments to an aide, August 1964.*[374]

Johnson was not completely convinced of the North Vietnamese attack on the U.S. destroyers *Maddox* and *Joy* on the night of 4 August 1964. Even with his doubts he initiated the retaliatory strikes against North Vietnam.

411 **Our national honor is at stake. We cannot and we will not shrink from defending it.**—*Senator Richard Russell of Georgia, speaking on the Senate floor, 6 August 1964.*[374]

Russell was speaking out in support of the Southeast Asia Resolution.

412 **[It is a] historic mistake.**—*Senator Wayne Morse, during debate of the Southeast Asia Resolution, 7 August 1964.*[731]

Morse's characterization of the Southeast Asia Resolution. He was one of two Senators who voted against the resolution.

413 **The votes prove our determination to defend our forces, to prevent aggression and to work firmly and steadily for peace and security in the area.**—*President Lyndon Johnson, comments to the press, 7 August 1964.*[518]

Johnson's response to the passage of the Southeast Asia Resolution, giving him Congressional approval to pursue the war in Vietnam. The vote in the House was unanimous. The Senate vote was 88-2.

414 **[This resolution is] a demonstration to all the world of the unity of all Americans.**—*President Lyndon Johnson, comments to the press, 7 August 1964.*[518]

Johnson's response to the passage of the Southeast Asia Resolution, giving him Congressional approval to pursue the war in Vietnam.

415 **How can he [General Khanh] talk about marching north when he cannot even control areas in the immediate vicinity of Saigon?**—*Comments made by Ho Chi Minh, President, Democratic Republic of Vietnam, 1964.*[374]

General Nguyen Khanh, leader of the GVN, publicly campaigned for a South Vietnamese invasion of North Vietnam. Khanh was attempting to turn the focus from his failing government policies to the enemy in the North. Ho viewed such a plan as "sheer stupidity." At the time 40-50 percent of South Vietnam was under the control of the VC.

416 **That the Congress approves and supports the determination of the President, as Commander in Chief, to take all necessary measures to repel any armed attack against the forces of the United States and to prevent further aggression. Section 2. The United States regards as vital to its national interest and to world peace the maintenance of international peace and security in Southeast Asia. Consonant with the Constitution of the United States and the Charter of the United Nations and in accordance with its obligations under the Southeast Asia Collective Defense Treaty, the United States is, therefore, prepared, as the President determines, to take all necessary steps, including the use of armed force, to assist any member or protocol state of the Southeast Asia Collective Defense Treaty requesting assistance in defense of its freedom. Section 3. This resolution shall expire when the President shall determine that the peace and security of the area is reasonably assured by international conditions created by action of the United Nations or otherwise, except that it may be terminated earlier by concurrent resolution of the Congress.**—*Southeast Asia Resolution (H.J. RES 1145), 7 August 1964.*[370]

The resolution approved by both houses of Congress authorized the President to take whatever action he deemed necessary to prevent further aggression against U.S. forces in Southeast Asia. Except for two dissenting votes, both houses of Congress unanimously approved the resolution.

417 **Aggression by the United States against (communist north) Vietnam means aggression against China ... the Chinese people will not sit idly by without lending a helping hand.**—*Statement by Communist China, as reported by United Press International, Tokyo, Japan, 7 August 1964.*[668]

418 **Review of action makes many reported contacts and torpedoes fired appear doubtful. ... No actual visual sightings by *Maddox*. Suggest complete evaluation before any further action**—*Captain Jon J. Herrick, Commander of the U.S.S. Maddox, in a cable to Washington, 4 August 1964.*[1021]

Herrick's doubts about the second attack by NVN gunboats against his ship in the Gulf of Tonkin reached Washington prior to the decision to launch air strikes against NVN.

419 **So my question is whether there is anything in the resolution which would authorize or recommend or approve the landing of large American armies in Vietnam or China?**—*Senator Daniel Brewster of Maryland, during debate of the Southeast Asia Resolution, 7 August 1964.*[731]

Brewster was afraid the Resolution would allow the President to introduce American combat troops into Southeast Asia. He was told, by senior members of Congress, that the resolution did not specifically authorize or deny the President such a move.

420 **I am sure the American people join me in expressing the deepest appreciation to the leaders and members of both parties in both houses of Congress for their patriotic, resolute and rapid action.**—*President Lyndon Johnson, comments to the press, 7 August 1964.*[518]

Congress overwhelmingly approved the Southeast Asia Resolution in the wake of reported North Vietnamese attacks on U.S. Navy destroyers in international waters in the Gulf of Tonkin. The resolution allowed Johnson to take whatever action he deemed necessary in Southeast Asia to protect U.S. forces and assist South Vietnam to maintain its freedom.

421 **[The Gulf of Tonkin Resolution was] like grandma's nightshirt — it covered everything.**—*President Lyndon Johnson comments on the Southeast Asia Resolution, August 1964.*[374]

Johnson's aides sent a draft of the resolution to Congress where it was fine tuned and almost unanimously passed. It gave the president authority to take whatever action he deemed necessary to protect U.S. forces and prevent further aggression as well as maintain security in the area. The resolution was officially known as the Southeast Asia Resolution.

422 **The American flag has been fired upon, we will not and cannot tolerate such things.**—*Representative Ross Adair, of Indiana, speaking in favor of the Southeast Asia Resolution, August 1964.*[257]

Adair was speaking of the Gulf of Tonkin incident in which NVN gunboats fired on the U.S. Navy destroyer *Maddox*, and later were suspected of firing on the *C. Turner Joy*.

423 **[The night of August the 4th was,] darker than the hubs of Hell.**—*Unidentified seaman of the USS C. Turner Joy, August 1964.*[347]

Comment made in reference to the night the *Joy* was reportedly attacked in the Gulf of Tonkin.

424 **Over the brink of war.**—*Announcement by the government of Communist China, 6 August 1964.*[517]

Peking was referring to U.S. air strikes against North Vietnam. The strikes were in response to the reported attacks by North Vietnamese PT boats on U.S. Navy destroyers operating in international waters in the Gulf of Tonkin. The attacks against the U.S. ships took place on the 2d and 4th of August. Peking characterized the retaliatory air strikes as surprise attacks.

425 **Our one desire — our one determination — is that the people of Southeast Asia be left in peace to work out their own destinies in their own way.**—*President Lyndon Johnson, Washington D.C., 10 August 1964.*[369]

426 **A predated declaration of war.**—*Senator Ernest Gruening of Alaska, August 1964.*[289]

Gruening's characterization of the Tonkin Resolution

(Southeast Asia Resolution). He was one of only two Senators who voted against the resolution.

427 **Our ships had absolutely no knowledge of it [GVN coastal operations against NVN], were not connected with it; in no sense of the word can be considered to have backstopped the effort.**—*Robert McNamara, Secretary of Defense, during Senate testimony, 1964.*[876]

McNamara was referring to the U.S. Navy's DeSoto surveillance patrols along the coast of North Vietnam. Independent of the DeSoto patrols the GVN, under OPLAN 34-A, conducted coastal raids against North Vietnamese facilities. Senator Morse tried to tie the DeSoto patrols with the GVN operations as a reason for the North Vietnamese attack on the *USS Maddox*. McNamara insisted the patrol commander knew nothing of OPLAN 34-A.

428 **The coming weeks will decide the destiny of our entire people. We will not accept becoming a minor province of Red China.**—*General Nguyen Khanh, Premier, South Vietnam, 7 August 1964.*[519]

With the political and military situation deteriorating in South Vietnam, Khanh declared a national emergency and attempted to rally the people behind his government. He tried to focus attention on North Vietnam's aggression and away from the turmoil in Saigon.

429 **The other side got a sting out of this. If they do it again, they'll get another sting.**—*Dean Rusk, Secretary of State, during press questions following a speech to the American Field Service, New York, August 1964.*[739]

Rusk was responding to questions about the North Vietnamese gunboat attacks against U.S. Navy destroyers in the Gulf of Tonkin and subsequent U.S. retaliatory attacks against North Vietnam.

430 **[The deployment of U.S. combat troops to Vietnam would provide] ammunition for Communist propaganda which falsely proclaims that the United States is conducting a "White man's war" against Asians.**—*Excerpt from a State Department booklet, August 1964.*[78]

The State and Defense departments collaborated to produce the pamphlet. Six months after the pamphlet was released the first American combat troops were deployed to South Vietnam.

431 **I have had advice to load our planes with bombs and to drop them on certain areas that I think would enlarge the war and escalate the war and result in our committing a good many American boys to fighting a war that I think ought to be fought by the boys of Asia to help protect their own land.**—*President Lyndon Johnson, from a speech in Stonewall, Texas, 29 August 1964.*[369]

The military constantly pressed the White House to use strong, decisive military force against North Vietnam. Johnson resisted and American military commanders were faced with target restrictions in North Vietnam until Johnson left office.

432 **This is a war for the confidence of the people, and the security of those people, and that kind of war is a long, hard war.**—*Robert McNamara, Secretary of Defense, during questions by reporters on his return from South Vietnam, May 1964.*[787]

433 **In every case ... every senior officer that I knew ... said we should never send ground combat forces into Southeast Asia.**—*General David Shoup, Commandant, U.S. Marine Corps, 1964.*[87]

Shoup, along with the members of the Joint Chiefs of Staff, did not advocate the use of American ground troops in South Vietnam in 1964.

434 **We seek no wider war...**—*President Lyndon Johnson, 1964.*[347]

Repeated in many of Johnson's speeches between 1964 and 1967.

435 **I do not wish to enter the patient in a 10-round bout, when he was in no shape to hold out for one round. We should get him ready for three or four rounds at least.**—*President Lyndon Johnson, during a White House meeting, 7 September 1964.*[147]

The meeting included discussions of the possibility of initiating a bombing campaign against North Vietnam to force them to stop supporting and directing the communist insurgency in South Vietnam. The political situation in Saigon was extremely fragile and Johnson and his advisers were afraid that such an air campaign could create a retaliatory backlash within South Vietnam that might be too much for the Saigon regime to deal with.

436 **[The Southeast Asia Resolution is] a functional equivalent of a declaration of war against North Vietnam.**—*U.S. State Department, 1964.*[555]

The Southeast Asia Resolution gave the President Congressional approval to take whatever action he deemed necessary in Vietnam to prevent further aggression by North Vietnam and the VC.

437 **I feel like a hitchhiker caught in a hailstorm on a Texas highway. I can't run. I can't hide. And I can't make it stop.**—*President Lyndon Johnson, comments to Bill Moyers, 1964.*[374]

Johnson was unable to goad Hanoi into submission by threats of military power. He was also unable to stabilize the Saigon government by threats of reduced aid and support. To withdraw from Vietnam would mean humiliation before the world and at home; he did not want to carry the brand of losing South Vietnam to the communists.

438 **Yesterday it was Korea, tonight it is Vietnam. Make no bones of this. Don't try to sweep this under the rug. We are at war in Vietnam. And yet the President, who is commander-in-chief of our forces, refuses to say — refuses to say, mind you — whether or not the objective there is victory, and his Secretary of Defense continues to mislead and misinform the American people, and enough of this has gone by.**—*Senator Barry Goldwater of Arizona, during his presidential campaign, July 1964.*[792]

439 **Mac, can't we be better protected from our friends? I know that everyone wants to help, but there's such a thing as killing with kindness.**—*Maxwell Taylor, Ambassador to South Vietnam, in a cable to McGeorge Bundy, 1964.*[629]

According to Nguyen Cao Ky, Taylor sent this cable to the White House because Johnson was considering introducing military–civil affairs personnel to participate in the air effort.

440 **If we leave Vietnam with our tail between our legs, the consequences of this defeat in the rest of Asia, Africa, and Latin America would be disastrous.**—*General Maxwell Taylor, Ambassador to South Vietnam, during a White House meeting, September 1964.*[374]

441 **A deeper military plunge neither was in the U.S. national interest nor would settle the question, it threatened to enlarge the morass in which we are now already on the verge of indefinite entrapment.**—*Senator Mike Mansfield of Montana, to President Johnson, 1964.*[374]

Mansfield was cautioning Johnson against further military involvement in Vietnam. Mansfield argued for a diplomatic solution along the lines of a neutral South Vietnam.

442 **The present authorized strength is about 20,000, which, in General Westmoreland's estimate, would last him. He foresaw no requirement beyond that in the coming year.**—*General Maxwell Taylor, U.S. Ambassador to South Vietnam, during testimony before Congress, 16 September 1964.*[241]

443 **It is not any problem to start a war.... I know some folks that I think could start one mighty easy. But it is a pretty difficult problem for us to prevent one, and that is what we are trying to do.**—*President Lyndon Johnson, from a speech in Manchester, New Hampshire, 28 September 1964.*[728]

444 **We are not going North and drop bombs at this stage of the game, and we are not going South and run out and leave it for the Communists to take over.**—*President Lyndon Johnson, from a speech in Manchester, New Hampshire, 28 September 1964.*[728]

445 **There are those that say you ought to go north and drop bombs, to try to wipe out the supply lines, and they think that would escalate the war. We don't want our American boys to do the fighting for Asian boys. We don't want to get involved in a nation with 700 million people and get tied down in a land war in Asia.**—*President Lyndon Johnson, Eufaula, Oklahoma, 25 September 1964.*[369]

446 **As your President I deal every day with the problems that affect your freedom and affect the peace of the world. Those problems may be remote from this peaceful site out here this afternoon. Not many of you get waked up in the night about Cyprus, or Zanzibar, or Vietnam. But I never send a reconnaissance mission out about 11 o'clock in our planes with our boys guiding them to take a look at what is developing, and realize they have to be back at 3:30 in the morning, but what promptly at 3:25 I wake up without an alarm clock, because I want to be sure my boys get back.**—*President Lyndon Johnson, Eufaula, Oklahoma, 25 September 1964.*[369]

447 **[The use of American combat troops in Vietnam] would be a mistake ... it is the Vietnamese's war.**—*General William Westmoreland, ComUSMACV, September 1964.*[87]

448 **I am completely tranquil, as I must be to have faith in this country's future. You know, we Asians are fatalistic. I believe in providential assistance.**—*Tran Van Huong, former Prime Minister of South Vietnam, 1964.*[728]

A group of military leaders, with Nguyen Khanh's agreement, dismantled the Khanh government and created a new civilian government for South Vietnam. Tran Van Huong was named prime minister and Phan Khac Suu, chief of state. This government lasted three months.

449 **We'd end up shooting at everything—men, women, kids, and the buffaloes.**—*John Paul Vann, former U.S. Army officer, comments on the possibility of U.S. troop deployments to South Vietnam, 1964.*[887]

Vann opposed the introduction of American combat troops to South Vietnam to carry on the war against the VC. He argued that the South Vietnamese had trouble distinguishing between friend and foe amongst the Vietnamese; for Americans, he thought it would be virtually impossible.

450 **I often wake up in the night and think about how many [men] I could lose if I made a misstep.**—*President Lyndon Johnson, from a speech in Manchester, New Hampshire, 28 September 1964.*[728]

Johnson, on the current loss of American troops in Vietnam—190 men killed, to date (September 1964).

451 **You mention the word nuclear, and all they can think of is the big mushroom cloud, the red blast and twenty million dead.**—*Senator Barry Goldwater of Arizona, during his 1964 presidential campaign.*[830]

Goldwater's musing on the possibility of using tactical nuclear weapons against the VC or North Vietnamese.

452 **For the moment I have not thought that we were ready for American boys to do the fighting for Asian boys. What I have been trying to do ... was to get the boys in Vietnam to do their own fighting with our advice and with our equipment. This is the course we are following.**—*President Lyndon Johnson, Manchester, New Hampshire, 28 September 1964.*[369]

453 **[An air effort against North Vietnam would cast the United States as] a great power raining destruction on a small power because we accused the small power of instigating what much of the world would quite wrongly regard as an indigenous rebellion.**—*George Ball, Under Secretary of State, in a memorandum, 5 October 1964.*[130]

Ball was one of the few Johnson administration officials who argued against the sustained bombing of North Vietnam.

454 **We are considering air action against the North as the means to a limited objective—the improvement of our bargaining position with the North Vietnamese. At the same time we are sending signals to the North Vietnamese that our limited purpose is to persuade them to stop harassing their neighbors, that we do not seek to bring down the Hanoi regime or to interfere with the independence of Hanoi.**—*George Ball, Under Secretary of State, in a paper on U.S. Vietnam policy, 5 October 1964.*[130]

455 **The VC are excellent at ambushes, but that's kind of a coward's way of fighting the war.**—*Unidentified senior military spokesman, Saigon, comment to the press, October 1964.*[886]

Throughout the war the American military hoped for large scale battles with the enemy, the set-piece battle. In such a battle American technology and sophistication of force would do severe damage to an enemy force which attempted large scale operations in the open, something the enemy did not do often.

456 **When one little old general in shirtsleeves can walk in and take Saigon, do you think I'm going to send American boys to fight 200 million Chinese waiting to come down those trails.**—*President Lyndon Johnson, onboard Air Force One, 1964.*[391]

Johnson was referring to the 1964 bloodless coup in Saigon in which General Nguyen Khanh came to power.

457 **The harsh fact ... is that, despite the use of overwhelming amounts of men, money and materiel, despite the quantity of well-meant American advice and despite the impressive statistics of casualties inflicted on the Viet Cong, the Communist subversive insurgents ... still retain the initiative to act at their will in the very areas of Viet Nam where Vietnamese and American efforts have been most concentrated.**—*General Edward G. Lansdale, former special adviser to President Diem, in a published article, October 1964.*[110]

458 **I didn't get us into Vietnam. I didn't ring up out there and say, "I want some trouble." I was out there in '61, one of the first things that I did. President Kennedy sent me out there when we were worried about the stability of the government there. We can't pick other people's governments. We have enough trouble picking our own.**—*President Lyndon Johnson, Louisville, Kentucky, 9 October 1964.*[369]

459 **As long as I am your President, I am not going to rattle our rockets, I am not going to bluff with our bombs. I am going to keep our guard up at all times and our hand out. But I am going to be willing to go anywhere, see anyone, talk anytime to try to bring peace to this world so these mothers will not have to give up their boys and have them wiped out in a nuclear holocaust.**—*President Lyndon Johnson, Casper, Wyoming, 12 October 1964.*[369]

460 **American boys will not be sent to do what Asian boys ought to be doing for themselves.**—*President Lyndon Johnson, 1964 campaign rhetoric.*[501]

461 **Some others are eager to enlarge the conflict. They call upon us to supply American boys to do the job that Asian boys should do. They ask us to take reckless action which might risk the lives of millions and engulf much of Asia and certainly threaten the peace of the entire world. Moreover, such action would offer no solution at all to the real problem of Vietnam.**—*President Lyndon Johnson, New York, New York, 12 August 1964.*[369]

Johnson was campaigning against Senator Barry Goldwater for the 1964 presidential election.

462 **The United States has not provided massive assistance to South Vietnam, in military equipment, economic resources, and personnel in order to subsidize continuing quarrels among South Vietnamese leaders.**—*Dean Rusk, Secretary of State, 1964.*[374]

Rusk's reference to the inability of Saigon's leaders to form a stable government due to infighting between rival military groups.

463 **The United States cannot substitute its presence for an effective South Vietnamese government ... over a sustained period of time.**—*George Ball, Under Secretary of State, in a memorandum to the President, October 1964.*[374]

Ball argued against the intervention of U.S. combat troops or initiation of a sustained air war against North Vietnam. He believed escalation would eventually lead to Communist China's direct entry into the war. He argued for a political solution at this early state of the conflict.

464 **What we might gain by establishing the steadfastness of our commitments, we could lose by an erosion of confidence in our judgments.**—*George Ball, Under Secretary of State, in a memorandum to the President, October 1964.*[374]

Ball opposed direct American military intervention in South Vietnam. He argued for a political solution as opposed to a military solution to the growing conflict.

465 **I want the mothers who must supply the boys, and I want the boys who must die in the wars, to know that no impulsive act of mine, no heat of emotion, is ever going to cause me to do a rash, dangerous, adventurous thing that might wipe out 300 million Americans.**—*President Lyndon Johnson, Memphis, Tennessee, 24 October 1964.*[369]

466 **When they lead your boy down to that railroad station to send him into boot camp and put a khaki uniform on him to send him some place [from] where he may never return, they don't ask you whether you are a Republican or a Democrat. They send you there to defend that flag, and you go.**—*President Lyndon Johnson, Pittsburgh, Pennsylvania, 27 October 1964.*[369]

467 **We don't want to get tied down in a land war in Asia.**—*President Lyndon Johnson, during the 1964 presidential campaign.*[79]

468 **The threat [of an air assault] may be as important as execution ... in producing desired Communist reactions.**—*Robert Johnson, State Department official, during a NSC planning session, November 1964.*[159]

Johnson was part of a NSC working group formulating options for the U.S. to take against Hanoi.

469 **We are in no hurry. The longer we wait, the greater will be the Americans' defeat.**—*General Vo Nguyen Giap, defense minister of North Vietnam, from an article published in Hanoi, 1964.*[949]

470 **Once on the tiger's back, we cannot be sure of picking the place to dismount.**—*George Ball, Under Secretary of State, comment to the President, 1964.*[278]

In late-1964 Ball argued against escalation of the U.S. military effort in South Vietnam. He cautioned the president against a sustained bombing campaign or the introduction of combat troops. The former would not deter North Vietnam from aggression in the South and in the latter, North Vietnam could match U.S. troop increases.

471 **Second place in our line of work is defeat of the unit on the battlefield, and death for the individual in combat.**—*Lt. Col. Harold G. Moore, Commander 1/7 Cavalry, speaking to his battalion, 1964.*[501]

472 **The ability of the Vietcong continuously to rebuild their units and to make good their losses is one of the mysteries of this guerrilla war...**—*General Maxwell Taylor, Ambassador to South Vietnam, during a White House meeting, late-1964.*[374]

473 **Not only do the Vietcong units have the recuperative powers of the phoenix, but they have an amazing ability to maintain their morale.**—*General Maxwell Taylor, Ambassador to South Vietnam, during a White House meeting, late-1964.*[374]

474 **We do not believe that attacks on industrial targets would so greatly exacerbate current economic difficulties as to create unmanageable control problems ... DRV leaders ... would probably be willing to suffer some damage to the country in the course of a test of wills with the U.S. over the course of events in South Vietnam.**—*William Bundy, Assistant Secretary of State, from a NSC memorandum, 17 November 1964.*[159]

The NSC working group was tasked with determining options for dealing with North Vietnam's continued support and direction of the communist insurgency in South Vietnam. Bundy chaired the committee.

475 **[The communists must be shown that] we are prepared to face down any form of escalation they might mount.**—*Walt Rostow, Department of State Counselor, recommendations, 1964.*[374]

Rostow argued for quick and forceful action in Vietnam.

476 **The DRV [Democratic Republic of Vietnam] contribution is substantial. The DRV manages the VC insurgency. It gives it guidance and direction [and] provides the VC [with] senior officers, key cadre, military specialists, and certain key military and communications equipment.... The DRV contribution may now be growing.**—*Excerpt from "NSC Working Group on Vietnam, Intelligence Assessment," 20 November 1964.*[925]

477 **Military action outside the country just as pure military action inside the country will not win in itself.**—*General Maxwell Taylor, American Ambassador to South Vietnam, during an interview released 23 November 1964.*[669]

Taylor opposed the introduction of U.S. combat troops to South Vietnam, but supported the bombing of North Vietnam to stop the flow of North Vietnamese men and materiel into South Vietnam. He believed a strong government in Saigon was necessary if the war against the communist insurgents was to be a success.

478 **It is absolutely inconceivable to me that the Viet Cong could ever militarily defeat the armed forces of South Vietnam.**—*General William Westmoreland, ComUSMACV, during an interview released 23 November 1964.*[669]

479 **We should delay China's swallowing up Southeast Asia until—she develops better table manners and—the food is somewhat more indigestible.**—*Michael Forrestal, Johnson administration adviser, in a memorandum to William Bundy, 23 November 1964.*[317]

Many in the Johnson administration argued for a sustained bombing campaign against North Vietnam. One line of reasoning was that it was necessary to stop the spread of communism to South Vietnam in an attempt to curb China's appetite. Many of the same advisers believed China was behind North Vietnam's push to take over the South.

480 **Communist strategy at present is designed toward bringing about a negotiation between some government in Saigon and their political arm which is the National Liberation Front...**—*Alexis Johnson, Deputy Ambassador to South Vietnam, in an interview, 23 November 1964.*[669]

Johnson believed the VC were incapable of winning militarily in South Vietnam and they were hoping to create a stalemate with the Saigon government that would result in a coalition government.

481 **[The United States must] first establish an adequate government in South Vietnam; second, improve the conduct of the counter-insurgency campaign; and, finally, persuade ... the DRV to stop supporting the Viet Cong.**—*General Maxwell Taylor, U.S. Ambassador to South Vietnam, during a briefing, 27 November 1964.*[925]

Taylor was appealing to the President, as the political and military situation in Saigon was fast deteriorating.

482 **You can only beat the other guy [VC/NVA] if you isolate him from the population.**—*Unidentified senior American Adviser, Saigon, December 1964.*[374]

483 **The Vietnamese are seeking triumph over communism manifested by insurgency, terrorism and aggression. Because we recognize the justice of their cause and its importance to all men, we provide them with support and assistance.**—*President Lyndon Johnson, during award ceremony, 5 December 1964.*[670]

Johnson awarded Captain Roger Donolon the Medal of Honor for actions in defense of the U.S. Special Forces camp at Nam Dong. He was the first Medal of Honor winner of the Vietnam War. The award was not posthumous.

484 **We are swatting flies when we ought to be going after the dunghill.**—*General Curtis E. LeMay, Commander, U.S. Air Force, December 1964.*[72]

LeMay was participating in a Pentagon computer wargame that simulated guerrilla war in Southeast Asia. Under the constraints of the game the Blue Team (representing SVN and U.S.) was unable to overcome the Red Team (VC and NVN). Constraints include guerrilla war, out of country sanctuaries, bombing restrictions and the threat of Chinese or Soviet intervention. LeMay believed all out bombing of NVN was the answer to stopping the insurgency in the South, and he was frustrated by the limitations place on his bombing campaign. In this case the dunghill was North Vietnam's POL facilities, Red River Valley dikes, port facilities, and air bases. Note: Some quote sources use "manure pile" instead of "dunghill."

485 **I have never felt that this war will be won from the air, and it seems to me that what is much more needed and would be more effective is a larger and stronger use of rangers and special forces and marines, or other appropriate military strength on the ground and on the scene ... know that it might involve the acceptance of larger American sacrifices [but] I myself am ready to substantially increase the number of Americans in Vietnam if it is necessary to provide this kind of fighting force against the Vietcong.**—*President Lyndon Johnson, in a cable to Ambassador Maxwell Taylor in Saigon, December 1964.*[374]

Because of escalated VC attacks in and around Saigon, Taylor pressed for retaliatory air strikes against North Vietnam. Johnson was hesitant to order widespread attacks at this time.

486 **All the world looks to this nation for its future, for the leadership that is required at this moment. And we cannot**

give that leadership and we cannot offer it if we are split up in guerrilla groups chewing on each other.—*President Lyndon Johnson, Washington, D.C., 10 August 1964.*[369]

487 **The Vietcong fought magnificently, as well as any infantry anywhere. But the big question ... is how its troops, a thousand or more of them, could wander around the countryside so close to Saigon without being discovered.**—*Unidentified senior American Adviser, Saigon, December 1964.*[374]

The adviser was referring to a series of major attacks by the VC on the outskirts of Saigon in December 1964. More than a thousand VC moved into position around Saigon to launch the attacks. The enemy troops traveled for several days from Tay Ninh, moving into position. Yet despite ARVN outpost, patrols and operations, the enemy troops moved into place without being detected.

488 **[A time comes] when the operation of the machine becomes so odious, makes you so sick at heart, that you can't take part; you can't even tacitly take part, and you've got to put your bodies upon the gears and upon the wheels, upon the levers, upon all the apparatus and you've got to make it stop.**—*Mario Savio, civil rights advocate, from a speech, December 1964.*[745]

Savio was speaking of civil rights at the time but his words came to apply to the war as well. It was continuing with no end in sight. Demonstrations against the war grew larger and more frequent.

489 **No matter which course is taken, it seems likely to us that we face years of involvement in South Vietnam.... We do not want a big war out there, but neither do we intend to back out of a 10-year-long commitment.**—*McGeorge Bundy, National Security Adviser, in a memorandum to President Johnson, 16 December 1964.*[231]

There was some argument within the Administration as to which course should be followed; bombing North Vietnam on a tit-for-tat basis, an all-out sustained air campaign, a gradually escalating campaign of bombing, or something else. Bundy believed that regardless of what was done we would be in Vietnam a long time.

490 **If Ambassador [Maxwell] Taylor [does] not act more intelligently, the United States will lose Southeast Asia and we will lose our freedom.**—*General Nguyen Khanh, Premier, South Vietnam, 22 December 1964.*[520]

Khanh made moves to dissolve the civilian government in Saigon, reinstating military rule. The U.S. cautioned Khanh against such a move through Ambassador Maxwell Taylor. In response to Khanh's moves the U.S. suspended ongoing aid talks between the two countries.

491 **We Americans are tired of coups.... We cannot carry you forever...**—*General Maxwell Taylor, Ambassador to South Vietnam, December 1964.*[374]

Taylor, reacting to a move by a group of South Vietnamese generals who arrested another group of generals who were planning a coup against the civilian Suu/Huong regime. Khanh, Thieu, and Ky headed the group supporting the regime. Taylor had cautioned the Khanh group against moves that did not demonstrate stability in the government; the arrests were seen as such a move.

492 **We should bomb them into the Stone Age.**—*General Curtis E. LeMay, Commander, U.S. Air Force, December 1963, during a reported exchange with McGeorge Bundy, December 1964.*[247]

The exchange between LeMay and Bundy supposedly took place during a Pentagon computer wargame simulating current conditions in Southeast Asia and Vietnam, and the conflict between the VC/NVA and the SVN/U.S. Rules of the game restricted American intervention and bombing of the North. LeMay, on the American team, wanted to bomb North Vietnam without limit, forcing it to end support and direction for the communists in the South. The flow of the wargame very closely unfolded as the actual war took place over the succeeding years. LeMay denied he made the "Stone Age" statement, saying he was misquoted.

493 **Our big advantage over the Americans is that they want to win the war more than we do.**—*Unidentified South Vietnamese government official's comments to correspondent, December 1964.*[374]

Description of the dilemma faced by the Johnson administration. The Administration was unable to stabilize the Saigon government, and threatened to cut off aid and or withdraw from South Vietnam if the political situation did not improve. But to withdraw from Vietnam was to admit defeat. The current leadership in Saigon realized this, rendering the American threats impotent.

494 **[The U.S. government is] the most hypocritical since the world began ... it was supposed to be a Democracy, supposed to be for freedom, but they want to draft you ... and send you to Saigon to fight for them while blacks still had to worry about getting a right to register and vote without being murdered.**—*Malcom X, black activist, from a speech in McComb, Mississippi, 31 December 1964.*[1005]

1965

Soldiers usually win the battles and generals get the credit for them.
—Napoleon Bonaparte

495 **No one has demonstrated that a white ground force of whatever size can win a guerrilla war—which is at the same time a civil war between Asians—in jungle terrain in the midst of a population that refuses cooperation to the white forces (and the South Vietnamese) and thus provides a great intelligence advantage to the other side.**—*George Ball, Under Secretary of State, in a memorandum to President Johnson, 1 July 1965.*[876]

Ball argued against increasing the U.S. ground force in Vietnam.

496 **Tonight Americans and Asians are dying for a world where each people may choose its own path to change. This is the principle for which our ancestors fought in the valleys of Pennsylvania. It is the principle for which our sons fight tonight in the jungles of Viet-Nam.**—*President Lyndon Johnson, address at Johns Hopkins University, 7 April 1965.*[365]

Johnson offered Hanoi $1 billion in reconstruction aid if it would stop its aggression against South Vietnam. He also offered unconditional discussions to reach a solution. North Vietnam's reply was there would be no negotiations as long as the U.S. remained in Vietnam.

497 **Hell, Vietnam is just like the Alamo. You damn well needed somebody.... Well, by God, I'm going to go, and I thank the Lord that I've got men who want to go with me, from McNamara right on down to the littlest private who's carrying a gun!**—*President Lyndon Johnson, 1965.*[403]

498 **Only significantly stronger military pressures against the Hanoi regime would give the Saigon government the relief and psychological boost it required to attain stability and viability.**—*Joint Chiefs of Staff, January 1965.*[374]

The JCS favored a heavy and sustained bombing campaign against North Vietnam to force them to stop the infiltration of men and materials into South Vietnam.

499 **This nation's commitment [in South Viet-Nam] in January, 1961 ... was not one that President Kennedy felt he could abandon without undesirable consequences throughout Asia and the world.**—*Theodore Sorensen, former Kennedy speech writer, in his book, Kennedy, 1965.*[81]

500 **The Indochina war cannot be considered a modern war since one of the opponents is entirely devoid of armor and air power.**—*Bernard Fall, historian and writer, 1965.*[13]

The first significant use of armor by the communists was in 1968. The first full use of armor by the NVA was during the 1972 Easter Offensive, the NVA invasion of South Vietnam. The communist air force played no role during battles in South Vietnam.

501 **Our goal is peace in Vietnam, that will come only when aggressors leave their neighbors in peace.**—*President Lyndon Johnson, State of the Union speech, 4 January 1965.*[768]

Speaking of North Vietnamese aggression against South Vietnam.

502 **We are presently on a losing track. To take no positive action now is to accept defeat in the fairly near future.**—*General Maxwell Taylor, U.S. Ambassador to South Vietnam, in messages to the White House, January 1965.*[374]

A series of VC attacks around and in Saigon intensified the deteriorating security situation in South Vietnam. VC terrorists bombed an American BOQ in Saigon to demonstrate the ineffectiveness of the Saigon regime and the impotence of America to protect its own soldiers.

503 **Our people in the north are bound to extend wholehearted support to the patriotic struggle waged by the people of the south.... Vietnam is one [and] the Vietnamese people are one.**—*Ho Chi Minh, President, Democratic Republic of Vietnam, during an interview, 1965.*[374]

Ho pronounced support for the struggle in the south, but all the time denied northern troops were in South Vietnam to assist the struggle.

504 **I could have ended the war in a month. I could have made North Vietnam look like a mud puddle.**—*Senator Barry Goldwater of Arizona, 1965.*[83]

505 **We ought to nuke the chinks.**—*General Curtis LeMay, U.S. Air Force Chief of Staff, 1965.*[729]

LeMay believed North Vietnam was the driving force behind the Viet Cong and the Chinese were the force behind the North Vietnamese.

506 **Victory for the Vietcong ... would mean ultimately the destruction of freedom of speech for all men for all time, not only in Asia but in the United States as well.**—*Richard Nixon, in a letter to The New York Times, 1965.*[474]

The Domino Theory taken to a new extreme.

507 **[It] is not that these cadres were exceptionally gifted.... The people were like a mound of straw, ready to be ignited.**—*Unidentified communist cadre, during interrogation, 1965.*[887]

This cadre was asked why the communist rebellion in South Vietnam had spread so quickly between 1955 and 1960. Many of the rural Vietnamese people were oppressed and under-served by the ruling Diem regime. They were ripe for revolution as they went from oppression under the French to more oppression under Diem. Because America backed Diem, America and Diem were seen as one.

508 **Outrages like this will only reinforce the determination of the American people and the government to continue and strengthen assistance and support of the people and government of Vietnam.**—*President Lyndon Johnson, 30 March 1965.*[1021]

Johnson was reacting to news of the VC terrorist bombing of the U.S. Embassy in Saigon. A car bomb exploded outside of the embassy killing two Americans and wounding 52 others. Twenty Vietnamese were also killed and 130 injured in the blast.

509 **The strength of the enemy offensive had completely overcome my former reluctance to use American ground troops in general combat.**—*General Maxwell Taylor, Ambassador to South Vietnam, 1965.*[307]

Taylor initially opposed the deployment of U.S. combat troops to South Vietnam in early 1965. The strength of the enemy continued to increase, unchecked by ARVN forces.

510 **[The United States can either negotiate and] salvage what little can be preserved, or resort to armed power to force a change of Communist strategy.**—*McGeorge Bundy, Special Assistant National Security Affairs, in a memorandum to President Johnson, January 1965.*[374]

The political and military situations were fast deteriorating in Vietnam. The VC had begun open conflict with the ARVN, and GVN control of the countryside was quickly shrinking to a few areas around the major towns and cities. Bundy recommended some move by the Johnson administration.

511 **We should not get involved militarily with North Vietnam and possibly Red China if our base in South Vietnam is insecure and Khanh's army is tied down everywhere by the Vietcong insurgency.**—*General Maxwell Taylor, Ambassador to South Vietnam, January 1965.*[374]

Taylor opposed the deployment of U.S. combat troops to Vietnam. At the time the Saigon regime had little control of South Vietnam and the military was insufficient to meet the internal communist threat, let alone deal with the threat from North Vietnam.

512 **[The homeless were] refugees from Communism who were voting with their feet.**—*Paraphrase of official U.S. explanation for the large numbers of South Vietnamese refugees, 1965.*[887]

By the end of 1965, Vietnamese refugees numbered in the tens of thousands. Many were the result of fighting between GVN troops and the VC, some as a result of political pressure by the VC or the GVN. Even more were physically displaced by the GVN program of creating strategic hamlets, where the people were forced out of their villes into government camps and hamlets to separate the people from the VC.

513 **The tragedy of Vietnam's revolutionary war for independence was that her "Benedict Arnold" was successful.**—*General Edward Lansdale, CIA specialist, 1965.*[887]

Lansdale likened Ho Chi Minh to America's Benedict Arnold, charging that Ho and his communist followers hijacked the Vietnamese nationalist movement for independence from the French, overlaying their goal of ruling all of Vietnam under communism.

514 **The army's tough, but it's good for us. We can get rank here where we can't even get jobs on the outside.**—*Unidentified black U.S. Army infantryman's comments to a journalist, 1965.*[860]

In the late-fifties and early-sixties the American military held more promise of advancement for blacks than they were likely to achieve in the civilian world.

515 **I have never seen any issue of significance which caused such uncertainty and questioning of policy.**—*Senator J. William Fulbright, Chairman, Senate Foreign Relations Committee, news conference, 24 January 1965.*[843]

Fulbright was expressing concern that the Senate should be consulted before resumption of the bombing of North Vietnam following the 1965 Christmas pause.

516 **We are losing the war in Vietnam. If our strategy is not changed we will be thrown out in a matter of months — certainly within the year.**—*Richard Nixon, former Vice President, to a group at the Hotel Roosevelt in New York City, 26 January 1965.*[810]

517 **Guerrilla warfare is in its use as a tool of political revolution — the single sure method by which an unarmed population can overcome mechanized armies, or, failing to overcome them, can stalemate them and make them**

irrelevant.—*Robert Taber, historian and author, from his writings, 1965.*[104]

518 **[It is a] courageous decision [by America] that Communism's advance must be stopped in Asia and that guerrilla war as a means to a political end must be finally discouraged.... This is the way it must be if we are to fulfill our pledge to ourselves and to others to stop Communist aggression wherever it raises its head.**—*Reporter and TV anchorman Walter Cronkite's comments on the war in Vietnam, 1965.*[652]

Cronkite backed the Administration's aims of stopping the spread of communism in Southeast Asia. He saw the combination of helping to build a new nation, while at the same time fighting communism to be a long term commitment.

519 **The crisis in Vietnam will not lead to war between the United States and Communist China so long as China itself is not attacked.**—*Mao Tse-tung, Chairman, Communist China, during an interview, January 1965.*[523]

The interview was conducted by Edgar Snow, released 11 February. Mao was responding to a question about the possibility of war between Red China and the U.S.

520 **If the RVNAF capability can be underwritten by political stability and durability, a significant turning point in the war could be forthcoming.**—*Excerpt from MACV Monthly Evaluation Report, January 1965.*[876]

The report was typically very optimistic about progress of the war. Items of negative interest were downplayed or discretely not included in the report. The report ultimately made it back to the White House and was one of the many tools used for formulating American policy and direction in Vietnam.

521 **There is only one means of defeating an insurgent people who will not surrender, and that is extermination. There is only one way to control a territory that harbors resistance, and that is to turn it into a desert. Where these means cannot, for whatever reason, be used, the war is lost.**—*Robert Taber, historian and author, from his writings, 1965.*[111]

The complete destruction of the VC would have required the destruction of North Vietnam. The U.S. did turn large tracts of South Vietnam into virtual deserts by killing vegetation with defoliants and declaring those areas free-fire zones.

522 **[TET holiday:] combination of All Souls' Day, a family celebration, a spring festival, a national holiday and an overall manifestation of a way of life.**—*Excerpt from U.S. Military Assistance Command Vietnam pamphlet, 1965.*[653]

An inadequate Western description of the TET holiday, the most important Vietnamese holiday celebration of the year.

523 **Pleikus are like streetcars.**—*McGeorge Bundy, Special Assistant to the President, 1965.*[258]

Bundy likened the dependability of a streetcar's schedule to the certainty of VC terrorist attacks. The Johnson administration used the VC attack against the U.S. installations at Pleiku as the reason for the start of sustained air strikes against North Vietnam. A contingency bombing program had been worked out in advance. Johnson determined that the next "spectacular" enemy event would serve as a trigger for U.S. air action against Hanoi. Pleiku was such a trigger.

524 **There's no place for families here now. There's a war going on.**—*Unidentified U.S. Marine Corps officer, Da Nang, February 1965.*[393]

Prior to the hostilities in South Vietnam in 1965, high ranking officers and Embassy employees posted to Vietnam were allowed the accompaniment of their dependents. Major VC attacks against Americans began in 1964 and continued into 1965. With the VC attack on the American base at Pleiku, President Johnson ordered the evacuation of all American dependents from Vietnam.

525 **[The North Vietnamese are a] bunch of stubborn bastards.**—*Unidentified aide to Aleksei Kosygin, following Soviet–North Vietnamese conference in Hanoi, February 1965.*[374]

The aide's description of the North Vietnamese during a conference between the Soviet Prime Minister and Hanoi leaders. Hanoi wanted more Soviet military aid, the Soviets wanted Hanoi to lean towards them rather than Red China. Hanoi was adamant about preserving its independence.

526 **I would never take advantage of my political position to resign for political reasons. That's not the way we play the game.**—*Adlai Stevenson, U.S. Ambassador to the United Nations, early 1965.*[849]

An anti-war group tried to shame Stevenson into resigning as U.N. Ambassador to protest the war.

527 **The judgment is that a regular program [of air strikes] will probably dampen VC activities in due course and will probably inspire the South Vietnamese to more effective efforts. The belief is widespread among the South Vietnamese that the U.S. is on the verge of bugging out.**—*John T. McNaughton, Assistant Secretary of Defense, in a cable to Robert McNamara, from Saigon, 7 February 1965.*[152]

McNaughton and McGeorge Bundy were on a fact finding mission to Vietnam when the VC attacked the U.S. base at Pleiku. They recommended the President launch retaliatory air strikes against North Vietnam.

528 **[The attack on the US base at Pleiku] was ordered and directed and masterminded directly from Hanoi.**—*Robert McNamara, Secretary of Defense, during a press announcement of retaliatory raids against NVN for the Pleiku attack, 7 February 1965.*[775]

529 **The Ministry of National Defense of the Democratic Republic of Vietnam severely warns the United States imperialists and their henchmen they must bear full responsibility for the extreme serious consequences of aggressive acts provoked by them.**—*Statement of the North Vietnam Defense Ministry, 7 February 1965.*[522]

Hanoi's response to U.S. air strikes against Dong Hoi. The strikes were in retaliation for the VC attack against the U.S. helicopter base and barracks at Pleiku, South Vietnam, 6 February 1965. The U.S. claimed North Vietnamese–backed communist guerrillas staged the attack which killed eight Americans and destroyed several aircraft.

530 **There is one grave weakness in our posture in Vietnam which is within our power to fix, and that is a widespread belief that we do not have the will and force and patience and determination to take the necessary action and stay the course.**—*McGeorge Bundy, Special Assis-*

tant to the President, in a memorandum to the President, 7 February 1965.[159]

Bundy had just completed a fact finding tour of South Vietnam with John McNaughton, and concluded that hard action was required to force Hanoi to stop its support and direction of the VC in South Vietnam.

531 **Suggesting heavy air attacks when the value of air action we have taken is sharply disputed and failing to examine the upper limit of U.S. liability [is] rash to the point of folly.**—*McGeorge Bundy, Special Assistant to the President, in a memorandum to Robert McNamara, 7 February 1965.*[153]

Bundy was commenting on McNamara's call for a heavy increase in the bombing of North Vietnam and the mining of harbors. There was some disagreement within the Johnson administration as to the actual effectiveness of the bombing thus far inflicted on North Vietnam. There was no indication that Hanoi's support to the South had slowed or stopped, and Hanoi was still defiantly refusing to negotiate.

532 **[The retaliatory attacks were] carefully limited to military areas which are supplying men and arms for attacks in South Vietnam ... the response is appropriate and fitting.**—*President Lyndon Johnson, White House statement, 7 February 1965.*[521]

The Administration claimed Hanoi planned and supported the VC attack against the U.S. helicopter base at Pleiku, South Vietnam. U.S. carrier–based aircraft struck enemy barracks and staging areas at Dong Hoi. Hanoi claimed the attacking aircraft strafed villages and the hospital at Dong Hoi.

533 **[US air raids against NVN are] a black page in American history.**—*Senator Wayne Morse of Oregon, speaking on the Senate floor, February 1965.*[751]

Morse opposed the air campaign against North Vietnam and Johnson's policy in Vietnam.

534 **I've had enough of this. I want three things. I want a joint attack. I want it to be prompt. I want it to be appropriate.**—*President Lyndon Johnson, speaking to the National Security Council, 6 February 1965.*[1021]

Johnson convened the NSC following the VC attack against the U.S. base at Pleiku. The surprise attack killed eight Americans and wounded 126 others. In retaliation Johnson authorized selective air attacks against North Vietnam. This Flaming Dart I strike was the start of the Rolling Thunder campaign against NVN.

535 **Get me a chisel and hammer and I will dig my own way out.**—*Unidentified American soldier, to rescue workers at the collapsed barracks in Qui Nhon, 10 February1965.*[671]

The soldier was trapped in the rubble of the building. On 10 February 1965 VC terrorist detonated bombs that collapsed a four-story barracks in Qui Nhon killing 23 Americans. The concrete BEQ housed American enlisted men.

536 **[The U.S. objective was to] give the people on the periphery of Asian Communism ... the confidence, and the help they needed to marshal their own resources in order eventually to live in peace and stability with their powerful neighbors.**—*President Lyndon Johnson, 1964.*[347]

Many in the Johnson administration associated Chinese communism directly with North Vietnam's communism.

537 **We have kept our guns over the mantel and our shells in the cupboard for a long time now. I can't ask our American soldiers out there to continue to fight with one hand behind their backs.**—*President Lyndon Johnson, during a meeting, February 1965.*[304]

Johnson discussed what the U.S. response would be to a VC attack against the U.S. facilities at Pleiku, 6 February 1965. Johnson ordered reprisal air strikes against NVA barracks locations in North Vietnam. These strikes were code named Flaming Dart.

538 **The United States can anticipate significant losses, yet the program [of sustained retaliation] seems cheap ... measured against the costs of defeat.**—*McGeorge Bundy, Special Assistant National Security Affairs, in a cable to President Johnson, 7 February 1965.*[374]

Bundy recommended sustained pressure against North Vietnam in the form of air strikes against military and industrial targets. He viewed American withdrawal, and defeat, as the only other alternative.

539 **China does not maintain any troops abroad, nor did it intend to fight as long as its own territory was not attacked.**—*Mao Tse-tung, Chairman, Communist China, during an interview, January 1965.*[523]

The interview was conducted by Edgar Snow, released 11 February. Mao was responding to a question about the possibility of war between Red China and the U.S.

540 **[To negotiate an American withdrawal] would mean surrender on the installment plan.**—*McGeorge Bundy, Special Assistant National Security Affairs, in a cable to President Johnson, 7 February 1965.*[374]

Bundy recommended sustained air strikes against North Vietnam to pressure them to stop their support of the VC in South Vietnam. He viewed withdrawal, and defeat, as the only other alternative at the time.

541 **The drumbeat of history is quickening.... We have had nine governments alone in Vietnam since I became President.**—*President Lyndon Johnson, Washington, D.C., 17 February 1965.*[369]

542 **Our primary objective ... was to communicate our political resolve ... future communications of resolve, however, will carry a hollow ring unless we accomplish more military damage than we have to date.**—*Robert McNamara, Secretary of Defense, in a memorandum to the JCS, 17 February 1965.*[925]

Early in the Rolling Thunder campaign against North Vietnam, McNamara complained that the air strikes were not sufficiently accurate to produce enough destruction to Hanoi's war making and supporting abilities.

543 **[We must] apply the maximum deterrent till he [North Vietnam] sobers up and unloads his pistol.**—*President Lyndon Johnson, February 1965.*[713]

Comments made by Johnson regarding VC attacks against American installations in Vietnam. Johnson held Hanoi responsible for the attacks because they were supporting and directing the communist insurgency in South Vietnam. The pressure Johnson chose to apply was a series of retaliatory air strikes against North Vietnamese facilities. These strikes were code named Operation Flaming Dart I & II.

544 **We should try to destroy the will of the DRV to continue their political interference and guerrilla activity. We should try to induce them to get out of the war without having their country destroyed and to realize that if they do not get out, their country will be destroyed.**—*Robert McNamara, Secretary of Defense, memorandum to JCS, 17 February 1965.*[159]

McNamara's desired results of a sustained bombing campaign against North Vietnam.

545 **Without new U.S. action defeat appears inevitable—probably not in a matter of weeks or perhaps even months, but within the next year or so.**—*McGeorge Bundy, Special Assistant to the President, in a report to President Johnson, February 1965.*[347]

Bundy's report was based on a fact finding trip to Vietnam in February. He saw the growing instability in South Vietnam and advised Johnson to implement sustained bombing against North Vietnam and their infiltration routes.

546 **[The bombing of North Vietnam] served to commit us deeply in Vietnam, and it is a commitment that must be carried through without hesitation or confusion of purpose.**—*Hedley Donovan, editor in chief, Time Inc., in Life magazine editorial, 19 February 1965.*[653]

Initially Time Inc. (*Life* and *Time* magazines) strongly backed Administration policy in Vietnam.

547 **We'll be at the conference table by September.**—*Unidentified Johnson administration official, early 1965.*[736]

The official did not believe North Vietnam could stand up to bombing by the U.S. Air Force and would be at the conference table discussing peace terms shortly after the bombing started.

548 **[Air] strikes—when they are carried out with bravery and resolution—can help force North Vietnam out of the military equation, and at the same time give new spirit to our friends in the South.**—*Life magazine editorial, 19 February 1965.*[394]

Life magazine's reaction to American retaliatory air strikes against North Vietnam, following VC attacks on U.S. installations in South Vietnam.

549 **[The use of American air power is to bring about] the cessation of infiltration from North Vietnam and the clear indication by the Hanoi regime that it is prepared to cease aggression against its neighbors.**—*President Lyndon Johnson, as quoted by Life magazine, 19 February 1965.*[394]

550 **Measured against the cost of defeat, the program [of sustained bombing of North Vietnam] would be cheap and even if it failed to turn the tide the value of the effort would exceed the cost.**—*John T. McNaughton, Assistant Secretary of Defense, during a report to President Johnson, February 1965.*[258]

McNaughton, having just returned from South Vietnam on a visit with McGeorge Bundy, urged the President to take strong action in Vietnam, commencing a sustained bombing campaign against North Vietnam.

551 **White-faced soldier armed, equipped and trained as he is [is] not suitable guerrilla fighter for Asia forests and jungles. French tried to adapt their forces to this mission and failed. I doubt that US forces could do much better.**—*General Maxwell Taylor, U.S. Ambassador to South Vietnam, in a cable to Washington, 22 February 1965.*[223]

Taylor opposed the deployment of U.S. combat troops to Vietnam. He argued that American troops were not trained in guerrilla warfare and were at a distinct disadvantage. He felt the guerrilla war should be fought on the guerrilla level, by the Vietnamese, who stood a better chance of discerning between Vietnamese friend and foe.

552 **We aim to raise the price of its [North Vietnam's] participation until the war no longer pays off for Ho Chi Minh.**—*Life magazine editorial, 19 February 1965.*[394]

Life magazine's reaction to American retaliatory air strikes against North Vietnam, following VC attacks on U.S. installations in South Vietnam.

553 **Purpose of a good shell is maximum maiming and bleeding effect, rather than outright mortality, since the aim is to create confusion and shock, lower morale and foul up the enemy's logistics.**—*Bill Mauldin, cartoonist turned correspondent, February 1965.*[393]

Discussing the sapper attack against the American compound at Pleiku, February 1965, and the merits of burdening your enemy with wounded as opposed to the easily disposable dead.

554 **In times of war and of hostilities, the first casualty is truth.**—*U Thant, Secretary-General of the United Nations, from a speech, 24 February 1965.*[808]

U Thant accused the U.S. of lying about the war in Vietnam and urged the U.S. to negotiate a settlement and withdraw from South Vietnam.

555 **I followed the President's advice a long time ago on not commenting on what dead men might have said or not said.**—*Bill Moyers, White House press secretary, response to the media, 24 February 1965.*[808]

Moyers was questioned by the press about an Eric Sevareid interview with Adlai Stevenson (Stevenson died in July 1965), who reported that U Thant had arranged for talks between the U.S. and Hanoi in late-1964, but the Johnson administration had declined to participate.

556 **There would be [the] ever present question of how [a] foreign soldier could distinguish between a VC and friendly Vietnamese farmer. When I view this array of difficulties, I am convinced that we should adhere to our past policy of keeping our ground forces out of direct counterinsurgency role.**—*General Maxwell Taylor, U.S. Ambassador to South Vietnam, in a cable to Washington, 22 February 1965.*[223]

Taylor opposed the deployment of U.S. combat troops to Vietnam. He argued that American troops were not trained in guerrilla warfare and would have a difficult job of distinguishing between Vietnamese friend or foe.

557 **I am sure that the great American people, if only they know the true facts and the background to the developments in South Vietnam, will agree with me that further bloodshed is unnecessary.**—*U Thant, Secretary General of the United Nations, during a news conference, 24 February 1965.*[524]

U Thant did not specify what the "true facts" were, which he eluded to during the news conference. He did urge the parties involved in the conflict in Vietnam to seek negotiations to settle the conflict.

558 **There are no authorized negotiations underway with Mr. Thant or any other government. I am not going into any diplomatic chitchat that may be going forth, or way-out feelers. But authorized or meaningful negotiations — no.**—*George Reedy, White House press secretary, to reporters, 24 February 1965.*[808]

Reedy was responding to reports that U Thant had arranged a meeting between the U.S. and Hanoi in late-1964, but the Johnson administration had declined to participate.

559 **Sure, Uncle Ho beat the French, but the Communists can never beat us — provided you remember that we turn out better boys at West Point than the French ever did in their military academy, St Cyr.**—*Unidentified American advisor, commenting to Nguyen Cao Ky, Prime Minister of South Vietnam, 1965.*[629]

The French originally trained a Vietnamese army to participate in the fight against the communists. When the U.S. became responsible for training the South Vietnamese they inherited this French-trained army, which required retraining of the Vietnamese in American tactics and methods. Many American officers believe that since the French lost in the first place their military training was not sufficient to stay the course in Vietnam.

560 **American aggressive actions have to cease in order to create conditions for the exploration of avenues leading to the normalization of the situation in Indochina.**—*Aleksei N. Kosygin, Premier, Soviet Union, 26 February 1965.*[525]

Kosygin stated the possibility of the war in Vietnam extending beyond the boundaries of the country if the U.S. continued attacks against North Vietnam. He hinted that the Soviets and the Communist Chinese could be drawn into the conflict.

561 **Ho Chi Minh has never doubted ultimate victory. To raise such a doubt would be our aim.**—*Admiral U.S. Grant Sharp, Commander-in-Chief, Pacific Command, in a message to the JCS, 27 February 1965.*[122]

Sharp proposed an intensified eight-week bombing campaign against North Vietnam, giving them notice that they would not be allowed to continue supplying and directing the insurgency in the South without pain and payment.

562 **A massive ground and air war in Southeast Asia would be a disaster for the United States.**—*Senator J. William Fulbright, of Arkansas, Chairman of the Senate Foreign Relations Committee, to President Johnson, March 1965.*[374]

A warning from Fulbright to Johnson. Fulbright had become increasingly concerned over the escalation of the war, citing the sustained air campaign against North Vietnam and the introduction of American combat troops in South Vietnam.

563 **[Rolling Thunder was designed] to apply a measured amount of strategic airpower in order to persuade the North Vietnamese leaders to cease their aggressive actions and to accede to President Johnson's offer of negotiating a peaceful settlement of the conflict.**—*General John P. McConnell, Chief of Staff, U.S. Air Force, 1965.*[713]

McConnell called this use of air power "strategic persuasion." This policy was also referred to within the Johnson administration as "measured response" or "graduated response" or "gradual response."

564 **[It is] difficult to strike a bite of food in the mouth without the flies riding in with it.**—*John Paul Vann, Hau Nghia Pacification Officer, in a letter, 1965.*[887]

Vann returned to Vietnam in March 1965 as an AID (U.S. Agency for International Development) officer. He was assigned to the Hau Nghia Province headquarters at Bao Tri. As a civilian he chose not to eat in the military advisers mess, but instead ate at local Vietnamese restaurants. These were mostly outdoors affairs, accordingly exposed to the elements.

565 **I want nothing more than to get our boys home. But I can't run and pull a Chamberlain at Munich.**—*President Lyndon Johnson, in a call to Washington Post columnist James A. Wechsler, 4 March 1965.*[750]

Johnson's reference was to British Prime Minister Chamberlain's appeasement of Hitler through concessions, in the hope of avoiding war in Europe.

566 **The limited mission of the Marines will be to relieve government of South Vietnam forces now engaged in security duties for action in the pacification program and in the offensive roles against communist guerrilla forces.**—*Department of Defense announcement on the deployment of U.S. Marines to Vietnam, 6 March 1965.*[672]

3,500 U.S. Marines deployed to Vietnam to protect the U.S. air base at Da Nang. The force was requested by General Westmoreland, who did not believe the South Vietnamese Army could provide sufficient security.

567 **A peace fraud and a big bluff.**—*Hanoi, official pronouncement, March 1965.*[452]

Marshal Tito of Yugoslavia called for unconditional peace talks to be held in Belgrade in March 1965. The U.S. agreed to attend, but the North Vietnamese refused.

568 **I fear to date that Rolling Thunder in [North Vietnamese] eyes has been merely a few isolated thunder claps.**—*Maxwell Taylor, U.S. Ambassador to South Vietnam, in a cable to President Johnson, 8 March 1965.*[159]

Taylor did not believe the initial Rolling Thunder air strikes were forceful enough to get Hanoi's attention. Johnson restricted the initial attacks and did not allow for multiple strikes against an already struck target.

569 **[Marshal Tito is] a stool pigeon of the United States.**—*Hanoi, official pronouncement, March 1965.*[452]

Hanoi's characterization of Yugoslavia's Marshal Tito. Tito called for unconditional peace talks to be held in Belgrade in March 1965. The U.S. agreed to attend, but the North Vietnamese refused.

570 **The whale in the sea and the eagle in the air cannot conquer the elephant in the jungle. We risk World War III in Vietnam. Even if we won, our own free institutions might not survive. So [do] we have to risk it to settle a pint-sized civil war in a feudal enclave 7,000 miles away?**—*Taylor Adams, letter to the editor, Life magazine, March 1965.*[396]

571 **The landing of the two infantry battalions is in its own way a far more significant act than the earlier attacks by U.S. airplanes, even though those attacks were directed against a country — North Vietnam — ostensibly not taking part in the direct war.**—*Tell Sell, Los Angeles Times journalist, writing for the Times, 10 March 1965.*[886]

The first sustained Rolling Thunder raids against North Vietnam commenced 2 March 1965, four days later the first U.S. ground combat troops deployed to Vietnam. The Marines' mission was to provide security for the air base at Da Nang, which was the primary airfield for land based aircraft striking North Vietnam and providing air support for the I Corps area. Many observers saw the deployment of ground troops as a change in administration policy for Vietnam.

572 **U.S. imperialists should get out of South Vietnam, taking their satellite troops and military equipment with them, and leave the true patriots of the NLF a decisive voice in settling the country's future.**—*Peace Program Announcement by the National Liberation Front, March 1965.*[452]

This announcement came after the Yugoslavian call for peace negotiations in Belgrade in mid–March 1965.

573 **Hanoi has not a good enough reason to negotiate — and the purpose of our air strikes, among other things, is exactly to give Hanoi such a reason.**—*Life magazine editorial, 12 March 1965.*[395]

574 **[The introduction of U.S. Marines would be the start of an] ever increasing U.S. combat involvement in an essentially hostile foreign country, it will be very difficult to hold the line once deployment begins.**—*General Maxwell Taylor, U.S. Ambassador to South Vietnam, in a message to President Johnson, March 1965.*[374]

Taylor's comment on General Westmoreland's request for two Marine battalions to protect American air facilities at Da Nang. Taylor opposed the introduction of U.S. combat troops into Vietnam.

575 **Ho is willing to enter negotiations only if there is an assurance in advance that the outcome will be on their terms and will, in effect, simply ratify the goals they have already stated.**—*Arthur Goldberg, U.S. Ambassador to the U.N., 1965.*[452]

Hanoi's conditions for the start of negotiations were so inflexible that they all but guaranteed there would be no peace talks. Two of the prime conditions for negotiations were the removal of Americans from South Vietnam, and the recognition of the NLF as the true government of South Vietnam.

576 **[There can be no peace until Hanoi] stops doing what it is doing and what it knows it is doing against its neighbors.**—*Dean Rusk, Secretary of State, in response to Hanoi's announcement of no peace, 1965.*[452]

Rusk was responding to Hanoi's announcement of no peace until the Americans withdrew from South Vietnam.

577 **A substantial U.S. troop commitment to Vietnam could be a quagmire ... without realistic hope of ultimate victory.**—*Clark Clifford, unofficial adviser to President Johnson, 1965.*[374]

578 **[U.S. policy in Vietnam could result in] lives lost, blood spilt and treasure wasted, [because] of fighting a war on a jungle front 7,000 miles from the coast of California.**—*The New York Times, editorial comments, 1965.*[347]

The *Times*, voicing concern over the bombing of North Vietnam and dispatch of U.S. combat troops to Vietnam.

579 **I have never discussed with a human being something he should say or shouldn't say on Vietnam. I think debate's healthy. It's good for us, provided it's responsible.**—*President Lyndon Johnson, news conference, LBJ Ranch, Texas, 20 March 1965.*[369]

580 **Talk of negotiations was a trick. Vietnam would settle its own political future and be reunited without any kind of foreign interference.**—*Ho Chi Minh, President of the Democratic Republic of Vietnam, 1965.*[452]

Ho rejected Johnson's peace feelers and rejected any attempts by third parties to arrange negotiations.

581 **[The conflict in Vietnam can be brought to an end only if the U.S. will] admit its mistakes without delay ... and immediately withdraw all its armed forces from South Vietnam.**—*Peking, People's Republic of China, in a broadcast announcement, 1965.*[452]

Hanoi's message to Washington was echoed by Peking. Washington responded that there could be no peace as long as Hanoi maintained its aggression against the South.

582 **[Justification for sending American soldiers to war in South Vietnam:]**

70%— To avoid a humiliating U.S. defeat (to our reputation as a guarantor).

20%— To keep SVN (and the adjacent) territory from Chinese hands.

10%— To permit the people of SVN to enjoy a better, freer way of life.—*John McNaughton, Assistant Secretary of Defense, in a memorandum to Robert McNamara, March 1965.*[887]

McNaughton's summarization of the Johnson administration's reasons for deploying U.S. combat troops to fight the communists in South Vietnam.

583 **How was it possible for an experienced Marxist such as Ho to get into war with America, without first assuring for himself the full political and military support of the Soviet Union? How could he only listen to the Chinese?**—*Pak Sung Chul, North Korean foreign minister, during an interview, 1965.*[450]

At this stage of history, North Korea was beginning to lean towards the Soviets and away from Mao's vision of communism.

584 **To win in Vietnam, we will have to exterminate a nation.**—*Dr. Benjamin Spock, noted pediatrician and anti-war activist.*[83]

585 **When we marched into the rice paddies on that damp March afternoon we carried, along with our packs and rifles, the implicit convictions that the Vietcong could be quickly beaten. We kept the packs and rifles; the convictions, we lost.**—*Philip Caputo, Lieutenant, U.S. Marine Corps, 1977.*[374]

U.S. Marines were the first regular American combat units deployed to Vietnam, March 1965.

586 **I thought that once they [the VC] ran up against our first team they wouldn't stand and fight. I made a miscalcu-**

lation.—*General Frederick Karch, U.S. Marine Corps, comments to the press, August 1965.*[887]

In the first major Marine operation of the war using armor, elements of the 3d and 4th Marine Regiments attacked the 1st Viet Cong Regiment near Chu Lai. The Marines claimed 614 VC KIA and had expected the VC to make a hasty retreat when the Marine force landed. Instead the VC put up stiff resistance. The Marines lost 51 men KIA, 203 WIA during Operation Starlite.

587 **Only American combat forces can prevent a humiliating U.S. defeat [in Vietnam].**—*John McNaughton, Assistant Secretary of Defense, during policy discussions on Vietnam, March 1965.*[374]

588 **If the American public must regard every loss as cause for "a new commitment" and expansion of the war, it appears that such commitments will eventually and inexorably amount to the commitment of suicide.**—*Rutherford H. Platt Jr., letter to the editor, Life magazine, March 1965.*[396]

589 **The type of gas that is a standard item in South Vietnamese military forces — anti-riot item — can be purchased by any individual from open stocks in this country just like you order something out of a Sears and Roebuck catalogue. I don't mean Sears and Roebuck's handling any gas, but it's the same — a catalogue almost that large — any of you can order it. If you felt that I was endangering your life and your family, you could use it on me right now in this room and it would bring some tears and it would nauseate me for — some of them three minutes and some five minutes, sometimes up to an hour. It would not kill me or kill you.**—*President Lyndon Johnson, during a news conference, Washington, D.C., 1 April 1965.*[369]

Johnson was responding to accusations of poison gas use by American forces in Vietnam.

590 **If the United States military forces were going to use poisonous gas, of course the Commander in Chief would know about it...**—*President Lyndon Johnson, news conference, Washington, D.C., 1 April 1965.*[369]

Johnson responding to press allegations of American units using poison gas in Vietnam.

591 **[The air campaign against North Vietnam had] not reduced in any major way North Vietnam's military capabilities or seriously damaged its economy, and the Hanoi regime continues to maintain, at least publicly, stoical determination.**—*General Earle Wheeler, Chairman, Joint Chiefs of Staff, to Robert McNamara, April 1965.*[374]

Results of several weeks of U.S. air strikes against North Vietnamese facilities, installations, and industrial areas, did not stop Hanoi's support for the VC guerrillas nor had it induced North Vietnam to sue for peace.

592 **I feel we must conduct our bombing attacks in a manner that will begin to hurt North Vietnam badly enough to cause the Hanoi regime to seek a political way out through negotiations rather than expose their economy to increasingly serious levels of destruction.**—*John McCone, Director, Central Intelligence, in a memorandum to the President, 2 April 1965.*[151]

593 **I think what we are doing in starting on a track which involves ground force operations ... [will mean] an ever-increasing commitment of U.S. personnel without materially improving the chances of victory.... In effect, we will find ourselves mired down in combat in the jungle in a military effort that we cannot win, and from which we will have extreme difficulty in extracting ourselves.**—*John McCone, Director, Central Intelligence Agency, in a memorandum, 2 April 1965.*[195]

McCone cautioned against the deployment of U.S. combat troops to SVN. Two Marine battalions deployed in March 1965 to protect the U.S. base at Da Nang, with an Army brigade planned for arrival in the III Corps area in April 1965.

594 **By limiting our attacks to targets like bridges, military installations, and lines of communication, in effect we signal to the Communists that our determination to win is significantly modified by our fear of widening the war.**—*John McCone, Director, Central Intelligence, in a memorandum to the President, 2 April 1965.*[151]

McCone recommended escalating the Rolling Thunder strikes to increase pressure on Hanoi to stop its support and direction of the VC in South Vietnam. McCone was just one of many in the Johnson administration who believed the Rolling Thunder strikes were not strong enough to obtain the desired effect.

595 **[War in Vietnam is due to] ... Communist attack which has increasingly been waged and directed from the North.**—*Representative Jeffrey Cohelan, California, from a speech on the House floor, 5 April 1965.*[850]

Cohelan's district included Berkeley and part of Oakland, both anti-war areas. He initially backed Johnson's war policy.

596 **I'm just not going to pull up my pants and run out on Vietnam. Don't you know the church is on fire over there, and we've got to find a way out?...**—*President Lyndon Johnson, during an animated discussion with Walter Lippmann, 6 April 1965.*[374]

Lippmann was one of the most outspoken media critics of American involvement in Vietnam. Johnson invited Lippmann to the White House to explain Administration policy and reasoning.

597 **Peace-loving nations will never forgive the United States imperialists barbarism...**—*Aleksei N. Kosygin, Premier, Soviet Union, in Poland, 7 April 1965.*[526]

598 **[Peace in Vietnam] demands an independent South Vietnam — securely guaranteed and able to shape its own relationships to all others — free from outside interference — tied to no alliance — a military base for no other country.**—*President Lyndon Johnson, from a speech at Johns Hopkins University, 7 April 1965.*[673]

During the speech Johnson stated the U.S. was open to unconditional discussions for peace in Vietnam. He also made an offer of $1 billion in development aid for Southeast Asia if the Hanoi regime would agree to negotiations.

599 **[As for the prospects of peace, I hope it will come swiftly] — but it is in the hands of others besides ourselves.**—*President Lyndon Johnson, from a speech at Johns Hopkins University, 7 April 1965.*[673]

600 **If the Communists can be persuaded to leave their neighbors alone, then peace is possible in South Vietnam and all of Southeast Asia.**—*Representative Jeffrey Cohelan, California, from a speech on the House floor, 5 April 1965.*[850]

601 **We fight because we must fight if we are to live in a world where every country can shape its own destiny. And only in such a world will our own freedom be finally secure.**—*President Lyndon Johnson, address at Johns Hopkins University, 7 April 1965.*[365]

602 **In recent months attacks on South Vietnam were stepped up. Thus, it became necessary for us to increase our response and to make attacks by air. This is not a change of purpose. It is a change in what we believe that purpose requires.**—*President Lyndon Johnson, Baltimore, Maryland, 7 April 1965.*[369]

603 **The confused nature of this conflict cannot mask the fact that it is the new face of an old enemy.**—*President Lyndon Johnson, from a speech at Johns Hopkins University, 7 April 1965.*[884]

Johnson, tying the aggression of North Vietnam and its support and direction of the communist insurgency in South Vietnam to the Communist Chinese. He accused Red China of being behind Hanoi's aggressive actions towards Saigon.

604 **We are becoming progressively divorced from reality in Vietnam ... and are proceeding with far more courage than wisdom.**—*Dr. Harold P. Ford, CIA Office of National Estimates, in a critique of U.S. policy in Vietnam, 8 April 1965.*[203]

Ford was one of several CIA analysts who believed the Johnson strategy of graduated response against North Vietnam would not bring the U.S. closer to its goals of a free, stable, and independent South Vietnam.

605 **We [must not] forget ... the VC insurrection remains essentially an indigenous phenomenon, the product of GVN fecklessness, VC power, and peasant hopelessness.**—*Dr. Harold P. Ford, CIA Office of National Estimates, in a critique of U.S. policy in Vietnam, 8 April 1965.*[203]

The CIA did not diminish the importance of Hanoi's influence and supply on the communist insurgency in South Vietnam, but many analysts concluded that bombing North Vietnam would not end the insurgency in the South. The feeling was that the introduction of American combat troops would not attain the Administration's goals for a free, independent South Vietnam, as long as the GVN was not stable and responsive to its people, especially the rural population which was at risk from communist influence.

606 **To abandon this small and brave nation to its enemies, and to the terror that must follow, would be an unforgivable wrong.**—*President Lyndon Johnson, from a speech at Johns Hopkins University, 7 April 1965.*[884]

Johnson was reaffirming the American pledge to stand beside, and behind, South Vietnam in its fight against the communists.

607 **Our objective is the independence of South Viet-Nam, and its freedom from attack. We want nothing for ourselves — only that the people of South Viet-Nam be allowed to guide their own country in their own way. We will do everything necessary to reach that objective. And we will do only what is absolutely necessary.**—*President Lyndon Johnson, address at Johns Hopkins University, 7 April 1965.*[365]

608 **The rulers in Hanoi are urged on by Peking. This is a regime which has destroyed freedom in Tibet, which has attacked India, and has been condemned by the United Nations for aggression in Korea. It is a nation which is helping the forces of violence in almost every continent.**—*President Lyndon Johnson, address at Johns Hopkins University, 7 April 1965.*[365]

Johnson, supporting the theory that North Vietnam was a tool of Communist China.

609 **They [Americans] are cowards. This is clear. The French used to lead the Vietnamese soldiers, but the Americans send them ahead while they come behind.**—*Huynh Tan Phat, General Secretary of the NLF, speaking to a photojournalist, April 1965.*[398]

The first American combat troops deployed to Vietnam in March and May 1965. Americans prior to this time were military advisers to the Vietnamese. Their role was advisory, not combat leadership for ARVN units. French officers led native troops (Vietnamese) against the Viet Minh during the First Indochina War.

610 **Old Ho can't turn me down.**—*President Lyndon Johnson, comments to Bill Moyers, 7 April 1965.*[374]

Johnson offered Hanoi a share in a multi-million dollar Mekong River development project for Vietnam, in exchange for Hanoi's participation in peace talks. He also promised increased military pressure if Hanoi did not cease its support of the southern guerrillas. With this carrot-and-stick approach, Johnson did not believe Ho could resist — Ho resisted.

611 **We must say in Southeast Asia — as we did in Europe — in the words of the Bible: "Hitherto shalt thou come, but no further."**—*President Lyndon Johnson, address at Johns Hopkins University, 7 April 1965.*[365]

612 **[The objective in Vietnam is] to break the will of the DRV/VC by depriving them of victory.**—*Robert McNamara, Secretary of Defense, in a memorandum, to President Johnson, April 1965.*[290]

At this point the plan was to continue the bombing of North Vietnam and send in 40,000 additional U.S. combat troops to deployed defensively around major U.S. bases, in an "enclave strategy." U.S. troops would provide security for the bases while the ARVN built up its forces and engaged the VC/NVA.

613 **We ... [support South Vietnam] ... to convince the leaders of North Viet-Nam — and all who seek to share their conquest — of a very simple fact: We will not be defeated. We will not grow tired. We will not withdraw, either openly or under the cloak of a meaningless agreement.... And we will remain ready ... for unconditional discussion.**—*President Lyndon Johnson, address at Johns Hopkins University, 7 April 1965.*[365]

614 **The enemy is brave, resourceful, skilled, and patient. He can shoot down our fancy aircraft, and he can shoot up and invest our bases.... Tough and hard-bitten, he has been**

at the job of subverting all of Indochina for over thirty years.—*Dr. Harold P. Ford, CIA Office of National Estimates, in a critique of U.S. policy in Vietnam, 8 April 1965.*[203]

Ford believed we could not expect to reason with the enemy because his thought patterns, priorities and values were completely different than ours.

615 **If the Americans want to fight us on equal terms, they'll need at least four million men.**—*Huynh Tan Phat, General Secretary of the NLF, speaking to photojournalist, April 1965.*[398]

The British determined, while fighting the communists in Malaysia, that they required a ratio of 10 troops/police for every communist guerrilla they were up against, in order to defeat the communist insurgency. If this ratio was used in Vietnam the Americans and their allies would have to total 2.8-4.3 million men to counter the estimated VC/NVA in South Vietnam.

616 **If I were Ho Chi Minh, I would never negotiate.**—*President Lyndon Johnson, comments to his staff, April 1965.*[374]

Johnson offered Hanoi a share in a multi-million dollar Mekong River development project for Vietnam, if they would consent to unconditional discussions on the future peace in Vietnam. The development project was Johnson's carrot in his 7 April 1965 carrot-and-stick speech, aimed at convincing Hanoi that he was willing to apply the necessary pressure if they were unwilling to yield. Johnson indicated to his staff that he respected Ho for his stand.

617 **Our men can live off the land, they can move freely. And above all, this is their land, and they'll die for it.**—*Huynh Tan Phat, General Secretary of the NLF, speaking to photojournalist, April 1965.*[398]

618 **[Okamura]—What type of government was planned if the Vietcong were successful?**

[Huynh Tan Phat]—Not Communist. A neutral government aligned with no one, but following a socialistic economic policy.—*Huynh Tan Phat, General Secretary of the NLF, speaking to photojournalist, April 1965.*[398]

Huynh Tan Phat became chairman of the NLF Central Committee in 1969. He was an ardent nationalist and socialist, but claimed not to be a communist.

619 **The further we explore the reality of what this country is doing ... in Vietnam, the more we are driven toward the conclusion of Senator Morse that the United States may well be the greatest threat to peace in the world today.**—*Paul Potter, peace activist and former SDS officer, speaking at a protest rally in Washington, D.C., April 1965.*[741]

620 **We're here to fight because it's in the interest of the United States that we do so.**—*James B. Stockdale, Wing Commander, U.S. Navy, speaking to his pilots, April 1965.*[120]

Stockdale was later shot down over North Vietnam and spent more than seven years as a prisoner of war in Hanoi.

621 **Until [their] independence is guaranteed there is no human power capable of forcing us from Vietnam.**—*President Lyndon Johnson, LBJ Ranch, Texas, 17 April 1965.*[369]

622 **The strikes to date have not caused a change in the North Vietnamese policy of directing Viet Cong insurgency, infiltrating cadres and supplying material. If anything, the strikes to date have hardened their attitude.**—*John A. McCone, Director, Central Intelligence, April 1965.*[713]

Excerpted from McCone's report on the initial effectiveness of the Rolling Thunder campaign.

623 **It is time that someone within the peace movement challenged activity which is in fact more hostile to America than to war.**—*Robert Pickus, peace activist, at a press conference, April 1965.*[734]

Pickus was responding to a planned peace march that was infiltrated by leftist factions, e.g., DuBois Clubs and May Second Movement.

624 **We must hit them harder, more frequently, and inflict greater damage. Instead of avoiding the [enemy jet fighters], we must go in and take them out. A bridge here and there will not do the job. We must strike their airfields, their petroleum resources, power stations and their military compounds.**—*John A. McCone, Director, Central Intelligence, April 1965.*[713]

McCone was not an advocate of the Johnson strategy of graduate response. He agreed with the JCS, who wanted swift, heavy, and decisive strikes against North Vietnam.

625 **[Demonstrations are a] stubborn disregard of plain facts by men who are supposed to be helping our young to learn ... how to think.**—*Dean Rusk, Secretary of State, from a speech to the American Society for International Law, April 1965.*[331]

An offended Rusk, responding to teach-ins conducted by resident professors at several university campuses. The teach-ins discussed U.S. policy in Vietnam and the escalation to war, and were highly critical of the Johnson administration.

626 **"Get Out of Vietnam"—That is not the way to end war in Southeast Asia or to help change America's mind about the use of national military power there.... America is involved in Vietnam. It should stay involved. The question is how...**—*Robert Pickus, peace activist, at a press conference, April 1965.*[741]

627 **We will never be second in the search for such a peaceful settlement in Viet-Nam.**—*President Lyndon Johnson, address at Johns Hopkins University, 7 April 1965.*[365]

628 **It is only when [the political] system is changed and brought under control that there can be any hope for stopping the forces that create a war in South Vietnam.**—*Paul Potter, peace activist and former SDS officer, speaking at a protest rally in Washington, D.C., April 1965.*[741]

629 **The Marines were not in Vietnam to sit on their ditty boxes, they were there to kill Viet Cong.**—*General Wallace M. Greene, Jr., Commandant of the Marine Corps, comments to the press, Da Nang, 28 April 1965.*[957]

When Marine ground combat units first deployed to Vietnam in March 1965, their role was designated as defensive only. Their mission, to protect the American facilities at the air base in Da Nang.

630 **They can't even bomb an outhouse without my approval.**—*President Lyndon Johnson, to the press, 1965.*[335]

Commenting on his tight personal control on the targets struck in North Vietnam, the ordnance used and in some cases, the routes to the targets.

631 **We're going to lose [this war] because of the moral degeneration in South Vietnam coupled with the excellent discipline of the VC. This country [South Vietnam] has pissed away its opportunities so long it is now force of habit — and apparently nothing is going to change them.**—*John Paul Vann, Hau Nghia Pacification Officer, in a letter, May 1965.*[887]

632 **My purpose in this plan is to begin to clear a path either toward restoration of peace or toward increased military action, depending upon the reaction of the communists.**—*President Lyndon Johnson, during an announced bombing pause, May 1965.*[713]

Johnson called a five-day pause in the bombing campaign against North Vietnam. He hoped Hanoi would respond by seeking negotiations or signal some repentance of their support and direction of the communist insurgency in South Vietnam.

633 **I'm bitter ... not at these ridiculous little Oriental play soldiers — but at our goddamn military geniuses and politicians for refusing to admit and act on the obvious — to take over command of this operation lock, stock, and barrel.... It is such a hopeless situation that nothing else will work.**—*John Paul Vann, Hau Nghia Pacification Officer, in a letter, May 1965.*[887]

634 **If they've been put there to fight, there are far too few. If they've been put there to be killed, there are far too many.**—*Ernest F. Hollings, Senator from South Carolina, 1965.*[83]

Comments on the deployment of U.S. Marines to protect the air base at Da Nang in 1965.

635 **So I warn you and I plead of you, if you have any suggestions or any views, or any differences, with your President — and all of you do at times, we don't see everything alike or we would all want the same wife — but communicate them to me through Uncle Sam, or Western Union, or directly, or through your friends. Don't send them through my intelligence bulletin via Peking or Hanoi or Moscow.**—*President Lyndon Johnson, Washington, D.C., 3 May 1965.*[369]

636 **The little bastard, General Ky, made a speech today demanding that we invade the North and liberate North Vietnam — the goddamn little fool can't even drive a mile outside of Saigon without an armed convoy and he wants to liberate the North! How damned ridiculous can you get?**—*John Paul Vann, Hau Nghia Pacification Officer, in a letter, May 1965.*[887]

General Ky (Premier Nguyen Cao Ky), as General Khanh before him, advocated taking the war to North Vietnam.

637 **Prime minister is not a profession; and being prime minister is certainly not my profession. My profession is pilot.**—*Nguyen Cao Ky, Prime Minister of South Vietnam, May 1965.*[629]

After the birth of his daughter, a nurse completing the paperwork asked him his profession.

638 **I am convinced that, even though the National Liberation Front is Communist-dominated, that the great majority of the people supporting it are doing so because it is their only hope to change and improve their living conditions and opportunities.**—*John Paul Vann, Hau Nghia Pacification Officer, in a letter to General Robert York, May 1965.*[887]

639 **[The United States must] not lose sight of the basically political aspect of the war. In the final analysis, it can only be won at the SVN hamlet level.**—*Admiral William F. Raborn, Jr., Director, Central Intelligence, in a memorandum to President Johnson, 6 May 1965.*[226]

Raborn became the director of Central Intelligence in April 1965, replacing John McCone.

640 **If I were a lad of eighteen faced with the same choice — whether to support the GVN or the NLF — and a member of a rural community, I would surely choose the NLF.**—*John Paul Vann, Hau Nghia Pacification Officer, in a letter to General Robert York, May 1965.*[887]

641 **[The US bombing pause is a] worn-out trick of deceit and threat.**—*North Vietnam spokesman, May 1965.*[347]

North Vietnam's response to a five-day bombing halt initiated by the U.S. In a Johnson message to Hanoi, he offered to back off on the air attacks against North Vietnam if the NVA/VC reduced their military activity in South Vietnam.

642 **We should hammer home the main theme of our intent to destroy their military capacity and our determination to continue until the military leave their cousins in peace.**—*Admiral U.S. Grant Sharp, Commander-in-Chief, Pacific Command, in a message to the JCS, 12 May 1965.*[123]

Sharp continued to press for more aggressive bombing of North Vietnam, feeling that when the damage was great enough, they would back away from their aggression in the South. The destruction caused by the bombing would focus Hanoi's efforts on the internal problems a massive bombing campaign would make on their industry, POLs and LOCs.

643 **Next time you need a dam in Idaho, ask Walter Lippmann for one.**—*President Lyndon Johnson, during a Congressional briefing in 1965.*[721]

Johnson's response to criticism of his Vietnam policy by Senator Frank Church of Idaho. Johnson asked Church, whom he had consulted for his anti-administration speeches, the Senator had responded: Walter Lippmann. Lippmann was an outspoken critic of Johnson's policy in Vietnam.

644 **The days of Buddha's birthday seem to me to provide an excellent opportunity for a pause in air attacks ... which I could use to good effect with world opinion.**—*President Lyndon Johnson, to Ambassador Maxwell Taylor, 1965.*[713]

The first bombing pause of the Rolling Thunder campaign took place in May 1965 and lasted five days. As the Administration expected, Hanoi rejected the call for negotiations as long as it was being attacked by the U.S.

645 **If we took the Marines now in the Dominican Republic and sent them to South Vietnam we would be a good deal better off in both countries.**—*Arthur Schlesinger, Jr., former Kennedy aide, speaking at a teach-in, 15 May 1965.*[748]

Schlesinger represented the government's view at the teach-in even though he was no fan of Johnson. In April 1965 Johnson ordered U.S. Marines to the Dominican Republic to restore order after perceived communist-led uprisings threatened to topple the government.

646 **Walter Lippmann is a fine man. I admire him. Next time you're in trouble out in Idaho, Frank, you ask Walter to come**

and help.—*President Lyndon Johnson, in an exchange with Senator Frank Church, March 1965.*[397]

Johnson told Church that some of his recent speeches against Administration policy in Vietnam weren't very helpful. He also reminded Church that he had come out to Idaho on occasion to support Church. Church responded that his speeches weren't much different than what columnist Walter Lippmann was writing about Vietnam. Lippmann was an opponent of Johnson's policy in Southeast Asia.

647 **There is a revolution going on in this country — and the principles, goals, and desires of the other side are much closer to what Americans believe in than those of the GVN [the Saigon Government].**—*John Paul Vann, Hau Nghia Pacification Officer, in a letter to General Robert York, May 1965.*[887]

York had commanded a special detachment in Vietnam in 1962 that experimented and tested equipment, weapons, and tactics for the Pentagon. York came to respect Vann's views on Vietnam and his capabilities.

648 **The time has come to call a spade a bloody shovel. This country is in an undeclared and unexplained war in Vietnam. Our masters have a lot of long and fancy names for it, like escalation and retaliation, but it is a war just the same.**—*James Reston, correspondent for The New York Times, 1965.*[374]

When Johnson initiated the sustained air strikes against North Vietnam, he made limited public disclosure of exactly why the strikes were taking place and the long term implications of escalation of force in Vietnam. Many in the media became skeptical of the Administration's policy in Vietnam.

649 **[Probe] every serious avenue leading to a possible settlement. It won't be what we want, but we can learn to live with it.**—*Clark Clifford, unofficial adviser to President Johnson, speaking to President Johnson, 17 May 1965.*[291]

Clifford opposed the deployment of large numbers of U.S. troops to South Vietnam. He agreed with George Ball that once troops were committed to Vietnam it would be very difficult to pull them out. He recommended seeking an early settlement of the war with the enemy.

650 **If it were not for the fact that Vietnam is but a pawn in the larger East-West confrontation, and that our presence here is essential to deny the resources of this area to Communist China, then it would be damned hard to justify our support of the existing government [of South Vietnam].**—*John Paul Vann, Hau Nghia Pacification Officer, in a letter to General Robert York, May 1965.*[887]

651 **[Nguyen Van Thieu, is a man of] considerable poise and judgment.**—*General Maxwell Taylor, Ambassador to South Vietnam, 1965.*[307]

Thieu and Ky came to power in a bloodless coup in May 1965. Ky as prime minister and Thieu as Commander-in-Chief of the armed forces and chief of state.

652 **The DRV Government resolutely exposes the U.S. government's trick in the so-called suspension of air raids against North Vietnam as a deceitful maneuver designed to pave the way for new U.S. acts of war.**—*Public statement from the Democratic Republic of Vietnam, 18 May 1965.*[875]

This was Hanoi's response to an announced American halt to the bombing of North Vietnam. Continuation of the halt was contingent on a cessation of attacks on ARVN and American facilities in South Vietnam. Hanoi rejected the offer. The bombing pause went into effect 12 May. In recognition of the U.S. announced bombing pause the VC attacked the U.S. compound at Song Be on 11 May 1965.

653 **When the Chinese brand of Communism takes over ... these "revolutionaries" are going to be sadly disappointed — but then it will be too late — for them; and too late for us to win them.**—*John Paul Vann, Hau Nghia Pacification Officer, in a letter to General Robert York, May 1965.*[887]

654 **[The Ky-Thieu directorate] seemed to all of us the bottom of the barrel, absolutely the bottom of the barrel.**—*William Bundy, Assistant Secretary of State, 1965.*[291]

Thieu and Ky came to power in a bloodless coup in May 1965. Ky as prime minister and Thieu as chief of state. It was the eighth South Vietnamese government since the coup against Diem in November 1963. Ky had a reputation as a playboy and hot-head. Thieu's political abilities were unknown.

655 **When the ground troops pushed the Viet Cong into the river, it was just like shooting sitting ducks...**—*James E. Horner, U.S. Marine helicopter door gunner, comments to a correspondent, 29 May 1965.*[674]

During an ARVN operation 25 miles south of Da Nang, a large group of Viet Cong were flushed into a river. When American gunships took the VC under fire, 85 VC were killed and 27 taken prisoner. U.S. casualties were one wounded; the ARVN lost one man killed and three wounded.

656 **American soldiers will begin to take heavy casualties in a war they are ill-equipped to fight in a non-cooperative if not downright hostile countryside; [to compensate for the losses, more troops will be sent out, and eventually the involvement will be] so great that we cannot — without national humiliation — stop.**—*George Ball, Under Secretary of State, recommendations to President Johnson, June 1965.*[374]

The bulk of American troops in 1965 were trained for war in Europe. Only a very small number of U.S. troops had jungle warfare training, and even smaller numbers had counterinsurgency training or experience.

657 **At this anguished, delicate and perhaps determining moment, I feel I'm serving you and our country best by not taking part in the White House Festival of the Arts.**—*Robert Lowell, poet, in a letter to President Johnson, 2 June 1965.*[728]

Lowell was reacting negatively to the bombing of North Vietnam and chose not to participate in the Festival even though he had originally accepted the invitation to the White House.

658 **Some of them insult me by staying away and some of them insult me by coming.**—*President Lyndon Johnson, off hand remark made within range of reporters, June 1965.*[728]

Johnson's reaction to some intellectuals who did not want to attend the White House Arts Festival; and those who wanted to use the occasion to voice their objection to the war.

659 **A change in DRV attitudes can probably be brought about only when, along with a sense of mounting pain from the bombings, there is also a conviction on their part that the tide has turned or soon will turn against them in the South.**—

Maxwell Taylor, U.S. Ambassador to South Vietnam, in a cable to George Ball, 3 June 1965.[153]

Taylor believed a maximum campaign of air power needed to be used against North Vietnamese lines of communications to stem the flow of support to the South and put Hanoi in a more receptive state for negotiations.

660 **Our ... intervention would appear to be turning the conflict into a white man's war, with the United States in the shoes of the French.**—*McGeorge Bundy, Special Assistant National Security Affairs, during policy discussions, June 1965.*[374]

Bundy recommended capping the American force in Vietnam at 100,000 men and trying for a stalemate. At which point Hanoi might consider negotiations to fend off further U.S. troop deployments or perhaps Saigon could come to some political arrangement with North Vietnam to end the conflict.

661 **The Vietnamese forces are carrying the brunt of combat operations. Those United States forces assigned as advisers to the armed forces of Vietnam remain in that capacity.**—*Robert J. McCloskey, State Department spokesman, during a press conference, 5 June 1965.*[957]

Regarding questions as to whether the role of U.S. ground combat forces had been changed since their deployment in March (Marines) and May (Army 173d Airborne Brigade). The press cited instances of Marine and Army combat units making small offensive operations around their base areas.

662 **The South Vietnamese armed forces cannot stand up to these pressures without substantial U.S. combat support on the ground.**—*General William Westmoreland, ComUSMACV, in a request for additional American troops, June 1965.*[374]

The VC unleashed another series of attacks across the country, further depleting South Vietnam's ineffective forces. Westmoreland requested the immediate deployment of an additional 180,000 U.S. troops to stem the collapse of South Vietnam.

663 **[If we are to avoid disaster in Vietnam there is] ... no solution ... other than to put our own finger in the dike.**—*General William Westmoreland, ComUSMACV, 1965.*[335]

The situation continued to deteriorate in South Vietnam. ARVN forces were insufficient to stop VC gains in the countryside. Westmoreland requested U.S. combat troops to shore up the situation and save South Vietnam from total collapse.

664 **We are in for the long pull. ... I see no likelihood of achieving a quick, favorable end to the war.**—*General William Westmoreland, ComUSMACV, in a request for additional American troops for Vietnam, June 1965.*[374]

665 **[The Communists can only be defeated by] a dedicated people and a strong government which dares to accept its responsibility before the nation and history.**—*Nguyen Van Thieu, Chief of State, June 1965.*[413]

In June 1965, a National Leadership Council of South Vietnamese generals established Thieu as Chief of State and Air Marshal Nguyen Cao Ky as Premier (Prime Minister) of South Vietnam. Ky and Thieu ruled in this capacity until 1967 when national elections were held and Thieu was elected president.

666 **[Further escalation of the war could drag the nation into] a bloody and protracted jungle war in which the strategic advantages would be with the other side.**—*Senator J. William Fulbright of Arkansas, Chairman of the Senate Foreign Relations Committee, during a Senate speech, June 1965.*[374]

Fulbright was opposed to escalating the war, but he was also opposed to unconditional retreat from Vietnam. His Senate speech stated the Administration's case for escalation, but he was unable to give the policy his unswerving, personal support.

667 **How many more secret, undebated Presidential decisions will it take to convince us that a constitutional crisis exists in America, that we have moved into a twilight zone between democratically delegated authority and something accurately called "Fascism?"**—*Professor Staughton Lynd, Yale professor, anti-war activist, in a published article, June 1965.*[742]

Johnson was able to raise troop levels and escalate the war in Vietnam without Congressional interference or approval, thus bypassing the normal avenues of political debate.

668 **It was obvious that neither the air war, nor the ground war, nor the political war was going well. The original hope, that with Americans securing major bases, the South Vietnamese could successfully carry the fight to the Viet Cong, was fading fast.**—*General Edwin H. Simmons, U.S. Marine Corps, 1965.*[893]

The situation in SVN in mid–1965 as reported during a meeting of the NSC.

669 **I am opposed to an unconditional American withdrawal from South Vietnam because such action would betray our obligation to people we have promised to defend, because it would weaken or destroy the credibility of American guarantees to other countries and because such a withdrawal would encourage the view in Peking and elsewhere that guerrilla wars supported from outside are relatively safe and inexpensive ways of expanding Communist power.**—*Senator J. William Fulbright, Chairman Senate Foreign Relations Committee, in a speech, 15 June 1965.*[737]

670 **If the Vietcong have anything to offer or negotiate, they would have no difficulty in finding a government with which to discuss it.**—*President Lyndon Johnson, during a press conference, 17 June 1965.*[527]

Johnson rejected the possibility of U.S. negotiations with the Vietcong on the grounds that the VC leadership consisted of men from North Vietnam, directed and sustained by Hanoi. Therefore negotiations should be between the U.S. and North Vietnam.

671 **We don't know anything about Communism, socialism and all that, but we do know that Negroes have caught hell here under this American Democracy.**—*From the McComb Freedom Democratic Party petition, circulated in summer, 1965.*[848]

This group and their petition called on blacks not to fight in Vietnam as long as their families were living under discrimination and oppression in Mississippi.

672 **[The plan is] rash to the point of folly.**—*McGeorge Bundy, Special Assistant National Security Affairs, during policy discussions, June 1965.*[374]

Bundy's description of a proposed plan of action recommended by the Pentagon and seconded by Robert McNamara. The plan called for the deployment of a large number of U.S.

combat troops, call-up of the Reserves, and a massive bombing campaign against North Vietnam (to include strikes against all their airfields, military, and industrial installations) and mining of the harbors. McNamara and the Pentagon wanted to demonstrate American military power so the communists would know they could not win when it came to actual war.

673 **[Deployment of large numbers of American combat troops was] a slippery slope toward total U.S. responsibility and corresponding fecklessness on the Vietnamese side.**—*McGeorge Bundy, Special Assistant National Security Affairs, during policy discussions, June 1965.*[374]

674 **The Viet Cong are capable of mounting regimental size operations in all four South Vietnam corps areas, desertion rates in the Vietnamese army are inordinately high. Battle losses have been higher than expected. I see no course of action open to us except to reinforce our efforts with additional United States or third country forces as rapidly as is practicable during the critical weeks ahead.**—*General William Westmoreland, ComUSMACV, reporting to Washington, June 1965.*[629]

The communists began a summer offensive in May and quickly increased their territorial control. Westmoreland requested an additional thirty-three American combat battalions for Vietnam.

675 **[The] objective is to cause the DRV to cease and desist in its support of the insurgency in Southeast Asia.**—*Admiral U.S. Grant Sharp, Commander-in-Chief, Pacific Command, in his orders initiating the Rolling Thunder campaign, June 1965.*[122]

Admiral Sharp was the operational director of the Rolling Thunder campaign, as well as all operations in the Pacific theater.

676 **I have, indeed, always believed that it is impossible for a great power which must take care of its prestige to admit, in so many words, that its policy has been mistaken during the last 10 years and leave the theater of operations.**—*Professor Hans Morgenthau, University of Chicago, during a televised debate on Vietnam, 21 June 1965.*[748]

Morgenthau debated McGeorge Bundy about the war and thought the U.S. should pull out of Vietnam as de Gaulle had done in Algeria.

677 **If help is requested by the appropriate Vietnamese commander, General Westmoreland also has authority within the assigned mission to employ those troops in support of Vietnamese forces faced with aggressive attack when other effective reserves are not available and when, in his judgment, the general military situation requires it.**—*Johnson administration, White House press release, June 1965.*[629]

The White House indicated the mission of U.S. combat troops in Vietnam had not changed, i.e., U.S. troops were to safeguard important U.S. military installations by means of area patrolling and security operations. The statement emphasized that there was no change in the mission and no orders from Johnson to Westmoreland to change the mission. But the statement also added the above quote, and by the end of June 1965 elements of the 173d Airborne and an Australian unit conducted a combined operation with the South Vietnamese, the first search and destroy operation using regular U.S. ground combat forces.

678 **I may have been dead wrong on Laos, but it doesn't prove that I am dead wrong on Vietnam.**—*Professor Hans Morgenthau, University of Chicago, during a televised debate on Vietnam, 21 June 1965.*[748]

Morgenthau's reaction to Bundy noting that he (Morgenthau) had been wrong about Laos. Morgenthau said in 1961 that "Communist domination of Laos is a foregone conclusion." At that point in time Laos had a coalition government and was not totally communist. Bundy was using this point to illustrate that Morgenthau had been wrong about Laos, and was also wrong about his views on Vietnam

679 **A wanton act of murder.**—*American Embassy statement, Saigon, South Vietnam, 25 June 1965.*[675]

U.S. Embassy reaction to an announcement by the Viet-cong that they had executed American Army Sgt. Harold G. Bennett. The execution was conducted in retaliation for the GVN execution of Tran Van Dang, a convicted VC agent. Sgt. Bennett was an adviser with a ARVN Ranger force. The force was overrun by the VC and Bennett was captured.

680 **We doubt if the Communists are likely to change their basic strategy in Vietnam unless and until two conditions prevail: (1) They are forced to accept a situation in the South which offers them no prospect of an early victory and no grounds for hope that they can simply outlast the U.S. and (2) North Vietnam itself is under continuing and increasingly damaging punitive attack.**—*Robert McNamara, Secretary of Defense, in a memorandum to the President, 26 June 1965.*[153]

In June 1965 McNamara called for increased bombing of North Vietnam and the mining of their harbors. Johnson and some of his advisers considered McNamara's call for escalation of the air war excessive.

681 **Perhaps next time we should keep going, occupying for a time the rooms from which orders issue and sending to the people of Vietnam and the Dominican Republic the profound apologies which are due; or quietly waiting on the Capitol steps until those who make policy for us, and who like ourselves are trapped by fear and pride, consent to enter into dialog with us and mankind.**—*Professor Staughton Lynd, Yale professor, anti-war activist, in a published article, June 1965.*[742]

Lynd was referring to the 17 April 1965 peace march in Washington, D.C.

682 **We have no basis for assuming that the Viet Cong will fight a war on our terms when they can continue to fight the kind of war they fought so well against both the French and the GVN [Government of South Vietnam].**—*George Ball, Under Secretary of State, in a memorandum to the President, 29 June 1965.*[153]

683 **The enemy will not be scared into quitting.**—*George Ball, Under Secretary of State, in a memorandum to the President, 29 June 1965.*[153]

Ball argued against the McNamara plan for increased bombing of North Vietnam. He believed the attempt to force Hanoi into submission would have the opposite effect.

684 **It is within our power to give much more drastic warnings to Hanoi than any we have yet given. If General Eisenhower is right in his belief that it was the prospect of nuclear attack which brought an armistice in Korea, we should at least consider what realistic threat of larger action is available to us for communication to Hanoi.**—*McGeorge Bundy, Special Assistant to the President, in a memorandum to Robert McNamara, 30 June 1965.*[153]

685 **The guns and the bombs, the rockets and the warships, are all symbols of human failure. They are necessary symbols. They protect what we cherish. But they are witness to human folly.**—*President Lyndon Johnson, address at Johns Hopkins University, 1965.*[365]

Lyndon B. Johnson Library—speech text.

686 **The South Vietnamese are losing the war to the Viet Cong. No one can assure you that we can beat the Viet Cong or even force them to the conference table on our terms, no matter how many hundred thousand white, foreign (U.S.) troops we deploy.**—*George Ball, Under Secretary of State, in a memorandum to President Johnson, 1 July 1965.*[876]

There were nearly 75,000 Americans in Vietnam at this time, including a brigade of Army airborne troops and several Marine battalions.

687 **The military task confronting us is to make it so expensive for the North Vietnamese that they will stop their aggression against South Viet Nam and Laos. If we make it too expensive for them, they will stop. They don't want to lose everything they have.**—*General Curtis E. LeMay, U.S. Air Force Chief of Staff, in his writings, July 1965.*[126]

LeMay advocated an all out bombing campaign against North Vietnam. He recommended completely disabling North Vietnam's air defense capability as part of the first series of targets.

688 **[If the United States pulled out of Vietnam] it might as well give up everywhere else—pull out of Berlin, Japan, South America.**—*President Lyndon Johnson, comments made during a conversation with John D. Pomfret, July 1965.*[291]

689 **[Deployment of large numbers of U.S. ground forces would lead to a] protracted war involving an open-ended commitment of U.S. forces, mounting U.S. casualties, no assurances of a satisfactory solution, and a serious danger of escalation at the end of the road.**—*George Ball, Under Secretary of State, comments to President Johnson, 1 July 1965.*[317]

Ball opposed deployment of U.S. ground forces to Vietnam.

690 **I am certainly as concerned about seeing the defeat of Communism as anyone else, but we won't defeat Communism by guns or bombs or gases. We will do it by making democracy work...**—*Dr. Martin Luther King, religious leader and civil rights activist, speaking in Petersburg, Virginia, 5 July 1965.*[844]

691 **Our involvement will be so great that we cannot—without national humiliation—stop short of achieving our complete objectives.**—*George Ball, Under Secretary of State, comments to President Johnson, 1 July 1965.*[317]

Ball and Clark Clifford opposed deployment of U.S. ground forces to Vietnam.

692 **The time has come for youth to guide the destiny of our nation.... This is youth's opportunity; everyone over fifty is finished.**—*Nguyen Cao Ky, Prime Minister of South Vietnam, from a speech shortly after taking office, 1965.*[629]

Ky was referring to the previous government (prime minister and chief of state) who were very old and had not moved the government forward.

693 **The war in Vietnam must be stopped. There must be a negotiated settlement even with the Vietcong.**—*Dr. Martin Luther King, religious minister and civil rights leader, speaking in Petersburg, Virginia, 5 July 1965.*[844]

694 **I think it is reasonable that if we must continue to fight wars, they ought to be fought by those people who really want to fight them. Since it seems to be the top half of the generation gap that is the most enthusiastic about going to war, why not send the Old Folks Brigade to Vietnam—with John Wayne leading them?**—*Dick Gregory, comedian and political activist.*[83]

695 **The university can best serve the cause of peace and morality by serving first the cause of rationality. In perspective, the good your committee can do for peace in Vietnam is, at best, doubtful; but the harm it can do the values of the university is quite certain.**—*An open letter from twenty-six U.C. Berkeley Faculty members, to the Vietnam Day Committee, 1965.*[742]

The Vietnam Day Committee advocated civil disobedience in their anti-war rallies.

696 **Once we suffer large casualties, we will have started a well-nigh irreversible process. Our involvement will be so great that we cannot—without national humiliation—stop short of achieving our complete objectives. Of the two possibilities I think humiliation would be more likely than the achievement of our objectives—even after we have paid terrible costs.**—*George Ball, Under Secretary of State, in a memorandum to President Johnson, 1 July 1965.*[876]

Towards the end of July 1965, Johnson announced a 50,000-man increase in American forces for South Vietnam.

697 **No, I don't think that the teach-ins and the differences of opinion have increased the strength of the North Vietnamese or the aggression that's taking place.**—*President Lyndon Johnson, news conference, Washington, D.C., 13 July 1965.*[369]

698 **I must say that candor compels me to tell you that there has not been the slightest indication that the other side is interested in negotiations or unconditional discussions, although the United States has made some dozen separate attempts to bring that about.**—*President Lyndon Johnson, press conference, 13 July 1965.*[786]

According to Ambassador Adlai Stevenson, the Administration declined a proposal for talks in Rangoon with Hanoi as brokered by U.N. Secretary U Thant in late 1964.

699 **U.S. killed-in-action might be in the vicinity of five hundred a month by the end of the year, but United States public opinion will support the course of action because it is a sensible and courageous military-political program designed to bring about a success in Vietnam.**—*Robert McNamara, Secretary of Defense, in a memorandum to President Johnson, July 1965.*[887]

700 **[I grant you authority to] commit U.S. troops to combat independent of or in conjunction with GVN forces in any situation ... when ... their use is necessary to strengthen the relative position of GVN forces.**—*President Lyndon Johnson, in orders to General William Westmoreland, July 1965.*[317]

701 **[Congressional debate on] that bitch of a war [would destroy] the woman I really loved — the Great Society.**—*President Lyndon Johnson, 1965.*[269]

Johnson did not bring his plans for escalation of the war to Congress for notification or debate. Escalation of the war through Congress would require funding and public debate. He wanted to avoid debate in the event Congress decided to make a choice between funding the war or his Great Society programs.

702 **[The] Goldwater crowd ... were more numerous, more powerful and dangerous than the fleabite professors...**—*President Lyndon Johnson, comments, July 1965.*[291]

Johnson was more concerned with the reaction from hawks than he was the fledgling anti-war movement.

703 **I am forced to conclude that we pursued McGeorge Bundy until he caught us.**—*Professor Stanley Diamond, University of Michigan, in a news letter of the Inter-University Committee, July 1965.*[748]

The committee pursued Bundy for two months to get him to have a public debate on Vietnam. When the debate was over Bundy and the government had not been as discredited for their position on Vietnam as the committee had expected.

704 **[American troop involvement would make a later decision to withdraw] even more difficult and costly than would be the case today.**—*Robert McNamara, Secretary of Defense, recommendations to President Johnson, July 1965.*[304]

McNamara explained that U.S. involvement at this stage would make it more difficult to get our troops out later, but that it was the only way to stop the VC/NVN in their quest for domination of the South, and could put the U.S. and Saigon in a better bargaining position for a political settlement at a later time. He reluctantly recommended an increase in U.S. combat troops to Vietnam.

705 **You must take the fight to the enemy, no one ever won a battle sitting on his ass.**—*General Earle Wheeler, Chairman, Joint Chiefs of Staff, 1965.*[285]

The JCS and Westmoreland strongly opposed the enclave policy and wanted to go on the offensive against the enemy. At this stage U.S. combat units in Vietnam were restricted to defensive operations.

706 **A commitment in South Vietnam is one thing, but a commitment to preserve another socialist state is quite another. This distinction we must bear in mind.**—*Dean Rusk, Secretary of State, during a White House meeting, 22 July 1965.*[121]

Rusk was arguing against the possibility of a U.S. land invasion of North Vietnam to end Hanoi's aggression in South Vietnam.

707 **No one could confuse him [Nguyen Cao Ky] with Uncle Ho.**—*An unidentified U.S. official, commenting on Nguyen Cao Ky's attire, July 1965.*[734]

South Vietnam's Prime Minister, Nguyen Cao Ky attended a Saigon dinner party along with such notable guest as Henry Cabot Lodge, Robert McNamara, and General Earle Wheeler. Ky entered, dressed in, "tight white jacket, tapered trousers, patent leather shoes, and red socks." A far cry from the loose white linen smock that hung on Ho Chi Minh.

708 **We entered into negotiations with the French colonialist on many occasions, and concluded with them several agreements in an effort to preserve peace. To them, however, the signing of peace agreements was only designed to gain time to prepare their military forces for further aggression.... This is a clear lesson of history, a lesson on relations with the imperialists, which our people will never forget.**—*Pham Van Dong, Prime Minister, Democratic Republic of Vietnam, 1965.*[374]

709 **[Escalation decisions shall be implemented in a] low-keyed manner in order to avoid an abrupt challenge to the Communist, and to avoid undue concern and excitement in the Congress and in domestic public opinion.**—*President Lyndon Johnson, memorandum to his staff, July 1965.*[259]

Johnson was avoiding debate in Congress of his early escalation of the war. Publicly he did not make known the full extent of the escalation.

710 **The overall situation continues to be serious. In many respects it has deteriorated since 15 months ago, when I was last here.**—*Robert McNamara, Secretary of Defense, during a press conference in Saigon, July 1965.*[957]

The press conference was held before McNamara's return to Washington. Several days after McNamara reported his finding on the deteriorating situation in Vietnam, President Johnson announced the deployment of an additional 50,000 American troops to South Vietnam and a doubling of the monthly draft.

711 **The President ... will do his very best on behalf of the country and leave no stone unturned to seek an honorable settlement that will safeguard Southeast Asia and allow it to go its own independent way.**—*Senator Mike Mansfield, of Montana, comments to the press, 27 July 1965.*[528]

712 **The United States was deeply enmeshed in a place we ought not to be; the situation is rapidly growing out of control and that every effort should be made to extricate ourselves.**—*Senator Mike Mansfield, Senate Majority Leader, to President Johnson, 27 July 1965.*[291]

713 **I do not believe that even a greatly extended program of bombing could be expected to produce significant North Vietnamese interest in a negotiated solution until they have been disappointed in their hopes for a quick military success in the South.**—*Robert McNamara, Secretary of Defense, in a memorandum to President Johnson, 28 July 1965.*[153]

McNamara changed his position on intensifying the bombing against North Vietnam after returning from a fact finding trip to South Vietnam in June 1965. He now proposed a gradual increase in the bombing, but placed more emphasis on stabilizing the situation in Saigon.

714 **I have today ordered to Vietnam the Airmobile Division and certain other forces which will raise our fighting strength from 75,000 to 125,000 men almost immediately. Additional forces will be needed later, and they will be sent**

as requested.—*President Lyndon Johnson, news conference, Washington, D.C., 28 July 1965.*[369]

715 **[The United States asks the United Nations] to employ its resources, energy and immense prestige in finding ways to halt aggression and to bring peace in Vietnam.**—*President Lyndon Johnson, in a letter to Secretary General U Thant, 28 July 1965.*[529]

Johnson indicated the United States was open to formal or informal talks that could lead to a negotiated settlement.

716 **We have every reason to believe that the strikes at infiltration routes have at least put a ceiling on what the North Vietnamese can pour into South Vietnam, thereby putting a ceiling on the size of the war that the enemy can wage there.**—*Robert McNamara, Secretary of Defense, in a memorandum to the President, 28 July 1965.*[153]

At the time, McNamara and the JCS wrongly believed the air interdiction campaign against the Ho Chi Minh Trail significantly stopped the flow of men and material from North Vietnam into South Vietnam.

717 **Retreat does not bring safety, or weakness, peace.**—*President Lyndon Johnson, from a televised speech, 28 July 1965.*[677]

718 **[Aggression in South Vietnam is] guided by North Vietnam and it is spurred by communist China. Its goal is to conquer the South, to defeat American power, and to extend the Asiatic domination of communism.**—*President Lyndon Johnson, from a televised speech, 28 July 1965.*[677]

719 **Most of the noncommunist nations of Asia cannot, by themselves, resist the growing might and grasping ambition of Asian communism. Our power is a vital shield. If we are driven from the fields in Vietnam, then no nation can ever again have the same confidence in our promise of protection.**—*President Lyndon Johnson, from a televised speech, 28 July 1965.*[677]

720 **I have asked ... General Westmoreland, what more he needs to meet this mounting aggression ... we will meet his needs. We cannot be defeated by force of arms. We will stand in Vietnam.**—*President Lyndon Johnson, in a televised announcement, 28 July 1965.*

721 **The loss of Vietnam would produce an even more explosive debate, a mean and destructive debate that would shatter my Presidency, kill my administration, and damage our democracy.**—*President Lyndon Johnson, comments, July 1965.*[374]

722 **A permanent abandonment of the [air] program would have a distinct depressing effect on morale in South Vietnam.**—*Robert McNamara, Secretary of Defense, in a memorandum to President Johnson, 30 July 1965.*[159]

McNamara believed the GVN was addicted to the U.S. air campaign against the North, and used it to boost morale in the country.

723 **This is really war [but not a] national emergency.**—*President Lyndon Johnson, 1965.*[399]

Johnson describing the conflict in Vietnam as war yet he refused to put the nation on a war footing, i.e., no call up of Reserve or National Guard units to support the war effort in Vietnam, nor price controls or a war tax.

724 **[We fight in Vietnam to force or induce a negotiated settlement, not to invite] an expanding struggle with consequences that no one can perceive.**—*President Lyndon Johnson, comments to the press, 1965.*[399]

Johnson believed the power and prestige of the United States would force the North Vietnamese into peace negotiations.

725 **[We are ready] for unconditional discussions with any government at any place at any time.**—*President Lyndon Johnson, comments to the press, 1965.*[399]

Johnson claimed his administration was ready to talk peace in Vietnam. His stated goal was to prevent the spread of communism in Asia and help South Vietnam get on its feet as a new, independent nation.

726 **All that is needed ... is the will to win — and the courage to use our power — now.**—*Richard Nixon, in an article for Reader's Digest, August 1964.*[374]

Nixon criticized Johnson's slow pace at escalating the war in Vietnam.

727 **You don't look like much, but from now on you're in the Army. From now on you belong to me. I'm your mother, father, doctor, chaplain, teacher, counselor — everything. You people got any problems — any problems at all — you come to me.**—*SSgt. Parker, Basic Training Center, Fort Knox, speaking to new recruits, August 1965.*[401]

The same speech heard at Army basic training centers around the country.

728 **I have never been able to see any strategic, political, or economic advantage to be gained by our involvement [in Vietnam].**—*Senator Richard B. Russell, of Georgia, Chairman, Senate Armed Services Committee, 1965.*[399]

Russell, a Democrat, was not a dove, but he questioned the administration's reasoning for pushing a war in Vietnam.

729 **Names like Phu Bai, Da Nang, Ban Me Thout [Ban Me Thuot], Kontum, Pleiku ... may some day be chiseled on monuments in Michigan and Kansas, under those other names, once also thought exotic, like Chateau-Thierry, Anzio, Tarawa, Pusan.**—*Life magazine editorial, 6 August 1965.*[653]

Initially Time Inc. (*Life* and *Time* magazines) strongly backed administration policy in Vietnam, including the bombing of North Vietnam and the use of American combat troops to stem the communists rush to take over South Vietnam.

730 **[Any peace conference] will find us at the appointed place at the appointed time, in the proper chair.**—*President Lyndon Johnson, speech outlining his proposed actions in Vietnam, August 1965.*[400]

Johnson decided not to call up the Reserves or institute wartime measures in the country. His comment indicated his willingness to participate in a negotiated settlement to the war that was expanding. During this speech he announced an increase in troops to be deployed to Vietnam and an increase in national draft calls.

731 **There is no substantial division in this country, in my judgment, and no substantial division in the Congress.**—*President Lyndon Johnson, comments to reporters, 6 August 1965.*[752]

Johnson responding to questions by the press about the growing anti-war movement in America and possible breaks in the support for the war in Congress.

732 **America has a purpose as well as interests in the world ... the purpose and the interests are not regional but global, and American freedom cannot be protected at the cost of those whose freedom we have promised to defend. Vietnam is the place where these beliefs once more are put to the test.**—*Life magazine editorial, 6 August 1965.*[399]

733 **The Marines could meet and defeat any force they might encounter.**—*General William Westmoreland, comments to the press, August 1965.*

Westmoreland praised the Marines for their successful mission during Operation Starlite, where they submitted a body count of 700 VC dead.

734 **Newsmen are told nothing or misleading information so they invent their own stories and they are wrong.**—*Captain Richard B. Sexton, U.S. Air Force pilot, writing in his journal, August 1965.*[886]

735 **I just ask him how useful or interesting or exciting his life right now really is.**—*General Lewis B. Hershey, Selective Service Director, interviewed by Susanna McBee, 1965.*[401]

Hershey's responds to potential draftee's complaints that two years of military service is two years down the drain.

736 **He was the most cautious man at the table.**—*Unnamed Johnson aide, August 1965.*[400]

Characterization of President Johnson during deliberations on the direction of the war. He was trying to decide if the country should go on a war footing, i.e., call up the Reserves, request new military appropriations from Congress, institute wartime economic controls (rent, wage, price), freeze military separations, etc. He decided not to seek a declaration of war from Congress.

737 **[The Army's] entire concept of fighting the war with conventional military tactics is wrong. They might win a battle once in a while ... but they will lose the war.**—*Captain Richard B. Sexton, U.S. Air Force pilot, writing in his journal, August 1965.*[886]

738 **It is a straightforward clear answer to those who would make a mockery of our efforts in South Vietnam by engaging in the mass destruction of draft cards.... If it can be proved that a person knowingly destroyed or mutilated his draft card, then ... he can be sent to prison, where he belongs. This is the least we can do for our men in South Vietnam fighting to preserve freedom, while a vocal minority in this country thumb their noses at their own government.**—*Representative L. Mendel Rivers, Chairman House Armed Services Committee, regarding anti-draft demonstrators, August 1965.*[716]

739 **A society that hasn't got the guts to make people do what they ought to do doesn't deserve to survive.**—*General Lewis B. Hershey, Selective Service Director, interviewed by Susanna McBee, 1965.*[401]

Responding to questions about the need for a compulsory draft during peace time.

740 **The presumption is that the citizen is responsible for his government. That means defending it.**—*General Lewis B. Hershey, Selective Service Director, interviewed by Susanna McBee, 1965.*[401]

Responding to questions about the validity of a military draft in peace time.

741 **A democracy has to make people do things for their own good — go to school, obey the law, respect the rights of others.**—*General Lewis B. Hershey, Selective Service Director, interviewed by Susanna McBee, 1965.*[401]

Responding to questions about the need for a draft in peace time.

742 **Catholics realize this is a war of extermination and will fight to the end. Buddhists are fatalists. They will endure whatever is their fate.**—*Captain Richard B. Sexton, U.S. Air Force pilot, writing in his journal, August 1965.*[886]

743 **I plead with my Cabinet — every time I see 'em, I say to Secretary McNamara, "You be sure that our men have the morale and have the equipment and have the necessary means of seeing that we keep our commitments in Vietnam. And we have the strength to do it. And Mr. Rusk, while he's working with his right hand of strength and stability there and doing the job we're committed to do, you and Mr. Goldberg and the rest of you use that left hand and be sure that you do everything to get us away from the battlefield and back at the conference table, if that's possible." So we're like a man in the ring — we're using our right and our left constantly.**—*President Lyndon Johnson, news conference, Washington, D.C., 25 August 1965.*[369]

744 **The Hanoi leaders believed that if they killed and wounded enough American soldiers over a period of time they would erode our national will and cause us to cease our support of the GVN.**—*General Victor Krulak, Commander, Fleet Marine Force, Pacific, 1965.*[887]

745 **80 days have September, April, June, and November. All the rest have 93, except the last month which has 140.**—*Captain Richard B. Sexton, U.S. Air Force pilot, writing in his journal, August 1965.*[886]

Sexton's rendition of the American GI's calendar during his tour of duty in South Vietnam.

746 **Too much thought is being given to the actual damage we do in the North and not enough thought to the signal we wish to send.**—*Walt Rostow of the State Department to Robert McNamara, 1965.*[925]

Rostow favored sending Hanoi and China a signal that they should change their policy of supporting the insurgency in South Vietnam. He was opposed to the all-out approach favored by the military. The military proposed heavy strikes against 94 key targets in North Vietnam.

747 **Revolutionary armed forces should not fight with reckless disregard for the consequences when there is a great disparity between their own strength and the enemy's. If they do they will suffer serious losses and bring heavy setbacks to the revolution. Guerrilla warfare is the only way to mobilize and apply the whole strength of the people against the enemy.**—*Lin Biao, Defense Minister, Communist China, in a published article, September 1965.*[374]

Red Chinese wisdom aimed at North Vietnam. Red China encouraged Hanoi to fight the U.S., but wanted to avoid the direct intervention of Chinese "volunteers" to assist the Vietnamese.

748 **It is a scathing indictment of our political awareness that we have sat idly by while many patriotic and non–Communist Vietnamese were literally forced to ally themselves with a Communist-dominated movement in the belief that it was their only chance to secure a better government.**—*John Paul Vann, Hau Nghia Pacification Officer, in a written strategy proposal, September 1965.*[887]

Vann wrote a strategy proposal detailing steps the U.S. could take to turn the nationalist revolution adopted by the communists into positive growth and security for the people of South Vietnam. Of prime importance was placing a government in Saigon that was responsive to the needs of the people.

749 **The understandable concern of the U.S. with the communist involvement in the revolution has obscured the fact that most of the objectives of the revolution are identical to those for which Americans have long fought and died.**—*John Paul Vann, AID adviser, in a position paper, September 1965.*[25]

The revolution Vann spoke of was the peasant population's move toward land reform and an end to exploitation by the government. A nationalist movement started against the French and continued against the GVN. This movement was taken over by the communists and offered as their own.

750 **[GVN officials] are incapable of surmounting a system of which they are both a product and a participant and have a vested interest in perpetuating.**—*John Paul Vann, AID adviser, in a position paper, September 1965.*[25]

Vann believed the GVN was incapable of reforming itself and that the U.S. would have to push the GVN to change in the form of creating programs that helped the people to develop and progress.

751 **She was challenged and didn't know the password.**—*Sgt. Maj. Basil L. Plumley, 1/7 Cavalry, reporting on the death of 1/9 Cavalry's mascot, September 1965.*[501]

Maggie, the 1/9 Cavalry's mule mascot, was transported with the squadron to Vietnam in 1965 and moved to the division base camp at An Khe. One night the mule went wandering in the dark and spooked a jumpy sentry who responded with a burst of rifle fire.

752 **We ... have naively expected an unsophisticated, relatively illiterate, rural population to recognize and oppose the evils of Communism, even when it is cleverly masked by front [NLF] organizations.**—*John Paul Vann, Hau Nghia Pacification Officer, in a written strategy proposal, September 1965.*[887]

Vann was referring to the U.S. government and by extension MAAGV/MACV.

753 **We wanted to lure the tiger out of the mountain. We would attack the ARVN — but we would be ready to fight the Americans.**—*General Chu Huy Man, Commander, NVA Central Highlands forces, 1965-66.*[501]

The battle of the Ia Drang Valley was the first major combat between NVA and American combat forces. The NVA plan involved attacking the USSF camp at Duc Co drawing the ARVN to reinforce. The ambush and destruction of the ARVN relief column would force the Americans to deploy their newly arrived combat units to relieve Duc Co.

754 **[Because of the demonstrations Hanoi might conclude] ... there is a real division of strengths in this country and that may tempt them to prolong the war.**—*General Maxwell Taylor, 1965.*[789]

Taylor believed the anti-war demonstrations in the U.S. were bolstering Hanoi's resolve, which would lead to prolonging the war.

755 **A successful military venture [in Vietnam] will be negated by a continuing failure of [the] GVN to win its own people.**—*John Paul Vann, Hau Nghia Pacification Officer, in a written strategy proposal, September 1965.*[887]

756 **Nearly every regimental plan is changed in many ways by the 25th Division headquarters, and virtually every change is such as to reduce the chance of contact or to allow the VC an avenue of escape.**—*Unidentified U.S. Adviser to the 25th ARVN Infantry Division, in a report, 1965.*[42]

The 25th ARVN was generally regarded as the worst division in the South Vietnamese Army. ARVN-initiated contact with the enemy was generally rare, or accidental.

757 **The situation is now too critical and the investment too great for us to longer tolerate a directionless and floundering effort that is losing the population, hence the war.**—*John Paul Vann, Hau Nghia Pacification Officer, in a written strategy proposal, September 1965.*[887]

Vann believed that if Saigon government could not be convinced to make policy changes favorable to its people, then the U.S. should be prepared to step in, colonial style, and make the changes necessary to get the government on track.

758 **[The time has come to] re-evaluate our position in Vietnam.**—*Senator Richard B. Russell of the Senate Armed Services Committee, 1965.*[374]

Some members in Congress were beginning to have doubts about American policy in Vietnam. Russell was one of them.

759 **The beginning of a new era in land warfare...**—*Robert McNamara, Secretary of Defense, 1965.*[249]

Commenting of the deployment of the 1st Cavalry Division (Airmobile) to Vietnam. This was the first U.S. Army unit to use the helicopter as its primary asset in the maneuver and support of the division's combat elements.

760 **For fear of tarnishing our own image, we have refused to become overtly involved in the internal affairs of governing to the extent necessary to insure the emergence of a government responsive to the majority of its people.**—*John Paul Vann, Hau Nghia Pacification Officer, in a written strategy proposal, September 1965.*[887]

761 **There are two hundred and twenty thousand people in Hau Nghia [Province], and two hundred thousand of them are ruled by the VC. I am not a province chief; I am a hamlet chief.**—*Province chief, Hau Nghia Province, comments to Daniel Ellsberg, 1965.*[41]

In 1965 Ellsberg was in Vietnam monitoring the pacification program. Hau Nghia was just northwest of Saigon, with a large NLF and VC presence.

762 **Each time you go into the fields and say "elections" the poor reply with one word, "food."**—*Nguyen Cao Ky, Prime Minister of South Vietnam, 1965.*[629]

The Americans were pushing the Ky government for free elections, but Ky said his priority was food for the people and victory over the communists.

763 **When you see a SAM coming up at you, it looks like a telephone pole on fire.**—*Jesse Randall, U.S. Navy A-6 pilot from VA-75, USS Independence, 1965.*[84]

North Vietnam used Soviet made SA-2, Surface to Air Missiles, as a part of their extensive air defenses. At the time it was not known if they were operated by Russian crews.

764 **The Vietcong comes forward with the demand that it be the sole representative of South Vietnam. But in South Vietnam live Buddhists, Catholics and various hill tribes. These are not represented by the Vietcong.**—*Dean Rusk, Secretary of State, speaking with Hungary's foreign minister, October 1965.*[450]

In addition to Hanoi's four demands for peace talks to start, they included another condition stating that the South Vietnamese people would resolve their internal issues according to the NLF program.

765 **There's only one thing's gonna do any good at all.... And that's everybody just look at it, look at the war, and turn your backs and say ... fuck it...**—*Ken Kesey, author of "One Flew Over the Cuckoo's Nest," at a teach-in at Berkeley, 15 October 1965.*[831]

766 **We are naturally aware of various noisy demonstrations that have taken place and are scheduled to take place but I would like to point out that these groups constitute an infinitesimal fraction of the American people, the vast majority of whom have indicated their strong support of President Johnson's policies in Vietnam.**—*Robert McCloskey, State Department spokesman, speaking to reporters 16 October 1965.*[789]

767 **They are not promoting peace but postponing it. They are not persuading the President or the Congress to end the war but deceiving Ho Chi Minh and General [Vo Nguyen] Giap into prolonging [it].... The problem of peace now lies not in Washington but in Hanoi...**—*James Reston, Reporter for The New York Times, 17 October 1965.*[789]

Reston was a Washington insider and often received information first-hand from those on Capitol Hill. He was speaking of the demonstrators and anti-war protesters in America.

768 **The war in Vietnam is most certainly a vital national issue, it both deserves and demands public thought and comment. But if this comment and participation is to be constructive it must be conducted in a lawful and responsible manner.**—*Representative Jeffrey Cohelan, California, 18 October 1965.*[850]

769 **[It's as] smooth as a golf course.**—*General John M. Wright, assistant division commander, 1st Cavalry Division, 1965.*[501]

The 1st Cavalry's base camp at An Khe was nicknamed the Golf Course. The camp covered six square kilometers and was the initial base of operations for more than 450 helicopters and 20,000 troops. The jungle and brush that occupied the area were cleared by hand by members of the 1st Cavalry Division.

770 **[The North Vietnamese] ... are on a sharp hook. They're looking for something to get them off and they may think this is it.**—*Henry Cabot Lodge, U.S. Ambassador to South Vietnam, to reporters, 16 October 1965.*[789]

Lodge saw anti-war demonstrations as benefiting the enemy.

771 **All we'll have to do if the draft keeps climbing is hire a few more clerks and some extra doctors.**—*General Lewis B. Hershey, Selective Service Director, interviewed by Susanna McBee, 1965.*[401]

Hershey, when asked what would happen if President Johnson continued to increase the draft. In August 1965 the draft was 17,000 men a month, by the end of 1965 it was up to 35,000 men a month.

772 **If you know what you want to be, then go to college. If not, go in the service. You'll find guys rich and poor, smart and stupid, decent and not so decent. And that's what life is all about.**—*General Lewis B. Hershey, Selective Service Director, interview, 1965.*[401]

Draft quotas were raised from 17,000 per month in August 1965, to 35,000 in October 1965.

773 **The commitment of SDS, and of the whole generation we represent, is clear: we are anxious to build villages; we refuse to burn them. We are anxious to help and change our country; we refuse to destroy someone else's country.**—*Paul Booth, an officer of SDS (Students for a Democratic Society), at a press conference in the National Press Club, Washington, D.C., 20 October 1965.*[734]

774 **We're going to be tighter on deferments. A lot of guys have been riding on velvet. The velvet's going to get thinner.**—*General Lewis B. Hershey, Selective Service Director, interviewed by Susanna McBee, 1965.*[401]

775 **I don't say total war is inevitable, but total peace is a long way from inevitable too.**—*General Lewis B. Hershey, Selective Service Director, interviewed by Susanna McBee, 1965.*[401]

776 **I consider this an unprecedented victory [—Battle of the Ia Drang Valley].**—*General William Westmoreland, ComUSMACV, October 1965.*[815]

MACV claimed 1,100 NVA killed in the valley, but for the two weeks that the Ia Drang made headlines U.S. casualties were 326 KIA.

777 **Caucasians cannot really imagine what ant labor can do.**—*Unidentified American officer, 1965.*[332]

Officer commenting on how quickly North Vietnamese labor crews were able to repair roads and bridges along the Ho Chi Minh Trail after they had been damaged or destroyed by American air strikes. There were thousands of labor crews, both forced and voluntary, who maintained the trail.

778 **One of the trademarks I had was that following bomb release, I would pull the airplane up and do a big barrel roll and state "Ho Chi Minh is a son of a bitch!" It use to frighten the new guys who did not know what to expect, because we would pull up into the SAM envelope, but I never did have SAMs fired at me during a barrel roll.**—*Jesse Randall, U.S. Navy A-6 pilot from VA-75, USS Independence, 1965.*[84]

779 **Anti-Vietnam demonstrators in the U.S. represent a minority for the most part composed of half way citizens who are neither morally, mentally nor emotionally mature. This is true whether the demonstrators be college professor or beatnik.**—*J. Edgar Hoover, Director of the FBI, 1 November 1965.*[758]

780 **We have stopped losing the war.**—*Robert McNamara, Secretary of Defense, during a press conference, November 1965.*[813]

McNamara's report after a fact finding trip to South Vietnam in November 1965.

781 **It isn't us who die in combat; it's those kids who die. Those kids we are responsible for training and leading. It's our job to get the job done and get those kids home safe.**—*Colonel Thomas W. Brown, Commander, 3d Brigade, 1st Cavalry Division, November 1965.*[501]

Brown was speaking of the high price American youth paid at the battle of LZ Albany in November 1965. American casualties: 155 killed, 124 wounded. Enemy casualties: 403 killed, estimated 150 wounded.

782 **This government is playing just like a piano without a sour note.**—*President Lyndon Johnson, commenting to the media. November 1965.*[403]

Johnson was commenting on the state of the government as he saw it at the end of his first two years in office. Under his administration Congress had passed seventy-five major bills, advancing his Great Society programs.

783 **They [NVA] could come when they were ready to fight and leave when they were ready to quit.**—*General Harry W.O. Kinnard, Commander, 1st Cavalry Division (Airmobile).*[501]

Kinnard, commenting on the ability of NVA/VC units to use base camps in Cambodia as staging areas to launch attacks into South Vietnam and as sanctuaries to retreat to in order to avoid American attacks.

784 **By God, they sent us over here to kill Communists and that's what we're doing.**—*Lt. Col. Harold Moore, Jr., Commander, 1st Battalion, 7th Cavalry, at LZ X-Ray, November 1965.*[887]

The Battle of the Ia Drang was initiated at LZ X-Ray. It represented the first major test of the Army's strategy of airmobility.

785 **You just don't run for office by sending Marines into Latin America. It's like arresting mothers.**—*President Lyndon Johnson, comments, November 1965.*[403]

In 1965 Johnson sent U.S. Marines into the Dominican Republic believing that a revolt by the "working class" and part of the Dominican Army was communist inspired. The Marines were there to keep the peace and restore order. Johnson knew the intervention would be unpopular, but he believed it necessary to prevent another communist foothold in the Western Hemisphere.

786 **We seek no wider war ... whether or not this course can be maintained lies with the North Vietnamese aggressors.**—*President Lyndon Johnson, White House statement, 7 February 1965.*[521]

The Administration claimed Hanoi planned and supported the VC attack against the U.S. helicopter base at Pleiku, South Vietnam. Retaliatory air strikes were launched against North Vietnam.

787 **[The decision was] based on strong instincts and flimsy intelligence.**—*General Richard T. Knowles, assistant division commander, 1st Air Cavalry Division, 1965.*[501]

Commenting on the decision making process he used to order 1st Cavalry troops into the Ia Drang Valley for their initial major encounter with NVA troops.

788 **I was always taught as an officer that in a pursuit situation you continued to pursue until you either kill the enemy or he surrenders. I saw the Ia Drang [battles] as a definite pursuit situation and I wanted to keep after them. Not to follow them into Cambodia violated every principle of warfare.**—*General Harry W.O. Kinnard, Commander, 1st Cavalry Division (Airmobile), 1965.*[501]

Battalions of three NVA regiments, mauled in the battles of the Ia Drang Valley, retreated to sanctuaries across the border into Cambodia. U.S. ground units were forbidden by Washington from crossing into Cambodia in hot pursuit of the enemy. The NVA regiments were repeatedly able to refit and receive reinforcements and later re-cross the border to stage further attacks.

789 **We saw nothing to indicate that Hanoi was prepared for peace talks and the Secretary of State said he would recognize it when it came. His antenna is sensitive.**—*Robert McCloskey, State Department spokesman, comments to the press, 15 November 1965.*[850]

State Department response to allegations that the Johnson administration turned down possible peace talk offers in 1964.

790 **You will never mention anything about Chinese soldiers in South Vietnam! Never!**—*General William Westmoreland, ComUSMACV, during a briefing on the battle at LZ X-Ray, November 1965.*[501]

Westmoreland was reacting to a report during the briefing that the body of a suspected Chinese soldier had been found among enemy dead at LZ X-Ray. His reaction reflected his attempts to downplay any mention of possible involvement of Chinese ground forces assisting the NVA.

791 **Although we have stated our intention to counter-demonstrate at this despicable, un-American activity, we believe that in the interest of public safety and the protection of the good name of Oakland, we would not justify the VDC by our presence ... because our patriotic concern for what these people are doing to a great nation may provoke us into violent acts...**—*Ralph "Sonny" Barger, President of the Oakland chapter of the Hell's Angels Motorcycle Club, from a public statement he released November 1965.*[735]

In October 1965 Hell's Angels had attacked a peace march in Berkeley. But before the second march took place in November 1965, the Angels were visited by Allen Ginsberg and Ken Kesey; they carried with them a supply of LSD. The statement from Sonny Barger was released the day after the meeting, the day before the next demonstration march was to take place.

792 **Fear comes, and once you recognize it and accept it, it passes just as fast as it comes, and you don't really think about**

it anymore. You just do what you have to do, but you [are] learning the real meaning of fear and life and death.—*SP/4 Bill Beck, machine gunner, A Company, 1st Battalion, 7th Cavalry, during an interview, 1965.*[501]

Beck was part of the 1st Cavalry's major battle with the NVA during the Battle of the Ia Drang Valley.

793 **We cannot defeat this armed enemy unless we win the people; yet unless we defeat the armed enemy, we cannot win the people.**—*Michael Mok, Associate Editor, Life magazine, on assignment in I Corps, November 1965.*[402]

Without the support of the people, the Viet Cong could not thrive; support coerced or volunteered, sustained them.

794 **We cut off the enemy's throat instead of just jabbing away at his stomach. This kind of operation is going to continue. This is just the beginning.**—*Unidentified 1st Cavalry Division officer, during the battle of the Ia Drang, November 1965.*[404]

The Ia Drang was the first combat test of the airmobile concept. The first large battle between regular U.S. Army units and NVA (PAVN) regulars. *Life* magazine reported the 1st Cavalry Division killed 2000 enemy, at a cost of 200 American troopers.

795 **It's too easy to be crisp, cool, and detached at 1,500 feet; too easy to demand the impossible of your troops; too easy to make mistakes that are fatal only to those souls far below in the mud, the blood and the confusion.**—*Lt. Col. Harold G. Moore, former Commander 1/7 Cavalry, during an interview released 1992.*[501]

Moore was speaking of the necessity of leading his men from the ground and not from a command and control helicopter above the troops on the ground.

796 **My dear young wife. When the troops come home after the victory, and you do not see me, please look at the proud colors. You will see me there, and you will feel warm under the shadow of the bamboo tree.**—*Anonymous NVA soldier, from writings in his diary, 1965.*[501]

Diary found by U.S. troops during the Battle of the Ia Drang.

797 **Some of the NVA were coming through the area killing all [the Americans] who were screaming and calling for medics.**—*PFC James Shadden, mortar platoon, D Company, 2d Battalion, 7th Cavalry Regiment, during an interview, released 1992.*[501]

Shadden was one of many American wounded during the ambush and attack against 7th Cavalry troops on LZ Albany in the Ia Drang Valley in 1965.

798 **True, it was a cliché camera shot from every war movie ever made, but there on LZ X-ray, in the midst of death, destruction and unbelievable heroism, its impact transcended the stereotype.**—*J.D. Coleman, writing of the Ia Drang battle at LZ X-ray, 1965.*[502]

The "cliché" was the display of a small American flag on the 7th Cavalry Regiment's perimeter around LZ X-ray during the Battle of the Ia Drang.

799 **Telling Lyndon Johnson no is like standing at the water's edge and shouting at the tide to go back.**—*Bill Moyers, Special Assistant to President Johnson, commenting during an interview, November 1965.*[403]

800 **When our infantry brothers called, we hauled.**—*Major Bruce Crandall, Commander A Company, 229th Assault Helicopter Company, during an interview released 1992.*[501]

The 229th AHC provided major slick (transport) and gunship support to the 7th Cavalry during the Battle of the Ia Drang.

801 **I'd rather see America save her soul than her face.**—*Norman Thomas, peace activist, at a peace rally, 27 November 1965.*[813]

Nearly blind, 80-year-old anti-war activist.

802 **After the Ia Drang campaign we concluded that we could fight and win against the [American] Cavalry troops.**—*General Vo Nguyen Giap.*[501]

The Battle of the Ia Drang was the first major engagement between American airmobile troops and NVA troops in South Vietnam. Westmoreland claimed 3,561 NVA dead (estimated) verses 305 Americans killed. Despite their losses, Hanoi considered the battle of the Ia Drang a victory.

803 **Cooks and bottle washers, the shit-burners, projectionists, club runners. Same Army, different species.**—*Captain Myron F. Diduryk, Commander, B Company, 2d Battalion, 7th Cavalry Regiment, 1965.*[501]

Uttered by Diduryk as he led his company as reinforcements in the relief of his battalion which had been badly cut up on LZ Albany, November 1965. The above mentioned rear-echelon personnel lined up along the road at Camp Holloway as the company made its way to the PZ (Pickup Zone) for extraction and insertion into LZ Albany.

804 **We have become a nation of young, bright-eyed, hard-hearted, slim-waisted, bullet-headed make-out artists. A nation — may I say it?— of beardless liberals.**—*Carl Oglesby, one of the presidents of SDS, speaking at a peace demonstration, 27 November 1965.*[723]

Oglesby blamed the war in Vietnam on liberals in Washington.

805 **[The North Vietnamese and the Vietcong] expressed a determination to carry on the conflict which can lead to only one conclusion — that it will be a long war.**—*Robert McNamara, Secretary of Defense, November 1965.*[813]

After a fact finding trip to Saigon in November, he concluded the bombing was not slowing down enemy infiltration into South Vietnam and the enemy was willing to fight American units on the ground.

806 **This battle [Ia Drang] is what the whole U.S. build-up has been about. The 1st Cavalry was designed to be able to react in a matter of minutes, not to hold real estate but to pursue and destroy the enemy.**—*Robert Morse, Life magazine correspondent, from a cable sent from Saigon, November 1965.*[404]

The Ia Drang was the first combat test of the airmobile concept. The first large battle between regular U.S. Army units and NVA (PAVN–People's Army of Vietnam) regulars.

807 **The original commitment in Vietnam was made by President Truman, a mainstream liberal. It was seconded by**

President Eisenhower, a moderate liberal. It was intensified by the late President Kennedy, a flaming liberal.—*Carl Oglesby, one of the presidents of SDS, speaking at a peace demonstration, 27 November 1965.*[723]

Oglesby blamed the war in Vietnam on liberals in Washington.

808 **The very substantial increase in strength here of U.S., Australian, New Zealand and Republic of Korea forces have denied the Viet Cong any victories they wanted during the recent monsoon season.**—*Robert McNamara, Secretary of Defense, speaking during a news conference in Saigon, 29 November 1965.*[678]

809 **Tide has turned but end not near...**—*Robert McNamara, Secretary of Defense, speaking during a news conference in Saigon, 29 November 1965.*[678]

He spoke of progress in the war against the communists.

810 **We should be aware that deployment of the kind [40 additional combat battalions] ... will not guarantee success. U.S. killed-in-action can be expected to reach 1,000 a month, and the odds are even that we will be faced in early 1967, with a no-decision at an even higher level.**—*Robert McNamara, Secretary of Defense, memorandum to President Johnson, November 1965.*[501]

811 **This [Albany] was the most savage battle in the Ia Drang campaign. We consider this our victory ... we defeated Americans, caused big American losses. As military men we realize it is very important to win the first battle. It raised our soldier's morale and gave us many good lessons.**—*General Nguyen Huu An, former deputy commander B-3 Front, November 1965.*[501]

The battle of LZ Albany was the second major battle of PAVN soldiers against an American combat unit. The first was the battle of LZ X-ray. The 8th Battalion, 66th NVA Regiment engaged the American 2d Battalion, 7th Cavalry Regiment of the 1st Cavalry Division in November 1965. Both sides claimed victory. NVA casualties were 1,519 KIA by body count, American casualties were 305 KIA and 524 WIA.

812 **It will be a long war.**—*Robert McNamara, Secretary of Defense, to reporters at Tan Son Nhut, November 1965.*[501]

McNamara had been briefed on the stiff enemy resistance encountered by the 1st Cavalry during the battles in the Ia Drang. He was in Saigon to get a firsthand look at the first major engagement between American and NVA troops in South Vietnam.

813 **When General Giap says he learned how to fight Americans and our helicopters at the Ia Drang, that's bullshit! What he learned was that we were not going to be allowed to chase him across a mythical line in the dirt [Cambodian Border].**—*General Harry W.O. Kinnard, Commander, 1st Cavalry Division (Airmobile), 1992.*[501]

Giap was able to attack at his discretion and retreat to sanctuaries across the border in Cambodia. Washington dictated the rules of engagement for American units, crossing into Cambodia in hot pursuit of the enemy was forbidden.

814 **He [the NVA] can bring us to battle when he wants and where he wants ... always within a few miles of the border, where his supply lines are the shortest, where the preponderance of forces is his, where he has scouted the terrain intensely and knows it better than we do.**—*General Harry W.O. Kinnard, Commander, 1st Cavalry Division (Airmobile), 1992.*[501]

Washington dictated the rules of engagement for American units. Crossing into Cambodia in hot pursuit of the enemy was forbidden. This allowed the NVA to mass across the border and strike on their terms.

815 **The fact that the Americans are making negotiation proposals demonstrates their weakness and their defeat.**—*Excerpt from a Viet Cong cadre propaganda program, Duc Hue district, December 1965.*[32]

816 **Make it inconvenient for them to take you, tell them you love them, tell them you slept with me.**—*Allen Ginsberg, poet and LSD use advocate, from his encounters with students in the mid-sixties.*[735]

Ginsberg advocated drug use as a means to enlightenment. He also advised students to stay out of the army.

817 **The enemy has only some technical advantages.... They're at a loss to choose among three paths: to withdraw from Vietnam, to go on, or to extend the war to the North.**—*Excerpt from a Viet Cong cadre propaganda program, Duc Hue district, December 1965.*[33]

818 **If the U.S. were willing to commit enough forces — perhaps 600,000 men or more — we could ultimately prevent the Democratic Republic of Vietnam/Viet Cong from sustaining the conflict at a significant level ... however, the question of Chinese intervention would become critical.**—*Robert McNamara, Secretary of Defense, memorandum to President Johnson, 6 December 1965.*[501]

819 **The odds are about even that, even with the recommended deployments, we will be faced in early 1967 with a military standoff at a much higher level.**—*Robert McNamara, Secretary of Defense, in a memorandum to President Johnson, 7 December 1965.*[72]

At that time the planned deployment was for an additional 150,000 U.S. troops to Vietnam. The enemy continued to raise his troop levels in South Vietnam countering the rise of American levels.

820 **This country should be mindful that our older partners, France and Great Britain, have found it possible to retire with honor from untenable positions.**—*Frank McGee, NBC correspondent, during an NBC news broadcast, December 1965.*[634]

McGee spent time in Vietnam and did not believe the Johnson administration was being completely open in its portrayal of the situation in Vietnam and American involvement.

821 **How devastating and poignant this war is! It has stolen the vernal spring of our lives, we fledglings who knew nothing except our schoolbooks. I didn't expect to be so wretched. If I see you again in the future, I will tell you everything in detail. If not, please calm your grief and do not mourn me.**—*Mai Van Hung, North Vietnamese soldier, from an unfinished letter home, Pleiku, 1965.*[374]

Mai Van Hung was killed near Pleiku.

822 **[The big-unit fighting with Main Force Viet Cong and the NVA] could move to another planet today, and we would still not have won the war, because the Vietnamese people are the prize.**—*General Victor Krulak, Commander, Fleet Marine Force Pacific, in a strategy paper, December 1965.*[887]

Krulak advocated a different approach to the war against the communists in Vietnam. He stressed the importance of winning the support of the Vietnamese population through pacification and economic reforms. His strategy was similar to that of John Paul Vann, and like Vann, his plan fell through the military-political cracks of the Administration's platform for success in Southeast Asia.

823 **I fear, with the escalation of the war, a cut-down and damage to the social programs here. Do we love the war on poverty, or do we love the war in Vietnam?**—*The Reverend Martin Luther King, SCLC leader, speaking in Chicago, late 1965.*[746]

There was increasing pressure and violence in the northern cities, where racist anger in the black ghettos was growing. King wanted money for Johnson's War on Poverty, but the war in Vietnam was swallowing the resources.

824 **These people really believe the President wants war. They have no idea of his anguish. They have no idea of my anguish. They don't like this big Texas swinger and that's that.**—*Representative Jeffrey Cohelan, California, 1966.*[847]

825 **[President Johnson]—Then no matter what we do in the military field there is no sure victory?**

[Secretary McNamara]—That's right. We have been too optimistic.—*Robert McNamara, Secretary of Defense, during conversation with President Johnson, 18 December 1965.*[72]

At the end of the 1965 Christmas bombing pause, the Johnson administration escalated the level of bombing against North Vietnam.

826 **The Communists are seeking to attrit U.S. forces through the process of violent, close-quarter combat which tends to diminish the effectiveness of our supporting arms.**—*General Victor Krulak, Commander Fleet Marine Force, Pacific, December 1965.*[887]

Krulak was commenting on the battle of the Ia Drang Valley, where troops of the U.S. 1st Cavalry Division engaged NVA regulars. This was the first major battle of the war involving the newly arrived American combat units and the NVA.

827 **You've seen some of those demonstrators.... Aren't you glad they're not on our side.**—*Bob Hope, comedian, actor, and U.S. troop entertainer, during a show at Tan Son Nhut Air Base, 24 December 1965.*[679]

828 **[Trying to interdict columns of men and supplies moving to the South] can be likened to fighting an alligator by chewing on his tail.**—*General Victor Krulak, Commander, Fleet Marine Force Pacific, in a strategy paper, December 1965.*[887]

829 **I have a feeling that the other side is not that tough...**—*Dean Rusk, Secretary of State, comments to President Johnson, December 1965.*[161]

Rusk's perception of the ability of North Vietnam to withstand U.S. military pressure.

830 **Damage has neither stopped nor curtailed movement of military supplies and created no evidence of serious problems due to shortages of equipment.**—*Excerpt from CIA/DIA intelligence appraisal, submitted to the White House, December 1965.*[925]

In reference to the air campaign against North Vietnam.

831 **The U.S. allocated the money for the villagers to rebuild their houses [damaged in combat], but there is some kind of regulation that says war claims can only be settled through the government [GVN]. So the money is turned over to the politicians in Saigon, who hate to let go of it and then it trickles down to the chiefs of the provinces who sit on it as long as they can and then it gets to the district chiefs. Eventually, some of it gets to the people for who it was meant all along.**—*Lt. James Smathers, U.S. Marine Corps, speaking to correspondent, in the village of Cam Ni, February 1965.*[402]

The reparations money was skimmed by Vietnamese officials at every level, so by the time it made it to the village level there was very little left. Some village chiefs used the money as an instrument of revenge, withholding it as they saw fit. So the villagers were angry with the Americans for the damage, angry with their government because it did not help them.

832 **I am a humanitarian and all that jazz, but I am not completely out of my mind.**—*Josiah Lucier, Hospitalman Second Class, U.S. Navy, to correspondent, at the village of Cam Ni, February 1965.*[402]

Lucier was a U.S. Navy corpsman deployed with a CAP squad. He was on his way to make his rounds. The correspondent commented that he was not carrying a weapon. Lucier produced a .45 automatic from his utility's cargo pocket.

833 **I will be glad to pray for his soul, but I will not pay for his plot...**—*Josiah Lucier, Hospitalman Second Class, U.S. Navy, to Vietnamese teacher, near the village of Dong Song, February 1965.*[402]

A VC was killed by Marines just outside the village of Dong Song. A relative claimed the body and asked the Marines if they wanted to contribute towards the burial cost. Lucier did the translating of the exchange and rendered the Marine's answer. The subject VC had wounded a Marine before being killed.

834 **There's just got to be something more than bullets. Until we start treating these people like human beings, they aren't going to want to help us.**—*Josiah Lucier, Hospitalman Second Class, U.S. Navy, to correspondent, at the village of Cam Ni, February 1965.*[402]

835 **If they fire at you from a cave, let them have it. But if no one shoots, hold your own fire and go down there with a flashlight and explore the damn thing...**—*Captain Phil Phelan, 1/7 Marines, USMC, to his men during the sweep of a fortified enemy village, February 1965.*[402]

In an effort to reduce civilian casualties, U.S. troops generally only returned fire when fired upon. Reconnaissance by fire in populated areas was prohibited.

836 **If they're dead, they're confirmed V.C., and if they're still breathing, they're suspects.**—*Unidentified Marine, B/1/7 Marines, to a correspondent, February 1965.*[402]

837 **No "front," no "rear" and it is absolutely impossible to tell friend from enemy without a program — even with one.**—*General Lewis Walt, Commander Marine Forces, Vietnam, to correspondent, November 1965.*[402]

838 **It's like everything else we do over here — we're damned if we do and damned if we don't.**—*General Lewis Walt, Commander, Marine Forces Vietnam, speaking to one of his battalion commanders, November 1965.*[402]

Reaction to news that during an operation 66 enemy soldiers had been killed in a cave by a Marine explosive charge. Enemy survivors of the blast indicated the cave was a hidden field hospital. Marines had taken fire from the cave when searching the area.

1966

When two elephants fight, it is the grass underneath that suffers.
—African proverb

839 **You got to hand it to those little mothers [VC]. They got the guts. If we had them on our side, we'd wrap up this war in about a month.**—*Unidentified Huey gunship pilot, overheard by a correspondent at Vinh Long, 1966.*[249]

840 **[The presence of North Vietnamese troops in South Vietnam is] a myth fabricated by the U.S. imperialist to justify their war of aggression.** *Pham Van Dong, Prime Minister, Democratic Republic of Vietnam, January 1966.*[374]

Hanoi's response to published reports and evidence of North Vietnamese troops in combat in South Vietnam.

841 **When a man is faced with death he takes a little different view of things.**—*Unidentified chaplain, commenting to Frank Harvey, 1966.*[249]

Harvey asked, what changed atheists into believers, in regard to the battlefield proverb that "there are no atheists in foxholes."

842 **You get hurt less when you hit the other guy harder than he hits you.**—*Major Jim Kasler, U.S. Air Force F-105 pilot, during an interview, 1966.*[249]

843 **There is a national paranoia, when a person is declared a Communist, he no longer is considered a human being and anything is all right to suppress him.**—*Harry Rubin, professor, University of California at Berkeley, 1966.*[414]

844 **I shot up a Charlie [VC] in the paddies today. I ran the little mother all over the place hosing him with guns but somehow or other we just didn't hit him. Finally he turned on us and stood there facing us with his rifle. We really busted his ass then. Blew him up like a balloon.**—*Unidentified Huey gunship pilot, overheard by a correspondent at Vinh Long, 1966.*[249]

845 **A man was really lucky if he just got one form of VD. Often as not, he'd come up with a pair of them, back to back.**—*Unidentified U.S. Air Force flight surgeon, during an interview with a correspondent, 1966.*[249]

Commenting on the high rate of venereal diseases in South Vietnam.

846 **If you go down in North Vietnam, your chances of being picked up by the chopper boys aren't really too good, but at least the North Vietnamese will treat you fairly well. In South Vietnam ... your chances of being picked up are excellent. But if the Vietcong catch you they kill you.**—*Unidentified U.S. Marine Corps pilot, during an interview, 1966.*[249]

The VC typically did not have facilities for prisoners and they were not usually disposed to maintain a captured pilot until they could turn him over to a NVA unit. It was easier to kill a pilot and move on.

847 **If you are shot down in South Vietnam, boys, don't badmouth Uncle Ho. He's the boy who threw out the French—and they still love him down here.**—*Major Young, Air Force escape and evasion specialist, during a briefing to U.S. Navy aircrews, 1966.*[249]

Most Vietnamese held Ho Chi Minh in high regard for leading the struggle to oust the French.

848 **News is a weapon. Secrets divulged by irresponsible newsman can give aid and comfort to the enemy.**—*Frank Harvey, free-lance writer and correspondent, 1966.*[249]

849 **Let them who talk of easy solutions through more soldiers and more bombs and more guns recognize that their past advice has only taken more of our soldiers to their deaths.**—*Senator George McGovern, of South Dakota, 1966.*[414]

850 **I'm sorry it is necessary to fight this kind of war, where civilians are bound to get hurt, but there's no way out of it. Civilians have always been hurt in wars and they probably always will be.**—*Major Frank Camp, U.S. Air Force doctor, during an interview, 1966.*[249]

Dr. Camp spent a good portion of his tour working on a military surgical team that supported the civilian Vietnamese hospital in Can Tho.

851 **I'm not going to fuss at you chaps about roots and tubers and that sort of thing. Fact is, you won't be able to escape and evade very well in this war. If you go down, one of two things will happen rather quickly: Either we'll get to you — or they will.**—*Major Young, Air Force escape and evasion specialist, during a briefing to U.S. Navy aircrews, 1966.*[249]

852 **We are in a posture for which there is no possible way to devise a sound moral defense. I think this does something very bad and cruel to you inside yourself.**—*Harvey Wheeler, author, during an interview, February 1966.*[414]

853 **Terroristic or indiscriminate bombing must involve the deaths of non-combatant men, women and children and merits the general condemnation of humanity. It cannot be justified as an instrument of U.S. foreign policy.**—*Mark O. Hatfield, Governor of Oregon, 1966.*[414]

Hatfield won a U.S. Senate seat in 1966.

854 **The war [in Vietnam] ... really started out as a war of liberation from colonial rule ... [which] became a civil war between the Diem government and the Vietcong. ... I think it is an oversimplication ... to say that this is a clear-cut aggression by North Vietnam.**—*Senator J. William Fulbright, chairman of the Senate Foreign Relations committee, during hearings on the war in Vietnam, March 1966.*[1027]

855 **[The Domino Theory] has not the slightest basis in history. It is an American version of the Communist theory of inevitability. For years Communists believed that their triumph in Russia was the beginning of world revolution. But revolutions succeed or fail because of local conditions, not on the basis of what happens in another country.**—*Hans J. Morgenthau, University of Chicago political science professor, 1966.*[414]

856 **We are the most hated outfit in Vietnam, nobody likes to see the trees and the crops killed. But we're in a war, and Ranch Hand is helping to win it.**—*Major Ralph Dresser, Commander, Operation Ranch Hand, during an interview, 1966.*[249]

857 **Just because you know what you don't like ... know what you hate, doesn't mean you automatically love the opposite.**—*Norman Thomas, former leader of the American Socialist Party, speaking during a Berkeley teach-in, January 1966.*[407]

Making the point that because the peace movement might be against the U.S. war in Vietnam, did not mean the movement supported the negative impact of communism. Many in the Administration attempted to tie the peace/anti-war movement to the communists.

858 **[The Johnson peace offensive is] a smoke screen to becloud world opinion.**—*Peking News Service, January 1966.*[408]

Peking's characterization of the Johnson administration's peace offensive during the 1966/67 bombing pause. Johnson sent Arthur Goldberg, Averell Harriman, Hubert Humphrey, and McGeorge Bundy around the globe to speak with dozens of international leaders in an attempt to get peace talks started between the U.S. and North Vietnam.

859 **The communists consider this a war for the minds of men. The military is actually secondary. It is a new kind of war for this day and age; different from Korea and World War II — different from anything in our current recollection or thinking. It is ten percent military, ninety percent psychological. We can win or lose through mass communications. This is a war of words as well as bullets.**—*Elaine Shepard, journalist and author, relating comments made by a Washington official, 1966.*[862]

This encounter took place shortly before she left the U.S. for South Vietnam.

860 **[The SNCC is] in sympathy with and supports the men in this country who are unwilling to respond to a military draft which would compel them to contribute their lives to United States aggression in Vietnam ... in the name of the "freedom" we find so false in this country.**—*John Lewis, official of the Student Nonviolent Coordinating Committee, during a press conference in Atlanta, 6 January 1966.*[987]

The SNCC advocated black civil rights.

861 **We believe that work in the civil rights movement is a valid alternative to the draft. We urge all Americans to seek this alternative, knowing full well that it may cost them their lives — as painfully as in Vietnam.**—*John Lewis, SNCC civil rights activist, public statement, 6 January 1966.*[738]

This statement was made following the murder of Samuel Younge in Alabama, 3 January 1966, when he tried to use the white restroom at a gas station. The SNCC advocated a struggle for civil rights in America over the struggle against communism in Southeast Asia.

862 **Nothing is more challenging than close air support.**—*Unidentified U.S. Marine Corps pilot, comments to a correspondent, Da Nang, 1966.*[249]

The primary mission for Marine pilots was tactical close air support of Marine ground units.

863 **Because I oppose what America is doing to the Vietcong doesn't mean I love the Vietcong or that I think terrorism is a virtue when used by them. I am no friend of violence on any side.**—*Norman Thomas, former leader of the American Socialist Party, speaking during a Berkeley teach-in, January 1966.*[407]

864 **I like a lot they do, but I wish they'd cut their hair.**—*Norman Thomas, former leader of the American Socialist Party, speaking during a Berkeley teach-in, January 1966.*[407]

Thomas's views on long-haired student demonstrators.

Thomas was 81 years old when he attended the Berkeley teach-in of January 1966.

865 **We simply cannot let the Communists arrive in South Vietnam with all that stuff intact.**—*Unidentified military source, Saigon, commenting to a correspondent, 8 January 1966.*[536]

Referencing the wisdom of heavy U.S. bombing of the Ho Chi Minh Trail in an attempt to restrict the flow of men and supplies from North Vietnam into South Vietnam. During bombing pauses, North Vietnam drastically increased the flow of men and materials south.

866 **To do any less would be madness...**—*Unidentified military source, Saigon, comments to correspondent, 8 January 1966.*[536]

Referencing the wisdom of heavy U.S. bombing of the Ho Chi Minh Trail in an attempt to restrict the flow of men and supplies from North Vietnam into South Vietnam. During bombing pauses, North Vietnam drastically increased the flow of men and materials south.

867 **It [defoliants] tastes like kerosene with chemical overtones — not good, but hardly a deadly poison unless you drink it, which nobody is likely to do.**—*Major Ralph Dresser, Commander, Operation Ranch Hand, during an interview, 1966.*[249]

In an effort to work up the peasants, the VC claimed the chemicals sprayed by American planes were deadly poisons. The Americans conducting the spray missions were told by the U.S. government that the defoliants being sprayed were only harmful to plants and trees.

868 **We have gone from a simple offer to assist the [South Vietnam] government to more than a quarter million Americans on land and off the coast in combat roles. Each extension of the war has resulted only in more troops from the other side.**—*Senator George McGovern, of South Dakota, 1966.*[414]

869 **The murder of Samuel Younge in Tuskegee, Alabama, is no different than the murder of people in Vietnam, for both Younge and the Vietnamese sought, and are seeking, to secure the rights guaranteed them by law. In each case, the United States government bears a great part of the responsibility for these deaths.**—*John Lewis, SNCC civil rights activist, public statement, 6 January 1966.*[738]

The SNCC faulted the government for not upholding the law in the South, and faulted the government for violation of international law in Vietnam.

870 **One or two napalm attacks can change the fighting spirit of a whole company.**—*Lt. Comdr. Fitch, U.S. Navy A-4 pilot, during an interview, 1966.*[249]

871 **[The New Left makes] few constructive suggestions. Freedom from dogmatism is a good thing. Lack of program is not.**—*Norman Thomas, former leader of the American Socialist Party, speaking during a Berkeley teach-in, January 1966.*[407]

Thomas believed the New Left's anti-American attitude was more anarchistic than socialistic. He complained they shouted revolution without a plan to replace the system they were revolting against.

872 **We have to stop Communism here — or face it later, closer to home.**—*Opinion expressed to interviewer by many pilots of the USS Constellation, 1966.*[249]

The *Constellation* was on Yankee Station, the pilots flying strikes against North Vietnam.

873 **We believe that the majority of the Vietnamese favor democracy, our style. This was, and is, our fallacy. I am not persuaded that even a bare majority of those who inhabit South Vietnam are on our side or know what democracy is.**—*Charles Warren, California Assemblyman, 1966.*[414]

874 **If you cannot learn to live with the Communists, then you might begin to think about dying with them.**—*Norman Thomas, former leader of the American Socialist Party, speaking during a Berkeley teach-in, January 1966.*[407]

Thomas, at 81 years of age, argued against U.S. intervention in Vietnam and spoke out for negotiations and U.S. withdrawal.

875 **Through triple-canopy jungle, where the tree layers of foliage are so intermeshed that whatever sunlight penetrates is but a diffused glow. After the heaviest downpour, rain doesn't even drip; it's absorbed by the overhead cover. The soldier fighting in this terrain is surrounded by the fetid, claustrophobic jungle, so that only the men immediately to his front and rear are visible. The infantryman finds himself slogging through foot-gripping mud with water lapping at his armpits, or enveloped in a cloud of dust, or stumbling across craggy mountains.**—*U.S. Army slide presentation on Vietnam, 1966.*[187]

876 **Guerrilla warfare requires the support of the countryside, and the Vietcong are now getting that support as regular as ever.**—*Charles Warren, California Assemblyman, 1966.*[414]

877 **If blood must be spilled let it be mine; if lives must be lost, let them be ours.**—*Norman Thomas, former leader of the American Socialist Party, speaking during a Berkeley teach-in, January 1966.*[407]

Thomas responding to a speaker at the teach-in who advocated arming canvassers collecting petition signatures to impeach Johnson.

878 **Move into a village. Run a daily Sick Call — real big — all day every day. Stay there. Guard the place so the VC can't come back, ever. Keep doing this in enough places and you'll win the war.**—*Sgt. Chuck Koscinski, U.S. Army Special Forces medic, during an interview, 1966.*[249]

879 **There were some in South Vietnam who wished to force Communist rule on their own people. But their progress was slight. Their hope of success dim. Then, little more than six years ago, North Vietnam decided on conquest and from that day to this, soldiers and supplies have moved from North to South in a swelling stream that swallowed the remnants of revolution in aggression.**—*President Johnson, State of the Union message, 12 January 1966.*[784]

880 **I am for all the goals of your revolution, but they aren't going to come about by your methods of revolution.**—*Norman Thomas, former leader of the American Socialist Party, speaking during a Berkeley teach-in, January 1966.*[407]

Thomas opposed the use of violence to obtain the goals of the anti-war and peace movement. Thomas was 81 years old at the time of this speech.

881 **Today we have sufficient force in South Vietnam to hold several enclaves on the coast, where sea and air power can be made fully effective.... However, we are [currently] stretching these resources beyond reason in our endeavors to secure the entire country of South Vietnam from Vietcong penetration.**—*General James Gavin, former ambassador, in a letter published by Harper's in January 1966.*[732]

Gavin did not think there were enough U.S. troops incountry to stem the tide against the VC. He believed that either more troops would be needed or the U.S. objectives would not be met. Gavin commanded the 82d Airborne during the Battle of the Bulge during World War II.

882 **We have sent our Secretary of State around the world to emphasize that our word is at stake and that if we do not hold the line in South Vietnam, then these other countries cannot depend on our commitment to them. Surely this is the most extraordinary diplomatic mission in our history.**—*Senator Frank Church of Idaho, during testimony before the Senate Foreign Relations Committee, February 1966.*[414]

883 **The world ought to understand that if we can achieve them [U.S. goals for the South Vietnamese] by negotiating we will. Otherwise we are fully prepared to go on fighting for them, as our build-up of forces should have made perfectly clear by now.**—*Life magazine editorial, 14 January 1966.*[406]

The U.S. goals for South Vietnam were stated in the U.N. as unconditional negotiations under the guidelines of the 1954 and 1962 Geneva agreements. South Vietnam should be in a position to determine its own future without outside interference, and seek free elections to determine if the two Vietnams should be unified.

884 **Sure I'm scared of the flak. We all are until we get in it. Then we're too busy.**—*Commander Jim Morin, U.S. Navy A-4 Squadron Leader, during an interview, 1966.*[249]

885 **[A great many people in South Vietnam] still think of Ho Chi Minh as a kind of George Washington; and it is our narrowness and lack of perspective and prejudicial interest that make it impossible for us to see that they have need of a revolution there ... even if that involves a form of Communism. I think it is our stupidity to let them be forced more and more toward China.**—*Dr. Dana McLean Greely, president, Unitarian Universalist Association of Boston, 1966.*[414]

886 **By shallow-flooding the rice, it leads after time to widespread starvation unless food is provided — which we could offer to do "at the conference table."**—*John T. McNaughton, Assistant Secretary of Defense, memorandum to Robert McNamara, 18 January 1966.*[159]

McNaughton proposed bombing the system of locks, dikes and dams that protected the rice growing region in the Red River Valley around Hanoi. The low-level flooding would destroy crops, yet not cause undue civilian casualties.

887 **In Southeast Asia we are facing revolutionary wars, which are indigenous. Our failure to distinguish between aggression and revolution had been the most serious defeat in our policy.**—*Senator Frank Church of Idaho, 1966.*[414]

Church argued against American intervention into civil wars. He saw the war in Laos and Vietnam as civil wars, as later was the war in Cambodia.

888 **I think we are running out of wiggle room. I think we are coming pretty close to the point of no return, and personally I am scared to death we are on our way to nuclear World War Three.**—*Senator Joseph Clark, Senate Foreign Relations Committee, during hearings, 28 January 1966.*[829]

Some members of Congress were worried that the U.S. escalation of the war would ultimately bring Chinese troops in on the side of North Vietnam, with a nuclear response by the U.S. that would no doubt be countered by nuclear weapons from the U.S.S.R. in support of China.

889 **The doctrines and policies espoused by Peking today constitute perhaps the most important single problem of peace.**—*Dean Rusk, Secretary of State, in hearings before the Senate Foreign Relations Committee, 28 January 1966.*[829]

Rusk believed Red China was really behind Hanoi's appetite for South Vietnam.

890 **We are in an escalating military stalemate.**—*John T. McNaughton, Assistant Secretary of Defense, January 1966.*[713]

Increases in American troop levels were being countered by North Vietnam increases. Such a high level of force would be required to stop the flow of men and material from North Vietnam that the Johnson administration feared there was a chance that the Soviets or Chinese would intervene on behalf of Hanoi.

891 **I'd be disappointed if they weren't eager to fly in combat for the first time. It's the eagerness to fly a second time that's more important.**—*Unidentified flight instructor, Fort Rucker, Alabama, January 1966.*[405]

Comments on new students at the Army's helicopter school at Fort Rucker.

892 **No mistake is so fundamental as to try to transplant our European experience to Asia, where white colonialism is well remembered.**—*Senator Frank Church of Idaho, 1966.*[414]

Church was a Democrat and against the use of U.S. troops in Vietnam. He likened U.S. involvement and occupation of Vietnam to colonialism.

893 **We thought we were tough and streetwise, but we were really ignorant. Most of us didn't really know where Vietnam was. If we were going to the Far East, why did we keep sailing west?**—*Robert Conner, enlisted member of the 25th Infantry Division, comments on his deployment, January 1966.*[42]

The 2d and 3d Brigades, 25th Infantry Division deployed by ship to Vietnam in January 1966. The brigades deployed from their bases in Hawaii.

894 **We have to reflect on how one builds peace. Do we build it by standing aside when aggression occurs or do we build it by meeting our commitments.**—*Dean Rusk, Secretary of State, in hearings before the Senate Foreign Relations Committee, 28 January 1966.*[829]

895 **There are Communist overtones but the Vietcong are inspired more by feelings of nationalism. It was this feeling that put the Vietnamese against the Japanese, also the French. ... I happen to think the white man no longer is a force in Asia.**—*John S. Knight, publisher of the Miami Herald, 1966.*[414]

896 **A bomb carried by a boy on a bicycle or mortar shells fired at the Da Nang base just three days ago are just as much**

bombs as those carried by planes to the North.—*Dean Rusk, Secretary of State, in an appearance before the House Foreign Affairs Committee, 26 January 1966.*[811]

Rusk was responding to questions from the Congress as to why the bombing of North Vietnam needed to be resumed.

897 **It is tragic that this problem could arise. It could end literally in twenty-four hours ... if these people in Hanoi should come to the conclusion that they are not going to seize Vietnam and Laos by force.**—*Dean Rusk, Secretary of State, in hearings before the Senate Foreign Relations Committee, 28 January 1966.*[829]

898 **If our boys were put in mortal conflict against the hordes of Red Chinese coolies, the United States should use every weapon we have.**—*Senator John Stennis of Mississippi, in a speech before the Mississippi Legislature, 27 January 1966.*[532]

Stennis proposed all-out air attacks against North Vietnam. In the event this pulled Red China into the war, he further advocated all-out war against the Chinese in support of American forces in Southeast Asia.

899 **I don't believe in correspondents killing people. I think it's a crummy thing for them to do. If they want to kill people they ought to jolly well join up, get a uniform and become a GI.**—*Frank Harvey, free-lance writer and correspondent, 1966.*[249]

Harvey had just come aboard a Navy PBR departing for a night patrol on the Bassac River. The PBR commander offered him a weapon for self-defense, should the need arise.

900 **We will lose some face no matter what we do. But what are we more concerned with, losing face or losing lives.**—*James Loder, student, University of Wisconsin, in an interview, February 1966.*[414]

901 **Many Vietnamese ... even in the [South Vietnamese] puppet army and administration ... now begin to see the [American imperialists'] true nature as aggressors and traitors.**—*General Vo Nguyen Giap, defense minister of North Vietnam, from an article published in Hanoi, 1966.*[410]

902 **Though they [the U.S.] may bring in hundreds of thousands of troops, they cannot avoid being driven into passivity in strategy, compelled to scatter their forces in the defensive as well as in the offensive, and cannot easily wrest back the initiative.**—*General Vo Nguyen Giap, Defense Minister of North Vietnam, from an article published in Hanoi, 1966.*[410]

The U.S. fielded approximately one combat soldier for every 6-10 American soldiers in Vietnam. This reduced the combat effectiveness of the overall American force. The rear support areas required large numbers of U.S. troops for protection and operation, furthering the diminution of troops available for offensive operations. The VC/NVA troops operated from sanctuaries along the border, reducing the forces required for protection of their base areas.

903 **A mission to kill crops is particularly serious. We have to take it right up to the American Ambassador himself for approval.**—*Major Ralph Dresser, Commander, Operation Ranch Hand, during an interview, 1966.*[249]

One of Ranch Hand's targets was enemy food crops.

904 **In training, they had told us the VC wore black pajamas. There were sampans all around the ship, and everyone wore black pajamas. Were they the enemy?**—*Robert Conner, enlisted member of the 25th Infantry Division, comments on his deployment, January 1966.*[42]

The 2d and 3d Brigades, 25th Infantry Division deployed by ship to Vietnam in January 1966.

905 **The notion that Communism is a monolithic system with a single set of aims is outdated. The Communist world is unraveling. Our policy should be to speed the process.**—*Senator Frank Church of Idaho, 1966.*[414]

906 **The enormous effort made in the last 34 days had produced nothing — no runs, no hits, no errors.**—*Dean Rusk, Secretary of State, during a National Security Council meeting, 29 January 1966.*[154]

Rusk was commenting on the results of the 37-day bombing halt called by Johnson in late December 1965. Soviet Ambassador Anatoly Dobrynin had indicated to the Johnson administration, that if the U.S. stopped the bombing of North Vietnam for a period of time, the Soviets would attempt to persuade Hanoi to seriously consider negotiations with the U.S. The extended bombing halt yielded no results other than North Vietnam's insistence that it would carry the war on to victory.

907 **It was a miserable couple of weeks. We did our pushups early in the morning to avoid burning our hands on the deck. The rest of the day we tried to stay on the shady side of the ship, avoided spitting windward, and read dirty books...**—*Robert Conner, enlisted member of the 25th Infantry Division, comments on his deployment, January 1966.*[42]

The 2d and 3d Brigades, 25th Infantry Division deployed by ship to Vietnam in January 1966.

908 **We'll go back and kill more of the sons of bitches.**—*General Stanley Larsen, Commander, U.S. Forces, II Corps, comments to correspondent, January 1966.*[887]

Larsen was responding to a press question as to why American troops were not remaining in the area following an operation, which allowed the enemy to filter back in once the American troops were gone. The 1st Cavalry operated against the enemy on the Bong Son plain during Operation Masher (White Wing). The Cavalry engaged elements of the 3d NVA Division, forcing them out of the area. When the operation was over the Cavalry departed. This type of engagement happened often. An area would be cleared of the enemy, then abandoned. The enemy would return, and eventually so would the U.S. troops.

909 **The situation in Vietnam has overtones of an indigenous civil war.**—*John S. Knight, publisher of the Miami Herald, 1966.*[414]

Knight's argument was that the war between North and South Vietnam was a civil war, and was not our concern.

910 **Now the world knows more clearly than ever who insists on aggression and who works for peace.**—*President Johnson, during a televised statement, 31 January 1966.*[837]

Johnson, on Hanoi's lack of response to the Administration's peace feelers during the January bombing pause. Johnson ordered the bombing of the North resumed 31 January 1966.

911 **It is possible that one of the obstacles to peace has been a failure on the part of Hanoi to understand that the United**

States will in fact meet its commitment.... If they are relying upon domestic differences among us to save their cause, they must understand that that will not occur.—*Dean Rusk, Secretary of State, during a press conference, 31 January 1966.*[837]

912 **[Any resolution adopted by the United Nations] intervening in the Vietnam question would be null and void.**—*Democratic Republic of Vietnam Foreign Ministry statement, 1 February 1966.*[531]

Hanoi rejected any intervention by the U.N. aimed at negotiating an end to the war. North Vietnam insisted that the 1954 Geneva Accords were at issue and the U.S. acts of war were in direct violation of the 1954 Accords.

913 **My personal feeling is that in this moment of crisis we all ought to support the President. He is the man who had all the information and knowledge of what we are up against.**—*Governor Nelson Rockefeller, New York, speaking to the press, 1 February 1966.*[755]

Most of the country still backed Johnson at this time, though the number of demonstrations against the administration were increasing and there was some erosion of support in Congress.

914 **No one wants to escalate the war and no one wants to lose any more men than is necessary. No one wants to surrender and get out. At least no one admits they do. So I don't see there is any great difference of opinion.**—*President Johnson, during a press conference during Senate Foreign Relations Committee hearings on Vietnam, 11 February 1966.*[840]

Referring to the ongoing Senate hearings on the Vietnam War.

915 **This is a lousy, stinking war. It's dirty and immoral. We're using—killing—the Vietnamese people for our own purposes. We're not rescuing or protecting them.**—*Henry Rubin, restaurant owner, Berkeley, California, in an interview, February 1966.*[414]

916 **Our only commitment is to ourselves. We would lose face at home [if we pulled out of Vietnam], and that is what the government is afraid of.**—*Dr. Harold Pickett, dentist, San Antonio, Texas, during an interview, February 1966.*[414]

917 **The U.S. expeditionary corps, deprived of an ideal to fight for, is possessed of a low morale ... it has to cope with a people's war. Its strategy and tactics based on the bourgeois military are of no use.**—*General Vo Nguyen Giap, defense minister of North Vietnam, from an article published in Hanoi, 1966.*[410]

918 **President Johnson ... objected ... because the connotation of violence provided a focus for carping war critics.**—*General William Westmoreland, ComUSMACV, comments on naming conventions, 1966.*[1019]

Johnson was angered at the name of Army Operation Masher, saying it did not reflect "pacification emphasis." The name was changed to White Wing. The operation was conducted by the 1st Cavalry Division on the Bong Son Plain, January 1966.

919 **Solutions for the terrible problems that exist in Asia and Africa might have to take forms not at all palatable to us. When a people who lead a miserable life see a way to improve their position, through Communism or whatever it takes, it is utter cynicism to say that we are trying to protect them from something evil.**—*Robert Treuhaft, California attorney, 1966.*[414]

920 **The United States can never triumph because it cannot win over the people of South Vietnam, occupy enough of its territory or create a viable army and government there.**—*General Vo Nguyen Giap, Defense Minister, Democratic Republic of Vietnam, to a correspondent, 1 February 1966.*[530]

921 **I cannot help feeling that a display of common sense by a proud and imperious nation would be a good moral investment for the future.**—*Walter Lippmann, columnist and author, 1966.*[414]

Lippmann argued for the withdrawal of American combat troops from Vietnam and an acknowledgement from the Johnson administration that the war in Vietnam was a lost American adventure.

922 **We have been escalating at the will of our opponents rather than on our own judgment.**—*James M. Gavin, U.S. Army General (Ret.), 1966.*[414]

Gavin commanded paratroops during W.W.II and was called upon to advise the President.

923 **A new development of the revolutionary military art ... is to rely mostly on man, on his patriotism and revolutionary spirit, to bring all weapons and techniques available to defeat an enemy with modern weapons and equipment.**—*General Vo Nguyen Giap, defense minister of North Vietnam, from an article published in Hanoi, 1966.*[410]

Hanoi believed at this point that it could still win the war militarily and that its staying power would outlast the Americans.

924 **If we fight the Americans in accordance with modern military tactics, we will be badly battered by them. We must fight the enemy as we would fight a tiger as he leaps at his prey. Only by inventing a special way of fighting can we defeat the Americans.**—*General Nguyen Chi Thanh, Senior Military Commander, South Vietnam, during a conference, 1966.*[653]

Thanh was Hanoi's commander in South Vietnam. He died in July 1967 as a result of wounds suffered from a B-52 strike near his headquarters.

925 **With it [leadership], we can take this revolution away from the Communists. We can show the people that we can give them more and better things than the Communists, not only material things but things the Communists do not even understand—such as justice and personal integrity.**—*Nguyen Cao Ky, Prime Minister, South Vietnam, February 1966.*[413]

926 **Of the $3 billion in aid we gave Vietnam from 1955 to 1961, a full 82% of the people actually received only 1.6% of the help. We are not interested in the people—we don't give aid that would do things for them.**—*Stanley K. Sheinbaum, economist with the Center for the Study of Democratic Institutions, California, 1966.*[414]

Sheinbaum was also a member of the Michigan State University technical assistance team sent to Vietnam in 1955.

927 **Special pleaders who counsel retreat...**—*President Johnson, in a speech welcoming South Vietnamese officials to a conference in Hawaii, 6 February 1966.*[838]

Johnson spoke of "special pleaders" as those who opposed his policy in Vietnam and sought to force the withdrawal of the U.S. from Vietnam.

928 **We are here to talk especially of the works of peace. We will leave here determined not only to achieve victory over aggression, but to win victory over hunger, disease, and despair. We are making a reality out of the hopes of the common people.**—*President Lyndon Johnson, from his speech at the opening of the Honolulu Conference, 6 February 1966.*[629]

Johnson's pledge to help the poor in Vietnam was not well received by anti-poverty forces at home. Johnson's Great Society programs were moving very slowly forward. Available budget funds had to be split between the Great Society programs and the war in Vietnam.

929 **We must create a society that will be able to withstand the false appeals of Communism. We must create a society where each individual can feel that he has a future, that he has respect and dignity, and that he has some chance for himself and for his children to live in an atmosphere where all is not disappointment, despair, and dejection.**—*Nguyen Cao Ky, Prime Minister of South Vietnam, during his opening speech at the Honolulu Conference, 6 February 1966.*[629]

930 **Boy, you speak just like an American.**—*President Lyndon Johnson, commenting to Nguyen Cao Ky on his speech at the Honolulu Conference, 6 February 1966.*[629]

Ky considered this high praise from President Johnson. His speech was tailored to give the Americans what they wanted to hear.

931 **We are brothers in arms. We will not tire. We will not flag. We intend to work with you, to fight with you in defeating the Communist aggressor.**—*President Johnson, in a speech at the Hawaii conference, 7 February 1966.*[839]

Johnson and his advisers met in Honolulu with members of the South Vietnamese government to discuss the progress of the war.

932 **I am fearful that if the war in Vietnam is not handled extremely well, the Chinese Communists will come in.**—*Senator J. William Fulbright, of Arkansas, Chairman of the Senate Foreign Relations Committee, speaking to the press, 7 February 1966.*[532]

933 **We have committed ourselves by constantly expanding the commitment. The original commitment was limited.**—*Senator Frank Church of Idaho, during testimony before the Foreign Relations Committee, February 1966.*[414]

934 **The United States is pledged to the principle of the self-determination of peoples and of government by the consent of the governed. We have helped and we will help to stabilize the Vietnamese economy, to increase the production of goods, to spread the light of education and stamp out disease.**—*Joint communiqué from the Honolulu Conference, 8 February 1966.*[629]

The communiqué was seen by some in the U.S. as putting more importance on the Vietnamese problems of poverty, disease, economic stability, than the same issues facing Americans at home.

935 **[The United States would not benefit from] ... the spectacle of Americans inflicting grievous injury on the lives of a poor and helpless people, and particularly a people of different race and color.**—*George F. Kennan, former U.S. ambassador to the Soviet Union, appearing before the Senate Foreign Relations Committee, 10 February 1966.*[834]

Kennan believed any serious attempt to win the war in Vietnam would damage relations with Russia and China, with no strategic, economic or military gain to be had from such a war.

936 **If we were not already involved as we are today in Vietnam, I would know of no reason why we should wish to become so involved and I could think of several reasons why we should wish not to.**—*George F. Kennan, former U.S. ambassador to the Soviet Union, appearing before the Senate Foreign Relations Committee, 10 February 1966.*[834]

Kennan believed any serious attempt to win the war in Vietnam would bring in the Chinese. For Kennan, South Vietnam was not of such economic or military value to the U.S. to warrant the expense it would take to win in Vietnam.

937 **Ky is an intelligent, dedicated young man whose only real weakness is inexperience. Every day he remains in office helps to overcome that weakness.**—*Unidentified American official in Saigon, to correspondent, February 1966.*[413]

Nguyen Cao Ky was 35 years old when he became Prime Minister.

938 **How can anyone believe that our all-out efforts for peace are serious when our own President insults Ho Chi Minh by naming his dog Ho Chi Him?**—*John C. George, Washington D.C., letter to the editors, Life magazine, 11 February 1966.*[409]

From a *Life* magazine reader who took exception to President Johnson's choice of nicknames. Johnson's pet beagles were officially named "Him" and "Her." After he became president and deeply involved with Vietnam he nicknamed "Him"—Ho Chi Him.

939 **If any country could ever afford to withdraw or mediate or conciliate, we can. Nobody's going to think we're a paper tiger because we make a settlement there [in Vietnam].**—*Senator J. William Fulbright of Arkansas, Chairman of the Senate Foreign Relations Committee, February 1966.*[414]

940 **I would like to know what that commitment really consists of, and how and when it was incurred.... If we did not incur such an obligation in any formal way, then I think we should not be inventing it for ourselves and assuring ourselves that we are bound by it today.**—*George F. Kennan, former U.S. ambassador to the Soviet Union, appearing before the Senate Foreign Relations Committee, 10 February 1966.*[834]

Regarding the Administration's repeated references to a "commitment" to South Vietnam.

941 **I do not believe it was tactful of the President of the United States to name a dog after the man who may well hold the future of the United States in his paws.**—*Charles F. Kreiner, Jr., Clinton, New York, letter to the editors, Life magazine, 11 February 1966.*[409]

Letter from a *Life* magazine reader who took tongue-in-cheek exception to President Johnson's choice of a nickname. Johnson's two pet beagles were named "Him" and "Her." He nicknamed his dog "Him"—Ho Chi Him.

942 **I hope we don't find out we only had one aces [sic].**—*President Lyndon Johnson, speaking to Prime Minister Nguyen Cao Ky in Hawaii, February 1966.*[70]

Johnson relating a story to Ky about two gamblers. One gambler asked the other what he had, he replied "aces." The other gambler then asked him how many, and the other replied, "one aces." Johnson had agreed to raise U.S. troop strength to 429,000 by the end of the year, this to stabilize the war militarily. He also pressed Prime Minister Ky to quickly institute a plan for free elections in South Vietnam, and a new constitution.

943 **There are men on the other side who know well that their only hope for success in this aggression lies in a weakening of the fiber and determination of the people of America.**—*President Johnson, speech at a fund-raising dinner in Chicago, 17 May 1966.*[794]

944 **If only we had had your helicopters, it might have been a different story.**—*Unidentified French veteran of the first Indochina War, speaking with U.S. helicopter pilots, February 1966.*[412]

By February 1966 there were 1,600 American helicopters operating in South Vietnam. The French had a small number of helicopters available, these sparingly used for medical evacuation.

945 **It is ... very plain that there is no readiness or willingness to talk [on the part of Hanoi]. No readiness for peace in that regime today.**—*President Lyndon Johnson, press comment, February 1966.*[410]

Johnson had halted the bombing of North Vietnam for 37 days, waiting for them to respond and possibly agree to negotiations. Hanoi rejected the bombing halt as a trick and continued its refusal to negotiate unless there was a permanent halt to the American attacks on North Vietnam.

946 **The "Paris of the East," [Saigon] has become—under the pressure of war—a grubby, frantic city, choked by a population boom, cheapened by greed and corruption, paralyzed by traffic that doesn't move, telephones that don't work and lights that go out without warning.**—*Sam Angeloff, Life magazine correspondent, February 1966.*[413]

Saigon was also called the Pearl of the Orient.

947 **[The enclave strategy, as proposed by General Gavin is] a formula for liquidating a mistake, for ending a war that cannot be won at any tolerable price, for cutting our losses before they escalate into bankruptcy.**—*Walter Lippmann, columnist and author, 1966.*[414]

The enclave strategy involved conducting the war from fortified, secure coastal areas. Protecting part of South Vietnam instead of failing to protect all of it.

948 **Prestige is a reflection of power and power depends on what is, and not on what is said.**—*O. Edmund Clubb, former U.S. Consul General to Peking, testifying before the Senate Foreign Relations Committee, February 1966.*[414]

There was talk that if the U.S. backed out of Vietnam it would be perceived around the world as a paper tiger and would lose prestige.

949 **The [Vietnam] war has no rational political purpose.**—*Hans J. Morgenthau, University of Chicago political science professor, 1966.*[414]

Morgenthau was the academic world's leading anti–Johnson administration spokesman.

950 **Where ... does the undoubted power of the President to make war collide with the sole constitutional power of the Congress to declare war.**—*David Nevin, Life magazine correspondent, February 1966.*[414]

Congress voted 7 August 1964 to authorized the President to "take all necessary steps" in regards to protecting American lives and interest in South Vietnam. The Southeast Asia Resolution was used by Johnson as a declaration of war, allowing him to pursue the war in Vietnam with Congressional support.

951 **It is difficult to believe that any decisive developments of the world situation would be determined in normal circumstances by what happens [in Vietnam]...**—*George Kennan, Princeton University professor and former U.S. Ambassador, testifying before the Senate Foreign Relations Committee, 1966.*[414]

The perspective that in the course of world events, Vietnam is very small potatoes.

952 **Our country should not be asked, and should not ask of itself, to shoulder the main burden of determining the political realities in any country—particularly not in one remote from our shores, from our culture and from the experience of our people.**—*George Kennan, Princeton University professor and former U.S. Ambassador, testifying before the Senate Foreign Relations Committee, 1966.*[414]

953 **An easy and incomplete answer [as to why Vietnam is so important] would be that it must be important to us since it is considered so by the other side.**—*General Maxwell Taylor, former U.S. ambassador to South Vietnam, in testimony before the Senate Foreign Relations Committee, 17 February 1966.*[834]

Taylor declared the conflict in Vietnam was a limited war for a specific end, and that if Hanoi won the war other communist inspired wars of liberation in the world would follow.

954 **[Morse]—You know we are engaged in a historic debate in this country, where there are honest differences of opinion. I happen to hold to the point of view that it isn't going to be too long before the American people as a people will repudiate our war in Southeast Asia.**

[Taylor]—That, of course, is good news to Hanoi, Senator.

[Morse]—I know that is the smear that you militarists give to those of us who have honest differences of opinion with you, but I don't intend to get down in the gutter with you and engage in that kind of debate, General.—*Senator Wayne Morse and General Maxwell Taylor, exchange during Senate Foreign Relations Committee hearings, 17 February 1966.*[834]

Morse voted against the Tonkin Gulf Resolution, and Taylor favored U.S. military action against North Vietnam.

955 **Number One young girl for you, GI.**—*Unidentified Saigon sidewalk pimp, February 1966.*[413]

Heard in every city in South Vietnam. The pimps ranged in age from chilren to adults.

956 **[The Ky government is] the first government which is solidly backed by the armed forces. As long as they are behind this government in the present sense, it is not going to be overturned by some noisy minority as some governments were overturned in the previous years. So I feel there is some encouragement, indicators of growing stability in the political scene.**—*General Maxwell Taylor, Special Advisor to President Johnson, in testimony before the Senate Foreign Relations Committee, February 1966.*[629]

In December 1964 Nguyen Cao Ky and several other South Vietnamese officers arrested several members of the High National Council who were involved in a coup plot against the standing GVN. Taylor, as Ambassador to South Vietnam, had sternly chastised the officers for creating instability in the GVN, initially believing Ky and the officers were behind the coup attempt.

957 **We are making a distinction though, [and] that is that South Vietnam is not Hanoi's country.**—*Dean Rusk, Secretary of State, during Senate Foreign Relations Committee hearings, 18 February 1966.*[834]

Rusk was arguing the case that Vietnam was two separate countries, while Senator Fulbright argued that Vietnam was one divided country.

958 **The Vietnamese were taught the rules of the road by the French — the most insouciant, single-minded drivers in the world.**—*Sam Angeloff, Life magazine correspondent, February 1966.*[413]

Some of the worst traffic in the world could be found in Saigon.

959 **Vietnam is their country. It is not our country. We do not even have the right the French did. We have no historical right. We are obviously intruders, from their point of view. We represent the old Western imperialism in their eyes.**—*Senator J. William Fulbright, Chairman Senate Foreign Relations Committee, during committee hearings 18 February 1966.*[834]

960 **We considered the advisability of entering the Hanoi delta ... we talked about the need for some eight divisions, plus 35 engineer battalions ... we finally decided, when we were through, what we were talking about doing was going to war with Red China under conditions that were appallingly disadvantageous.**—*General James Gavin, appearing before the Senate Foreign Relations Committee, February 1966.*[834]

Gavin was discussing a plan to go to the aid of the French in 1954. He believed any invasion of the North by the U.S. would bring China directly into the war, and if that happened nuclear weapons would be required, and most likely the U.S.S.R. would assist China. He did not believe South Vietnam was that important.

961 **We can turn blue expounding our peace-loving natures, our righteousness and superiority, and yet we can find no way but war to achieve our objectives. Who says our objectives are right for others? Who says God is an American?**—*Susan Pressly, housewife, Haddonfield, New Jersey, in an interview, February 1966.*[414]

962 **Our policy is to hold the line on left-wing revolutions.... Most underdeveloped countries have decided that capitalism as we know it won't work for them. The U.S. doesn't like this, but it should accept it.**—*Morris W. Hirsch, professor, University of California at Berkeley, in an interview, February 1966.*[414]

963 **If the armed attack against South Vietnam is brought to an end, peace can come very quickly.**—*Dean Rusk, Secretary of State, during Senate Foreign Relations Committee hearings, 18 February 1966.*[834]

Rusk was defending administration policy and pointing to North Vietnam as the aggressor.

964 **We have done much and spent much in Vietnam, we have not done it or spent it in the right way.**—*David Nevin, Life magazine correspondent, February 1966.*[414]

965 **Keep your head down, don't get tangled up in a row over Vietnam if you want to come through the 1966 election.**—*Representative Wayne Hayes of Ohio, advice given to Democratic candidates, February 1966.*[747]

To publicly go against the President's war policy was considered at the time an act of political suicide.

966 **[Vietnam] ... is in one sense a relatively minor matter. In another sense it seems to be the trigger that may result in a world war, and I do not want that to happen, and that is what we are really concerned with.**—*Senator J. William Fulbright, Chairman Senate Foreign Relations Committee, during committee hearings 18 February 1966.*[834]

967 **Don't send me any niggers. Be careful, however, not to give the impression we are prejudiced in the Special Forces. You won't find it hard to reject them. Most will be to [sic] dumb to pass the written test. If they luck up on that and get by the physical testing, you'll find that they have some sort of criminal record.**—*Unidentified U.S. Army recruiting officer's instructions to his recruiting sergeant, February 1966.*[986]

The recruiting sergeant was Green Beret Master Sergeant Donald Duncan, U.S. Special Forces. Duncan spent 18 months with the Special Forces in Vietnam.

968 **If there is no democracy we lose not only the reason for our struggle but our principal means of victory.**—*Nguyen Cao Ky, Prime Minister, South Vietnam, in an interview, February 1966.*[413]

969 **It is dangerous to commit yourself 100% to the Americans because they reverse their policies so completely.**—*Nguyen Cao Ky, Prime Minister, South Vietnam, February 1966.*[413]

Ky used the example that under Diem America said democracy was more important than stability, and under the Ky-Thieu regime America said stability was more important than democracy.

970 **Our military units had many advantages: they didn't have to carry rice and could carry more ammo. They also didn't have to warn a village in advance of their arrival and thus safeguarded the security of the operations.**—*Unidentified NLF rallier, during an interview, February 1966.*[31]

Cadre explaining the benefit of food and weapons caches secreted throughout their operational area.

971 **Once you decide you've got the right to intervene when you think it's necessary, you've reduced morality to doing**

what you want to do when you want to do it.—*William A. Williams, professor, University of Wisconsin, in an interview, February 1966.*[414]

972 **[The balance of power] is a very delicate matter in which many things must be kept balanced. The way we work is that my colleagues decide what they want done and then I try to carry it out.**—*Nguyen Cao Ky, Prime Minister of South Vietnam, in an interview, February 1966.*[413]

Ky was one of ten military men on the National Leadership Committee. These men led South Vietnam until a constitution was written and elections for President and Vice President were held.

973 **It is our misfortune that in North Vietnam, the authentic vehicle of nationalism was a Communist.**—*Senator Frank Church of Idaho, during testimony before the Foreign Relations Committee, February 1966.*[414]

Speaking of Ho Chi Minh.

974 **Everything is for sale and almost anything will find a buyer. More than with her refuse, Saigon stinks with her corruption.**—*Unidentified Vietnamese official in Saigon, to correspondent, February 1966.*[413]

975 **Anyone who says the present government [in Saigon] represents the people is all wet. It's too bad the American people, who really started the peoples' revolutions, should be on the side of trying to stop them.**—*Madelene Van Arsdell, housewife, Phoenix, Arizona, during an interview, February 1966.*[414]

976 **We have no commitment there that justifies the sacrifice of American troops on a scale necessary to win a military decision.**—*Senator George McGovern of South Dakota, 1966.*[414]

McGovern first supported the "enclave strategy," which would lead to a negotiated settlement. These enclaves would be fortified bastions of anti-communist zones of control, which the communist would have to deal with. The VC/NVA controlled the countryside, while the U.S./ARVN controlled the major city areas.

977 **Our motives [in Vietnam] are widely misinterpreted in the spectacle ... of America inflicting grievous injury on the lives of a poor and helpless people.... A victory purchased at the price of further such damage would be a hollow one...**—*George Kennan, Princeton University professor and former U.S. Ambassador, testifying before the Senate Foreign Relations Committee, 1966.*[414]

978 **[Our government has assumed] an obligation on our part not only to defend the frontiers of a certain political entity against outside attack, but to assure the internal security of its government in circumstances where that government is unable to assure that security by its own means.**—*George Kennan, Princeton University professor and former U.S. Ambassador, testifying before the Senate Foreign Relations Committee, 1966.*[414]

This is Kennan's view that the U.S. was defending South Vietnam from attack by North Vietnam and at the same time propping up the government(s) in Saigon that were not fully representative of the people of South Vietnam.

979 **However justified our action may be in our own eyes, it has failed to win either enthusiasm or confidence even among peoples normally friendly to us.**—*George Kennan, Princeton University professor and former U.S. Ambassador, testifying before the Senate Foreign Relations Committee, 1966.*[414]

980 **The repeated U.S. assurances that we do not seek to overthrow the North Vietnamese regime would surely be the first casualty of any all-out attack from the North.**—*Hedley Donovan, Editor-in-Chief, Time, Inc., Life editorial, 25 February 1966.*[411]

Donovan believed the Johnson administration would not tolerate any invasion or large-scale military offensive by the VC/NVA. In 1968 VC/NVA units attacked all across South Vietnam during the TET Offensive. In 1972 NVA troops invaded South Vietnam crossing the DMZ and from sanctuaries along the Cambodian border, in large numbers, with supporting armor. Neither of these events triggered a U.S. invasion of North Vietnam.

981 **The ground resembled lunar landscape for miles on end, so close together were the shell holes.**—*Unidentified American Army officer, 1966.*[42]

The officer was in a helicopter flying over Hau Nghia Province, northwest of Saigon.

982 **The secret to driving in Saigon is to drive as if you intended to go through a place and as if you could not see the other vehicles involved.**—*Frank Harvey, free-lance writer and correspondent, Saigon, 1966.*[249]

Saigon, infamous for some of the worst traffic in the world.

983 **[Free-fire zone:] It's a place where we practice up trying to kill VC, and they practice up trying to shoot down choppers.**—*Major Hube Merritt, U.S. Army gunship pilot, comments to a correspondent, Vinh Long Province, 1966.*[249]

A free-fire zone was an area in which any person, animal, or structure could be fired on without clearance from a higher authority. Under the Rules of Engagement all American fire on a target usually had to be cleared through a higher headquarters. The exception was in a free-fire zone.

984 **To turn the South over to Communism, which would almost certainly be the consequences of a peace negotiated from a few enclaves, would be "defeat."**—*Hedley Donovan, Editor-in-Chief, Time, Inc., Life editorial, 25 February 1966.*[411]

In 1966 U.S. units operated from several enclaves along the coast.

985 **[The F-4 is] the outstanding airplane for the job. When you're faced with a situation where you need both air-to-air and air-to-ground capability, the F-4 is the finest airplane in the free world today...**—*Unidentified U.S. Marine Corps pilot, comments to a correspondent, Da Nang, 1966.*[249]

986 **The Directory hangs together by the grace of God, baling wire, glue — and the American dollar.**—*Unidentified American Adviser, in an interview, February 1966.*[413]

The Directory was also know as the National Leadership Committee, ten military officers that led the Government of Vietnam. Thieu was the chairman and country's Chief of State, Ky was also one of the ten, and Prime Minister.

987 **We are trying to run the Vietcong — Vietnamese themselves — out of Vietnam.**—*Ernest Gwinn, finance company president, Seattle, Washington, during an interview, February 1966.*[414]

988 **This ugly, maddening, big-little war may some day be remembered as a historic turning point. Many peoples of the West as well as Asia could have reason for gratitude to the extraordinary generation of Americans now serving in Vietnam (their harassed chiefs in Washington might even rate a word or two of thanks), and to the long-suffering troops and people of South Vietnam.**—*Hedley Donovan, Editor-in-Chief, Time, Inc., Life editorial, 25 February 1966.*[411]

989 **I have a simple solution to this war. We just take all the other planes off the carrier, load it with A-6s.... We wait for dark nights and heavy rains. We go out and wipe out the targets. We come home and land and spend the rest of the time in Singapore on R and R.**—*Lt.Comdr. Pete Garber, U.S. Navy A-6 pilot, during an interview, 1966.*[249]

In praise of the night/all-weather bombing capabilities of the Grumman A-6 Intruder.

990 **We should start at the DMZ and kill every man, woman and child in North Vietnam.**—*Unidentified American pilot, Da Nang, commenting to a correspondent, 1966.*[249]

One solution to end North Vietnam's support for the war in South Vietnam.

991 **[The Nungs.] They really like to shoot people, that's what makes them such good guards.**—*Major George Larrieux, U.S. Air Force photography officer, 1966.*[249]

The Nungs were an ancestral mix of Thai-Chinese-Muong-Tibetan. The were American paid mercenaries who generally despised the Vietnamese. The Nungs were used for security work with the Special Forces and as private guards at many facilities and American lodgings in Saigon.

992 **[Ranch Hand C-123] operated at all times on the ultimate edge of the airplane's performance envelope.**—*Unidentified Ranch Hand pilot, during an interview, 1966.*[249]

Ranch Hand C-123s sprayed herbicides from an altitude of 150 feet at a speed of 130 knots. At this speed the aircraft was operating just above stall speed and insufficient altitude to recover from an emergency.

993 **[Bombing a Russian ship in Hai Phong harbor would be] just too damn bad.**—*Senator Barry Goldwater, commenting to the press, 1966.*[249]

President Johnson refused to allow Hai Phong to be targeted for air strikes until April 1967.

994 **It's patently a contradiction for us to talk about our support of the U.N. when even a high school freshman can look at the U.N. Charter and see we are in flagrant contradiction of it in Vietnam.**—*W.H. Ferry, vice president, Center for the Study of Democratic Institutions, 1966.*[414]

995 **Go ahead and have your fun, boys. Just remember that if you develop symptoms [of V.D.] after you're shot down in North Vietnam, forget the penicillin. It isn't on the room-service list at the Hanoi Hilton. That holds the little bastards.**—*Unidentified U.S. Air Force flight surgeon, during an interview with a correspondent, 1966.*[249]

996 **To win we must have true leadership, and leadership is not simply a matter of being in power ... it is a matter of being accepted by the people.**—*Nguyen Cao Ky, Prime Minister, South Vietnam, February 1966.*[413]

997 **The American people are turning against the escalation of this conflict. If President Johnson accepts the recommendation of General Westmoreland and Ambassador Lodge [for more troops], I believe we will lose 75 seats in Congress in the next election.**—*Senator Joseph S. Clark, of Pennsylvania, at a press conference in San Francisco, 26 February 1966.*[809]

Clark was afraid voters would identify the escalating war with the President's party and vote against the Democrats in the next election.

998 **Despite the advanced handwringing in the U.S., the fears early last year that China might "come in" if the U.S. bombed North Vietnam or put ground combat units in South Vietnam, China did not come in.**—*Hedley Donovan, Editor-in-Chief, Time, Inc., Life editorial, 25 February 1966.*[411]

One of the main reasons for the Administration's slow approach to Vietnam was the fear that the Chinese might come in on the side of North Vietnam, much as they had during the Korean War.

999 **It isn't considered desirable to make a crash landing in the vicinity of folks you have just been strafing. They tend to be antisocial.**—*Commander Jim Morin, U.S. Navy A-4 pilot, during an interview, 1966.*[249]

1000 **There is a reasonably good chance the present phase of the war can be successfully wound up in 1967, or even in late 1966.**—*Hedley Donovan, Editor-in-Chief, Time, Inc., Life editorial, 25 February 1966.*[411]

1001 **Only you can prevent forest.**—*Operation Ranch Hand motto, on a placard over their Ready Room door, 1966.*[249]

A paraphrase of the U.S. Forest Service Smoky Bear campaign. Operation Ranch Hand was the USAF defoliation mission. Millions of gallons of herbicides were sprayed from Air Force C-123 aircraft along trails and river banks in an attempt to kill the vegetation and eliminate enemy ambush cover.

1002 **The likeliest ending [to the war] is not around a conference table, however, but in a quiet withdrawal of main-force North Vietnamese units, after they have been hurt enough, back to the North, and a gradual tapering off of the Vietcong military effort in the South.**—*Hedley Donovan, Editor-in-Chief, Time, Inc., Life editorial, 25 February 1966.*[411]

Donovan believed the war effort was going well for the U.S.

1003 **The VC need ten days to transfer three battalions, we manage five battalions in a day.**—*General William E. DePuy, Commander, 1st Infantry Division, 1966.*[249]

Comments on the mobility of the 1st Cavalry.

1004 **But you're driving the President crazy.**—*Hubert Humphrey, Vice President, in an exchange between Humphrey and Senator Joseph S. Clark, March 1966.*[823]

Humphrey was counseling the Senator after Clark's public prediction that Johnson's escalation of the war would result in democratic election loses at the polls.

1005 **We accept the fact that there are degrees of victory and that each degree must be defined in terms of political, economic, and military objectives, as well as the aggregate price that must be paid to achieve them.**—*General Harold K. Johnson, Army Chief of Staff, from a speech, 1966.*[713]

By 1966 the U.S. had stopped the downward slide of South Vietnamese deterioration, but the war approached a stalemate as increases in American troops were offset by increases in NVA troops and increased VC recruiting. A quantifiable definition of victory in Vietnam had not been stated before the war of escalation began.

1006 **I think it's great that a country like the U.S. will back up with force what it says it believes. You can't sit behind your fortress and let things like that happen just because it's 10,000 miles away.**—*George H. Witchell, former U.S. Marine Corps F-4 pilot, during an interview, 1966.*[249]

1007 **He was not fighting a second class war and did not die a second class death.... My son was not a shoeshine boy like his father. He was a soldier, a paratrooper in the Green Berets.... My son died fighting on the front for all of us. He didn't die a segregated death and he'll not be buried in a segregated cemetery.**—*Mrs. Williams, mother of a U.S. Special Forces soldier who was killed in action, 1966.*[983]

PFC Jimmy Williams, of the U.S. Special Forces died of fragmentation wounds in Vietnam, 19 May 1966. His mother attempted to bury him in the public cemetery in their home town of Wetumpa, Alabama. Town officials would not allow the soldier to be buried in the white cemetery because he was black, and they would not allow burial in the black cemetery on the grounds that it was full. Jimmy Williams was eventually buried at Andersonville National Military Cemetery, Georgia, one hundred miles from his home in Alabama.

1008 **I've seen some things happen here that have moved me so much that I've changed my whole outlook on life. I feel different now after seeing some horrible things, and I'll never forget them. I can't say what I mean, but some of the things you see here can really change a man or turn a boy into a man. Any combat GI that comes here doesn't leave the same.**—*PFC George J. Robinson, U.S. Army, HHC, 2d Battalion, 28th Infantry Regiment, in a letter home, 1966.*[187]

1009 **[The NLF must be recognized] as the sole genuine representative of the South Vietnamese people.**—*Ho Chi Minh, President Democratic Republic of Vietnam, 1966.*[452]

Ho Chi Minh added this to the conditions necessary for peace negotiations to take place. At this point the NLF was not recognized as the legitimate government of South Vietnam by any countries other than the Soviet Bloc and Red China.

1010 **[The U.S. will stop bombing] the moment we are assured privately or otherwise that this step will be answered promptly by a corresponding and appropriate de-escalation on the other side.**—*Arthur Goldberg, U.S. Ambassador to the United Nations, in a speech at the U.N., 1966.*[452]

The U.N. repeatedly called for de-escalation and peace talks, but Hanoi refused unless its demands were met and warned the U.N. to keep its nose out of Vietnamese affairs.

1011 **Put away all the childish divisive things, if you want the maturity and the unity that is the mortar of a nation's greatness. I do not think that those men who are out there fighting for us tonight think we should enjoy the luxury of fighting each other back home.**—*President Lyndon Johnson, Chicago, Illinois, 17 May 1966.*[369]

1012 **We have an arrangement with the Colts. When they have a player with a military problem, they send him to us.**—*Unidentified, Maryland National Guard commander, 1966.*[420]

If a member of the Baltimore Colts football team was unable to avoid the draft on physical or other grounds he was likely to be enlisted in the National Guard, thus avoiding overseas duty and not missing any Colt games in the bargain. At the time, Guard units had long lists of men waiting to join the Guard. The Guard and Reserves were excellent ways of avoiding overseas duty with the regular military.

1013 **So I would say that the reports from the front are good. We must not be too optimistic and we must not exaggerate what is taking place. But I get about one hundred letters a week from them, and I would say they are my greatest source of strength. If I get real depressed when I read how everything has gone bad here, I just ask for the letters from Vietnam so I can cheer up.**—*President Lyndon Johnson, news conference, Washington, D.C., 22 March 1966.*[369]

1014 **By escalating our activity and protests we can de-escalate the war.**—*A.J. Muste, peace activist and chairman of the Spring Mobilization to End the War in Vietnam, speaking at a peace rally in Central Park, 26 March 1966.*[846]

One of several protest that took place in several cities around the country.

1015 **The current struggle in South Vietnam is an historically rooted phenomenon of infinite complexity, particularly since it involves an externally directed Communist drive for power ... with a genuine indigenous social revolution. In analyzing such a phenomenon, truth is often a function of one's angle of vision, and myth is not always easy to distinguish from reality.**—*Attributed to George Carver, special assistant to director, CIA, by PFC Carl D. Rogers, U.S. Army, March 1966.*[853]

1016 **The bombing [of North Vietnam] clearly strengthened popular support of the [Hanoi] regime by engendering patriotic and nationalistic enthusiasm to resist the attacks.**—*From the Jason Study, 1966.*[374]

The Jason Study was commissioned by the Department of Defense to study the effects of the U.S. bombing campaign against North Vietnam. The study, conducted by a group of academics using a wide variety of source material, concluded that the bombing was having no measurable effect on North Vietnamese military activities in North Vietnam nor the ultimate support it provided to troops in South Vietnam.

1017 **We should be wary of experts, who feel they can correctly interpret Chinese intentions and can predict how they will react to any move of ours. We know what the Chinese are capable of in Southeast Asia. This is the knowledge that should guide us in appraising our strategy.**—*General Matthew Ridgeway, former Army Chief of staff and commander of U.S. forces during the Korean War, from a magazine article, 5 April 1966.*[715]

1018 **If the Americans do leave I will have achieved passively what the Viet Cong have been unable to do by killing people.**—*Tri Quang, Leader of the Buddhist High Clerical Association, speaking to the media, 1966.*[629]

Tri Quang urged his followers to protest against the Nguyen Cao Ky government and the Americans. They called

Ky an American puppet and demonstrated vigorously in early 1966.

1019 **The United States is in danger of losing its perspective on what exactly is within the realm of its power and what is beyond it.**—*Senator J. William Fulbright of Arkansas, Chairman of the Senate Foreign Relations Committee, from a speech at Johns Hopkins University, April 1966.*[374]

1020 **We should concentrate our attention on cutting our losses.... There are no attractive options open to us.**—*George W. Ball, Under Secretary of State, during policy steering meetings at the White House, April 1966.*[629]

Specific meetings April 9 through 20 covered new problems in South Vietnam and their impact on U.S. policy with an outlook to possible options the Administration could take. There was severe unrest between the Ky government and Buddhist factions. The meetings dealt with the possibility of the overthrow of the Ky government and the installation of neutralist Buddhist government at a time when the communists were making a military push in the country.

1021 **Bully boys, armed with crowbars and waiting for the propitious moment to move in and destroy the weakening building. Only by eliminating the bully boys ... was there a possibility of eliminating the termites or enticing them for our side, an essential though systematic and tedious process.**—*General William Westmoreland, ComUSMACV, 1966.*[22]

In his metaphor Westmoreland compared political subversives and the VC to termites destroying the building (the GVN). Supporting the termites were even bigger termites, his "bully boys" (the NVA and main force VC units). By eliminating or at least keeping the bully boys away from the GVN-building, there was a chance the building would stand and grow stronger over time.

1022 **The war could well become an albatross around the administration's neck at least equal to what Korea was for President Truman in 1952.**—*William Bundy, Assistant Secretary of State for Far Eastern Affairs, during policy steering meetings at the White House, April 1966.*[629]

The meeting covered U.S. options in South Vietnam in the event unrest between the Buddhists and the GVN resulted in the overthrow of the Ky regime. If the Buddhists were to take over the government it was believed they would declare South Vietnam politically neutral and order the U.S. out of the country. The result of the meeting was a decision by the administration for no change in the current U.S. policy at the time.

1023 **The President didn't ask for a "situation" report, he asked for a "progress" report. And that's what I've given him — not a report on the situation, but a report on the progress we've made.**—*Robert Komer, special assistant to the President, during a news conference with the press, 1966.*[374]

1024 **Air power could knock North Vietnam out of the war in a matter of days.**—*Air Force Association, April 1966.*[917]

A military belief that bombing of North Vietnam could force Hanoi to stop its supply and direction of the insurgency in South Vietnam.

1025 **[Lewis B. Hershey is] a terribly misinformed and senile man.**—*Jack Helms, Grand Dragon of the Ku Klux Klan and chairman of a local Louisiana draft board, April 1966.*[988]

Helms chaired a local draft board from 1957 to 1966. At that time the racist aspects of some draft boards surfaced and changes were made by the director of Selective Service, General Lewis B. Hershey.

1026 **We frequently do not have the right kind of bombs — specifically, sufficient time-delay bombs for the Ho Chi Minh Trail.**—*Major Theodore J. Shorack, Jr., U.S. Air Force A-1 pilot, in a letter home, 14 April 1966.*[853]

The major's comments regard the aircraft bomb shortage of 1966. At the time, some air units were experiencing shortages of 500- and 750-pound bombs. Shorack blamed the shortage on the Secretary of Defense's cost cutting measures in 1964 and 1965. Major Shorack was killed in action, 9 June 1966.

1027 **The Seabee Team has been called the military peace corps and the reasons for that comparison are obvious. Like the Peace Corps, the Seabee Teams put something into the country: They develop human resources. Such a contribution is valuable indeed.**—*Hubert Humphrey, Vice President, speaking before the U.S. Senate in 1966.*[958]

Besides thousands of military construction projects, the Seabees worked on a wide variety of public works projects that directly benefited the civilian population of South Vietnam.

1028 **[The war in Vietnam offered an opportunity] ... for realizing the dream of the Great Society in the great area of Asia...**—*Hubert Humphrey, Vice President, speaking during a televised news interview, 19 April 1966.*[718]

1029 **I don't mind killing VC; they are a sickness that needs to be cut out. American demonstrators make me sick. They don't need to collect blood for the VC. The VC can get all they need by washing it off their hands.**—*Captain Richard B. Sexton, U.S. Air Force pilot, writing in his journal, April 1966.*[878]

1030 **It is only when the Congress fails to challenge the Executive, when the opposition fails to oppose, when politicians join in a spurious consensus behind controversial policies, that the campuses and streets and public squares of America are likely to become the forums of a direct and disorderly democracy.**—*Senator J. William Fulbright, speaking at John Hopkins University, 22 April 1966.*[799]

Fulbright was speaking of the value of dissent.

1031 **America is showing some signs of that fatal presumption, that over-extension of power and mission, which brought ruin to ancient Athens, to Napoleonic France and to Nazi Germany.**—*Senator J. William Fulbright, speaking at Johns Hopkins University, 22 April 1966.*[814]

1032 **[The war in Vietnam] ... is the stirring up of a war fever in the minds of our people and leaders; it is only just now getting under way, but, as the war goes on, as the casualty lists grow larger and affect more and more American homes, the fever will rise and the patience of the American people will give way to mounting demands for an expanded war, for a lightning blow that will get it over with at a stroke. The first demand might be a blockade of Hai Phong; then, if that doesn't work, a strike against China; and then we will**

have global war.—*Senator J. William Fulbright, speaking at Johns Hopkins University, 22 April 1966.*[814]

1033 **I have every reason to believe that we'll be successful [in Vietnam], that a stable democratic society will be built.**—*President Lyndon Johnson, news conference, Washington, D.C., 22 April 1966.*[369]

1034 **Gradually but unmistakably America is succumbing to that arrogance of power which has afflicted, weakened and in some cases destroyed, great nations in the past.**—*Senator J. William Fulbright, speaking at Johns Hopkins University, 22 April 1966.*[799]

Fulbright eluding to U.S. intervention in Vietnam, as he saw it, a war between the Vietnamese.

1035 **You have to hit enemy supply to break their backs. The war could go on for years if you don't take out the supply lines.**—*Unidentified U.S. Marine Corps pilot, during an interview, 1966.*[249]

1036 **If we gave up bombing in order to start discussions, we would not have the coins necessary to pay for all the concessions required for a satisfactory settlement.**—*General Maxwell Taylor, Special Military Adviser to the President, in a memorandum to the President, 27 April 1966.*[159]

In early April 1966 several officials from various countries called on the U.S. to initiate a bombing halt in an effort to entice North Vietnam to consider negotiations. Johnson's advisers cautioned him against such a halt.

1037 **We had not forced Hanoi to the peace table. We had not scared Hanoi out of the war. We had not caused any diminution whatsoever of his carrying the war into South Vietnam.... It was evident to me that Ho Chi Minh intended to continue to support the Viet Cong until he was denied the capability to do so.**—*Admiral U.S. Grant Sharp, U.S. Navy, Commander in Chief, Pacific, speaking to the JCS, January 1966.*[964]

These comments were made during discussion of the early results of the sustained bombing campaign against North Vietnam.

1038 **The current battle for the villagers of South Vietnam may well be one of the most important and decisive conflicts in world history. PROVN focuses on this central battle; all other military aspects of the war are secondary.**—*Excerpt from the PROVN study, May 1966.*[19]

The PROVN study, commissioned July 1965, reviewed the history of Vietnam, interaction between the GVN and the people, and American involvement. The study concluded that America should make the necessary moves to stabilize the country and force the GVN to be responsive and supportive of its people.

1039 **The weakest chink in our armor is American public opinion. Our people won't stand firm in the face of heavy losses, and they can bring down the government.**—*President Lyndon Johnson, comments to his staff, 1966.*[374]

1040 **[The government may consider] asking every young person in the U.S. to give two years of service to his country—whether in one of the military services, in the Peace Corps or in some other developmental work at home or abroad.**—*Robert McNamara, Secretary of Defense, May 1966.*[420]

1041 **We will stay until aggression has stopped, because in Asia and around the world are countries whose independence rests, in large measure, on confidence in American's word and in America's protection.**—*President Lyndon Johnson, 1966.*[374]

1042 **Remove an American division.**—*John Paul Vann, AID adviser, in response to a question posed to him during an interview in South Vietnam in 1966.*[25]

Vann's stock answer to the question: what immediate action could the United States take to strengthen the war effort in Vietnam?

1043 **If Americans start to shoot down our planes, destroy the [American] marine base. That is an order.**—*Nguyen Cao Ky, Prime Minister of South Vietnam, in orders to his ground commanders in the I Corps area around Da Nang Air Base, 14 May 1966.*[629]

During a Buddhists uprising in Da Nang, Ky ordered South Vietnamese Marines and Airborne units to retake control of the city from pro–Buddhist ARVN units defending Da Nang. Ky also ordered VNAF aircraft to support the Marines and Airborne units. General Walt was not aware of the situation between the pro-GVN units and the pro–Buddhist ARVN units. He believed Ky planned to indiscriminately attack the I Corps ARVN units and their American advisers. He issued orders to American units in Da Nang to shoot down any VNAF planes that attacked any ARVN positions. With this development Ky flew to Da Nang to personally take command of the retaking of Da Nang. He issued the order to destroy the U.S. Marine base at Da Nang if they interfered with his actions. This was the situation until Ky explained to Walt exactly what was happening.

1044 **If you fire one single round [into Da Nang Air Base], I will destroy every gun in the artillery base.**—*Nguyen Cao Ky, Prime Minister of South Vietnam, in a message to an ARVN artillery base commander, 14 May 1966.*[629]

Ky decided to use military force against the Buddhist uprising in Da Nang. A pro–Buddhist commander at a nearby ARVN artillery base trained his guns on the base at Da Nang in response to the arrival of VNAF aircraft (sent to support the government's move against the Buddhist). Ky's note was dropped from a plane that flew over the base. Many of the ARVN troops in I Corps supported the Buddhist, thus Ky sent in Marine and Airborne units to take back control of I Corps.

1045 **Airpower is doing all it's presently being called upon to do in Vietnam. But with superior technology the key to military strength, and airpower as the cutting edge, airpower is not being called upon to do enough.**—*Air Force Association policy statement, as delivered at a convention in Dallas, May 1966.*[796]

The military component conducting the air war against North Vietnam wanted fewer restrictions on targeting and the ability to apply more force against North Vietnam; to include the mining of ports, destruction of POL and storage facilities, rail links to China, and air facilities supporting MiG operations.

1046 **I can spare you five minutes.**—*Nguyen Cao Ky, Prime Minister of South Vietnam, in reply to General Walt, 14 May 1966.*[629]

General Walt requested to meet with Ky to discuss the possible confrontation between U.S. forces and pro–Saigon forces led by Ky. The pro–Saigon force was assembled to retake Da Nang from pro–Buddhist ARVN units that were holding the city. Walt had threatened to shoot down Ky's aircraft if they moved on Da Nang, and Ky had issued an order to bomb the Marine base if the Americans fired on Ky's planes. Ky put off meeting with Walt until he was ready to talk with him, at that time the situation was explained to Walt and the confrontation avoided.

1047 **I do not genuinely believe that there's any single person anywhere in the world that wants peace as much as I want it.**—*President Lyndon Johnson, Chicago, Illinois, 17 May 1966.*[369]

1048 **There will be some Nervous Nellies and some who will become frustrated and bothered and break ranks under the strain. And some will turn on their leaders and their own country and on their own fighting men.**—*President Johnson, speech at a fund-raising dinner in Chicago, 17 May 1966.*[794]

Johnson making a patriotic appeal for party unity and loyalty.

1049 **Tell 'em they have no sanctuaries!**—*Dwight Eisenhower, former President, in counsel with President Johnson, 1966.*[713]

Johnson chose to allow the VC/NVA to establish and maintain sanctuaries along South Vietnam's border. Many within his administration advocated striking the enemy wherever he gathered, regardless of which side of the border they were on. Johnson feared that widening the ground war into Laos or Cambodia would eventually draw the Red Chinese into the war. Eisenhower advocated striking enemy base areas regardless of their location.

1050 **For all intents and purposes, race is irrelevant [in Vietnam].**—*Whitney Young, Jr., writing in the Baltimore Afro-American, 1966.*[1015]

1051 **[They are] professional non-students who are either drugged on LSD or on Marxist theory.**—*Robert Scheer, 1966 peace candidate, 1966.*[850]

Scheer's characterization of the student radicals who supported his bid for a seat in the California Congress. Scheer ran for the California's 7th Congressional District in 1966.

1052 **We regret any diversion from ... efforts to defeat the Communists' attempt to take over South Vietnam.**—*President Lyndon Johnson, speaking to the press, 21 May 1966.*[533]

Johnson was commenting on the confrontation between the Saigon government and the Buddhists demonstrators in Da Nang. The Buddhists were demonstrating against the Ky military government demanding a return to civilian rule. Ky sent Vietnamese marines to Da Nang to put down the demonstrations. This internal struggle temporarily shifted Vietnamese focus away the war against the communists.

1053 **Our goals cannot be achieved by Vietnamese leaders who are identified as U.S. puppets. The U.S. will must be asserted, but we cannot afford to overwhelm the structure we are attempting to develop.**—*General William Westmoreland, ComUSMACV, in a report to the JCS, May 1966.*[36]

MACV's response to a suggestion by the PROVN study that the U.S. take a more active hand in making changes within the GVN to accomplish the goal of improving conditions for the South Vietnamese people, thus winning their support. The PROVN study was commissioned by the JCS in an attempt to develop a direction for the American effort in Vietnam.

1054 **The killing of Americans and Vietnamese will not stop unless opponents of this war and of the bankrupt foreign policy which it reflects can turn their dissent into real political power.**—*National Conference for New Politics, anti-war group, from their ad in The New York Times, 22 May 1966.*[802]

1055 **We're going to tell them what is being done in their name and we are going to make them either take responsibility for it or repudiate it.**—*Robert Scheer, 1966 peace candidate, from pre-election speeches, 1966.*[850]

Scheer attacked the war in Vietnam as immoral.

1056 **The U.S. should never have gone into Vietnam, should not have stayed there and should now get out.**—*Robert Scheer, 1966 peace candidate, from pre-election speeches, 1966.*[850]

Scheer was preaching the immorality of the war and its high cost (morally and financially)—he denounced the war budget and wanted that money spent on anti-poverty programs.

1057 **There's something terribly personal about the SAM; it means to kill you and I'll tell you right now, it rearranges your priorities...**—*Colonel Robin Olds, U.S. Air Force pilot and commander of the 8th Tactical Fighter Wing, 1966.*[189]

Olds took command of the 8th TFW in September 1966, based at Ubon Royal Thai Air Base. During his tour he shot down four enemy MiGs as his wing flew missions against North Vietnam.

1058 **The fellows who are optimistic are not so much those in the field, as the chaps in headquarters in Washington and Saigon who ... tend to take a happier view than perhaps the objective circumstances might indicate.**—*Chester L. Cooper, former O/NE and NSC analyst, during an oral history interview, June 1966.*[200]

1059 **It is the most exciting thing I guess a human being could experience, diving through the flak at a target. It's best if you have the lead, because you don't see the stuff that is bursting behind you.... But it looks pretty bad to the number-two man.... The sky seems so full of it you couldn't possibly escape.**—*Captain Jim Mitchell, U.S. Air Force F-105 pilot, during an interview, 1966.*[249]

Describing an attack on a target in North Vietnam.

1060 **I don't want to put that albatross around the civil rights movement.**—*One of the section chairman of civil rights leaders during a civil rights conference hosted at the White House, June 1966.*[824]

CORE leader Floyd McKissick wanted the conference to draw up a resolution against the war in Vietnam, but the chairman ruled McKissick out of order. A vote was taken on his resolution though and it lost by a wide margin. Leaders at the conference did not want to antagonize the President with an anti-war resolution at a time when they were attempting to get the government to move more forcefully on civil rights.

1061 **When the guns are quiet, destructive combat power is dormant; the commander limited to only this dimension of warfare is hobbled. Here civic action, the constructive aspect of combat power, gains increased significance.**—*Major William Holmberg, U.S. Marine Corps, June 1966.*[349]

1062 **There is one language Johnson understands — it is the language of political power. Election of Scheer would be the most effective protest against the war yet mounted in this country.**—*Robert Scheer, 1966 peace candidate, from his election campaign ad, 6 June 1966.*[850]

He lost the primary nomination for a California Congressional seat, but did receive 45 percent of the vote.

1063 **If he were a real Buddhist priest, then perhaps he would die, but Tri Quang is a politician and his doctor friend is feeding him secretly ... for a politician death is the end. Tri Quang must survive if he wants to carry on his political career.**—*Nguyen Cao Ky, Prime Minister of South Vietnam, in comments to an American adviser, May 1966.*[629]

Buddhist leader Tri Quang was arrested in Da Nang and held under house arrest in a hospital in Saigon. He immediately declared a hunger strike. Ky said he was not losing any weight, even after several months of arrest. His arrest and removal from the Buddhist centers of Hue and Da Nang quieted the Buddhists anti-government demonstrations. Tri Quang led anti-government protest in Da Nang in April 1966 with the goal of overthrowing the Ky regime.

1064 **I can assure you of one thing, if you choose the way of the sword to take over, I will not hesitate to kill every Buddhist leader before I relinquish office.**—*Nguyen Cao Ky, Prime Minister of South Vietnam, speaking to Buddhist leaders, June 1966.*[629]

Ky was speaking to Buddhist leaders who threatened to overthrow the Ky regime by force to achieve a change in the government to one more favorable to the Buddhists (i.e., controlled by the Buddhists).

1065 **If the government says it's goin' to do, it ought to quit politickin' and do. We poor folks need help now.**—*Floyd Robertson, speaking at the White House civil rights conference, June 1966.*[824]

Robertson was a sharecropper who attended the conference. There was rhetoric coming out of Washington but a lack of substantial progress.

1066 **If you believe in the destiny of South Vietnam, if you want us to survive against Communism, which is an enemy of your religion, surely it's time we united against the common foe. What I can't understand is why you have to organize demonstrations, cause trouble, and generally weaken our cause against Communism.**—*Nguyen Cao Ky, Prime Minister of South Vietnam, speaking to Buddhist leaders, June 1966.*[629]

Buddhist unrest had increased after the fall of the Diem regime and they continued to hold demonstrations against the governments that followed.

1067 **The raw figure of VC killed ... can be a dubious index of success since, if their killing is accompanied by devastation of friendly areas, we may end up having done more harm than good.**—*General Victor Krulak, Commander, Fleet Marine Force Pacific, in a letter to Robert McNamara, June 1966.*[887]

Krulak advocated a greater pacification role for American troops, citing that winning the support of the people would be more productive than just killing the enemy. Westmoreland's strategy was a war of attrition and he did not put much faith in the pacification program. McNamara saw the merits of pacification but believed the process, as utilized by the Marines, was too slow to accomplish the U.S. goals in the time allotted.

1068 **We're asking Negroes not to go to Vietnam and fight but to stay in Greenwood and fight here.... We need black power.**—*Stokley Carmichael, SNCC leader, speaking at a Greenwood, Mississippi rally, 17 June 1966.*[821]

This was the birth of the "Black Power" phrase and a new militancy in the SNCC.

1069 **We risked eight guys, when we could have hung the whole [bomb] load on one plane — risking only two people — and done the job better.**—*Unidentified pilot, Da Nang, commenting to a correspondent, 1966.*[249]

During 1966 there were reports of bomb shortages for missions in Vietnam. The Navy and Air Force denied the rumors, stating that there were temporary shortages in some ordnance types, but overall their was a sufficient supply. Many pilots had a different reading on the situation, sometimes taking off with much less than a full bomb load for a target.

1070 **The destruction of petrol facilities won't deter infiltration. It may slow it down for the time being, but the end result may be increased infiltration that will make the road to the negotiating table that much more difficult.**—*Senator Mike Mansfield of Montana, speaking to the press, 29 June 1966.*[534]

This was Mansfield's reaction to U.S. bombing of North Vietnam POL targets, less than five miles from the center of Hai Phong and Hanoi. The attacks against oil storage facilities marked the first time U.S. aircraft had been allowed to hit targets so close to North Vietnam's two largest cities. Administration opponents claimed the oil facilities were in populated areas. The Johnson administration insisted U.S. planes only struck military targets.

1071 **It seems to me we have exhausted every effort to arrive at negotiations. Any further delay in drying up the sources of supply for the Vietcong and the North Vietnamese troops in the South could only increase the casualty lists of American dead and wounded.**—*Senator Richard B. Russell of Georgia, comments to the press, 29 June 1966.*[534]

Russell's reaction to U.S. strikes against North Vietnam targets less than five miles from the center of Hai Phong and Hanoi was favorable. The attacks against oil storage facilities marked the first time U.S. aircraft had been allowed to hit targets so close to North Vietnam's two largest cities. Administration opponents claimed the oil facilities were in populated areas. The Johnson administration insisted U.S. planes only struck military targets.

1072 **Now there are many, many, many who can recommend and advise and sometimes a few of them consent. But there is only one who has been chosen by the American people to decide.**—*President Johnson, speaking in Omaha, Nebraska, 30 June 1966.*[756]

Johnson speaking about his decision to bomb targets in the Hanoi–Hai Phong area. The initial raids on these targets took place in late-June and early-July 1966.

1073 **The ingenuity, energy and resources of this country must be redirected and devoted to the building of new towns [in the South] and not to villages in Vietnam.**—*Resolution* *adopted by civil rights leaders during a civil rights conference hosted at the White House, June 1966.*[824]

Civil rights leaders wanted more emphasis by the government on civil rights, believing that the war in Vietnam was overshadowing and detracting from successes of the civil rights program.

1074 **An awesome curtain of exploding steel.**—*Unidentified U.S. Air Force pilot, comments to a correspondent, 1966.*[249]

Description of the concentrated anti-aircraft barrages American pilots faced while striking targets in North Vietnam. Rated as the most concentrated anti-aircraft defenses in the short history of air warfare.

1075 **You cannot win militarily [in Vietnam]. You have to win totally, or you are not winning at all.**—*General Victor Krulak, Commander, Fleet Marine Force Pacific, in a letter to General Lewis Walt, July 1966.*[887]

Krulak was referring to a remark made by a MACV Army general, that "the U.S. was winning militarily in Vietnam." To win totally was to win the lasting support of the people as well as the military war against the VC and the NVA.

1076 **In some cases ... optimum weapons necessary for achievement of maximum damage per sortie were not used when local shortages required substitution of alternate weapons for those preferred.**—*Admiral U.S. Grant Sharp, former Commander-in-Chief, Pacific Command, 1966.*[923]

In early 1966 there was a shortage of 500- and 750-pound general purpose bombs. The Department of Defense had not planned on extensive use of conventional bombs as the military moved towards the nuclear battlefield in the late-fifties. It took the DoD several months to raise bomb supply levels, alleviating the shortage.

1077 **The U.S. imperialists must restrict the U.S. forces participating in a local war because otherwise their global strategy would be hampered and their influence throughout the world would diminish.**—*General Vo Nguyen Giap, defense minister of North Vietnam, from an article published in Hanoi, 1966.*[129]

The North Vietnamese never took veiled American threats of "total destruction" of their country seriously, because the U.S. repeated publicly that it was not their intention to destroy North Vietnam, bring down the Hanoi regime, or interfere with its independence.

1078 **[Harold Wilson is] a man not to go to the well with.**—*William Bundy, Assistant Secretary of State, describing President Johnson's impression of Wilson, July 1966.*[139]

This statement indicated the feeling of distrust President Johnson had for British Prime Minister Harold Wilson after Wilson began to distance himself from support of the American administration. Wilson was put off by a series of intensive attacks against North Vietnam POL facilities in June and July 1966.

1079 **[They are] ham-handed and clumsy attempts to win over the people.**—*Lt.Col. Andrew Rutherford, Hau Nghia Province Senior Adviser, comments on Country Fair operations, 1966.*[42]

Rutherford's description of the 25th Infantry Division's Country Fair operations. Country Fair involved American and ARVN units surrounding a ville, then sweeping through it, searching for enemy soldiers, arms and caches of supplies. Draft age males or any other suspicious villagers were removed for questioning. After this, an Army band would be trucked in to give the villagers a concert, South Vietnamese officials made speeches and a crew of Army cooks would make a late lunch for the entire ville. The villagers were a captive audience, though hardly receptive.

1080 **It is better to face them (the Communist Chinese) right now than in 5 or 10 years.**—*Nguyen Cao Ky, Premier, South Vietnam, during a press conference, July 1966.*[676]

Ky called for an invasion of North Vietnam and a military showdown with Communist China. As previous South Vietnamese governments had done, Ky tried to focus South Vietnam's attention outside the country. The U.S. denied any plans to invade North Vietnam nor encouraged South Vietnam to do so.

1081 **[Hanoi] ... will never deter or defeat us.**—*President Johnson, from a speech in Atlanta, 16 February 1966.*[842]

1082 **There is nothing more demoralizing than the sight of an F-4 taxiing out with nothing but a pair of bombs nestled among its ejector racks.**—*Unidentified U.S. Air Force pilot, July 1966.*[143]

For several months in 1966 there were unconfirmed reports of iron bomb shortages. McNamara never officially acknowledged the temporary shortage, but he did indicate in 1966 that there was a brief shortage of the 750-pound bombs that were used by B-52s. He denied any other shortages. A typical bomb load for an F-4 was eight to twelve 500-pound bombs or some combination of bombs and CBUs. Many pilots reported sorties with only one or two bombs, until the "unconfirmed" bomb shortage went away.

1083 **It takes two sides to negotiate, and what the other side makes plain is that all it wants is total victory. What the Viet Cong and Hanoi want is peace at no price, and what Peking wants is no peace whatsoever.**—*Cyrus L. Sulzberger, columnist, New York Times, editorial comment, 1966.*[862]

1084 **It is good to report that many of the things which we used to hope for — and dream about — are taking place.... In Hau Nghia today we are winning; they are losing. Our side is clearly coasting along as the Americans say.**—*Henry Cabot Lodge, Jr., American Ambassador to South Vietnam, in a cable to President Johnson, August 1966.*[37]

Lodge believed the pacification effort in Hau Nghia Province was making substantial progress. His evaluation of progress in the province did not coincide with the views of the American advisory team working in Hau Nghia.

1085 **[Civilian casualties are] a problem, but it does deprive the enemy of the population, doesn't it?**—*General William Westmoreland, ComUSMACV, in response to a correspondent's question, August 1966.*[887]

Correspondent Neil Sheehan asked General Westmoreland if "he was worried about the large number of civilian casualties from air strikes and the shelling."

1086 **How would you feel if a bunch of burly foreigners invaded your hamlet, took away your men, and played weird**

foreign music to entertain you?—*As related by American relief worker, from a conversation with a Vietnamese villager, 1966.*[27]

The villager asked this question after a U.S. Army Country Fair operation. Country Fair involved American and ARVN units surrounding a ville, then sweeping through it, searching for enemy soldiers, arms and caches of supplies. Draft age males or any other suspicious villagers were removed for questioning. After this, an Army band would be trucked in to give the villagers a concert, South Vietnamese officials made speeches, and a crew of Army cooks would make a late lunch for the entire ville. The villagers were a captive and confused audience.

1087 **I don't think the whole of Southeast Asia, as related to the present and future safety and freedom of the people of this country, is worth the life or limb of a single American.**—*General David Shoup, former commandant of the U.S. Marine Corps, May 1966.*[1027]

1088 **[I see] no indication that the resolve of the leadership in Hanoi has been reduced.**—*General William Westmoreland, ComUSMACV, August 1966.*[374]

After over a year of Rolling Thunder Hanoi, was not contrite.

1089 **[The war in South Vietnam had evolved into] a protracted war of attrition.**—*General William Westmoreland, ComUSMACV, August 1966.*[713]

The American strategy of war was primarily defensive in nature. The source of support and direction for the insurgency in the South was from North Vietnam and could not be cut based on the restrictions under which the U.S. military operated. Enemy sanctuaries along the border could not be entered. The only strategy left was to try to kill the enemy faster than they could be replaced by local recruitment or NVA infiltration.

1090 **[Hanoi is counting on] the possibility that American public opinion will become jaded with the war, as French public opinion did. The other is the expectation that American casualties will, within a short time, reach the level of the Korean War, and then the Americans will be compelled to bring the war to an end.**—*Janos Peter, Hungarian foreign minister in conversation with Janos Radvanyi, August 1966.*[450]

Hanoi's position was relayed to Janos during his visit to Hanoi in August 1966.

1091 **In terms of its morale effects, the U.S. campaign may have presented the [North Vietnamese] regime with a near-ideal mix of intended restraint and accidental gore.**—*Oleg Hoeffding, RAND Corporation analyst, from a memorandum, 1966.*[161]

The bomb threat posed by the U.S. against North Vietnam allowed the Hanoi regime to institute tighter population controls, while at the same time blaming such controls on a foreign power. The Hanoi regime had the added benefit of knowing the ineffectual bombing campaign would not result in a U.S. invasion of North Vietnam.

1092 **[Johnson is] the most disagreeable individual ever to have occupied the White House.**—*Walter Lippmann, Washington newspaper columnist, 1966.*[374]

Lippmann opposed Johnson's policy in Vietnam.

1093 **The [North] Vietnamese are doing well by being unwilling to talk to the Americans. In the end the Yankees will give up Vietnam just as the French did.**—*Janos Peter, Hungarian foreign minister in conversation with Janos Radvanyi, August 1966.*[450]

Radvanyi was the chargé d'affaires of the Hungarian legation in Washington.

1094 **The Chinese are fighting to the last Vietnamese soldier.**—*Janos Radvanyi, Hungarian legation Chargé d'Affaires, in conversation with Janos Peter, August 1966.*[450]

Radvanyi was eluding to the Chinese ploy of using a third party to blood their opponent, rather than a direct confrontation with the opponent. In this case the Chinese opponent was the U.S.

1095 **The Chinese offered to help Hanoi with an army of 500,000 on condition that the DRV should launch simultaneous general attacks against South Vietnam and Laos.**—*Janos Peter, Hungarian foreign minister in conversation with Janos Radvanyi, August 1966.*[450]

Hanoi declined the offer of Chinese troops, but continued to accept Chinese technical advisers and Chinese labor battalions.

1096 **We have to stop Communism and we'd rather do it here in Vietnam than on the coast of California.**—*American GI's response to question posed by correspondent, "How do you feel about the war?" 1966.*[249]

Ninety percent of those the correspondent polled agreed with the GI.

1097 **I don't think any President in any wartime situation has generally had as clear sailing as I have had.**—*President Johnson, speaking to a reporter, September 1966.*[819]

Johnson was citing Scheer's recent loss in the California primary and several other losses by peace candidates in primaries in other states. Based on these losses he believed he had the full backing of the people and the anti-war demonstrations were mere bumps in the road.

1098 **In accessing the Air Force's achievements in Southeast Asia, there is one factor that stands out: that is the impressive margin by which air power has exceeded many early estimates of its usefulness in limited conflicts.**—*General John P. McConnell, Chief of Staff, U.S. Air Force, writing in Air Force Magazine, September 1966.*[928]

By this time in the air campaign McNamara discovered that the bombing and interdiction campaign against North Vietnam was not stopping the flow of men and materiel into South Vietnam. The flow had been reduced, but not enough to affect the VC/NVA war effort in South Vietnam.

1099 **I have tossed and turned in the night and gagged in the morning when I brushed my teeth. I have worried about myself and worried about the missions of others. I have seen men go to God and men go to booze. I have not seen a hero. I have seen men doing a given task because it was their profession. I have seen a man for what he is and a war for what it brings and recognize that restful, peaceful sleep is one of the most precious things in the world.**—*Captain Edward W. O'Neil, Jr., U.S. Air Force, 20th Tactical Reconnaissance Squadron, 1966.*[84]

1100 **[The war in Vietnam is] predominantly an infantry war. More than this, it is a light infantry war. What you can take to the fight is what counts.**—*Colonel Y.Y. Philipps, writing in Army Magazine, September 1966.*[97]

U.S. Army and Marine infantry companies typically operated in the field without their normal organic heavy weapons (recoilless rifles, antitank missiles, medium mortars). The heavy weapons were used for battalion base defense or flown to the field for use at a company base camp.

1101 **The greatest indifference to the war effort is found among Vietnam's young people.**—*Excerpt from a Newsweek article, 12 September 1966.*[77]

1102 **There is a callous unconcern [by the Vietnamese people] for the welfare of the Vietnamese soldiers who lack incentive to fight aggressively.**—*Excerpt from a Newsweek article by the Saigon bureau chief, 12 September 1966.*[77]

1103 **When you're at Khe Sanh, you're not really anywhere.**—*General Lowell English, Assistant Commander, 3d Marine Division. Comment, 1966.*[887]

Khe Sanh was located in an isolated mountain jungle area in the northwest corner of South Vietnam, near the border junctions of Laos, North Vietnam, and South Vietnam.

1104 **In this war, the battle lines are not clear. But our goals are very clear.**—*President Lyndon Johnson, from a speech during an awards ceremony, 15 September 1966.*[680]

Johnson posthumously awarded the Medal of Honor to U.S. Navy Seabee Marvin G. Shields. Shields was instrumental in the defense of the Special Forces camp at Dong Xoai, 10 June 1965.

1105 **[Vietnam] is a war fought, not to gain territory or dominion, but to prove that despots cannot work their will by spreading fires of violence.**—*President Lyndon Johnson, from a speech during an awards ceremony, 15 September 1966.*[680]

Johnson posthumously awarded the Medal of Honor to U.S. Navy Seabee Marvin G. Shields. Shields was instrumental in the defense of the Special Forces camp at Dong Xoai, 10 June 1965.

1106 **It may be that the main thing we [America] have succeeded in doing in Vietnam over the past fifteen years — or, anyway, the last ten — has been to inhibit a natural revolutionary development that might have evolved on its own.**—*Robert Shaplen, American writer, 1966.*[628]

Indicating that if left to its own devises South Vietnam may have come up with the leaders to counter the communist threat. But time restrictions did not support this theory as the communist's move in the South was very swift and the element of political turmoil so high.

1107 **Our most important job is eliminating the guerrilla. I believe in all my heart that we are on the right track ... but there are no dramatic changes in this war. It is slow because you are changing minds. That takes time.**—*General Lewis Walt, Commander, III Marine Amphibious Force, 1966.*[957]

Stressing the importance of the pacification program as conducted by the Marines.

1108 **We intend to make it possible for a young nation to begin its experiment with democracy without staring down the barrel of an aggressor's gun.**—*President Lyndon Johnson, from a speech during an awards ceremony, 15 September 1966.*[680]

Johnson, speaking during awards ceremony in which he posthumously awarded the Medal of Honor to U.S. Navy Seabee Marvin G. Shields. Shields was instrumental in the defense of the Special Forces camp at Dong Xoai, 10 June 1965.

1109 **A fighter without a gun ... is like an airplane without a wing.**—*Colonel Robin Olds, U.S. Air Force pilot and commander of the 8th Tactical Fighter Wing, 1966.*[189]

Initially the F-4 Phantoms used by the Air Force in Vietnam were not equipped with cannons. This restricted their air-to-air dogfights to missile combat only. Later in the war U.S. Air Force F-4s were equipped with guns or gun pods. U.S. Navy F-4s were equipped with organic (built-in) cannons.

1110 **The great power of the people's war will overcome the so-called superiority of the U.S. Air Force.**—*General Vo Nguyen Giap, defense minister of North Vietnam, from an article published in Hanoi, 1966.*[129]

1111 **The solution in Vietnam is more bombs, more shells, more napalm ... till the other side cracks and gives up.**—*General William E. DePuy, Commander, 1st Infantry Division, during a conversation with Daniel Ellsberg, 1966.*[887]

DePuy was a firm believer in the "bullets for bodies" maxim — the use of air and artillery support to reduce enemy resistance and limit friendly casualties.

1112 **We deliberately spread out Negroes in component units at a ratio pretty much according to the division total. We don't want to risk having a platoon or company that has more Negroes than whites overrun or wiped out.**—*Unidentified U.S. Army general, during an interview, 1966.*[981]

The death rate for American blacks killed in Vietnam in 1965 through 1966, was 20 percent, while blacks represented about 11 percent of the general population and only 9.3 percent of the military population.

1113 **[The Vietcong] were rough, tricky, brave and they could stand living conditions Americans couldn't ... they were better soldiers than the Arvins [ARVN]; their discipline was better, their fighting spirit better.**—*Chief Ed Canby, U.S. Navy, Can Tho PBR group, during an interview, 1966.*[249]

1114 **Stabilize the Rolling Thunder program against the North at the current monthly level of 12,000 sorties because to bomb the North sufficiently to make a radical impact on Hanoi's political, economic and social structure, would require an effort which we could make but which would not be stomached either by our own people or by world opinion; and it would involve a serious risk of drawing us into open war with China.**—*Robert McNamara, Secretary of Defense, in a report to President Johnson, October 1966.*[185]

McNamara proposed that the bombing against North Vietnam not be increased. His reports indicated the bombing was not severely adversely affecting the enemy's war in the south, nor undercutting Hanoi's defiance.

1115 **Pacification is a bad disappointment.... Pacification has, if anything, gone backward ... enemy full-time regional forces and part-time guerrilla forces are larger; attacks, terrorism, and sabotage have increased in scope and intensity**

... we control little, if any, more of the population; the VC political infrastructure thrives in most of the country, continuing to give the enemy his enormous intelligence advantage; full security exists nowhere; in the countryside, the enemy almost completely controls the night.—*Robert McNamara, Secretary of Defense, in a report to President Johnson, October 1966.*[37]

McNamara made an inspection visit to Vietnam in October 1966. Publicly he indicated that progress was being made in the war against the communists. In private he told the President that the air war was not stopping North Vietnamese support for the VC, pacification was not working, and the enemy was growing stronger.

1116 **No matter how much we might hope for something, our commitment is not ... to guarantee that the self-chosen government [of South Vietnam] is non–Communist ... and to insist that the independent South Vietnam remain separate from North Vietnam.**—*Robert McNamara, Secretary of Defense, to President Johnson, 1966.*[159]

By 1966 McNamara has lost sight of the goal of an independent, non-communist South Vietnam that was self-sufficient and able to hold out against communist pressure from the North.

1117 **I'll give you one week to re-supply the market with enough rice at a reasonable and stable price. If you cannot do this by the deadline, I shall draw lots and the first man whose name I pick out of my cap will be shot. At the end of the second week, if my ultimatum is still not satisfied, I shall draw a second name out of my cap and that man will be shot; and I shall do this until there is enough rice for everyone.**—*Nguyen Cao Ky, Prime Minister of South Vietnam, speaking to a group of rice distributors, 1966.*[629]

Ten of the leading rice merchants began a campaign to drive up the price of rice and collapse the Ky government. In response Ky confronted the group. Within three days of his ultimatum, rice was again plentiful on the street and at reasonable and stable prices.

1118 **[We should] take steps to increase the credibility of our peace gestures in the minds of the enemy through both political and military moves.**—*Robert McNamara, Secretary of Defense, in a report to President Johnson, October 1966.*[185]

McNamara proposed a reduction in the American war effort and increased moves to obtain a political settlement.

1119 **All we can do is massage the heart.**—*Robert McNamara, Secretary of Defense, in a report to the President, 14 October 1966.*[44]

McNamara was speaking of the conditions in South Vietnam, lack of progress on winning the support of the people for the GVN and the inability of the ARVN as a viable security force. With U.S. troops in country, the GVN was able to continue its existence, but it was not an existence supported by the people it was supposed to represent.

1120 **We must continue to press the enemy militarily; we must make demonstrable progress in pacification; at the same time, we must add a new ingredient forced on us by the facts. Specifically, we must improve our position by getting ourselves into a military posture that we credibly would maintain indefinitely—a posture that makes trying to "wait us out" less attractive.**—*Robert McNamara, Secretary of Defense, in a report to the President, 14 October 1966.*[44]

McNamara proposed escalating the war, realizing that Hanoi would try to drag out the war in hopes the U.S. would be drained by the effort and back out of South Vietnam.

1121 **We do not want to conquer North Vietnam, and we don't want to maintain military bases in South Vietnam.**—*Dean Rusk, Secretary of State, in conversation with Hungarian foreign minister Janos Peter, October 1966.*[450]

Peter was attempting to broker a meeting between the U.S. and Hanoi. He told the Americans he was in direct contact with Hanoi and was speaking for them. In fact he was working on his own and Hanoi was not involved, nor favorably impressed by his efforts.

1122 **We came with victory in mind, to leave with sorrow in our hearts.**—*Michael Pipkin, former U.S. Navy Corpsman, who served with 2d Battalion, 1st Marines, 1966.*[975]

1123 **Success in pacification depends on the interrelated functions of providing physical security, destroying the VC apparatus, motivating the people to cooperate and establishing responsive local government.**—*Robert McNamara, Secretary of Defense, in a memorandum to President Johnson, 14 October 1966.*[899]

McNamara was stressing the importance of the pacification program, a program which to date had been unsuccessful.

1124 **Mountains like Korea, jungles like Guadalcanal, only thing missing is snow.**—*Unidentified Marine, along the DMZ, October 1966.*[415]

A U.S. Marine comparing the terrain faced during the Korean War and World War II, with the terrain southwest of the DMZ.

1125 **[The installation of an infiltration barrier] would hinder enemy efforts, would permit more efficient use of the limited number of friendly troops, and would be persuasive evidence both that our sole aim is to protect the South from the North and that we intend to see the job through.**—*Robert McNamara in a memo to President Johnson, October 1966.*[899]

1126 **The discouraging truth is that, as was the case in 1961 and 1963 and 1965, we have not found the formula, the catalyst, for training and inspiring them [South Vietnamese] into effective action.**—*Robert McNamara, Secretary of Defense, in a report to the President, 14 October 1966.*[44]

McNamara had just returned from a fact finding trip to South Vietnam.

1127 **We find ourselves—from the point of view of the important war (for the complicity of the people)—no better, and if anything worse off. This important war must be fought and won by the Vietnamese themselves...**—*Robert S. McNamara, Secretary of Defense, in a report to the President, 14 October 1966.*[44]

McNamara had just returned from a fact finding trip to Saigon, and stressed the importance of pacification.

1128 **The large-unit operations war, which we know best how to fight and where we have had our successes, is largely irrelevant to pacification as long as we do not have it.**—*Robert*

McNamara, Secretary of Defense, in memorandum to President Johnson, 14 October 1966.[899]

McNamara was stressing the difference in tactics between the war against the communist, and pacification to win the support of the people.

1129 **... Fortas doesn't know anything about Vietnam ... but he knows a lot about Lyndon Johnson.**—*Unidentified senior State Department official to author Stanley Karnow, 1966.*[374]

Abe Fortas was one of President Johnson's closest unofficial advisors. At the time he advocated increased military pressure against NVN to force them into negotiations and to cease their infiltration and support of the VC insurgency in SVN.

1130 **I see no reasonable way to bring the war to an end soon.**—*Robert McNamara, Secretary of Defense, in a memo to President Johnson, 14 October 1966.*[72]

McNamara saw the war as a stalemate at this point. To withdraw would result in South Vietnam being overrun by the North, to stay would require high American troop levels, long term commitment, and continuing casualties.

1131 **A North Vietnamese victory [Giap believed] would help demoralize Americans and elect "doves" to a peace-seeking Congress that would yank the U.S. out of Vietnam.**—*Unidentified Western official, interviewed, October 1966.*[415]

Giap attempted to attack south across the DMZ rolling U.S. Marine units stationed along the DMZ beneath his forces. His plan was executed in mid–1967, but his attempt to roll the Marines beneath his forces failed.

1132 **[Hanoi] knows we can't achieve our goals. The prognosis is bad ... that the war can be brought to a satisfactory conclusion within the next two years. The large-unit operations probably will not do it; negotiations probably will not do it.**—*Robert McNamara, Secretary of Defense, in a memorandum to President Johnson, 14 October 1966.*[72]

The rapid influx of U.S. troops and bombing of the North stopped the communist takeover of South Vietnam, but McNamara did not believe the war could be won militarily. To leave would result in South Vietnam being overrun by the North, to stay would require high American troop levels, and commensurate casualties.

1133 **Disputes settled by other than peaceful means are disputes that will remain unsettled.**—*President Lyndon Johnson, in a speech in Manila, October 1966.*[416]

1134 **In Vietnam, only the Communists represent revolution and social change, for better or worse according to a man's politics ... the Communists, despite their brutality and deceit, remain the only Vietnamese capable of rallying millions of their countrymen to sacrifice and hardship in the name of the nation and the only group not dependent on foreign bayonets for survival.**—*Neil Sheehan, journalist, writing in The New York Times Magazine, October 1966.*[75]

1135 **I believe there is a light at the end of what has been a long and lonely tunnel.**—*President Lyndon Johnson, while speaking in Australia, October 1966.*[957]

Johnson was on his way to the Manila Conference.

1136 **We should in no case unilaterally quit bombing. Infiltration continues. The price of infiltration has definitely been raised.**—*General William Westmoreland, ComUSMACV, in response to questions from President Johnson during the Manila conference, October 1966.*[72]

Westmoreland favored increased air strikes against North Vietnam and infiltration routes in Laos.

1137 **While there was light at the end of the tunnel, we had to be geared for the long pull. The enemy is relying on his greater staying power. It is only his will and resolve that are sustaining him now, and his faith that his will is stronger than ours.**—*General William Westmoreland, ComUSMACV, in response to questions from President Johnson during the Manila Conference, October 1966.*[72]

That light at the end of the tunnel again. General Henri Navarre first uttered this in 1953 when he revealed his Navarre Plan for winning the war against the Viet Minh. Navarre commanded French forces in Indochina at the time.

1138 **We are not able to garrison a locality and then move on to another place. That is the reason that the so-called march-and-destroy tactics are employed. ... They have not undertaken to hold the ground that they have taken. We have taken some areas two or three times. ... We turn [an area] over to the South Vietnamese. ... We appoint the Governor of the village and give him a half dozen armed villagers, and they do not last too long if the Vietcong come back.**—*Senator Richard B. Russell of Georgia during a Senate speech, 21 March 1966.*[1025]

Russell was the chairman of the Senate Armed Services committee. Throughout the course of the war the pattern was frequently repeated. American troops would clear an area of the enemy and soon afterward the enemy would filter back into the area and resume operations. Several months would pass and American troops would be sent back into the area to clear it once again. This process was repeated by the U.S. Marines and the Army in places like the Bong Son Plain and the coastal valleys that emptied into the South China Sea.

1139 **If I'm ever banished, I want to go to Australia.... The way I feel about Australians is that they are good men to go to the well with, good ones to get behind a log with.**—*President Lyndon Johnson, speaking to correspondents at the White House, October 1966.*[416]

Johnson kept the Australians in high regard. Australia sent advisory units, a ground combat force, and several naval vessels to support the South Vietnamese during the war.

1140 **Political power held by a few and the rich within a nation is power that will not survive.**—*President Lyndon Johnson, in a speech during his Asian tour, October 1966.*[416]

Johnson went to Manila to confer with several Pacific region countries, formulating policy and discussing the needs of the region.

1141 **Our current actions in Quang Tri are probably agreeable to NVN. I believe they are glad we have a battalion invested in the defense of Khe Sanh, and that we have five other battalions operating in the inhospitable jungle which might otherwise be engaged in Revolutionary Development Support [the official term for pacification].... We may expect him [the enemy] to hang on to our forces in Quang Tri as long as he can.**—*General Victor Krulak, Commander, Fleet Marine Force Pacific, in a cable to General Lewis Walt, October 1966.*[887]

Khe Sanh is located in the northwest corner of South Vietnam, near the border junctions of North Vietnam, South Vietnam and Laos. Westmoreland ordered the establishment of a fortified base to be manned by Marines. In addition to the battalion at Khe Sanh there were five Marine battalions operating along the DMZ in Quang Tri Province. Walt and Krulak believed the Marine position at Khe Sanh was an unwise move, but as Westmoreland was the commander for U.S. forces in Vietnam, the Marines had no choice. The deployment of six battalions in the wilderness areas of northern I Corps reduced the Marines available for pacification operations in the remainder of I Corps.

1142 **All of you have said so much of my speech, there is very little of it left.**—*President Lyndon Johnson, in his opening statement to the members of the Manila Conference, October 1966.*[418]

Johnson was emphatic that the U.S. presence at the conference remain low profile. He did not want the conference to appear to be an American-run show.

1143 **It's not our conference. We're not even number 2, we're number 7.**—*President Lyndon Johnson, instructions to his staff during the Manila Conference, October 1966.*[418]

Johnson was emphatic that the U.S. presence at the conference remain low profile. He did not want the conference to appear to be an American-run show. He repeatedly impressed this upon his aides at the conference.

1144 **We must improve our information, get to the people, give them the facts, enlarge the open arms program. Then they will come back to us.**—*Nguyen Cao Ky, Prime Minister of South Vietnam, during the Manila Conference, October 1966.*[43]

The open arms program (Hoi Chanh—Chieu Hoi) encouraged VC/NVA soldiers to defect to the Government of South Vietnam.

1145 **[Johnson]—What is in the mind of the Viet Cong—do they expect to win?**

[Nguyen Cao Ky]—No, I don't think so. I believe they will very soon collapse—if we can get to them the facts.—*Exchange between President Johnson and Prime Minister Nguyen Cao Ky, during the Manila Conference, October 1966.*[43]

The facts Ky was talking about were that Diem was no longer leading the government of South Vietnam and things were changing for the better under the Ky-Thieu regime.

1146 **The Rolling Thunder program of bombing the north has not significantly affected infiltration or crushed the morale of Hanoi ... at the proper time we should consider terminating bombing in all of North Vietnam.**—*Robert McNamara, Secretary of Defense, in a memorandum to President Johnson, 19 October 1966.*[925]

McNamara's disillusionment with the bombing campaign was backed by the findings of the Jason Study (commissioned by the DoD and conducted by the IDA). The study concluded the bombing campaign against North Vietnam was not effective in stopping the infiltration into South Vietnam, nor was it adversely affecting North Vietnam's will to fight.

1147 **The Australians were better to me than anybody has ever been to me except my mother and my wife...**—*President Lyndon Johnson, speaking to correspondents at the White House, October 1966.*[416]

During World War II Johnson crash landed his plane in Australia. The Australians took very good care of him until he was reunited with his unit.

1148 **This is not an American show.**—*President Lyndon Johnson, speaking to a meeting of the National Security Council, October 1966.*[418]

Johnson emphasizing that the upcoming Manila Conference was not to take on the appearance of an American controlled meeting. He wanted his entourage to maintain a low profile and not be the center of attention, and most emphatically not play the part of the "ugly American."

1149 **The American people, our allies and our enemies alike, are increasingly uncertain as to our resolution to pursue the war to a successful conclusion.**—*Joint Chiefs of Staff, in a memorandum to Secretary of Defense McNamara and the President, October 1966.*[374]

The JCS were responding to McNamara's call for a stabilizing of the American war effort in Vietnam. McNamara called for a reduction in the bombing of the North and a cap on the number of American troops deployed to South Vietnam. The JCS wanted all-out war against North Vietnam and the VC, to complete the war in the shortest time frame.

1150 **After a year of increasing escalation, the area controlled by the Viet Cong is larger today than it was a year ago, and the North Vietnamese have replied to the bombing not by ceasing to intervene in South Vietnam, but by doing what it was plain that they would do if we bombed them, by sending in more and more of their trained troops.**—*Walter Lippmann in a San Francisco Chronicle article, 2 January 1966.*[1023]

Lippmann staunchly opposed President Johnson's policy in Vietnam.

1151 **If I die before this terrible war is ended, I will feel that my whole life's work for decency has been a failure.**—*Norman Thomas, peace activist, during an anti-war speech, October 1966.*[826]

Thomas was in his eighties at the time.

1152 **We will not fail you.**—*President Lyndon Johnson, speaking to American troops at Cam Ranh Bay, October 1966.*[975]

Johnson's final words to troops as he prepared to depart the Army base at Cam Ranh Bay. Johnson had made the secret trip during a break in the Manila Conference. He returned to Manila after his short visit to U.S. troops in South Vietnam.

1153 **The Joint Chiefs of Staff believe that the likelihood of the war being settled by negotiation is small; and that, far from inducing negotiations, another bombing pause will be regarded by North Vietnamese leaders, and our Allies, as renewed evidence of lack of U.S. determination to press the war to a successful conclusion.**—*General Earle Wheeler, Chairman, Joint Chiefs of Staff, in a memorandum to Secretary of Defense McNamara, October 1966.*[44]

McNamara wanted to continue to use bombing followed by pauses as an inducement to Hanoi to seek negotiations. The JCS were much opposed to any pauses in the bombing. All indications were that Hanoi used the pauses to increase infiltration of South Vietnam.

1154 **Communist leaders in both North and South Vietnam expect to win this war in Washington, just as they won the war**

with France in Paris.—*General Earle Wheeler, Chairman, Joint Chiefs of Staff, in a memorandum to Secretary of Defense McNamara, October 1966.*[44]

The U.S. realized Hanoi's strategy was to wait America out in hopes that American casualties, cost, and time would weaken American resolve to remain in South Vietnam.

1155 **When I thought of all the power that man [Johnson] has at his command, telling those six nations he was going to stand by them, I could feel my skin tingle. It was very effective and very moving.**—*Unidentified American official attending the Manila Conference, October 1966.*[419]

The Manila Conference encompassed the nations of Australia, New Zealand, South Vietnam, Philippines, South Korea, Thailand and the United States. Johnson pledged the U.S. would stand by those nations represented at the conference, in their opposition of communist encroachment.

1156 **Give us this day our daily rice, deliver us from Mao Tse-tung.**—*Filipino phrase displayed in the Philippines during the Manila Conference, October 1966.*[419]

Filipinos demonstrated in support of a stronger Pacific pact between the nations of the conference in order to keep China from exerting pressure on Pacific rim countries.

1157 **Don't let the newspapermen divide us.**—*President Lyndon Johnson, speaking at the Manila Conference, October 1966.*[72]

Johnson suspected that the press might destroy his Administration, and cautioned the members of the conference accordingly.

1158 **[I regret] that I could not begin to personally thank every man in Vietnam for what he is doing.**—*President Lyndon Johnson, speaking to troops at Cam Ranh Bay, October 1966.*[419]

Johnson visited U.S. troops in Cam Ranh Bay. He was warmly received and moved by their admiration. Johnson made the secret trip during a break in the Manila Conference. He returned to Manila after his visit to Cam Ranh Bay.

1159 **Asia and Asians must lead, but we are prepared to help.**—*President Lyndon Johnson, speaking on his arrival in Manila, 23 October 1966.*[43]

Seven Pacific rim nations met in Manila for a summit: South Vietnam, Thailand, South Korea, Australia, New Zealand, Philippines, United States.

1160 **I thank you, I salute you, may the Good Lord look over you and keep you until you come home with the coonskin on the wall.**—*President Johnson, speaking to military personnel at a Cam Ranh Bay officer's club, October 1966.*[733]

Johnson paid a special visit to U.S. troops at Cam Ranh Bay in Vietnam. He made the two hour stopover during a break in the Manila Conference (October 1966). While at Cam Ranh Bay, Johnson presented medals to several soldiers including Westmoreland and was warmly received by the American troops.

1161 **The bombing campaign is one of two trump cards in the hands of the President (the other being the presence of US troops in SVN). It should not be given up without an end to NVN aggression in SVN.**—*General Earle Wheeler, Chairman, Joint Chiefs of Staff, in a memorandum to Secretary of Defense McNamara, October 1966.*[44]

The JCS did not want bombing pauses unless there was indication that Hanoi did not use the pauses to move additional men and materiel into South Vietnam.

1162 **Our commitment was to a "legitimate government" and what we have in Saigon is neither "legitimate" nor a "government." ... Our promise was to help South Vietnam, not destroy it.**—*Editorial comment by James Reston in the New York Times, 18 May 1966.*[1024]

1163 **You want a man that has guts enough to stand up and tell Washington yonder that we're tired of that no-win policy.**—*James "Justice Jim" Johnson, Democratic candidate for Arkansas governor, during campaigning, October 1966.*[417]

Hawkish Democrat on the war in Vietnam.

1164 **I give you my pledge. We shall never let you down, nor your fighting comrades, nor the 15 million people of South Vietnam, nor the hundreds of millions of Asians who are counting on us to show here in Vietnam that aggression does not pay, and that aggression cannot succeed.**—*President Lyndon Johnson, speaking to U.S. troops at Cam Ranh Bay, 26 October 1966.*[535]

During the Manila Conference in the Philippines Johnson made a surprise visit to Cam Ranh Bay, where he was warmly received by U.S. troops.

1165 **I came here today for one good reason, simply because I could not come to this part of the world and not come to see you.**—*President Lyndon Johnson, speaking to U.S. troops at Cam Ranh Bay, 26 October 1966.*[535]

During the Manila Conference in the Philippines Johnson made a surprise visit to Cam Ranh Bay. Following the two and a half hour visit he returned to Manila.

1166 **I never saw him so emotional.**—*Jack Valenti, Special Assistant to the President, commenting on the President's visit with American troops in Vietnam, October 1966.*[419]

Johnson was moved by the reception he received from American troops who greeted him at Cam Ranh Bay.

1167 **Johnson's war ... a wishy-washy war killing our best young men.**—*Howard "Bo" Callaway, Republican candidate for Georgia's Governor, during campaigning, October 1966.*[417]

Callaway's description of the war in Vietnam.

1168 **There are 100 boys a week brought back in canvas sacks ... 18-year-old boys who have never known a woman's love, never known the joy of holding a son in his arms.**—*Winthrop Rockefeller, Republican candidate for governor of Arkansas, during a campaign speech, October 1966.*[417]

1169 **Allied forces are in the Republic of Vietnam because that country is the object of aggression and its government requested support in the resistance of its people to aggression. They shall be withdrawn as the other side withdraws its forces to the North, ceases infiltration and the level of violence thus subsides. Those forces will be withdrawn as soon as possible and not later than six months after the above conditions have been fulfilled.**—*From a joint communiqué by the Allied forces providing combat support to South Vietnam, 25 October 1966.*[722]

The announcement of a pledge to withdraw in six months

made headlines — the pledge made no statement about how long the war could go on until the above conditions were met.

1170 **I do not pretend to speak for Asia. Let us listen when the Asians speak for themselves.**—*President Lyndon Johnson, speaking to the press in Auckland, New Zealand, October 1966.*[416]

Johnson was on his way to Manila for a summit conference with ministers from South Vietnam, Australia, New Zealand, South Korea, and the Philippines.

1171 **I wanted to tell them [American troops] how their President and most of their countrymen felt about what they were doing, I have never been more moved by any group I have talked to, never in my life.**—*President Lyndon Johnson, writing about his encounter with American troops at Cam Ranh Bay, October 1966.*[66]

Johnson made a special trip to Cam Ranh Bay to visit with U.S. troops. He spent nearly two and a half hours on the ground with the troops before his return to Manila to complete a conference with Asia-Pacific allies.

1172 **Slow, painful, and incredibly expensive though it may be — we're beginning to win the war.**—*Robert Komer, Special Assistant to the President, late-1966.*[374]

Komer indicated that the U.S. intervention was countering the NVA buildup in South Vietnam, but a greater allied force would be required to move from countering the enemy to overcoming the enemy.

1173 **Enemy morale has not broken — he apparently has adjusted to our stopping his drive for military victory and has adopted a strategy of keeping us busy and waiting us out (a strategy of attriting our national will).**—*Robert McNamara, Secretary of Defense, late-1966.*[713]

1174 **The administration's current policy resigns America and the free Asian nations to a war which could last five years and cost more casualties than Korea.**—*Richard Nixon, former Vice-President, during campaign support speeches, 3 November 1966.*[766]

Nixon criticized the Manila Communiqué which stated the Allies would withdraw from Vietnam in six months if the conditions set by the communiqué were met (withdrawal of NVA forces, end of NV support for the insurgent forces, and a reduction in the level of violence). He criticized the open-ended nature of the communiqué. U.S. KIAs during the Korean War were 35,000+, at this point, U.S. KIAs in Vietnam were at 5,700+.

1175 **[Nixon is a] chronic campaigner.**—*President Johnson, during a news conference, 4 November 1966.*[850]

Johnson was referring to Nixon's campaign losses for governor in 1962, and Republican presidential nomination in 1964. He was implying that Nixon did not know what was going on when he was VP and still didn't know what was going on.

1176 **I don't like the word "class," but it's a fact that the burden of the draft falls on people of lower economic or educational class. That is morally wrong.**—*Henry Drummonds, student body president at the University of Oregon, 1966.*[420]

Drummonds relinquished his 2-S education deferment and was promptly classified 1-A.

1177 **We have explained that we would pull out just as soon as the infiltration ceases. We made the statement and we set a time limit on it. Why would we want to stay there if there was no aggression, if there was no infiltration, and the violence ceased? We wouldn't want to stay there as tourists.**—*President Johnson, during a news conference, 4 November 1966.*[769]

1178 **[The] American Vietnam War [is] misguided and immoral.**—*Henry Drummonds, student body president at the University of Oregon, 1966.*[420]

1179 **The frequent, broadly-based public offers made by the President to settle the war by peaceful means on a generous basis, which would take from NVN nothing it now has, have been admirable. Certainly no one — American or foreigner — except those who are determined not to be convinced, can doubt the sincerity, the generosity, the altruism of the U.S. actions and objectives. In the opinion of the Joint Chiefs of Staff the time has come when further overt actions and offers on our part are not only nonproductive, they are counterproductive. A logical case can be made that the American people, our allies, and our enemies alike are increasingly uncertain as to our resolution to pursue the war to a successful conclusion.**—*Joint Chiefs of Staff, in a memorandum to the Secretary of Defense, late 1966.*[185]

The JCS, unhappy with the progress of the war and Secretary of Defense's apparent softening towards the war effort.

1180 **I went to school at Berkeley and spent four years there doing a lot of the same things you here are doing. I was doing the same things as you are, but there were two big differences. I was tougher, and I was more courteous. And I'm still tougher!**—*Robert S McNamara, Secretary of Defense, in an exchange with students, Quincy House, 7 November 1966.*[850]

Following a campus debate students surrounded McNamara's car and refused to let him leave until he answered more questions.

1181 **I had about two hundred fifty [SAMs] shot at me and the last one was as inspiring as the first. Sure I got cagey, and I was able to wait longer and longer, but I never got overconfident. I mean, if you're one or two seconds too slow, you've had the schnitzel.**—*General Robin Olds, U.S. Air Force pilot and commander of the 8th Tactical Fighter Wing, 1966.*[189]

1182 **[Nixon hoped it would be] ... absolutely clear to Hanoi and Peking that the new House of Representatives will be much stronger than its predecessor as a bulwark of support for a United States policy of "no reward for aggression."**—*Richard Nixon, former Vice President, from a public statement following the November 1966 elections, 5 November 1966.*[780]

1183 **The sharpest rebuff of a President in a generation.**—*Richard Nixon, former Vice President, comments on the 1966 off-year elections, 5 November 1966.*[780]

The Democrats lost 47 seats in the House, 3 seats in the Senate to Republicans and also lost eight governorships to Republicans. These were higher than average losses for the incumbent party in an off year election. Nixon attributed the results of the election as an indication of voter discontent with President Johnson's Vietnam War policy.

1184 **The United States Air Force has bombed the North Vietnamese city of Vinh out of existence. I think it's time to start calling LBJ the "Butcher of Vinh."**—*Robert Sheer, peace* *activist, from a speech at Quincy House, on the Harvard Campus, 7 November 1966.*[826]

The POL facilities near the North Vietnam town of Vinh were struck during the U.S. retaliatory raids against North Vietnam in 1964. Many anti-war activists perpetuated the rumor that Vinh was "wiped out" in the raid. Anti-war protesters nicknamed President Johnson, the Butcher of Vinh.

1185 **Cambodia is now a real source of manpower and supplies for the VC. It was not merely a supply route but an actual storage area.**—*Unidentified NLF rallier, during an interview, 1966.*[35]

There were many small Vietnamese hamlets and villages along and on both sides of the South Vietnam-Cambodian border. The villes provided storage areas, recruits and laborers for the VC.

1186 **I propose ... that everybody including the President and his ... our vast hordes of generals, executives, judges and legislators of these states go to nature, find a kindly teacher or Indian peyote chief or guru guide and assay their consciousness with LSD.**—*Allen Ginsberg, poet and LSD use advocate, from a speech in Boston's Arlington Street Church, 12 November 1966.*[740]

1187 **There are rights and privileges in any society, also obligations. If I'm willing to give up the rights and privileges, I should be able to give up the obligations.**—*Gregory Roman, draft dodger, in an interview, November 1966.*[420]

Roman fled to Canada rather than face prosecution for draft evasion.

1188 **I don't dig patriotism or nationalism, it leads to war.**—*Gregory Roman, draft dodger, in an interview, November 1966.*[420]

Roman escaped to Canada rather than face prosecution for draft evasion.

1189 **By and large, the people in rural areas believe that the GVN when it comes will not stay but that the VC will; that cooperation with the GVN will be punished by the VC; that GVN is really indifferent to the people's welfare; that the low-level GVN are tools of the local rich; and that the GVN is ridden with corruption.**—*Robert Komer, Special Assistant to the President, 1966.*[876]

Komer was stressing the need for a successful pacification program. One that would provide the villagers with security and at the same time address their needs.

1190 **Are you in favor of an immediate ceasefire and withdrawal of United States troops from Vietnam so the Vietnamese people can settle their own problems?**—*Dearborn, Michigan referendum ballot measure, placed by Mayor Orville Hubbard, November 1966.*[757]

The vote was 14,134 in favor of U.S. withdrawal, and 20,628 opposing unilateral U.S. withdrawal from Vietnam.

1191 **The Joint Chiefs of Staff do not concur in your [Secretary of Defense, Robert McNamara] recommendation that there should be no increase in level of bombing effort and no modification in areas and targets subject to attack. They believe our air campaign against NVN to be an integral and indispensable part of our over all war effort. To be effective, the air campaign should be conducted with only minimal constraints necessary to avoid indiscriminate killing of population. The Joint Chiefs of Staff believe that the war has reached a stage at which decisions taken over the next sixty days can determine the outcome of the war, and, consequently, can affect the overall security interest of the United States for years to come.**—*Joint Chiefs of Staff, in a memorandum to the Secretary of Defense, late 1966.*[185]

JCS predicted dire consequences for the U.S. if the application of military pressure against North Vietnam was not intensified. They were at odds with McNamara's recommendation to stop the increase in military pressure against North Vietnam in favor of a political settlement.

1192 **[Political stability of the Saigon regime did not] translated itself into political achievements at Province level or below. Pacification has if anything gone backward.**—*Robert McNamara, Secretary of Defense, late-1966.*[713]

A semblance of political stability had come about in the GVN in 1965 when Nguyen Cao Ky became the prime minister and Nguyen Van Thieu chief of state. This arrangement held until 1967, when public elections took place in South Vietnam, resulting in Thieu becoming president and Ky, vice president. The focus of the war during the period 1965 and 1966 was on the destruction of the VC/NVA, with minimal attention directed to the rural pacification program.

1193 **These latest figures [enemy strength levels] indicate that the communists by now ought to be in really serious trouble. ... If the present trend continues, however,—and this is always a big if—I do not see how they can possibly hold out beyond the summer of 1969.**—*Colonel Robert Ginsburgh, NSC liaison to the JCS, in a report to Walt Rostow, 21 November 1966.*[72]

These results were based on MACV figures of some 300,000 enemy in South Vietnam, with an infiltration rate of less than 9,000 men a month. The actual number of enemy was closer to 500,000 in South Vietnam, and a much higher rate of infiltration.

1194 **The draft is not universal and everybody does not serve. I find this very wrong.**—*William F. Wild, Chairman, Draft Board No. 66, in an interview, November 1966.*[420]

Wild was speaking of the Universal Military Training and Service Act—the military draft.

1195 **I suspect that we have reached the point where we are killing, defecting, or otherwise attriting more VC/NVA strength than the enemy can build up.**—*George Carver, Special Assistant to director CIA, in a memo to Robert Komer, 22 November 1966.*[64]

Westmoreland was waging a war of attrition on the communist. The goal, to grind down the enemy until he gave up the fight.

1196 **A reappraisal of the strength of communist regular forces which is currently underway indicates that accepted (i.e. MACV) estimates of the strength of Viet Cong irregular forces may have drastically underestimated their growth, possibly by as much as 200,000 persons.**—*George Carver, Special Assistant to director CIA, in a memo to Robert Komer, 22 November 1966.*[72]

After studying captured enemy documents, CIA analyst Samuel Adams believed the number of enemy troops in South Vietnam was much higher than current intelligence reports from MACV were indicating. He notified George Carver, who passed the information on to Komer, presidential assistant.

1197 **The poor will feel they have been shortchanged. They will feel they have been double-crossed. The poor will feel that democracy is only for the rich.**—*Sargent Shriver, Director, Office of Economic Opportunity, during a news conference, 22 November 1966.*[805]

Reacting to continued reductions in funding of the War on Poverty, the cutbacks were a direct result of the rising cost of the war in Vietnam.

1198 **Every male who is physically capable should put in two years in the armed forces.**—*William F. Wild, Chairman, Draft Board No. 66, in an interview, November 1966.*[420]

Wild was speaking of the Universal Military Training and Service Act—the military draft.

1199 **It's a gross breach of democracy to give a youngster educational advantages and then have him avoid service. Educate the man—fine. But soon as he's educated make him fulfill his obligations.**—*William F. Wild, Chairman, Draft Board No. 66, in an interview, November 1966.*[420]

Wild was speaking of the Universal Military Training and Service Act—the military draft.

1200 **If they [Americans] come to teach or to help us build we would welcome them, but they come to our country to kill us, so we have no other choice but to kill them.**—*Ho Chi Minh, President, Democratic Republic of Vietnam, during a meeting with black radicals visiting Hanoi, December 1966.*[1018]

Ho was speaking with Diane Nash Bevel, a civil rights activist, who spent eleven days in North Vietnam. She spoke out against the war in Vietnam on Radio Hanoi, preaching black solidarity with the Vietnamese against "American colonialism."

1201 **[A successful pacification program would depend] on the extent to which the South Vietnamese can be shocked out of their present [indifferent] pattern of behavior.**—*Robert McNamara, Secretary of Defense, 1966.*[713]

Prior to the TET Offensive, the pacification program made very limited headway in rural areas. After TET the pacification effort was renewed and began to make progress. An important factor in that progress was the fact that large numbers of VC troops and NLF cadre had been killed, captured, or defected as a result of the TET Offensive. The reduction in the local VC and VCI forces greatly improved the survivability of GVN pacification teams.

1202 **It got more exciting with each war. I mean the planes were going faster than hell when I was flying a Mustang, but by the time I got to Nam, it scared the piss out of a lot of guys just to fly the damn jets at full speed. Let alone do it in combat.**—*General Robin Olds, U.S. Air Force pilot and commander of the 8th Tactical Fighter Wing, 1966.*[189]

1203 **We're going to get left of Karl Marx and left of Lenin, we're going to get way out there, up on that cross with Jesus.**—*Reverend James Bevel, member of the SCLC and director of the Spring Mobilization in January, during a meeting of anti-war activists, December 1966.*[626]

Bevel's reaction to criticism that this particular group and the organization of the upcoming demonstration was leaning too far to the left. Leftist factions from the Progressive Labor Party, Communist Party, Youth Against War and Fascism, and the Socialist Workers Party were in attendance for the demonstration planning session led by Bevel.

1204 **I shot and killed a little 8- or 9-year-old girl, with the sweetest, most innocent little face, and the nastiest grenade in her hand, that you ever saw.**—*Unidentified American soldier, in a letter home, 1966.*[74]

The soldier, walking with a group of other soldiers, was confronted by the child when she ran into their path to throw a grenade at the group.

1205 **The Vietnam War is a colonial war. If you fight in it, you are fighting Asian brothers who are determined to prevent their country from becoming owned and managed by racist-capitalist white men.**—*Diane Nash Bevel, civil rights activist, speaking over Radio Hanoi, December 1966.*[995]

Bevel was just one of several black radicals and civil rights activists who made political broadcasts for North Vietnam over Radio Hanoi or South Vietnam Liberation Radio (NLF). The broadcasts were aimed at turning black troops against the war. They emphasized racial problems in the U.S. and the military, and black solidarity with the Vietnamese "struggle" against America in Southeast Asia.

1206 **Progress in pacification, more than anything else, will persuade the enemy to negotiate or withdraw.**—*Robert Komer, Special Assistant to the President, 1966.*[876]

Pacification efforts tended to hamper normal activity of the communist cadre and recruitment for VC units. One of the major targets of the enemy 1968 TET Offensive was the disruption of the pacification program. The program as a whole was not widely successful, but in districts it was making modest gains, posing a threat to the VC and VC infrastructure.

1207 **In this war, when we have beaten the army of North Vietnam and the main force battalions of the Viet Cong, we have simply won the opportunity to get to the heart of the matter, which is more than 150,000 terrorist guerrillas highly organized throughout the country and looking exactly like civilians.**—*Henry Cabot Lodge, U.S. Ambassador to South Vietnam, December 1966.*[957]

1208 **Despite our interdiction, the enemy has accommodated to our lines of communications (LOC) attacks by ingeniously hiding and dispersing his logistic activity. His recuperative capability along these lines has been remarkable.** —*Admiral U.S. Grant Sharp, U.S. Navy, Commander in Chief, Pacific, in a report to the JCS, December 1966.*[964]

1209 **The military solution to the problem is not certain.... Ultimately we must find alternative solutions. We must perforce find a diplomatic solution.... We need to explore other means. Our military approach is an unacceptable way to a successful conclusion.**—*Robert McNamara, Secretary of Defense, during strategy a meeting, December 1966.*[374]

1210 **Johnson and the war machine are things to be faced, to stand up to, not to stand in awe of or cringe before.**—*A.J. Muste, peace activist and chairman of the Spring Mobilization to End the War in Vietnam, in an article appearing in Liberation magazine, December 1966.*[850]

Muste, responding to comments that anti-war demonstrations were having little impact on stopping the war in Vietnam.

1211 **I would feel just like the KKK over there. Denying those people freedom of choice, just like black people are denied freedom of choice in the U.S.**—*John Otis Sumrall, black activist, speaking at an anti-draft conference in Chicago, December 1966.*[716]

1212 **I am not looked upon as an equal citizen in everyday life. Why am I looked upon as an equal citizen when it comes time to report for induction?**—*John Otis Sumrall, black activist, speaking at an anti-draft conference in Chicago, December 1966.*[716]

Blacks were asking the question, why am I good enough to die for America, but not good enough to drink from the same water fountain as whites, or enjoy the same rights a white would enjoy.

1213 **If the show were going to the Vietcong or even to the moon, I would go.**—*Reita Faria, 1996 Miss World, commenting during tour of U.S. bases in South Vietnam, December 1966.*[421]

Faria represented India when she won the Miss World beauty pageant. She accompanied the Bob Hope Christmas tour to Vietnam.

1214 **Civilian areas are unavoidably hit when they are located next to military targets.**—*Unidentified Pentagon spokesman, December 1966.*[421]

The spokesman was reacting to the issue of rising civilian casualties as reported by the North Vietnamese. Hanoi routinely claimed high civilian casualties caused by American bombing raids.

1215 **It appears relatively certain to me that this [war] will be escalated to a point where we will force North Vietnam to negotiate and then, at the negotiating table, we will throw away all that has been purchased at the cost of U.S. and Vietnamese lives, not to mention the many billions of dollars of U.S. taxpayers' money.**—*John Paul Vann, Director, III Corps Office of Civil Operations, in a letter, 23 December 1966.*[887]

1216 **The prospect of large scale reinforcements in men and defense budget increases for the next eighteen-month period requires solid preparation of the American public. A crucial element will be a clear demonstration that we have explored fully every alternative but that the aggressor has left us no choice.**—*Dean Rusk, Secretary of State, in a cable to Ambassador Henry Cabot Lodge, 28 December 1966.*

1217 **Unless this conflict can be eased the United States will find some of her most loyal and courageous young people choosing to go to jail rather than to bear their country's arms....**—*From an open letter to President Johnson, released to the press, 29 December 1966, signed by 100 student leaders.*[816]

A White House aide remarked there could be some question as to just how courageous these students saw themselves. They benefited from what America had to offer, but were reluctant to support it during the war in Vietnam.

1967

No one can guarantee success in war, but only deserve it.
—Winston Churchill

1218 **I was one of those who told McNamara in 1964 that the war would be over by the end of 1965; I swear I thought it would be. But don't dare you print my name.**—*Unidentified Marine officer, comments to correspondent, January 1967.*[424]

In 1963 McNamara predicted the withdrawal of American advisers to Vietnam could probably begin the end of 1963, with all American advisers to be out of the country by the end of 1965.

1219 **I wish that I could report to you that the conflict is almost over. This I cannot do. We face more cost, more loss, and more agony. For the end is not yet. I cannot promise you that it will come this year — or come next year. Our adversary still believes, I think, tonight that he can go on fighting longer than we can, longer than we and our allies will be prepared to stand up and resist.**—*President Lyndon Johnson, State of the Union speech, January 1967.*[72]

Johnson also mentioned that Westmoreland believed the VC/NVA could not succeed militarily.

1220 **Ho Chi Minh has said he can hold out for 10 years because he knows very well the American people will not stand for another decade of war in Vietnam.**—*Ho Chi Minh, as related by Robert Sherrod, 1967.*[424]

Ho's strategy was to outlast the Americans. He knew that in a war of attrition he had the edge. He was willing to sacrifice more of his people than America was willing to sacrifice the lives of its soldiers.

1221 **Vietnam will never get well unless the Americans take over or the Vietcong take over.**—*Doctor, from an unnamed British Commonwealth country, speaking to a correspondent, January 1967.*[424]

In hospital, the Vietnamese received more support from the Americans than they did from their own government, even though America provided the funding to the government for their care and rehabilitation. Corruption within the GVN diverted many of the resources supplied by America for Vietnamese support services.

1222 **The chemical reaction of this napalm does melt the flesh, and the flesh runs right down their faces onto their chests and it sits there and grows there...**—*Unidentified New Jersey woman, interviewed for Ladies' Home Journal, January 1967.*[850]

This particular housewife was visiting the Vietnamese children she had adopted under the Foster Parents Plan. She went to Vietnam to visit them and paid a visit to the children's wing of a civilian hospital in Saigon.

1223 **[We will continue our present course in Vietnam, until the quest for negotiations succeeds,] or until infiltration ceases, or until the conflict subsides.**—*President Lyndon Johnson, State of the Union Message, as quoted by Life magazine, January 1967.*[423]

1224 **I do not for one minute believe the infiltration rate is 8,400 a month. I believe it is a MACV balancing figure to give**

them what I strongly suspect is an inflated order of battle. They are being excessively conservative both as an insurance policy and to protect themselves against what they regard as excessive pressure to allocate more forces to pacification.—*Walt Rostow, Special Assistant to the President, in a memorandum to the President, 3 January 1967.*[72]

Rostow accused Westmoreland of inflating enemy numbers, yet later, CIA and CBS would accuse him of under reporting enemy numbers.

1225 **How are you going to get democracy to these people? They have no sense of nationality, they think only of the village that they have always lived in.**—*Unidentified American battalion commander, to correspondent, January 1967.*[424]

For many Vietnamese peasants the land and their ancestors were their world. Many never left the immediate area of their hamlet. They felt no allegiance to the local or national government or any interest in what the governments did as long as it did not impact their hamlet.

1226 **Whether it's a big war or a small war, when you're dead, you're very dead.**—*Colonel Charles Davis, U.S. Army, ARVN advisor, to correspondent, January 1967.*[424]

Davis was a veteran of World War II and Korea, at the time he was working with the ARVNs in IV Corps.

1227 **The only thing that can defeat us is for the American people to get tired of the war.**—*Admiral Ulysses S. Grant Sharp, U.S. Navy Commander in Chief, Pacific, in an interview, January 1967.*[424]

Hanoi's strategy in Vietnam was partly based on the possibility that America would get tired of the war and withdraw before Hanoi gave up the fight to unite all of Vietnam under communism. Hanoi believed America would follow the path of the French.

1228 **The more the war of aggression is Americanized, the more disintegrated the Saigon puppet army and administration become.**—*General Vo Nguyen Giap, Defense Minister of the Democratic Republic of Vietnam, 1967.*[713]

Giap predicted the Saigon regime and its troops (the ARVN) would grow steadily weaker and increasingly ineffective as America took over the fighting in South Vietnam.

1229 **We ought to take over the country — the hell with these Vietnamese generals and politicians — win the war, then give it back, like we did in Korea.**—*Unidentified U.S. Army sergeant in Cu Chi, January 1967.*[424]

1230 **Pity the poor peasant. The villagers are supposed to be warned to get out before the bombing starts, but it is a lie to say that this is done even half of the time.... If they leave their villages, they go to refugee camps where they're supposed to get enough money to live on, but the piasters disappear into someone's pocket. If they stay and miraculously survive the bombing and shelling, the infantry comes in and shoots them as V.C.**—*Doctor, from an unnamed British Commonwealth country, speaking to a correspondent, January 1967.*[424]

1231 **Whether we can fight a war of limited objectives over a period of time, and keep alive the hope of independence and stability for people other than ourselves; whether we can continue to act with restraint when the temptation to "get it over with" is inviting, but dangerous; whether we can accept the necessity of choosing "a great evil in order to ward off a greater"; whether we can do these without arousing the hatreds and the passions that are ordinarily loosed in the time of war — on all these questions so much turns.**—*President Lyndon Johnson, State of the Union Message, as quoted by Life magazine, January 1967.*[423]

1232 **From the purely military standpoint there are good reasons to believe that the Communists will persevere.**—*CIA report to the White House, 9 January 1967.*[72]

The war of attrition was not reducing enemy numbers faster than the enemy was able to recruit within South Vietnam and infiltrate more troops from North Vietnam.

1233 **There is no evidence of a diminution of Communist will to continue the war. We do not know how long the Communists will remain determined to persist.**—*CIA report to the White House, 9 January 1967.*[72]

The report also indicated pacification efforts were making little progress and the ARVN military capabilities were still poor. U.S. combat efforts to find and fix the enemy were still dependent on the enemy's willingness to engage in combat.

1234 **[Enemy strength estimates were] far too low and should be raised, perhaps doubled to a more realistic level [that] would allow the intelligence community to make a better-informed appraisal of what we are up against and would enable it to grapple more effectively with such nuts and bolts problems as communist manpower allocations, desertion rates, casualties, and logistics.**—*George Carver, CIA Special Assistant for Vietnamese Affairs, in a memorandum to Richard Helms, 11 January 1967.*[72]

Order of Battle figures were calculated based on intelligence gathered in the field from a variety of sources (direct observations, air reconnaissance, photo reconnaissance, captured documents, agent reports, interrogations, etc.). It was an estimate of enemy force capabilities and components.

1235 **If we can't win this war in the Delta, we can't win the war.**—*Unidentified U.S. official in Saigon, to a correspondent, January 1967.*[422]

U.S. units began operations in the Delta in mid–1966, expanding those operations as the war progressed. The Mekong Delta of IV Corps produced more than half the food consumed by South Vietnam's population.

1236 **The days may become months and the months may become years, but we will stay as long as aggression commands us to battle.**—*President Lyndon Johnson, during his State of the Union Address, 12 January 1967.*[374]

1237 **A major portion of the enemy's base and control center for operations against the Capital Military District has been destroyed. This represents the loss of an investment of twenty years.**—*General Jonathan Seaman, Commander, II Field Force, comments on Operation Cedar Falls, January 1967.*[42]

Cedar Falls was conducted in the Iron Triangle, 25 miles northwest of Saigon. Thirty thousand allied troops attempted, unsuccessfully, to bring the 9th VC Division to battle. The VC retreated from the area, then flowed back in after the operation was over.

1238 **[Our self-restraint is] trading American lives for public opinion.**—*Senator Richard B. Russell, Leader of the Senate Armed Services Committee, 1967.*[423]

Russell decried the Johnson administration's policy of target restrictions for U.S. forces in Vietnam. Because of target restrictions and limited rules of engagement U.S. forces were more vulnerable to enemy fire, suffering higher casualty rates.

1239 **I personally [hope] that our leaders have no illusions ... that they do not entertain ambitions going beyond a minimum face-saving roll-back which will permit our withdrawal without undue loss of military prestige. Anything more is wishful thinking, and any attempt to achieve it would be to compound past folly with future folly.**—*Douglas Ramsey, Foreign Service Officer and captive of the Vietcong, in a letter to his parents, January 1967.*[887]

Ramsey was captured by the VC, 17 January 1966, near Trung Lap in III Corps. He was held prisoner until 1973. Before his capture Ramsey worked with John Vann in Hau Nghia Province in the pacification program.

1240 **Our ground forces must take the field on long term, sustained combat operations. We must be prepared to accept heavier casualties in our initial operations and not permit our hesitance to take greater losses to inhibit our tactical aggressiveness. If greater hardships are accepted now we will, in the long run, achieve a military success sooner and at less overall cost in lives and money.**—*Admiral U.S. Grant Sharp, U.S. Navy, Commander in Chief, Pacific, cable to General Westmoreland in Vietnam, January 1967.*[59]

Advising Westmoreland of the importance of increasing operations at the ground level against the VC/NVA.

1241 **We, unintentionally, are killing and wounding three or four times more people than the Vietcong do. ... We are not maniacs and monsters; but our planes range the sky all day and all night and our artillery is lavish, and we have much more deadly stuff to kill with. The people are there on the ground, sometimes destroyed by accident, sometimes destroyed because Vietcong are reported to be among them. This is indeed a new kind of war...**—*From an advertisement posted in The New York Times, 15 January 1967.*[76]

The ad was the work of a group of American lawyers who opposed the escalating destruction in South Vietnam.

1242 **[We should] avoid devoting too great a measure of our effort to anti-infiltration at the expense of more important operations. We should continue and, if possible, expand our air and naval interdiction of his infiltration system.**—*Admiral U.S. Grant Sharp, U.S. Navy, Commander in Chief, Pacific, cable to General Westmoreland in Vietnam, January 1967.*[59]

Sharp wanted to increase the interdiction campaign in Laos and along the coast of South Vietnam.

1243 **We are going to have to be very discriminating with our firepower.**—*General William R. Desorby, Senior American Advisor, IV Corps, in an interview, January 1967.*[422]

The Delta of IV Corps was home to some 5 million Vietnamese; the entire population of Vietnam was around 30,000 people. American firepower had the potential to devastate the civilian population if not carefully controlled.

1244 **These people aren't going to stand up and fight until they have an overwhelming advantage.... They know every inch of every trail; they can cover in 15 minutes what would take us four hours, so they just melt into the heavy woods.**—*Lt.Col. Lewis Goad, battalion commander, 173d Airborne Brigade, to correspondent, January 1967.*[424]

A common VC tactic was not to attack unless they had the advantage in numbers, terrain and or surprise. One of the most difficult parts of the war was engaging the enemy. If he did not want to be found, he was difficult to find.

1245 **It is virtually impossible to stop or appreciably impede infiltration into South Vietnam with ground forces now available or programmed for the theater, especially in light of the contiguous sanctuaries the enemy now enjoys. Although it would be desirable to stop or measurably impede infiltration, such action is not imperative to our winning military victory....**—*Admiral U.S. Grant Sharp, U.S. Navy, Commander in Chief, Pacific, cable to General Westmoreland in Vietnam, January 1967.*[59]

In October 1966 McNamara proposed installing an electronic barrier and monitoring system along the DMZ to counter NVA infiltration. Sharp was pointing out the futility of such a barrier. Westmoreland believed that the only way to close the Ho Chi Minh trail was to put Allied troops across it, which would mean a line of troops from the South China Sea to the Thai border.

1246 **Our air and naval interdiction operations must be continued at the present level and, if possible, they must be expanded. Although not in themselves capable of quelling infiltration, their effects against the enemy and his movement of personnel and equipment to the South are appreciable.**—*Admiral U.S. Grant Sharp, U.S. Navy, Commander in Chief, Pacific, cable to General Westmoreland in Vietnam, January 1967.*[59]

Sharp argued for expansion of the air campaign against North Vietnam and the Ho Chi Minh Trail.

1247 **If our Asian boys had lived up to their American advisers' estimates, we wouldn't be involved in South Vietnam now....**—*Robert Sherrod, correspondent, January 1967.*[424]

In 1964 Johnson believed the South Vietnamese Army would be able to battle the communists, but events proved otherwise. On average, ARVN performance was poor, they lacked discipline and motivation, and most importantly—leadership.

1248 **Our country harbors a natural desire to ease hardships in the Vietnam conflict. The military, however, must press to go all out at all levels in SVN if we are to win.**—*Admiral U.S. Grant Sharp, U.S. Navy, Commander in Chief, Pacific, cable to General Westmoreland in Vietnam, January 1967.*[59]

1249 **What motivates the men who must do the killing? The foremost incentive, I believe, is revenge on the cunning, ruthless enemy who kills a man's friends or blows their legs off with booby traps. This comradeship factor probably has been underestimated in previous wars and should be ranked above flag, honor, duty or Mom's apple pie.**—*Robert Sherrod, correspondent, January 1967.*[424]

Sherrod spent two months in the field with American troops.

1250 **This is not a military war; it's a political war. If the villagers will tell us who the Vietcong are, things will get better.**—*Lt.Col. Lewis Goad, battalion commander, 173d Airborne Brigade, to correspondent, January 1967.*[424]

On average, American troops received little support from the local populace. Those villagers who weren't opposed to the Americans were afraid of retaliation by the Vietcong.

1251 **The only thing to do is kill everybody in the country over five years old.**—*Unidentified U.S. Army private, comments to correspondent, January 1967.*[424]

His opinion was shared by many GIs, practiced by some.

1252 **The official statistics now show for the first time a net decline in both VC main force and North Vietnam army units for the fourth quarter of 1966. This is the first reversal of the upward trend since 1960.**—*Walt Rostow, Special Assistant to the President, in a letter to the President, 20 January 1967.*[72]

Rostow mentioned the debate on actual enemy strength, but overall it was concluded that the total enemy numbers were declining—an indication that America was winning in Vietnam.

1253 **If you count the combat-fatigue factor in World War II as 25 and Korea as five, then the Vietnamese war would be one.**—*Unidentified military psychiatrist commenting to Robert Sherrod, 1967.*[424]

In 1967 morale was considered very good.

1254 **The Pentagon's primary purpose in bombing the North is to restrict the flow of men and supplies to the South. Its secondary hope is that by thus raising the cost of war to Hanoi, we may give Ho Chi Minh enough reason to stop the infiltration, perhaps even to negotiate a truce.**—*Life magazine editorial, 20 January 1967.*[423]

1255 **Hai Phong port facilities and Red River dikes would be much more rewarding targets, but they are off our self-imposed limits, partly to avoid involving Chinese or Russians.**—*Life magazine editorial, 20 January 1967.*[423]

Fear of hitting Soviet or Chinese ships delivering war materiel to North Vietnam via Hai Phong was a major concern during the Johnson targeting sessions. Hitting the dikes would flood much of the Red River Valley, inundating the low-lying cropland for miles around Hanoi, and so were not official targets under consideration.

1256 **The hundred-a-week killed-in-action rate is militarily acceptable (though this is small consolation to those platoons which occasionally must take heavy casualties).**—*Robert Sherrod, journalist, 1967.*[424]

U.S. losses were considered low in comparison to reported enemy losses and the number of American troops incountry.

1257 **What we have achieved in Vietnam is the equivalent of a half-million-man Foreign Legion.**—*Robert Sherrod, journalist, 1967.*[424]

The U.S. Army in Vietnam represented a distinct foreign presence, tolerated by the Vietnamese who were able to profit from the Army's presence, unaccepted by the average Vietnamese.

1258 **If we are to reach an acceptable military decision in Vietnam, we must not permit our operational tactics to reflect the reticence which currently characterizes some bodies of public and official opinion.**—*Admiral U.S. Grant Sharp, U.S. Navy, Commander in Chief, Pacific, cable to General Westmoreland in Vietnam, January 1967.*[59]

Sharp was pressing for a military solution to the war.

1259 **Pretty soon we'll have the country paved over. Then we won't have to worry about it any more.**—*Unidentified U.S. Navy sailor in My Tho, January 1967.*[424]

1260 **[Correspondent]—Doesn't the bombing sometimes kill civilians?**

[Sergeant]—What does it matter? They're all Vietnamese.—*Unidentified American Sergeant, from comments to correspondent, 1967.*[292]

1261 **Charlie may be little, but he carries a big gun.**—*Tony de Vargas, Corporal U.S. Marine Corps, to reporter, January 1967.*[424]

1262 **Our men may die, but our children will carry on. We can take it.**—*Dang Doan, Senior Captain commanding a battalion of the 2d Vietcong Regiment, to correspondent, January 1967.*[424]

1263 **Your mission is to help the Vietnamese people and to defeat the enemy. Never before in history have soldiers been called upon to help build a nation while fighting.**—*General William Westmoreland, American commander in Vietnam, speaking to newly arrived troops, January 1967.*[424]

American troops were involved in nation building while at the same time fighting the communist. It was indeed a double edged sword. In previous American wars the enemy was defeated, then the nation rebuilt.

1264 **Only the United States would undertake this thing [civilian education and training programs]. The diplomats here think we're nuts. But we had to start somewhere.**—*William Porter, U.S. Deputy Ambassador, January 1967.*[424]

Porter was in charge of the American effort to train and educate Vietnamese civilians. Because of cultural attitudes of the Vietnamese, the programs were not very successful.

1265 **General Westmoreland, there are 15 million people in South Vietnam. We put that many people in uniform in World War II. Why not mobilize enough troops to give every South Vietnamese a personal American bodyguard?**—*Facetious reporter, to General William Westmoreland, January 1967.*[424]

1266 **I find this the most hateful war we have ever fought. Surely, we never would have got into it if we had known how deep was the well, but we are the victims of one tragic miscalculation after another. We find ourselves supporting a government of mandarins with little basis of popular support, fighting for an army that has little inclination to do its own fighting.**—*Robert Sherrod, reporting in a Life magazine article, 27 January 1967.*[850]

1267 **There is no substitute, in a matter of this kind, for the President's personal, lonely judgment.**—*Clark Clifford, unofficial adviser to the President, in a conversation with Walt Rostow, January 1967.*[72]

President Johnson instructed Rostow to convene a secret committee to independently evaluate the air campaign against

North Vietnam, i.e., seek outside advice. Clifford believed such a secret committee to be a mistake. It would indicate to the world the uncertainty of the President and his lack of trust in his Secretary of Defense and the Joint Chiefs of Staff.

1268 **I wish we had the North Vietnamese on our side....**—*Unidentified American civilian political officer, January 1967.*[424]

As a rule, the North Vietnamese were perceived as better workers, less likely to be lazy, and more structure and discipline oriented.

1269 **There is only one Vietnam nation. There is only one Vietnamese People.... Therefore when the Americans come to Vietnam, it is the duty of the Vietnamese people to throw them out of the country. They come here as aggressors. They come to invade Vietnam ... the Vietnamese people are determined to chase them out of the country, to liberate the South and to unify the nation.**—*NLF propaganda phrase, from an enemy interview, January 1967.*[10]

This was taught in NLF schools in their controlled areas, and repeated in hamlets across the country during propaganda sessions.

1270 **[The resumption of the bombing of North Vietnam] may become the first in a series of steps on a road from which there is no turning back — a road that leads to catastrophe for all mankind.**—*Senator Robert Kennedy of New York, from a speech, 31 January 1967.*[374]

Kennedy feared the war in Vietnam would continue to escalate, eventually drawing Red China and possibly the Soviet Union into direct conflict with the United States. He supported a complete halt to the bombing of North Vietnam, breaking with President Johnson's decision to resume the bombing after a 37-day pause (December 1966–January 1967).

1271 **The agrarian nature of [North Vietnam's] economy precludes an economic collapse as a result of the bombing.**—*Robert McNamara, Secretary of Defense, from statement to Congress, 1 February 1967.*[159]

1272 **Prime Minister, I think you've made it. This is going to be the biggest diplomatic coup of this century.**—*David Bruce, American Ambassador to Great Britain, speaking to Prime Minister Harold Wilson, February 1967.*[479]

In 1967 Prime Minister Harold Wilson worked secretly with Soviet Premier Aleksei Kosygin to bring the U.S. and North Vietnam into negotiations. Wilson worked with Bruce as his contact to the Johnson administration, while Kosygin worked through his sources to Hanoi. After several meetings, tentative agreement was reached that the U.S. would extend the 1967 TET bombing halt. In exchange North Vietnam would agree to stop moving troops into South Vietnam. When there was proof of this stop in the infiltration, the U.S. would stop sending additional troops to Vietnam.

1273 **The authorities in Washington were suffering from a degree of confusion about possible and unfortunate juxtaposition of certain parts of their anatomy, one of which was their elbow.**—*Prime Minister Harold Wilson, commenting on secret peace feelers, February 1967.*[479]

Wilson's paraphrasing of his response to the sudden change in Washington's direction. Wilson and Kosygin worked out a secret deal between the U.S. and North Vietnam, based on terms the U.S. and North Vietnam would agree to in order to facilitate peace negotiations. Wilson and Kosygin had worked out the details, but at the last minute there was a change in the terms from Washington. The hawks advising the President insisted that the infiltration by North Vietnam had to cease and become public knowledge before the negotiations could begin. Prior to this the terms were that the bombing halt would be extended (February 1967) and Hanoi would secretly insure that infiltration South would stop (verifiable by the U.S.). The U.S. in turn would not reinforce its troops in South Vietnam.

1274 **We call ourselves CADRE. We speak of squads, escalation, campaigns. The terminology is no accident — it fits our attitude. We are no longer interested in merely protesting the war; we are out to stop it.**—*Gary Rader, anti-war activist, from a report on the Chicago Area Draft Resistance, 1967.*[743]

1275 **Despite our many successful spoiling attacks and base area searches, and despite the heavy interdiction campaign in North Vietnam and Laos, VC/NVA combat capability and offensive activity throughout 1966 and now in 1967 has been increasing steadily, with the January 1967 level some two and one-half times above the average of the first three months in 1966.**—*General Earle Wheeler, Chairman Joint Chiefs of Staff, in a cable to General Westmoreland and Admiral Sharp, February 1967.*[72]

Wheeler was responding to the end-of-year enemy initiated action report from MACV, which after one and one-half years of reports indicating enemy numbers and incidents of attack were declining suddenly jumped up.

1276 **Whatever one may think of the "domino theory," it is beyond question that without the American commitment in Vietnam, Asia would be a far different place today.**—*Richard Nixon, former Vice President, commenting to the press, 1967.*[320]

1277 **The North Vietnamese could not be expected to abandon the South or to stop all movement of supplies to the South, for it would imperil the security of 100,000 of their fighting men there.**—*Aleksei Kosygin, Premier of the Soviet Union, as repeated by Prime Minister Harold Wilson, February 1967.*[479]

Kosygin and Wilson secretly worked to bring the U.S. and Hanoi to negotiations. Just as they neared agreement on terms to be met for negotiations to begin, the White House changed the terms they would accept to initiate the negotiations. Washington set a time limit as to when Hanoi had to agree to stop sending troops and supplies South. The time limit was in a matter of hours. Wilson and Kosygin considered this time limit insufficient for Hanoi to react, and they were correct. Hanoi did not respond and the U.S. resumed the bombing of North Vietnam following the February (TET 1967) bombing halt. This represented the first time Kosygin or any other communist leader had quoted the number of NVA troops in South Vietnam. Note that Hanoi continued to insist that they had no troops in South Vietnam.

1278 **This "Korean trauma" of American military planning in Viet Nam was utterly disastrous, for it created a road-bound, over-motorized, hard-to-supply battle force totally**

incapable of besting the real enemy on his own ground.—*Bernard Fall, historian and writer, 1967.*[14]

Initial American training of the South Vietnamese army was in large unit tactics, similar to the training American units underwent for Europe. Large unit tactics were not effective against small enemy guerrilla forces.

1279 **You have worked nobly this week to bring about what all humanity wants: a decisive move towards peace. It is an effort that will be long remembered. I feel a responsibility to give you this further chance to make that effort bear fruit....**—*President Lyndon Johnson in a telegram to Prime Minister Harold Wilson, February 1967.*[479]

Kosygin and Wilson secretly worked to bring the U.S. and Hanoi into negotiations. Just as they neared agreement on terms to be met for negotiations to begin, the White House changed the terms they would accept to initiate the negotiations. Washington set a time limit as to when Hanoi had to agree to stop sending troops and supplies South. Hanoi had to notify the U.S. directly or through the Wilson and Kosygin connection of their willingness to agree to the stated American terms. The time limit was in a matter of hours. Kosygin passed the U.S. proposal (Kosygin called it an ultimatum) on to Hanoi. Wilson and Kosygin considered this time limit insufficient for Hanoi to react, and they were correct. Hanoi did not respond and the U.S. resumed the bombing of North Vietnam following the February (TET 1967) bombing halt.

1280 **Wastefully, expensively, but nonetheless indisputably, we are winning the war in the South. Few of our programs—civil or military—are very efficient but we are grinding the enemy down by sheer weight and mass. And the cumulative impact of all we have set in motion is beginning to tell.**—*Robert Komer, Special Assistant to the President, February 1967*[185]

Komer's view of the war was decidedly different than McNamara's even though they had both visited South Vietnam within the same six month period, late-1965 and early-1967. Komer became the head of CORDS, the U.S. pacification effort in South Vietnam, and was publicly optimistic about the progress of the war.

1281 **I am prepared to order a cessation of bombing against your country and the stopping of further augmentation of U.S. forces in South Vietnam as soon as I am assured that infiltration into South Vietnam by land and by sea has been stopped.**—*President Johnson, in a secret letter to Ho Chi Minh, 8 February 1967.*[726]

The letter sent during the 8–12 February bombing pause. This phrase has been interpreted by some to mean that Hanoi had to abandon its troops in South Vietnam before the U.S. would stop the bombing. The letter was delivered to the North Vietnamese embassy in Moscow, while other Administration officials were talking to Wilson and Kosygin about what it would take to get peace negotiations going. In effect the U.S. was sending mixed signals.

1282 **We must know the military consequences of such a military action [bombing halt] on our part. They must not expect us to stop our military action by bombing while they continue their military action by invasion.**—*Dean Rusk, Secretary of State, to the press, 9 February 1967.*[760]

Rusk was responding to questions of whether the U.S. would consider a bombing halt without a reciprocal commitment from North Vietnam. Hanoi demanded a halt in the bombing before they would consider talking peace, but they made no mention of stopping or reducing their support for their war effort in the South.

1283 **The object of this [operation] is not to kill Viet Cong. It is to remove the population from the enemy's control.**—*Comments from an American infantry officer during Operation Cedar Falls, January 1967.*[1021]

Part of the operation involved the relocation of the 6,000 inhabitants of the village of Ben Suc, located in the Iron Triangle northwest of Saigon. After the people and their livestock were removed the village was leveled and the tunnel complex beneath it destroyed.

1284 **The Vietnamese people will never submit to force; they will never accept talks under the threat of bombs.**—*Ho Chi Minh, President, Democratic Republic of Vietnam, in a letter to President Johnson, 10 February 1967.*[927]

Ho was responding to President Johnson's offer to stop the bombing of North Vietnam in exchange for Hanoi's agreement to open negotiations.

1285 **Despite the deeply held differences in the attitudes of the major participants, the gap is not unbridgeable, given a realistic appreciation of the political and military factors involved and above all given a belief on each side that the other desires a negotiated settlement.**—*Harold Wilson, British Prime Minister, speaking before the House of Commons, 13 February 1967.*[538]

Wilson and Soviet Premier Aleksei N. Kosygin attempted to secretly broker the initiation of talks between Hanoi and the U.S. The plan fell through because of the inflexibility of both Hanoi and the U.S.

1286 **At no time was the draft message [Hilsman Cable] ever discussed with me, shown to me, or concurred in by me ... [the cable was] ill-conceived, ill-timed, and inadequately coordinated.**—*Marshall Carter, Deputy Director Central Intelligence, in a memorandum, 1967.*[195]

Carter was reacting to a Roger Hilsman book published in 1967. Carter denounced reference in the book to CIA approval/agreement in the forming of the "Hilsman Cable." The cable told Ambassador Lodge to pass on approval of America's tacit support for a South Vietnamese military junta which planned to overthrow the Diem regime. The coup generals wanted American support before they moved against Diem.

1287 **Despite our efforts and those of third parties, no other response has yet to come from Hanoi. In fairness to our troops and those of our allies, we have no alternative but to resume full-scale hostilities after the cease-fire period.**—*President Lyndon Johnson, in a press statement, 13 February 1967.*[538]

Bombing of North Vietnam and combat in general was suspended in recognition of the Vietnamese TET holiday. The truce started 7 February and was due to expire 11 February. The truce was extended in support of attempts made by the British Prime Minister and the Soviet Premier to coordinate the initiation of peace talks between the U.S. and Hanoi. When these attempts broke down the U.S. resumed normal combat operations in the face of increased infiltration and actions by the NVA and the VC.

1288 **It's almost impossible to throw a net they can't exfiltrate through. Whatever they do, we've got to go into these [enemy] base areas and make them useless. It's a damned rough game.**—*Unidentified military planner, 173d Airborne Brigade, February 1967.*[425]

Commenting on Operation Junction City in which elements of the 1st, 4th, 9th, 25th, Infantry Divisions, 196th, and 173d Brigades, and the 11th Armored Cavalry cordoned off War Zone C and attempted to pin the enemy in the area. Expected large scale battles with the enemy did not take place as most enemy units slipped from the area rather than engage U.S. forces.

1289 **The President has never defined our national purpose except in the vaguest, most ambiguous generalities about aggression and freedom. Gestures, propaganda, public relations, and bombing and more bombing will not work.**—*Walter Lippmann, Washington newspaper columnist, February 1967.*[374]

1290 **Vietnam is situated thousands of miles from the United States. The Vietnamese people have never done any harm to the United States.**—*Ho Chi Minh, President of the Democratic Republic of Vietnam in a letter to President Johnson, 15 February 1967.*[850]

Ho's response to Johnson's peace feeler, based on stopping the infiltration and supply of its troops in South Vietnam. In return, the U.S. would stop bombing North Vietnam and not send more U.S. troops to South Vietnam.

1291 **The division of the country [over Vietnam] will simply grow as the casualties and costs increase, and the attainment of our aims and the end of the fighting continues to elude us.**—*Walter Lippmann, Washington newspaper columnist, February 1967.*[374]

1292 **If President John F. Kennedy were alive today he would be doing exactly what the Johnson administration is doing at this very hour.**—*Hubert Humphrey, Vice President, in a speech at Stanford University, California, 20 February 1967.*[788]

1293 **[Preventing a communist victory in Vietnam has been] the great and central achievement of these last two years. The fact that South Vietnam has not been lost and is not going to be lost is a fact of truly massive importance in the history of Asia, the Pacific, and the U.S.**—*McGeorge Bundy, Special Assistant to the President for National Security Affairs, writing in 1967.*[713]

1294 **It is estimated that we spend $322,000 for every enemy we kill [in Vietnam], while we spend in the so-called war on poverty in America only about $53 for each person classified as "poor."**—*Reverend Martin Luther King, religious leader and civil rights activist, speaking at a meeting in Los Angeles, 25 February 1967.*[844]

1295 **Today we're not just reading history—we're making it.**—*PFC William D. Kuhl, 2d Battalion, 503d Airborne, to correspondent, February 1967.*[425]

First U.S. combat jump of the Vietnam War, by 2/503/173d Airborne Brigade, during Operation Junction City.

1296 **We must combine the furor of the civil rights movement with the peace movement. We must demonstrate, teach and preach until the very foundations of our nation are shaken.**—*Reverend Martin Luther King, religious leader and civil rights activist, speaking at a meeting in Los Angeles, 25 February 1967.*[844]

King, declaring that the civil rights movement and the war on poverty should join with the peace/anti-war movement to end the war in Vietnam and use the money at home.

1297 **Peace was in our grasp.**—*British Prime Minister Harold Wilson, in comments in London, February 1967.*[722]

Wilson, reflecting on secret attempts between Soviet Premier Alexei Kosygin and himself to establish a meeting between the U.S. and Hanoi. Wilson believed the Johnson administration missed an opportunity when they resumed bombing 13 February 1967. During the halt there were exchanges between Washington and London and between the Soviets (Kosygin) and Hanoi. North Vietnam would not consider negotiations unless the U.S. ended bombing. The U.S. paused the bombing to see if they got a positive reaction form Hanoi; when they did not, the bombing resumed. The reasoning from Hanoi was the U.S. bombing had to stop, not pause, before any negotiations could be considered.

1298 **Our men are there because of aggression from the North, and in accordance with a treaty commitment approved by the United States Senate with only one negative vote.**—*Dean Rusk, Secretary of State, in a Department of State Bulletin, 28 Febuary 67.*[243]

Rusk was speaking about the SEATO Treaty.

1299 **The size of the problem in Vietnam will diminish, and fewer U.S. resources will be needed.**—*Robert Komer, Special Assistant to the President, during a White House meeting, 1 March 1967.*[238]

1300 **The armies of the United States have, through conscription, already oppressed or destroyed the lives and consciences of millions of Americans and Vietnamese.**—*Policy statement from an organized group of Cornell University students opposed to the draft, 2 March 1967.*[730]

The Cornell group opposed the war in Vietnam and the draft.

1301 **It should be clear by now that the bombing of the North cannot bring an end to the war in the South; that, indeed, it may well prolong that war.**—*Senator Robert Kennedy, from a speech on the Senate floor, 2 March 1967.*[762]

1302 **The opposition to President Johnson [on the war] has its active center in his own party.**—*Walter Lippmann, Washington columnist, March 1967.*[850]

Some Democrats within the party wanted to oppose Johnson in the 1968 Presidential election but found it difficult to do without splitting the party, thus giving an advantage to the Republicans. They were stuck at the time with backing Johnson and his policies in order to maintain control. Democratic opposition to the war was stymied because the rules of the party stipulated that the incumbent President would not be denied the nomination of his party, if he wanted the nomination.

1303 **It would be too much to say that our side scents victory, but there is certainly no atmosphere of defeat or impending disaster.**—*George Carver, Special Assistant for Vietnamese Affairs, CIA, in a memorandum, 2 March 1967.*[314]

1304 **The bombing of North Vietnam makes the war more costly and difficult for North Vietnam. It is harsh punishment indeed.**—*Senator Robert Kennedy, from a speech on the Senate floor, 2 March 1967.*[763]

Kennedy proposed an indefinite bombing halt and that the Johnson administration immediately enter into peace negotiations with Hanoi.

1305 **We have argued and demonstrated to stop this destruction. We have not succeeded. Murderers do not respond to reason. Powerful resistance is now demanded: radical, illegal, unpleasant and sustained.**—*Policy statement from an organized group of Cornell University students opposed to the draft, 2 March 1967.*[730]

The group opposed the draft and its direct tie to the war in Vietnam.

1306 **[Only such a government can tap the long-ignored but desperately needed] rich wellsprings of leadership inherent in the Vietnamese people.**—*Edward G. Lansdale, Special Assistant to Ambassador Lodge, speaking to the press, March 1967.*[428]

Referring to the Ky-Thieu government, the improving economy in South Vietnam, and the stability of the current government. The Ky-Thieu government was in its 21st month of control without a coup.

1307 **We are in the wrong place, fighting the wrong war.**—*Senator Mike Mansfield of Montana, March 1967.*[374]

Mansfield was commenting on the possibility of the war escalating again, based on leaked reports of General Westmoreland's request for additional troops for Vietnam.

1308 **[There could be no talks until the United States stopped bombing] and all other acts of war ... definitely and unconditionally.**—*Ho Chi Minh, President of the Democratic Republic of Vietnam (North Vietnam), March 1967.*[427]

This was Ho's reply to a secret letter from Johnson offering to stop the bombing of North Vietnam and stop U.S. troop reinforcements if Ho stopped infiltration of men and supplies into South Vietnam. Johnson sent the letter in secret; Ho made Johnson's letter and his reply public.

1309 **I do not favor a [draft] lottery.**—*Representative L. Mendel Rivers of South Carolina, during an interview, 6 March 1967.*[539]

Rivers was reacting to a proposed plan by President Johnson to set up the national draft lottery. Some in Congress balked at the plan, complaining that it was Congress' constitutional duty to raise and maintain military forces.

1310 **The American Government [is] ... trying to camouflage its aggressive intentions, it hastened to set forth ultimatums that were absolutely unacceptable to the Vietnamese people.**—*Aleksei N. Kosygin, Soviet Premier, speaking in Moscow, 6 March 1967.*[540]

Kosygin and British Prime Minister Harold Wilson attempted to broker a secret agreement between Hanoi and Washington to initiate peace talks. Hanoi demanded an unconditional halt to all attacks against North Vietnam, and the U.S. insisted that Hanoi agree to show some outward sign that they would reduce or stop the flow of men and materiel into South Vietnam if the U.S. halted bombing of North Vietnam.

1311 **We do not yet have the answer [to the war].**—*President Lyndon Johnson, from a speech in Guam, March 1967.*[427]

During the bomb halt for the 1967 TET holiday, North Vietnam increased their rate of infiltration and supply South. This was taken into account at the Guam talks between the U.S. and South Vietnam, resulting in an increase in U.S. bombing of North Vietnam.

1312 **I chase every peace feeler just like my little beagle chases a squirrel.**—*President Lyndon Johnson, as quoted by Hugh Sidey, Life magazine, 17 February 1967.*[426]

Life magazine reader Herbert Gans in "Letters to the Editor," made the point that beagles do not chase squirrels with an intent to negotiate. He was responding to the quote in Sidey's piece, "The Presidency."

1313 **If these figures [enemy initiated actions] should reach the public domain, they would, literally, blow the lid off of Washington. Please do whatever is necessary to insure these figures are not repeated nor released to news media or otherwise exposed to public knowledge...**—*General Earle Wheeler, Chairman Joint Chiefs of Staff, in a cable to General Westmoreland, 11 March 1967.*[72]

The military was under pressure from the White House to show progress in Vietnam and the system used was the numbers generated for the enemy order of battle. Emphasis was placed on the body count which the military perceived as a direct indicator of progress against the enemy. Also factored in were desertions/defectors, captures, as well as the number of friendly and enemy initiated contacts. Washington had the impression that things were improving in Vietnam based on the numbers submitted by MACV—the CIA Order of Battle numbers indicated otherwise.

1314 **Their proud looks at Guam said: We have done what we said we would, even though many people thought it was impossible.**—*President Lyndon Johnson, speaking at the Guam Conference, March 1967.*[53]

Johnson was praising the Ky-Thieu government for completion of a constitution for South Vietnam and the scheduling of their country's first free elections. During the Honolulu Conference in 1966 Ky and Thieu promised the world that South Vietnam would soon have a new constitution and free elections. The media and political experts had been skeptical.

1315 **[It is vital to] saturate the minds of the people with some socially conscious and attractive ideology, which is susceptible of being carried out.**—*Henry Cabot Lodge, Jr., American Ambassador to South Vietnam, to President Johnson, March 1967.*[36]

The ideology Lodge spoke of was never defined. But the communists followed a similar vein using communism and nationalism as the ideology of choice.

1316 **If present trends continue I think we might arrive at the cross-over point. Perhaps this month or next month ... by the cross-over point I mean where their loses are greater**

than their gains.—*General William Westmoreland, ComUSMACV, to President Johnson, March 1967.*[72]

Westmoreland's reports to the JCS indicated the enemy numbers were growing steadily. This exchange with Johnson indicated a brighter outlook for the war of attrition against the enemy. The cross-over indicated that Hanoi would be losing more troops than they could supply through infiltration or recruitment within South Vietnam.

1317 **[Ky]—Those [North Vietnamese airfields] are the targets that should be bombed.**

[Johnson]—Mac, tell the Vice President why we can't bomb those airfields.

[McNamara]—We studied the possibility but the trouble is that those fields are extremely well defended by flak and if we tried to attack them we would suffer enormously heavy losses.—*Exchange between Nguyen Cao Ky, President Johnson, Robert McNamara, during the Guam Conference, March 1967.*[629]

Ky wanted to bomb several North Vietnamese air bases from which MiGs operated. Later in the war, under Nixon, these bases were destroyed.

1318 **America is committed to the defense of South Vietnam until an honorable peace can be negotiated.**—*President Lyndon Johnson, speaking in Nashville, Tennessee, 15 March 1967.*[185]

1319 **[We are] ready tomorrow as need be to send a volunteer army into North Vietnam if Hanoi made such a request.** —*Chou En-Lai, Premier of the People's Republic of China, during a Chicago Daily News interview, March 1967.*[73]

This was the Chinese reaction to media talk of the need for an invasion of North Vietnam to cut the supply of men and materiel feeding into South Vietnam. The interview was released in May 1967. When the interview was made public the Red Chinese Foreign Minister denied such an interview was ever conducted.

1320 **The conclusion seems inescapable that the effort to maintain an approximation of the American standard of living in the Army and even in the combat zones diverted an excessive amount of manpower away from the essential combat units of the Army.**—*Russell F. Weigley, historian, from his writings, 1967.*[712]

The tooth-to-tail ratio for American troops was approximately 1:5-8, that is, 5-8 support troops were required for each combat soldier in the field. The ratio for World War II was about 1:4. The result was that even though there were more than 500,000 U.S. troops in Vietnam less than 70,000 were in the field available for maneuvering against the enemy.

1321 **Military success alone will not achieve the U.S. objectives in Vietnam. Political, economic and psychological victory is equally important, and support of Revolutionary Development (RD) program is mandatory. The basic precept for the role of the military support of Revolutionary Development is to provide a secure environment for the population so the civil aspects of RD can progress.**—*General William Westmoreland, in a memorandum to Secretary of Defense McNamara, 18 March 1967.*[185]

Westmoreland planned to request additional troops, bringing the number to more than 670,000. His plan was to use U.S. troops to expel NVA/VC troops from South Vietnam while ARVN troops focused on nation building and internal security (elimination of the VC).

1322 **There's a lot of plain and fancy screwing going on around here, but I suppose it's all in the interest of the war effort.**—*Ellsworth Bunker, Ambassador to South Vietnam, in comments to a correspondent, 1967.*[887]

Bunker's reflections on the loose sexual mores that, for many, typified the war in Vietnam.

1323 **Our operations were primarily holding actions characterized by border surveillance, reconnaissance to locate enemy forces, and spoiling attacks to disrupt the enemy offensive. As a result of our buildup and successes, we were able to plan and initiate a general offensive. We now have gained the tactical initiative, and are conducting continuous small and occasional large-scale offensive operations to decimate the enemy forces; to destroy enemy base areas and disrupt his infrastructure; to interdict his land and water LOC's and to convince him, through the vigor of our offensive and accompanying psychological operations, that he faces inevitable defeat.**—*General William Westmoreland, in a memorandum to Secretary of Defense McNamara, 18 March 1967.*[185]

Westmoreland was projecting that the battlefield successes of 1966 would continue into 1967 and 1968.

1324 **If victory is not in sight, it is on the way.**—*Walt Rostow, Special Assistant to the President, in a letter to the President, 18 March 1967.*[72]

Rostow was very optimistic about the war effort.

1325 **The graduated use of military force, which has been an essential characteristic of our strategy, has compounded the difficulties of explaining to our people what we were doing [in Vietnam] and why it takes so long.**—*General Maxwell Taylor, special consultant to the President, 1967.*[713]

The strategy of graduated response was a strategy of reaction, with the U.S. reacting to the VC/NVA. This effectively took the initiative away from America, allowing the enemy to determine where and when a particular battle might take place.

1326 **[Bombing] had not stopped infiltration, but no one ever thought it would. It had made Communist infiltration immensely more difficult and costly for the Communists and also exerted a constant pressure on the North Vietnamese regime.**—*Admiral U.S. Grant Sharp, Commander, Pacific, speaking at the Guam Conference, March 1967.*[72]

Sharp was arguing against any future bombing pauses, indicating that the bombing had been successful, given the limited scope it encompassed.

1327 **If you can get your friends to come to the table at this point I think I can get mine.**—*British Prime Minister Harold Wilson, in a suggestion to Soviet Premier Aleksei Kosygin, February 1967.*[452]

Wilson and Kosygin attempted to bring the U.S. and Hanoi together but failed. Wilson was to represent the U.S. and Kosygin represented Hanoi.

1328 **[The Vietcong are] on the run and North Vietnam's supply system [is] in near paralysis.**—*Nguyen Cao Ky, Premier, South Vietnam, comments to the press, Guam, 21 March 1967.*[542]

President Johnson met with South Vietnamese government leaders on Guam to discuss progress of the war and future plans. In press releases the GVN and President Johnson indicated progress in the war against the communists and progress in stabilizing the government in Saigon.

1329 **I am greatly impressed by the fact that the Chieu Hoi [desertion] figures have remained over 1,000 per week for 5 weeks. If it can be sustained for say, 6 months, I find it hard to believe that the VC infrastructure can hold up.**—*Walt Rostow, Special Assistant to the President, in a memorandum to the President, 22 March 1967.*[72]

Many members of the Administration were working with numbers indicating the enemy infiltration rate South was 7,000 men a month. In reality the figure was much higher.

1330 **It was a sheer physical impossibility to keep him [the enemy] from slipping away whenever he wished if he were in terrain with which he was familiar — the jungle is usually just too thick and too widespread to hope ever to keep him from getting away; thus the option to fight was usually his.**—*General Bernard Rogers, 25th Infantry Division, in his after-action report, March 1967.*[26]

One of the major problems for American combat units was forcing the enemy to stand his ground. On those occasions when the enemy did not slip away or was unable to retreat, he was pounded by artillery and air strikes, often resulting in major casualties.

1331 **MACV's success (which means the success of the United States and of all of us) will ... willy-nilly, be judged not so much on the brilliant performance of the U.S. troops as on its success in getting ARVN, RF and PF quickly to function as a first-class counter-terror, counter-guerrilla force.**—*Henry Cabot Lodge, U.S. Ambassador to South Vietnam, in a message to President Johnson, March 1967.*[876]

1332 **With respect to the enemy ... we found most of them dedicated, well-disciplined, persistent, tenacious, and courageous, often displaying more "guts" than sense.**—*General Bernard Rogers, 25th Infantry Division, in his after-action report, for Operation Cedar Falls, March 1967.*[26]

Operation Cedar Falls was conducted in the Iron Triangle in January 1967.

1333 **There is legitimate and growing hope that the long-awaited "light at the end of the tunnel" has begun to glimmer.**—*Life magazine editorial, 31 March 1967.*[428]

Life reported that military situation in South Vietnam had improved, the nation's economy had begun to stabilize, and the Saigon government had gone 21 months without a coup, and Saigon had formed a new constitution. The "light at the end of the tunnel" was the point at which North Vietnam would actively enter into peace negotiations. It was also looked upon by the military as the point where the end of the war was near, with a U.S. victory at the end of that tunnel.

1334 **We're up against an enemy who just may have found a dangerously clever strategy for licking the United States ... to wait us out, keeping their losses at a level low enough to be sustained indefinitely, but high enough to tempt us to increase our forces to the point of U.S. public rejection of the war.**—*Alain Enthoven, Assistant Secretary of Defense, in a memorandum to Robert McNamara, April 1967.*[374]

1335 **We have hurt them [North Vietnam] with our bombing, and we can hurt them more. But we can't hurt them so badly as to destroy their society or, more to the point, their hope, not only for regaining the material things they sacrifice today, but the whole of South Vietnam.**—*Alain Enthoven, Assistant Secretary of Defense, in a memorandum to Robert McNamara, April 1967.*[72]

North Vietnam was determined to reunite North and South Vietnam under communist rule from Hanoi.

1336 **I would encourage all ministers of draft age to give up their ministerial exemptions and seek status as conscientious objectors....**—*Reverend Martin Luther King, Jr., religious leader and civil rights activist, speaking at Riverside Church, 4 April 1967.*[767]

1337 **We'll just go on bleeding them until Hanoi wakes up to the fact that they have bled their country to the point of national disaster for generations.**—*General William Westmoreland, ComUSMACV, comments, April 1967.*[887]

Westmoreland directed the Marines to establish a series of fire support bases along the DMZ to counter North Vietnam moves south across the DMZ into South Vietnam. Westmoreland believed the enemy attrition rate would significantly rise as NVA troops moving south were engaged by the Marines along the DMZ.

1338 **With the [American] troops now in country, we are not going to lose, but progress will be slowed down. This is not an encouraging outlook, but it is a realistic one.**—*General William Westmoreland, ComUSMACV, to President Johnson, April 1967.*[59]

1339 **The most careful, self-limited air war in history.**—*President Lyndon Johnson, comments to the press, 1967.*[374]

One of Johnson's rebuttals to claims by correspondent Harrison Salisbury, that U.S. bombing of North Vietnam was causing wide spread civilian damage and casualties. Salisbury visited North Vietnam in late-1966 and reported on the conditions he was shown by his North Vietnamese guides.

1340 **Nobody, but nobody!, badmouths the Jolly Greens — unless he wants to get five propelled by an outraged right arm in his teeth.**—*Frank Harvey, free-lance writer and correspondent, 1967.*[249]

Jolly Green crews (HH-3/HH-53) were highly respected throughout Vietnam for their dedication in retrieving down aircraft crews, even in bad weather or heavy enemy fire.

1341 **We are fighting a war of attrition in Southeast Asia.**—*General William Westmoreland, ComUSMACV, to President Johnson, April 1967.*[59]

Westmoreland's strategy from the beginning had been to make the war so costly for Hanoi that they would reconsider their aggression.

1342 **Somehow this madness must cease. We must stop now.... I speak for the poor of America who are paying the double price of smashed hopes at home and death and corruption in Vietnam. The great initiative in this war is ours. The initiative to stop it must be ours....**—*Reverend Martin*

Luther King, Jr., religious leader and civil rights activist, speaking at Riverside Church, 4 April 1967.[844]

1343 **We fly a limited aircraft, drop limited ordnance, on rare targets in a severely limited amount of time. Worst of all, we do all this in a limited and highly unpopular war. ... All theories aside, what I've got is personal pride pushing against a tangled web of frustration.**—*Lt. Eliot Tozer III, U.S. Navy A-4 pilot, from his diary, 1967.*[148]

Tozer was expressing his frustration at the air campaign waged against North Vietnam. He was not alone in his views. Target restrictions, narrow rules of engagement, the weather, and operational controls were but a few of the factors that made the Rolling Thunder campaign difficult for American pilots.

1344 **[Without additional forces] we will not be in danger of being defeated, but it will be nip and tuck to oppose the reinforcements the enemy is capable of providing.**—*General William Westmoreland, ComUSMACV, to President Johnson, April 1967.*[59]

Westmoreland sought an additional 200,000 troops over the next two years (1968–1969). He wanted 100,000 troops immediately to allow him to go on the offensive against the enemy, with the additional troops to follow in 1969.

1345 **Hanoi is betting that we'll lose public support in the United States before we can build a nation in South Vietnam.**—*Alain Enthoven, Assistant Secretary of Defense, in a memorandum to Robert McNamara, April 1967.*[72]

The weak, ineffectual government in Saigon had to be built up to the point that the South Vietnamese people had confidence in their government, and at the same time the VC/NVA had to be kept from overrunning the country.

1346 **Honestly, if I had to confront this problem I would be a conscientious objector. I would not even serve as a chaplain.** —*Reverend Martin Luther King, Jr., religious leader and civil rights activist, at a news conference in New York, 4 April 1967.*[844]

Reverend King's view of the problem of participating in the Vietnam War.

1347 **Ho Chi Minh is a tough old S.O.B., and he won't quit no matter how much bombing we do.**—*Robert McNamara, Secretary of Defense, 1967.*[286]

The air campaign against North Vietnam had not forced Hanoi into negotiations, nor had it stopped NVA infiltration of supplies and manpower into South Vietnam. McNamara had come to believe increased bombing and more U.S. troops would not significantly change the situation in Vietnam.

1348 **As we [clergymen] counsel young men concerning military service we must clarify for them our nation's role in Vietnam and challenge them with the alternative of conscientious objection.... I recommend it to all who find the American course in Vietnam a dishonorable and unjust one.**—*Reverend Martin Luther King, Jr., religious leader and civil rights activist, speaking at Riverside Church, 4 April 1967.*[767]

King, actively telling his followers not to support the government's Vietnam War policy.

1349 **What I was trying to find out was how the hell the war went on year after year after year when we stopped the infiltration or shrunk it and when we had very high body count and so on. It just didn't make sense.**—*Robert McNamara, Secretary of Defense, April 1967.*[72]

The infiltration rate and enemy troop totals were higher than reported to Washington via the military reporting channels.

1350 **I must be concerned for the thousands of our men in Vietnam, many of whom, I am sure, are just as opposed to this war, philosophically, as you are.**—*Judge Harold Tyler, Jr., during sentencing of David Miller for refusing his draft card, 6 April 1967.*[771]

Miller burned his first draft card in public then refused a new one. Judge Tyler sentenced him to 2.5 years in federal prison.

1351 **The Hanoi leaders may be holding out in the desperate hope that America will tire of the struggle, that our purpose will falter, that disillusionment and discord here at home will somehow induce us to abandon our friends and dishonor our commitments by pulling back or pulling out. That is a false hope and I for one will not contribute to it....**—*George Romney, Governor of Michigan, from a speech, 7 April 1967.*[774]

Romney was a moderate Republican and though he opposed the President, he did not want to stand out as being the only major republican in opposition to the war effort.

1352 **Every man of human convictions must decide on the protest that best suits his convictions, but we must all protest.**—*Reverend Martin Luther King, Jr., religious leader and civil rights activist, speaking at Riverside Church, 4 April 1967.*[767]

1353 **[Romney] deserves the gratitude of the American people for maintaining our great tradition that politics stops at the water's edge.**—*George Christian, White House spokesman, 7 April 1967.*[774]

Christian was speaking of Romney's speech in which he backed the Administration's position on the war.

1354 **I could never again raise my voice against the violence of the oppressed in the ghettos without having first spoken clearly to the greatest purveyor of violence in the world today — my own government...**—*Reverend Martin Luther King, Jr., religious leader and civil rights activist, speaking at Riverside Church, 4 April 1967.*[767]

King, speaking out against the war and the government controlling the war in Vietnam.

1355 **What am I going to tell Congress? What is the press going to do with this? What am I going to tell the President?**—*General William Westmoreland, ComUSMACV, to one of his intelligence briefing officers, April 1967.*[72]

Westmoreland had just returned to Vietnam from briefing the Congress and the President on how well the war was going against the communists. On his return to Saigon he was met with the news that the enemy totals he had just delivered were not accurate. There was a conflict between the low numbers MACV reported and the higher numbers calculated by the CIA and other intelligence agencies.

1356 **If we continue to add forces to Americanize the war, we will only erode whatever incentives the South Vietnamese**

people may now have to help themselves in this fight.—*Alain Enthoven, Assistant Secretary of Defense, in a memorandum to Robert McNamara, April 1967.*[374]

Enthoven argued for a cap on U.S. forces deployed to Vietnam, followed by a reduction of American forces in Vietnam and a greater emphasis on the pacification program.

1357 **If we allow ourselves to be split we will be chewed up, fragment by fragment, because we have powerful and relentless enemies.**—*Dr. Benjamin Spock, from a speech during an anti-war rally in New York, 15 April 1967.*[820]

Spock was speaking of the infighting between the various peace and anti-war groups. He wanted the groups to band together and fight the Administration, not each other.

1358 **If we heard that 100,000 people were marching in Hanoi for peace, we would draw very important conclusions from it.**—*Dean Rusk, Secretary of State, during a broadcast of Meet the Press, 16 April 1967.*[726]

1359 **I am concerned ... that the authorities in Hanoi may misunderstand this sort of thing and that the net effect of these demonstrations will be to prolong the war and not shorten it.**—*Dean Rusk, Secretary of State, during a broadcast of Meet the Press, 16 April 1967.*[726]

Rusk was commenting on nationwide anti-war demonstrations in several cities on 15 April. He indicated that the demonstrations were strengthening Hanoi's resolve by indicating weakness in American popular support for the war.

1360 **A tremendously important intensification ... of the air war.**—*Unnamed Senior American official, Saigon, 20 April 1967.*[543]

On 20 April U.S. aircraft struck power plants inside the North Vietnamese port city of Hai Phong. These attacks represented the first attacks on Hai Phong proper. According to the unnamed source, the escalation in attacks was in response to Hanoi's continued rejection of negotiations.

1361 **Now we don't know whether Hanoi is sufficiently sophisticated to understand that this [anti-war demonstration] is not the way the American people come to their decisions and that these demonstrations will not affect the conduct of the war.**—*Dean Rusk, Secretary of State, during a broadcast of Meet the Press, 16 April 1967.*[726]

1362 **I ain't got no quarrel with those Vietcong, anyway. They never called me nigger.**—*Muhammad Ali, Heavyweight Champion of the World, shouting at the press, 1967.*[654]

Ali, formerly Cassius Clay, was drafted in April 1967. He refused induction citing religious grounds, was tried and convicted of Selective Service Act violations in June 1967. He received a five-year prison sentence. His conviction was overturned by the U.S. Supreme Court in October 1970. Ali was stripped of his championship title, but regained it in 1974 when he knocked out George Foreman.

1363 **The end is not in sight ... we will have to grind him down. In effect we are fighting a war of attrition. The only alternative is a war of annihilation.**—*General William Westmoreland, from a speech in New York, April 1967.*[101]

1364 **We helped to elect this administration because it promised peace. We did not intentionally elect a vice president to walk arm in arm with either Marshal Ky or Lester Maddox.**—*Alex J. Rosenberg, Leader Sixty-fifth Assembly District, in a speech to the Ansonia Independent Democrats, 23 April 1967.*[806]

Some Democrats saw the Johnson policy in Vietnam as a problem for their individual runs for office and tried to distance themselves from him and his policy. The reference to Maddox was because of his anti-black attitude, which was becoming out of vogue in 1967 as a public pronouncement.

1365 **Despite staggering combat losses, he clings to the belief that he will defeat us. And through a clever combination of psychological and political warfare, both here and abroad, he has gained support which gives him hope that he can win politically that which he cannot accomplish militarily....**—*General William Westmoreland, ComUSMACV, from a speech to the Associated Press, 24 April 1967.*[807]

1366 **I do not see any end in sight.**—*General William Westmoreland, ComUSMACV, from a speech in New York, 24 April 1967.*[544]

1367 **If we began bombing North Vietnamese airfields, the planes would seek sanctuary in Red China and this would expand China's role in the war.**—*Senator Charles H. Percy of Illinois, from a speech in New York, 24 April 1967.*[544]

Two North Vietnamese MiG airfields were hit by U.S. air strikes 25 April 1967. Up to this point attacks against North Vietnamese airfields had been forbidden by President Johnson. It was expected that North Vietnam would ferry their MiGs to Chinese airfields to keep them from being destroyed on the ground. According to Percy the information about possible Chinese involvement had come from the U.S. State Department.

1368 **Backed at home by resolve, confidence, patience, determination, and continued support, we will prevail in Vietnam over the Communist aggressor.**—*General William Westmoreland, ComUSMACV, speaking before a joint session of Congress, 28 April 1967.*[47]

1369 **Although war is evil, it is occasionally the lesser of two evils.**—*McGeorge Bundy, National Security Adviser to presidents Kennedy and Johnson.*[83]

1370 **In evaluating the enemy strategy it is evident to me that he believes our Achilles' heel is our resolve.**—*General William Westmoreland, ComUSMACV, speaking before a joint session of Congress, 28 April 1967.*[47]

Westmoreland believed the war in Vietnam could be lost at home.

1371 **[America must promote a strong sense of nationalism in South Vietnam] ... without that, we will have lost everything we have invested ... no matter what military success we may achieve.**—*Alain Enthoven, Assistant Secretary of Defense, in a memorandum to Robert McNamara, April 1967.*[374]

North Vietnam's tenacity stemmed from an extremely strong sense of nationalism. This drove Hanoi to achieve ultimate control of all of Vietnam.

1372 **It appears that last month [March 1967] we reached the cross-over point. In areas excluding the two northern provinces, attrition will be greater than additions to the**

[enemy] force.—*General William Westmoreland, ComUSMACV, to President Johnson, April 1967.*[59]

At this point Westmoreland's figure of enemy strength was at 285,000 men. His own force was at 470,000 men. Unpublished CIA figures for the enemy force were in the 400,000+ range.

1373 **Only unrelenting—but discriminating—military, political and psychological pressure can defeat the Communist foe in Vietnam.**—*General William Westmoreland, speaking before a joint session of Congress, 28 April 1967.*[680]

1374 **[U.S. troops] are dismayed, and so am I, by recent unpatriotic acts here at home. Regrettably, I see signs of success in that world arena which [the enemy] cannot match on the battlefield. He does not understand that American democracy is founded on debate, and he sees every protest as evidence of crumbling morale and diminishing resolve. Thus, discouraged by repeated military defeats but encouraged by what he believes to be popular opposition to our effort in Vietnam, he is determined to continue his aggression from the North. This, inevitably, will cost lives....**—*General William Westmoreland, ComUSMACV, from a speech to the Associated Press, 24 April 1967.*[807]

1375 **The enemy believes our Achilles' heel is our resolve.**—*Alain Enthoven, Assistant Secretary of Defense, in a memorandum to Robert McNamara, 1 May 1967.*[37]

Enthoven believed Hanoi was dragging out the war to a point where the American public would force the recall of U.S. troops from Vietnam through a loss of public support for the war. The military initiative was with the enemy, while American troops were forced to react to communist actions.

1376 **Only atomic bombs could really knock them out (an invasion of North Vietnam would not do it in two years, and is of course ruled out on other grounds), they [North Vietnam] have it in their power to "prove" that military escalation does not bring peace—at least over the next two years. ... However much they may be hurting, they are not going to do us any favors before November 1968.**—*McGeorge Bundy, former Special Assistant to the President for National Security Affairs, in a letter to the President, 4 May 1967.*[72]

Bundy was addressing the political reality of the war and Johnson's choices. Johnson was escalating the war in Vietnam to force Hanoi to negotiate. North Vietnam held out to show that they would not be forced into talks.

1377 **Hai Phong is the single most vulnerable and important point in the lines of [the] communications system of North Vietnam.**—*General Earle Wheeler, Chairman, Joint Chiefs of Staff, memorandum to President Johnson, 5 May 1967.*[72]

The JCS wanted to close the port of Hai Phong, but the Johnson administration was afraid of the reaction from the Soviets and China. They were also concerned with the VC/NVA reciprocating by mining the passage from the South China Sea to Saigon (the Saigon River and the larger, Song Nha Be).

1378 **I think there is no one on earth who could win an argument that an active deployment of some 500,000 men, firmly supported by tactical bombing in both South and North Vietnam, represented an under commitment at this time. I would not want to be the politician, or, the general, who whined about such a limitation.**—*McGeorge Bundy, former Special Assistant to the President for National Security Affairs, in a letter to the President, 4 May 1967.*[72]

Bundy was advising the president to set a limit on U.S. troop levels. Johnson recently received a request from Westmoreland and the JCS for 200,000 additional troops. Half of which were to deploy to Vietnam immediately, the remainder to become part of the strategic reserve and deploy to Vietnam a year later.

1379 **I can't tell you how I feel.... I'm so sick of it. ... I have never been so goddamned frustrated by it all.**—*General John P. McConnell, U.S. Air Force Chief of Staff, commenting after a Rolling Thunder briefing, 1967.*[131]

McConnell, as were many other air commanders, was frustrated by the progress and the handling of the air war against North Vietnam. The micro-management from Washington was perhaps the biggest factor in the general's frustrations.

1380 **The fact that South Vietnam has not been lost and is not going to be lost is a fact of truly massive importance in the history of Asia, the Pacific, and the U.S.**—*McGeorge Bundy, Special Assistant to the President for National Security Affairs, in a memorandum to the President, 4 May 1967.*[72]

By 1968 the war in Vietnam was a stalemate, and South Vietnam was lost to the communists in April 1975.

1381 **Unless and until we find some means of constricting and reducing the flow of war-supporting material through Hai Phong, the North Vietnamese will continue to be able to support their war effort in both North Vietnam and South Vietnam.**—*General Earle Wheeler, Chairman, Joint Chiefs of Staff, memorandum to President Johnson, 5 May 1967.*[72]

1382 **To stop the bombing today would give the Communists something for nothing.**—*McGeorge Bundy, to the President, 4 May 1967.*[317]

Bundy advised against a bombing halt without some reciprocal action from Hanoi indicating a willingness to negotiate and a reduction in the flow of men and material into South Vietnam.

1383 **If the present trend continues, I am afraid direct confrontation, first of all between Washington and Peking, is inevitable.**—*U.N. Secretary General U Thant, 11 May 1967.*[73]

1384 **If he has hatred, even a child can kill Americans.**—*Unidentified seventeen year old guerrilla, 1967.*[653]

1385 **The enemy has us "stalemated" and has the capacity to tailor his actions to his supplies and manpower, by hit-and-run terror, to make government and pacification very difficult in large parts of the country almost without regard to the size of US forces there. And ... the enemy can and almost certainly will maintain the military "stalemate" by matching our added deployments as necessary.**—*Robert McNamara, Secretary of Defense, to President Johnson, May 1967.*[72]

1386 **There is rot in the fabric. Our efforts to enliven the moribund political infrastructure have been matched by VC efforts—more now through coercion than was formerly the case.**—*Robert McNamara, Secretary of Defense, to President Johnson, 19 May 1967.*[72]

McNamara was speaking to the fact that the government

of South Vietnam was not making any headway in winning the hearts and minds of its people. The GVN was corrupt and inefficient and unresponsive to the people's needs. It was easily being countered by the VC and the NLF.

1387 **Most Americans do not know how we got where we are, and most, without knowing why ... are convinced that somehow we should not have gotten this deeply in. All want the war ended and expect their President to end it. Successfully. Or else.**—*Robert McNamara, Secretary of Defense, to President Johnson, 19 May 1967.*[72]

1388 **I think it is going to have minimum effectiveness for the cost that has been associated with it.... My own description of it is that it is like closing the window and leaving open the door.**—*General Harold K. Johnson, U.S. Army Chief of Staff, during Senate subcommittee hearings, August 1967.*[893]

General Johnson was speaking against McNamara's decision to construct an electronic and barbed wire barrier along the DMZ. McNamara planned for the Marines to clear a 35 mile long strip along the DMZ, west from Con Thien. The electronic barbed wire wall was nicknamed McNamara's Wall, and the idea was not enthusiastically received by the Marines, who would have to construct and man the barrier. There were no provisions to extend the wall into Laos to cut the Ho Chi Minh Trail.

1389 **With respect to interdiction of men and materiel, it now appears that no combination of actions against the North short of destruction of the regime or occupation of North Vietnamese territory will physically reduce the flow of men and materiel below the relatively small amount needed by enemy forces to continue the war in the South.**—*Robert McNamara, Secretary of Defense, in a report to President Johnson, 19 May 1967.*[185]

1390 **The war in Vietnam is acquiring a momentum of its own that must be stopped.**—*Robert McNamara, Secretary of Defense, to President Johnson, 19 May 1967.*[72]

The escalation of the bombing campaign and the rising American troop numbers were not forcing North Vietnam to the negotiating table, nor did it cause them to reduce their supply and direction of the war in South Vietnam.

1391 **Those thoroughly professional men in Hanoi, would, I believe, be profoundly impressed by a call-up [of U.S. Reserves].**—*Walt Rostow, Special Assistant to the President, in a memorandum to the President, 21 May 1967.*[72]

Rostow recommended the call-up of Reserves to the President, a move which the JCS continually pressed for.

1392 **Dramatic increases in U.S. troop deployments, in attacks on the North, or in ground actions in Laos and Cambodia are not necessary and are not the answer.**—*Robert McNamara, Secretary of Defense, in a memorandum to the President, 19 May 1967.*[155]

At this stage of the war McNamara no longer believed bombing would force Hanoi to negotiate and that the war was perhaps escalating out of control. He proposed a limit to the size of the U.S. force commitment in Vietnam and a reduction and ultimate halt to the bombing of North Vietnam. He also advised an increased effort to establish negotiations with the enemy.

1393 **[Should the Chinese intervene overtly with major combat forces in Vietnam,] it might be necessary to establish a strategic defense in South Vietnam and use tactical nuclear weapons against bases and LOCs in South China.**—*Joint Chiefs of Staff, in a report to President Johnson, 20 May 1967.*[59]

The JCS were pushing for a call up of Reserves. Troops had been pulled from many areas of the world to maintain troop levels in Vietnam. This thinning of the forces would make a move by North Korea, backed by China, or a move by China into Thailand difficult to contain without an increase in manpower. The use of tactical "nukes" could be used to equalize the enemy's advantage in numbers and part of the reserves would be used to fill the ranks around the world and increase the U.S. forces in Vietnam.

1394 **Application of US power in Southeast Asia, incrementally and with restraint, has inhibited the effective exploitation of the superiority of US military forces and allowed the enemy to accommodate to the military measures taken. This has contributed to the extension of the war.**—*Joint Chiefs of Staff, in a report to President Johnson, 20 May 1967.*[59]

The JCS argued for an increased military effort against North Vietnam, to include mining North Vietnam coastal and port facilities, intensified bombing of North Vietnamese LOCs, and call up of some U.S. Reserve forces.

1395 **[McNamara's Wall:] They'll just walk around it...**—*Unidentified Marine Lance Corporal, commenting on McNamara's Wall, 1967.*[893]

McNamara's Wall was the Secretary of Defense's decision to build an electronic and barbed wired barrier across the DMZ, but not extend it to cut the Ho Chi Minh Trail.

1396 **They [North Vietnamese Army] have been hitting our bases with rockets, mortars and artillery and then going back into the DMZ. We got sick of it, and we're going in to get them.**—*Unidentified U.S. Marine officer, comments to correspondent, 21 May 1967.*[681]

The Marines and ARVN troops conducted an operation into the South Vietnam side of the DMZ in an effort to dislodge NVA units in the zone. Officially the DMZ was off-limits to any military usage or occupation. The NVA used the DMZ on a regular basis, launching artillery and ground attacks from within the zone against Marine and ARVN positions located on the edge of the DMZ.

1397 **I think it would be unwise for us to go into the 1967-68 shooting season without some forces in reserve.**—*Walt Rostow, special assistant to the President, in a memorandum to the President, 21 May 1967.*[72]

Rostow recommended the call-up of Reserves to the President. Such units could have been available for duty in Vietnam before the end of 1967.

1398 **The use of tactical nuclear and area-denial radiological-bacteriological chemical weapons would probably be suggested at some point if the Chinese entered the war in Vietnam or Korea or if U.S. losses were running high while conventional efforts were not producing desired results.**—*Robert McNamara, Secretary of Defense, in a memorandum, 19 May 1967.*[72]

McNamara was outlining possible future actions the war could necessitate if it continued to escalate with the continuing poor results.

1399 **The rate at which US power has been applied has permitted North Vietnamese and Viet Cong reinforcements and force posture improvements to keep pace with the graduated increases in US military actions. It is fundamental to the successful conduct of warfare that every reasonable measure be taken to widen the differential between the capabilities of the opposing forces.**—*Joint Chiefs of Staff, in a report to President Johnson, 20 May 1967.*[59]

The JCS and military leaders wanted to maximize the use of U.S. military power. The gradual increases in U.S. forces levels were being matched by the enemy. Sanctuaries and bombing restrictions gave the enemy a decided edge. And the strategy of "graduated response" allowed the enemy time to match American escalation of the war.

1400 **I have a feeling that it would be wise to have some sort of Reserve call-up this summer if you judge it politically possible.**—*Walt Rostow, special assistant to the President, in a memorandum to the President, 21 May 1967.*[72]

Rostow advised the President that he should call-up some Reserve units. He believed it would signal to Hanoi that America was serious about Vietnam and able to marshal more forces for the effort. Rostow was also aware of the political considerations a call-up would have at home.

1401 **The most popular chant was: "What do you want?" "Victory!" "When do you want it?" "Now!" ... The next time some $3.90 an hour AFL type workers go on strike for a 50 cent raise, I'll remember the day they chanted "Burn Hanoi, not our flag" and so help me I'll cross their fucking picket line.**—*Marvin Garson, co-leader of the Free Speech Movement, in his column for the Berkeley Barb, 19-25 May 1967.*[850]

Garson was commenting on the May 1967 "March to Support Our Boys in Vietnam," organized by a coalition of patriotic groups to support the troops in Vietnam. The demonstration was a counter event to the anti-war and peace protests that were rampant at the time.

1402 **A withdrawal from Hanoi–Hai Phong bombing would stir deep resentment at home, among our troops, and be regarded by the Communist as an aerial Dien Bien Phu.**—*Walt Rostow, special assistant to the President, paraphrasing General Earle Wheeler, in a memorandum to the President, 21 May 1967.*[72]

Rostow, along with the JCS, argued for increased bombing of North Vietnam to include the restricted areas of Hanoi and Hai Phong. McNamara and Rusk felt the bombing of Hanoi–Hai Phong was not cost effective in comparison to the effect it would have on supplies infiltrated south.

1403 **The war in Vietnam is alienating a sufficient number of Democratic voters to cause the defeat of local and state, as well as national Democratic candidates [i.e., the President himself] in next year's Presidential election.**—*Resolution of the Committee for Democratic Voters (part of the Reform Democratic movement of New York), May 1967.*[777]

The perception that Johnson's position and involvement with the war in Vietnam would be detrimental to other democratic candidates right down to the local level. The committee could not vote to support the president and wanted a candidate other than Johnson for the 1968 Presidential race.

1404 **When we add divisions, can't the enemy add divisions? If so, where does it all end?**—*President Lyndon Johnson, during a White House meeting, 1967.*[629]

Johnson responding to a request by General Westmoreland for additional American troops for Vietnam. The JCS requested 200,000 troops, half of which were destined for Vietnam, the rest for the strategic reserve.

1405 **Hanoi shows no signs of ending the large war and [is] advising the VC to melt into the jungles. ... [The North Vietnamese] believe the world is with them and that the American public will not have staying power against them.... They believe that, in the long run, they are stronger than we are for the purpose.**—*Robert McNamara, Secretary of Defense, mid-1967.*[713]

1406 **[The M-16 rifle,] a reliable hard-hitting weapon — a big improvement over any we've had.**—*General Wallace Greene, Marine Corps Commandant, at a news conference, June 1967.*[429]

Greene, responding to a Congressional inquiry about problems with the M-16 rifle. Marines, first issued the M-16s in Vietnam, complained bitterly about the weapon jamming and not being user friendly, to the extent of costing Marine lives in combat. It was later discovered that there were problems with the newly issued rifles and the ammunition used.

1407 **[President Johnson] has poured out his own strength to renew the strength of the country.**—*Senator Robert Kennedy of New York, speaking in New York, 3 May 1967.*[765]

Kennedy at this point was publicly trying to keep the Democratic Party united and had not yet publicly split from supporting Johnson.

1408 **I don't think you have any real choice in the matter. When the President asks you to do something, it is the only thing you can do.**—*Ellsworth Bunker, Ambassador to South Vietnam, comments to the press, June 1967.*[430]

Bunker replaced Henry Cabot Lodge as the U.S. Ambassador to South Vietnam in 1967.

1409 **What inspires great respect and admiration is the sagacity of age combined with the vigor and endurance of youth.**—*Editorial from a leading political columnist in Saigon, 1967.*[430]

Columnist complimenting Ellsworth Bunker, who was 73 years old when appointed ambassador to South Vietnam.

1410 **To destroy the enemy you first have to find him — the classical problem against irregulars, the goal of all our reconnaissance activity.**—*Frank Harvey, free-lance writer and correspondent, 1967.*[249]

The U.S. was able to bring massive amounts of firepower against the enemy, but the biggest problem was identifying and finding the enemy in large enough concentrations to make our firepower effective.

1411 **Many of us within the party have been vocally opposed to the President's policy. Suddenly we're asked to participate in a "Salute to Johnson." This is asking too much of us.**—*Theodore Weiss, New York City Councilman, to the press during* *a demonstration outside a Democratic party fund-raising dinner, 3 May 1967.*[765]

He was part of a large group of demonstrators outside the hotel protesting against Johnson and the Vietnam War.

1412 **CDC has been told that its opposition is divisive — to the Democratic Party and the nation. That's nonsense! The war is dividing my party. The war has turned the hopes of a massive war on poverty into prolonged frustration. The war has divorced America from advancement of civil rights and economic opportunity for all Americans. And the war is killing peasants and young Americans in Southeast Asia.**—*Gerald Hill, leader of the California Democratic Party, in a speech, June 1967.*[717]

There was much talk in mid–1967 about the weakening chances of the Democratic Party to win the presidential election because the various factions within the party were not united behind Johnson and his Vietnam War policy.

1413 **The limited over-all US objective, in terms of the narrow US commitment and not of wider US preferences, is to take action (so long as they [the South Vietnamese] continue to help themselves) to see that the people of South Vietnam are permitted to determine their own future.**—*Robert McNamara, Secretary of Defense, in a draft memorandum to President Johnson, 12 June 1967.*[72]

1414 **Neither the extermination by the People's Army of Vietnam of entire southern communities nor the massacres in the north during land reform distracted American intellectuals from the prospect of humiliating, if not butchering, their own country.**—*John Colvin, British Consul-General, 1967.*[886]

The media and various anti-war factions in America did not draw much attention to Hanoi's excesses, or those carried out by the NVA and VC in South Vietnam. The intellectual elements arguing against U.S. presence in Vietnam turned a blind eye to the methods the communists used to mark progress in the war.

1415 **[Corruption now] dominates and paralyzes [Vietnamese] society.**—*David Halberstam, correspondent, 1967.*[265]

Corruption infected South Vietnamese society at all levels.

1416 **The real damage [in bombing the Hanoi–Hai Phong and mining NVN ports] ... rests in the inexorable pressure towards further escalation and in the serious risk of enlarging the war into one with the Soviet Union and China.**—*Robert McNamara, Secretary of Defense, in a draft memorandum to President Johnson, 12 June 1967.*[72]

McNamara opposed the recommendations by the JCS for increased operations against North Vietnam. He also opposed the JCS recommendation of mining North Vietnam ports, closing North Vietnam's border with Red China, and the striking of targets in Hanoi and Hai Phong.

1417 **[The South Vietnamese government] is still largely corrupt, incompetent and unresponsive to the needs and wishes of the people.**—*Robert McNamara, Secretary of Defense, in a draft memorandum to President Johnson, 12 June 1967.*[72]

One of the indicators of progress in Vietnam was the GVN's ability to attract support from their people. They were highly unsuccessful at doing so.

1418 **Our commitment is to stop (or generously to offset when we cannot stop) North Vietnamese military intervention in the South, so that "the board will not be tilted" against Saigon in an internal South Vietnamese contest for control.**—*Robert McNamara, Secretary of Defense, in a draft memorandum to President Johnson, 12 June 1967.*[72]

1419 **I feel the fate of Asia — Southeast Asia — will be decided in the next few years by what happens out in Viet-Nam.**—*Lee Kuan Yew, Prime Minister of Singapore, 1967.*[82]

1420 ANDREWS: **Do you have enough equipment?**
OFFICER: **Yes sir.**
ANDREWS: **Do you have enough planes?**
OFFICER: **Yes sir.**
ANDREWS: **Do you have enough guns and ammunition?**
OFFICER: **Yes sir.**
ANDREWS: **Well, why can you not whip that little country of North Vietnam? What do you need to do it?**
OFFICER: **Targets — targets.**

—*An exchange between Congressman George Andrews of Alabama and unidentified Pentagon official, during testimony, 13 May 1967.*[640]

Underscoring the fact that North Vietnam was not an industrial nation, but a small country with an agricultural-based economy.

1421 **There may be a limit beyond which many Americans and much of the world will not permit the United States to go. The picture of the world's greatest superpower killing or seriously injuring more than 1,000 non-combatants a week while trying to pound a tiny backward nation into submission on an issue whose merits are hotly disputed, is not a pretty one. It could conceivably produce a costly distortion in the American national consciousness and in the world image of the United States — especially if we increase the damage to North Vietnam greatly in an effort to achieve their capitulation.**—*Robert McNamara, Secretary of Defense, in a draft memorandum to President Johnson, 12 June 1967.*[72]

McNamara had serious doubts that the U.S. could win militarily in Vietnam without destroying or occupying North Vietnam. He believed such destruction would not have been tolerated by the American people or the world community.

1422 **Most of the generals are corrupt. Most of the senior officials in the provinces are corrupt ... corruption exists everywhere, and people can live with some of it. You live with it in Chicago and New York.**—*Vice President Nguyen Cao Ky, as quoted to President Johnson by Harry McPherson, 13 June 1967.*[291]

Corruption was a way of life for many in South Vietnam. Bribery and threat were the tender of action.

1423 **[Nothing] short of destruction of the regime or occupation of North Vietnamese territory will with high confidence reduce the flow of men and materiel below the relatively small amount needed by enemy forces to continue the war in the South.**—*Robert McNamara, Secretary of Defense, in a draft memorandum to President Johnson, 12 June 1967.*[72]

A few hundred tons of materiel infiltrated in to South Vietnam and Cambodia daily was sufficient to sustain several thousand VC/NVA troops. Cutting off all supply from North

Vietnam would have been required to greatly affect NVA combat operations in the South.

1424 **Implicit in the [JCS] recommendation is a conviction that nothing short of toppling the Hanoi regime will pressure North Vietnam to settle so long as they believe they have a chance to win the "war of attrition" in the south.**—*Robert McNamara, Secretary of Defense, in a draft memorandum to President Johnson, 12 June 1967.*[72]

McNamara was at odds with the JCS's recommendation of increasing the bombing of North Vietnam, mining of the harbors, and dramatically increasing U.S. troop strength in Vietnam.

1425 **The riots are actually a good deal for us. They wouldn't dare send us to Vietnam now.**—*Unidentified National Guard soldier, Cleveland, Ohio, 1967.*[440]

Because of a series of riots in large American cities over a three year period, Guard units were often deployed to support local police forces. For the most part, Guard and Reserve units were not deployed to Vietnam.

1426 **Students who deny Dow the freedom to recruit are denying Dow the freedom to kill....**—*Excerpt from an SDS leaflet handed out at anti-war demonstrations on many university campuses across the nation, 1967.*[727]

Dow was the focus of attacks and accusations of genocide because they manufactured the napalm used in Vietnam. Dow recruited heavily on campuses across the nation.

1427 **It is wrong for the U.S.A. to be the sole judge in the Vietnam conflict.**—*Public declaration of the General Board of the National Council of Churches of Christ, June 1967.*[653]

The churches opposed the war on moral grounds.

1428 **It makes me feel very humble. It makes me realize how little I've done for my country.**—*General Lewis Walt, Commander 3d Marine Amphibious Force, during an interview, June 1967.*[431]

Walt, much moved after visiting Marine wounded in a Da Nang Naval hospital.

1429 **Everybody considered him [President Johnson] to be the most cruel and most incapable President that has ever ruled in the United States.**—*Lord Bertrand Russell, British philosopher, 1967.*[969]

1430 **Current teen-agers are a generation lost to another cause.**—*General Lewis Walt, Commander 3d Marine Amphibious Force, during an interview, June 1967.*[431]

Walt was speaking of the current generation of Vietnamese teen-agers. He hoped that the next generation of Vietnamese, educated and self-sufficient, would be able to stabilize South Vietnam and be able to resist North Vietnam.

1431 **[If the war in Vietnam should fail] I hope that I, as one who has supported the policy, will be prompt to admit that we had attempted something beyond our powers.**—*Hedley Donovan, editor in chief, Time Inc., during a New York University commencement address, June 1967.*[653]

In 1967 Donovan became less supportive of the war and entertained the possibility that his faith in Administration policy may have been misdirected. He did not doubt the goals of America in Vietnam, but he had doubts about the means used to obtain those goals.

1432 **Now, let's look at some other education we're getting from protesting and expressing dissent in this country: During a week a short time ago our newspapers, our TV programs and our radio commentators informed us fully about the protesters and the peaceniks who invaded the Pentagon. They came there to stay. They walked over the tulips. They sat down on the steps. They slept in the halls.... Unfortunately a student carrying a sign, or a protester wearing a beard, or an attention seeker burning a draft card in front of a camera, can get more attention and more billing than all 10,000 of these [armed forces] volunteers.**—*President Lyndon Johnson, Baltimore, Maryland, 27 May 1967.*[369]

1433 **We are not in the business of legislating honor, dignity, good taste or good sense. I do not believe we have to rise to meet the bait of every irresponsible [individual] who finds a new way of making a bloody fool out of himself.**—*James Scheuer, Democratic Congressman of New York, during debate over a flag burning bill, July 1967.*[433]

A rash of American flag burning during anti-war demonstrations prompted the House of Representatives to pass a bill subjecting those who would desecrate the American flag to fines and or imprisonment.

1434 **[Dixie Station was where] young pilots could get their first taste of combat under the direction of a forward air controller over a flat country in bright sunshine where nobody was shooting back with high-powered ack-ack. He learns how it feels to drop bombs on human beings and watch huts go up in a boil of orange flame when his aluminum napalm tanks tumble into them. He gets hardened to pressing the firing button and cutting people down like little cloth dummies, as they sprint frantically under him. He gets his sword bloodied for the rough things to come.**—*Frank Harvey, free-lance writer and correspondent, July 1967.*[249]

U.S. Navy aircraft carriers supporting operations in South Vietnam launched from Dixie Station. Navy carrier operations against North Vietnam were conducted from Yankee Station. Dixie Station was due east of Saigon in the South China Sea. Yankee Station was located in the Gulf of Tonkin.

1435 **We have reached a meeting of the minds. The troops that General Westmoreland needs and requests, as we feel it necessary, will be supplied.**—*President Lyndon Johnson, during a press conference, July 1967.*[72]

Johnson was referring to Westmoreland's request for 200,000 additional troops (over a two year period). U.S. troop levels in South Vietnam at that time were 430,000+. The press conference was intended to show the media that Johnson's principle advisors on the war effort were in agreement on the troop request. In attendance were Westmoreland, McNamara, and Wheeler.

1436 **I don't think I'll be talking to you again — we are being overrun.**—*Captain Warren O. Keneipp, Jr., Forward Air Controller, from U.S. Marine Corps Squadron VMF (AW)-232, 2 July 1967.*[84]

Keneipp, a Marine pilot, was attached to two companies of the 1st Battalion, 9th Marine Regiment, as forward air controller. During a sweep east of Con Thien the two Marine companies were engaged by several NVA battalions. Keneipp did not survive. The NVA staked him out and beheaded him.

1437 **Compromise has no place and opposition of any kind must of necessity be subversive and must be suppressed with all the vigor the system is capable of.**—*Bernard Fall, historian and author, 1967.*[260]

Fall echoed Diem's beliefs of absolute power to guide the nation, and that Diem, as the leader, knew what was best for South Vietnam.

1438 **It is demonstrable that interferences close to the source have a greater effect, not a lesser effect, than the same interferences close to the output.**—*Harold Brown, Secretary of the Air Force, in a memorandum to Robert McNamara, 3 July 1967.*[925]

Brown was referencing the Rolling Thunder air campaign against North Vietnam, and the debate of its effectiveness. In this case Brown was saying bombing closer to the source of supply was more effective than bombing at the end or middle of the supply pipeline.

1439 **A man — or a nation — allows itself to grow weak at its peril; horrors, injustices and tragedies notwithstanding.**—*Frank Harvey, free-lance writer and correspondent, July 1967.*[249]

1440 **Whenever we catch a V.C. now, we behead him. Then we spread the word that the boys who crossed over [Chieu Hoi'd] did it. They can't go back.**—*Unidentified Vietnamese District Chief, III Corps, speaking to a reporter, July 1967.*[432]

Viet Cong who had rallied to the Saigon government were sometimes placed in resettlement villages to provide security or used as scouts or guides for U.S. units. Many of them returned to the ranks of the VC.

1441 **All reports of stalemate were completely fiction and completely unrealistic.**—*General William Westmoreland, ComUSMACV, during a White House press conference, July 1967.*[72]

Westmoreland was sensitive to criticism that the war in Vietnam was a stalemate. He continually spoke of progress in the war against the communists. The press asked Westmoreland why more troops were needed if there was so much progress in the war effort.

1442 **We are gaining momentum and by the end of next winter it will be clear for all to see that we gained the upper hand.**—*Robert Komer, Special Assistant to the President, in a report to the President, July 1967.*[72]

Komer went to Vietnam in June 1967 to study the U.S. situation. He reported that progress was being made against the enemy. Komer thought it was not a matter of if the U.S. would win, but when.

1443 **Aerial bombardment ... though extremely important, has neither interdicted infiltration nor broken the will of the North Vietnamese, and it is doubtful that it can accomplish either.**—*Ellsworth Bunker, U.S. Ambassador to South Vietnam, during discussions on Vietnam, 1967.*[918]

1444 **The war is not a stalemate. We are winning slowly but steadily. North Vietnam is paying a tremendous price with nothing to show for it in return.**—*General William Westmoreland, ComUSMACV, during a conference at MACV Headquarters, 7 July 1967.*[72]

The media and some Administration officials spoke of a stalemate in Vietnam. The NVA/VC were not able to militarily take control of South Vietnam, but the U.S. and the ARVN were not able to eject the enemy or stop his growth in South Vietnam. Westmoreland insisted that stalemate was not the case. He requested 200,000 more troops to increase the pace of progress.

1445 **We've begun to turn defeat into victory. ... There is no truth to the stalemate theory.**—*President Lyndon Johnson, during an interview with Peter Lisagor, correspondent, Chicago Daily News, 12 July 1967.*[55]

McNamara had made it clear to Johnson that in his opinion (McNamara's) the U.S. war effort was not stalemated by North Vietnam and that progress was being made. Very slow progress, but progress all the same.

1446 **After listening to their side of the story for a year and a half, I've decided that Rusk and McNamara and the rest of them are wrong.**—*Congressman Thomas P. O'Neill of Massachusetts, to reporters, 1967.*[653]

One of several members of Congress who changed from supporting Administration policy in Vietnam, to seeking a change in that policy. O'Neill advocated the enclave strategy and settlement of the war through the United Nations.

1447 **The real question is not whether we need more US troops to "win" the war in the South, but rather how fast we want to win it.**—*Robert Komer, Special Assistant to the President, in a report to the President, July 1967.*[72]

Komer went to Vietnam in June 1967 to study the U.S. situation. He reported that progress was being made against the enemy. Komer thought it was not a matter of if the U.S. would win, but when.

1448 **We are making progress. We are deeply conscious of the heavy burden you bear. Please be assured you can count on us.**—*Ellsworth Bunker, Ambassador to South Vietnam, in a cable to President Johnson, 14 July 1967.*[72]

Bunker was responding to Johnson's dispatch of Wheeler and McNamara to South Vietnam for an evaluation of the situation there.

1449 **We are dropping $20,000-bombs every time somebody thinks he sees four Viet Cong in a bush. And it isn't working.**—*Congressman Thomas P. O'Neill of Massachusetts, to reporters, 1967.*[653]

One of several members of Congress who changed from supporting Administration policy in Vietnam, to seeking a change in that policy, O'Neill advocated the enclave strategy and settlement of the war through the United Nations. As a Democrat he initially supported the Johnson policy in Vietnam.

1450 **Who will say that a third world war is not already incubating in the ever-deepening and expanding struggle in Southeast Asia?**—*Senator Mike Mansfield of Montana, July 1967.*[782]

Mansfield worried that the increasing escalation of the war would pull China and perhaps the Soviet Union into the war, thus starting World War III.

1451 **I am concerned about the charge that we cannot kill enough people in Vietnam, so we go out and shoot civilians in Detroit.**—*President Lyndon Johnson in a comment to his advisors, 24 July 1967.*[72]

Johnson commenting on the announcement that federal troops called out to control the riots in Detroit would be issued live ammunition.

1452 **I do not believe ... that there is any evidence that things are in a "stalemate" here or that we have lapsed into a static situation ... we are moving steadily ahead and moving in the right direction. I do think we need to do more intensive work in educating the press here and I intend to concentrate on this.**—*Ellsworth Bunker, Ambassador to South Vietnam, in a cable to President Johnson, 27 July 1967.*[72]

The ambassador and his team reported positive progress in the war against the VC/NVA.

1453 **Withdraw our forces immediately from South Vietnam for the sake of reconciliation.**—*Archbishop Fulton J. Sheen of Rochester, New York, in a public plea to President Johnson, 30 July 1967.*[73]

1454 **General attitude appears to be that the Thieu-Ky ticket will win, that the election will not reflect the true views of the majority, and that the results will have little or no effect on the current prevailing conditions in the country.**—*American, Province Senior Adviser, detailed from the Hau Nghia Province Report, August 1967.*[8]

South Vietnam's first presidential election took place in September 1967. Thieu and Ky did win the election with 35 percent of the popular vote.

1455 **We're winning the war ... this was the first trip where I could see significant evidence of progress.**—*General Harold K. Johnson, Army Chief of Staff, during a press conference, August 1967.*[72]

General Johnson had recently returned from a fact finding visit to South Vietnam and was optimistic about the U.S. war effort.

1456 **Communist armed strength is falling, not spectacularly and not mathematically provable, but every indication suggests this.... There is evidence that we may have reached the crossover point.**—*General William Westmoreland, ComUSMACV, during a press briefing, August 1967.*[887]

The cross-over point was that point at which enemy losses (through death, desertion, and lack of recruitment) were increasing faster than could be replaced.

1457 **I believe the United States should get out of Vietnam at the earliest possible time, and on the best possible basis; because with his [Robert McNamara's] premises, there would appear to be no chance for any true "success" in this long war.**—*Senator Stuart Symington of Missouri, to reporters, August 1967.*[653]

Comments to the press following Senate testimony by Robert McNamara which indicated the air war against North Vietnam was not successful. It had neither stopped nor significantly reduced the flow of men and materiel from North to South Vietnam, nor increased Hanoi's willingness to negotiate. McNamara indicated the monetary cost of U.S. aircraft in destroying North Vietnam was nearly three times the value of what was being destroyed.

1458 **We must make haste carefully in order to avoid charges that the military establishment is conducting an organized propaganda campaign, either overt or covert.**—*General William Westmoreland, ComUSMACV, in a memorandum to his superior commanders, 2 August 1967.*[72]

The perception in the high ranks of the military was that America was winning the war. The public perception and that of the media was that the war was a stalemate. Westmoreland's memorandum was dispatched to Wheeler (JCS), Johnson (Army Chief of Staff), and Sharp (CINCPAC).

1459 **All of the evidence is so far that we have not been able to destroy a sufficient quantity [of war materiel in North Vietnam] to limit the activity in the South below present level, and I do not know [if] we can in the future.**—*Robert McNamara, Secretary of State, in Senate testimony, August 1967.*[961]

The Navy and Air Force countered McNamara's claims with the fact that Washington-imposed restrictions placed on the pilots and targeting greatly restricted the effectiveness of the bombing campaign.

1460 **While we work on the nerve ends here we hope that careful attention will be paid to the roots there — the confused or unknowledgeable pundits who serve as sources for each other.**—*General William Westmoreland, ComUSMACV, in a memorandum to his superior commanders, 2 August 1967.*[72]

Westmoreland was to take steps to explain to the media in Vietnam what progress the U.S. was making in the war. He asked that like steps be taken in the U.S. to explain the progress gained. Westmoreland's memorandum was dispatched to Wheeler (JCS), Johnson (Army Chief of Staff), and Sharp (CINCPAC).

1461 **It is impossible to fight the Communists the way we are now. It would be better to have a shouting war rather than a shooting war. We must de-escalate.**—*Dr. Phan Quang Dan, physician and South Vietnamese Vice Presidential candidate, to the press, 3 August 1967.*[545]

Phan Quang Dan and Phan Khac Suu were running together for president and vice president of South Vietnam. Suu and Dan proposed to open immediate negotiations with Hanoi if they were elected. Elections were held in September 1967.

1462 **Our strategy of attrition has not worked....**—*Alain Enthoven, Assistant Secretary of Department of Defense, in a Pentagon document, 1967.*[60]

Enthoven's paper was one of many documents that comprised the secret *Pentagon Papers*, which were eventually published by *The New York Times*. The report, commissioned by McNamara in June 1967, was a review of the military policy regarding Vietnam covering a 22 year period.

1463 **All the evidence we have indicates bombing North Vietnam (and Laos) helps cut down the level of infiltration below the level it would otherwise attain.**—*Walt Rostow, Special Assistant to the President, in a report, 7 August 1967.*[72]

Rostow reportedly had other evidence indicating that the bombing was not as effective as he was reporting, but he chose to use the most optimistic assessment.

1464 **The evidence is that the Vietcong are having severe manpower problems in the south and [are] facing real difficulties in maintaining both their guerrilla and their main-force units.... All the evidence we have indicates that**

Hanoi does not now expect to win the war in the South on the battlefield.—*Walt Rostow, Special Assistant to the President, in a report to the President, 7 August 1967.*[72]

Rostow was very optimistic about the progress of the war against the VC/NVA. He tended to favor good news over bad when reporting to the President.

1465 **I wish somebody would stop saying what President Johnson should do and spend a little time trying to get Ho to do something. Don't put the heat on me. I'm doing everything I can.**—*President Lyndon Johnson, during a meeting with labor leaders at the State Department, 7 August 1967.*[72]

1466 **They [North Vietnam] are hanging on hoping that there will be a break in the will of the U.S. to continue the war.**—*Walt Rostow, Special Assistant to the President, in a report to the President, 7 August 1967.*[72]

Based on Rostow's interpretation of reports from Vietnam, he concluded that the enemy was weakening and had resolved to hold out for a political victory instead of a military victory.

1467 **We became mesmerized by statistics of known doubtful validity, choosing to place our faith only in the ones that showed progress. We judged the enemy's intentions rather than his capabilities because we trusted captured documents too much....**—*Alain Enthoven, Assistant Secretary of Department of Defense, in a Pentagon document.*[60]

Enthoven's paper was one of many documents that comprised the secret *Pentagon Papers*, which were eventually published by *The New York Times*. The report, commissioned by McNamara in June 1967, was a review of the military policy regarding Vietnam covering a 22 year period.

1468 **The possibility of major Chinese Communist intervention could be kept to a minimum so long as we made it clear at all times, both by word and deed, that our objective was confined solely to freeing South Viet-Nam from external interference and that we did not threaten Communist China....**—*William P. Bundy, Assistant Secretary for East Asian and Pacific Affairs, during a public address in College Park, Maryland, 15 August 1967.*[82]

1469 **If free elections [in Vietnam] are not possible ... we have every right, once the elections take place, to begin to consider phasing out our commitment.**—*Senator Jacob Javits, Republican Senator from New York, speaking to the press, August 1967.*[434]

Free election of a president was to take place in South Vietnam September 1965. There were charges by opposition candidates that the election might not be so free (harassment by the police, etc). U.S. critics of the war argued that if free elections could not take place because of political restrictions by the current military government, then we should consider getting out of Vietnam. And that once elections took place and the South Vietnamese had determined their leader, America should begin phasing itself out of South Vietnam.

1470 **Every indicator belies either stalemate or loss of initiative.**—*General William Westmoreland, ComUSMACV, in a memorandum to his superior commanders, 2 August 1967.*[72]

Public perception was that in 1967 the war in Vietnam was at a stalemate. The enemy numbers Westmoreland offered as proof that there was progress against the enemy were not the same numbers offered by the CIA. Westmoreland's memorandum was dispatched to Wheeler (JCS), Johnson (Army Chief of Staff), and Sharp (CINCPAC).

1471 **Every time Westy [Westmoreland] makes a speech about how good the South Vietnamese army is, I want to ask him why he keeps calling for more Americans. His need for reinforcement is a measure of our failure with the Vietnamese.**—*Unidentified military source, as quoted by correspondent R.W. Apple, New York Times, August 1967.*[72]

Prior to this Westmoreland had requested additional troops and was granted 45,000 by the President.

1472 **I feel like a hound bitch in heat in the country. If you run, they chew your tail off, if you stand still, they slip it to you.**—*President Lyndon Johnson, comment to a friend, 1967.*[72]

Johnson's view of his relationship with the American press.

1473 **[Some administration officials had] ... overestimated the persuasive and disruptive effects of the bombing [of North Vietnam], and correspondingly, underestimated the tenacity and recuperative capabilities of the North Vietnamese.**—*Jason Study findings, 1967.*[72]

The Jason Study was commissioned by the Department of Defense to study the effects of the bombing campaign against North Vietnam. There was a previous report in 1966 with similar findings. The studies found the bombing was having no measurable direct effect on the enemy's ability to support his war effort in South Vietnam. The Jason group was part of the IDA (Institute for Defense Analysis) and was independent of the Department of Defense.

1474 **We knew ... that North Viet-Nam would resist any Communist trespassing on areas it controlled.**—*William P. Bundy, Assistant Secretary for East Asian and Pacific Affairs, during a public address in College Park, Maryland, 15 August 1967.*[82]

Bundy acknowledged that the Administration knew that Hanoi was acting with Chinese support, but that China and Vietnam were not partners in the conquest of South Vietnam. Hanoi wanted sole control of all of Vietnam, not shared control under communism with China.

1475 **We've got no place for gook-haters here.**—*William R. Corson, Lt. Colonel, USMC, during an interview on the CAP program, August 1967.*[435]

According to Corson, CAP troops were carefully selected because they worked closely with Vietnamese civilians and the village's defense force (PFs).

1476 **Since he must deal with so many bastards, it would be comforting to know that he is as good at it as they are.**—*Unidentified Georgetown lady resident, 1967.*[441]

She was speaking of Johnson's trend in 1967 of taking a tougher stand against his opposition — his attempt to gain public respect as opposed to the people's affection.

1477 **We don't use a gunnery sergeant — he looks like a tough old pro. We don't use officers because the people associate them with corruption. But our young corporals and sergeants look like they have succeeded in the same way that the best of the village boys, who can only aspire to becoming corporals and sergeants, might hope to succeed.**—*William R Corson, Lt. Colonel, USMC, during an interview on the CAP program, August 1967.*[435]

Combined Action Platoon (CAP) squads of Marine infantry took up residence in a village where they assisted the residents with civil projects, provided basic medical services and worked with the village defense force (Popular Forces) to provide security and training. Typically the PFs were not well trained or armed, poorly paid, and usually not motivated.

1478 **The spring of 1954 brought French defeat, in spirit if not in military terms, and left non–Communist nationalism in Viet-Nam almost bankrupt.**—*William P. Bundy, Assistant Secretary for East Asian and Pacific Affairs, during public address in College Park, Maryland, 15 August 1967.*[82]

In reference to the French defeat at Dien Bien Phu.

1479 **A statement of appeasing the Communists and if no-win ... if we follow what you have recommended, we ought to get out of Vietnam at once, because we have no chance to win.**—*Senator Strom Thurmond of South Carolina, during Senate hearings, August 1967.*[640]

Thurmond's response was to Robert McNamara's testimony of the effectiveness of the air campaign against North Vietnam. McNamara testified that American bombardment of North Vietnam was not effective in stopping or significantly reducing the flow of enemy men and materiel into South Vietnam, and it had not intimidated Hanoi into ending its support and direction of the war in the South.

1480 **We knew ... that the actions against South Viet-Nam reflected deeply held ambitions by Hanoi to unify Viet-Nam under Communist control and that Hanoi needed and wanted only Chinese aid to this end and wished to be its own master.**—*William P. Bundy, Assistant Secretary for East Asian and Pacific Affairs, during a public address in College Park, Maryland, 15 August 1967.*[82]

1481 **Airpower, in affording this advantage, exerts the influence that is most likely to force the enemy to reconsider his avowed hard line.**—*General John McConnel, U.S. Air Force Chief of Staff, during testimony before the Senate Armed Services Preparedness Investigating Subcommittee, August 1967.*[185]

The Air Force reported the air campaign against North Vietnam inflicted heavy material losses, and by extension, would mean a reduction in U.S. casualties.

1482 **We are taking out half of the infiltration with our bombing ... we are reducing infiltration, but we haven't stopped it.**—*Congressman Lester Wolff of New York, speaking to President Johnson during a lobbying conference, August 1967.*[72]

Johnson was lobbying for a tax bill to allow him to fund some of his Great Society programs. Wolff was one of many in Congress who did not see the progress in the war that the Johnson administration tried to convince them was there.

1483 **It is regrettable that a senior officer felt compelled to respond to a press query of this type and tragic that he was disloyal to his commander in the process.**—*General Earle Wheeler, Chairman, Joint Chiefs of Staff, August 1967.*[72]

Wheeler was responding to a quote in *The New York Times* by an unidentified officer, that Westmoreland's request for more U.S. troops was indication of the failure of the Vietnamese army to pull its own weight in the war.

1484 **Nobody sees the light at the end of the tunnel in Vietnam. We are the victims of a poor public relations program.**—*Congressman Lester Wolff of New York, speaking to President Johnson during a lobbying conference, August 1967.*[72]

Johnson was lobbying for a tax bill to allow him to fund some of his Great Society programs. Wolff was one of many in Congress who did not see the progress in the war that the Johnson administration tried to convince them was there.

1485 **Despite some mis-givings [sic], non–Communist leaders from Tokyo to Tehran largely support United States policies in South [Asia] and Southeast Asia.**—*Drew Middleton, New York Times columnist, as quoted by William Bundy, August 1967.*[82]

Middleton reported after an Asia trip that several countries feared the results should North Vietnam or China succeed in Vietnam.

1486 **Do not, under any circumstances, fly low-level down a trail or a river. If you do fly low-level down a trail or a river, you will die. You will deserve to die because the stupid do not deserve to live.**—*Douglas W. Nelms, U.S. Army gunship pilot, 1st Squadron, 9th Cavalry Regiment, August 1967.*[84]

Nelms repeating the watch word for new helicopter pilots operating in Vietnam.

1487 **The more we do, the less they [the South Vietnamese] do.**—*George Romney, Governor of Michigan, addressing the media, 16 August 1967.*[790]

Romney was commenting on the lack of effective participation by the South Vietnamese in their own war.

1488 **I do not think [the bombing] has in any significant way affected their war making capability ... the North Vietnamese still retain the capability to support activities in South Vietnam and Laos at present or increased combat levels and force structure.**—*Robert McNamara, Secretary of State, in Senate testimony, August 1967.*[961]

The Navy and Air Force countered McNamara's claims with the fact that Washington-imposed restrictions placed on the pilots and targeting greatly restricted the effectiveness of the bombing campaign.

1489 **Didn't that resolution [Southeast Asia Resolution] authorize the President to use the Armed Forces of the United States in whatever way was necessary? ... What could a declaration of war have done that would have given the President more authority and a clearer voice of Congress than that did?**—*Nicholas Katzenbach, Under Secretary of State, in hearings before the Senate Foreign Relations Committee, 17 August 1967.*[793]

Katzenbach argued that the resolution was the equivalent of a declaration of war and that the war effort to date had not exceeded the limits of the resolution.

1490 **The Marines had to show the people that they were going to fight, they were going to die—above all that they were going to stay.**—*William R. Corson, Lt. Colonel, U.S. Marine Corps, during an interview about the CAP program, August 1967.*[435]

CAP units frequently came under attack by VC units. The CAP program, though small in scope, was successful and a thorn in the side of local VC units.

1491 **Hanoi ... had taken major steps to raise the level of the war before the bombing [of NVN] began.**—*William P. Bundy, Assistant Secretary for East Asian and Pacific Affairs, during a public address in College Park, Maryland, 15 August 1967.*[82]

Hanoi claimed it only moved troops into South Vietnam as a result of U.S. bombing of the North. According to Bundy, the first documented NVA regiment entered South Vietnam before December 1964, followed by other regiments in early 1965. At this stage of the war, transit down the Ho Chi Minh Trail on foot took approximately four months. The first U.S. air strikes hit North Vietnam in August 1964. This would indicate NVA regular troops were in motion down the trail before the first U.S. retaliatory air strikes against North Vietnam took place.

1492 **Ford is not asking for an escalation but for more effective bombing. I don't think bombing is the answer, and I don't think he thinks bombing is the answer, but if there's going to be bombing, we should bomb in a more effective way.**—*George Romney, Governor of Michigan, addressing the media, 16 August 1967.*[790]

Representative Gerald Ford publicly attacked proposed limitations on the bombing campaign against North Vietnam.

1493 **He [R.W. Apple] is pessimistic and suspicious.... [He] still is convinced that we are not honest about casualties and are manipulating the figures.**—*General William Westmoreland, ComUSMACV, in a cable to the JCS and CINCPAC, August 1967.*[72]

Westmoreland was responding to a quote in *The New York Times* by an unidentified officer that Westmoreland's request for more U.S. troops was indication of the failure of the Vietnamese army to pull its own weight in the war. Westmoreland believed Apple was bucking for a Pulitzer Prize for his disclosures about the war.

1494 **The generals are ready to bomb there [along the Chinese–North Vietnamese border] but I'm not—there's a difference in judgment.**—*President Lyndon Johnson, during lobbying efforts for an administration tax bill, August 1967.*[72]

Johnson imposed restrictions against American air attacks against North Vietnamese targets along the Chinese-Vietnamese border. He did not want to provoke the Chinese into entering the war on the side of Hanoi. The military argued for striking the restricted area.

1495 **Get a colorful general to go to Saigon and argue with them [the press]. We've got to do something dramatic.**—*President Lyndon Johnson, comment made to Walt Rostow during a White House meeting, July 1967.*[54]

Johnson was referring to convincingly getting across to the media the message of U.S. progress in the war. He wanted a spokesman who would capture the media's attention and from there get the point across.

1496 **What is desperately needed is a strong, dynamic, ruthless, colonialist-type ambassador with the authority to relieve generals, mission chiefs and every other bastard who does not follow a stated, clear-cut policy which, in itself, at a minimum, involves the U.S. in the hiring and firing of Vietnamese leaders.**—*John Paul Vann, Deputy, II Field Force CORDS, in a letter, 19 August 1967.*[887]

1497 **In war, politics stops at the water's edge.**—*President Lyndon Johnson, during a meeting, 19 August 1967.*[72]

Johnson was commenting on the lack of political support his Administration was receiving regarding the war in Vietnam.

1498 **I cannot see [a] case for including vague estimates of low-grade part time hamlet self-defense groups, mostly weaponless, in new O/B [enemy Order of Battle].**—*Robert Komer, Special Assistant to the President, in a cable to George Carver, 19 August 1967.*[72]

The "low-grade groups" referred to were the enemy Self-defense and Secret Self-defense forces. These numbers were at the heart of the O/B controversy between MACV and the CIA. MACV claimed these groups were not offensive in nature, rarely armed, poorly disciplined, and local by nature and not a military threat. The CIA claimed these groups as local combatants, defending their villages, planting mines and booby-traps, and capable of supporting regular VC and NVA units. The discrepancy in numbers amounted to nearly 250,000 men.

1499 **I think we are on the road to doom and we must change direction and change soon.**—*John Paul Vann, Deputy, II Field Force CORDS, in a letter, 19 August 1967.*[887]

The level of corruption and ineptness was so great in the South Vietnamese government and military that Vann advocated U.S. control of South Vietnam in an attempt to get the country on track supporting the people of South Vietnam through a responsive and accountable government. Such a government, supported by the people, was the only way to defeat the communists.

1500 **There is no limit to what he [Katzenbach] says the President could do. There is only one thing to do—take it to the country.**—*Senator Eugene McCarthy of Minnesota, speaking to a reporter from The New York Times, 17 August 1967.*[793]

McCarthy was reacting to testimony given by Nicholas Katzenbach during Senate hearings, stating that under the Tonkin Gulf Resolution Johnson could take whatever action he deemed necessary in regards to the war in Vietnam. McCarthy was outraged. Several weeks later McCarthy threw his hat into the ring as a presidential candidate.

1501 **It seems like with all the South Vietnamese and all the Americans troops we could whip 'em.**—*President Lyndon Johnson, comment made to Walt Rostow during a White House meeting, August 1967.*[54]

Johnson was comparing the MACV numbers on enemy strength (nearly 300,000) to the rough total of South Vietnam and American troops in Vietnam (nearly 1.2 million). Sir Robert Thompson believed a 10:1 ratio of regular forces opposing guerrilla forces was required for victory over the guerrillas. Thompson was a British counterinsurgency specialist with extensive experience gained during the communist insurgency in Malaya.

1502 **I do not concur in the inclusion of strength figures for self-defense and secret self-defense. It distorts the situation and makes no sense. No amount of caveats will prevent the erroneous conclusion that will result.**—*General William Westmoreland, ComUSMACV, in a cable to General Earle Wheeler, 20 August 1967.*[72]

Westmoreland complained about the release of the CIA estimates of enemy Order of Battle, which indicated enemy strength at 175,000-242,000 more men than the publicly released MACV estimate. MACV used the Order of Battle as a reference of overall enemy strength and also as indicator of success in the war. But the perceived jump from the MACV numbers of 279,000-299,000 to the CIA numbers of 456,000-541,000 indicated a credibility gap.

1503 **There is something wrong with our system when our leaders are testifying instead of thinking about the war.**—*President Lyndon Johnson, during a meeting, 19 August 1967.*[72]

McNamara and members of the JCS had been called to testify before the Senate.

1504 **I just don't see an end to this conflict.**—*Senator Henry M. Jackson of Washington, during Senate hearings, August 1967.*[640]

Jackson's response to McNamara's testimony that the bombing campaign against North Vietnam and the Ho Chi Minh Trail was neither stopping nor significantly reducing the flow of men and materiel from North Vietnam into South Vietnam.

1505 **Westmoreland has turned defeat into what we believe will be a victory. It's only a matter now of will.**—*President Lyndon Johnson, during lobbying efforts for an administration tax bill, August 1967.*[72]

Johnson was trying to gather support for a new tax increase to help finance some of his Great Society programs.

1506 **Enemy operations in the south cannot, on the basis of any reports I have seen, be stopped by air bombardment—short ... of the virtual annihilation of North Vietnam and its people.**—*Robert McNamara, Secretary of Defense, during Senate hearings, August 1967.*[374]

1507 **We recommended what we called a sharp, sudden blow which would have, in our opinion, done much to paralyze the enemy's capability to move his equipment around and supply people in the South.**—*General John P. McConnell, U.S. Air Force Chief of Staff, in testimony before Senate subcommittee, 22 August 1967.*[171]

The Secretary of Defense asked the JCS for a program of graduated response to be applied against North Vietnam. The JCS formulated a plan that called for a full, swift strike against North Vietnam's munitions and POL facilities, military air bases, bridges, junction points, and industry. They also called for the mining of North Vietnamese harbors to keep replacement materials from entering the country.

1508 **General Westmoreland also reports progress in the very difficult but absolutely essential task of destroying the Viet Cong infrastructure which for many years has been working under deep cover in the villages and hamlets.**—*Ellsworth Bunker, Ambassador to South Vietnam, in a cable to President Johnson, 23 August 1967.*[72]

Bunker was one of the Administration's proponents of progress in the war against the enemy.

1509 **The guerrilla infra-structure is on the verge of collapse. All I can say to that is that if there is a stalemate, as the press reports, then every single one of our men we have out there is wrong.**—*President Lyndon Johnson, speaking to the press, 24 August 1967.*[72]

Johnson based his opinion on the Order of Battle figures from MACV, which indicated progress in the war.

1510 **We have now run out of targets [in North Vietnam] but Republican hawks keep calling for more [bombing] which produces useless casualties and encourages some Air Force fire-eaters to urge population bombing.**—*Dean Acheson, former Secretary of State, in a letter to Anthony Eden, August 1967.*[72]

1511 **We have hit two ships [in Hai Phong Harbor]. You know how emotions run in this country when ships are hit. Remember the *Lusitania*. We do not want to get the Soviet Union and China into this war.**—*President Lyndon Johnson, during lobbying efforts for an administration tax bill, August 1967.*[72]

Hawks pressed the President for more intense bombing of North Vietnam, closing the ports and the lines of communications between China and North Vietnam. The Soviet freighter *Mikhail Frunze* (June 1967) and the British freighter *Dartford* (April 1967) were reported hit during American air strikes against Hai Phong harbor. In addition the Soviets reported the freighter *Turkestan* was hit during a U.S. strike against the port of Cam Pha. The U.S. claimed the damage was from anti-aircraft fire against the American planes.

1512 **The decision to hit or not hit [a target] is a function of three primary elements: the value of the target, the risk of U.S. pilot loss, and the risk of widening the war....**—*Robert McNamara, Secretary of Defense, in Senate testimony, 25 August 1967.*[182]

McNamara was describing part of the methodology used at the White House to select targets for Rolling Thunder.

1513 **There can be no question that the bombing campaign has and is hurting North Vietnam's war-making ability.**—*Robert McNamara, Secretary of Defense, during Senate testimony, 25 August 1967.*[164]

McNamara reasoned it was not hurting North Vietnam sufficiently to force them to stop their supply and direction of the war in the South, nor sufficiently for them to seek negotiations.

1514 **The diametrically opposed views of the Joint Chiefs and Secretary McNamara had created the unsatisfactory progress of the war.**—*Excerpt from "Senate Armed Services Subcommittee Report on the Air War Against North Vietnam," August 1967.*[72]

McNamara opposed escalation of the bombing of the North. The JCS argued for increased bombing, and mining of Hai Phong Harbor.

1515 **This command cannot support these latest NIE figures with the intelligence at hand.**—*General William Westmoreland, ComUSMACV, in a cable to General Earle Wheeler, 26 August 1967.*[72]

The NIE indicated enemy troop strength at 461,000, while published MACV estimates were listed as under 300,000. The NIE was based on the CIA estimates. It should be noted that the NIE was to be made public 1 September 1967, while the MACV numbers were released June 1967.

1516 **[Nothing offered] any confidence that they [North Vietnam] can be bombed to the negotiating table.**—*Robert*

McNamara, Secretary of Defense, during testimony, Senate hearings, August 1967.[374]

McNamara's contention was that the air war was not designed to take the place of ground combat, but was supplemental to the overall campaign to keep South Vietnam independent.

1517 **It is not our intention to point a finger or to second guess those who determine this policy. But the cold fact is this policy has not done the job and it has been contrary to the best military judgment.**—*Excerpt from "Senate Armed Services Subcommittee Report on the Air War Against North Vietnam," August 1967.*[72]

The subcommittee consisted of a good many hawks at the time of the hearing and they blamed the civilian control of the bombing campaign for the lack of results.

1518 **[McNamara's] report [to Congress] is the truth, but not the whole truth. Rather, a loyal lieutenant putting the best face on a poor situation.**—*Dean Acheson, former Secretary of State, in a letter to Anthony Eden, August 1967.*[72]

Acheson was writing to former British Prime Minister Eden regarding McNamara's testimony before the Senate Armed Services Subcommittee in August 1967.

1519 **Despite our successes in grinding down VC/NVA ... CIA figures are used to show that they are really much stronger than ever ... the credibility gap would be enormous, and is quite inconsistent with all the hard evidence we have about growing enemy losses, declining VC recruitment and the like.**—*Ellsworth Bunker, Ambassador to South Vietnam, in a cable to Walt Rostow, 29 August 1967.*[72]

The CIA figures were used in the NIE report with a release date of September 1967. These figures indicated enemy strength to be 161,000 men higher than the MACV estimates.

1520 **What is needed now is the hard decision to do whatever is necessary, take the risks that have to be taken, and apply the force that is required to see the job through.**—*Excerpt from "Senate Armed Services Subcommittee Report on the Air War Against North Vietnam," August 1967.*[72]

The Senate subcommittee sided with the military, indicating a need for greater pressure on North Vietnam. The Secretary of Defense argued against escalation on the grounds that the current air campaign was not stopping the infiltration nor coercing North Vietnam into negotiations. McNamara backed a proposal to limit the bombing of North Vietnam to targets below the 20th Parallel. The military argued strongly against those restrictions and for a significant increase in the bombing campaign against North Vietnam.

1521 **I just had the greatest brainwashing that anyone can get when you go over to Vietnam, not only by the generals but also by the diplomatic corps over there, and they do a very thorough job.**—*George Romney, Governor of Michigan, during a TV interview, 31 August 1967.*[770]

Romney was talking about an official Vietnam tour the White House sent him and nine other governors on in November 1965. He described the trip as "shallow, misleading, and self-serving."

1522 **If gradualism does not pay off early, then the enemy must be regarded as the enemy and fought with all resources, with no sanctuary or quarter given.**—*Dwight Eisenhower, as quoted by President Lyndon Johnson during a meeting, September 1967.*[72]

Gradualism as used in Vietnam saw the steady escalation of force used by both sides in the war. Johnson incrementally increased U.S. pressure in Vietnam, which was matched by Hanoi.

1523 **If they increase their troops by another 50,000, 100,000 or more, they cannot extricate themselves from their comprehensive stalemate in the southern part of our country.**—*General Vo Nguyen Giap, defense minister of North Vietnam, from an article published in Hanoi's Armed Forces newspaper, September 1967.*[892]

Giap claimed the U.S. had reached a stalemate in the war and their only options were to either invade North Vietnam or continue on the present, stalemated course. He had no doubts the U.S. would not invade and risk direct Soviet and or Chinese intervention.

1524 **[The opposition is probably] correct in holding that the war has brought stalemate to government efforts on behalf of Negroes at home, but they are wrong, I would think, in their proposed solution, which is for the government to get out of Vietnam.**—*Senator Daniel Patrick Moynihan of New York, in a speech to the Americans for Democratic Action, September 1967.*[833]

1525 **[Westmoreland's O/B figures had been] a monument of deceit, and that the Agency's retreat had been an acquiescence to MACV half-truths, distortions, and sometimes outright falsehoods.**—*Sam Adams, CIA Analyst, comments to George Carver, 1967*[195]

1526 **Guerrilla warfare [in South Vietnam] was not a spontaneous revolution, as Communist propaganda would have it, but a contrived, deliberate campaign directed and managed from Hanoi.**—*Roger Hilsman, as quoted by William P. Bundy, September 1967.*[80]

1527 **The people in Washington were not sophisticated enough to understand and evaluate this [O/B values] thing and neither was the media.**—*General William Westmoreland, ComUSMACV, 1967.*[72]

When Westmoreland submitted enemy troop numbers to Washington he did not include their cadre and self defense forces in the totals. He considered such forces not a military threat. He did not think Washington would understand the distinction.

1528 **[South] Vietnam was in the throes of a true revolution, a social and nationalistic revolution very much akin to the "new nationalisms" that pervaded both the Congo crisis and Indonesia's confrontation with Malaysia.**—*Roger Hilsman, former Assistant Secretary of State for Intelligence and Research, as quoted by William P. Bundy, September 1967.*[80]

1529 **The elections thus constitute the successful end of one process and the beginning of another important one, namely the successful prosecution of the war and the conclusion of an acceptable settlement.**—*Ellsworth Bunker, Ambassador to South Vietnam, in a cable to President Johnson, 5 September 1967.*[72]

South Vietnam held elections 3 September 1967, in which Thieu was voted President and Ky Vice President. This was the first national election under South Vietnam's new constitution. Thieu-Ky won 35 percent of the popular vote.

1530 **All in all, while the elections have taken a considerable step farther down the road, there are still plenty of potholes ahead.**—*Ellsworth Bunker, Ambassador to South Vietnam, in a memorandum to President Johnson, 5 September 1967.*[72]

1531 **We are in a war that we cannot win and, even more important, one we should not wish to win.**—*John Kenneth Galbraith, former U.S. Ambassador to India and economist, from his book, 1967.*[243]

Galbraith made the claim that Americanization of the war in Vietnam looked more like colonialization to the average Vietnamese.

1532 **I think we have made two mistakes in Vietnam. ... First, our posture at home and abroad may have been too moderate, too balanced, not strong or assertive enough from the first.... Second, we may have helped to create mistrust or misinterpretation of our peace proposals. If the sincerity of our overtures are questioned, it could be that we have crawled too often.**—*President Lyndon Johnson, during a White House meeting, September 1967.*[72]

Johnson strategy in the war was to gradually increase pressure on Hanoi to coerce them to negotiate. Hanoi repeatedly rejected American peace overtures, calling for an unconditional halt of U.S. bombing of North Vietnam before they would even consider diplomatic talks.

1533 **There is not the slightest doubt in his mind [Bradley] that the war is not stalemated. We are moving forward.**—*General Omar Bradley, as rephrased by Walt Rostow, special assistant to the President, in a report to the President, 8 September 1967.*[72]

Bradley issued a report on his inspection trip to South Vietnam indicating that he was optimistic about the U.S. war effort and that we were on the way to winning the war in Vietnam.

1534 **If you want to get into a discussion of who's been brainwashing whom ... look at what the administration has been telling the American people. The information has not been accurate.**—*Governor George Romney of Michigan, during questioning by the press, 9 September 1967.*[682]

Romney claimed to have been brainwashed by the Johnson administration during an information tour of South Vietnam in 1965. He said the "rosy" picture of progress painted for him when he was in South Vietnam was a distortion of the true situation in Vietnam at the time. The Administration countered that Romney was "blind to the truth."

1535 **We can't hunker down like a jackass in a hailstorm.**—*President Lyndon Johnson, 1967.*[261]

Johnson refused to consider staff recommendations that would reduce U.S. troop levels in South Vietnam or falling back to an enclave strategy which would leave large areas of the country in uncontested control of the enemy.

1536 **Put our best man in there to see if there are any ships, and if not, hit the ports.**—*President Lyndon Johnson, to General Harold Johnson, during a White House meeting, 12 September 1967.*[72]

General Johnson was acting chairman of the JCS. President Johnson authorized strikes against the North Vietnamese ports of Cam Pha and Hong Gai, provided there were no foreign ships in those ports at the time of the strike.

1537 **[It was] Chicago politics, but with circumspection.**—*Unidentified American official, as quoted by The New York Times, September 1967.*[56]

Times correspondent's view of the 1967 South Vietnamese election for president. Communist or pro-communist names did not appear on the ballot. The governors of the outer provinces around Saigon were appointed by the Ky-Thieu regime. Many of these governors were suspected of "directing" some of the balloting of major ethnic groups within their provinces.

1538 **You guys simply have to back off. Whatever the true O/B [Order of Battle] figure is, is beside the point. [If a much larger figure should be published] ... some dove in State will leak it to the press; that will create a public disaster and undo everything we've been trying to accomplish out here.**—*Robert Komer, Director of CORDS, during a conversation with George Carver, September 1967.*[223]

Carver headed a Washington team of intelligence analysts who attended a conference with MACV intelligence officers. The conference was to resolve the difference between MACV's enemy Order of Battle and the CIA's enemy O/B. MACV refused to include enemy irregular (self-defense and secret self-defense) forces in the O/B because adding them in would have increased the total enemy strength in South Vietnam to well above 420,000 men. By the end of the conference CIA had backed off and the extra enemy was not counted in the totals which would be officially released to the press.

1539 **Americans like to kill as well as the next man and they do it more effectively than most. It happens to be a built-in factor in the basic nature of all men, like sex, food and alcohol.**—*Frank Harvey, free-lance writer and correspondent, 1967.*[249]

Harvey responding to the argument that Americans killed in Vietnam out of "reluctant necessity." His short response to that was "bull shit."

1540 **[A] higher [enemy strength] figure would not be sufficiently optimistic and would generate [an] unacceptable level of criticism from the press.**—*George Carver, Special Assistant for Vietnamese Affairs, CIA, in a report to Richard Helms, 12 September 1967.*[72]

Carver was in Vietnam to resolve the O/B dispute between MACV and the CIA. He informed Helms (Director of the CIA) that it appeared that pressure came from Westmoreland to keep the enemy O/B numbers low by not including enemy irregular forces as well as lower numbers of enemy main force and guerrilla units.

1541 **I think he is trying to tell us something ... every time he comes I get the feeling that I should have been born white.**—*David Parks, former U.S. Army infantryman, from his diary, 1967.*[1001]

Parks was relating the story of his racist sergeant who would pick the "Negroes and Puerto Ricans" for patrol every time there was a hazardous mission.

1542 **What is the use of barbed-wire fences, when we can penetrate even Tan Son Nhut Air Base outside Saigon?**—*General Tran Do, Deputy Commander, Communist Forces in South Vietnam, as quoted by Time magazine, 15 September 1967.*[112]

Tran Do's reaction to Robert McNamara's plan to install an anti-infiltration barrier across the DMZ, more widely known as McNamara's Wall or McNamara's Fence.

1543 **Search for imaginative ideas to put pressure to bring this war to a conclusion — he [LBJ] did not want them to just recommend more men or that we drop the Atom bomb. He [LBJ] could think of those ideas.**—*President Lyndon Johnson, to General Harold Johnson, from the notes of a White House meeting, 15 September 1967.*[45]

General Harold Johnson was the Army Chief of Staff and at the time was the acting Chairman of the Joint Chiefs of Staff.

1544 **Hanoi's leaders are elderly men. They are living on their French Indo-china memories. They are hanging on. They lost their winning strategy between the 1964 buildup and now ... they are just hoping we cave in. Hanoi is suffering a manpower shortage.**—*Walt Rostow, Special Assistant to the President, in a report to the President, 20 September 1967.*[72]

Rostow was of the opinion that a reduction in guerrilla attacks and large unit enemy operations indicated America was winning the war in Vietnam.

1545 **Cambodia takes great pride in supporting the struggle carried out by the Front [NLF] and the South Viet Nam people right from the outset and we will continue to support you.**—*Norodom Sihanouk, Cambodian Head of State, speaking in Cambodia, 17 September 1967.*[969]

Sihanouk continually claimed Cambodian neutrality in the Vietnam War yet he sanctioned the transport of war materiel to the VC/NVA through the Cambodian port of Sihanoukville as well as VC/NVA base areas along the Cambodian border.

1546 **As a matter of high national policy there should be a publicly stated ceiling to the level of American participation in Vietnam, as long as there is no further marked escalation on the enemy side.**—*McGeorge Bundy, Special Assistant to the President for National Security Affairs, 1967.*[713]

Bundy and other Johnson administration advisers proposed setting a troop ceiling limit to the number of American troops that would be sent to Vietnam. This debate surfaced when General Westmoreland requested an additional 200,000 troops for Vietnam. By the end of 1966, American troop strength was approximately 385,000 men.

1547 **The agency's [CIA] analysts ... could not expect to compare in depth and quality to that of MACV.**—*Robert Komer, Special Assistant to the President, during a meeting with George Carver, September 1967.*[72]

Komer, on why the CIA numbers were not as accurate as MACV enemy strength numbers. The discrepancy was in the range of more than 130,000 troops, CIA claiming the larger number.

1548 **NBC and the *New York Times* are committed to an editorial policy of making us surrender.**—*President Lyndon Johnson, during a New York Times interview, 20 September 1967.*[72]

Johnson attacked the American press for displaying a bias towards Ho Chi Minh.

1549 **I can prove that Ho is a son-of-a-bitch if you let me put it on the screen — but they want me to be the son-of-a-bitch.**—*President Lyndon Johnson, during a New York Times interview, 20 September 1967.*[72]

Johnson argued that media coverage of the war was unfairly biased against the American side, and specifically against him. The daily atrocities of the Viet Cong did not make the headlines as often as a misstep by American troops.

1550 **The Armed Services will ... one day realize with sorrow that one of the costs of the Vietnam war has been the widespread alienation of public opinion on which they depend.**—*John Kenneth Galbraith, former U.S. Ambassador to India and economist, from his book, 1967.*[243]

1551 **It is possible that we may have moved into Vietnam too slowly — that we have been too restrained in our bombing policy — too gradual across the board.**—*President Lyndon Johnson, during a White House meeting, September 1967.*[72]

Johnson, speaking to an Australian Broadcasting Group visiting the White House. His comments came after Ho Chi Minh had again rejected his San Antonio peace feeler.

1552 **A feeling is widely and strongly held that "the Establishment" is out of its mind ... that we are trying to impose some U.S. image on distant peoples we cannot understand, and that we are carrying the thing to absurd lengths. Related to this feeling is the increased polarization that is taking place in the United States, with seeds of the worst split in our people in more than a century.**—*John T. McNaughton, Assistant Secretary of Defense, in comments to Robert McNamara, 1967.*[374]

1553 **Press coverage of Vietnam is a reflection of broader and deeper public attitudes, a refusal by many Americans "to see the enemy as the enemy."**—*President Lyndon Johnson, during a New York Times interview, 20 September 1967.*[72]

Johnson objected to the media's narrow focus on the war in Vietnam, so narrow that it focused on the American conduct of the war, limiting coverage of enemy failures and misconduct.

1554 **[The *New York Times*] plays a leading part in prejudicing people against [me]. Editors won't use the words "President Johnson" in anything that is good. Bigotry is born in some of the *New York Times* people.**—*President Lyndon Johnson, during a New York Times interview, 20 September 1967.*[72]

1555 **Those who kill for pleasure are sadists.... Those who kill for money are professionals.... Those who kill for both are Gunslingers.**—*The Slogan of the Gunslingers of the 128th Assault Helicopter Company, recorded by the press, 1967.*[371]

The Gunslingers was the company's gunship platoon. The 128th AHC was part of the 1st Aviation Brigade.

1556 **We strongly suggest that white civilizing committees be established immediately in all white communities to civilize and humanize the savage and beast-like character that runs rampant throughout America, as exemplified by George Lincoln Rockwells and Lyndon Baines Johnsons.**—*Publicized resolution of the Black Caucus during the National Conference for New Politics, Chicago, September 1967.*[719]

This was one of thirteen resolutions put before the conference. The Caucus threatened to leave the conference if their resolutions were not accepted by the conference. The conference attempted to ally the various political factions (left-wing and activist groups) in to one political focus group to increase their political power and voice their opposition to the war.

1557 **Our problem is not that the public has not been exposed to this kind of material before. The problem is that they do not accept this evidence as sufficient. Better statistics will help, but not enough to meet the basic problem.**—*Philip Habib, Deputy Assistant Secretary of State, reporting to Harold Kaplan, 26 September 1967*.[72]

Discussing the credibility gap between the information that was coming out of Washington and MACV as compared to what the public was receiving from the media and seeing on TV. Harold Kaplan was Deputy Assistant Secretary of State for Public Affairs.

1558 **No force can be conscripted to oppose the nationalist instinct of its own people, and all experience with the South Vietnamese army is consistent with this expectation.**—*John Kenneth Galbraith, former U.S. Ambassador to India and economist, from his book, 1967*.[243]

1559 **The [Administration's statistical] data do not explain away dismay at our own casualty figures (the level and cumulative total) ... do not answer charges of Vietnamese corruption, inefficiency, and inadequate performance ... do not answer the question of how much longer we will be required to maintain our effort ... do not answer those who doubt that it is in our national interest to do what we are doing at the price we are paying ... do not satisfy those who are not looking for military success but who are hoping for a short-run political solution.**—*Philip Habib, Deputy Assistant Secretary of State, reporting to Harold Kaplan, 26 September 1967*.[72]

Harold Kaplan was Deputy Assistant Secretary of State for Public Affairs.

1560 **[The brigade commander] spends firepower as if he is a millionaire and husbands his men's lives as if he is a pauper ... during search and destroy operations, commanders should look upon infantry as the principal combat reconnaissance force and supporting fires as the principal destructive force.**—*Colonel Sidney B. Berry, Jr., experienced brigade commander, writing in a military training pamphlet, 1967*.[713]

Prior to the Vietnam War the Army taught "fire and maneuver." The tactic of firing on the enemy, pinning him in place as your troops close and destroy him. In Vietnam, the tactic was often reversed. Troops were maneuvered to locate the enemy, at which point they were pulled back to allow heavy firepower to destroy the enemy (artillery, air strikes).

1561 **As we have told Hanoi time and time again, the heart of the matter is this: the United States is willing immediately to stop all aerial and naval bombardment of North Vietnam when this will lead promptly to productive discussion. We of course would assume that while discussions proceed, North Vietnam would not take advantage of the bombing cessation or limitation.**—*President Johnson, in a speech in San Antonio, Texas, 29 September 1967*.[817]

This was known as the San Antonio Formula. Previously the Administration demanded that North Vietnam stop all infiltration of men and supplies before a bombing halt would be called. The new formula allowed for a bombing halt on an indication that Hanoi was ready to talk.

1562 **[He is] being-the-bastard-he-really-can-be...**—*Unidentified Johnson aide, 1967*.[441]

Alluding to President Johnson's get tough attitude in dealing with his detractors.

1563 **I know their character from the past. There's something kind of marvelous about them; it's their simplicity, their generosity, their casual sharing of everything they have.**—*David Douglas Duncan, photojournalist, October 1967*.[439]

Duncan was speaking of the U.S. Marines.... He was a Marine combat photographer in World War II. As a photojournalist he was with the Marines at Khe Sanh and Con Thien.

1564 **It's a miserable war and we've got a miserable part of it.**—*GySgt. Joseph Welock, K Battery, 11th Marines, 1st Marine division, to correspondent, October 1967*.[384]

K Battery was an M109, self-propelled, 155mm howitzer battery. It fired in support of USMC and Allied units in the Da Nang area.

1565 **The war is the tough frustrating slow struggle in the south, on the ground, in the villages, and in the Saigon government. If we can't win that war and can bomb the North into ruble we won't have won a thing.**—*Harry C. McPherson, Jr., Special Counsel to the President, to the President, 27 October 1967*.[72]

Some in the White House perceived that media coverage of the air war against North Vietnam was what the public believed was the "real" war in Vietnam — the perception of a large military power bombing a small backward nation into submission.

1566 **Saigon [Report #] 7867 presents powerful evidence of solid progress.**—*Dean Rusk, Secretary of State, October 1967*.[72]

The report by the American Embassy in South Vietnam on the progress of the war, released October 1967, submitted to the President, and eventually to the press, was heavily documented with indications that the U.S. was winning the war in Vietnam.

1567 **That's the most beautiful noise on this earth.**—*Unidentified Marine, in a bunker at Con Thien, October 1967*.[438]

The noise was an air strike by B-52s on enemy positions across the DMZ during the siege of Con Thien in 1967.

1568 **There are some pictures which are not easy to bear — of men wounded and killed. But they are all professionals, practicing a trade for which they volunteered.**—*David Douglas Duncan, photojournalist, with the U.S. Marines at Con Thien, October 1967*.[438]

Duncan spent ten days with the Marines at Con Thien, then under siege from NVA guns from across the DMZ.

1569 **[Con Thien was] a symbol of cumulative frustrations in a complex war.**—*Time magazine, 6 October 1967*.[653]

Con Thien was a Marine base on the southern edge of the DMZ. In late-1967 the base was subjected to intense bombardment by NVA guns in and across the DMZ. Several NVA ground assaults were launched against and near Con Thien, gaining it the title, "The Meatgrinder."

1570 **The war in Vietnam is not, and must not become a political issue.... It would be wrong for the loyal opposition so to misconceive its role as to become a "peace at any price" party.**—*Senator Hugh Scott of Pennsylvania, speaking 9 October 1967.*[780]

Scott was trying to tell other Republicans not to use the Vietnam War as a political issue in the upcoming 1968 election. Romney made the mistake of making the war a public, political issue, dooming his chances at a nomination for the Republican candidacy.

1571 **I have yet to hear anyone tell us if we did stop the bombing they could definitely deliver Hanoi to the conference table.**—*Dean Rusk, Secretary of State, to the media, 1967.*[436]

The U.S. initiated bombing pauses, seeking a response from Hanoi, which would indicate a willingness to talk. The response from Hanoi was either silence or a rejection of the American terms, and a restatement of their conditions, i.e., an unconditional halt of the bombardment of North Vietnam and the withdrawal of American forces from South Vietnam.

1572 **This briefing [Saigon Report #7867] and similar fictions that MACV proposes to present in the near future, present a series of vulnerable intelligence judgments that cannot be substantiated at this time and promise almost certainly to lead to even graver credibility problems than the current debate over Orders of Battle.**—*Paul Walsh, Acting Deputy Director for Economic Research, CIA, in a cable to George Carver, 11 October 1967.*[72]

SR #7867 was a U.S. Embassy report on the progress of the war in South Vietnam, pre-released in October 1967.

1573 **We have achieved stalemate [in Vietnam] at a high commitment.**—*Alain Enthoven, Assistant Secretary of Department of Defense, in a Pentagon document.*[60]

Enthoven's paper was one of many documents that comprised the secret *Pentagon Papers*, which were eventually published by *The New York Times*. The report, commissioned by McNamara in June 1967, was a review of the military policy regarding Vietnam covering a 22 year period.

1574 **Takes real courage going day to day and not even knowing that there's a warm body over there.**—*Alice Stratton, wife of Lt.Comdr. Richard Stratton, POW in Hanoi, during Life magazine interview, October 1967.*[437]

She had recently received word that her husband was being held by North Vietnam.

1575 **I might sweat a little more than the younger Marines, but I keep up with them.**—*Corporal Walter S. Stanley, B Company, 1st Battalion, 1st Marine Regiment, to a Marine reporter, October 1967.*[383]

Corporal Stanley rejoined the Marine Corps after eleven years as a civilian. At 39, he was the oldest Marine in his company. Stanley deployed to Vietnam as an infantryman.

1576 **[The Vietnam War is] the most sophisticated war in history.**—*General William Westmoreland, ComUSMACV, 1967.*[347]

1577 **Our setbacks [in Vietnam] were due to wishful thinking compounded by a massive intelligence collection and/or intelligence failure.**—*Alain Enthoven, Assistant Secretary of Department of Defense, in a Pentagon document.*[60]

Enthoven's paper was one of many documents that comprised the secret *Pentagon Papers*, which were eventually published by *The New York Times*. The report, commissioned by McNamara in June 1967, was a review of the military policy regarding Vietnam covering a 22 year period.

1578 **[It's like] pouring bombs into a funnel.**—*Anonymous, 1967.*[931]

The phrase coined by the Rolling Thunder advocates in reference to a plan under consideration at the White House in mid–1967, which would restrict the bombing campaign against North Vietnam to targets below the 20th Parallel. The Air Force and Navy strenuously objected to the proposal which was backed by Robert McNamara.

1579 **Bomb, bomb, bomb — that's all they know.**—*President Lyndon Johnson, comments on the JCS, 1967.*[302]

Johnson is said to have complained on several occasions about the JCS continual recommendation to increase the bombing of North Vietnam in order to force Hanoi to negotiate and reduce its support to the VC in the South.

1580 **One can't help but wonder what a man thinks about, after he'd set fire to 50 square miles of jungle from high altitude with a rain of fire bombs, and wakes up in his room in the darkness — and lies awake watching the shadows on the ceiling...**—*Frank Harvey, free-lance writer and correspondent, 1967.*[249]

Harvey commenting on the bombing campaign carried on by B-52s.

1581 **Let me say, as solemnly as I can, that those who would place in question the credibility of the pledged word of the United States under our mutual security treaties would subject this nation to mortal danger.... Within the next decade or two there will be a billion Chinese on the mainland, armed with nuclear weapons, with no certainty about what their attitude toward the rest of Asia will be.**—*Dean Rusk, Secretary of State, during a press conference, 12 October 1967.*[785]

Rusk, defending the war effort in Vietnam as being of vital interest to the U.S., not just the defense of Saigon, but stopping the spread of communism in Asia.

1582 **...one of the greatest snow jobs since Potemkin constructed his village.**—*Paul Walsh, Acting Deputy Director for Economic Research, CIA, in a cable to George Carver, 11 October 1967.*[72]

Walsh was referring to the "Measurements of Progress in South Vietnam" report pre-released in October 1967. The report was the Administration's statistical proof of progress in Vietnam. The report was compiled by the U.S. Embassy in Saigon from a variety of sources. Potemkin constructed fake villages along the tour route of Empress Catherine in 1787, giving her the impression that all was well in the countryside.

1583 **This is not Johnson's war. This is America's war. If I drop dead tomorrow, this war will still be with you.**—*President Lyndon Johnson during an interview at the White House, 13 October 1967.*[72]

1584 **All "H and I" fire accomplishes is to harass me and interdict my sleep.**—*Ronald W. Knox, ammo humper, K Battery, 11th Marines, 1st Marine Division, speaking to a correspondent, October 1967.*[384]

Knox was an ammo humper for one of the self-propelled 155mm howitzers of the battery. The H & I (harassment and interdiction) fire was randomly fired against suspected enemy LOCs, staging areas, and base locations.

1585 **The picture is of a war which has reached its peak and is beginning to decelerate slowly.**—*Walt Rostow, Special Assistant to the President, in a memorandum to the President, 14 October 1967.*[72]

Rostow promoted the MACV version of the enemy strength based on the O/B, showing progress on the battlefield through a reduction in total enemy troops in South Vietnam. The CIA did not agree with the MACV numbers, but did not seriously challenge Westmoreland on the issue.

1586 **We cannot and will not permit South Vietnam to be a monument to freedom's defeat — or a franchise to infiltration and subversion.**—*Abe Fortas, Supreme Court Justice, in a letter to President Johnson, 14 October 1967.*[72]

Fortas was a long-time personal friend of Johnson's and he advised him to step up the war in Vietnam to a successful conclusion.

1587 **I am not going to spit in China's face.**—*President Lyndon Johnson in comments to one of his aides, 1967.*[261]

Johnson resisted his military advisers' calls for escalation of the war to the point of mining and attacking North Vietnamese ports and harbors, as well as increased strikes against LOCs along the North Vietnam–China border. His advisers also called for a large increase in U.S. troop strength in Vietnam, with a call up of Reserve units to support the manpower increase.

1588 **[Vietnamese prisons:] hotels for unasked guests.** —*Unidentified North Vietnamese prison guard, Hanoi, 1967.*[437]

What the North Vietnamese publicly call their American POW prisons. This remark was made to an East German film crew filming the conditions of American POWs in Hanoi.

1589 ***Life*** **believes that the U.S. is in Vietnam for honorable and sensible purposes. What the U. S. had undertaken there is obviously harder, longer, more complicated than the U.S. leadership foresaw.... We are trying to defend not a fully born nation but a situation and a people from which an independent nation might emerge. We are also trying to maintain a highly important — but in the last analysis not absolutely imperative — strategic interest of the U.S. and the free world. This is a tough combination to ask young Americans to die for.**—*Life magazine editorial, 13 October 1967.*[653]

Time Inc. shifted from support of the war to neutrality in mid–1967, and later on to guarded opposition to the manner in which the war was being waged.

1590 **The most powerful nation on earth [is] pouring World War II–scale bomb loads onto a primitive little country.**—*Life magazine, editorial, 20 October 1967.*[436]

1591 **[The war in Vietnam] may well be a costly exercise in futility.**—*Senator Eugene McCarthy, of Minnesota, during a Senate speech, 16 October 1967.*[822]

McCarthy was of the opinion that even if the war could be won in Vietnam it would have no impact on the threat the Administration indicated was posed by China. Dean Rusk repeatedly indicated that the first step in stopping the spread of communism in Asia was a victory over communism in South Vietnam.

1592 **I feel we (the CIA in general and SAVA in particular) ... misinformed policy-makers of the strength of the enemy.... The Agency's and the office's failing concerning Viet Cong manpower ... has been its acquiescence to MACV half-truths, distortions, and sometimes outright falsehoods. We have occasionally protested, but neither long enough, nor loud enough.**—*Sam Adams, CIA analyst, in a department transfer request, 1967.*[72]

Adams complained that the true enemy strength figures were not being passed on to the Administration. The low enemy numbers indicated by MACV gave a false sense of progress in the war of attrition.

1593 **The American Selective Service System will continue to send young men out to the slaughter.**—*Michael Ferber, member of the anti-draft/anti-war group, The Resistance, in a speech during a demonstration in Boston, 16 October 1967.*[736]

The Resistance organized a nationwide draft card turn-in where more than a thousand draft cards were collected, and on 20 October an unsuccessful attempt was made to give the cards to Assistant Deputy Attorney General John R. McDonough of the Justice Department.

1594 **We shall apply the minimum of the tremendous force available to us — the minimum necessary to protect freedom — to resist a Communist victory — to obtain the modest goal that we seek and must obtain. But obtain it, we shall.**—*Abe Fortas, Supreme Court Justice, in a letter to President Johnson, 14 October 1967.*[72]

Fortas was a long-time personal friend of Johnson's and he advised him to step up the war in Vietnam to a successful conclusion.

1595 **Were it not for the Marines who guard the bridges, our hope would be as bright as a candle under a basket.**—*Father Nguyen Kiem, Vietnamese Catholic priest, Da Nang, to a correspondent, October 1967.*[385]

Father Kiem was speaking of the two bridges that span the Song Han River on the eastern edge of Da Nang. The USMC guarded the two bridges linking Da Nang to the Monkey Mountain peninsula.

1596 **This country has never left the field of battle in abject surrender of cause for which it fought. We shall not do so now.**—*Abe Fortas, Supreme Court Justice, in a letter to President Johnson, 14 October 1967.*[72]

Fortas was a long-time personal friend of Johnson's and he advised him to step up the war in Vietnam to a successful conclusion.

1597 **[It would be a major mistake to marshal] any elaborate effort to show by new facts and figures that we are "winning"**

the war in Vietnam.—*McGeorge Bundy, former Special Assistant to the President, in a letter, 18 October 1967.*[72]

Bundy caution Johnson against aligning himself with hawks who were calling for increased bombing of the North and increased military action in South Vietnam.

1598 **[The doves and protesters would not] know a Communist if they tripped over one.**—*President Lyndon Johnson, comments about youthful dissenters, 1967.*[269]

Johnson often complained that those opposed to the war did not have a real understanding of what was going on in Vietnam and the terror and turmoil wrought by the communists.

1599 **Given the overriding need to demonstrate our progress in grinding down the enemy, it is essential that we do not drag too many red herrings across the trail.**—*Ellsworth Bunker, Ambassador to South Vietnam, in a cable to Walt Rostow, October 1967.*[72]

Bunker's reference was to the exclusion of enemy irregular forces from the total enemy force numbers given to the press. He was concerned that the O/B discrepancy between MACV and CIA would surface, indicating a reversal in the progress he promoted.

1600 **[I have posed this question to a number of governments.] All right, if we stop the bombing, what can you deliver? I get no response.**—*Dean Rusk, Secretary of State, to the media, 1967.*[436]

As of October 1967 there had been six bombing pauses.

1601 **[It] truly says something about [the government's] own convictions — that it doesn't have enough morality on its side to carry through with such a moral confrontation.**—*Reverend William Sloane Coffin, Jr., chaplain of Yale University, comments to reporters, 20 October 1967.*[724]

Sloane was one of the leaders of a group that attempted to turn in draft cards to the Justice Department to protest the draft, and the war in Vietnam. The Justice Department refused to accept the cards or confront the demonstrators. Coffin and four others were later indicted 8 January 1968, in Boston, on charges of "conspiring to violate the Selective Service Act." They were loosely known as the Boston Five. They were members or supporters of the group, The Resistance, which was anti-draft and anti-war.

1602 **[Hanoi is] in no mood for concessions or bargaining, and there is an absolute refusal to offer anything except talks for cessation of the bombardment.**—*Wilfred Burchett, Australian Communist journalist, interviewing North Vietnam Foreign Minister Trinh, 21 October 1967.*[452]

Hanoi once again insisted that their demands be met. In this case indicating that they would only consider talks when the bombing stopped.

1603 **The bombing [of North Vietnam] has isolated the U.S. from most of its friends and allies throughout the world (there are a few stout exceptions in Asia), and in this country the bombing is the focus and catalyst of most of the opposition to the war.**—*Life magazine, editorial, 20 October 1967.*[436]

The perception encouraged by Hanoi was that of a world power pounding a small backward nation into submission.

1604 **Don't stop the bombing. If anything, step it up. Anytime you want to lose a war you can. If we lose Vietnam we lose influence in this entire area of the world. We must make a stand here.**—*Senator Russell Long of Louisiana, during a White House meeting, 23 October 1967.*[72]

Long was the majority whip in the Senate.

1605 **There is a strong probability that a bombing pause would improve the posture of the U.S. in Vietnam, in the eyes of many other nations and indeed of many Americans, and ultimately improve our chances of achieving our purposes in Vietnam.**—*Life magazine, editorial, 20 October 1967.*[436]

The editorial proposed that the Johnson administration institute a bombing halt without including the usual statement that the bombing would resume unless there was some reciprocal movement by Hanoi towards reducing or stopping infiltration into the South.

1606 **United States bombing attacks on North Vietnam would never break the will of its people to help the Vietcong in South Vietnam achieve victory. The Vietnamese are ready to pay any price for victory.**—*General Vo Nguyen Giap, Defense Minister, Democratic Republic of Vietnam, comments published in a Moscow newspaper, 21 October 1967.*[546]

Hanoi rejected American terms for initiating peace talks. They insisted no talks could begin unless the U.S. conceded to their demands.

1607 **The strategic air war ... does not affect the real contest, which is in the South. Its political costs are rising each week.**—*McGeorge Bundy, former Special Assistant to the President, in a letter, 18 October 1967.*[72]

Bundy conferred with the CIA and came to the conclusion that the bombing of Hanoi–Hai Phong would not significantly affect the supplies reaching South Vietnam, nor would increased bombing break the will of North Vietnam to resist.

1608 **We could bomb North Vietnam into the stone age if we wanted to. I do not believe we have reached the objective which was stopping the flow of men and materiel into the South.**—*Senator Mike Mansfield, of Montana, during a White House meeting, 23 October 1967.*[72]

Senate majority leader Mansfield did not believe the bombing of North Vietnam was effective in stopping Hanoi's support for the war in the South.

1609 **We have everything to gain politically and almost nothing to lose militarily if we will firmly hold our bombing to demonstrably useful target areas.**—*McGeorge Bundy, former Special Assistant to the President, in a letter, 18 October 1967.*[72]

Bundy arguing against the bombing escalation hawks were clamoring for.

1610 **While those most opposed to the war have been silenced, the [Selective Service] system that provides the personnel for war crimes continues to function smoothly.**—*David Harris, member of group called The Resistance, in an anti-draft speech in San Francisco, 1967.*[730]

Harris was the student body president at Stanford University in Palo Alto, California, before co-founding The Resistance. The group advocated draft resistance and called for a nationwide draft card turn-in, in October 1967.

1611 **At best, it [anti-infiltration barrier] is a costly undertaking which could impede some infiltration; at worst, it is an unwise, costly scheme fraught with severe political and military disadvantages, and one whose potential value is greatly outweighed by its cost and its inherent disadvantages.**—*Lt. Col. William D. Barnes, in a USAWC essay, 27 October 1967.*[96]

McNamara authorized construction of a barbed-wire and electronic sensor barrier to be installed along the DMZ, for the purpose of detecting and hampering NVA infiltration across the DMZ. The barrier, would extend along the southern edge of the DMZ, from the South China Sea to the South Vietnamese border with Laos. As the barrier would not extend into Laos, the North Vietnamese could simply bypass the barrier by continuing to move through Laos.

1612 **We can no longer passively acquiesce to the Selective Service System by accepting its deferments. The American military system depends upon students, those opposed to war, and those with anti–Vietnam war politics wrangling for the respective deferments.**—*David Harris, member of a group called The Resistance, in an anti-draft speech in San Francisco, 1967.*[730]

Harris was the student body president at Stanford University in Palo Alto, California, before co-founding The Resistance. The group advocated draft resistance and called for a nationwide draft card turn-in in October 1967.

1613 **[The M109 looks like] somebody pried the turret off a tank, replaced it with a chicken coop and ran a stove pipe out the front window.**—*Unidentified Marine Corps rifleman, commenting to a correspondent, October 1967.*[384]

The M109 was a self-propelled 155mm howitzer. It was equipped with a turret housing the 155mm howitzer tube. The turret was mounted on a fully tracked carriage.

1614 **...we do not seek jail, but we do this [draft card turn-in] because as individuals we know of no justifiable alternative and we believe in time many other American men will also choose to resist the crimes done in their names.**—*David Harris, member of group called The Resistance, in an anti-draft speech in San Francisco, 1967.*[730]

Harris was the student body president at Stanford University in Palo Alto, California, before co-founding The Resistance. The group advocated draft resistance and called for a nationwide draft card turn-in, in October 1967. He attacked the morality of the war and the perceived U.S. war crimes of the war in Vietnam.

1615 **The concept and objective planned for our forces ... portrays to the American people some light at the end of the tunnel.**—*General William Westmoreland, ComUSMACV, in a message to his staff, November 1967.*[653]

During Westmoreland's PR campaign in Washington he outlined America's four-phase program for success in Vietnam. He reiterated the planned program to his staff. Phase one and two were the rescue of South Vietnam and the buildup of forces, then turning to the offensive. Phase three was the training and equipping of the South Vietnamese military and their gradual assumption of the dwindling war effort. Phase four was the "final mopping up" of the enemy and the withdrawal of American troops from Vietnam.

1616 **We're not going to yield. And we're not going to shimmy. We are going to wind up with a peace with honor which all Americans seek.**—*President Lyndon Johnson, speaking to American troops at Cam Ranh Bay, 1967.*[347]

Johnson flew to Cam Ranh Bay during a break in the Manila Conference. He spent a few hours with the troops before returning to Manila.

1617 **It is not at all clear that the image of performance of this government [South Vietnam] over the next 15 months will make it appear to the US public to [be] a government worthy of continued US support in blood and treasure.**—*Robert McNamara, Secretary of Defense, in a memorandum to President Johnson, 1 November 1967.*[72]

The recent elections of Thieu and Ky had not bolstered Vietnamese public support for the government.

1618 **The public would be outraged if we got out [of Vietnam].**—*Abe Fortas, Supreme Court Justice and unofficial advisor to the President, during a meeting of the Wise Men, 2 November 1967.*[48]

The President posed the question whether the U.S. should withdraw from Vietnam, even though the goals there had not been met.

1619 **No nation has been more enlightenedly [sic] served under Secretaries Rusk and McNamara.**—*President Lyndon Johnson, during a meeting of his official and unofficial advisors, 2 November 1967.*[48]

1620 **The Viet Cong has been defeated from Da Nang all the way down in the populated areas. He can't get food and he can't recruit. He has been forced to change his strategy from trying to control the people on the coast to trying to survive in the mountains.**—*General Bruce Palmer, Deputy Commander, U.S. Army Vietnam, commenting to journalist Orr Kelly, November 1967.*[653]

1621 **Although we have redoubled our efforts, we have lost sight of our objective.**—*Unidentified American officer, 1967.*[501]

1622 **I accept ... the prospect that U.S. forces will reach 525,000, other free world forces will reach 59–75,000, and South Vietnamese forces can be increased by 60,000. I do not agree that these increased forces cannot bring the North Vietnamese and the Viet Cong forces visibly closer to collapse during the next 15 months. The indicators point in the other direction.**—*Dean Rusk, Secretary of State, in a memorandum to President Johnson, 1 November 1967.*[72]

Rusk did not agree with McNamara's position that increased force in Vietnam would not yield a military victory or force Hanoi to negotiate.

1623 **I am very, very encouraged.... We are making real progress.**—*General William Westmoreland, ComUSMACV, comments to the press, Washington D.C., November 1967.*[269]

Westmoreland spoke before Congress and the news media during a visit to Washington.

1624 **In no case is there a clear, direct or broadly-accepted relationship between the statistical progress and the end of the war ... the upward trend in the statistics is almost**

universally accepted. It is the sweeping conclusions being drawn from those figures that are in doubt.—*Don Oberdorfer, Washington Post reporter, November 1967.*[72]

The Administration concluded from their (MACV) statistics that the enemy threat was diminishing and pacification was increasing.

1625 **We must resist pressure to take direct action against foreign shipping entering Hai Phong or to bomb irrigation dikes.**—*Dean Rusk, Secretary of State, in a memorandum to President Johnson, 1 November 1967.*[72]

Rusk did not want to bomb Hai Phong or seal it with mines for fear of damage to Soviet or Chinese shipping, which could escalate the war and bring more sophisticated Soviet weapons or Chinese troops to the aid of North Vietnam. The military proposed closure of Hai Phong harbor and increased pressure on North Vietnam.

1626 **I am like the steering wheel of a car without any control.**—*President Lyndon Johnson, speaking with his advisors, November 1967.*[72]

Johnson, on the expanding quicksand that had become the war in Vietnam. He sought peace but could not get the other side to agree to peace on his terms.

1627 **I could not free myself from the continuing nagging doubt left over from that August [1967] trip, that if the nations living in the shadow of Viet Nam were not now persuaded by the "Domino Theory," perhaps it was time for us to take another look.**—*Clark Clifford, adviser to President Johnson, 1967.*[199]

1628 **The bombing has no effect on negotiations. When these fellows decide they can't defeat the South, then they will give up.... This is the way the Communists operate.**—*Dean Acheson, former Secretary of State, during a meeting of the Wise Men, 2 November 1967.*[48]

Acheson advised the President that there would be no negotiations as long as Hanoi believed they could outlast the U.S.

1629 **There are ways to guide the press to show the light at the end of the tunnel.**—*Walt Rostow, Special Assistant to the President, during a meeting of the Wise Men, 2 November 1967.*[48]

Rostow wanted to steer the media is such a way that they would support the war and the Administration. The media would then pass this on to the public.

1630 **An excessive eagerness to negotiate or a broad humanitarian gesture to the Communists is interpreted as a sign of weakness by Communists.**—*Arthur Dean, lawyer and unofficial advisor to President Johnson, during a meeting of the Wise Men, 1 November 1967.*[72]

The Wise Men, along with several other Johnson advisors met to discuss Vietnam and options available to the President. This group met with the President on 2 November.

1631 **Our troubles can be blamed on the communications media.... If it wasn't for all the protesters, the North Vietnamese would give up....**—*General Omar Bradley, former Chairman of the JCS, during a meeting of the Wise Men, 2 November 1967.*[48]

1632 **[A McCarthy campaign for President] would allow Americans to take out their frustration in talk instead of violence.**—*Senator Robert Kennedy of New York, speaking at Marymount College, New York, 18 November 1967.*[796]

At this point Kennedy insisted he was not a candidate for President, but he did say he would back whoever the Democratic candidate was. He did not specifically mention Johnson.

1633 **[An unconditional bombing halt] would give an enormous lift to the spirits and morale of the North, and an equally grave setback to the will and determination of the South Vietnamese and our other allies fighting with us.**—*Clark Clifford, unofficial advisor to President Johnson, in a letter to the President, 7 November 1967.*[72]

Clifford's reaction to McNamara's call for an end to the bombing of North Vietnam.

1634 **I'm going to take the man's blood pressure and make sure he is loyal. It doesn't do any good to win the fight over there and lose it over here.**—*President Lyndon Johnson, during a meeting, 4 November 1967.*[72]

In regards to the selection of a new commander for the III Marine Amphibious Force in Vietnam. Johnson wanted his commanders' loyalty.

1635 **We in the Administration do not expect negotiations in the next year. Public support is eroded because people see dying with no picture of result in sight. If we can prove to the public that we are seeing the results at the end of the road, this will be helpful.**—*McGeorge Bundy, former Special Assistant to the President, during the meeting of the Wise Men, 2 November 1967.*[48]

Most of the senior Johnson advisers did not foresee peace negotiations taking place in the near future.

1636 **They get ice cream about three times a week. Only two out of a thousand that I and my wife visited disliked being there or did not understand why they were there.**—*General Omar Bradley, former Chairman of the JCS, during a meeting of the Wise Men, 2 November 1967.*[48]

Bradley had recently returned from South Vietnam where he had been on a fact finding mission for President Johnson.

1637 **We need to raise patriotism. We never had a war without patriotic slogans. "Patience," 100 years means nothing to a Chinaman, but we do not have their patience.**—*General Omar Bradley, former Chairman of the JCS, during a meeting of the Wise Men, 2 November 1967.*[48]

1638 **Of the alternatives (pull-out, pull-back, all-out, stick-it-out) ... the pull-back alternative ... would probably degenerate into pull-out.**—*General Maxwell Taylor, Special Consultant to the President, November 1967.*[72]

Taylor, addressing McNamara's suggestion that the U.S. stop the bombing of North Vietnam and limit the number of American troops, in an effort to coax Hanoi into negotiations. Taylor proposed vigorous prosecution of the war to a successful conclusion.

1639 **Don't let communications people in New York set the tone of the debate. Emphasize the "light at the end of the tunnel" instead of the battles, deaths and danger.**—*McGeorge*

Bundy, former Special Assistant to the President, during the meeting of the Wise Men, 2 November 1967.[48]

1640 **Hanoi will never seek a cessation of the conflict if they think our determination is lessening ... if our pressure is unremitting and their losses continue to grow, and hope fades for any sign of weakening on our part, then some day they will conclude that the game is not worth the candle.**—*Clark Clifford, unofficial advisor to President Johnson, in a letter to the President, 7 November 1967.*[72]

1641 **There is a good deal of over-reaction to what appears to be the public attitude of the United States. This opposition exists in only a small group of the community, primarily the intellectuals or so-called intellectuals and the press.**—*Abe Fortas, Supreme Court Justice and unofficial advisor to the President, during a meeting of the Wise Men, 2 November 1967.*[48]

1642 **When you must go to the bunkers from a sound sleep that is the most frightening of all. You are not sure where they [enemy rockets] are hitting; and know that you are awfully slow and confused (though in fact you have probably never moved faster) and that in a second you will be blown to pieces.**—*PFC Chester McMullen, U.S. Marine Corps, in a letter home, 7 November 1967.*[853]

1643 **Because of the unique position we occupy in the world today, we cannot expect other countries and other peoples to love us, but with courage and determination, and the help of God, we can make them respect us.**—*Clark Clifford, unofficial advisor to President Johnson, in a letter to the President, 7 November 1967.*[72]

Clifford responding to McNamara's proposal that the U.S. unilaterally scale down or stabilize efforts in South Vietnam with no reciprocal action from Hanoi.

1644 **The American people ... do not want us to achieve less than our objectives — namely, to prevent North Vietnamese domination of South Vietnam by military force or subversion; and to continue to exert such influence as we reasonably can in Asia to prevent an ultimate Communist takeover.**—*Abe Fortas, Supreme Court Justice and unofficial advisor to the President, in a letter to the President, 9 November 1967.*[72]

1645 **An invitation to slaughter.**—*Abe Fortas, Supreme Court Justice and unofficial advisor to the President, in a letter to the President, 9 November 1967.*[72]

Fortas's opinion of McNamara's suggestion that the U.S. stop the bombing of North Vietnam and limit the number of American troops in Vietnam in an effort to coax Hanoi into negotiations.

1646 **The prospect of endless inconclusive fighting is the most serious single cause of domestic disquiet about the war.**—*McGeorge Bundy, advisor to President Johnson, in a letter to the President, 10 November 1967.*[72]

Bundy's comments about the 2 November meeting of the President's advisors, where most of them urged him to continue the war in Vietnam to a successful conclusion.

1647 **We've been fortunate so far that North Vietnam has rejected our [peace] offer.... To continue to talk about negotiations only signals to the communists that they are succeeding in winning over American public opinion.**—*Abe Fortas, Supreme Court Justice and unofficial advisor to the President, during a meeting of the Wise Men, 2 November 1967.*[48]

1648 **The chortles of unholy glee issuing from Hanoi would be audible in every capital in the world.**—*Clark Clifford, unofficial advisor to President Johnson, in a letter to the President, 7 November 1967.*[72]

Clifford's reaction to McNamara's proposal to stabilize the American war effort by halting the bombing of North Vietnam and setting a ceiling on U.S. troop levels in Vietnam.

1649 **One of the measures of the success that history will look very favorably upon is that both President Kennedy and Johnson didn't wait for public opinion to catch up with them. They went ahead with what was right, and because of that the war is a success today.**—*Clark Clifford, unofficial advisor to President Johnson, during a meeting of the Wise Men, 2 November 1967.*[43]

Clifford was one of the "Wise Men," and later became Secretary of Defense. He urged Johnson to continue to press the war against North Vietnam, advising against any consideration of unilateral withdrawal from Vietnam.

1650 **I believe that, with a little luck and reasonable performance by the South Vietnamese under the new government, the evidence of solid progress will become increasingly clear to one and all.**—*Walt Rostow, Special Assistant to the President, 4 November 1967.*[72]

Rostow continued to be optimistic about the war, citing the newly elected Thieu-Ky government in South Vietnam as influential in the outcome of the war.

1651 **We are beginning to win this struggle. We are on the offensive. Territory is being gained. We are making steady progress.**—*Vice President Hubert Humphrey, during an interview, November 1967.*[653]

Humphrey had recently returned from a visit to Vietnam and was being interviewed on the NBC *Today Show.*

1652 **You're like a flock of buzzards sitting on a fence, sending the young men off to be killed. You ought to be ashamed of yourselves.**—*George Ball, former Under Secretary of State, during a meeting of President Johnson's advisors, 2 November 1967.*[49]

Ball made this statement to several of Johnson's advisors as the meeting was breaking up.

1653 **The [concern of this White House] group ... was with opinion manipulation and political persuasion, with the aim of altering perceptions to make them coincide with specific notions, whether those notions were supportable by evidence or not.**—*Walt Rostow, Special Assistant to the President, during White House meeting, 1967.*[204]

Rostow chaired the White House group, their focus putting the best face on progress reports from Vietnam indicating an improving and winning situation.

1654 **I think we have tried too hard to convert public opinion by statistics and by spectacular visits of all sorts.... I think public discontent with the war is now wide and deep. ... I think people are getting fed up with the endlessness of the fighting.**—*McGeorge Bundy, advisor to President Johnson, in a letter to the President, 10 November 1967.*[72]

1655 **I am not convinced that our military program in South Vietnam is as flexible or ingenious as it could be.**—*Abe Fortas, Supreme Court Justice and unofficial advisor to the President, in a letter to the President, 9 November 1967.*[72]

Fortas was questioning the hawk-dove nature of Johnson's administration in respect to the conduct of the war, tending to be critical towards McNamara's recent dove-leanings.

1656 **We are making progress. We are pleased with the results we are getting. We are inflicting greater losses than we are taking.**—*President Lyndon Johnson, during a press conference, 13 November 1967.*[72]

1657 **[The war will continue] not many more nights ... not while we stand as one family, and one nation, united in one purpose.**—*President Lyndon Johnson, from a speech to crewman of the USS Enterprise, November 1967.*[653]

Johnson was on a morale boosting visit during Veteran's Day observances.

1658 **Success is cumulative—and so is failure. The enemy has problems which are growing.**—*Dean Rusk, Secretary of State, in a memorandum to President Johnson, 1 November 1967.*[72]

Rusk's evaluation of the progress of the U.S. war effort, based on information received from General Westmoreland.

1659 **What really hurts ... is not the arguments of the doves but the cost of the war in lives and money, coupled with the lack of light at the end of the tunnel.**—*McGeorge Bundy, advisor to President Johnson, in a letter to the President, 10 November 1967.*[72]

1660 **It is clear from the [Harris poll] results that the American people are not particularly concerned at this juncture over keeping a strong civilian authority in the Pentagon.**—*Louis Harris, pollster, in a Washington Post article, November 1967.*[72]

The poll rated McNamara and Westmoreland on their job performance. McNamara received a 45 percent negative, and a 42 percent positive ratings. Westmoreland received 16 percent negative and 68 percent positive ratings.

1661 **Our American people, when we get in a contest of any kind ... want it decided and decided quickly; get in or get out.**—*President Lyndon Johnson, during a press conference, 13 November 1967.*[72]

1662 **Hanoi uses time the way the Russians used terrain before Napoleon's advance on Moscow, always retreating, losing every battle, but eventually creating conditions in which the enemy can no longer function.**—*Nicholas Katzenbach, Under Secretary of State, in a memorandum to the President, 16 November 1967.*[72]

For Napoleon, the closer he got to Moscow the longer and more fragile his lines of supply, and when the winter set in he was stranded. For the U.S., the length of the war, the mounting dissension and frustration with the lack of real progress, all worked to Hanoi's advantage, even though militarily they were unable to force the U.S. out of South Vietnam.

1663 **Airpower alone didn't do the job. It never has, but we give it a chance in every war.**—*General William Westmoreland, ComUSMACV, from a speech given at West Point, 1967.*[713]

Westmoreland was referring to the Rolling Thunder air campaign against North Vietnam. The campaign was designed to stop or greatly reduce the flow of men and materiel from North Vietnam to South Vietnam, and also to force Hanoi into peace negotiations.

1664 **The country isn't against you, Mr. President, it's just confused.**—*Comment from an unidentified presidential adviser, November 1967.*[653]

The unnamed source was one of a group of close advisers to the president called the "Wise (Old) Men." After reviewing documentation on the progress of the war, the advisers concluded that government policy in Vietnam was proper, but there was a problem with the public's perception of the war and its goals.

1665 **We're going to win this war if it takes our lives to do it.**—*President Lyndon Johnson, from a speech at Fort Benning, quote attributed to an unknown GI in Vietnam, November 1967.*[653]

President Johnson told his audience the quote was from a man in a foxhole in Vietnam, written on the side of a ham and lima bean C-ration box.

1666 **Even a rapid acceleration of progress [in Vietnam] would not bring the light at the end of the tunnel.**—*Nicholas Katzenbach, Under Secretary of State, in a memorandum to the President, 16 November 1967.*[72]

1667 **The rioting at the Pentagon will look like a panty-waist tea party.... We've got to turn this horrible frustration from the streets to the ballot box.**—*Joseph L Raul, leader of Americans for Democratic Action, from a speech, 16 November 1967.*[744]

Raul, an ardent liberal, was troubled by the war yet supported the Johnson Great Society plan. He believed the government direction on the war needed to be altered at the ballot box, not by demonstrations in the street.

1668 **Can the tortoise of progress in Vietnam stay ahead of the hare of dissent at home?**—*Nicholas Katzenbach, Under Secretary of State, in a memorandum to the President, 16 November 1967.*[72]

By all administration indications progress in pacification and reduction of the enemy was going very slowly, if going forward at all. Yet in America, dissent against the war was growing faster and becoming more widespread.

1669 **Communist strategy is to sustain protracted war of attrition and to persuade the United States that it must pull out or settle on Hanoi's terms.**—*Walt Rostow, Special Assistant to the President, in a memorandum, 14 November 1967.*[72]

1670 **Indeed, the very fact that those who have access to all relevant intelligence [of the U.S. bombing campaign] continually disagree about its value should be proof at least that its value is dubious.... Nobody really believes that the war can be won with bombs in the North.**—*Nicholas Katzenbach, Under Secretary of State, in a memorandum to the President, 16 November 1967.*[72]

Katzenbach expressed reservations about the effectiveness of the bombing campaign against North Vietnam. As a moral issue he believed it was costing the U.S. more at home and internationally than its effects on the war in South Vietnam.

1671 **The cross you have to bear is a lousy Senate Foreign Relations Committee. You have a dilettante fool [J. William**

Fulbright] at the head of the committee.—*Dean Acheson, former Secretary of State, during a meeting of the "Wise Men," 2 November 1967.*[48]

Acheson was one of the "Wise Men." Fulbright no longer fully supported the American war effort in Vietnam or the foreign policy that brought it about.

1672 **The war is in no sense over.... There won't be any collapse.... But U.S. and South Vietnamese forces are doing well ... the war is going in our favor.**—*Richard M. Helms, Director, CIA, during a Cabinet a briefing, November 1967.*[72]

Helms briefed the President and the Cabinet on the most recent National Intelligence Estimate which covered the situation in Vietnam. He was cautiously optimistic but pointed out there were still discrepancies in the O/B numbers.

1673 **The fact that the population under free control has constantly risen ... is a very encouraging sign ... over all we are making progress.**—*President Lyndon Johnson, during a news conference, 17 November 1967.*[29]

Pre-TET 1968 evaluation of the situation in Vietnam, as announced to the American people.

1674 **We have no alternative. We don't want Ronnie Reagan, we want Lyndon Baines Johnson.**—*Unidentified speaker during the National Young Democrats convention in Hollywood, Florida, 17 November 1967.*[797]

Many in the convention voiced their opinion that they would rather have Johnson as president than Ronald Reagan. When the full convention finally voted, they endorsed McCarthy as their candidate.

1675 **In approximately two years or less the Vietnamese Armed Forces should be ready to take over an increasing share of the war thereby permitting us to start phasing down the level of our effort.**—*General William Westmoreland, during a briefing of the Joint Chiefs of Staff, 20 November 1967.*[72]

The briefing, in substance, was repeated several times in Washington before Westmoreland returned to Vietnam.

1676 **If we don't act soon we will wreck the Republic.**—*President Lyndon Johnson, speaking to Congressional leaders, 18 November 1967.*[72]

Attempting to fight the war in Vietnam and support his Great Society reforms in the U.S. was slowly tearing Johnson's administration apart, as well as separating the nation.

1677 **In two years or less, American forces will be able to begin to shift the combat burden to ARVN and disengage.**—*President Lyndon Johnson, during a news conference, 17 November 1967.*[29]

1678 **In Vietnam the military has been handicapped by civilians who won't let them go all out.**—*Louis Harris, pollster, in a Washington Post article, November 1967.*[72]

Those polled were asked how they felt about civilian control of the U.S. war effort in Vietnam; 65 percent believed the military was handicapped by civilian authority, while 10 percent thought the military was not handicapped.

1679 **The ranks of the Vietcong are thinning.**—*General William Westmoreland, ComUSMACV, during comments at the Pentagon.*[374]

Westmoreland was on a PR campaign in Washington to generate support for the Administration's policy in Vietnam.

1680 **[The Vietnam war is Johnson's] colossal mistake....**—*George Romney, Governor of Michigan, during an interview on Face the Nation, 18 November 1967.*[798]

Romney's characterization of the Vietnam War in late 1967. Romney initially backed the Johnson administration's war policy in Vietnam, but changed his views in 1967.

1681 **Infiltration will slow; the Communist infrastructure will be cut up and near collapse; the Vietnamese Government will prove its stability, and the Vietnamese army will show that it can handle the Vietcong; United States units can begin to phase down.**—*General William Westmoreland, ComUSMACV, from a speech at the National Press Club, 20 November 1967.*[219]

Westmoreland's "selling" the success of the war in Vietnam against the communists in 1967, less than three months before nationwide attacks by communist forces across South Vietnam.

1682 **I don't think it will be a case of [political] suicide. It might be an execution.**—*Senator Eugene McCarthy of Minnesota, commenting to the media, November 1967.*[836]

When McCarthy announced his intention to run for the Democratic nomination for president against President Johnson a reporter asked him if he was "committing political suicide," due to the historical difficulty of a challenge to an incumbent President for his party's nomination.

1683 **Well, we simply must tell everyone that Johnson is a man of peace.**—*Edwin Weisl, Democratic National Committee member and personal friend of President Johnson, late 1967.*[717]

Members of the group told Weisl they could not back the President and wanted another candidate. Weisl was a personal friend of Johnson and was reacting to challenges from the New York Reform Democratic movement. This represented deterioration of support for the President within his own party.

1684 **[We are] winning a war of attrition...[it is] conceivable that within 2 years or less the enemy will be so weakened that the Vietnamese will be able to cope with a greater share of the war burden. We will be able to phase down the level of our military effort, withdraw some troops....**—*General William Westmoreland, during an interview on Meet the Press, 19 November 1967.*[72]

1685 **I know of no better way to prolong the war than to stop the bombing of the North.**—*General William Westmoreland, during a meeting of the Joint Chiefs of Staff, 20 November 1967.*[72]

Westmoreland wanted to maintain military pressure on North Vietnam. He argued against McNamara's calls for an end or reduction to the bombing of North Vietnam.

1686 **We are making progress.... It lies within our grasp—the enemy's hopes are bankrupt. With your support we will give you a success that will impact not only on South Vietnam, but on every emerging nation in the world.**—*General William Westmoreland, ComUSMACV, from a speech at the National Press Club, 21 November 1967.*[887]

1687 **The enemy has many problems: ... he is losing control of the scattered population under his influence ... he is**

losing credibility with the population ... he is alienating the people by his increased demands and taxes ... he sees the strength of his forces steadily declining ... he can no longer recruit in the South to any meaningful extent ... his monsoon offensives have been failures ... he was dealt a mortal blow by the installation of a freely elected representative government. ... And he failed in his desperate effort to take the world's headlines from the inauguration by a military victory.—*General William Westmoreland, ComUSMACV, during a televised speech, 21 November 1967.*[857]

Westmoreland outlined U.S./GVN successes in Vietnam, rendering the impression that the war was under control. Less than three months later the enemy launched a nationwide offensive at TET in which 28 of the country's 48 cities and provincial towns were attacked. A result of the offensive caused an abrupt re-evaluation of the U.S. effort in Vietnam and the credibility of past information received regarding the war.

1688 **Fighting efficiency of the VC/NVA has progressively deteriorated.**—*General William Westmoreland, ComUSMACV, during a press briefing, 22 November 1967.*[72]

Westmoreland was specifically speaking about the enemy's condition between June and November 1967. This was based on a reduction in enemy numbers reflecting deaths, defections, reduced recruiting, and captures.

1689 **I am absolutely certain that whereas in 1965 the enemy was winning, today he is certainly losing. ... It is significant that the enemy has not won a major battle in more than a year.**—*General William Westmoreland, from a speech at the National Press Club, 21 November 1967.*[72]

1690 **Hundreds and thousands of people in Vietnam are being killed on our responsibility. You've got to think of the implications to your own conscience.**—*Senator Robert Kennedy of New York, speaking at Marymount College, New York, 18 November 1967.*[796]

Kennedy was speaking to students, some of whom advocated an increase in the bombing of Vietnam.

1691 **We are fighting a limited war for limited objectives and ... we will not need more than 525,000 U.S. forces.**—*Ellsworth Bunker, Ambassador to South Vietnam, in a cable to Walt Rostow, 21 November 1967.*[72]

1692 **We have reached an important point when the end begins to come into view.**—*General William Westmoreland, from a speech at the National Press Club, 21 November 1967.*[374]

Westmoreland was on a PR campaign in Washington to gather support for Administration policy in Vietnam. During Westmoreland's November visit to Washington he indicated enemy numbers and the ability to launch major offensives was on the decline. He voiced public optimism that "we" were winning the war against the communists in Vietnam and that the end of the war was in sight.

1693 **[The] enemy's purpose — seems to be to prolong the war and by psychological and military action weaken our resolve.**—*General William Westmoreland, ComUSMACV, from Westmoreland's briefing notes, November 1967.*[653]

The war of attrition as applied by the VC/NVA was to drag the war out until America became tired of the drain in blood and treasure. This tactic had been successful against the French.

1694 **For the first time in the history of naval warfare a combat commander could launch one aircraft carrying one weapon with a high degree of confidence that significant damage could be inflicted on a selected target.**—*Admiral Thomas J. Walker, Commander, Carrier Division Three, 1967.*[961]

Walker was referring to the first use of "smart bombs" by the U.S. Navy in Vietnam. Walleye, TV-guided air-to-surface glide bombs were first used in combat by aircraft from the USS *Bon Homme Richard* against targets in North Vietnam.

1695 **I hope they [the VC/NVA] try something, because we are looking for a fight.**—*General William Westmoreland, ComUSMACV, comments to a Time correspondent, November 1967.*[374]

Westmoreland painted a picture of progress against communist forces in Vietnam. Based on the reported decline in enemy numbers, he challenged them to try a massive attack. The massive attack took place over TET 1968.

1696 **Emphasize the "light at the end of the tunnel" instead of the battles, deaths, and danger.**—*McGeorge Bundy, president, Ford Foundation and unofficial adviser to President Johnson, advice to the President, November 1967.*[887]

Bundy was one of the "Wise Men" who advised President Johnson. There was a big push toward the end of 1967 to emphasize to the public that the U.S. was winning the war in Vietnam.

1697 **I didn't believe we had reached a crossover point. I didn't believe the [enemy] strength would decline. I didn't believe that the bombing would prevent North Vietnam from supplying the forces in South Vietnam with whatever strength North Vietnam wished to have there.**—*Robert McNamara, former Secretary of Defense, 27 November 1967.*[72]

The cross-over point was the point at which enemy losses (through death, desertion, and lack of recruitment) were increasing faster than could be replaced by the enemy.

1698 **The government is not likely to prosecute us. Its bankruptcy in the moral sense is proved by its refusal to move against those of us who have placed ourselves between the young people and the draft.**—*Dr. Benjamin Spock, speaking at a press conference in Penn Garden Hotel, New York, 30 November 1967.*[754]

At the conference Spock announced that several anti-war groups would attempt to shut down the Whitehall Induction Center. They were trying to get arrested so they could be heard in court. They were forcing a confrontation with the government so they could legally open the issue of the draft in the courts.

1699 **My decision to challenge the President's position, and the administration's position, has been strengthened by recent announcements out of the administration — the evident intention to intensify the war in Vietnam and, on the other hand, the absence of any positive indications or suggestions for a compromise or for a negotiated political settlement. I am concerned that the administration seems to have set no limits to the price that it is willing to pay for a military victory.**—*Senator Eugene McCarthy of Minnesota, in an announcement in Washington, 30 November 1967.*[796]

McCarthy announcing his run for the Democratic nomination for President, based on his belief that the Administration planned to escalate the war as opposed to seeking a negotiated settlement.

1700 **There is growing evidence of a deepening moral crisis in America; discontent and frustration, and a disposition to take extra-legal — if not illegal — action to manifest protest. I am hopeful that this challenge I am making ... may alleviate to at least some degree this sense of political helplessness, and restore to many people a belief in the process of American politics and American government.**—*Senator Eugene McCarthy of Minnesota, in an announcement in Washington, 30 November 1967.*[796]

McCarthy was appealing to the protesters and demonstrators to support him as a means of voicing their opposition to the war and Administration policy.

1701 **[The man has deteriorated into] an emotional basket case.**—*President Lyndon Johnson, speaking to his press secretary about Robert McNamara, November 1967.*[887]

Johnson appointed Robert McNamara to president of the World Bank. McNamara found out about the appointment through a press leak. Johnson had lost confidence in McNamara because of his change of view on the Vietnam War. McNamara advocated a reduction in the U.S. role, a stop to the bombing of North Vietnam, and a political settlement with Hanoi.

1702 **We military people are all very optimistic. We see the situation getting steadily better. ... He [the enemy] just isn't going to make it.... By next year this time, he's going to be in bad shape. ... I have doubts that he can hang on....**—*General A.R. Brownfield, Deputy Chief of Staff, American Command Vietnam, during an interview, November 1967.*[653]

1703 **If you need conscription to have an army, then you will need an army to have conscription.**—*Marvin Garson, anti-war activist, December 1967.*[720]

In 1967 anti-war protests were continuing and anti-draft demonstrations were becoming more frequent with more violent encounters between demonstrators and police.

1704 **Thirty-one million Vietnamese, young and old, men and women, must be thirty-one million resistance fighters, fearing neither hardships nor sacrifice, going forward in the wake of their victories to accomplish even greater feats of battle.**—*Ho Chi Minh, President, Democratic Republic of Vietnam, from a speech, December 1967.*[636]

Ho was speaking to all Vietnamese, calling for them to rise and resist the Americans and the "puppet regime" in Saigon. The speech was later seen as groundwork for the proposed general uprising Hanoi expected to take place during the planned 1968 TET Offensive.

1705 **We are a country caught between the hammer and the anvil, a country that would very much like to remain the last haven of peace in Southeast Asia.**—*Prince Norodom Sihanouk, Cambodian head of state, in an interview, December 1967.*[373]

In late-1967 and early-1968 Sihanouk made overtures to the Johnson administration, offering to allow American units to make hot pursuit of the NVA/VC into the Cambodian border areas, provided they did no harm to the Cambodians in those areas. Westmoreland had publicly pressed Johnson to allow American troops to go into the enemy sanctuaries in Cambodia. Johnson did not move on the Sihanouk offer, and did not authorize hot pursuit into Cambodia.

1706 **Men and materiel needed for the level of combat now prevailing in South Vietnam continue to flow despite our attacks on LOCs, we have made it very costly to the enemy in terms of materiel, manpower, management, and distribution.**—*Admiral U.S. Grant Sharp, Commander-in-Chief, Pacific Command, in a report to the JCS, December 1967.*[120]

Sharp's findings on the bombing were contrary to a study commissioned by McNamara, which indicated the Rolling Thunder bombing campaign was not effective against the enemy and could not affect Hanoi's will to fight.

1707 **The only real loyalty that exists in the American teenager today is to his music. He doesn't give an actual damn about his country or his mother or his government or his religion. He has more actual patriotism in terms of how he feels about his music than in anything else.**—*Frank Zappa, musician and leader of the rock group, Mothers of Invention, in an interview, 1967.*[812]

1708 **For the Viet Cong, there isn't any distinction; the Viet Cong are the people.**—*Excerpt from a secret report, commissioned by General William Westmoreland, late-1967.*[887]

The report was a rebuttal to an article written by journalist Jonathan Schell. The article was read by Robert McNamara and forwarded to Ambassador Lodge and Westmoreland. Schell detailed the destruction of hamlets and high civilian casualties caused by U.S. operations designed to root out the VC/NVA in the area in Quang Ngai Province. The VC routinely used the civilian population, and their homes, as shelter, storage, and ambush positions, ignoring American rules of war against such use of civilians or their property.

1709 **I don't want to press the point but I did want to know if I can assume that the Pope will try to bring the South Vietnamese to informal talks — and will immediately help out the prisoner problem.**—*President Lyndon Johnson, speaking to the Pope Paul VI, 23 December 1967.*[63]

In response to Johnson's request the Pope had said he'd pray for Johnson and his peace efforts. Johnson sought a more substantial commitment from the Pope on the issues.

1710 **I was an all-out hawk. I was all for the bombing; I thought once we started, the war would be over in six months. I was wrong. Our country has been planted into a corner out there. There's going to have to be a change.**—*Senator Thurston B. Morton of Kentucky, during an interview, December 1967.*[653]

Morton's change from hawk to dove took place after many complaints from his constituents about the new "war tax" proposed by President Johnson. Johnson announced the proposed surtax of 10 percent in August 1967 to assist in paying for the war and Great Society programs.

1711 **[Reporter] — You have leveled virtually every enemy village and hamlet [on the Bong Son Plain], killed or driven more than 50,000 peasants off the land with your fire power. My question is, how do you intend to go about winning the hearts and minds of these people?**

[Briefing Officer] — I'm afraid you'll have to take that up with the S-5, Sir, but jeeze, it's a real good question.—

Unidentified briefing officer, during a question/answer exchange with reporter Desmond Smith, 1967.[850]

During the briefing the officer explained that during Operation Pershing (in progress) there were 600+ air strikes and millions of pounds of artillery detonated, yet only six tons of rice and salt were captured along with a couple dozen hand grenades and four large calibre rounds.

1712 **This system lives by murdering in Vietnam, exploiting the world, and killing black people at home; and we say to hell with middle class "security and phony status games, we are going to screw up this society."**—*Jerry Rubin, Co-founder of the Vietnam Day Committee, 1967.*[827]

Rubin was speaking about the demonstrations and unrest eventually bringing down American society and the U.S. government along with it.

1713 **In every case in the past, cessation of the bombing has been used by the other side to accelerate the movement of supplies and men to the South.**—*President Lyndon Johnson, from a letter to the Pope Paul VI, December 1967.*[72]

A pause in the bombing translated to higher American casualties, as Hanoi increased the flow of men and materiel during such pauses.

1714 **The intelligence and reporting problems during this period cannot be explained away.... In retrospect [the estimators] were not only wrong, but more importantly, they were influential.**—*Conclusion by the authors of the Pentagon Papers, 1967.*[201]

Secretary of Defense McNamara commissioned a study of the background and prosecution of American involvement in Vietnam. The study came to be known as the *Pentagon Papers.* It documented the government's actions regarding Vietnam from 1947 to 1967.

1715 **We haven't had our primaries. We haven't had our convention. So there's really no way of guessing who the candidate will be. But I do want to say this: I fully intend to support him.**—*President Lyndon Johnson, speaking to a Democratic party gathering in Charleston, West Virginia, 2 December 1967.*[759]

1716 **You cannot have imperialistic war abroad and social peace at home.**—*Marvin Garson, anti-war activist, December 1967.*[720]

Garson was eluding to the increasing numbers of people demonstrating against the draft and its direct connection to the war in Vietnam.

1717 **I cannot tell you how much longer it may take to achieve peace in Vietnam ... [but] the situation in South Vietnam is not a stalemate. And what has been done by the splendid Americans who are there has already yielded dividends of historic significance. Behind the shield which we have helped to provide, a new Asia is arising.**—*Dean Rusk, Secretary of State, speaking to a meeting of the National Association of Manufacturers, in New York City, 6 December 1967.*[772]

At the time Rusk was speaking, demonstrations were going on in the area in an attempt to block the Army induction center at Whitehall Street.

1718 **[The enemy has] met their master in the field.**—*President Lyndon Johnson, speaking to U.S. troops at Cam Ranh Bay, December 1967.*[72]

Johnson stopped off at Cam Ranh Bay on his return to Washington following the funeral of Australia's Prime Minister Harold Holt.

1719 **The war is probably nearing a turning point and the outcome of the 1967-68 winter-spring campaign will in all likelihood determine the future direction of the war.**—*Bob Layton, CIA analyst, in an intelligence estimate, 8 December 1967.*[195]

Layton served at the CIA's Saigon Station. Based on documentation and interviews with enemy prisoners of war and Chieu Hois, he and other analysts at the station concluded the enemy was going to conduct a widespread campaign to inflict damage and casualties on the U.S./GVN, in hopes of forcing the GVN to collapse, and ultimately forcing the U.S. out of Vietnam.

1720 **Those who would belittle or even condemn the haste, the extravagance or the corn of some of Mr. Johnson's performances, had best begin therefore with the new signs last week that he remains one of the most formidable political showmen in American history.**—*New York Times editorial, December 1967.*[57]

Johnson completed a 27,000 mile trip before Christmas, with stops in Australia, Thailand, Cam Ranh Bay, and Vatican City in Rome.

1721 **[You have brought our Vietnam policy] from the valleys and depths of despondence to the cliffs and heights where we know now that the enemy can never win.**—*President Lyndon Johnson, during an awards decoration ceremony at Cam Ranh Bay, December 1967.*[61]

Johnson was awarding General Westmoreland the Distinguished Service Medal.

1722 **The VC/NVN ... appear to have committed themselves to unattainable ends within a very specific and short period of time, [which included] a serious effort to inflict unacceptable military and political losses on the Allies regardless of VC casualties during a US election year, in the hope that the US will be forced to yield to resulting domestic and international pressure and withdraw from South Vietnam.**—*Bob Layton, CIA analyst, in an intelligence estimate, 8 December 1967.*[195]

Layton and other CIA analysts at the Saigon Station developed this analysis based on information gathered from the field and current trends. They anticipated a large offensive by the enemy around the TET holiday, the end of January. The CIA in Washington was notified of the station's estimate, but did not necessarily agree with the their conclusions.

1723 **He has wit, charm and grace. But he seems to lack heart and guts.**—*I.F. Stone, political commentator, from his publication, Weekly, 11 December 1967.*[850]

Eugene McCarthy's announcement of his candidacy was less than rousing causing some political observers to doubt his sincerity and conviction.

1724 **The fact that President Johnson has decided to extend, on a large scale, the war in Viet Nam, proved that he had no regard for world opinion.**—*Lord Bertrand Russell, British philosopher, 1967.*[969]

1725 **Watching him [Eugene McCarthy] at the press conference here at which he launched his candidacy, one began to wonder why he was running at all. A certain cynicism and defeatism seemed basic to the man. This is no way to embark on a fight. His hero, Adlai [Stevenson], was a Hamlet. McCarthy gives one the uneasy feeling that he doesn't really give a damn.**—*I.F. Stone, political commentator, from his publication, Weekly, 11 December 1967.*[850]

1726 **The low-level night missions flown by the A-6 over Hanoi and Hai Phong were the most demanding missions we have ever asked our aircrews to fly. Fortunately, there is an abundance of talent, courage, and aggressive leadership in these A-6 squadrons.**—*Admiral William F. Bringle, Commander Seventh Fleet, 1967.*[961]

The A-6 Intruder was the Navy's all-weather, night capable bomber. It was so successful and accurate that it often flew solo missions against a specific target. It could deliver up to 15,000 pounds of bombs deep into North Vietnam, at night or in bad weather, without escort or MiG-CAP (Combat Air Patrol).

1727 **There is no prospect of peace, no promise of stability, no hope for the better in the policies of this [Johnson] Administration.**—*Senator Everett M. Dirksen of Illinois, as entered in the Congressional Record, 15 December 1967.*[548]

Dirksen, formerly a strong supporter of Johnson's policy in Vietnam, sharply attacked the President's policy on the war.

1728 **If we go across the border, there will always be one more sanctuary just beyond the one we clean out.**—*John Paul Vann, Deputy, II Field Force CORDS, during a press interview, December 1967.*[887]

In 1967 Vann opposed cross border operations to attack communist sanctuaries along the Cambodian and Laotian borders. By 1970 he had reversed himself, favoring the incursion into Cambodia in May 1970.

1729 **Gutless bureaucrats who leaked defeatist information to simpleton reporters; it's gotten so you can't have intercourse with your wife without it being spread around by traitors.**—*President Lyndon Johnson, comments to historian Dr. Henry F. Graff, 1967.*[374]

Johnson, reported response to the pressures of his position, which included a seeming stalemate in the Vietnam War, domestic programs squeezed for lack of funds, racial turmoil within the country, and challenge on the horizon to his bid for re-election. Graff, a historian from Columbia University, was visiting Johnson at the White House.

1730 **As our casualties mount daily, the skyrocketing costs of combat soar beyond sight, the unpopularity of the war among our people intensifies hourly and there is little evident reason to hope for victory in the foreseeable future.**—*Senator Everett M. Dirksen of Illinois, as entered in the Congressional Record, 15 December 1967.*[548]

Dirksen, formerly a strong supporter of Johnson's policy in Vietnam, sharply attacked the President's policy on the war.

1731 **The Congress and the people have seen all too little evidence of genuine effort to explore and exploit the diplomatic opportunities available to us....**—*Senator Everett M. Dirksen, of Illinois, as entered in the Congressional Record, 15 December 1967.*[548]

Dirksen, formerly a strong supporter of Johnson's policy in Vietnam, sharply attacked the President's policy on the war and diplomacy.

1732 **I really think the whole issue of Vietnam is kind of beyond debate now. Most of the facts and the kind of intellectual judgments people are going to make about Vietnam really have been made.... It becomes almost a matter of will at that point. Do you want to take a chance on some kind of de-escalation, on easing up with some form of less violent effort? Or do you think the way to do it is to intensify the military action?**—*Senator Eugene McCarthy of Minnesota, during an interview for America magazine, 16 December 1967.*[850]

McCarthy was running a one-issue campaign based solely on the situation in Vietnam and how it should be handled.

1733 **The enemy is building his forces in the south. We must try very hard to be ready. We may face dark days ahead.**—*President Lyndon Johnson, speaking to the Australian Cabinet, 22 December 1967.*[65]

Johnson was in Australia for the funeral of Prime Minister Harold Holt. At the time the Australians had several thousand combat troops and advisors in South Vietnam.

1734 **The enemy has already made a crucial decision concerning the conduct of the war ... to undertake an intensified countrywide effort, perhaps a maximum effort, over a relatively short period of time.**—*General William Westmoreland, ComUSMACV, in a cable to Washington, 20 December 1967.*[653]

Westmoreland's warning was based on the possibility of widespread enemy attacks, gleaned from conclusions gathered from enemy interrogations, captured documents, and other intelligence intercepts and assets. The possibly of such an offensive was considered remote by MACV.

1735 **Peace in South Vietnam for South Vietnam and by South Vietnamese.**—*President Lyndon Johnson, comments to Pope Paul VI, the Vatican, December 1967.*[72]

Johnson visited the Pope in Rome following the funeral of Australian Prime Minister Harold Holt. John asked the Pope for assistance in bringing Hanoi to the conference table.

1736 **Hanoi is ignoring and violating the Geneva convention prisoner rules. If the Pope can call on both sides to accord just and humane treatment to prisoners and ask for permission to visit both sides, we would be willing to open our doors immediately.**—*President Lyndon Johnson, speaking to Pope Paul VI, 23 December 1967.*[63]

Johnson appealed to the Pope for assistance, intervening on behalf of the prisoners held on both sides. He also asked the Pope to use his influence to coax President Thieu into seeking separate peace negotiations with the NLF.

1737 **80% of the U.S. either follows the President or wants to do more [in Vietnam]. Twenty percent make all the noise and mislead Hanoi into believing we will give up.**—*President Lyndon Johnson, speaking to the Pope Paul VI, 23 December 1967.*[63]

By Johnson's reckoning, 50 percent of the people wanted to do more in Vietnam, 30 percent wanted to follow the moderate course. The moderate course was the President's current policy.

1738 **Hanoi has great problems but they believe the U.S. will tire and fail just like the French did — and they can win by default what they lost on the battlefield.**—*President Lyndon Johnson, speaking to Pope Paul VI, 23 December 1967.*[63]

1739 **[Rostow]—Vann, I know your pitch; I read all the reports, but don't you agree that the war will be over by July?**

[Vann]—Oh, hell, no, Mr. Rostow; I'm a born optimist — I think we can hold out a little longer than that.—*Reported exchange between John Paul Vann and Walt Rostow, December 1967.*[29]

Vann's report on the situation in South Vietnam indicated a different picture than the encouraging one painted by MACV and the Johnson administration. Vann attempted to dispel the notion that the war was going well in Vietnam and the VC/NVA were in retreat.

1740 **Hanoi ... is not going to the conference table because Hanoi believes they will win this war in Washington.**—*President Lyndon Johnson, speaking to Pope Paul VI, 23 December 1967.*[63]

1741 **I have this problem of keeping the pressure on without widening a war. My right hand keeps the pressure steady and with my left hand we seek negotiations.**—*President Lyndon Johnson, speaking to Pope Paul VI, 23 December 1967.*[63]

1742 **P.S. Send some Kool-Aid. Water here tastes like hell.**—*Cpl. Dennis W. Lane, U.S. Army, A Company, 4th Battalion, 3d Infantry, in a letter home, December 1967.*[187]

In the field, treated water was potable, but the chemical taste left by the iodine water purification tablets was barely tolerable. Adding unsweetened Kool-Aid to a canteen of treated water made it a little easier to drink. The iodine chemically treated the water but did nothing about the grit and debris that was also collected when the canteen was refilled from a stream or bomb crater.

1743 **If the U.S. would stop bombing [North Vietnam] for good, Hanoi will take part in talks.**—*North Vietnam Foreign Minister Nguyen Duy Trinh, announcement 29 December 1967.*[452]

This was the first softening of Hanoi's hard line position. In response the U.S. resumed bombing after the Christmas bombing pause. On 30 January 1968 the VC/NVA launched the 1968 TET Offensive during the cease-fire to observe the holiday. The offensive had been planned months in advance.

1744 **The words of Uncle Ho are like a trumpet announcing battle.... The solemn appeal of Chairman Ho is the mobilization order to the fatherland passed to one after another of the thirty-one million fighters.**—*Excerpt from Quan Doi Nhan Dan, the NVA newspaper, December 1967.*[641]

NVA response to Ho's call for all Vietnam to rise up against the Americans and the Saigon regime. This call preceded the January 1968 TET Offensive.

1745 **If there were serious [American] raids or bombings against frontier areas inhabited by Cambodians or Vietnamese who had been living there for a long time, Cambodian troops would strike back as strongly as possible.**—*Prince Norodom Sihanouk, Chief of State, Cambodia, in reply to questions from the Washington Post, 28 December 1967.*[547]

He was asked the response of Cambodian troops should American troops pursue VC/NVA troops into Cambodia. Sihanouk responded that Cambodian troops would not interfere in such hot pursuit, provided VC/NVA troops had illegally entered uninhabited areas along the Cambodian border. He also warned the U.S. against taking the Vietnam War into inhabited areas of Cambodia.

1746 **We are unable to devise a bombing campaign in the North to reduce the flow of infiltrating personnel into SVN [South Vietnam].**—*Excerpted from the Jason Study group, December 1967.*[925]

The Jason Study was commissioned by the DoD to study the effects of the bombing campaign against North Vietnam. There were previous reports in 1966 and early 1967 with similar findings. The study group re-evaluated the bombing campaign in September 1967. Again their conclusions were the same: the bombing was not stopping the flow of men and materiel south, and was not disrupting life in North Vietnam sufficiently to cause Hanoi to agree to negotiations.

1747 **We shall pray for you and we shall pray for your efforts for peace.**—*Pope Paul VI, during an audience with President Johnson at the Vatican, December 1967.*[63]

Pope Paul was responding to a request made by Johnson that he use his influence to encourage President Thieu to seek separate negotiations with the NLF and that the Pope intercede on behalf of the prisoners of war held in North and South Vietnam.

1748 **The United States Government has unceasingly claimed that it wants to talk with Hanoi but has received no response. If the United States Government truly wants to talk it must, as was made clear in our statement of 28 January 1967, first of all stop unconditionally the bombing and all other acts of war against the Democratic Republic of Vietnam [North Vietnam]. After the United States has ended unconditionally the bombing and all other acts of war, the Democratic Republic of Vietnam will hold talks with the United States on questions concerned.**—*Nguyen Duy Trinh, North Vietnam's Foreign Minister, in a press statement, 30 December 1967.*[761]

North Vietnam was still insisting the U.S. unilaterally cease attacks against North Vietnam before any talks could take place. They mention no concessions towards stopping or lessening their infiltration of men and supplies into South Vietnam should negotiations be initiated. They took a hard line and successfully maintained it.

1968

All warfare is based on deception.
—Sun Tzu

1749 **For those who fight for it, life has a flavor the protected never know.**—*Anonymous Marine, Khe Sanh, 1968.*[976]

1750 **I do believe that with all RVNAF [Republic of Vietnam Armed Forces] and Free World Forces taking the offensive in 1968, together with greatly stepped-up operations against the VC infrastructure, victory will come within our grasp.**—*Robert Komer, Director of CORDS, in a cable to the III Corps Commander, 1 January 1968.*[18]

The South Vietnamese III Corps commander was General Le Nguyen Khang. CORDS, Civil Operations and Revolutionary Development, had overall control of the American aspect of the pacification efforts.

1751 **The year [1967] ended with the enemy increasingly resorting to desperation tactics in attempting to achieve military/psychological victory; and he has experienced only failure in these attempts.... The friendly picture gives rise to optimism for increased successes in 1968.**—*General William Westmoreland, ComUSMACV, in his 1967 year-end report, January 1968.*[224]

Westmoreland's optimistic outlook for the progress of the war, less than a month before nationwide attacks by communist forces across South Vietnam.

1752 **If you exclude the two northernmost provinces of South Vietnam, just south of the Demilitarized Zone, you will find that all the major forces of the enemy have already been largely broken up. They will have an occasional ability to mount an attack in a force of up to 2,500 in poorly coordinated attacks. But this will be periodic and somewhat spasmodic, because I do not believe that they any longer have the capability of regular, planned reinforcement.**—*General Harold Johnson, U.S. Army Chief of Staff, during an interview with journalists, January 1968.*[29]

1753 **[Viet Cong forces are] poorly motivated, poorly trained and ... the South Vietnamese Army has the upper hand completely.**—*General William R. Desobry, Senior Military Adviser, IV Corps, during a news conference, January 1968.*[645]

Less than a month after the news conference the VC/NVA launched the TET Offensive.

1754 **[The Vietnamese people defeated the Japanese,] the most barbarous fascist aggressors of Asia, and the French, the shrewdest colonialism of Europe, and are currently crushing the cruel new colonialism of America, which is playing the role of an international gendarme.**—*Editorial comment from the communist party paper, Nhan Dan, 1 January 1968.*[653]

Nhan Dan was calling the Vietnamese (North and South) to support the movement to oust America and the Saigon regime from Vietnam. This was considered part of the opening moves toward the TET Offensive which started less than a month later.

1755 **All for complete victory over the U.S. Aggressors.**—*Official North Vietnamese government slogan for TET, 1968.*[652]

The slogan was created by North Vietnam's prime minister as the official slogan celebrating the new year, the Year of the Monkey, TET 1968.

1756 **I'm not sure that they are anywhere near the point of being ready to yield. There is no indication of when they would talk — no indication, no mention of whether they themselves would exercise any kind of restraint.**—*William Bundy, Assistant Secretary of State for Far Eastern Affairs, speaking during a TV interview, 7 January 1968.*[776]

In the past Hanoi took advantage of the temporary bomb halts to increase the flow of men and materiel into South Vietnam.

1757 **The second set of [O/B] numbers were what some of us worried about.**—*Richard Moose, assistant to Walt Rostow, in a deposition to Larry Berman.*[72]

Moose became disillusioned with the conduct of the war and his perception was that one set of enemy strength numbers (MACV version) was made public, while a second, higher numbered (CIA version) set was held privately by the Administration. He resigned in March 1968.

1758 **Vietnam may be the Rhineland of the Third World War.... I'm not sure it's so, but you're not sure it isn't so.**—*Louis Nizer, lawyer and Lyndon Johnson supporter, speaking at a meeting of the Village Independent Democrats, New York, January 1968.*[835]

Nizer comparing the Johnson administration's fight against communism in Vietnam with the spread of Fascism at the start of World War II and Hitler's seizure of the Rhineland.

1759 **I consider this area [Khe Sanh] critical to us from a tactical standpoint ... it is even more critical from a psychological point of view.**—*General William Westmoreland, in a cable to General Earle Wheeler, 12 January 1968.*[72]

The American high command in South Vietnam confirmed a massive enemy buildup in the border area of Laos, near the Marine Base at Khe Sanh. The base was occupied by approximately 6,000 Marines. There was evidence of three NVA divisions in the area around the base.

1760 **Senator McCarthy spoke with a subdued but almost tangible fervor lacking in previous speeches.**—*E.W. Kenworthy, New York Times reporter, reporting on a speech by Eugene McCarthy, 12 January 1968.*[749]

One of the few speeches during his campaign that McCarthy spoke with enthusiasm and conviction which was recognizable by political observers.

1761 **To relinquish ... [Khe Sanh] ... would be a major propaganda victory for the enemy. Its loss would seriously affect Vietnamese and U.S. morale.**—*General William Westmoreland, in a cable to General Earl Wheeler, 12 January 1968.*[72]

The American high command in South Vietnam had confirmed a massive enemy buildup in the border area of Laos, near the Marine base at Khe Sanh. The base was occupied by approximately 6,000 Marines. There was evidence of three NVA divisions, 15-20,000 men in the area around the base.

1762 **Our actions and words must be judged by the human consequences, and political consequences be damned.**—*Jesse Unruh, a California Democratic Party leader, during a party meeting in Fresno, California, January 1968.*[818]

At this date Unruh had not made a decision whether to back Johnson or McCarthy. He was holding out hope that Robert Kennedy would reconsider and throw his hat into the ring for the Democratic Party's nomination for president. Unruh felt the war and its impact on American society was too important to stick with the party line of backing the incumbent.

1763 **I do not recall a time when Americans seemed so beset, so discouraged, and so confused or when there was such profound dissension, distrust and even hatred. Even in the depths of the Great Depression or in the darkest days after Pearl Harbor, when our country was in much deeper trouble than it is now, Americans were held together by a sense of common purpose which seems lacking today.**—*Congressman Jonathan B. Bingham, of New York, in and open letter to his constituents, January 1968.*[653]

1764 **[The government of South Vietnam] is a small handful of Saigon generals who are of absolutely no value to society and are a bunch of dregs.**—*Aleksei Kosygin, Premier of the Soviet Union, from a Life magazine interview, 19 January 1968.*[442]

1765 **I would not object to designating this an act of war in terms of the category of actions to be construed. My strong advice to North Korea is to cool it.**—*Dean Rusk, Secretary of State, during a press conference, January 1968.*[72]

When American attention was focused on the siege of the Marines at Khe Sanh, North Korea seized the USS *Pueblo*. It was in international waters, 26 miles off the coast of Korea at the time. There was some conjecture at the time that the seizure might have been timed to coincide with the North Vietnamese push at Khe Sanh, forcing the U.S. to split its resources between two possible wars.

1766 **From this war you have gained absolutely nothing.**—*Aleksei Kosygin, Premier of the Soviet Union, from a Life magazine interview, 19 January 1968.*[442]

1767 **For the sake of Almighty God and those men who have fallen in Vietnam and those that shall fall in Vietnam, let's go ahead and win the war there if we have a justifiable cause to wage war there; if not, let's apologize to the peoples of the world and get out of there....**—*Excerpt from a resolution by Veterans of Foreign Wars No. 4585, 18 January 1968.*[648]

1768 **The U.S. cannot defeat Vietnam. And we, for our part, will do all we can so that the U.S. does not defeat Vietnam.**—*Aleksei Kosygin, Premier of the Soviet Union, from a Life Magazine interview, 19 January 1968.*[442]

Approximately $1.5 billion of Soviet military aid was supplied to North Vietnam for the years 1965–1967.

1769 **I don't want no Damn Dien Bien Phu.**—*President Lyndon Johnson speaking to the JCS as reported by the news media, January 1968.*[62]

This quote was carried by the news media who attributed it to Johnson. According to the press, Johnson confronted the members of the JCS wanting assurance that all that could be done to protect Khe Sanh was being done. Johnson later stated that he never made the statement above and had one of his aides check meeting notes for late-January 1968 to verify he had not made the quote. Tom Johnson checked the notes and confirmed no such phrase was uttered by the President.

1770 **History will never forgive the U.S. [for Vietnam].**—*Aleksei Kosygin, Premier of the Soviet Union, from a Life magazine interview, 19 January 1968.*[442]

1771 **Intelligence reports show a great similarity between what is happening at Khe Sanh and what happened at Dien Bien Phu.**—*President Lyndon Johnson, speaking during a White House meeting, 23 January 1968.*[72]

The analogy between Dien Bien Phu and Khe Sanh was often stressed by the media and the Administration. But there were notable differences between the two. The 6,000 Marines at Khe Sanh were surrounded by 20,000 NVA; at Dien Bien Phu, 13,000 French forces were surrounded by 100,000 Viet Minh. Air support for the French was 175 aircraft, the Marines had the possible support of 5,000 aircraft.

1772 **To a Western, so-called developed society, cutting our electricity means something. It doesn't mean very much in Vietnam. The Vietnamese for years and years have been used to living by candlelight or oil lamps.**—*Oliver Todd, journalist, from an article, 1968.*[156]

The Rolling Thunder air campaign against North Vietnam destroyed 59 percent of their power plants and 80 percent of their POL facilities, yet it had little effect on the North Vietnamese's ability to supply men and materiel to the Southern front.

1773 **Quit playing around with the war.... How long are we going to wait? ... How many more Americans have to be killed before we take that firm, decisive action we should have taken several years ago?**—*Senator Strom Thurmond of South Carolina, from a speech in the Senate, 30 January 1968.*[639]

Thurmond was responding to reports of the attack on the U.S. Embassy and the widespread communist offensive during the cease-fire period of the TET holiday. He implored President Johnson to act with all force to end the war and stop the loss of American troops.

1774 **Yeah, we're winning.**—*Senator Robert Kennedy of New York, comment to UPI correspondent, 30 January 1968.*[653]

Kennedy's response was to a teletype message passed to him by a UPI reporter. The message was from the Saigon UPI office, reporting on "a wave of coordinated surprise attacks" by the VC/NVA against several cities in South Vietnam. The attacks were characterized by UPI as "the greatest enemy offensive of the war."

1775 **[The Vietnam War is] one of the great disasters of all time for the United States.**—*Senator Robert Kennedy of New York, during a press conference, 30 January 1968.*[653]

Kennedy called the conference to announce he would not run against President Johnson for the Democratic nomination for president. His reasoning was that he did not want to split the Democratic Party.

1776 **In many areas the enemy has been driven away from the population centers; in others he has been compelled to disperse and evade contact, thus nullifying much of his potential.**—*General William Westmoreland, ComUSMACV, in his 1967 year-end report, January 1968.*[222]

Westmoreland's report on the progress of the war was released a few days before the Administration's optimistic reports were shattered by the communists TET Offensive.

1777 **The Vietcong seized part of the U.S. Embassy in Saigon early Wednesday, Vietnam time. Snipers are in the buildings and on roof tops near the Embassy and are firing on American personnel inside the compound. Twenty suicide commandos are reported to be holding the first floor of the Embassy.**—*An excerpt from a news report read on the NBC Huntley-Brinkley Report, 30 January 1968*[653]

NBC initially mis-reported the facts of the VC attack on the U.S. Embassy. This was the first news many Americans heard of the 1968 TET Offensive. The VC attack force entered the Embassy grounds, most of them dying in the courtyard. They never entered the Embassy building or made it to the roof in the six hours of the attack.

1778 **Use your power to bomb them so that they cannot take it—the kind of bombing we did in World War II, if necessary. Whatever is necessary to bring this war to an end should be done to save American lives.**—*Senator Strom Thurmond of South Carolina, from a speech in the Senate, 30 January 1968.*[639]

Thurmond implored President Johnson to take swift and harsh action against the VC/NVA to end the war in South Vietnam. He was responding to the initial reports of the communist TET Offensive, and the reported seizure of the U.S. Embassy by the VC.

1779 **A piddling platoon action.**—*Unidentified U.S. Army officer, comments to the press, 31 January 1968.*[653]

The officer was describing the VC attack on the U.S. Embassy in Saigon, 31 January 1968. A VC suicide team of 21 men blasted through the Embassy wall and entered the court yard. They were unable to enter the Embassy building, but 19 of the team died in the attempt, most in the Embassy courtyard. Four U.S. Army MPs and a Marine Embassy guard died in defense of the Chancellery. By military standards it was a small action, but it made world news.

1780 **Suddenly a long strip of earth just erupts, dirt and debris flying five hundred feet into the air. Then a few seconds later another nearby strip erupts the same way.... It was as if a little part of the world blew up for no apparent reason.**—*General Rathvon Tompkins, commander, 3d Marine Division, January 1968.*[653]

Tompkins was describing a B-52 Arc Light strike. The Bombers flew too high to be heard or seen. The only indication of their passing was when the ground exploded.

1781 **The enemy exposed himself by virtue of his strategy and he suffered great casualties.... As soon as President Thieu, with our agreement, called off the truce, American troops went on the offensive and pursued the enemy aggressively.**—*General William Westmoreland, ComUSMACV, speaking to the press outside the U.S. Embassy in Saigon, 31 January 1968.*[653]

The VC/NVA launched their nationwide offensive during the agreed upon cease-fire observing the Vietnamese TET holiday.

1782 **The biggest fact is that the stated purposes of the general uprising have failed.... I do not believe when the American people know the facts, when the world knows the facts and when the results are laid out for them to examine, I do not believe they will achieve a psychological victory.**—*President Lyndon Johnson, comments to reporters during a news conference, 31 January 1968.*[216]

MACV claimed the communist TET Offensive was a military victory for the Allies. Opponents of the Johnson administration claimed TET was a psychological defeat for the U.S.

1783 **The enemy's well-laid plans went afoul. Some superficial damage was done to the building. All of the enemy that entered the compound so far as I can determine were killed. Nineteen bodies have been found on the premises — enemy bodies.**—*General William Westmoreland, ComUSMACV, speaking to the press, outside the U.S. Embassy in Saigon, 31 January 1968.*[653]

Westmoreland was speaking of the VC attack on the U.S. Embassy in Saigon. The VC blew a hole in the Embassy wall and entered the compound, but never entered the Embassy building.

1784 **A few bandits can do that in any city.**—*President Lyndon Johnson, during a news conference, 1 February 1968.*[72]

Johnson was commenting on the initial enemy attacks in Saigon during the TET Offensive. He likened it to the Detroit riots. His evaluation of the enemy attacks changed considerably when the full scope of the offensive became known.

1785 **As floor after floor was captured, the fighting became harder and harder.... Dawn came as they reached the fifth floor.... They had suffered practically no losses [casualties].... They had killed over 200 enemy personnel, most of them holding key posts in the American ruling machinery in Saigon.... The detachment had quietly withdrawn, after raining hard blows on the enemy for two days and nights.**—*Excerpt of a news report in the Vietnam Courier, 10 June 1968.*[653]

This was the North Vietnamese's skewed account of the VC attack on the U.S. Embassy in Saigon. In reality the VC entered the Embassy compound but were unable to break into the building. Less than seven hours after the VC breached the Embassy wall nineteen of the attacking force were dead and the Embassy secured. Five American soldiers died in defense of the Embassy. The *Vietnam Courier* was an English-language newspaper printed in Hanoi and used as a propaganda instrument by the Hanoi regime.

1786 **The enemy will fail again and again because we Americans will never yield.**—*President Lyndon Johnson, comments to the press, 1 February 1968.*[550]

Johnson was responding to widespread enemy attacks during the Vietnamese TET holiday. The VC and NVA launched an offensive that struck 26 of South Vietnam's 44 provincial capitals and various military installations.

1787 **For twenty years we have been wrong. The history of conflict among nations does not record another such lengthy and consistent chronicle of error. It is time to discard so proven a fallacy and face the reality that a military victory is not in sight, and that it probably will never come.**—*Senator Robert Kennedy of New York, from a speech in Chicago, 8 February 1968.*[640]

Kennedy was repudiating the Administration's claims of progress and near victory in the war against the communists in Vietnam.

1788 **Let those who would stop the bombing answer this question: What would the North Vietnamese be doing if we stopped the bombing and let them alone?**—*President Lyndon Johnson, comments to the press, 1 February 1968.*[550]

Johnson was commenting on widespread enemy attacks during the Vietnamese TET holiday. The VC and NVA launched an offensive that struck 26 of South Vietnam's 44 provincial capitals as well as various military installations. Johnson argued that enemy capabilities would be even greater and the terrorism and aggression even greater if it weren't for the bombing campaign.

1789 **We have assumed that the [draft] laws are constitutional, regardless of how unwise or unjust they may be from the viewpoint of the individual who violates them.**—*ACLU statement concerning legal aid to draft violators, 1 February 1968.*[549]

The ACLU declined to provide legal defense for those accused of draft law violations as a means of protest against the Vietnam War or the Selective Service System.

1790 **If taking over a section of the American Embassy, a good part of Hue, Dalat and major cities of the Fourth Corps area constitutes complete failure, I suppose by this logic that if the Viet Cong captured the entire country, the Administration would be claiming their total collapse.**—*Senator Eugene McCarthy of Minnesota, to the press, 1 February 1968.*[644]

During a news conference held on 31 January, President Johnson proclaimed that the enemy TET Offensive "has been a complete failure." The enemy did not succeed in holding most of the cities he had attacked, and failed to have the South Vietnamese people follow the VC in a general uprising against the Americans and the Saigon government.

1791 **I'm not going to start anything I can't finish.**—*President Lyndon Johnson, comments, February 1968.*[444]

Johnson's response to an advisor's recommendation that the U.S. fleet be sent in after the USS *Pueblo* and her crew.

1792 ***Des grandes queules au coeur d'or.***—*Cathy Leroy, freelance correspondent, in an interview with Life magazine, 1968.*[447]

"Bigmouths with hearts of gold." This was the nickname the French had for their Foreign Legion troops. Leroy gave the U.S. Marines this nickname after accompanying them as they took Hill 881, near Khe Sanh.

1793 **What the hell is going on, I thought we were winning the war!**—*Walter Cronkite, CBS News anchor, commenting on the TET Offensive, February 1968.*[268]

Cronkite was totally surprised by the strength and scope of the enemy offensive at TET. Like many others he had listened to the optimistic reports of progress coming from the Johnson administration and from Westmoreland, the U.S. commander in Vietnam.

1794 **[The Front has staged the] most all-out and widespread attacks ever known.**—*Nguyen Phu Xoai, Spokesman for the National Liberation Front (Viet Cong), during a news conference in Hanoi, 1 February 1968.*[551]

The Vietcong, with NVA support, launched an all-out offensive during the Vietnamese TET holiday. The VC attacked many provincial capitals, towns and ARVN/U.S. military installations, in an attempt to overthrow the Thieu-Ky regime and force Free World Forces to withdraw from Vietnam.

1795 **We are determined to overthrow the Thieu-Ky puppet administration.**—*Radio Hanoi, during a broadcast, 2 February 1968.*[551]

The VC/NVA expected many ARVN troops to rally to the support of the VC. The civilian population was also expected to stage a general uprising against the Saigon government, throwing their support to the VC. VC expectations were not realized.

1796 **Power is of no value unless you use it to accomplish something.**—*Robert McNamara, Secretary of Defense, February 1968.*[449]

Quoted from McNamara in his final days as Secretary of Defense.

1797 **[The 1968 enemy TET Offensive is] a complete failure....**—*President Lyndon Johnson, during a news conference, 2 February 1968.*[552]

Johnson viewed the enemy attacks at TET as a military failure. With the exception of Hue, the enemy was unable to effectively maintain control of any of the towns they attacked for longer than a few hours to a few days. There was no general uprising of the South Vietnamese people in support of the VC offensive. And the South Vietnamese military did not defect in significant numbers to the VC/NVA as a result of the offensive.

1798 **Prometheus Bound ... a tenth-rate country [had] abruptly confront[ed] Lyndon B. Johnson with one of the most delicate and intractable emergencies of his crisis-wracked Administration.**—*Newsweek, 2 February 1968.*[58]

This quote appeared in a *Newsweek* article on the seizure of the USS *Pueblo* in international waters, by the North Koreans. The seizure of the USS *Pueblo* coincided with the NVA siege at Khe Sanh in South Vietnam.

1799 **The Administration's reports of progress are the products of their own self deception.... Their [the Communists'] attacks on the cities of South Vietnam show that we don't have the country under any kind of control and that we are in much worse position than we were in two years ago.**—*Senator Eugene J. McCarthy of Minnesota, to the press, 1 February 1968.*[644]

McCarthy was referring to the nationwide attacks by the VC/NVA during the TET Offensive. Weeks before the offensive the Administration claimed progress in the war against the communists and a marked decline in their offensive capabilities.

1800 **I can count. It looks like somebody has paid a very dear price for the temporary encouragement that some of our enemies had.**—*President Lyndon Johnson, during a news conference, 2 February 1968.*[552]

The enemy TET Offensive began 31 March (Vietnam time), and by the date of the news conference MACV was reporting 12,000+ enemy soldiers killed, with the loss of 983 Free World Forces killed (318 Americans).

1801 **The Communist propagandists have a unique genius for smearing the jam on someone else's face when they steal the jar.**—*Reverend Jess C. Moody, D.D., First Baptist Church, West Palm Beach, Florida, from an address to his congregation, February 1968.*[448]

Moody's response to a *Life* magazine interview of Soviet Premier Aleksei N. Kosygin in which he (Kosygin) condemned U.S. actions in Vietnam and claimed Russia had a deep desire for peace. Yet Russia continued to supply North Vietnam with arms and equipment and they were not instrumental in convincing Hanoi to negotiate an end to the war.

1802 **The aim of the Vietcong struggle is to win independence for the nation, peace for our country and democracy and happiness for the people, and to build a political power entirely for the fatherland and the people.**—*Radio Hanoi, during a broadcast, 2 February 1968.*[551]

The VC/NVA expected many ARVN troops to rally to the support of the VC. The civilian population was also expected to stage a general uprising against the Saigon government, throwing their support to the VC. The uprising didn't happen.

1803 **We have been suckers and we are going to quit being suckers. There is no point in this kind of negotiation. The next time they come to us, they had better mean it. San Antonio is the final formula — the furthest we can go.**—*Clark Clifford, unofficial adviser to the President, in remarks to the President, February 1968.*[653]

The San Antonio Formula was Johnson's latest offer to Hanoi to get negotiations started. He offered to stop the bombing of North Vietnam if Hanoi would show some positive signal that they were ready to talk and also that they would not take advantage of a bombing halt to increase their position in South Vietnam. In January, the bombing of North Vietnam was stopped because Romania indicated Hanoi might be willing to talk. The NVA used the halt to increase preparations for the February TET Offensive, and after some time, denied any willingness to negotiate. Hanoi said the Romanians had misread their signals.

1804 **I am fed up to the teeth with the activities of the North Vietnamese and the Viet Cong. We apply rigid restrictions to ourselves and try to operate in a humanitarian manner with concern for civilians at all times. They apply a double standard. Look at what they did in South Vietnam [during TET].**—*General Earle Wheeler, Chairman, Joint Chiefs of Staff, during a meeting, 5 February 1968.*[72]

Wheeler recommended lifting some of the bombing restrictions placed around Hanoi and Hai Phong. McNamara raised the issue that he believed such an action would increase civilian casualties. Wheeler pointed out that Hanoi was not very concerned about civilian casualties as evidenced by the actions they repeatedly took.

1805 **I have never under-estimated the Viet Cong. They are not push-overs.**—*President Lyndon Johnson, during a meeting with Democratic leaders, 6 February 1968.*[72]

Senator Robert Byrd broached the question whether the President and the Administration had under-estimated the VC.

1806 **General George Custer said today in an exclusive interview with this correspondent that the Battle of Little Big Horn had just turned the corner and he could now see the light at the end of the tunnel. ... "We have the Sioux on the run.... Of course we will have some cleaning up to do, but the Redskins are hurting badly and it will only be a matter of time before they give in."**—*Art Buchwald, political satirist, 6 February 1968.*[235]

Buchwald's satirical parallel of General Westmoreland and his claims of diminished enemy activity, progress in the war against the communists, and claims that the shining light at the end of the conflict was near — only to have it all go up in smoke when the communists launched the 1968 TET Offensive.

1807 **Should we ask for a declaration of war?**—*President Lyndon Johnson, during a meeting with his advisers, February 1968.*[72]

Weighing the full impact of the enemy TET attacks, Johnson feared the enemy might launch even more attacks. The majority of casualties suffered by the enemy were VC; that left many NVA battalions still available and seemingly uncommitted to the TET attacks. Johnson asked his advisers if a declaration of war would allow them to increase the resources available to escalate the war to match the latest round of North Vietnamese escalations.

1808 **That thing had more holes in it than Swiss cheese.**—*Robert Burkhardt, former U.S. Marine.*[350]

Burkhardt, describing the Catholic church in Hue. It had been riddled with shells as the allies retook the city from the VC/NVA.

1809 **It is as if James Madison were able to claim a great victory in 1812 because the British only burned Washington instead of annexing it to the British Empire.**—*Senator Robert Kennedy of New York, from a speech in Chicago, 8 February 1968.*[640]

Kennedy's response to the claims of victory from the Administration and Saigon over the enemy TET Offensive.

1810 **America has changed completely since World War II. During the war you struggled for the liberation of the white people in France and England, but now in Asia you have come to implant yourselves as a neo-colonialist power.**—*Prince Norodom Sihanouk, Cambodian head of state, in an interview, February 1968.*[446]

Sihanouk berating America for the war against North Vietnam.

1811 **In the past ... the problem was finding the enemy. Now that the enemy has come to us I am sure many will ask why aren't we doing better under these circumstances, now that we know where they are.**—*Dean Rusk, Secretary of State, during a meeting with the President and his advisers, 8 February 1968.*[72]

1812 **Our enemy, savagely striking at will across all of South Vietnam, has finally shattered the mask of official illusion from which we have concealed our true circumstances even from ourselves.**—*Senator Robert Kennedy of New York, from a speech in Chicago, 8 February 1968.*[640]

1813 **[Hanoi] may have estimated that the impact of the TET attacks would at the very least greatly discourage the United States and cause other countries to put more pressure on us to negotiate on Hanoi's terms.**—*Ellsworth Bunker, Ambassador to South Vietnam, in a cable to President Johnson, 8 February 1968.*[72]

1814 **I do not recommend a declaration of war. ... It might be a direct challenge to Moscow or Peking in a way we never challenged them before. There would be very severe international effects.**—*Dean Rusk, Secretary of State, during a meeting with the President and his advisers, 8 February 1968.*[72]

1815 **War is an ugly thing, but not the ugliest: the decayed and degraded state of moral and patriotic feeling which thinks nothing worth a war is worse.... A man who has nothing which he cares about more than his personal safety is a miserable creature who has no chance of being free, unless made and kept so by the exertions of better men than himself.**—*John Stuart Mill, philosopher (1806-1873), this quote was sent by President Johnson to three of his top advisors and the JCS, 8 February 1968.*[72]

Mill was a 19th century English philosopher/economist. Johnson sent the quote to Rusk, McNamara, Clifford and the JCS.

1816 **When two elephants are fighting, an ant should step aside.**—*Prince Norodom Sihanouk, Cambodian head of state, in an interview, February 1968.*[446]

Sihanouk spoke of the tight rope he walked between the war of the U.S./SVN and Soviet/Chinese backed North Vietnam.

1817 **All that is needed to start negotiations is assurance that the talks will begin promptly, and that they will be meaningful and directed in good faith to a peaceful settlement.**—*Harold Wilson, Prime Minister of Britain, speaking to the press, 9 February 1968.*[553]

During a visit to Washington, Wilson spoke hopefully of getting negotiations started between Hanoi and the U.S.

1818 **One fortunate by-product of Kim's [Il Sung] outrage [seizure of the USS *Pueblo*] is that Johnson could call up 15,000 air and naval reserves without arousing cries of escalation.**—*Life magazine editorial, 9 February 1968.*[443]

Kim Il Sung, leader of North Korea, ordered the seizure of the U.S. intelligence ship *Pueblo* in international waters off the coast of North Korea. The crew was held captive for 11 months. The JCS argued for a call up of military Reserves to support a request for 206,000 additional troops for Vietnam. The call-up would also help bolster American troop levels worldwide in the event it was necessary for U.S. troops to deploy in force to South Korea.

1819 **[Hanoi scored] a psychological blow, possibly greater in Washington than in South Vietnam, since there are tentative signs that the populace is turning against the Viet Cong as a result of these [TET] attacks.**—*General William Westmoreland, ComUSMACV, in a cable to General Earle Wheeler, 9 February 1968.*[72]

Hanoi expected the South Vietnamese people to rise up against the Thieu-Ky government and rally to the side of the VC/NVA, a great general uprising against the GVN and the Americans. This did not happen. The brutality of the attacks and their timing (during the Vietnamese's most sacred holiday) turned many South Vietnamese against the attackers.

1820 **I come here today as your President to tell you that on your journey the hearts of this nation and the hopes of men in many nations fly with you and will follow you until this duty is done. Those duties may become more demanding, the trials may become more difficult, the tests more challenging, before we or the world shall know again that peace on this planet is once more secure.**—*President Lyndon Johnson, addressing troops of the 82d Airborne at Fort Bragg, February 1968.*[653]

A brigade of the 82d Airborne Division was deployed to Vietnam as reinforcements following the start of the enemy

TET Offensive. Johnson flew to North Carolina to address the Airborne troops as they were departing for Vietnam. Johnson also flew to California to address men of the 27th Marine Regiment who were also deploying to Vietnam as reinforcements.

1821 **Hanoi may well have reasoned that in the event that the TET attacks did not bring the outright victory they hoped for, they could still hope for political and psychological gains of such dimensions that they could come to the negotiating table with a greatly strengthened hand.**—*Ellsworth Bunker, Ambassador to South Vietnam, in a cable to President Johnson, 8 February 1968.*[72]

1822 **There can be no peace because the enemy still wants war. And those who talk of peace only cause the enemy to redouble his attacks on our men in Vietnam.**—*Walt Rostow, Special Assistant to the President, speaking to the President, February 1968.*[72]

1823 **If we proceed on our present course, it promises only years and decades of further draining conflict on the mainland of Asia — conflict which, as our finest military leaders have always warned, could lead us only to national tragedy.**—*Senator Robert Kennedy of New York, from a speech in Chicago, 8 February 1968.*[640]

Kennedy broke with the Administration's war policy, but still refused to run for the Democratic nomination for president.

1824 **America is trying to fight Chinese Communism and is destroying Vietnamese Communism.... You [America] are working for China by stamping out the only barrier to Communist China's aggression — Vietnamese nationalism.**—*Prince Norodom Sihanouk, Cambodian head of state, in an interview, February 1968.*[446]

Sihanouk was secure in the historical knowledge of the Vietnamese and their dislike and mistrust of the Chinese.

1825 **[As a result of TET 1968] subsequent events showed, The Vietcong were broken as a military threat and the North Vietnamese Army did not recover for two years.**—*Sir Robert Thompson, British authority on counterinsurgency.*[627]

Thompson estimates the losses to the VC/NVA were about 30 percent of its force. This would be the equivalent of a five million man Army if the U.S. suffered such a loss.

1826 **You [America] should let these people [the Vietnamese] develop themselves and it would be an excellent barrier to Chinese expansionism.**—*Prince Norodom Sihanouk, Cambodian head of state, in an interview, February 1968.*[446]

1827 **The Australians are fighting there [in Vietnam] because they are not yellow, they are part of the white Western world. They claim to be part of Asia but they are not. They are fighting for their own white Western bourgeois comforts.**—*Prince Norodom Sihanouk, Cambodian head of state, in an interview, February 1968.*[446]

Sihanouk's philosophy on what he saw as Western imperialist motives.

1828 **The enemy has suffered very substantially, but he still has sizable uncommitted reserves. He displays a tenacity which we have not seen before in this war.**—*General Earle Wheeler, Chairman, Joint Chiefs of Staff, in a cable to President Johnson, February 1968.*[72]

1829 **By destroying Vietnam you have made her so weak she cannot bother us along the frontier. But I will not thank America for this. I cannot thank America for destroying Vietnam.**—*Prince Norodom Sihanouk, Cambodian head of state, in an interview, February 1968.*[446]

Cambodia and Vietnam have been enemies for centuries. Shortly after the fall of Saigon in 1975, a united Vietnam, under Hanoi's control, invaded Cambodia.

1830 **It was a powerful revelation that these people [VC/NVA] were everywhere and they weren't going to be defeated.** —*James Carroll.*[350]

Carroll was speaking of the communist's TET Offensive in 1968.

1831 **Nothing is as dirty as to violate a truce during the holidays. But nobody says anything bad about Ho [Chi Minh]. They call me a murderer. But Ho has a great image.**—*President Lyndon Johnson, during a meeting with Democratic leaders, 6 February 1968.*[72]

The media made much of the TET attacks, about the performance of the ARVN and lack of preparedness, and the ability of the enemy to launch such attacks. But little was reported on the fact that the attacks came in the middle of the truce, in celebration of the Vietnamese holiday, which Hanoi had agreed to.

1832 **Enemy losses have been heavy; he has failed to achieve his prime objectives of mass uprisings and capture of a large number of capital cities and towns. The South Vietnamese Army held up against the initial assault with gratifying, and in a way, surprising strength and fortitude. They were not badly hurt physically — they should recover strength and equipment rather quickly. Their problems are more psychological than physical. U.S. forces have lost none of their pre–TET capability.**—*General Earle Wheeler, in a memorandum to President Johnson, February 1968.*[185]

The widespread TET attack by NVA/VC troops was considered a military failure for the enemy. But the mere fact that the attacks were launched cast grave doubt on military reports of an improving military situation in Vietnam.

1833 **I [do not] fear defeat if I am not reinforced.... I do not feel I can fully grasp the initiative from the recently reinforced enemy without them.**—*General William Westmoreland, ComUSMACV, to the JCS, 12 February 1968.*[653]

By 12 February the situation had begun to stabilize following the initial wave of attacks during the communist TET Offensive. Westmoreland wanted additional troops in South Vietnam, which would allow him to go on the offensive against the retreating enemy. His request was approved 12 February 1968, and an additional 10,000 troops were dispatched to Vietnam (3d Bde/82d Airborne + 27th Marines).

1834 **Nearly every option open to us is worse than what we are doing.**—*President Lyndon Johnson's comments to a group visiting the White House, 12 February 1968.*[653]

Johnson anguished over Vietnam and the inability to find a solution that did not involve the total destruction of North Vietnam of the abandonment of South Vietnam.

1835 **The nights are very long. The winds are very chilly. Our spirits grow weary and restive as the springtime of man**

seems farther and farther away. I can, and I do, tell you that in these long nights your President prays.—*President Lyndon Johnson, speaking at a presidential prayer breakfast, February 1968.*[72]

1836 **We are going through the worst fucking flak in the history of man, and for what—to knock out some twelve-foot wooden bridge they can build back a couple hours later. We can't hit the docks (at Hai Phong) where they unload the war materiel because we might hit the ships, and we can't hit the ships because some of them might be Russian.... We've got a great big country with sophisticated equipment, trained pilots, expensive aircraft and it's not worth a damn, it's not worth the loss of planes or the loss of a single pilot—and plenty are being lost, believe me.**—*Unidentified U.S. Navy pilot aboard the USS Constellation, during discussion, February 1968.*[653]

President Johnson paid a visit to sailors and officers of the USS *Constellation*. While there some of Johnson's aides met with several of the carrier's pilots to hear their views of the war.

1837 **[The enemy] had launched a major campaign signaling a change of strategy of protracted war to one quick military/political victory during the American election year.**—*General William Westmoreland, ComUSMACV, in a cable to General Earle Wheeler, 12 February 1968.*[72]

1838 **When Spooky was working, everything stopped while that solid stream of violent red poured down out of the black sky. If you watched from a great distance, the stream would seem to dry up between bursts, vanishing slowly from air to ground like a comet tail, the sound of the guns disappearing too, a few seconds later. If you watched at close range, you couldn't believe that anyone would have the courage to deal with that night after night, week after week, and you cultivated a respect for the Viet Cong and NVA who had crouched under it every night now for months.**—*Michael Herr, journalist, writing in Dispatches of Khe Sanh in 1968.*[870]

The Vietnam Spooky was a piston-engine, C-47 transport plane fitted with three, fixed firing 7.62mm miniguns. The guns were fired simultaneously, 18,000 rounds per minute, and were aimed by the position of the aircraft. Every fifth round fired was a red tracer round, which accounted for the red ribbon that spewed forth when the ship fired. A burst of less than a minute was sufficient to put a round in every inch of an area the size of a football field.

1839 **We are now in a new ball game where we face a determined, highly disciplined enemy, fully mobilized to achieve a quick victory. He is in the process of throwing in all his "military chips to go for broke."**—*General William Westmoreland, ComUSMACV, in a cable to General Earle Wheeler, 12 February 1968.*[72]

Referring to the communist TET Offensive.

1840 **I would feel greatly relieved if the Joint Chiefs of Staff would see fit to send General Westmoreland guidance which would provide Westmoreland with a way out of Khe Sanh.**—*Walt Rostow, Special Assistant to the President, to the President, February 1968.*[72]

Some of Johnson's advisers argued for a re-deployment of the Marines at Khe Sanh, allowing them to be used against the enemy, who exposed himself to conventional military tactics during the TET Offensive. As the Marines were under siege in Khe Sanh a plan was required to raise the siege and put the Marines in action.

1841 **Hills 861, 881 North, and 881 South, named for their height in meters but remembered for the lives they cost.**—*Life magazine, Khe Sanh, February 1968.*[445]

The Marines took these hills from the NVA, hills which were part of the protective ring around Khe Sanh Combat Base. In the process the Marines lost 155 men killed and 424 wounded. Enemy casualties were reported as 940 NVA killed.

1842 **[The seizure of the USS *Pueblo* is] a dastardly act of piracy.**—*Congressman William Bates of Massachusetts, February 1968.*[72]

Bates was speaking out on the seizure of the USS *Pueblo* by the North Koreans during a time when America was focused on the siege of Marines at Khe Sanh. There was some speculation at the time that the North Korean move against the *Pueblo* had been coordinated to coincide with the NVA move against Khe Sanh, and the TET Offensive.

1843 **The use of tactical nuclear weapons should not be required in the present situation. [However, should the situation change], I visualize that either tactical nuclear weapons or chemical agents would be active candidates for employment.**—*General William Westmoreland, ComUSMACV, in a cable to General Earle Wheeler, February 1968.*[72]

Westmoreland was responding to a query by Wheeler as to whether nuclear weapons should be considered for use at Khe Sanh.

1844 **The parallels [between Khe Sanh and Dien Bien Phu] are there for all to see.**—*Walter Cronkite, Anchorman for CBS News, during a national telecast, February 1968.*[374]

Cronkite likened the Marine position at Khe Sanh to the French at Dien Bien Phu. The only real similarities were that the Marines were in a position on the floor of the valley, surrounded by several hills which were occupied by the enemy and the road into the base was under enemy control. Beyond that the similarity ends. The Marines were supported by a massive array of air power; there was a large artillery presence on the base and within supporting range; and Khe Sanh was never completely isolated from resupply.

1845 **It became necessary to destroy the town to save it.**—*Unidentified U.S. Army major, comment to correspondent, February 1968.*[887]

This statement was reported by correspondent Peter Arnett. During the communist offensive of TET 1968, the VC captured the town of Ben Tre, the capital of Kien Hoa Province, IV Corps. During the retaking of Ben Tre by ARVN units, much of the town was destroyed in the process. A popular variant of the phrase surfaced as: "We had to destroy the town in order to save it."

1846 **I am not white and I will not struggle for the whites against the yellows.**—*Prince Norodom Sihanouk, Cambodian head of state, in an interview, February 1968.*[446]

Sihanouk, showcasing the public neutrality he maintained for Cambodia, yet in private he allowed Hanoi to establish bases along his border and move men and supplies through Cambodia along the frontier with South Vietnam. He also allowed the transshipment of war materiel from the Cambodian port of Sihanoukville to VC/NVA sanctuaries along the border.

1847 **A setback is fully possible if I am not reinforced. I desperately need reinforcements. Time is of the essence.**—*General William Westmoreland, ComUSMACV, in a cabled request to the JCS, February 1968.*[374]

Westmoreland requested additional troops for Vietnam, ostensibly to allow him to "regain the initiative and go on the offensive" against the retreating enemy.

1848 **[Our Vietnamese had] pulled up their socks.**—*Walt Rostow, Special Assistant to the President, comments picked up by the press, February 1968.*[42]

Rostow indicating that the ARVN had recovered quickly from the initial communist attacks and fought well to restore security and clear the contested cities of the enemy. Facts later indicated that this had not often been the case.

1849 **All through the night, we could hear the enemy dragging their dead away. When we could get a direction on the sound we would open up on them.**—*Captain Armon I. DeDescare, Commander, C Company, 4th Battalion, 39th Infantry Regiment, during an interview, 15 February 1968.*[895]

From a three-day battle around Dong Phu, six miles southeast of Saigon.

1850 **[The Secretaries of State and Defense and the Joint Chiefs of Staff] have at no time even considered or made recommendations in any respect to the employment of nuclear weapons.**—*President Lyndon Johnson, during a White House news conference, 16 February 1968.*[555]

Johnson, responding to press questions as to whether or not he was considering, or had been recommended, the use of nuclear weapons against the large build up of enemy forces surrounding Khe Sanh.

1851 **They know what they're doing. They know how to do it—and they don't mind doing it.**—*Captain James O. Lawson, Commander, B Company, 4th Battalion, 39th Infantry Regiment, during an interview near Dong Phu, 15 February 1968.*[898]

Lawson was talking about the men of his company and their combat abilities against the enemy. The unit was heavily engaged during a sweep of the area. The battle lasted two days resulting in 83 enemy killed.

1852 **It seems that [the enemy] is pushing all his chips into the middle of the table. Ours are there also. It is not credible to think in terms of a peak of effort followed by subsidence and a return to the status quo ante. Vietnam will never be the same again.**—*General William E. DePuy, MACV J-3, February 1968.*[72]

Many in MACV believed the TET attacks were a go-for-broke push by the enemy. DePuy was MACV's operations and training officer.

1853 **I do not like what I am smelling from those cables from Vietnam and my discussions with outside advisers.**—*President Lyndon Johnson, during a meeting with his advisers, February 1968.*[72]

This was during the TET battles and Johnson was worried that the enemy might launch more attacks.

1854 **This is serious—very grave ... it does not lend itself to any emotional irresponsibility ... the consequences are too horrible...**—*President Lyndon Johnson, comments, February 1968.*[444]

Johnson commenting on the tense situations of the North Korean capture of the *USS Pueblo* and the communist TET Offensive in South Vietnam.

1855 **Westy's forces are stretched too thin.... I believe that we must reinforce him promptly and substantially.**—*General Earle Wheeler, Chairman, Joint Chiefs of Staff, in a cable to President Johnson, February 1968.*[72]

After a meeting with Westmoreland, Wheeler requested additional American troops for Vietnam, in light of the communists TET Offensive.

1856 **The Viet Cong suffered a military defeat [but on the other hand] the TET Offensive has widened a credibility gap which exists here too between what the people are told and what they see about them.**—*Walter Cronkite, reporter and TV anchorman, in a news report from Saigon, February 1968.*[653]

Cronkite arrived in Saigon 11 February 1968 to report on thc TET Offensive.

1857 **When the Vietcong come [into Cambodia], the Americans are guilty of pushing them here. If you are not capable of restraining the Vietcong from coming into Cambodia, it is more your fault than ours.**—*Prince Norodom Sihanouk, Cambodian head of state, in an interview, February 1968.*[446]

Sihanouk not only allowed NVA/VC bases along the border, he also sanctioned the transport of North Vietnamese supplies through the Cambodian port of Sihanoukville on the Gulf of Thailand. The communist base areas along the border were established before U.S. combat troops deployed to South Vietnam.

1858 **[General Westmoreland has] the greatest responsibility of any general I have ever known in history.**—*Dwight Eisenhower, former President, during a meeting with President Johnson, February 1968.*[653]

Eisenhower insisted that Westmoreland's direction of half a million Americans in Vietnam was far more difficult that his direction of five million men during W.W.II. When Eisenhower was asked why, he answered, "I always knew where the enemy was."

1859 **Give me the lesser of two evils.**—*President Lyndon Johnson, in a directive to Secretary of Defense Clark Clifford, February 1968.*[72]

Johnson tasked Clifford with evaluating General Westmoreland's and the JCS's request for 206,000 addition American troops for Vietnam. The deadline for the evaluation was 4 March 1968.

1860 **One is almost embarrassed to be the messenger of such bad news. The situation is so obvious: the optimism of the military men was unfounded, pacification is not working, political stability is further away than ever. It's distressing that the situation had to deteriorate so far before the country woke up.**—*Senator Eugene McCarthy of Minnesota, commenting on the 1968 TET Offensive, February 1968.*[749]

McCarthy did not beat up the President over TET 1968, but quietly stated the obvious. TET helped to make McCarthy more appealing to the voting public.

1861 **Do you really believe America is fighting for the South Vietnamese? No, she is fighting for herself.**—*Prince Norodom Sihanouk, Cambodian head of state, in an interview, February 1968.*[446]

Sihanouk's philosophy on what he saw as Western imperialist motives.

1862 **If what we have seen in the past week is a Viet Cong failure, then I hope they never have a victory.**—*Governor George Romney of Michigan, during a meeting with newspaper editors in New York, February 1968.*[652]

Romney's reaction to the enemy TET Offensive of 1968.

1863 **Sometimes they will change "will" to "would" or "shall" to "should" or something of that kind, but the answer is all the same.**—*President Johnson, responding to the latest North Vietnamese statement on conditions for holding formal talks, 16 February 1968.*[791]

The latest statement from Hanoi showed a slight change from previous statements. Accordingly, they said they would talk if the bombing was stopped. They did not agree to reciprocate, de-escalate or commit to any kind of reduction or halt in the infiltration south. The Johnson administration saw Hanoi's answer as more of the same.

1864 **We don't want a wider war. They [the North Vietnamese] have two big brothers that have more weight and people than I have.**—*President Lyndon Johnson, speaking with the crew of the USS Constellation, 19 February 1968.*[168]

1865 **The well laid plans of the North Vietnamese and Vietcong have failed.... The enemy exposed himself by virtue of his strategy and he suffered heavy casualties.**—*General William Westmoreland, ComUSMACV, comments on the TET Offensive, February 1968.*[347]

1866 **I'd rather be slow and right than smart and dead.**—*President Lyndon Johnson, comments, February 1968.*[444]

1867 **It continues to amaze me that the Vietcong's 15,000 political murders and kidnappings, the traditional Communist technique of disruption and power takeover is considered by even a minority of U.S. citizens as not worth resisting.**—*Malcolm Marshall, Newton, Massachusetts, in a letter to the editor of Life magazine, February 1968.*[448]

The depth of Viet Cong political murders, harassment, and kidnappings did not receive much coverage in the Western press.

1868 **If this is a failure, I hope the Viet Cong never have a major success.**—*Senator George Aiken of Vermont, February 1968.*[72]

Aiken was responding to Administration claims that the enemy TET Offensive was a defeat and a failure for the VC/NVA.

1869 **Whose side are you on? ... I'm on our side! ... None of your papers or broadcasting apparatuses are worth a damn unless the United States succeeds. They are trivial compared to that question. So I don't know why people have to be probing for things that one can bitch about, when there are two thousand stories on the same day about things that are more constructive.**—*Dean Rusk, Secretary of State, during a press conference, February 1968.*[374]

Rusk was reacting to repeated questions by the press as to why the enemy TET Offensive had not been detected in advance and prepared for accordingly. Rusk was generally unhappy with the press reporting of TET which leaned heavily towards showing the VC in a stronger light than their military position warranted. After a few days of the offensive most of the enemy captured areas had been cleared, yet the press was slow to indicate that in their reports because good news was less spectacular.

1870 **[It was] against the national interest to carry on discussions about the employment of nuclear weapons with respect to Khesanh [sic].**—*President Lyndon Johnson, during a press conference, 16 February 1968.*[72]

Johnson was responding to questions by the press that nuclear weapons were being considered for use against the NVA.

1871 **We have looked at that damn North Vietnamese flag all day, and now we are going to take it down.**—*Captain Ron Christmas, Commander, H Company, 2d Battalion, 5th Marine Regiment, to his troops at the Citadel, Hue City, February 1968.*[500]

H Company was in the lead of the 2d Battalion's attack on the Citadel in Hue. The Citadel held by enemy troops flew the NVA flag. The capture of Hue was part of the 1968 TET Offensive. After heavy fighting the Marines forced the NVA out of the Citadel, struck their flag and temporarily raised the American flag in its place. The South Vietnamese flag was later raised, and they took credit for clearing the Citadel.

1872 **The enemy has never been more vulnerable to effective military action than he is today.**—*John Paul Vann, Deputy, II Field Force CORDS, during a CORDS meeting, February 1968.*[887]

Casualties among the communists who launched the TET Offensive were very high. The communist temporarily abandoned their guerrilla war tactics in exchange for the set piece battles of the offensive. They could not match American fire power in such battles. By the end of February most enemy units had been driven from the towns and cities, and were in retreat. Vann encouraged his CORDS advisers to press the South Vietnamese forces to take the offensive and attack the weakened enemy forces in their retreat.

1873 **If I've lost Walter Cronkite, I've lost Mr. Average Citizen.**—*President Lyndon Johnson, comment to his staff, February 1968.*[362]

Johnson's response to a comment by CBS anchor Walter Cronkite that "It seems now more certain than ever that the bloody experience of Vietnam is to end in a stalemate." Cronkite no longer supported the Administration's claims of progress in Vietnam, due in large part to the widespread offensive launched by the VC/NVA during TET 1968.

1874 **The President is a distraught man, a tired man, a very worried man, a very sincere man.**—*General Matthew B. Ridgeway, former Chairman of JCS, comments to his wife, February 1968.*[643]

Ridgeway had conferred with the president on the situation in Vietnam (TET Offensive) and Korea (capture of the USS *Pueblo*).

1875 **You should keep them [the Vietcong and North Vietnamese Army] in Vietnam — it's your colony.**—*Prince Norodom Sihanouk, Cambodian head of state, in an interview, February 1968.*[446]

Sihanouk's answer to American complaints of VC/NVA

base camps and lines of communication along the eastern Cambodian border.

1876 **It is hard for a proud nation such as this to admit defeat and error. But if we are a moral, honorable nation with a sense of duty and destiny, we cannot go on killing and destroying to perpetuate an error and deepen it.**—*Austin Whitley, editor of the Salina Journal, in an editorial, February 1968.*[638]

Whitley was reacting to the communist TET Offensive, February 1968

1877 **The only honorable and wise course is to de-escalate the war and prepare to withdraw from Vietnam in the best order and with the fewest casualties possible. If President Johnson finds his personal pride too stubborn, the weight of defeat too grievous, then Congress should reassert its Constitutional authority, if necessary remove him from office, and put this nation back of the paths of peace.**—*Austin Whitley, editor of the Salina Journal, in an editorial, February 1968.*[638]

Whitley was reacting to the communist TET Offensive, February 1968

1878 **The more you lick Chinese boots, the more they scorn you.**—*Prince Norodom Sihanouk, Cambodian head of state, in an interview, February 1968.*[446]

Sihanouk preached neutrality, but he tended to lean toward the PRC. Most of the weapons of his small army were of Chinese or Soviet origin.

1879 **I have never served the Chinese, though sooner or later all Asia will be Chinese.**—*Prince Norodom Sihanouk, Cambodian head of state, in an interview, February 1968.*[446]

1880 **There will be blood, sweat and tears shed. The weak will drop from the lines, their feet sore and their voices loud. Persevere in Vietnam we will and we must. There, too, today, we stand at a turning point.**—*President Lyndon Johnson, comments to the press, February 1968.*[72]

Johnson referring to the turn of events posed by the widespread enemy attacks at TET.

1881 **They were talking strategy and tactics with no consideration of the bigger job of pacifying and restoring the country. This had come to be total war, not a counterinsurgency or an effort to get the North Vietnamese out so we could support the indigenous effort. This was a World War II battlefield. The ideas I had talked about in 1965 were gone.**—*Walter Cronkite, reporter and TV anchorman, comments on his trip to Vietnam during TET 1968.*[653]

During the Cronkite visit to Vietnam in February 1968, he sat in on an informal conference of Deputy MACV commander General Creighton Abrams and his staff, at the Corps headquarters near Phu Bai. There was lengthy discussion on the military situation brought about by the communists TET Offensive, and the required action to crush the enemy and restore security.

1882 **The Soviets were importing revolution into South Vietnam before there was one American soldier or one American dollar committed to that country.**—*Reverend Jess C. Moody, D.D., First Baptist Church, West Palm Beach, Florida, from an address to his congregation, February 1968.*[448]

Ho studied communist doctrine and Marxism in the Soviet Union before organizing the Vietnamese Nationalist Party in China in 1925. Ho later founded the Communist Party of Vietnam in 1930, again in China. In 1941 he finally organized the Vietnam Independence League in Vietnam, which became known as the Viet Minh.

1883 **The American people should be getting ready to accept, if they haven't already, the prospect that the whole Vietnam effort may be doomed, that it may be falling apart beneath our feet.**—*John Evans, chief editorial writer for the Wall Street Journal, in an editorial, 23 February 1968.*[651]

Evans was reacting to the communist TET Offensive, February 1968.

1884 **We believe the Administration is duty-bound to recognize that no battle and no war is worth any price, no matter how ruinous, and that in the case of Vietnam it may be failing for the simple reason that the whole place and cause is collapsing from within.**—*John Evans, chief editorial writer for the Wall Street Journal, in an editorial, 23 February 1968.*[651]

Evans was reacting to the communist TET Offensive, February 1968.

1885 **[The war in Vietnam, as viewed by most Europeans, is] unnecessary, unjustified, stupid and impossible to win.**—*Henry Tanner, reporting for The New York Times, Paris, France, 24 February 1968.*[554]

The Europeans believed the U.S. was the stumbling block to peace negotiations by its refusal to stop the bombing of North Vietnam. Some also viewed Administration policy in Vietnam as a tool to aid Johnson in the upcoming presidential election.

1886 **This Division, while destroying those who would oppress the Vietnamese people, will strive to create and build the conditions which make for a peaceful, prosperous and free Vietnamese nation.**—*General Julian J. Ewell, Commander 9th Infantry Division, in an open letter to his division, 25 February 1968.*[898]

Ewell replaced General G.G. O'Connor. This open letter was his introduction to his new command.

1887 **It will be difficult to convince critics that we are not simply destroying South Vietnam in order to "save" it.**—*Clark M. Clifford, Adviser to President Johnson, 1968.*[629]

Clifford's reaction to Westmoreland's and the JCS's request for an additional 206,000 troops in the face of the TET Offensive and the offensive's negative results on popular support for the war.

1888 **[The call-up of Reserves] would serve as a reminder to our people at home that, while we are not technically at war, we are in a situation of similar emergency which places on our citizens duties and responsibilities analogous to those in a state of declared war.**—*Maxwell Taylor, adviser to President Johnson, February 1968.*[72]

Many Johnson advisers recommended that he call up the Reserves. Reserves could help to meet Westmoreland's request for additional U.S. troops for Vietnam and replenish the national reserve.

1889 **The United States is at a cross-road. It must choose between using its power without restriction to achieve victory ... or retreating in defeat from Southeast Asia, leaving**

its allies to face the Communist alone.—*Admiral U.S. Grant Sharp, Commander-in-Chief, Pacific Forces, 1968.*[287]

1890 **Whatever the past value of the position [Khe Sanh], it is a positive liability now. We are allowing the enemy to arrange at his leisure a set-piece attack on ground and in weather favorable to him and under conditions which allow us little opportunity to punish him except by our air power.**—*Maxwell Taylor, adviser to President Johnson, February 1968.*[72]

There were more than 6,000 American troops committed to Khe Sanh. In addition, there was a large number of aircraft assigned to support them. These troops and resources were effectively unavailable to the TET action, and unable to leave the base to pursue or attack the enemy surrounding them.

1891 **Your alertness, aggressiveness, professionalism and courage — individually, by team and by unit — add new luster to our outstanding reputation.**—*General William Westmoreland, ComUSMACV, in a message of congratulations to the 9th Infantry Division, February 1968.*[896]

The 9th Infantry Division fought several major battles during the 1968 TET Offensive, listing a body count of more than 1225 enemy KIA.

1892 **The war in Vietnam is at a stalemate which neither side can convert into a military victory without leaving the country — and perhaps the world — in ruins.**—*Senator Joseph Clark of Pennsylvania, in a report on Vietnam, February 1968.*[72]

Clark conducted an investigation of the Vietnam War as part of the Senate Committee on Foreign Relations. He believed the U.S. land war in Asia was a mistake.

1893 **In a city like Saigon people can infiltrate easily. They carry in rounds of ammunition and mortars. They fire and run. It is impossible to stop this entirely. This is about as tough to stop as it is to protect against an individual mugging in Washington, D.C.**—*General Earle Wheeler, Chairman, Joint Chiefs of Staff, during a White House meeting, February 1968.*[72]

1894 **Never, never again, should we commit a ground army on the mainland of Asia.**—*Senator Joseph Clark of Pennsylvania, in a report on Vietnam, February 1968.*[72]

Clark, a Democrat, made this conclusion after a detailed study of America and the Vietnam War.

1895 **It is increasingly clear to this reporter that the only rational way out [of the war in Vietnam] ... will be to negotiate, not as victors but as honorable people who lived up to their pledge to defend democracy, and did the best they could.**— *Walter Cronkite, reporter and TV anchorman, televised personal comments on the war, 27 February 1968.*[653]

1896 **They were throwing everything at us but Chieu Hoi leaflets.**—*SP/4 John Iannucci, Squad Leader , 3d Battalion, 60th Infantry Regiment, during an interview, 27 February 1968.*[897]

The 3d/60th was engaged by a VC battalion in a battle lasting two days. The American battalion suffered 22 KIA and 83 WIA and listed enemy dead at more than 85. A single U.S. company encountered the enemy unit and was reinforced by sister companies of the battalion. Chieu Hoi leaflets were safe-conduct passes dropped in enemy areas. The passes allowed enemy soldiers to surrender to Allied forces with a reduced likelihood of being shot in the process.

1897 **205,000 [sic] men ... it is neither enough to do the job, nor an indication that our role must change.**—*Robert McNamara, Secretary of Defense, during a strategy meeting, 27 February 1968.*[55]

Westmoreland requested an additional 206,000 men for Vietnam. Clark Clifford, McNamara's replacement, initially suggested deploying 500,000 men at once to support Westmoreland.

1898 **We have been too often disappointed by the optimism of the American leaders, both in Vietnam and Washington, to have faith any longer in the silver linings they find in the darkest clouds.... For it seems now more certain than ever that the bloody experience of Vietnam is to end in stalemate.... To say that we are mired in stalemate seems the only realistic, yet unsatisfactory, conclusion.**— *Walter Cronkite, reporter and anchorman for CBS News, during a national telecast, 27 February 1968.*[72]

Cronkite's broadcast was seen by many as the turning point in public support for the war. Cronkite had supported Administration policy on Vietnam since 1965. The communists' TET Offensive collapsed that support.

1899 **There must be no weakening of the will that would encourage the enemy or would prolong the bloody conflict. Peace will come of that response, of our unshakable and our untiring resolve, and only of that. The peace of Asia and the peace of America will turn on it. I do not believe that we will ever buckle.**—*President Lyndon Johnson, from a speech in Dallas, Texas, 27 February 1968.*[653]

President Johnson gave the speech at the National Rural Electric Cooperative Association Convention. He announced the war had reached a turning point, but he publicly stated the U.S. was holding firm to its commitment.

1900 **If the Kommunists [sic] want to take over the world, I would rather wait and fight them in my backyard than in this hole.**—*PFC Chester McMullen, U.S. Marine Corps, in a letter home, 27 February 1968.*[853]

1901 **Ho Chi Minh never got elected to anything. ... He is like Hitler in many ways...**—*President Lyndon Johnson, during a meeting of his advisers, 28 February 1968.*[72]

Johnson chaffed under criticism at home while the critics said little or nothing about Ho Chi Minh's treachery of launching the TET attacks during the mutually agreed upon TET holiday truce.

1902 **The predominant sentiment here is — I'd rather save my ass than Johnson's face.**—*PFC Chester McMullen, U.S. Marine Corps, in a letter home, 27 February 1968.*[853]

1903 **We have to be careful about statements like Westmoreland's ... that he saw "the light at the end of the tunnel."** —*President Lyndon Johnson, during a meeting of his advisers, 28 February 1968.*[72]

Johnson was referring to Westmoreland's optimistic appraisal of the war in late-1967. Within three months of Westmoreland's optimistic view that the end of the war was in sight, communist forces launched nation-wide attacks during the TET Offensive.

1904 **If we stick with it, I am confident we shall come out all right in the end.**—*Ellsworth Bunker, Ambassador to South Vietnam, in a cable to President Johnson, 29 February 1968.*[72]

1905 **I believe that every American will answer now for his future and the future of his children. I believe he will say, "I did not retreat when the going got rough. I did not fall back when the enemy advanced and things got tough, when the terrorists attacked, when the cities were stormed, the villages assaulted and the people massacred."**—*President Lyndon Johnson, from a speech in Dallas, Texas, 27 February 1968.*[653]

President Johnson gave the speech at the National Rural Electric Cooperative Association Convention.

1906 **Don't vote for fuzzy thinking and surrender.**—*New Hampshire radio ad delivered prior to the New Hampshire primary, 6 March 1968.*[773]

Part of the anti-McCarthy campaign, which projected McCarthy's views on the Vietnam War as unpatriotic and defeatist.

1907 **The signs are all over here. They all say "Stop the War," but you never see any of them over there [in North Vietnam].**—*President Lyndon Johnson, during a meeting of his advisers, 28 February 1968.*[72]

1908 **The Communist in Vietnam are watching the New Hampshire primary. They're watching to see if we at home have the same determination as our soldiers in Vietnam. To vote for weakness and indecision would not be in the best interests of our nation. We urge you to support our fighting men in Vietnam. Write-in President Johnson on your ballot on Tuesday.**—*An ad placed in a New Hampshire newspaper by a group of anti-McCarthy Democratic leaders, 6 March 1968.*[850]

Some saw McCarthy's call for a political solution in Vietnam as defeatist amounting to surrender to the Communist. They also saw it as a lack of support for the American soldier on the nation's business involved in Vietnam. Johnson was so confident of the support of his party that he did not enter the New Hampshire primary.

1909 **Something is definitely wrong when the leader of our so-called enemy makes more sense than our own President.**—*Hamish Davey, Lowville, New York, in a letter to the editor of Life magazine, February 1968.*[448]

Reader's response to an interview conducted by *Life* magazine with Aleksei Kosygin, Premier of the Soviet Union.

1910 **There is considerable doubt about the accuracy of the Allied claim of thirty-six thousand Communists killed between January 29th and February 18th.**—*Excerpt from an article in The New Yorker magazine, 2 March 1968.*[107]

Based on a history of sometimes inflated enemy body counts, some media correspondents were skeptical of the enemy casualty figures issued by MACV and accepted by the Johnson administration.

1911 **It looks as if all of you have counseled, advised, consulted and then — as usual — placed the monkey on my back again...**—*President Lyndon Johnson, during a meeting with his advisers, February 1968.*[72]

1912 **For Kosygin to protest that the Soviets have no influence over Ho Chi Minh is as hypocritical as our saying we have no influence over [Nguyen Van] Thieu.**—*Reverend Jess C. Moody, D.D., First Baptist Church, West Palm Beach, Florida, from an address to his congregation, February 1968.*[448]

Kosygin claimed the Soviets could not persuade Hanoi to negotiate.

1913 **For a while, we thought and had the feeling that we understood the strength of the Viet Cong and the North Vietnamese ... it came as a shock that the Vietcong–North Vietnamese had the strength of force and skill to mount the TET offensive — as they did.**—*Clark Clifford, Secretary of Defense, during a meeting with the President, March 1968.*[46]

1914 **An unprecedented victory of scientific quality.**—*General Vo Nguyen Giap, defense minister of North Vietnam, in a message to a subordinate headquarters, March 1968.*[653]

Hanoi characterized the battle of Hue as a huge communist military and political victory. Ten-thousand VC/NVA were entrenched in Hue for 25 days before they were forced out by American and ARVN forces. This amounted to the longest single battle of the war. In Hue the VC/NVA lost more than 5,000 men killed. American losses were 142 killed; ARVN, 384 killed. Communist forces were neither able to permanently hold the city after they captured it or rally the population of 140,000 people to their side.

1915 **It has become abundantly clear that no level of bombing can prevent the North Vietnamese from supplying the necessary forces and material necessary to maintain their military operations in the South.**—*Clark Clifford, Secretary of Defense, in a memorandum to the President, 4 March 1968.*[925]

The daily needs of the enemy in South Vietnam were so small that the reduced quantities of supplies surviving the U.S. bombing campaign were sufficient to maintain the enemy troops.

1916 **The President wants General Westmoreland to know that he has freedom of action to conduct his military operations as he thinks wise from a military point of view without being inhibited by political or psychological factors originating in the United States...**—*President Lyndon Johnson, in a public statement of support for General Westmoreland, February 1968.*[72]

1917 **This has been a limited war with limited objectives, fought with limited means and programmed for the utilization of limited resources. This was a feasible position on the assumption that the enemy was to fight a protracted war. We are now in a new ball game where we face a determined, highly disciplined enemy, fully mobilized to achieve a quick victory.**—*General William Westmoreland, ComUSMACV, February 1968.*[653]

Westmoreland viewed the communist TET Offensive as a change in enemy strategy from small unit guerrilla action to large scale unit war. Such a change would allow the U.S. to bring more of its technology to bear against the enemy. More American troops and larger operations against the enemy would be required and desired.

1918 **If in November this war is not over, after all of this power has been at their disposal, then I say the American people will be justified to elect new leadership. And I pledge to you the new leadership will end the war and win the peace in**

the Pacific — and that is what America wants.—*Richard Nixon, former Vice President, during campaign for Republican presidential nomination, Nashua, New Hampshire, 5 March 1968.*[556]

1919 **The South Vietnamese as well as the North Vietnamese are now at war with the United States.**—*Maurice Couve de Murville, French Foreign Minister, speaking before the French National Assembly, February 1968.*[554]

The reference was to the communists TET Offensive and the widespread nature of the attacks.

1920 **If General Westmoreland wishes to defend Khe Sanh he will be supported; if he wishes to avoid a major engagement in a fixed position which does not utilize the peculiar mobility of the U.S. forces, he will also be supported.**—*President Lyndon Johnson, in a public statement of support for General Westmoreland, February 1968.*[72]

1921 **Mining [North Vietnamese ports] is the best way of satisfying that part of the US public opposed to sending more of our boys to South Vietnam, without increasing pressure on North Vietnam.**—*Walt Rostow, adviser to President Johnson, in a memorandum to the President, 6 March 1968.*[72]

1922 **We seem to have a sinkhole. We put in more [troops]—they match it.... I see more and more fighting with more and more casualties on the US side and no end in sight to the action.**—*Clark Clifford, Secretary of Defense, during a meeting with the President, March 1968.*[46]

After discussions with the military leadership, Clifford discovered there was no plan to win the war in Vietnam. The military blamed the lack of a plan on Administration restrictions (e.g., no invasion of North Vietnam, no ground incursions into Laos/Cambodia to block enemy LOCs, etc.). In addition, North Vietnam had a large manpower pool available which could be used to increase their troop strength in South Vietnam to match U.S. increases.

1923 **The war can be ended if we mobilize our economic and political and diplomatic leadership.**—*Richard Nixon, former Vice President, during his campaign for Republican presidential nomination, Nashua, New Hampshire, 5 March 1968.*[556]

1924 **[Even with 206,000 additional troops, the current strategy could] promise no early end to the conflict, nor any success in attriting the enemy or eroding Hanoi's will to fight.**—*Alain Enthoven, Assistant Secretary of Defense, in a report, 1968.*[317]

Enthoven and other analysts evaluated Westmoreland's immediate request for 100,000 additional troops and found that adding more troops would simply raise the level of stalemate, as North Vietnam was able to raise their own troop levels to counter any U.S. troop increases.

1925 **[Hue is] a shattered, stinking hulk, its streets choked with ruble and rotting bodies.**—*Unidentified news reporter, 1968.*[263]

Hue was held for three weeks by the VC/NVA. During the operation to force the enemy from Hue, large sections of the city were destroyed leaving more than 100,000 civilians homeless. In addition, more than 2800 South Vietnamese were found executed in mass graves in and around Hue, and more than 2000 civilians missing and presumed dead. These civilians and GVN workers and administrators were victims of the VC.

1926 **The major concern of the people is that they do not see victory ahead. The military has not come up with a plan for victory. The people were discouraged as more men go in and are chewed up in a bottomless pit.**—*Clark Clifford, Secretary of Defense, during a meeting with the President, March 1968.*[72]

Clifford, who made the transition from hawk to dove, was advising the President to stop the bombing of North Vietnam and seek negotiations to end the war in Vietnam.

1927 **The grand objective — the building of a free nation — is not nearer, but further from realization. In short, the war, as the Administration has defined it, is being lost.**—*Frank McGee, NBC correspondent, during an NBC News special report, 10 March 1968.*[633]

The hour long report on NBC highlighted major events leading to the TET enemy offensive in South Vietnam. The show made many references to past declarations by the Administration of progress and success against the enemy, contrasted with the current situation during the nationwide enemy TET Offensive.

1928 **Those were the most important moments of my life.**—*SP/4 Charles J. Fleming, 3d Battalion, 60th Infantry Regiment, during an interview, March 1968.*[898]

Recounting to a Army reporter how he single-handedly attacked and knocked out an enemy machinegun position after being separated from the rest of his company. Fleming was under intense enemy fire when he moved against the enemy position.

1929 **The time is at hand when we must decide whether it is futile to destroy Vietnam in the effort to save it.**—*Frank McGee, NBC correspondent, during an NBC News special report, 10 March 1968.*[633]

The hour-long report on NBC highlighted major events leading to the TET enemy offensive, with high-point coverage of the ongoing offensive. McGee notified his TV audience of the pending military request for an additional 206,000 troops for Vietnam.

1930 **I don't know what would happen to the peace of the world if it should be discovered that our treaties do not mean anything.**—*Dean Rusk, Secretary of State, responding to questions during Senate Foreign Relations Committee hearings, 11 March 1968.*[783]

Rusk, emphasizing that the U.S. had a treaty with South Vietnam and was bound to uphold that treaty.

1931 **The war cannot be won by military means without tearing apart the whole fabric of [the United States] national life and international relations.**—*Newsweek editorial comment, 11 March 1968.*[646]

1932 **Unless it [the United States] is prepared to indulge in the ultimate, horrifying escalation — the use of nuclear weapons — it now appears that the U.S. must accept the fact that it will never be able to achieve decisive military superiority in Vietnam.**—*Newsweek editorial comment, 11 March 1968.*[646]

Newsweek recommended the Johnson administration seek a political settlement and begin immediate de-escalation of the war.

1933 **Perhaps in purely financial terms we can afford it [the war], although I for one am far from convinced. But even if we can afford the money, can we afford the sacrifice of American lives in so dubious a cause? Can we afford the horrors which are being inflicted on the people of a poor and backward land to say nothing of our own people? Can we afford the alienation of our allies, the neglect of our own deep domestic problems and the disillusionment of our youth? Can we afford the loss of confidence in our government and institutions, the fading of hope and optimism and the betrayal of our traditional values?**—*Senator J. William Fulbright, Chairman Senate Foreign Relations Committee, in his opening statement of hearings, 11 March 1968.*[783]

1934 **It's like the dance of the Seven Veils. Four or maybe five, have been peeled away. Whether we like it or not, there are still a couple to go.**—*William P. Bundy, Assistant Secretary of State for East Asian and Pacific Affairs, 1968.*[452]

Speaking of the various peace feelers and failures to date.

1935 **Here I take four million people out of poverty, and all I ever hear about is Hoopees.**—*President Lyndon Johnson, comment to his aides, March 1968.*[374]

On 10 March 1968, the *Times* broke the story of Westmoreland's request to President Johnson for 206,000 additional troops. A White House investigation traced the leak to Townsend Hoopees, under secretary of the Air Force. The *Times* disclosure was not accurate, in that it did not explain in the headlines that approximately half of the manpower requested would go immediately to Vietnam, the rest going into the strategic reserve.

1936 **A strategy of more of the same is no longer acceptable.**—*Newsweek editorial comment, 11 March 1968.*[646]

Newsweek recommended the Johnson administration seek a political settlement and begin immediate de-escalation of the war. *Newsweek* declared the addition of the 206,000 American troops requested by MACV would lead to a matching increase by the enemy resulting in a continued stalemate.

1937 **Unless we "win" in Vietnam, our total national personality will ... change — and for the worst. If we do not "win" here, we will not participate elsewhere in the world on a substantial scale. If we do not "win" here, I think that a long period of national self-doubt and timidity will be reflected in our economy, our social programs, etc.; and our nation will be sufficiently shaken so as to be in real danger from a demagogue (who is not likely to have even the virtues of de Gaulle).**—*Abe Fortas, Supreme Court Justice, in a letter to President Johnson, 12 March 1968.*[72]

Fortas was a close friend and unofficial adviser to President Johnson. He argued for hitting North Vietnam harder, pounding them into submission.

1938 **[The New Hampshire primary is] the only race where anybody can enter and everybody can win.**—*President Lyndon Johnson, comments at a Veterans of Foreign Wars dinner, March 1968.*[841]

Johnson attempted to downplay Eugene McCarthy's strong showing in the New Hampshire primary. McCarthy won 42 percent of the Democratic vote. Johnson did not enter the primary.

1939 **[New Hampshire—]where a candidate can claim 20 per cent is a landslide and 40 per cent is a mandate and 60 per cent is unanimous.**—*President Lyndon Johnson, comments at a Veterans of Foreign Wars dinner, March 1968.*[841]

Johnson attempted to downplay Eugene McCarthy's strong showing in the New Hampshire primary. McCarthy won 42 percent of the Democratic vote. Johnson did not enter the primary.

1940 **The best way to prevent further erosion of public support from taking place is to make a new and fresh move toward a political solution at this time.**—*Arthur Goldberg, U.S. Ambassador to the United Nations, in a cable to President Johnson, 15 March 1968.*[72]

Goldberg recommended a bombing halt and intensified attempts to negotiate with Hanoi.

1941 **I believe that now, no less than when the decade began, this generation of Americans is willing to "pay any price, bear any burden, meet any hardship, support any friend, oppose any foe to assure the survival and the success of liberty."**—*President Lyndon Johnson, address to the nation, quoting John F. Kennedy, 31 March 1968.*[365]

1942 **[The Johnson administration's Vietnam policy is] a massive miscalculation and error of policy, an error for which it is hard to find any parallels in our history.**—*George Kennan, Presidential advisor, March 1968.*[72]

Kennan was recognized as the author of the Containment Doctrine, formulated at the end of W.W.II. The doctrine was used successfully in Europe to limit Soviet expansion and was used to form the basis for U.S. policy in Southeast Asia.

1943 **I was convinced that the military course we were pursuing ... was not only endless, but hopeless ... our primary goal should be to level off our involvement, and to work toward gradual disengagement.**—*Clark Clifford, Secretary of Defense, 1968.*[347]

The military could not outline a winning strategy that met with Clifford's approval.

1944 **This growing disaffection accompanied, as it will be, by increased defiance of the draft and growing unrest in the cities because of the belief that we are neglecting domestic problems, runs great risks of provoking a domestic crisis of unprecedented proportions.**—*Memorandum to President Johnson, by a group of his private advisers (the Wise Men), 1968.*[629]

Reaction to Westmoreland's and the JCS's request for an additional 206,000 troops in the face of the TET Offensive, and the offensive's negative results on popular support for the war.

1945 **The United States is ready to send its representatives to any forum, at any time, to discuss the means of bringing this ugly war to an end.**—*President Lyndon Johnson, address to the nation, 31 March 1968.*[365]

1946 **Destroy Pinkville and everything in it.... Kill everything that moves...**—*Captain Ernest Medina, Commander, C Company, 11th Infantry Brigade, Americal Division, as related by Lenny Lagunoy, 16 March 1968.*[934]

This is how several members of C Company, 1st Battalion, 20th Infantry Regiment remember the orders issued by Medina before being inserted into the My Lai area. Other members of the company do not remember the orders worded that exact way. A court-martial could not settle the controversy.

1947 **A great many people — even very determined and loyal people — have begun to think that Vietnam really is a bottomless pit.**—*McGeorge Bundy, Special Assistant to the President for National Security Affairs, during a strategy meeting with the President, March 1968.*[72]

1948 **These are not ordinary times, and this is not an ordinary election.**—*Senator Robert Kennedy, of New York, speaking to the press, 16 March 1968.*[72]

Kennedy announced his candidacy for the Democratic nomination for president. Based on the strong showing of McCarthy in the New Hampshire primary, Kennedy decided the public was ready to back a candidate who would move the country away from the stalemate in Vietnam.

1949 **So long as he [Hanoi] feels that he can win something by propaganda in the country, that he can undermine the leadership, that he can bring down the government, that he can get something in the capital that he can't get from our men out there, he is going to keep on trying.**—*President Johnson, speaking to the National Farmers Union, Minnesota, 18 March 1968.*[795]

1950 **If peace does not come now through negotiations, it will come when Hanoi understands that our common resolve is unshakable, and our common strength is invincible.**—*President Lyndon Johnson, address to the nation, 31 March 1968.*[365]

1951 **I am concerned that, at the end of it all, there will only be more Americans killed, more of our treasure spilled out; and because of the bitterness and hatred on every side of this war, more hundreds of thousands of Vietnamese slaughtered, so that they say, as Tacitus said of Rome: "They made a desert, and called it peace."... Can we ordain to ourselves the awful majesty of God — to decide what cities and villages are to be destroyed, who will live and who will die, and who will join the refugees of our creation?**—*Senator Robert Kennedy, speaking at Kansas State University, 18 March 1968.*[795]

Kennedy entered the Presidential race 16 March 1968, and hammered the President and his conduct of the war.

1952 **The most outstanding feature [of the battle of Hue] was that we won an overall success, militarily and politically ... typical example of our tactic on how to occupy and defend a city.**—*Excerpted from a communist report on the Battle of Hue, March 1968.*[637]

The communists claimed the Battle of Hue was their political and military victory. The 10,000-man VC/NVA force that held the city for 25 days suffered more than 5,000 killed. The VC executed more than 2,700 Vietnamese inhabitants of Hue, depositing them in mass graves in and around the city.

1953 **We and our allies can only help to provide a shield behind which the people of South Vietnam can survive and can grow and develop. On their efforts — on their determination and resourcefulness — the outcome will ultimately depend.**—*President Lyndon Johnson, address to the nation, 31 March 1968.*[365]

1954 **The most significant fact was that we were masters for an extended period of time and completely reversed the economic and political balance in our favor, rendering the enemy helpless.**—*Excerpted from a communist report on the Battle of Hue, March 1968.*[637]

Communists forces held the City of Hue for 25 days until forced to retreat by counterattacking American and South Vietnamese forces. The communists never completely controlled Hue due to ARVN and U.S. pockets of resistance still active within the city.

1955 **What most people want is for the Vietnamese to do more and us do less.**—*McGeorge Bundy, Special Assistant to the President for National Security Affairs, during a strategy meeting with the President, March 1968.*[72]

The focus of the meeting was the text of a speech to be delivered by the President to the public. Some of his advisers cautioned him to avoid using words about escalating the war, others wanted him to be more pointed about what the war really was about. Bundy wanted Johnson to focus on explaining Vietnam to the people, to gain their support, putting emphasis on the Vietnamese taking up more of their own defense.

1956 **[General Wheeler]—...this is the worst time to negotiate.**

[Henry Cabot Lodge]— Yes, because we are in worse shape militarily than we have ever been.—*Comments made during a strategy meeting, 25 March 1968.*[1027]

Johnson's top advisors were evaluating the U.S. position in Vietnam following the communist TET offensive. Talk centered around seeking negotiations with NVN.

1957 **We don't plan to surrender or let people divide our nation in time of national peril.... The time has come when we ought to stand up and be counted, when we ought to support our leaders, or government, or men, and our allies until aggression is stopped, wherever it has occurred.**—*President Lyndon Johnson, from a speech at National Farmers Union convention, 18 March 1968.*[653]

1958 **I don't believe the enemy has any great capacity to assume any general offensive in the near future. He has been hurt and hurt badly. He is tired.**—*General William Westmoreland, ComUSMACV, comments quoted as background by the press, March 1968.*[653]

Westmoreland's background statement was widely publicized and appeared contrary to his request for 206,000 additional troops for Vietnam. Opponents of the request pointed out that if the enemy had suffered such a great defeat and everything was under control, why the need for the additional 206,000 troops?

1959 **[The US military effort in Vietnam was] grievously unsound, devoid throughout of a plausible, coherent and realistic object.**—*George Kennan, Presidential advisor, comments, March 1968.*[72]

Kennan was recognized as the author of the Containment Doctrine, formulated at the end of World War II. The Doctrine was used successfully in Europe to limit Soviet expansion and was used to form the basis for U.S. policy in Southeast Asia.

1960 **[You are the] natural defender of the status quo. You represent things as they are ... the man who is not calling for change, but resisting it.**—*Harry McPherson, President Johnson's speech writer, in a memorandum to the President, 18 March 1968.*[72]

The other candidates in the presidential race all called for a definite change in American policy in Vietnam, but none talked of taking stronger action to force North Vietnam to negotiate.

1961 **I think the course we seem to be taking now will lead either to Kennedy's nomination or Nixon's election, or both.**—*Harry McPherson, President Johnson's speech writer, in a memorandum to the President, 18 March 1968.*[72]

1962 **We hope to achieve an honorable peace and a just peace at the negotiating table. But wanting peace, praying for peace, and desiring peace, as Chamberlain found out, doesn't always give you peace.**—*President Lyndon Johnson, from a speech at National Farmers Union convention, 18 March 1968.*[72]

1963 **If [the enemy] insists, as he does now, that the outcome must be determined on the battlefield, then we will win peace on the battlefield by supporting our men who are doing that job there now.**—*President Lyndon Johnson, from a speech at the National Farmers Union Convention, 18 March 1968.*[72]

1964 **Hue was the place where reactionary spirit had existed for over ten years. However, it took us only a short time to drain it to its roots.**—*Excerpted from a communist report on the Battle of Hue, March 1968.*[637]

The "reactionary spirit" referred to was the control and administration of Hue by the Saigon regime. The most effective measure of draining the spirit of Hue was the execution of thousands of the city's residents by communist occupation forces. Members of the GVN, ARVN soldiers, intellectuals, GVN employees, those employed by the Americans, or anyone else with a history of anticommunist activity were subjected to execution and burial in mass graves.

1965 **[The Vietnam War is] a controversial and expensive military effort in a faraway place.**—*Tony Dechant, President of the Farmers Union, speaking at their convention, 18 March 1968.*[653]

Dechant spoke out against the war telling members of the union that continued escalation of the war would lead to higher interest rates, increased production costs, and lower profits. President Johnson spoke at the same convention and asked for the Farmers Union's support.

1966 **We know that we constantly underestimated the enemy's capacity and his will to fight and overestimated our progress. We know now that all we thought we had constructed was built on sand.**—*Unidentified Pentagon official, in a leak to The New York Times, March 1968.*[72]

The *Times* broke the story of Westmoreland's request for 206,000 additional troops for Vietnam. If the request was honored it would have raised U.S. troop strength in Vietnam to more than 700,000.

1967 **From the people I've talked to I've come up with some new ideas on the war. For the most part nobody is particularly wild with patriotic feeling. There are, of course, those who just get a real charge out of killing people. One lieutenant I talked to said what a kick it had been to roll a gook 100 yards down the beach with his machine gun. But most people generate their enthusiasm for two reasons: one is self-preservation — if I don't shoot him, he'll eventually shoot me — and the other is revenge. It's apparently quite something to see a good friend blown apart by a VC booby trap, and you want to retaliate in kind.**—*Lt. Robert C. Ransom, Jr., U.S. Army, A Company, 4th Battalion, 3d Infantry, in a letter home, March 1968.*[187]

1968 **If we do not talk in terms of Communism, it is like a production of Hamlet without the prince.**—*Abe Fortas, Supreme Court Justice, during a meeting with President Johnson and his advisers, March 1968.*[72]

The focus of the meeting was the text of a speech to be delivered by the President to the public. Some of his advisers cautioned him to avoid using words about escalating the war, others wanted him to be more pointed about what the war really was about. Fortas recommended that Johnson speak of the communists and what they had done in South Vietnam and Laos.

1969 **I'm not going to stop the bombing.... I've heard every argument. I'm not going to stop.**—*President Lyndon Johnson, during a meeting with his aides, March 1968.*[51]

Johnson refused to halt the bombing of North Vietnam. He was concerned that such a halt would result in more American casualties as North Vietnam used the halt to step-up the flow of men and material into South Vietnam.

1970 **We must meet our commitments in Vietnam and the world. We shall and we are going to win.**—*President Lyndon Johnson, speaking to his staff, March 1968.*[287]

Johnson's Secretary of State urged him to continue existing Administration policy in Vietnam, while his Secretary of Defense recommended a bombing halt of North Vietnam and concessions to get Hanoi to negotiate.

1971 **In our judgement, the only action which can avert major Democratic Party losses in this state in 1968 is an immediate all-out effort to secure a non-military settlement of the Vietnam war.**—*California Democratic Central Committee, in a telegram to President Johnson, March 1968.*[828]

Support for Johnson's nomination as the Democratic Party's candidate for president was weak in California, with a slight edge going to Kennedy. The party believed they would lose local political positions based on their link, as Democrats, to Johnson and the war.

1972 **We have no intention of widening this war. But the United States will never accept a fake solution to this long and arduous struggle and call it peace.**—*President Lyndon Johnson, address to the nation, 31 March 1968.*[365]

1973 **It is our fervent hope that North Vietnam, after years of fighting that have left the issue unresolved, will now cease its efforts to achieve a military victory and will join with us in moving toward the peace table.**—*President Lyndon Johnson, address to the nation, 31 March 1968.*[365]

1974 **[The draft is] a totalitarian instrument used to practice genocide against black people.**—*Walter Collins, SNCC spokesman and activist, 1968.*[978]

1975 **We must make greater efforts and accept more sacrifices because, as I have said many times, this is our country. The existence of our nation is at stake, and this is mainly a Vietnamese responsibility.**—*Nguyen Van Thieu, President, Republic of Vietnam, from a speech, March 1968.*[366]

1976 **If I were betting, I'd bet we win a third at least [of the New York delegates in a three-way Johnson-Kennedy-**

McCarthy race], and have a better than 50-50 chance for a majority when the chips are down.—*Edwin Weisl, New York state Democratic Party national committeeman, speaking to the press, 20 March 1968.*[801]

It must be remembered that up to this point Johnson had not yet officially announced his candidacy for his party's nomination.

1977 **Hardly anyone today is interested in winning the war. Everyone wants to get out, and the only question is how.**—*James L. Rowe, long-time Democratic party leader, in a memorandum to President Johnson, 19 March 1968.*[374]

Rowe informed Johnson that within the party, two of the three Democratic candidates for the presidential nomination (Kennedy and McCarthy) were peace candidates, while Johnson appeared as the war candidate. Rowe advised Johnson that he needed to be seen as pursuing peace, without surrender.

1978 **General [Harold K] Johnson's term expires as Chief of Staff of the Army in July, 1968. He plans to retire. He has notified us of his desire to retire. He will be succeeded by General Westmoreland.**—*President Lyndon Johnson, during a press conference, 22 March 1968.*[803]

Westmoreland, as the U.S. commander of MACV was the architect of the American war in Vietnam. He was to be replaced by his deputy, General Abrams. Westmoreland had championed the effort in Vietnam and publicly stated that the war was under control. Many saw the replacement of Westmoreland as indication of a rejection of his search and destroy strategy of dealing with the enemy.

1979 **Over more than 20 years I had seen many bodies with fresh blood of Asians, whites, blacks, by the dozens, the hundreds. Sometimes I hated it, sometimes I was moved, but never before was I so moved, did I hate it so much, was I so fed up as at this time, even though the scene was only brought by television.**—*Tran Ngoc Chau, South Vietnamese Assemblyman, 1968.*[649]

Chau was commenting of the extensive TV coverage of the war in Vietnam and especially the battle for Hue during the communist TET Offensive.

1980 **Our objective in South Vietnam has never been the annihilation of the enemy. It has been to bring about a recognition in Hanoi that its objective — taking over the South by force — could not be achieved.**—*President Lyndon Johnson, address to the nation, 31 March 1968.*[365]

1981 **Here, while the sun shines, our brave young men are dying in the swamps of Southeast Asia. Which of them might have written a poem? Which of them might have cured cancer? Which of them might have played in a World Series or given us the gift of laughter from a stage or helped build a bridge or university? Which of them would have taught a child to read? It is our responsibility to let these men live.**—*Senator Robert Kennedy, campaigning in Los Angeles, California, 23 March 1968.*[795]

1982 **The single most important psychological event in race-relations in the nineteen-sixties was the appearance of the Negro fighting men on the TV screens of the nation, acquiring a reputation for military valor is one of the oldest known routes to social equity.**—*Daniel P. Moynihan, Director of the Joint Center for Urban Studies at Harvard University, quoted in New York Times Magazine, 24 March 1968.*[1006]

The war in Vietnam was the first American war where blacks were fully integrated into the armed forces, in positions of field command and decision, as well as throughout the ranks.

1983 **If the North Vietnamese were to be expelled from the South and the country pacified, it would ... take at least five to ten years.**—*George Ball, unofficial adviser to President Johnson, during a meeting of his advisers, 25 March 1968.*[49]

Ball was estimating the time of U.S. involvement in Vietnam — if the conditions were right.

1984 **General, I am not a great mathematician, but with 80,000 [enemy] killed and a wounded ratio of three to one, or 240,000 [enemy wounded], for a total of 320,000, who the hell are we fighting?**—*Arthur Goldberg, U.S. Ambassador to the United Nations, during a meeting of President Johnson's advisers, 25 March 1968.*[50]

Goldberg was reacting to a military briefing that indicated 320,000 enemy soldiers were put out of action during TET, yet MACV claimed total enemy strength in South Vietnam was in the 230,000-280,000 range.

1985 **What in the name of God have we got five hundred thousand troops out there for — chasing girls? You know damned well this is what we are trying to do — to force the enemy to sue for peace. It won't happen — at least not in any time the American people will permit.**—*Dean Acheson, former Secretary of State and unofficial Johnson adviser, during a meeting of the Wise Men, 25 March 1968.*[374]

The meeting was held as a strategy session, the results to be presented to President Johnson. The meeting was called to review the situation in Vietnam and recommend options to the President.

1986 **We can no longer do the job we set out to do in the time we have left and we must begin to take steps to disengage.**—*Dean Acheson, during a meeting with the President, as related by McGeorge Bundy, 26 March 1968.*[887]

Acheson and Bundy were members of the "Wise Men," who informally advised President Johnson. Based on the mood of the country after the communist TET Offensive, the "Wise Men" advised Johnson that it was time for a change in the direction of the war.

1987 **We have not really gone out to win the war.**—*Admiral Thomas H. Moorer, U.S. Navy Chief of Staff, March 1968.*[72]

Moorer favored an expansion of the bombing campaign in North Vietnam.

1988 **Our gross national product now soars above $800 billion a year. But that counts air pollution and cigarette advertising, and ambulances to clear our streets of carnage. It counts the special locks for our doors and jails for the people who break them. It counts the destruction of our redwoods and the loss of natural wonder to chaotic sprawl. It counts napalm and nuclear warheads and armored cars for the police to fight riots in our cities. It counts Whitman's rifle and Speck's knife, and television programs which glorify violence to sell toys to our children.**—*Senator Robert Kennedy's speech at a fund raiser in Des Moines, Iowa, March 1968.*[781]

Kennedy attacked not only the war but the whole breakdown in our society, as he saw it.

1989 **The establishment bastards have bailed out.**—*President Lyndon Johnson, remarks made following a meeting of his advisers, the "Wise Men," 26 March 1968.*[325]

Johnson's comment followed a strategy meeting with his official/unofficial advisers, the Wise Men, in which the majority recommended the United States begin unilateral de-escalation of the war effort. The same group had previously backed escalation of the war.

1990 **Less stress on search and destroy would mean fewer casualties, less destruction, fewer refugees, less ill will and more public support at home.**—*Henry Cabot Lodge, U.S. Ambassador to South Vietnam, during a White House meeting, 26 March 1968.*[653]

Lodge advocated movement away from large offensive operations (search and destroy operations), instead using American units in screening operations to keep the enemy away from the population and agricultural centers. This was contrary to the way the war had been conducted under Westmoreland where search and destroy operations where his primary weapon against the enemy.

1991 **Can we by military means keep North Vietnam off the South Vietnamese. I do not think we can. They can slip around and end-run them and crack them up.**—*Dean Acheson, former Secretary of State, during a meeting with President Johnson, 26 March 1968.*[887]

Acheson was one of the "Wise Men" who advised President Johnson. After the widespread attacks of the communist TET Offensive the "Wise Men" concluded that a change in American policy for Vietnam was necessary since the military approach had not had the desired effect.

1992 **Unless we do something quick, the mood in this country may lead us to withdraw.**—*Cyrus Vance, former Deputy Secretary of Defense, during a meeting of the President's advisers, March 1968.*[887]

Vance was sounding a warning that the mood of the country was definitely turning against the war in Vietnam as a result of the communist TET Offensive. An offensive that the Johnson administration had believed was not probable because the enemy numbers were on the decline, he was weakening, and had become a reduced threat.

1993 **What seems not to be understood is that major elements of the national constituency — the business community, the press, the churches, professional groups, college presidents, students and most of the intellectual community — have turned against this war. What the President needs is not a war speech, but a peace speech.**—*Clark Clifford, advisor to President Johnson and later Secretary of Defense, during discussions on an upcoming Presidential speech, 28 March 1968.*[832]

Clark had been an early and avid supporter of the war in Vietnam, but by late '67 he evaluated the change in the national attitude towards the war and advised Johnson accordingly.

1994 **People's feeling of discontent is over whether the effort is being prosecuted intelligently and firmly. Our combination of war and peace is confusing.**—*Abe Fortas, Supreme Court Justice, during a meeting with President Johnson and his advisers, March 1968.*[72]

1995 **We have found that the best treatment for simple combat reaction is a few days rest and return to duty. ... This new treatment has been found to be 100 percent effective.**—*SP/4 Dennis E. Hengen, clinical psychology specialist, 2d Brigade, 9th Infantry Division, 1968.*[894]

Combat Reaction was the Vietnam War era name for the condition called "shell shock" in WWI and "combat fatigue" in W.W.II. A man so diagnosed was pulled off the line for a few days then returned to his unit in the field.

1996 **I would ask all Americans to guard against divisiveness and all its ugly consequences.**—*President Lyndon Johnson, address to the nation, 31 March 1968.*[683]

1997 **There are no military conclusions in this war — or any military end in the near future, [the conflict should be de-escalated].**—*This was the majority consensus of Johnson's unofficial advisers, the "Wise Men," March 1968.*[314]

The Wise Men consisted of Johnson's highest level, official/unofficial, advisers. They were thoroughly briefed by the CIA, State Department and the Pentagon before discussing the situation in Vietnam, and making recommendations to the President.

1998 **Fighter by day ... Lover by night ... Drunkard by choice ... Army by mistake.**—*Inscription from a Zippo lighter owned by an infantryman of the 4th Infantry Division, 1968.*[1026]

1999 **I renew the offer I made last August — to stop the bombardment of North Vietnam. We ask that talks begin promptly, that they be serious talks on the substance of peace. We assume that during those talks Hanoi will not take advantage of our restraint.**—*President Lyndon Johnson, address to the nation, 31 March 1968.*[365]

Johnson announced a halt to the bombing of North Vietnam above the 20th Parallel. In the past Hanoi took advantage of bombing halts to increase the flow of men and materiel into South Vietnam. Johnson hoped Hanoi would show restraint in acknowledgement of America's move towards peace.

2000 **They [North Vietnam and the Vietcong] are, it appears, trying to make 1968 the year of decision in South Vietnam — the year that brings, if not final victory or defeat, at least a turning point in the struggle.**—*President Lyndon Johnson, address to the nation, 31 March 1968.*[365]

2001 **Tonight, in the hope that this action will lead to early talks, I am taking the first step to de-escalate the conflict. We are ... substantially reducing ... the present level of hostilities. And we are doing so unilaterally and at once.**—*President Lyndon Johnson, from a televised speech, 31 March 1968.*[557]

Johnson ordered a halt to all air strikes against North Vietnam except for the area immediately north of the DMZ (south of the 20th Parallel).

2002 **I have concluded that I should not permit the Presidency to become involved in the partisan divisions that are developing in this political year. With America's sons in the fields far away, with America's future under challenge right here at home, with our hopes and the world's hopes for peace in the balance every day, I do not believe that I should devote**

an hour or a day of my time to any personal partisan causes or to any duties other than the awesome duties of this office — the Presidency of your country. Accordingly, I shall not seek, and I will not accept, the nomination of my party for another term as your President.—*President Lyndon Johnson, address to the nation, 31 March 1968.*[365]

2003 **The VC [stage attacks] more efficiently than we do.... And the reason is that they usually know what they're aiming at, and we usually don't — they have good intelligence.**—*Bill Johnson, CIA counterintelligence analyst, in a conversation with Sam Adams, 1968.*[3]

Johnson was referring to the effectiveness of VC attacks on U.S. installations. VC attacks were preplanned and based on a large amount of collected information on the American facility. This was compared to the weak and dated information American intelligence units most often were able to collect and use for targeting of the enemy.

2004 **The ultimate strength of our country and our cause will lie not in powerful weapons or infinite resources or boundless wealth, but will lie in the unity of our people.... What we won when all of our people united just must not now be lost in suspicion, distrust, selfishness and politics among any of our people.**—*President Lyndon Johnson, during a nationally televised speech, 31 March 1968.*[753]

2005 **We have turned the corner... — Gen. Westmoreland.**—*From a cartoon caption, Washington Daily News, 31 January 1968.*[653]

The cartoon pictured Westmoreland colliding with a VC guerrilla at the corner of a building labeled "U.S. Embassy Saigon." The VC's rifle was jammed into Westmoreland's stomach, the general's stars (insignia) were falling off his uniform and his gun was slipping from his hand. Weeks prior to the TET Offensive Westmoreland had indicated the Allies were making progress in the war against the communists, having "turned the corner" towards winning the war.

2006 **Let men everywhere know ... that a strong, a confident, and a vigilant America stands ready tonight to seek an honorable peace — and stands ready tonight to defend an honored cause — whatever the price, whatever the burden, whatever the sacrifice that duty may require.**—*President Lyndon Johnson, address to the nation, 31 March 1968.*[365]

2007 **In these times as in times before, it is true that a house divided against itself by the spirit of faction, of party, of region, of religion, of race, is a house that cannot stand.**—*President Lyndon Johnson, during nationally televised speech, 31 March 1968.*[859]

In this speech Johnson announced a halt to the bombing of North Vietnam above the 20th Parallel, and announced he would not seek re-election in the 1968 presidential campaign.

2008 **I remembered the way a Phantom pilot had talked about how beautiful the surface-to-air missiles looked as they drifted up toward his plane to kill him, and remembered myself how lovely .50-caliber tracers could be, coming at you as you flew at night in a helicopter, how slow and graceful, arching up easily, a dream, so remote from anything that could harm you. It could make you feel a total serenity, an elevation that put you above death, but that never lasted very long. One hit anywhere in the chopper would bring you back, bitten lips, white knuckles and all, and then you knew where you were.**—*Michael Herr, journalist, writing in Dispatches, Khe Sanh in 1968.*[870]

2009 **I call upon the United Kingdom and I call upon the Soviet Union — as co-chairmen of the Geneva Conferences, and as permanent members of the United Nations Security Council — to do all they can to move from the unilateral act of de-escalation that I have just announced toward genuine peace in Southeast Asia.**—*President Lyndon Johnson, address to the nation, 31 March 1968.*[365]

2010 **The United States is planning a new plot to maintain its new colonialism and increasing its troops to reconstruct the South Vietnamese puppet regime and troops.**—*Quan Doi Nhan Dan, North Vietnamese Army newspaper, 2 April 1968.*[558]

Hanoi's response to the bombing halt called by President Johnson on 31 March 1968. Johnson halted all bombing of North Vietnam except for the area immediately south of the 20th Parallel.

2011 **Of those to whom much is given, much is asked. I cannot say and no man could say that no more will be asked of us.**—*President Lyndon Johnson, address to the nation, 31 March 1968.*[365]

2012 **Peace will come because Asians were willing to work for it — and to sacrifice for it — and to die by the thousands for it. But let it never be forgotten: Peace will come also because America sent her sons to help secure it.**—*President Lyndon Johnson, address to the nation, 31 March 1968.*[365]

2013 **One day, my fellow citizens, there will be peace in Southeast Asia.**—*President Lyndon Johnson, address to the nation, 31 March 1968.*[365]

2014 **The General Offensive and Uprising of the South Vietnam Armed Forces [communist] and people early this year have inflicted on the U.S. aggressors and their lackeys a fatal blow.... The Vietnamese people's fight for independence and freedom has entered a new period. The U.S. defeat is already evident.**—*Excerpt from an official announcement by Hanoi, 2 April 1968.*[653]

Hanoi announced that it was ready to discuss negotiations based on President Johnson's 31 March announcement that he was suspending bombing of North Vietnam above the 20th Parallel. Hanoi had refused any consideration of negotiations as long as the U.S. was bombing North Vietnam.

2015 **The Government of the Democratic Republic of Vietnam declares its readiness to appoint its representative to contact the United States representative with a view to determining with the American side the unconditional cessation of the United States bombing raids and all other acts of war against the Democratic Republic of Vietnam. So the talks may start.**—*Statement from the government of the Democratic Republic of Vietnam, as read by President Johnson to the press, 3 April 1968.*[561]

2016 **The war in Vietnam is unwinnable, and the longer it goes on the more the Americans will be subjected to losses and humiliation.**—*Joseph Kraft, correspondent, 1968.*[347]

Comments after the enemy TET Offensive.

2017 **You're sitting out in the open in a foxhole, and you put out your magazines, you put all your grenades, you check the radio, you check the batteries. And then you wait. And the sky gets a little darker ... and in that twilight gloom, you used to just shiver and shake with nervousness and fear because you couldn't do anything. And then it would be totally dark, and then you'd hear noise, you'd hear a probe and they'd start firing. You'd get movement. And then you weren't as afraid anymore because then there was something to do.**—*Dennis Mannion, former U.S. Marine.*[350]

Mannion survived the North Vietnamese siege of Khe Sanh and the "Hill fights" of 1968.

2018 **[Khe Sanh was] a trap laid by the enemy to force you into the expenditure of absolutely unreasonable amounts of men and material to defend a piece of terrain that wasn't worth a damn.**—*General Lowell English, U.S. Marine Commander at Khe Sanh, 1968.*[374]

English, at the time, believed the siege of Khe Sanh to be an enemy diversionary tactic. Westmoreland, on the other hand, initially believed the attack against Khe Sanh was eminent, and Khe Sanh was the main aim of the enemy TET Offensive.

2019 **The Marines had defeated the enemy in the place he had chosen to fight. It was the Marine, with his rifle in his hand and perhaps, a tight knot in the pit of his stomach, who had routed the invader from Hue.**—*Leatherneck Magazine in a story about the Battle of Hue, May 1968.*[642]

The VC/NVA seized much of Hue in the early hours of the 1968 TET Offensive. The enemy held the city for 25 days before American and ARVN units cleared the city of the last enemy units. Much of the fighting was house to house as streets were methodically cleared of the enemy.

2020 **Every press conference reeks with these two words [body count]. It is inescapable, insidious, corrosive.... Someone decided there must be a way to keep score in a war where there are no victories.**—*David Douglas Duncan, correspondent, comments in Life magazine, 5 April 1968.*[94]

2021 **I remember General Westmoreland and Robert McNamara saying, "We're winning this thing. There's light at the end of the tunnel." And then all of a sudden, [the VC] they're in downtown Saigon.... They will not be stopped because they're fighting for their homes. So you had this feeling that these people who are representing us, they're lying to us. They've been lying to us all along.**—*Julian Bond.*[350]

Speaking of the communist 1968 TET Offensive and the credibility gap.

2022 **We cannot wage war in Vietnam and at the same time alleviate the hopelessness that leads to riots.**—*Senator Eugene J. McCarthy from Minnesota, during campaigning for the Democratic nomination for President, 1968.*[72]

McCarthy made a very strong bid for the Democratic nomination for president early in the campaign.

2023 **[It is] an act of reason and political courage.**—*Charles de Gaulle, President of France, during a French Cabinet meeting, 3 April 1968.*[560]

De Gaulle's praise was for President Johnson's announcement of the planned halt to the bombing of North Vietnam, 31 March 1968.

2024 **I call it the Madman Theory.... I want the North Vietnamese to believe that I've reached the point where I might do anything to stop the war. We'll just slip the word to them that, "for God's sake, you know Nixon is obsessed about Communists. We can't restrain him when he's angry—and he has his hand on the nuclear button"—and Ho Chi Minh himself will be in Paris in two days begging for peace.**—*Richard Nixon, presidential candidate, speaking to H.R. Haldeman, 1968.*[374]

The "Madman Theory" was one of several plans Nixon considered during the final months before the 1968 presidential election. In March 1968, following a speech by Nixon in New Hampshire, a reporter wrote of the speech, that Nixon had a secret plan for Vietnam. From that point on the press asked Nixon what his plan was for Vietnam.

2025 **Let's declare that we have achieved our objectives in Vietnam and go home.**—*Senator George Aiken of Vermont, 1968.*[72]

2026 **We have fought bravely but victory in Vietnam is nowhere in sight ... with the President's proposal, Hanoi can only see things as going its way.**—*General James M. Gavin, U.S. Army (Retired), comments to the press, April 1968.*[453]

Gavin was referring to President Johnson's decision to stop attacks against North Vietnam, north of the 20th Parallel, capping American troop levels in Vietnam, and not seeking another term as president. Gavin was a longtime opponent of the introduction of American combat troops into Vietnam.

2027 **This war was going to be won or lost in the hamlets.**—*General James M. Gavin, U.S. Army (Retired), comments during an interview, April 1968.*[453]

Gavin proposed an enclave policy for fighting the VC in Vietnam. Under this policy the U.S. troops would help protect a group of enclaves centered on several South Vietnamese coastal cities. The ARVN would work outward from the enclave clearing the countryside of the VC, strengthening the position of the Saigon regime while at the same time clearing larger areas of the country of the enemy.

2028 **We feel sorry they got King.... He's a martyr now, and his people will probably follow the Rap Browns and the Stokley Carmichaels. We have 300 Americans dying here each week.... King was one man. What about the people out here who are dying.**—*Unidentified U.S. Army MP, comments to a correspondent in Vietnam, April 1968.*[989]

2029 **The awesomeness of the American buildup is staggering ... all altering the fabric of Vietnamese society. They would have been better off if we had never gone in. So would we.**—*General James M. Gavin, U.S. Army (Retired), comments during an interview, April 1968.*[453]

2030 **[Peace must not be a] cheap peace, a giveaway peace, a peace at any price.**—*President Lyndon Johnson, comments on possible peace talks, 1968.*[303]

Johnson was not overly hopeful that Hanoi would negotiate in good faith at the opening of peace talks in May 1968.

2031 **Ho Chi Minh attempts to project the kindly, scholarly grandfather image, when, in fact, he must rank among the bloodiest despots in history.**—*A.J. Donahue, III of Milford, Connecticut, in a letter to the editor, April 1968.*[454]

By some estimates 40,000 North Vietnamese died as Ho Chi Minh consolidated his power in Hanoi after the French departed in 1954. Many of those who died were teachers, land owners, and local village leaders who resisted communist rule.

2032 **I feel good about it [high death rate among blacks in Vietnam]. Not that I like the bloodshed, but the performance of the Negro in Vietnam tends to offset the fact that the Negro wasn't considered worthy of being a front-line soldier in other wars.**—*Lt.Col. George Shoffer, U.S. Army, during an interview, 1968.*[1006]

The death rate among blacks in Vietnam was higher than their statistical representation in the general population until about 1968. After 1967, changes were made in the organization of units, which by the end of the war had dropped the black casualty rate to a more representative ratio of the general population.

2033 **I know a lot of brothers who will stay in the Army, because they're afraid to get out and face what's out there.**—*Pvt. James Williams, U.S. Army, during an interview, 1968.*[1006]

For many blacks from poor educational backgrounds, the military provided a chance for education, security, and advancement that was sometimes more difficult to achieve outside of the military.

2034 **Confidence in the ability of the GVN to furnish security must be given to the people of this province before any significant progress in pacification can be made.**—*Unidentified member of the U.S. Hau Nghia Province Advisory Team, in the monthly province report, April 1968.*[7]

The South Vietnamese RD Cadres were responsible for working with the villages to which they were assigned. In addition to their civic duties and pacification, they were also tasked with the defense of the village, incorporating the villagers into a self-defense force. With the enemy offensive of TET 1968, the RD Cadre program came to a halt.

2035 **No matter how effective our actions, the prevalent strategy could no longer achieve its objectives within a period or with force levels politically acceptable to the American people.**—*Henry Kissinger, consultant to the U.S. State Department, 1968.*[374]

Kissinger was referring to the enemy TET offensive, which erupted at a time when the U.S. was supposedly winning the war and grinding the enemy down.

2036 **The only difference between the Kennedy assassination and mine is that I am alive and it has been more torturous.**—*President Lyndon Johnson, comment to journalists at the White House, 5 May 1968.*[653]

Johnson was referring to the difficulty he was having in getting "good press" from the news media reporting on his policies and the war in Vietnam.

2037 **If you took out all the United States ... forces now, the Government [of South Vietnam] would have to settle for a piece of Vietnam.**—*General Creighton W. Abrams, ComUSMACV, from comments to a correspondent, May 1968.*[254]

Abrams was responding to questions whether or not the ARVN was ready to take up the fight against the communist. There were large areas of South Vietnam not under the control of the government of South Vietnam and Abrams did not believe it likely that those areas could be recovered without the support of American troops.

2038 **In any war, the military group is always superior, the ones who handle military forces. A good leader is one who concentrates the most troops. People have more affection for the military man, the one, who in their minds, sacrifices more.**—*Unidentified, high-ranking Vietcong prisoner of war, from a speech, May 1968.*[30]

2039 **Our strategy is based on the people. Our basic means [are] the people. But if the people all went to safe areas, we lost the basic means—especially the means for conducting the military indoctrination missions and for the political struggle.**—*Unidentified, high-ranking Vietcong prisoner of war, from a speech, May 1968.*[30]

The PW was emphasizing the importance of the people and the necessity for disrupting the U.S./SVN pacification program.

2040 **The main force that truly wants to defeat us is the U.S. force, not the RVNAF.**—*Unidentified, high-ranking Vietcong prisoner of war, from a speech, May 1968.*[30]

The PW had been a corps commander and was the COSVN assistant to the Chief of Indoctrination at the time of his capture in October 1967. Hanoi and COSVN did not consider the ARVN as a force to be reckoned with.

2041 **We Americans left the highest standard of living in the world, came ten thousand miles to one of the most fucked-up countries there ever was to save these people from communist brutality and to show them how to raise themselves to our level of civilization. We Americans are doing these Vietnamese a favor by just coming over here and the least they could do to show their appreciation is put out with a little nooky now and then and keep their mouths shut.**—*U.S. Marine Corps Sergeant voicing his personal opinion to Charles Anderson, 1968.*[4]

2042 **If we can attack the cities and can overthrow the South Vietnam government and remain in those cities, the Americans cannot muster sufficient reaction to overcome that situation; if we cannot get a victory in this TET Offensive, we can at least make an echo in international opinions—especially in American public opinions. In this case, we participate directly in the antiwar movement in the United States...**—*Unidentified, high-ranking Vietcong prisoner of war, from a speech, May 1968.*[30]

The VC/NVA expected the South Vietnamese to rise up against the GVN, backing the VC in their attacks on the cities during TET. Once entrenched in the cities and supported by the populace, the Americans would have had little alternative but to withdraw from Vietnam. The TET Offensive of 1968 failed to rally the people to the support of the VC and except for Hue, the length of time they were able to hold the cities was measured in hours.

2043 **By its neglect, by its insensitivity, by its arrogance, our present leadership has caused an unprecedented chasm to develop in our society.**—*Richard Nixon, Republican presidential candidate, in speeches during the 1968 campaign.*[939]

2044 **The Communists do not measure victory or defeat by body counts ... [but by whether or not their interests were furthered through their sacrifice].**—*Hanson W. Baldwin, in a magazine article, 9 June 1968.*[99]

The body count was use by the American military in Vietnam to gage the progress of the war. A high enemy body count was used as an indication of success in the progress of the war against the communists. The communists were willing to sacrifice troops to inflict casualties on American units, many American commanders were not so willing to use their troops to simply further the enemy body count to impress higher headquarters.

2045 **We have decided to continue the mobile posture we adopted in western Quang Tri Province with Operation Pegasus in April. This decision makes the operation of the base at Khe Sanh unnecessary.**—*From a MACV press release, June 1968.*[893]

Operation Pegasus was a joint Army and Marine operation to open Route 9 to the Marine base at Khe Sanh. Pegasus was a highly mobile operation. According to MACV, sufficient troops and air assets were operating in the I Corps area to allow for more mobile operations, thus the fixed base at Khe Sanh could be abandoned. Khe Sanh was originally established astride one of the main East-West infiltration routes between the Laotian border and the northern I Corps coastal area.

2046 **(Reporter)—General, can the war be won militarily? (Westmoreland)—Not in a classic sense, because of our national policy of not expanding the war. But, even if the United States could not win a classic victory, the enemy can be attrited, the price can be raised—and is being raised to the point that it could be intolerable to the enemy.**—*General William Westmoreland, ComUSMACV, during his final news conference in South Vietnam, 10 June 1968.*[893]

Westmoreland was replaced as MACV commander by General Creighton W. Abrams. Westmoreland continued his career as Chairman of the JCS.

2047 **Even had I known exactly what was to take place [at TET], it was so preposterous that I probably would have been unable to sell it to anybody.**—*Unidentified MACV intelligence officer, 1968.*[335]

MACV had bits and pieces of the planned offensive, but not an exact time table or all the targets the enemy planned to strike.

2048 **They had the usual abilities of those in the vast middle ranges of the world's many hierarchies—they could look very busy and deeply concerned when they were perfectly idle and thoroughly apathetic.**—*Charles R. Anderson, Lieutenant, USMC, in June 1968.*[4]

Commenting on the mentality and ability of a significant number of officers in the military.

2049 **Vietnam was a nine-to-five war, and from five in the afternoon until curfew tens of thousands of Americans in Vietnam were looking for something to do.**—*Charles R. Anderson, Lieutenant, U.S. Marine Corps, in June 1968.*[4]

In general, U.S. combat units were on the offensive during the day and defensive at night. Many of the men in major base and rear areas had idle time during off-duty hours. With 6–10 troops supporting each soldier in the field there were a lot of men with time on their hands.

2050 **The fall of Khe Sanh is a grave defeat for the Americans, with disastrous political and psychological consequences.**—*Nguyen Thanh Le, spokesman for the North Vietnamese delegation to the Paris peace talks, speaking to the press, June 1968.*[893]

The North Vietnamese view of the U.S. decision to abandon the combat base at Khe Sanh.

2051 **America is the greatest country in the history of the world; the duty of every American citizen is to do all in his or her power to keep America the greatest; the best way to help keep America the greatest and to show one's love of country is to serve in the military; the line between dissent and treason is so vague that it can safely be ignored; communists and hippies are the most despicable forms of life on earth and should be locked up forever if they can't be killed on sight.**—*Group of U.S. Marine Corps senior NCO's lament as related by Charles R. Anderson, Lieutenant, USMC, in June 1968.*[4]

A "lifer's" view of the war.

2052 **We must listen to the voices of dissent because the protester may have something to say worth listening to. If we dismiss dissent as coming from "rebels without a cause," we will soon find ourselves becoming leaders without an effect.**—*Richard Nixon, Republican presidential candidate, in speeches during the 1968 campaign.*[939]

2053 **Sour grapes.**—*Nguyen Thanh Le, spokesman for the North Vietnamese delegation to the Paris peace talks, speaking to the press, June 1968.*[893]

Hanoi's opinion of the reasoning behind the abandoning of the U.S. combat base at Khe Sanh. According to MACV their were sufficient troops and air assets in the northern I Corps area to allow U.S. units to resume mobile operations to interdict enemy use of the infiltration routes and bases in the area. The fixed base at Khe Sanh was no longer required since mobility had been re-established.

2054 **The [NVA] are nearly as alien in this country as are our U.S. forces and receive only that support and assistance from the population that they are able to coerce through fear.**—*John Paul Vann, Deputy, II Field Force CORDS, in a letter, June 1968.*[887]

Vann was emphasizing the point that the NVA troops were not warmly accepted by the South Vietnamese. Because of heavy losses sustained by the VC during the TET Offensive, the ranks of many VC units were filled by large numbers of NVA troops.

2055 **This Vietnam war is a great patriotic crusade that got off to a good start but recently turned into a chickenshit no-win thing because the pinko socialistic professors and politicians back in Washington won't get their hands off it and let us invade North Vietnam and atom-bomb Hanoi, Peking, and Moscow so we could end the war right and straighten out the world.**—*Generic class of U.S. Marine Corps senior NCO's lament as related by Charles R. Anderson, Lieutenant, U.S. Marine Corps, in June 1968.*[4]

A "Lifer's" view of the war.

2056 **In the battle fought at Trang Bang, Go Dau, elements of the 2d Brigade, 25th U.S. Infantry Division, were ordered to go to the aid of a U.S. unit there. They ran away to hide themselves, refusing to get aboard the planes. Their commanders pursued and caught them, beat them mercilessly, and shaved their heads. A number of others struggled against the order, cried, and fasted.**—*Excerpt from a captured enemy operations report for Cu Chi District. 30 June 1968.*[16]

This fictionalized report was indication of the depth of misconception that enemy sometimes operated under. The report also claimed the district VC force, consisting of less than 1000 men, claimed a body count of nearly 6,000 Americans of the 25th Infantry Division during the TET 1968 fighting. Actual American casualties for the entire 25th Infantry Division between January and July were 883 killed and 3,679 wounded. The division consisted of three brigades at the time.

2057 **Those who do not battle for their country do not know with what ease they accept their citizenship in America.**—*Dean Brelis, reporter and author, 1968.*[502]

2058 **[American military action] was like a sledgehammer on a floating cork. Somehow the cork refused to stay down.**—*Malcolm Browne, author, 1968.*[305]

2059 **The VC are right to bet the GVN and U.S. will fail to exploit any such "opportunies" and fanatics like you, me (before), [and] our friends were always wrong to imagine otherwise.**—*Daniel Ellsberg, Pentagon analyst, writing to John Paul Vann, mid-1968.*[887]

The "opportunities" Ellsberg spoke of was the weakening of the VC as a result of heavy losses during the TET Offensive. Pacification experts advocated stepped-up pacification attempts during the enemy's weakness.

2060 **I recommend that the air campaign against North Vietnam be resumed.... Postponement of a decision will prevent initiation of a concerted air and naval campaign against North Vietnam until spring of 1969.... It will then require us to engage an enemy whose defenses have been reconstituted, whose resolve to continue the war will be strengthened, and whose war-making potential will have been substantially enhanced through Soviet and Chicom military and technical assistance.**—*Admiral U.S. Grant Sharp, CINCPAC, in a report to Secretary of Defense Clark Clifford in Saigon, July 1968.*[185]

This was Sharp's argument for resuming air strikes against North Vietnam. The strikes were halted, above the 20th Parallel, by President Johnson in April 1968.

2061 **Things are so bad now that a guy almost has to get a petition signed by all members of Congress and approved by the President before he can return fire when the VC take a shot at him! The strongest, greatest country in the history of the world is letting a half-assed, backward, worthless little country push it around while the whole world looks on and cheers the wrong side.**—*Unidentified (and enraged) Gunnery Sergeant, I Corps, 1968.*[4]

Commenting on the restrictive rules of engagement placed on the U.S. war effort in Vietnam.

2062 **The draft is white people sending black people to fight yellow people to protect the country they stole from the red people.**—*From the musical, HAIR, 1968.*[246]

The musical was anti-war and anti-establishment.

2063 **He who has no country should not fight for it.**—*Leonard Henderson, militant black activist, 1968.*[1001]

Henderson argued against blacks fighting in the Vietnam War because he felt blacks in the U.S. did not enjoy the same benefits of society as did whites.

2064 **It is extremely difficult for a party to a negotiation to achieve by diplomacy objectives which it has conspicuously failed to win by warfare.**—*Senator J. William Fulbright, Chairman Senate Foreign Relations Committee, speech in 1968.*[737]

2065 **The hard fact of the matter is that our bargaining position is at present a weak one; and until the equation of advantages between the two sides has been substantially altered in our favor, there can be little prospect of a negotiated settlement which would secure independence for a non–Communist South Vietnam.**—*Senator J. William Fulbright, Chairman Senate Foreign Relations Committee, speech in 1968.*[737]

Fulbright was referring to the U.S. position, post–TET.

2066 **Racial differences between blacks and whites have disappeared on the fighting fronts. At the front, the main thing is to stay alive and you do this most often by depending on the man next to you.**—*Thomas Johnson, correspondent, August 1968.*[1011]

2067 **[The internal affairs of South Vietnam must be resolved by the South Vietnamese themselves] in accordance with the program of the National Liberation Front.**—*Hanoi, 1968.*[276]

This was one of the conditions the U.S. had to meet before Hanoi would consider peace talks. This position did not allow the existing South Vietnamese government any part in the determination of its future. With the Viet Cong deciding the politics of South Vietnam, there would be unification with the North into one communist Vietnam.

2068 **We rate a ville friendly if they don't shoot at us and if they talk to us.**—*Civic Action Officer (S-5), I Corps, 1968.*[4]

2069 **He is his own Nhu.**—*Unidentified American staff official, Saigon, 1968.*[323]

After TET President Nguyen Van Thieu became more withdrawn and more resistive of instituting the kinds of changes required to gain public support and trust. Diem's brother Nhu had similar attitudes until he was deposed in the 1963 coup.

2070 **The first 100,000 Americans to leave would be for free. They are the clerks, the laundry men, the engineer battalions building officers' clubs.... So many extraneous things are soaking up people not essential.**—*John Paul Vann, Deputy, II Field Force CORDS, during an interview with a correspondent, September 1968.*[887]

Vann advocated a plan of phased withdrawal of 300,000 U.S. troops from South Vietnam over the course of three years. Under his plan, conduct of the war would gradually be turned over to the South Vietnamese, who, with the backing of the remaining U.S. troops, should be able to hold South Vietnam through an increased pacification plan and strengthening of the GVN. General Abrams was highly insulted by Vann's plan and unsuccessfully attempted to have him fired from his CORDS position.

2071 **[Vietnam is no longer] an unlimited drain on our resources ... the so-called bottomless pit has been capped.**—*Clark Clifford, Secretary of Defense, September 1968.*[374]

2072 **I didn't think Mr. McNamara understood air power nor its applications very well. ... In fact, I don't think there was at that time anybody in the Office of the Secretary of Defense who understood the application of tactical and strategic powers. At least, not the way I understood it.**—*General John P. McConnell, U.S. Air Force Chief of Staff, 1968.*[69]

2073 **Hell, I wish they would let us go North again! You can't win any medals bombing South Vietnam!**—*Unidentified Navy pilot, aboard the USS Kitty Hawk, 1968.*[185]

Regarding Johnson's blanket bombing halt of North Vietnam, above the 20th parallel.

2074 **I will not be the first president of the United States to lose a war.**—*Richard Nixon, commenting to his aide during presidential campaigning, 1968.*[374]

2075 **We must seek to de-escalate.**—*Hubert H. Humphrey, Vice President, during a televised speech, 30 September 1968.*[684]

Humphrey, the Democratic candidate for President, vowed to immediately de-escalate the war in Vietnam.

2076 **People here say that when the bombing of North Vietnam stops, then peace will come. The North and South are both Vietnamese, and to stop the bombing means no more Vietnamese get killed.**—*Unidentified Vietnamese village elder, speaking to a correspondent, An Dien, October 1968.*[455]

An Dien was near Lai Khe in III Corps. It was a GVN resettlement village. Most of the inhabitants had been relocated to An Dien from their home villages in nearby enemy active or controlled areas.

2077 **I am certain that the United States has never fought a war in which our young men have been as courageous—as competent—as they have in this one.**—*Admiral Ralph W. Cousins, U.S. Navy Commander, Task Force 77, 1968.*[961]

Task Force 77 was the component of the 7th Fleet that operated off the coast of Vietnam. It provided naval support during operations in Southeast Asia.

2078 **Don't call it a compensation. It's just something we try to do on the spot—something. How can you compensate someone for this?**—*Unidentified officer, 1st Infantry Division, during an interview, October 1968.*[455]

The officer was speaking of a $35 solatium payment made to the family of a 12-year old Vietnamese girl who was shot by a U.S. helicopter crew as she moved through a free fire zone near her village. She survived, but lost her right leg. At the time $35 was the most that could be officially paid for such an injury.

2079 **End the war and win the peace.**—*Richard Nixon often repeated campaign pledge, 1968.*[374]

2080 **You are a mother too, although you have had daughters and not sons. I am a mother and I know the feeling of having a baby come out of my gut. I have a baby and then you send him off to war. No wonder the kids rebel.**—*Eartha Kitt, singer and entertainer was talking to Mrs. Lyndon (Lady Bird) Johnson during a White House luncheon, 1968.*[653]

Eartha Kitt, one of several dozen guests at the luncheon, confronted Lady Bird about the war in Vietnam.

2081 **We were rich. We had water buffalo, cows, pigs, our old house. We got much rice.**—*Unidentified Vietnamese mother of four, during an interview, October 1968.*[455]

Speaking of her life in her home village before it was razed and the family evacuated to the government resettlement village of An Dien. There the houses were made of cardboard, corrugated sheet metal, and tin. In the forced evacuation they lost their home, land, and animals—their way of life.

2082 **We did not surmise the true nature or scope of the countrywide attack.**—*General William Westmoreland, Chairman JCS, 1968.*[713]

Based on intelligence reports, MACV was aware of a possible enemy offensive to be launched sometime in February, but many of the MACV staff, including Westmoreland, did not believe that the VC/NVA could launch the widespread attacks that constituted the 1968 TET Offensive.

2083 **We fight with bullets—not bodies.**—*Personal motto of General Ellis Williamson, Commander, 25th Infantry Division, 1968.*[42]

The concept of using firepower against the enemy to reduce friendly casualties. This concept was used extensively by American forces throughout the Vietnam War.

2084 **I became thoroughly convinced that it was immoral for a commander to throw the bodies of his men at an enemy that was still firing weapons.**—*General Ellis Williamson, Commander, 25th Infantry Division, 1968.*[42]

He was a firm believer of his motto, "We fight with bullets-not bodies."

2085 **If the Americans want to withdraw, they can go ahead. We only want people who want to stay.**—*Nguyen Cao Ky, Premier, South Vietnam, speaking to the press, 1968.*[933]

Ky was speaking in regard to press questions about what his government would do if the U.S. decided to unilaterally retreat from Vietnam.

2086 **What we now expect—what we have a right to expect, are prompt, productive, serious and intensive negotiations in an atmosphere that is conducive to progress.**—*President Lyndon Johnson, speaking during a national broadcast, 31 October 1968.*[280]

Johnson announced the complete cessation of all attacks against North Vietnam. There was no announcement of any reciprocal action by North Vietnam to reduce the flow of NVA troops or materials into South Vietnam.

2087 **The United States has been forced to end the bombing [of North Vietnam] because it was facing great defeats in Vietnam and increasing condemnation and pressure from peoples throughout the world.**—*Hanoi Radio broadcast, 1 November 1968.*[566]

2088 **Beaucoups deaths—women, children, men.**—*Reverend Nguyen Van Tri, priest of the Xom Catholic Church, speaking to reporters, 1 November 1968.*[563]

The priest was describing the results of a VC rocket attack that struck the church. Several other rocket attacks took place against South Vietnamese population centers. The attacks coincided with President Johnson's announcement of the halt to all bombing and attacks against North Vietnam.

2089 **The Administration has finally chosen to alter its discredited policies in Vietnam and to seek instead a genuine political settlement of the war.**—*Paul O'Dwyer, Democratic Candidate for the Senate, during a press conference, 1 November 1968.*[564]

Dwyer was a Democratic peace activists who continually attacked the Johnson administration's policies on Vietnam.

2090 **We can't trust the Americans no longer — they are just a band of crooks.**—*Nguyen Cao Ky, Vice President of South Vietnam, speaking to Vietnamese legislators, 2 November 1968.*[73]

Ky's reaction was to Johnson's decision, on 31 October 1968, to halt all American bombing of North Vietnam.

2091 **So long as a single aggressor remains in our country, we must continue the fight and wipe him out.**—*Ho Chi Minh, public appeal posted in the Vietnam Courier, 3 November 1968.*[970]

The *Vietnam Courier* was a weekly paper published in Hanoi, in English, reflecting North Vietnam's Communist Party's rhetoric.

2092 **[People of Vietnam resolve] to liberate the South, defend the North and proceed toward the peaceful reunification of the fatherland.**—*Ho Chi Minh, President, Democratic Republic of Vietnam, in a nationwide appeal, 2 November 1968.*[566]

2093 **You sweep into a village and sweep out, and all you remember are these blank uncomprehending faces.**—*Larry Burrows, Life magazine correspondent, 1968.*[456]

Burrows was in his sixth year of covering the war in South Vietnam. He was speaking of the villagers that remained behind when the GVN/American forces left a village.

2094 **It will definitely hurt us. I don't think Hanoi will stop the war because of the bomb halt. The NVA will be able to move in more supplies and set up more artillery and rocket sites in North and South Vietnam.**—*SP/4 Rudolph Meeks, U.S. Army, during a street interview, Saigon, 3 November 1968.*[685]

Meeks was referring to the total bombing halt against North Vietnam, called by President Johnson on 30 October 1968. Most American troops in Vietnam believed North Vietnam would step up their build-up in South Vietnam and in the sanctuaries along the border.

2095 **The Government of South Vietnam deeply regrets not to be able to participate in the present exploratory talks.**—*Nguyen Van Thieu, President, South Vietnam, Speaking to the National Assembly, 2 November 1968.*[565]

The Thieu regime refused to attend the initial peace talks because Hanoi stipulated that the NLF must take part in the negotiations.

2096 **There's no point in stopping the bombing unless you're going to pull the troops out. This way, it's not getting us anywhere. The NVA aren't going to stop just because we quit bombing.**—*Unidentified American soldier, during a street interview, Saigon, 3 November 1968.*[685]

The soldier was referring to the total bombing halt against North Vietnam, called by President Johnson on 30 October 1968. Most American troops in Vietnam believed North Vietnam would step up their build up in South Vietnam and in the sanctuaries along the border.

2097 **The Republic of Vietnam has reminded its allies of the harmful acts by which North Vietnam can profit through the cessation of the bombing, so precautionary measures have been taken and have been applied by the Republic of Vietnam and its allies.**—*Nguyen Van Thieu, President, South Vietnam, in a press statement, 3 November 1968.*[685]

Thieu and the Saigon government did not agree with the full bombing halt announced by President Johnson on 30 October 1968. Thieu contended that the Saigon government did not participate in the decision making process which led to the bomb halt.

2098 **...their hearts in Moscow but their stomachs in Peking.**—*Averell Harriman, Leading U.S. negotiator at the Paris peace talks, 1968.*[451]

Commenting on the fact that Ho Chi Minh and his immediate leaders never committed to the two major Communist factions in the world, the Soviets and the Chinese.

2099 **Last night I killed and everyone has been patting me on the back.... It isn't all that horrifying.**—*Lt. Jim M. Simmen, U.S. Army, 5th Battalion, 60th Infantry (Mechanized), in a letter home, 1968.*[187]

2100 **[The fighting in Vietnam produced] a defensive, stereotype, tactical philosophy, [called] firebase psychosis.**—*General William Westmoreland, Chairman Joint Chiefs of Staff, 1968.*[713]

Firebase psychosis was the tactical philosophy in which a unit operating in the field was reluctant to move beyond the range of supporting guns of a firebase. The heavy reliance on firepower to kill the enemy — once he was found — reinforced this tendency. As the war progressed it became increasing difficult to motivate units to operate beyond the range of supporting artillery.

2101 **We have not attained peace ... only the possibility of peace. All of our efforts are bent to that pursuit ... [however] other bitter days and battles lie ahead.**—*President Lyndon Johnson, during awards ceremony, 19 November 1968.*[686]

2102 **When one starts to enjoy the sickness of war, he is sick...**—*Lt. Jim M. Simmen, U.S. Army, 5th Battalion, 60th Infantry (Mechanized), in a letter home, 1968.*[187]

2103 **[National Guardsmen are] Sergeant Bilkos — trying to look brave while making sure that someone else does the fighting.**—*An unidentified Pentagon official's comment to the press, 1968.*[493]

Official's description of National Guardsmen and military reservists. Of the 27-million men of draft age during the Vietnam War, one million of them served in the Guard or Reserves. During the height of the Vietnam War there were more than 100,000 names on the waiting list to join the Army National Guard.

2104 **Used as it was in Vietnam, the naval power of the United States did not succeed either in improving the military and political situation there or in reducing the cost of the war.**—*Admiral John D. Hayes, U.S. Navy, in a Naval Review article, 1968.*[960]

2105 **We will never set up a coalition government with the NLF and we will never recognize it as a political entity equal to us, with which we must negotiate on an equal footing.**—*Nguyen Van Thieu, President of South Vietnam, 1968.*[629]

Thieu refused to participate in the peace negotiations in Paris. His attitude of defiance lasted several months. By the end of 1968, Nguyen Cao Ky was leading a delegation to the peace talks.

2106 **Camp Holloway in Pleiku attacked: 42 helicopters destroyed or damage, 350 GI's killed or wounded.**—*Vietnam Courier, 16 December 1968.*[965]

The *Vietnam Courier* was the English version of the "news" distributed by Hanoi. U.S. casualties and damage reported by the free world media was 8 Americans killed, 48 wounded, and 7 Army aircraft destroyed.

2107 **The South Vietnamese armed forces [Vietcong] and the people have been gaining increasing victories. They have successively smashed two U.S. dry-season counter-offensives, successfully preserved the liberated zones, wiping out 800,000 adverse troops including nearly 300,000 GI's and mercenaries of satellite countries...**—*Vietnam Courier, 16 December 1968.*[968]

The *Vietnam Courier* was the English language version of "news" distributed by Hanoi. Within the same article the *Vietnam Courier* makes the claim that the U.S. had built up an army of one million men, half of which were American troops. At the time, there were 536,000 American troops in Vietnam.

2108 **The NLF is the genuine representative of the South Vietnamese people ... not only does it enjoy the affection and the confidence of the South Vietnamese people, but it has been recognised [sic] and supported by many governments and by all progressives in the world.**—*Vietnam Courier, 16 December 1968.*[967]

The *Vietnam Courier* was the English version of the "news" distributed by Hanoi. The population of South Vietnam was about 15 million. The NLF claimed control of 4/5s of the country and 14 million of the people.

2109 **The de-Americanization of the war must proceed with all deliberate speed.**—*President-elect Richard Nixon, in a letter to John Paul Vann, 1968.*[887]

Nixon agreed with Vann that the South Vietnamese should gradually take full responsibility for the conduct of the war against the communists in Vietnam.

2110 **Washington had to admit its failure: Johnson ... withdrew from the race to the White House; Khe Sanh was evacuated in haste; Westmoreland was replaced by Abrams. ...; Komer, the specialist in "pacification" was sacked ... the decision by Johnson ... to halt unconditionally all bombings on the whole North Vietnamese territory and to agree to a quadripartite conference in Paris...**—*Vietnam Courier, 16 December 1968.*[966]

The *Vietnam Courier* was the English version of the "news" distributed by Hanoi.

2111 **[Ap Bac] ... striking demonstration of the ineffectiveness of the "modern" U.S. "heliborne" and "amphibious cars" tactics, in front of the PLAF [Viet Cong].**—*Vietnam Courier, 16 December 1968.*[965]

The *Vietnam Courier* was the English version of the "news" distributed by Hanoi. The battle of Ap Bac was a major humiliation for ARVN forces. The ARVN had 2000 troops on the ground, surrounding 400 VC. The VC inflicted heavy casualties on the ARVN and then withdrew unmolested.

2112 **Total of U.S. planes shot down over the DRV [NVN] since August 5, 1964 [has been brought] to 3,255.**—*Vietnam Courier, news item, 16 December 1968.*[970]

The *Vietnam Courier* was the English version of the "news" distributed by Hanoi. The *Courier* claims 3000+ aircraft downed in four years. While the U.S. government has released a figure of 3,720 fixed wing aircraft lost to enemy fire for the entire period of the war, 1964–1975.

1969

In war there is no substitute for victory.
— General Douglas MacArthur

2113 **Vietnam is four walls around the President. Every day those walls move in a little bit closer and press him tighter.**—*An unidentified member of Johnson's staff, January 1969.*[464]

A member of Johnson's staff was remarking to the staff of the incoming Nixon administration.

2114 **However we got into Vietnam, whatever the judgement of our actions, ending the war honorably is essential for the peace of the world. Any other solution may unloose forces that would complicate the prospects of international order.**—*Henry Kissinger, President Nixon's National Security Adviser, during an interview, 1969.*[282]

2115 **I want a precise report on what the enemy has in Cambodia and what, if anything, we are doing to destroy the buildup there. I think a very definite change of policy toward Cambodia probably should be one of the first orders of business when we get in.**—*Richard Nixon, President-elect, in a note to Henry Kissinger, 8 January 1969.*[885]

Early plans to address the issue of enemy sanctuaries along the Cambodian border.

2116 **We will not make the same old mistakes, we will make our own.**—*Henry Kissinger, National Security Adviser, 1969.*[325]

When asked by the press how the new Nixon administration would handle the situation in Vietnam.

2117 **[The war in Vietnam] hasn't been a success because it couldn't be! We went soberly about making a rabbit stew without the guest of honor. The beast in the bag is not a rabbit. And its been a pretty odd dish ever since. We hire a new chef from time to time, and we buy a new potion and mix it in and tell the folks who are paying the bill that "it's almost ready!" But, it still is not what we think it should be—because the ingredients are not what we have labeled them.**—*Lt.Col. Carl F. Bernard, former Province Senior Advisor, 1969.*[95]

2118 **I've got a hundred-odd generals, and only two of them understand this war!**—*General Creighton Abrams, ComUSMACV, commenting to Lt.Col. Donald Marshall, 1969.*[325]

Abrams did not specify the names of the "two" generals.

2119 **We can continue our present management methods and lose the war, or make a massive reevaluation and take action with some brighter hopes!**—*Lt.Col. Carl F. Bernard, former Province Senior Advisor, 1969.*[95]

Bernard was not unique in his observations. Other officers and civilians in Vietnam held similar views, and expressed them at various levels of the command structure.

2120 **To all those who would be tempted by weakness, let us leave no doubt that we will be as strong as we need be for as long as we need be.**—*President Richard Nixon, inaugural speech, January 1969.*[185]

Peace negotiations started in 1968 but North Vietnam did not seriously apply themselves to the talks. There is speculation that they were waiting to see who would win the U.S. Presidential race and perhaps get a better deal than was offered by the Johnson administration. Nixon put Hanoi on notice that he wanted fruitful peace negotiations but not at the expense of security in Southeast Asia.

2121 **They'll believe any threat of force Nixon makes because it's Nixon.**—*President Richard Nixon, comments to one of his advisers, 1969.*[281]

Nixon believed his past reputation as a hard-line anti-communist would give sufficient weight to his threats to Hanoi.

2122 **Past favorable publicity about integration of U.S. troops in Vietnam has shimmered and disappeared like paddy water under a tropic sun.**—*Zalin B. Grant, former U.S. Army intelligence officer, turned correspondent, writing in the New Republic, January 1969.*[1017]

Reflecting the increasing racial tensions in the military.

2123 **[The idea of a coalition government would] destroy the existing political structure and thus lead to a Communist takeover.**—*Henry Kissinger, President Nixon's National Security Adviser, during an interview, 1969.*[336]

In 1969 Nixon and Kissinger established a goal of ending the war in Vietnam by means of a political settlement. The settlement was not to include recognition of the NLF as part of a coalition government in South Vietnam.

2124 **It would be instructive, but depressing, to contrast the total cost of resources devoted to programs to eliminate the VCI [Viet Cong Infrastructure] and improve the RF/PF [Regional Forces/Popular Forces] with the cost to support one U.S. Division. We may recognize the importance — but we still deny the priority.**—*Lt.Col. Carl F. Bernard, former Province Senior Advisor, 1969.*[95]

Bernard was pointing out the importance of the pacification program and its supporting structures in the war against communist insurgency.

2125 **The commitment of five hundred thousand Americans has settled the issue of the importance of Vietnam. For what is involved now is confidence in American promises.**—*Henry Kissinger, President Nixon's National Security Adviser, 1969.*[338]

2126 **[The war in Vietnam has become] a bone in the nation's throat.**—*Unidentified speech writer to President Richard Nixon, 1969.*[347]

2127 **I've heard some good things about you, mainly that you don't get along with the 25th Division. Any province senior advisor who gets along with that division isn't doing his job.**—*John Paul Vann, AID adviser, in conversation with Province Senior Adviser Lt.Col. James Bremer, March 1969.*[42]

Bremer became Hau Nghia PSA in March 1969. Through the course of the war there was a major feud between the 25th Infantry Division and the American advisory elements assigned to the provinces in which the 25th operated. The 25th Infantry relied heavily on firepower to clear enemy positions, which led to much collateral civilian damage. Many of the areas the division operated within were heavily populated, and the 25th Division's tactics generating a large number of refugees and anti-American sentiment.

2128 **[We (the United States) should not be] committed to the endless support of a group of men in Saigon [who] could not remain in power for more than a few months without our large-scale presence.**—*Townsend Hoopes, Former Air Force Under Secretary, in his writings, 1969.*[471]

Hoopes did not think the Thieu-Ky regime could last without American support, and he did not think we should provide that support indefinitely.

2129 **I was outraged by what I saw in Vietnam — the corruption, the filth, the thievery, the profiteering on other people's misery. But when I reported what was happening, I was told to shut up, to quit being a trouble maker...**—*Cornelius Hawkridge, former consultant, currency manipulator, and whistle-blower, in testimony to the U.S. Senate subcommittee, March 1969.*[466]

Senate Subcommittee on Investigations regarding the widespread graft and corruption in Vietnam.

2130 **The United States will not tolerate continued attacks on South Vietnam cities ... appropriate response will be made to these attacks if they continue.**—*President Richard Nixon, during a White House news conference, 4 March 1969.*[567]

Nixon was responding to a wave of VC/NVA attacks against South Vietnamese cities, spanning a period of several weeks.

2131 **I do agree with why we are here. I just happen to totally disagree with how we are going about it.**—*Major Mark Berent, U.S. Air Force pilot, in a letter to a friend, 4 March 1969.*[886]

2132 **The only way [to get the Communists to negotiate is] to do something on the military front ... something they will understand.**—*President Richard Nixon, during a meeting at the White House, 16 March 1969.*[374]

A result of the meeting was the authorization for the secret bombing of enemy sanctuaries along the Cambodian border. The bombing was called Operation Menu.

2133 **We are not angry at the Americans and the army. It is only natural that when the enemy comes here the Americans must come and fight them.**—*Father Thao, Pastor of the Catholic church at Dong Lach, March 1969.*[457]

A battalion of NVA entered the village of Dong Lach during the 1969 TET Offensive. ARVN and U.S. units attempted to push the NVA out. When they were unable to move them out of the ville the ARVN commander called in an air strike. Much of the ville was destroyed as was most of the NVA battalion. Civilian casualties were minimal as the villagers had moved out when the NVA moved in. Dong Lach was 20 miles NE of Saigon, in sight of the Bien Hoa air base runways. The 2,000 people who had lived in the ville became refugees after the battle.

2134 **In Vietnam, we failed to convince our foes that for us the stake — the control of South Vietnam — was worth sacrificing such other American interest as moderate relations with Russia, peace with China, the preservation of NATO, harmony at home. We failed because we did not convince ourselves that this was so.**—*Stanley Hoffman, Harvard professor, in a Life magazine article, 21 March 1969.*[458]

Hoffman's reasoning for the U.S. failure in Vietnam at the time.

2135 **The public no longer wants its army to police the world, or to catch every sparrow of a nation that might fall on enemy ground.**—*Life magazine editorial, 21 March 1969.*[459]

2136 **The future of Western civilization is at stake in the way you handle yourselves in Vietnam.**—*Sir Robert Thompson, British authority on counterinsurgency, in council to President Nixon, 1969.*[374]

Thompson urged Nixon to maintain a firm stand against the communist in Vietnam.

2137 **The initial U.S. withdrawal would be unilateral, but should be accompanied by a statement that if there were reciprocal de-escalation by Hanoi, the U.S. would be willing to withdraw more troops by early 1970.**—*Life magazine editorial, 28 March 1969.*[460]

Shortly after Nixon became president he announced the planned withdrawal of 50,000 U.S. troops in mid-1969. He voiced a hope that Hanoi would respond by showing a withdrawal of their own, or at least a reduction in the infiltration and some progress at the peace table. There was neither from Hanoi.

2138 **If it should turn out that the enemy does not want peace, a carefully phased, moderate troop withdrawal would give the U.S. plenty of leeway for second thoughts in case of Communist bad faith — and is a far wiser way of smoking out Hanoi's intentions than a new round of potentially self-fulfilling threats of escalation.**—*Life magazine editorial, 28 March 1969.*[460]

The editorial counted on some reaction from Hanoi. Hanoi increased its infiltration of the South and stalled at the peace table, while U.S. troop numbers continued to decrease over subsequent years.

2139 **The precipitate withdrawal of all American forces from Vietnam would be a disaster, not only for the South Vietnamese but for the United States and the cause of peace.**—*President Richard Nixon, from a speech, 1969.*[629]

Nixon directed a slow withdrawal of American forces from Vietnam combined with an effort to prepare the ARVN for defending themselves.

2140 **Despite what many people thought 15 years ago, the Koreans have turned out to be tremendous soldiers. The Vietnamese can do it too. They have all the potential.**—*General Creighton Abrams, Commander, US forces in Vietnam, in an interview, April 1969.*[461]

Abrams voiced the opinion that given enough time the Vietnamese could hold their own against North Vietnam.

2141 **We had nothing to do with it. The [National Liberation] Front put it on.**—*General Vo Nguyen Giap, Minister of Defense, during an interview, published 6 April 1969.*[647]

Giap's response was to a journalist's question about Hanoi's involvement in the 1968 TET Offensive in South Vietnam. Supplemental evidence indicates Hanoi ordered preparations for the offensive in July 1967 and Giap was the planner of the offensive. The brunt of the attack was borne by the VC with support from a number of NVA units. The majority of the casualties were suffered by the VC.

2142 **The Americans still have a considerable role to play. We have to go on dealing with the North Vietnamese and the Vietcong main forces. It's an essential part of the war, but not the most important part. We must also have an interest in the people. That has to be our front burner.**—*General Creighton Abrams, ComUSMACV, during an interview, April 1969.*[461]

Abrams was tasked with Vietnamizing the war to facilitate American troop withdrawals.

2143 **The Vietnamese are as patriotic and as brave as anybody in the world.**—*General Creighton Abrams, ComUSMACV, during an interview, April 1969.*[461]

Abrams seemed to have closer ties with the Vietnamese people than his predecessor, William Westmoreland.

2144 **[The Red River Valley is] the center of hell with Hanoi as its hub.**—*Colonel Jack Broughton, former Deputy Commander, 355th Tactical Fighter Wing, 1969.*[142]

Broughton was speaking of the impressive anti-aircraft defenses in the Red River Valley and especially surrounding Hanoi. By 1967 there were more than two-hundred SAM missile sites, seven thousand AA-guns and approximately eighty MiGs based around Hanoi.

2145 **A man wants to relax, really relax, when he's off duty. He doesn't want to listen with half an ear to hear if some drunken whites are going to call him a nigger.** —*Sgt. Jack Smedley, U.S. Air Force, during an interview, April 1969.*[1009]

This was one of the reasons given by some blacks for their self-segregation during off-duty hours or when returning to base for standdown after operations in the field.

2146 **If we're not sophisticated and sensible we could suffocate these people with [our] good works.**—*General Creighton Abrams, ComUSMACV, in an interview, April 1969.*[461]

Abrams, commenting on the effort to pacify the rural Vietnamese and attempts to bring their living standard closer to that of America's.

2147 **The Vietnamese have a wonderful history as a people, proud, gallant and heroic. What comes out of here must be Vietnamese in character, founded on Vietnamese pride — in fact it must be Vietnamese.**—*General Creighton Abrams, ComUSMACV, in an interview, April 1969.*[461]

Abrams was stating the obvious and the original idea posed by President Johnson — that the Vietnamese need to fight and win their own war.

2148 **Whenever blacks seem to unite, whites panic.**—*Emmett Doe, former U.S. Army sergeant, 1969.*[1012]

Because of racial tensions, some commanders attempted to break up groups of blacks who met to socialize or talk. Some whites felt threatened by a group of black soldiers grouping together. These demonstrations of black solidarity and camaraderie were something some unit commanders were not comfortable with.

2149 **One day the Vietnamese will go it alone.**—*General Creighton Abrams, ComUSMACV, in an interview, April 1969.*[461]

2150 **Practically everything in North Vietnam has been rebuilt. All the highways, the bridges, the trans-shipment points that were destroyed, and what little industry they have, which is not much.**—*General John P. McConnell, U.S. Air Force Chief of Staff, during Senate testimony, 16 April 1969.*[687]

McConnell was testifying before the Senate Armed Services Committee on the rapid recovery of North Vietnam following the bombing halt. President Johnson ordered a full halt to the bombing of North Vietnam the end of October.

2151 **The police charge was beautiful. They accomplished their mission — to clear the building — in 20 minutes. But the way they did it reminded me of those Search and Destroy missions in Vietnam, where a "successful" one often throws more people into the Vietcong camp.**—*Colin Leinster, reporter and editor, 1969.*[462]

Leinster was covering the student demonstrations and their takeover of the Harvard University administration building. The police were called in to clear the building. Leinster got in the way of the clearing operation and was beaten by police. The building was cleared and more than 150 arrest made.

2152 **The friendship formed between whites and Negroes in Vietnam will never die because of what we went through together.**—*Sgt. Melvin Murrel Smith, U.S. Marine Corps, during an interview, 1969.*[1010]

2153 **When we assumed the burden of helping defend South Vietnam, millions of South Vietnamese men, women, and children placed their trust in us. To abandon them now would risk a massacre.... Abandoning the South Vietnamese people ... would threaten our long-term hopes for peace in the world. A great nation cannot renege on its pledges. A great nation must be worthy of trust.... If we simply abandoned our effort in Vietnam, the cause of peace might not survive the damage that would be done to other nations' confidence in our reliability.**—*President Richard Nixon, 1969.*[713]

Part of the Nixon's reasoning for his decision not to immediately withdraw America from Vietnam. Peace and anti-war advocates clamored for U.S. withdrawal from Vietnam to be one of Nixon's first actions when he took office as President.

2154 **More VCI are killed by Honda accidents than by the Phoenix Program.**—*American Province Senior Adviser, Hau Nghia Province, 1969.*[42]

The Phoenix Program was considered by many U.S. advisers as a failure. Many VCI were "neutralized" as a result of Phoenix, but there were many other Vietnamese neutralized under the program that were the victims of jealousy, revenge, and poor investigative techniques.

2155 **If Hanoi were to succeed in taking over South Vietnam by force — even after the power of the United States had been engaged — it would greatly strengthen those leaders who scorn negotiation, who advocate aggression, who minimize the risks of confrontation with the United States. It would bring peace now but it would enormously increase the danger of a bigger war later.**—*President Richard Nixon, 1969.*[713]

Part of Nixon's reasoning for his decision not to immediately withdraw America from Vietnam. Peace and anti-war advocates clamored for U.S. withdrawal from Vietnam to be one of Nixon's first actions when he took office as President.

2156 **You may not be able to read this. I am writing it in a hurry. I see death coming up the hill.**—*Unidentified Army infantryman, in a note home, written before his death on Hamburger Hill, May 1969.*[465]

The battle for Hamburger Hill (Ap Bia Mountain-Hill 937) took place in May 1969, when elements of the 187th Infantry (Airborne) battled two battalions of NVA entrenched on the hill. Other than destruction of the entrenched enemy, Hill 937 had no other significance. After eleven bloody assaults the Americans took the hill. A week later American units abandoned the hill. More than 400 American troops were wounded or killed in the assaults, nearly 600 NVA troops were reported killed. At one point some U.S. units had stopped near the top of the hill only to be attacked from the rear by NVA hidden in a series of tunnels and trenches honeycombing the hill.

2157 **Being held in an unfavorable strategic position, the enemy can only use a small part of his troops. Though numerous, he is outnumbered; though strong, he is weak.**—*General Vo Nguyen Giap, Defense Minister of North Vietnam, from an article published in Hanoi, 1969.*[947]

This was the tactic he later used in the 1972 Easter Offensive, in which South Vietnam's nearly one million men under arms were tied down across the country while NVA invasion forces struck in a three pronged attack.

2158 **When discipline goes, men die needlessly.**—*General Lewis Walt, Assistant Commandant of the Marine Corps, during an interview, May 1969.*[463]

General Walt was referring to the problems the lack of military discipline posed by dissenters within the military.

2159 **The Army is obsessed with us, but they deny our existence.**—*Andrew Stapp, head of American Servicemen's Union, during an interview, May 1969.*[463]

ASU was formed by military servicemen seeking reform in some of the military regulations and as a vehicle to protest their views about the military and its direction. Because of fears of harassment by the military leadership most of the ASU's military members did not openly acknowledge their membership.

2160 **We rolled in on three women on a gunship — three women running down a dike ... the orders were we didn't have time to move them, so knock them down. I wasn't serving [my country]; they just needed someone to pull the trigger.**—*Tom Doyle, U.S. Army, during an interview with a correspondent, May 1969.*[463]

Doyle was a helicopter door gunner during his tour of duty in Vietnam.

2161 **The main goal of fighting must be the destruction of enemy manpower.**—*General Vo Nguyen Giap, defense minister of North Vietnam, from an article published in Hanoi, 1969.*[947]

2162 **I volunteered for Vietnam ... they would tell us to destroy a village because there were VC suspects, and the next day tell us to rebuild it because there weren't any.**—*Robert Bower, U.S. Army, during an interview with a correspondent at Fort Hood, Texas, May 1969.*[463]

2163 **So many of our people were dead at the end of each week, you begin to feel you've been in Vietnam all your life.**—*Ken Willis, U.S. Army, during an interview at Fort Dix, May 1969.*[463]

2164 **Dissent [within the military] and the system are totally incompatible: given one, the other cannot work.**—*Re-phrase of General Lewis Walt by correspondent Frank McCulloch, May 1969.*[463]

Walt was expressing the point that the military leaders must select the appropriate action and lead their men to carry out that action. Such actions should not be subject to majority rule, discussion, or resistance from the soldiers being led.

2165 **When you're in Vietnam, it doesn't matter what you believe. You can be dead set against it [the war], but when you're 20 clicks out of Dak To there isn't much you can do. You shoot — and as straight as you can because they're trying to kill you. I'd run before I'd go back. They'd give me a leave and I'd have a 14-day head start.**—*Robert Mall, U.S. Army, during an interview at Fort Bragg, May 1969.*[463]

2166 **I'm not going to end up like LBJ, holed up in the White House afraid to show my face on the street. I'm going to stop that war. Fast.**—*President Richard Nixon, 1969.*[336]

2167 **In combat, a unit's discipline and casualties are almost in inverse ratio — the higher the discipline, the lower the casualties. And dissent of any kind erodes discipline.**—*Re-phrase of General Lewis Walt by correspondent Frank McCulloch, May 1969.*[463]

2168 **It sounds like a great idea [South Vietnamese troops fighting on their own], but do you think your boys can fight? I have heard reports they're not that good.**—*Spiro T. Agnew, Vice President, speaking to Nguyen Cao Ky, 1969.*[629]

Ky reportedly pressed for a more active part in the war effort. Past experiences of the ARVN's fighting abilities indicated that, on average, they were not up to the challenge.

2169 **[Dissenters] are violating the oaths they have taken and, more seriously, they are endangering the security and welfare of their nation. They are involved in a dangerous, self-destructive process. Few if any great nations have fallen to enemies from without. They fall because of dissension within.**—*General Lewis Walt, Assistant Commandant of the Marine Corps, during an interview, May 1969.*[463]

General Walt on dissenters within the military.

2170 **What the dissenter is doing is placing not only his own life but the lives of everyone around him in unnecessary jeopardy.**—*General Lewis Walt, Assistant Commandant of the Marine Corps, during an interview, May 1969.*[463]

Walt's comments on the destructiveness of dissent in the military.

2171 **It is my conviction that the disruptive impact of the military draft on individual lives should be minimized as much as possible, consistent with the national security.**—*President Richard Nixon, in a message to Congress, 13 May 1969.*[567]

Nixon proposed a draft lottery and the eventual discontinuation of the draft.

2172 **Phung Hoang is still an American-inspired, American-style program that is accepted without enthusiasm by the Vietnamese. Phung Hoang has little momentum and, if left to the Vietnamese, would soon grind to a halt.**—*Excerpt from CORDS III Corps overview, May 1969.*[9]

Phung Hoang was the Vietnamese name for the Phoenix Program, established in 1967 as an extension of the CORDS-CIA program, ICEX. ICEX operated against the NLF and the VCI. With the inclusion of South Vietnamese security agencies ICEX was renamed Phoenix, and billed as a South Vietnamese program with U.S. support and assistance.

2173 **[Ho Chi Minh was] one of the greatest Marxist-Leninists of all times...**—*Excerpt from the Black Panther newspaper, May 1969.*[982]

The Black Panther Party identified with the Vietnamese struggle against America, much as the Black Panthers struggled against white America. The North Vietnamese praised the Black Panther movement and publicly announced solidarity with them.

2174 **We would destroy ourselves if we pulled out [of Vietnam] in a way that wasn't really honorable.**—*President Richard Nixon, comments to a journalist, May 1969.*[281]

Nixon was responding to a question about an immediate pull out of American troops from Vietnam

2175 **American troop withdrawals must be balanced against a declining enemy capability and a rising South Vietnamese capability; they must not be so fast that they allow the North Vietnamese army to stage an all-out offensive before the South Vietnamese are ready to cope with it; they must not be so slow that they encourage the South Vietnamese to think that American combat forces will be around forever.**—*Sir Robert Thompson, British counterinsurgency specialist.*[713]

His recommendations for Vietnamization.

2176 **[Vietnam] Is a war for peace.... The true objective of this war is peace.**—*President Richard Nixon, comments to a journalist, May 1969.*[261]

2177 **We never forget that the blood and human life are precious to anyone, to any people, at any time.**—*Nguyen Van Thieu, President, South Vietnam, from a speech on Midway Island, 8 June 1969.*[568]

2178 **Here it's been five months and everyone knows the draft is unfair to young people. My God, why don't we do something about it.**—*President Richard Nixon, speaking to the press, 1969.*[468]

Nixon commenting on Congress' slow movement to change the draft laws.

2179 **[It is the] constant duty of the Vietnamese people to take over more responsibility [of the war] and to alleviate the burden of the United States people to support us and defend freedom in Vietnam.**—*Nguyen Van Thieu, President, South Vietnam, from a speech on Midway Island, 8 June 1969.*[568]

Thieu met with Nixon on Midway for a conference and a show of solidarity.

2180 **The first thing to understand about Giap's TET Offensive is that it was an Allied intelligence failure ranking with Pearl Harbor in 1941 or the Ardennes Offensive in 1944. The North Vietnamese gained complete surprise.**—*An excerpt from a military history book used at West Point Military Academy, 1969.*[713]

Prior to the TET Offensive of February 1968 the Allies had captured several documents referring to a planned offensive. They also had interviews from Chieu Hois and interrogations from captured prisoners which indicated a large scale offensive was scheduled. Yet, neither MACV nor Washington believed the VC/NVA capable of such an offensive.

2181 **The frightening thing about it all is that it is so very easy to kill in war. There's no remorse, no theatrical "washing of the hands" to get rid of nonexistent blood, not even any regrets. When it happens, you are more afraid [than] you've ever been in your life.... You kill because that little SOB**

is doing his best to kill you and you desperately want to live, to go home, to get drunk or walk down the street on a date again.—*SP/4 George Olsen, U.S. Army, G Company, 75th Infantry (Rangers), 1969.*[187]

2182 **Our Vietnamese Socialist friends are ... overtly Vietnamizing our territory. ... Cambodia will fight to maintain territorial integrity.**—*Prince Norodom Sihanouk, Cambodian head of state, in a public announcement, 11 June 1969.*[886]

Sihanouk softened his stand against U.S. hot pursuit of the VC/NVA into Cambodian territory. For many years, he denied the VC/NVA had established bases along the Cambodian border and publicly denied permission for American hot pursuit of the VC/NVA into Cambodian territory.

2183 **They reacted to me like a flu victim — someone who has undergone an unfortunate experience and then recovered.**—*Robert Hammer, Vietnam War veteran, during an interview, June 1969.*[932]

Hammer was relating his treatment from civilian Americans on his return from duty in Vietnam. Some returning veterans were met with open hostility, most were simply ignored by the American public.

2184 **I won't say the ARVNs won't do nothing, but you got to kick 'em in the ass to fight. When you go on a sweep with them, they spend their time picking fruit and stealing chickens.**—*PFC Willis V. Tapscott, U.S. Army, commenting to a reporter, June 1969.*[932]

Tapscott was commenting on Nixon's announcement of the first incremental withdrawal of 25,000 American troops from Vietnam.

2185 **All the political speeches and stuff don't mean anything when you're over here ... they were talking about Viet Nam when I was 15.**—*PFC Jimmy Poston, U.S. Army, comments to a reporter, June 1969.*[932]

Poston was expressing his thoughts about Nixon's announcement of the first incremental withdrawal of 25,000 American troops from Vietnam.

2186 **This is a replacement, not a withdrawal. The first order of business is the reduction of violence.... How can we expect the enemy to end their fighting if we don't. We should be taking a more defensive position and at the same time demand that the other side respond. I believe they will.**—*Averell Harriman, Chief American negotiator at the Paris peace talks, June 1969.*[932]

2187 **[B]y their effective teamwork, aggressive fighting spirit and individual acts of heroism and daring, the men of the First Marines ... soundly defeated a numerically superior enemy force and achieved an illustrious record of courage and skill which was in keeping with the highest traditions of the Marine Corps and the United States Naval Service.**—*Excerpted from a Presidential Unit Citation, to the 1st Marine Regiment, U.S. Marine Corps, for the Battle of Hue, awarded 13 June 1969.*[653]

U.S. Marine Corps battalions involved in the ground fighting to free Hue were 1/1st Marines, 1/5th and 2/5th Marine Regiments. The Marines suffered 142 killed and 857 wounded. U.S. Army units also participated in the battle, sealing the city against NVA's reinforcement's attempts to enter Hue. The Army lost 74 killed and 507 wounded during the battle for Hue.

2188 **It's like a man learning to ride a bicycle. We think we can do it, but you never know until the man running alongside takes his hand away.**—*Unidentified South Vietnamese official in a conversation with the American Secretary of State, William P. Rogers, 1969.*[932]

The official was commenting on the pregnant question as to whether or not the South Vietnamese military would be able to take up the slack left by the departure of American units from Vietnam.

2189 **[I doubt that] South Vietnamese forces will be able to rapidly assume this burden of fighting and be effective.**—*Senator John Stennis of Mississippi, commenting on Vietnamization, June 1969.*[932]

Stennis's comments followed the Nixon announcement of the withdrawal of 25,000 American troops from Vietnam.

2190 **Man, it doesn't mean nothing...**—*Unidentified U.S. Army soldier of the 25th Infantry Division, comments to reporter, June 1969.*[932]

The trooper was commenting on Nixon's announced withdrawal of 25,000 American troops from Vietnam. The first increment of the withdrawal was from the Army's 9th Infantry Division and the Marine Corps 3d Marine Division. When the first planned withdrawal was complete, 512,000 Americans would still be in Vietnam. This phrase, also known as "don't mean nothing," another way of expressing a "don't-give-a-shit-attitude."

2191 **I think our biggest mistake was stopping the bombing up North. As soon as we pull out, there's going to be beaucoup trouble.**—*SP/4 Francis E. Rodriquez, U.S. Army infantryman of the 2d Brigade, 9th Infantry Division, in comments to a reporter, June 1969.*[932]

Rodriquez was commenting on the first withdrawal of American troops from Vietnam, announced by President Nixon in early June. Many other GI's believed the war against NVA and the VC should be won and completed before the withdrawal of U.S. troops began.

2192 **[The Provisional Revolutionary Government is] a fabrication concocted by a group of people who take cover in jungles without daring to disclose their location ... it is a propaganda trick that has changed nothing.**—*Nguyen Van Thieu, President, South Viet Nam, comments to the press, June 1969.*[932]

Thieu was commenting on a communist announcement that the NLF had established an absentee government, the PRG (Provisional Revolutionary Government). The PRG declared itself to be the legitimate government of the South Vietnamese people. The formation of the PRG was done in a secret location and no "capitol" of the new government was identified. Thieu and the U.S. refused to acknowledge the PRG's claim as the sole government of South Vietnam, but other communist and socialist countries immediately recognized the PRG.

2193 **We have done enough.**—*Senator John Sherman Cooper of Kentucky, comments on U.S. troop withdrawal, June 1969.*[932]

Cooper was commenting on the announced withdrawal of 25,000 American troops to be completed by 1 September 1969. He favored the swift withdrawal of American forces from Vietnam.

2194 **During the first 6 months of 1969, the [VC/NVA] South Vietnamese Army and people wiped out or captured 330,000 of the enemy including 145,000 U.S. and satellite troops.**—*Lao Dong Party report on progress in South Vietnam, June 1969.*[868]

These statistics were maintained in the DRV Communist's Party records. U.S. Department of Defense differed significantly for the same period: 3,074 Americans KIA, 25,785 WIA, Free World Forces (excluding American and South Vietnam), 396 KIA, 1,025 WIA.

2195 **Since U.S. troop strength in South Viet Nam amounts to over half a million, the withdrawal of 25,000 means nothing.**—*Le Duc Tho, special adviser to North Vietnam's chief negotiator at the Paris peace talks, June 1969.*[932]

Tho's response to President Nixon's announcement of the withdrawal of 25,000 American troops from Vietnam. Nixon challenged Hanoi to reciprocate with a troop reduction of their own or progress at the Paris peace negotiations. Hanoi did neither, choosing to escalate attacks.

2196 **I have decided to order the immediate redeployment from Viet Nam of the divisional equivalent of approximately 25,000 men...**—*President Richard Nixon, from a speech during the Midway Conference, June 1969.*[932]

Nixon's announcement of the unilateral withdrawal of American troops from South Vietnam. The 25,000 men would come from Army and Marine units and the withdrawal was to be completed by the end of August 1969. Nixon also called upon Hanoi to reciprocate and/or enter into serious peace negotiations at the Paris peace talks.

2197 **We have opened wide the door to peace, and now we invite the leaders of North Viet Nam to walk with us through that door either by withdrawing their forces from South Viet Nam as we have withdrawn ours, or by negotiating in Paris ... we believe this is the time for them to act.**—*President Richard Nixon, from a speech at Midway Island, June 1969.*[932]

Nixon announced the unilateral withdrawal of 25,000 American troops from Vietnam. He called on North Vietnam to reciprocate or bargain in good faith in Paris toward a peaceful solution of the war in Vietnam. In acknowledgement of the President's move, the NVA launched a series of heavy attacks in the midst of a lull on the battlefield.

2198 **I don't see the [withdrawal of 25,000 American troops] as anything more than token action.**—*Senator George McGovern of South Dakota, comments to the press, June 1969.*[932]

McGovern believed if the President was serious about troop withdrawal from Vietnam, more troops should have been involved. He wanted a rapid American disengagement from Vietnam.

2199 **Ultimately, the South Vietnamese will have to bear the major part of their own military and political burdens.**—*Time magazine, 20 June 1969.*[932]

2200 **As far as Vietnam is concerned, the train has just left the station and is now headed down the track.**—*Henry Kissinger, President Nixon's National Security Adviser, speaking with Soviet Ambassador Anatoly Dobrynin, July 1969.*[321]

Kissinger was speaking of a new round of Nixon threats to use additional force against North Vietnam in an attempt to coerce them into establishing a channel for secret peace talks. Kissinger had confidence that Dobrynin would pass the word on to Hanoi.

2201 **If there is one lesson to come out of this war, it must be a reaffirmation of the axiom—don't get in a fight unless you are prepared to do whatever is necessary to win.**—*General William W. Momyer, Commander, U.S. 7th Air Force, in a letter to General McConnell, 3 July 1969.*[160]

Momyer and McConnell were both frustrated by the restrictions placed on the air campaign against North Vietnam. They held the opinion that the war could have been won, the President's objectives met, if the air commanders had been allowed to pursue the war to win.

2202 **My regret is we didn't win the war. We had the force, skill, and intelligence, but our civilian betters wouldn't turn us loose.**—*General William W. Momyer, Commander, U.S. 7th Air Force, in a letter to General McConnell, 3 July 1969.*[160]

2203 **[American antiwar protests, acclaimed as a] noble reflection of the American public's desire to save its sons from a useless death in Vietnam.**—*Pham Van Dong, Prime Minister, Democratic Republic of Vietnam, in an open letter to the American anti-war movement, 1969.*[374]

This broadcast was the first public acknowledgment by the North Vietnamese of the importance of the American anti-war movement in the achievement of their goals for Vietnam. Some in the Nixon administration interpreted this praise by Hanoi for the American anti-war movement as an indication of the movement's communist leanings or inspiration.

2204 **I realize that it is difficult to communicate meaningfully across the gulf of four years of war. But precisely because of this gulf, I wanted to take this opportunity to reaffirm in all solemnity my desire to work for a just peace.... As I have said repeatedly, there is nothing to be gained by waiting.... You will find us forthcoming and open-minded in a common effort to bring the blessings of peace to the brave people of Vietnam. Let history record that at this critical juncture, both sides turned their face toward peace rather than toward conflict and war.**—*President Richard Nixon, in a hand-carried letter to Ho Chin Minh, July 1969.*[185]

Within days of the receipt of this letter, secret peace negotiations between the U.S. and North Vietnam were initiated.

2205 **The Americans have all along been wrong in their evaluation of the abilities and capacities of the Vietnamese people.**—*Nguyen Cao Ky, Prime Minister of South Vietnam, luncheon speech, July 1969.*[629]

Ky's statement is highly suspect based on the poor showing the ARVNs demonstrated during their incursion into Laos in 1971 and their final defense of South Vietnam in 1975. They did eventually make a good showing in 1972 when North Vietnam openly invaded South Vietnam, but a massive effort by U.S. air support was critical to stopping the invasion.

2206 **The V.C. were stealing the stuff [C-rations and medical supplies] and squirreling it away, so when the [1969] TET offensive came, we fed 'em, shot 'em and then we provided the medicine to treat 'em.**—*Unidentified transport foreman in Saigon, during an interview, July 1969.*[466]

Referring to an increase in the theft of supplies and material prior to the TET offensive, much of which went to the enemy. The communists launched a series of offensives in February 1969 which was referred to by the U.S. military as TET 1969. This series of attacks had neither the surprise or impact of the 1968 TET Offensive.

2207 **You get a flat tire in one of those villages between here [Saigon] and Cuchi [*sic*] and in five minutes you got an empty truck. The villagers ... swarm over you like ants. You can yell and stomp all you like, it doesn't do any good. What the hell are you going to do anyway — shoot them?**—*Unidentified civilian trucking supervisor, during an interview in Saigon, July 1969.*[466]

2208 **Any objective and carefully prepared account of the history of Vietnam must conclude with the fact that the United States must bear the responsibility for the torture of an entire nation since the end of the Second World War.**—*Gabriel Kolko, historian, writing in 1969.*[91]

2209 **[In a free election between the Nationalist and the Communist,] the people of South Vietnam know that they still have the cherished right to criticize us, even to insult us, but Communism would never tolerate that, and that is what we would win in a free election tomorrow.**—*Nguyen Cao Ky, Vice President of South Vietnam, speaking to President Nixon, July 1969.*[629]

Nixon posed the Question to Ky, "Who would win in a free election held tomorrow?"

2210 **[You] will be confronted by those who will degrade your performance in Vietnam.**—*General William Westmoreland, Chairman, Joint Chiefs of Staff, speaking to troops at McCord Air Force Base, 10 July 1969.*[687]

Westmoreland met the first group of American troops withdrawn from Vietnam. In his speech he warned them that they might not be well-received by some Americans. He was eluding to incidents of Vietnam veterans being spit upon, called baby killers, and other terms demeaning their service to their country.

2211 **An effete corps of impudent snobs who characterize themselves as intellectuals.**—*Spiro T. Agnew, Vice President, comments on the anti-war movement, 1969.*[374]

Agnew was referring to the anti-war movement's refusal to denounce the verbal support it received from North Vietnam in an open letter from Pham Van Dong. This new, open support by Hanoi, was hailed as indication of the anti-war movement's communist leanings.

2212 **[You will find yourselves] more mature, more dedicated to the service of others, more compassionate, more responsible, more realistic and more practical than [your] contemporaries who have not served.**—*General William Westmoreland, Chairman, Joint Chiefs of Staff, speaking to troops at McCord AFB, 10 July 1969.*[687]

Westmoreland met the first group of American troops withdrawn from Vietnam. During his speech he praised them for their service and warned them that they might experience problems adjusting to American society, but told them they were stronger for their military service.

2213 **I realized that the sole hope of this nation lies in it's youth. The elders, the parents, are tired. They've lived with war, and the hardships involved, for too long. They no longer believe another kind of life is possible. The children do, though. They want to learn. They want to do things the way we do, have things like we have. They have hope for their future.**—*CWO Bruce L. McInnes, U.S. Army, 155th Assault Helicopter Company, 10th Combat Assault Battalion, in a letter home, July 1969.*[187]

2214 **[Unless some progress toward a settlement is made I have no choice but to resort to] measures of great consequence and force.**—*President Richard Nixon, in a personal message to Ho Chi Minh, July 1969.*[321]

Nixon's attempts at secret diplomacy through intermediaries such as the Russians and the French did not gain any concessions or agreement from the North Vietnamese. Nixon threatened more direct force unless North Vietnam negotiated in good faith.

2215 **The first [component] is the strengthening of the armed forces of the South Vietnamese in numbers, equipment, leadership and combat skills, and overall capability. The second component is the extension of the pacification program in South Vietnam.**—*President Richard Nixon, from a speech during the Guam Conference, 25 July 1969.*[713]

Nixon was summarizing his Vietnamization program.

2216 **I can't believe that a fourth-rate power like North Vietnam doesn't have a breaking point.**—*Henry Kissinger, National Security Adviser, from comments to his staff, 1969.*[374]

Kissinger favored increased military pressure on Hanoi to force them to back-off their demand for the removal of the Thieu regime in Saigon. In 1969 Hanoi was adamant about the removal of Thieu, and the establishment of the NLF as the true representative government of South Vietnam.

2217 **[America would still] furnish military and economic assistance when requested and as appropriate. But we shall look to the nation directly threatened to assume the primary responsibility of providing the manpower for its defense.**—*President Richard Nixon, from a speech in Guam, 25 July 1969.*[713]

This was Nixon's formal introduction of his policy of Vietnamization. Under his policy the South Vietnamese would increase their involvement in the war against the communists until they were completely responsible for their own defense. During the process American troops would be withdrawn. South Vietnam would still have the backing and material support of America, but the war against the communists would be carried on by the Vietnamese.

2218 **We have gone as far as we can or should go in opening the door of negotiations which will bring peace.**—*President Richard Nixon, speaking to the press during a visit to Saigon, 1 August 1969.*[688]

Nixon paid a short visit to South Vietnam where he held a conference with President Nguyen Van Thieu. Following the conference he made a brief stopover at the U.S. 1st Infantry Division base camp to visit with American troops.

2219 **[It is now time for the North Vietnamese and the Viet Cong] to sit down with us and talk seriously about ways to stop the killing.**—*President Richard Nixon, speaking to the press during a visit to Saigon, 1 August 1969.*[688]

Nixon made a brief visit to South Vietnam where he held

a conference with President Nguyen Van Thieu. Following the conference he made a brief stopover at the U.S. 1st Infantry Division base camp to visit with American troops.

2220 **Out here in this dreary difficult war, I think history will record that this may have been one of America's finest hours, because we took a difficult task and we succeeded.**—*President Richard Nixon, speaking to American troops at Di An, South Vietnam, 1 August 1969.*[688]

2221 **We feel boundless grief in informing the entire party and the entire Vietnamese people that Comrade Ho Chi Minh ... passed away...**—*Hanoi communiqué, 4 September 1969.*[569]

Ho reportedly died of a heart attack at age 79, he was succeeded by Vice President Ton Duc Thang.

2222 **A small and unelected elite that do not—I repeat not—represent the view of America.**—*Spiro T. Agnew, Vice President, comments regarding the media, 1969.*[374]

Agnew's view of the liberal news media.

2223 **To a large and vocal portion of the dissenters in this country, the strength of the allied position is irrelevant—they want an end to the war at any price.**—*Henry Kissinger, National Security Adviser, in a memorandum to President Nixon, 10 September 1969.*[866]

Shortly after Nixon took office, Kissinger formulated a possible plan of action for the Nixon administration to follow. He stressed the importance of timely resolution of the Vietnam issue as the patience of the country was wearing thin, and the enemy was prolonging the conflict to further antagonize the anti-war movement against the Administration.

2224 **Try to imagine grass 8 to 15 feet high so thick as to cut visibility to one yard, possessing razor-sharp edges. Then try to imagine walking through it while all around you are men possessing the latest automatic weapons who desperately want to kill you. You'd be amazed at how such a man can age on one patrol.**—*SP/4 George Olsen, U.S. Army, G Company, 75th Infantry (Rangers), in a letter home, September 1969.*[187]

Olsen was describing patrolling through elephant grass.

2225 **We see the president sinking deeper into the Johnsonian bog.**—*Roger Morris, Kissinger aide, comments on the Vietnam War, 1969.*[374]

The aide, as well as several others on Kissinger's staff, argued that no amount of military pressure, acceptable to the American people, could force Hanoi to negotiate. They argued for a political settlement that would install a coalition government in Saigon and allow American troops to withdraw. Kissinger did not agree and wanted to increase military pressure on North Vietnam.

2226 **The border area is a very important area which we are striving to secure in order to protect our agencies and forces which are located there to support the battlefield.**—*Excerpt from captured South Vietnamese [Communist] Liberation Army document, September 1969.*[886]

The VC/NVA had several base areas along the 900+ kilometer-long border between South Vietnam and Cambodia. Between the major base areas were smaller bases and way stations.

2227 **It will take more than soul music on the EM club juke box and Afro haircuts to satisfy the legitimate demands of black service personnel.**—*Bobby Seale, Chairman, Black Panther Party, in a Black Panther publication, September 1969.*[991]

In an effort to make military service more acceptable to minorities, the DoD initiated reforms in regard to military housing discrimination, more balance in the type of music played on Armed Forces Radio and the music available on EM club juke boxes, black hair and cosmetic products at the PX, allowance for Afro haircuts, etc. Bobby Seale did not think the DoD went far enough.

2228 **Most whites stay home and argue about the immorality of the war while the minorities are sent off to fight.**—*Linda Quint, anti-draft activist, quoted in an article, September 1969.*[1000]

Most of the militant black organizations were anti-draft. They believed the draft was geared toward inducting the poor and minorities. Those who could least financially or educationally afford to beat the draft. In 1964 there was a 30 percent chance of a black male being drafted, while there was an 18 percent chance for a white male. By 1967 there was a 63 percent chance for a black, and a 32 percent chance for a white.

2229 **To quash the court-martial of these men, would, in my view, be both immoral and political dynamite. It is bad enough we are over there [in Vietnam] fighting an immoral war.**—*Stanley Resor, Secretary of the Army, September 1969.*[188]

Resor was referring to the courts-martial of Colonel Robert Rheault and six fellow officers, who were charged with the murder of a Vietnamese double agent in their employ. Rheault was the commanding officer of U.S. Special Forces in Vietnam at the time of the murder. Rheault resigned from the Army following dismissal of the charges for "implied expediency reasons."

2230 **We're all scared. One can easily see this emotion in the eyes of each individual. One might hide it with his mouth, while another might hide it with his actions, but there is no way around it—we are all scared. They say when fear is in a man, he is prepared for anything. When fear possesses the man, he is prepared for nothing. As of now, fear is in me. I hope I can keep it from possessing me.**—*PFC William A. Maguire, Jr., U.S. Marine Corps, 2d Battalion, 5th Marine Regiment, in a letter home, September 1969.*[187]

2231 **A President must not feel unable to go to war when he believes that it's necessary, and I genuinely felt that L.B.J. could minimize it. I thought that he knew something I didn't.**—*David Moss, realtor, Dallas, Texas, during an interview, October 1969.*[469]

Moss was a liberal Democrat who made the transition from hawk to dove.

2232 **We must understand that the struggle in South Vietnam is not our war. We went there to help the South Vietnamese.**—*Hubert H. Humphrey, former Vice President, during an interview with a correspondent, October 1969.*[469]

2233 **Even if a guy isn't a sensitive person, he can't help being affected by all the death and pain he sees over here. And once you have seen that, you don't want anyone, anywhere to ever hurt again.**—*PFC Saul Sindell, U.S. Army, during an interview with a correspondent, October 1969.*[469]

2234 **[Antiwar demonstrators] have the right, but they are wrong.**—*Hascal Dennison, 1st Infantry Division, during an interview with a correspondent, October 1969.*[469]

Commenting on the peace and anti-war demonstrations at home.

2235 **I don't see the threat to these people if they do have a Communist government. They're going to be rice farmers regardless of who is running Saigon.**—*SP/4 Richard Beshel, 25th Infantry Division, during an interview with a correspondent, October 1969.*[469]

2236 **Outside our families, I think the protesters may be the only ones who really give a damn about what's happening.**—*PFC Chris Yapp, 4th Infantry Division, during an interview, October 1969.*[469]

Regarding the Vietnam Moratorium Day demonstration in various cities across the U.S..

2237 **While you are here [in Vietnam], it's just your own private war.**—*SP/4 Joseph Williams, U.S. Army, during an interview with a correspondent, October 1969.*[469]

2238 **A person must tell the government to change. I intend to state my case, and even when they spit at me, I mean to stand there.**—*David Moss, realtor, Dallas, Texas, during an interview, October 1969.*[469]

2239 **The U.S. today ... is so great a country that it can neither wage a little war nor suffer a little defeat. The war is big because the U.S. is a party to it; a defeat would be great because it would reveal the extent of our internal weakness — with no external power capable of defeating us, our loss would be clearly self-imposed.**—*Maxwell Taylor, former Chairman, Joint Chiefs of Staff, during an interview with a correspondent, October 1969.*[469]

2240 **I've never marched, rallied, picketed, demonstrated or otherwise created a public fuss in my life — but this war has gone on too long.**—*Alan Coburn, Washington D.C., during an interview, October 1969.*[469]

A moderate Republican, he initially backed the war and Nixon. But later decided the U.S. was trying to impose its will on the Vietnamese, and he disagreed with such strategy.

2241 **Who persuaded the U.S. to nullify the sacrifice of the thousands of Americans killed in action and to abandon an ally on the battlefield with the issue still in doubt?**—*Maxwell Taylor, former Chairman, Joint Chiefs of Staff, during an interview with a correspondent, October 1969.*[469]

2242 **The wonder is not that there is protest but that there is so much willingness to serve and sacrifice.**—*Hedley Donovan, Editor-in-Chief, Life magazine editorial, 24 October 1969.*[467]

Based on the length of the war, casualties, lack of progress and growing anti-war sentiment, the military was still able to field troops to Vietnam. Of the 27 million American men that were of draft age during the war 2.8 million men went to Vietnam.

2243 **Our withdrawal from this civil war [in Vietnam] in which we have no security interest of our own would be a clear indication not of American defeat but of civilized restraint, of belated awakening to our own best interests, and of the strength and self-confidence to acknowledge a mistake.**—*Senator J. William Fulbright, Chairman, Foreign Relations Committee, during an interview with a correspondent, October 1969.*[469]

2244 **I was against the war all along but too lazy to speak up. When I saw the war on TV, I could always turn it off and go out. But you can't do that here and when you see what is happening, you know you have to protest.**—*PFC James Petrillo, 101st Air Cavalry Division, during an interview with a correspondent, October 1969.*[469]

2245 **Everyone knows that we can destroy North Vietnam tomorrow.**—*Senator J. William Fulbright, Chairman, Foreign Relations Committee, during an interview with a correspondent, October 1969.*[469]

Fulbright did not see the U.S. withdrawal from Vietnam as a defeat, but as a realization of the correct path for the United States to pursue.

2246 **The Johnson administration tried to escalate, then bomb, then negotiate Hanoi into a state of enlightenment. The Nixon administration has changed the emphasis.**—*Senator Hugh Scott from Pennsylvania, during an interview with a correspondent, October 1969.*[469]

Scott was Republican Senate Minority Leader at the time. He said only the President could be the chief foreign policy spokesman for the nation and Nixon's policy was more realistic than Johnson's.

2247 **Red is for the blood he's never spilled, blue for the ocean he's never crossed, white is for the eyes he's never seen, yellow is the reason why.**—*Verse AWOL soldiers were reportedly forced to recite at the Camp Pendleton Brig, October 1969.*[491]

AWOL Marines were reportedly forced to scream the above verse while facing a picture of the National Defense Ribbon. The ribbon was awarded for honorable active military service. This shouting of verse was one of several harassment and tortures Marine AWOLs were reportedly subjected to in the late-sixties. The design of the ribbon featured vertical color bars of red, white, blue and yellow.

2248 **I don't even know what I'm fighting for. I'm just in the bushes getting shot at.**—*PFC Sam Benson, U.S. Marine Corps, during an interview with a correspondent, October 1969.*[469]

2249 **There has to be a new and different government in South Vietnam which is reasonably acceptable to the United States, to South Vietnam, to the National Liberation Front and also Hanoi.**—*Senator Eugene J. McCarthy from Minnesota, during an interview with a correspondent, October 1969.*[469]

2250 **This country will suffer a loss in its reputation and self-respect if we leave the South Vietnamese defenseless, with arbitrary timetables of withdrawal, etc., as some have suggested.**—*Senator Hugh Scott from Pennsylvania, during an interview with a correspondent, October 1969.*[469]

He claimed Nixon's Vietnamization program would leave South Vietnam able to defend itself against North Vietnam, something they historically had not been able to do.

2251 **I do not think our self-respect has grown in the course of this war, and it is my opinion that withdrawal would do it**

no harm.—*Senator Eugene J. McCarthy, from Minnesota, during an interview with a correspondent, October 1969.*[469]

McCarthy opposed U.S. policy in Vietnam and nearly defeated President Johnson in the New Hampshire primary for the Democratic presidential nomination.

2252 **We are firmly confident that with the solidarity and bravery of the peoples of our two countries and with the approval and support of peace-loving people in the world, the struggle of the Vietnamese people and U.S. progressive people against U.S. aggression will certainly be crowned with total victory. May your fall offensive succeed splendidly.**—*Pham Van Dong, Premier, Democratic Republic of Vietnam, in an open letter, 14 October 1969.*[874]

Hanoi published an open letter to American anti-war protesters giving them the support of Hanoi in their demonstrations and protest against the American government. Congressman Rogers Morton of Maryland, read Dong's letter into the Congressional record.

2253 **Why should I get knocked down in a white folks' march?**—*Unidentified, black Washington D.C. resident, during a street interview, 15 October 1969.*[933]

The man was asked why there were so few blacks participating the in the Moratorium Day demonstration against the war in Vietnam.

2254 **I could never see the sense in this war, but I enlisted partly because I wanted to get the true picture on what is happening. I'll go back now and carry my sign on the campus. Maybe I can influence somebody.**—*SP/5 Raul Torres, 4th Infantry Division, during an interview with a correspondent, October 1969.*[469]

2255 **The Administration's Vietnamization policies are increasing their [South Vietnam's] strength and their ability to defend themselves.**—*Senator Hugh Scott from Pennsylvania, during an interview with a correspondent, October 1969.*[469]

2256 **America's reputation around the world will be helped by almost any action we take to bring an end to our participation in the war in Vietnam.**—*Senator Eugene J. McCarthy, of Minnesota, during an interview with a correspondent, October 1969.*[469]

2257 **The threat of death changes many things, but comradeship doesn't last after you get [back] ... to the village.**—*Unidentified U.S. Army colonel, 1969.*[1017]

Blacks and whites who were often very close in the field, tended to separate and self-segregate when they returned to their base camp on standdown.

2258 **It's [Paris peace talks] the biggest hoax of the war, a big joke.**—*Darryl Logsdon, U.S. Air Force security police, during an interview with a correspondent, October 1969.*[469]

2259 **The pacification program which previously had not been taken seriously, gradually assumed major significance for the communists. A full scale attack on it is now underway...**—*Douglas Pike, historian, 1969.*[713]

The pacification operations were a major threat to the communists in South Vietnam because it put the people in direct contact with representatives of the Saigon government and made recruiting among the villagers very difficult. Because of heavy losses of VC soldiers and NLF cadre during the 1968 TET Offensive, the GVN pacification efforts were more successful. The VC and NVA targeted pacification villages in an effort to undermine the program.

2260 **I came partly for revenge, but now I have lost all faith. The demonstrators are right to speak up because this war is wrong and it must be stopped.**—*Pvt. Jim Beck, 101st Air Cavalry Division, during an interview with a correspondent, October 1969.*[469]

2261 **I don't believe Hanoi intends to negotiate anything that isn't already settled in the battlefield.**—*Hubert H. Humphrey, former Vice President, during an interview with a correspondent, October 1969.*[469]

2262 **I feel that the U.S. is a strong enough country to undertake [an immediate withdrawal from Vietnam]. Of course, it would hardly be seen as a U.S. victory, but it would be interpreted as an act of political wisdom and boldness.**—*Yuri Arbatov of the Soviet Academy of Science's Institute of American Studies, comments to an interviewer, October 1969.*[933]

2263 **[The Vietnam Moratorium Day protest] was like pushing against a door you think is locked and finding that it is not locked, that there is no adversary.**—*Henry Graff, Columbia University historian, comments to the press, October 1969.*[469]

There was no overt violence at the protest in Washington, the 30,000 participants did not confront police and they were not unduly harassed by the authorities.

2264 **When I see something on the front page about Paris talks, I just think they have put the comics on the front page again.**—*SP/4 Horace, U.S. Army, during an interview with a correspondent, October 1969.*[469]

Horace was commenting on the lack of progress at the Paris peace talks.

2265 **This war is one that no one can afford to say he lost and everyone will try to say he won.**—*Hubert H. Humphrey, former Vice President, during an interview with a correspondent, October 1969.*[469]

In the end Hanoi claimed victory over the United States and Nixon claimed victory in Vietnam and peace with honor.

2266 **Americans have no culture, unless you call beer and big bosoms culture.**—*An unidentified South Vietnamese intellectual's comments to an interviewer, October 1969.*[933]

The interviewer had raised the issue of growing anti-American sentiment in South Vietnam amongst the very people the Americans were there to assist. The French-educated Vietnamese considered themselves the Vietnamese elite and generally looked down upon Americans as a group.

2267 **We should stop expecting anything out of the Paris peace talks. We should proceed on the assumption that there will be no formal settlement with the North.**—*Hedley Donovan, Editor-in-Chief, Life magazine editorial, 24 October 1969.*[467]

2268 **We went there [to Vietnam] to stop the success of aggression, to help protect the right of self-determination. We have accomplished both.**—*Hubert H. Humphrey, former Vice President, during an interview with a correspondent, October 1969.*[469]

2269 **I do not ask the U.S. troops to stay here for 100 years. I only ask the Americans to have the courage and the clear sight to remain here until we nationalists have enough military, economic and political strength.**—*Nguyen Van Thieu, President, South Vietnam, October 1969.*[933]

Thieu was responding to media questions regarding an immediate pull-out of American troops from South Vietnam. Anti-war demonstrators in the U.S. called for the immediate withdrawal of American troops, a move not supported by the Nixon administration.

2270 **People who haven't been here and suffered have no right to bitch and moan about what is going on.**—*Sgt. Howard Clarke, U.S. Marine Corps, during an interview with a correspondent, October 1969.*[469]

Clarke was commenting on anti-war demonstrators at home.

2271 **The Communist side hasn't given the least sign of a desire to conduct serious negotiations.**—*Pham Dang Lam, South Vietnam's Ambassador to the Paris peace talks, comments to the press, 25 October 1969.*[689]

Pham Dang Lam was speaking about the lack of progress in the peace talks. In Vietnam, North Vietnam and the VC stepped up attacks against U.S. and ARVN installations across the country, while at the same time American troop withdrawals continued.

2272 **...systematic troop withdrawal through 1970 will not represent defeat or abandonment of our commitment. It will represent a response to American public opinion on the one hand and, on the other, a recognition that we have fulfilled our commitment to aid an ally which can now undertake its own self-defense.**—*Hubert H. Humphrey, former Vice President, during an interview with a correspondent, October 1969.*[469]

2273 **If we have not ended the war by six months from now, you can come back and tear down the White House fence.**—*Henry Kissinger, President Nixon's National Security Adviser, speaking to anti-war protesters, 1969.*[949]

2274 **I could blame the defeat [on L.B.J.] and come out as a peacemaker, and from a political standpoint this would have been a popular and easy course.**—*President Richard Nixon, from a speech on the Vietnam War, November 1969.*[471]

During the speech he said he could have ordered the withdrawal of U.S. troops immediately on taking office, but he didn't.

2275 **Challenge is what life is all about, without it, there is no meaning.**—*Colonel Robert Rheault, Special Forces, November 1969.*[470]

Rheault was the commanding officer of U.S. Special Forces in Vietnam when a Vietnamese double agent was (allegedly) killed by a group of Special Forces officers. Rheault resigned from the Army following dismissal of the charges. The charges were dropped for "implied expediency reasons."

2276 **A nation cannot remain great if it betrays its allies and lets down its friends.**—*President Richard Nixon, televised speech on Vietnamization, 3 November 1969.*[354]

2277 **North Viet Nam cannot defeat or humiliate the United States. Only Americans can do that.**—*President Richard Nixon, during a televised Presidential address, 3 November 1969.*[934]

Nixon appealed to Americans for support of his peace initiative, and for patience. No progress was being made at the Paris peace talks, and enemy military activity was steadily increasing, jeopardizing Nixon's schedule for American troop withdrawals.

2278 **If a President — any President — allowed his course to be set by those who demonstrate, he would betray the trust of all the rest. Whatever the issue, to allow government policy to be made in the streets would destroy the democratic process. It would give the decision, not to the majority, and not to those with the strongest arguments, but to those with the loudest voices.... It would allow every group to test its strength not at the ballot box but through confrontation in the streets.**—*Richard Nixon, foreign policy speech, 3 November 1969.*[185]

Nixon's reaction to continued anti-war demonstrations and the Vietnam Moratorium demonstration in October 1969.

2279 **A precipitate withdrawal would be a prescription for a disaster of immense magnitude.**—*President Richard Nixon, in a national message, 3 November 1969.*[570]

No progress was made during the peace negotiations in Paris and the war in Vietnam continued. Anti-war activists pressed for immediate withdrawal of U.S. forces.

2280 **[Those who urge such immediate withdrawal from Vietnam are only a] vocal minority [who are trying to] prevail over reason and the will of the majority.**—*President Richard Nixon, from a speech on the Vietnam War, November 1969.*[471]

During the speech Nixon made no announcement of troop withdrawals or other initiatives to resolve the Vietnam question. During presidential campaigning he eluded to a plan to end the Vietnam War.

2281 **I pledged in my campaign for the Presidency to end the war in a way that we could win the peace. I have initiated a plan of action which will enable me to keep that pledge.**—*President Richard Nixon, in a national message, 3 November 1969.*[570]

2282 **The more support I can have from the American people, the sooner that pledge [to end the war] can be redeemed, for the more divided we are at home, the less likely the enemy is to negotiate in Paris.**—*President Richard Nixon, in a national message, 3 November 1969.*[570]

Nixon asked for public support for his Vietnam policy. No progress was made during the peace negotiations in Paris and the war in Vietnam continued. Anti-war activists pressed for immediate withdrawal of U.S. forces

2283 **It [a trial] would have been a travesty of justice to try dedicated soldiers for doing their job, carrying out their mission, and protecting the lives of the men entrusted to them in a wartime situation.**—*Colonel Robert Rheault, Special Forces, November 1969.*[470]

Rheault believed there should not have been a trial because vital information concerning the secret operations of the Special Forces in Vietnam would have to be publicized in order for the Special Forces soldiers charged to receive a fair trial. The officers were arrested for the murder of a Vietnamese double agent in their employ.

2284 **Withdrawal will be made from strength and not from weakness...**—*President Richard Nixon, Vietnam speech, November 1969.*[471]

Nixon, outlining conditions for the phased withdrawal of U.S. troops from Vietnam.

2285 **I thought that's what Dad was in Vietnam for—to kill the Vietcong.**—*Robert Rheault Jr., son of Special Forces Colonel Robert Rheault, October 1969.*[470]

Reacting to the news that his father, along with several other soldiers, had been arrested in Vietnam for conspiracy to commit murder in the death of a Vietnamese double agent in the employ of the U.S. Special Forces.

2286 **If you accept the Nixon and Johnson assumptions, there is no justification for winding down the war.**—*Senator J. William Fulbright, of Arkansas, Chairman of the Senate Foreign Relations Committee, November 1969.*[471]

During the Nixon speech about Vietnam in November 1969 he spoke of the Communist threat but did not speak about ending the war or announce more troop withdrawals.

2287 **[The American air campaign against North Vietnam is] the product of defeat on the Southern battlefield [and will never affect the Communists' initiative in the South].**—*General Van Tien Dung, North Vietnamese Chief of Staff, commenting on Saigon's predicament.*[173]

The U.S. military believed that by cutting the VC off from their supply and support in North Vietnam, they could eventually win the battle against the insurgents. But they were never able to cut the VC off from North Vietnam.

2288 **Stop the picnic! Start the Revolution!**—*A call from a small group of radicals that were part of the anti-war, Moratorium Day demonstration in Washington, D.C., 15 November 1969.*[886]

The slogan of a small group of radicals that were part of the anti-war, Moratorium Day demonstration in Washington, D.C., 15 November 1969. The radicals advocated revolution to overthrow the current government system. The radicals numbered less than ten of the estimated 250,000+ people that participated in the demonstration.

2289 **We anti-war people may occasionally throw rocks, but the government drops six-ton bombs on Vietnam.**—*Jerry Rubin, New Left activist and Yippie co-founder, during an anti-war demonstration at the Justice Department, 15 November 1969.*[886]

Some of the 250,000 people who participated in the Moratorium Day anti-war demonstrations threw rocks and bottles at police, the police returned tear-gas in exchange, followed by the use of batons and nightsticks.

2290 **The Corps says it treats all men just one way—as a Marine. What it actually has done is treat everybody like a white Marine.**—*Lt.Col. Hurdle L. Maxwell, one of the highest ranking black Marines in the Corps, 1969.*[1007]

Treating all Marines as "green" ignored the cultural differences of Marine personnel. The technique worked very well in the field under combat conditions, but the policy was lacking when it came to off duty hours, standdowns, or duty stations outside of the war zone.

2291 **We've got those liberal bastards on the run now ... and we're going to keep them on the run.**—*President Richard Nixon, comments to his aids, November 1969.*[329]

Nixon was responding to polls indicating solid and stable public support for his policy in Vietnam. The policy he outlined in a speech 3 November 1969, indicated increased progress and support for Vietnamization of the war and increased numbers of American troops being withdrawn.

2292 **A mantle of almost complete secrecy descended on American officialdom in Viet Nam, both military and civilian.**—*Marsh Clark, Time magazine, in a cable to the home office, November 1969.*[935]

Clark was investigating the revelations of the My Lai massacre.

2293 **If it had been me out there, I would have swung my rifle around and shot Calley instead—right between the goddam eyes.**—*Tony Meadlo, during an interview, 1969.*[934]

Tony was the father of Paul Meadlo, one of Lt. Calley's platoon. Calley was charged with the massacre of civilians at the Vietnamese hamlet of My Lai, March 1968.

2294 **The reason you people are so tight, is because of needs in the past. We [whites] don't have this, we can act as individuals.**—*Unidentified white U.S. Marine Corps private, to a black correspondent, 1969.*[1007]

The Marine was attempting to explain why, if a white was attacked by blacks, he would report the incident to the base authorities, whereas, if a black was attacked by whites, he was more likely to go to the barracks to seek back-up, and return to the scene of the attack to retaliate and finish the fight.

2295 **A simplistic, deliberate act of inhumanity—one of the darkest days in American history.**—*Senator Richard Schweiker of Pennsylvania, during testimony before the Senate and House Armed Services Committees, December 1969.*[934]

Schweiker was speaking of the My Lai massacre. Secretary of the Army, Stanley Resor entered photographs of massacred victims into the record.

2296 **[My Lai was] ... a normal act of war.**—*Statement by the Government of South Vietnam, 1969.*[934]

This was the initial statement released by the Saigon government after the massacre at My Lai when the story broke in 1969.

2297 **A lot of time we get our butts chewed out and we need a crutch to fall back on. Prejudice.**—*Master Sergeant Thomas A. Roberson, U.S. Marine Corps, during an interview, December 1969.*[1007]

Roberson blamed the lack of more black representation in the higher enlisted ranks on the black individuals. The blacks claimed they were not promoted or allowed to advance at the same rate as whites. In 1972 Department of Defense studies indicated that though blacks made up 17 percent of the enlisted ranks they were predominantly grouped in higher percentages in the lower ranks.

2298 **None of the funds appropriated by this Act shall be used to finance the introduction of American ground combat troops into Laos or Thailand.**—*Excerpted from the Cooper-Church Amendment, 15 December 1969.*[855]

The amendment was attached to the Defense Appropriations bill for fiscal year 1970. The bill funded the U.S. military for the coming year. It effectively kept President Nixon from sending combat troops into Laos or Thailand. This was an attempt by Congress to curtail some of the war making powers of the presidency.

2299 **The tools of the Viet Cong are primarily non-military — political subversion by use of persuasion, explanations to the foreign and domestic press, propaganda, and terror — all calculated to gain control over people. The tools [of the United States] overwhelmingly are military — bombs, artillery and infantry battalions.**—*Lt.Col. Carl F. Bernard, former Province Senior Advisor, 1969.*[95]

1970

The object of war is not to die for your country,
but to make the other bastard die for his.
— General George S. Patton

2300 **For those of you staying on in "Nam," here's a little advice regarding our Vietnamese friends. As you know, they are kind of jumpy now, so please remember the golden rule. Never pat a Vietnamese on the head. Stand on low ground when you talk to them. They kind of resent looking up to you. Okay?**—*AFVN—Armed Forces, Radio Vietnam, 1970. As related by Nguyen Cao Ky, 1976.*[629]

For most GI's it was considered normal to pat a Vietnamese child on the head. The Vietnamese took offense at such. It was years before the message got across to the GIs, that patting a Vietnamese kid on the head was not acceptable behavior in Vietnam.

2301 **Unplanned, unwanted, undeclared, and unpopular war.**—*C. J. Merdinger, 1970.*[891]

View of the Vietnam War held by many of its American participants. A variant of the "UUUU" ("The unwilling, led by the unqualified, doing the unnecessary for the ungrateful.") phrase.

2302 **When he had done his best for his country, his country was still doing its worst for him.**—*Father Eugene Farrell, speaking at the funeral of Private Bill Terry, Jr., January 1970.*[979]

Terry was killed in action in South Vietnam 3 July 1969. Prior to his death he had requested burial in an all white cemetery near his home in Birmingham, Alabama. Because Terry was black, the cemetery refused his burial and was taken to court. The U.S. district court ruled that racial restrictions in any cemetery were void and of "no legal effect." Private Terry was buried at the cemetery of his choice in January 1970.

2303 **Treat the men as human beings, pay them the respect they deserve, regardless of rank.**—*General DeWitt Smith, Commander 4th Infantry Division, Fort Carson Colorado, during an interview, January 1970.*[476]

The New Army's direction to liberalize policy and prepare for an all-volunteer army.

2304 **They say I am just a Marine, but how can I forget eighteen years of being black and all that being black means in this country?**—*Pvt. Allen E. Jones, U.S. Marine Corps, during an interview, January 1970.*[984]

2305 **The enemy would rather kill a white soldier than a black one.**—*Arthur Westbrook, former U.S. Army sergeant, during an interview, January 1970.*[985]

North Vietnam proclaimed solidarity with the black civil rights movement in the U.S. The aim was to create dissension in the ranks of the American military at a time when racial problems were increasing.

2306 **Join the Army and see the world, meet interesting people, and kill them.**—*Anonymous, 1970.*[245]

Parody of Army recruiting ads.

2307 **It was as if we were trying to build a house with a bulldozer and wrecking crane.**—*Unidentified American official, 1970.*[323]

Large scale U.S. operations, forced relocations of Vietnamese rural populations, and heavy-handed combat practices,

GVN corruption and abuses, alienated much of the Vietnamese population in the midst of American efforts to build a self-sufficient South Vietnam.

2308 **The General Offensive and Uprising is a process. Throughout 1968, the South Vietnamese [communist] Army and people knocked out of action 630,000 of the enemy, including 230,000 U.S. and satellite troops.**—*Lao Dong Party Central Committee, January 1970 report on the events of 1968.*[868]

This was Hanoi's version of their claimed victory during the TET Offensive and the rest of the year, 1968. It should be noted that American casualties for all of 1968 were reported, by the U.S. Government, as 14,589 Americans killed in action; South Vietnamese (non-communist) 27,915 killed in action; other Free World Forces 979 killed in action.

2309 **There are no American ground combat troops in Laos.... We have no plans for introducing ground combat forces into Laos.... No American stationed in Laos has ever been killed in ground combat operations...**—*President Richard Nixon, from a speech regarding Laos, 6 March 1970.*[886]

Clandestine cross-border operations and covert ground support of the RLG and Meo forces—excluded.

2310 **I told the ambassador from North Vietnam last year that we will accept the use of the [Ho Chi Minh] trail by North Vietnamese troops with the condition that those troops withdraw from the important regions of Laos.**—*Souvanna Phouma, Prime Minister of Laos, at a press conference, 6 March 1970.*[474]

The Laotian government gave consent to the use of the trail by North Vietnam after the fact, since North Vietnam had been using the trail since the late-fifties. In any event, Laos was militarily powerless to stop North Vietnam's use of eastern Laos.

2311 **We don't anticipate that any request will be made...**—*William P. Rogers, Secretary of State, responding to press questions, 23 March 1970.*[374]

Roger's was asked if the Lon Nol government in Cambodia might request U.S. military assistance in its fight against communist rebel forces. The communist Khmer Rouge were fully supported by the North Vietnamese and were aligned with the former leader of Cambodia, Prince Norodom Sihanouk. The Khmer Rouge were increasing their attacks against the small Cambodian Army forces.

2312 **May this be the great turning point in the worldwide crusade against Communism.**—*Reverend Carl McIntire from Bible Presbyterian Church, New Jersey, speaking during a support march in Washington, D.C., 4 April 1970.*[571]

McIntire organized the rally and march in support of a U.S. victory in Vietnam over communism. The crowd of 50,000 included anti-communist and a mixture of small right wing groups advocating an end to school busing, the restoration of segregation, prayer in public schools, and the South shall rise again.

2313 **The most pusillanimous little nitpicker I ever saw.**—*President Richard Nixon's comments on a proposed plan by the Secretary of Defense, April 1970.*[374]

Nixon was referring to a plan proposed by Melvin Laird to assist the Lon Nol government in their struggle against the Khmer Rouge. Under the Laird plan South Vietnamese forces would strike communist base areas in the Parrot's Beak area of Cambodia. A more expansive plan involving South Vietnamese and American troops was later adopted.

2314 **We can now say with confidence that pacification is succeeding. We can say with confidence that the South Vietnamese can develop the capability for their own defense. We can say with confidence that all American forces can and will be withdrawn.**—*President Richard Nixon, from a nationally televised speech, 20 April 1970.*[690]

2315 **The president wants you to know if this doesn't work, Henry, it's your ass.**—*Charles "Bebe" Rebozo, close Nixon friend, in a phone conversation with Henry Kissinger, April 1970.*[374]

Rebozo was referring to the Nixon/Kissinger plan to use American troops in Cambodia. It was hoped the use of American troops would bolster the Lon Nol regime and send a message to Hanoi that Nixon was serious about a settlement in Vietnam. Kissinger was the unofficial shepherd of the plan and was under pressure to make the scheme work. Nixon gave this message to Rebozo to pass to Kissinger.

2316 **We finally have in sight the just peace we are seeking...**—*President Richard Nixon, from a nationally televised speech, 20 April 1970.*[690]

During the speech Nixon announced the withdrawal of 150,000 additional American troops from South Vietnam, dropping the total American force remaining in Vietnam to 284,000, from a peak of 549,500 in 1968.

2317 **We have no incentive to escalate. Our whole incentive is to de-escalate. We recognize that if we escalate and get involved in Cambodia with out ground troops, that our whole program [Vietnamization] is defeated.**—*William P. Rogers, Secretary of State, Congressional testimony, 23 April 1970.*[474]

Rogers appeared before Congress on 23 April, and Nixon announced on 30 April that American troops were crossing into Cambodia .

2318 **We need a bold move in Cambodia to show we stand with Lon Nol ... we must do something symbolic for the only Cambodian regime in twenty-five years with the guts to take a pro-Western and pro-American stand.**—*President Richard Nixon, in a memorandum to Henry Kissinger, 22 April 1970.*[374]

Under the rule of Prince Norodom Sihanouk, Cambodia steered a somewhat neutral course, accepting limited western aid, but larger amounts of aid from Red China. With the ouster of Sihanouk by Lon Nol, Cambodia took a decided turn to the west. In response to this turn communist rebel forces sought to overthrow the Lon Nol regime.

2319 **I think the one lesson that the war in Viet Nam has taught us is that if you are going to fight a war of this kind satisfactorily, you need public support and congressional support.**—*William Rogers, Secretary of State, in testimony before a House subcommittee, 23 April 1970.*[939]

Rogers made this statement a few days before Nixon ordered American ground troops in Vietnam to strike into Cambodia against enemy sanctuaries. The contradiction between what some Nixon cabinet members were saying and what the Administration was doing, was not lost on the press.

2320 **The North Vietnamese may have been going on a pussycat theory about Nixon. Now they know they have a tiger.**—*Senator Hugh Scott, Jr. of Pennsylvania, comments to the press, 30 April 1970.*[937]

Scott's comments were made after President Nixon's speech notifying the country that he had ordered U.S. troops into Cambodia for a limited expedition to clean out enemy sanctuaries.

2321 **We will not allow American men by the thousands to be killed by an enemy from privileged sanctuaries.**—*President Richard Nixon, from a televised speech, 30 April 1970.*[866]

Nixon was announcing the start of the American incursion into Cambodia, with the target of destroying enemy sanctuaries along the border and capture of COSVN.

2322 **This could be a turning point in the war for us for the good. I do not believe in itself it is an escalation — not yet...**—*Senator John Stennis, of Mississippi, comments on ARVN operations in Cambodia, 29 April 1970.*[572]

Stennis was referring to the South Vietnamese incursion into Cambodia, supported by American troops. Word did not come out until the following day that U.S. troops would also be attacking enemy base areas in Cambodia.

2323 **Once enemy forces are driven out of these sanctuaries and their military supplies destroyed, we will withdraw.**—*President Richard Nixon, from a televised announcement, 30 April 1970.*[574]

Nixon announced that some 30,000 American combat troops would be joining a larger force of South Vietnamese troops attacking VC/NVA sanctuaries along the border, inside Cambodia. This was the first incursion into Cambodia by regular U.S. combat units.

2324 **Most felt that something had to be done to eliminate the Communist sanctuaries [in Cambodia].**—*Unidentified Congressional leader in comments to the press, 30 April 1970.*[573]

Forty Congressional leaders were briefed by the White House on the Nixon decision to send American combat troops into Cambodia to destroy enemy sanctuaries. The strike into Cambodia by 70,000+ American and South Vietnamese troops was generally well received by the Congressional leadership.

2325 **If when the chips are down the world's most powerful nation acts like a pitiful helpless giant, the forces of totalitarianism and anarchy will threaten free nations and free institutions throughout the world.**—*President Richard Nixon, from a televised speech, 30 April 1970.*[347]

2326 **His burden is awesome. The final responsibility is his. It was a gesture by a bunch of humans to another human.**—*Senator Mike Mansfield of Montana, during a White House meeting, 30 April 1970.*[937]

Mansfield was one of forty congressional leaders called to the White House for a preview of Nixon's "Cambodian Incursion" speech. After Nixon expressed his reasoning for sending American troops into Cambodia and asking for Congressional support, he received a standing ovation by the Congressional party.

2327 **This is not an invasion of Cambodia but a necessary extension of the Vietnam war designed to eliminate a major Communist staging and communications area.**—*President Richard Nixon, from a televised announcement, 30 April 1970.*[574]

The operation against enemy sanctuaries was an effort to deflate a large buildup of enemy units which posed a threat to U.S. and allied troops in the III Corps area. Another goal of the operation was to capture COSVN, the Communist's southern headquarters for the enemy's war effort in South Vietnam.

2328 **One of the cruelest tactics of the war in Vietnam is the Communists' refusal to identify all prisoners of war, to provide information about them and to permit their families to communicate with them regularly.**—*President Richard Nixon, during a public declaration, 1 May 1970.*[691]

Nixon declared Sunday, 3 May 1970, as a national day of prayer for American service personnel missing in action or prisoners of war in Vietnam.

2329 **I would rather be a one-term President and do what I believe is right than to be a two-term President at the cost of seeing America become a second-rate power and to see this nation accept the first defeat in its proud 190-year history.**—*President Richard Nixon, announcing the launch of U.S. combat operations into Cambodia, 30 April 1970.*[574]

30,000 American combat troops joined a larger force of South Vietnamese troops attacking VC/NVA sanctuaries along the border inside Cambodia.

2330 **If the U.S. lets Lon Nol go down the drain, the Russians will conclude that the Americans have gone soft. It will also be very bad news for us.**—*Unidentified Israeli diplomat, comments to the press, 30 April 1970.*[937]

The Israeli diplomat was commenting on the Nixon speech which notified the American public, and the world, of Nixon's decision to send American troops into Cambodia with the mission of cleaning out enemy sanctuaries. In the speech Nixon warned the communist powers against any retaliatory moves, and reaffirmed American support for its commitments to other treaties and agreements. A notable commitment was to Israel, who was under pressure from Soviet armed Arab states.

2331 **In order to avoid a wider war and keep the casualties of our brave men in Vietnam at an absolute minimum, I have ordered American troops to invade Cambodia.**—*President Richard Nixon, in a televised address, 30 April 1970.*[631]

Nixon's announcement of the American/South Vietnamese incursion into Cambodia. The object of the incursion was to destroy enemy sanctuaries along the border and the capture or elimination of COSVN, the communist headquarters in South Vietnam.

2332 **The Cambodians sent in a request for enough stuff to equip an army of 200,000. We asked them to take it back and reconsider ... and then they came in with a request for enough stuff to equip an army of 400,000.**—*Henry Kissinger, President Nixon's National Security Adviser, during a briefing for White House staff members, May 1970.*[937]

At this time the Cambodian army stood at 35,000 men. The Nixon administration had asked the Lon Nol government what equipment they needed to fight the communist in Cambodia.

2333 **Having drawn the sword, don't take it out — stick it in hard.**—*President Richard Nixon, instructions to his staff, May 1970.*[283]

There was much public and political outrage when Nixon announced to the nation he had committed American troops to the incursion of Cambodia. The outcry of criticism angered Nixon. He ordered his staff to step up investigations of peace and anti-war groups and to find links between them and communist or subversive groups overseas. He was especially critical of the negative reaction he received from Congress.

2334 **The criminal left is not a problem to be solved by the department of philosophy or the department of English — it is a problem for the Department of Justice.**—*Spiro T. Agnew, Vice President, from a speech in Fort Lauderdale, Florida, May 1970.*[937]

Agnew spoke out strongly against student unrest on university and college campuses, equating them to spawning grounds for rebellion, revolution, and violence. The criminal left was his description of student, radical, and activists groups that advocated the use of violence to achieve their agendas. The agendas covered the war in Vietnam, poverty, racial inequity, destruction of the "establishment," etc.

2335 **You see these bums ... blowing up the college campuses ... the boys on the college campuses today are the luckiest people in the world — going to the greatest universities — and here they are burning up the books.**—*President Richard Nixon, comments to a group of Pentagon staffers, 3 May 1970.*[691]

Nixon was commenting on campus unrest and the protester's use of violence to protest the war.

2336 **Out there [in Vietnam], we've got kids who are just doing their duty. And I've seen them, and they stand tall and they're proud.**—*President Richard Nixon, comments to a group of Pentagon staffers, 3 May 1970.*[691]

Nixon personally visited with U.S. troops in Saigon and at the 1st Infantry Division base camp, Di An, in August 1969. Nixon contrasted young American troops serving in Vietnam against protesting college students on campus. He labeled such students who turned to violent protest as "bums."

2337 **We're sinking deeper into the morass. The feeling of gloom in the Senate is so thick that you could cut it with a knife. A dull knife.**—*Senator Mike Mansfield of Montana, comments to the press, May 1970.*[937]

These comments followed Nixon's speech, notifying the nation of his decision to send U.S. combat troops into Cambodia to clean out enemy sanctuaries.

2338 **My God, this is for real.**—*Charles Brill, professor, Kent State University, 4 May 1970.*[939]

Realization that National Guard troops, confronted by demonstrating students, were not firing blanks.

2339 **[Over the years the executive branch has been] conducting a constitutionally unauthorized, Presidential war in Indochina.**—*Senate Foreign Relations Committee, in a complaint to President Nixon, 4 May 1970.*[577]

The Nixon White House rejected the Senate's complaint on the grounds that he was acting within his constitutional authority as Commander-in-Chief of the armed forces. He argued that he had neither invaded nor declared war.

2340 **Sending American troops into Cambodia without the consent or knowledge of Congress was usurping the war-making powers of Congress.**—*Senate Foreign Relations Committee, in a complaint to President Nixon, 4 May 1970.*[577]

The Nixon White House rejected the Senate's complaint on the grounds that he was acting within his constitutional authority as Commander-in-Chief of the armed forces.

2341 **You can't fight pigs with bricks.**—*Fred Kirsch, Columbia University student, speaking at an anti-war rally, May 1970.*[939]

Kirsh had been one of many protesters who advocated violence to stop the war, including the overthrow of the Nixon government. The student deaths at Kent State gave him a new perspective on violence. His anti-war rhetoric after Kent State endorsed peaceful demonstrations and nonviolent rebellion.

2342 **We implore you to consider the incalculable dangers of an unprecedented alienation of America's youth and to take immediate action to demonstrate unequivocally your determination to end the war quickly.**—*James M. Hester, President, New York University, in a letter to President Nixon, 5 May 1970.*[578]

Hester drafted the letter that was signed by thirty-seven of America's college presidents. The letter called for Nixon to move quickly to complete the peace in Vietnam. It also requested a meeting with the President. The college presidents were responding to the backlash at hundreds of college campuses, where students took great exception to Nixon's orders to resume the bombing of North Vietnam, and authorized the U.S. incursion into Cambodia.

2343 **We're not bums and we don't like to be called bums. We'd like to show Mr. Nixon that we can work within the system.**—*Ted Gup, student and member of the National Lobby Committee, speaking during an anti-war demonstration, May 1970.*[939]

On 3 May Nixon referred to anti-war demonstrators who used violence to voice their opposition to the war and the government, as "bums."

2344 **They were organized. It was not scattered. They all waited and they all pointed their rifles at the same time. It was like a firing squad.**—*Charles Brill, professor, Kent State University, 4 May 1970.*[939]

Brill's perceptions of the firing by National Guardsmen into the ranks of students during a demonstration on the campus of Kent State University. The resulting Guard fire killed four students and wounded nine.

2345 **This should remind us all once again that when dissent turns to violence it invites tragedy. It is my hope that this tragic and unfortunate incident will strengthen the determination of all the nation's campuses, administrators, faculty and students alike to stand firmly for the right which exists in this country of peaceful dissent and just as strongly against the resort to violence as a means of such expression.**—*President Richard Nixon, in a statement on the Kent State deaths, 4 May 1970.*[575]

Four Kent State students were shot and killed by Ohio National Guardsmen during an anti-war rally on the university campus. The Guardsmen, under attack by rocks and bottles, reportedly believed they were taking sniper fire, and returned fire on the crowd. Further investigation could not validate the Guard's claim of incoming sniper fire.

2346 **The Nixon Administration has the mouth of Buddha and the heart of a serpent.**—*An unidentified spokesman for* *the Hanoi government, comments to the press, Paris, May 1970.*[937]

Hanoi's comment on the Nixon decision to send American troops into Cambodia to clean out NVA/VC sanctuaries.

2347 **If Congress undertakes to restrict me, Congress will have to assume the consequences.**—*President Richard Nixon, a warning to Congress, May 1970.*[283]

Many in Congress were highly critical of Nixon's escalation of the war in the form of the American incursion into Cambodia. In response, the Senate voted to terminate the Tonkin Gulf Resolution and other bills were introduced to further limit the President's war powers to act in Vietnam.

2348 **The floating crap game.**—*Anonymous description of COSVN, 1970.*[937]

COSVN, identified as the Central Office for South Vietnam, was Hanoi's operational headquarters for military and political activity in South Vietnam. One of the reasons for the U.S. incursion into Cambodia in 1970 was to capture COSVN. COSVN continually changed locations. The Americans were looking for a large command structure, when in fact, it consisted of a number of small groups which easily dispersed and regrouped for action at a later time and location.

2349 **And I trust you bums have learned a lesson from all this.**—*Cartoon caption in the British newspaper The Guardian, May 1970.*[939]

The cartoon depicted Nixon standing in front of four white crosses in a cemetery, he is wagging his extended finger saying, "And I trust you bums have learned a lesson from all this." This cartoon bringing into play Nixon's criticism of violent student protest and the killing of four students at Kent State during an anti-war protest.

2350 **It is not the Americans who have brought the war to Cambodia, but the communists. For years, North Vietnam has violated the neutrality of this country—with barely a chirp of protest from the rest of the world.... To condemn the United States for "invading" neutral Cambodia is about as rational as to condemn Britain for "invading" formally neutral Holland in 1944.**—*From the British Magazine The Economist, May 1970.*[185]

Regarding the worldwide hue and cry against the U.S. incursion into Cambodia in May 1970.

2351 **We cannot continue to fight the war in Vietnam without doing serious and irreparable injury to our country.**—*Clark Clifford, former Secretary of Defense, published views, 22 May 1970.*[474]

Clifford was citing the tear in the fabric of American society caused by the war in Vietnam. A tear between those forces that wanted to fight communism in Asia and those that did not want to be a part of that fight.

2352 **What is the value of international agreements which the United States is or intends to be a party to if it so unceremoniously violates its obligations?**—*Aleksei N. Kosygin, Premier, Soviet Union, during a press conference in Moscow, 4 May 1970.*[576]

Kosygin attacked Nixon for the American incursion into Cambodia. Kosygin's attacks raised questions of doubt about the President's ability to keep his word on international agreements. It should be noted that the U.S. was not a signatory to the 1954 Geneva Agreements on Vietnam.

2353 **President Nixon continues to give priority to policy in Indochina and to ignore its consequences at home. His actions are dividing the nation when we need desperately to be united and to devote our energies to our critical domestic problems.**—*Clark Clifford, former Secretary of Defense, published views, 22 May 1970.*[474]

Clifford speaking of national domestic problems (education, poverty, pollution, housing, crime, etc.) suffering because of the efforts to maintain the war in Vietnam due to diversion of funding and focus.

2354 **Is it possible to speak seriously about the desire of the United States President for fruitful negotiations to solve pressing international problems while the United States is grossly flouting the Geneva Agreement of 1954 and 1962 to which it is a party, and undertaking one new act after another undermining the foundations of international security?**—*Aleksei N. Kosygin, Premier, Soviet Union, during a press conference in Moscow, 4 May 1970.*[576]

Kosygin attacked Nixon for the American incursion into Cambodia. Kosygin's attacks raised questions of doubt about the President's ability to keep his word on international agreements. It should be noted that the U.S. was not a signatory to the 1954 Geneva Agreements on Vietnam.

2355 **We can make this system responsive from within instead of trying to destroy it from without.**—*Senator Birch Bayh of Indiana, speaking to a student delegation in Washington, D.C., May 1970.*[939]

Bayh referred to using the constitutional process of the vote to make changes in government policy as opposed to the violent method of change proposed at some anti-war rallies and demonstrations.

2356 **I want to stop the war as much as you do. I have been fighting this war for twenty-four years, risking my life every moment of every day.... All I want to do is enjoy life. So, more than any of you people here, I want peace. Without peace no one can enjoy life. I don't see why you should protest against me. I know what the war is about.**—*Nguyen Cao Ky, Vice President of South Vietnam, during a visit to the U.S., 1970.*[629]

Ky was speaking to a group of peace demonstrators protesting outside his hotel in Williamsburg, Virginia.

2357 **I think we have warned the leaders of North Viet-Nam ... several times, and because we have warned them I do not believe they will move across the DMZ.**—*President Richard Nixon, during a news conference, 8 May 1970.*[886]

A reporter asked Nixon about the American reaction if NVA troops should cross the DMZ to invade South Vietnam.

2358 **If the North Vietnamese ... move a massive force of 250,000 to 300,000 across the DMZ against our Marine Corps people who are there—I would certainly not allow those men to be massacred without using more force, and more effective force, against North Viet-Nam.**—*President Richard Nixon, during a news conference, 8 May 1970.*[886]

A reporter asked Nixon about the American reaction if North Vietnam should cross the DMZ to invade South Vietnam.

2359 **If it works, it's a stroke of genius. If it doesn't, he strikes out.**—*Senator Robert Dole of Kansas, comments to the press, May 1970.*[937]

Dole was referring to the American incursion into Cambodia ordered by President Nixon.

2360 **[There will likely be] racial violence, widespread destruction and even assassination at New Haven.**—*An unidentified federal government official, comments to the press, New Haven, Connecticut, May 1970.*[937]

The official was commenting on the protest rally to be held at Yale University on 1 May 1970. The rally was for anti-war elements to denounce the use of American troops in Cambodia, as announced by Richard Nixon. The expected violence and mayhem did not occur.

2361 **When the action is hot, keep the rhetoric cool.**—*President Richard Nixon, to his staff, May 1970.*[939]

In this case Nixon was referring to the surge of anti-war activism that followed his announcement of U.S. troops entering Cambodia, and the National Guard shooting of students at Kent State.

2362 **I feel the way we Vietnam veterans are being treated is abnormal. I regret having to say this, but now I have nothing but disgust for my country. I used to hate the guys who ran off to Canada to avoid the draft. Now I don't hate them. I don't like them, but I respect them for what they did. If I had known what I know now, I would have never enlisted. I don't mean just my injury, but the insensitivity and lack of care. They would have to drag me into the service kicking. It makes me wonder about Vietnam — about whether the people I saw die, and the people like me who are half dead, fought for nothing.**—*Marke Dumpert, former Marine Lance Corporal, in an interview at Bronx VA Hospital, May 1970.*[473]

Dumpert was wounded in Vietnam, resulting in paralysis from the neck down. VA hospitals were under-staffed and under-funded and unable to support the large number of casualties generated by the war in Vietnam.

2363 **The enemy continues to symbolize the forces of nationalism. The regime which we [America] support is a narrowly based military dictatorship.**—*Clark Clifford, former Secretary of Defense, published views, 22 May 1970.*[474]

Hanoi claimed they were supporting the NLF in its war to remove foreign interference in the internal affairs of Vietnam and that foreign interference was backing a regime in Saigon that was not "of the people." Hanoi's stated design was to unite all of Vietnam under Communist rule from Hanoi.

2364 **Those who protest want peace. I know that what I have done will accomplish the goals they want. I agree with everything they are trying to accomplish.**—*President Richard Nixon, during a televised press conference, May 1970.*[939]

Nixon spoke the day before a nation-wide protest.

2365 **The alternatives in Vietnam are not military victory on the one hand, or defeat and humiliation on the other.**—*Clark Clifford, former Secretary of Defense, published views, 22 May 1970.*[474]

Clifford was responding to President Nixon's assertion that America's only alternatives in Vietnam are military victory through Vietnamization or unilateral withdrawal from Vietnam and the attendant defeat such a move would carry. Clifford sought a re-evaluation of the American commitment to Vietnam in light of the realities of the war and the two prime participants.

2366 **Is dissent a crime? Is this a reason for killing her? Have we come to such a state in this country that a young girl has to be shot because she disagrees deeply with the actions of her Government?**—*Arthur Krause, Father of slain Kent State student, comments to the press, May 1970.*[939]

Allison Krause was one of four Kent University students killed by National Guard fire 4 May 1970, on the university campus.

2367 **The criminal left ... belongs not in a dormitory but in a penitentiary.**—*Spiro T. Agnew, Vice President, from a speech in Fort Lauderdale, Florida, May 1970.*[937]

Agnew spoke out strongly against student unrest on university and college campuses, equating them to spawning grounds for rebellion, revolution, and violence. The criminal left was his description of student, radical, and activists groups that advocated the use of violence to achieve their agendas. The agendas covered the war in Vietnam, poverty, racial inequity, destruction of the "establishment," etc.

2368 **We have to decide whether you and I will liberate this country from the inside or whether it will be liberated from abroad.**—*Michael Tigar, UCLA Law professor, speaking at a Berkeley anti-war rally, May 1970.*[939]

2369 **Four kids are dead — he gave no comfort. Nixon acts as if the kids had it coming.**—*Elaine Miller, mother of student killed at Kent State. Comments from an interview, May 1970.*[472]

Miller's son Jeffrey was one of four students killed on the Kent State University campus when National Guard troops opened fire on an advancing crowd of demonstrators.

2370 **In 1939 I thought Neville Chamberlain was the greatest man living and that Winston Churchill was a madman ... years later I realized that Churchill was right.**—*President Richard Nixon, speaking to a group of anti-war demonstrators, Washington, D.C., May 1970.*[939]

Chamberlain was the British prime minister at the start of World War II who pursued a policy of appeasement in an attempt to maintain peace in Europe with Hitler and Mussolini. Churchill, a member of Parliament, advocated a hard line against Hitler, believing the fascists appetite too great to be appeased.

2371 **A [American] program for orderly disengagement will create the conditions in which productive negotiations become possible. Such a program is the only way to peace, and peace in Southeast Asia is the only victory that we should seek.**—*Clark Clifford, former Secretary of Defense, published views, 22 May 1970.*[474]

Clifford was referring to the Johnson and Nixon administration's quest for a victory in Vietnam.

2372 **When peace comes through appeasement and capitulation — that sellout is intellectual treason.**—*Spiro T. Agnew, Vice President, from a speech in Fort Lauderdale, Florida, May 1970.*[937]

2373 **We did not intervene to conquer North Vietnam ... but to extend a shield to South Vietnam. We did not intervene**

to impose any particular government on South Vietnam. The interest of the South Vietnamese people will be served and our objectives will be achieved by a realistic political settlement.—*Clark Clifford, former Secretary of Defense, published views, 22 May 1970.*[474]

Clifford believed that the "orderly disengagement" of America from Vietnam would make negotiations and settlement possible. He tended to overlook the certainty that once America removed the shield, the North Vietnamese and communism would flood into and devour the South.

2374 **[Once weapons are loaded] you have effectively lost control of that unit. You have given them license to fire.**—*Unidentified Pentagon officer, commenting on the Kent State shooting, May 1970.*[939]

The National Guard units that deployed for riot control were issued live ammunition and given the order to lock and load their weapons prior to the confrontation with student demonstrators on 4 May 1970.

2375 **We're just not being funded in a way that can adequately give and fulfill our services. We can't take care of patients as we would like.**—*Dr. Abraham M. Kleinman, Director, Bronx VA Hospital, in an interview, May 1970.*[473]

VA hospitals were under-staffed and under-funded and unable to support the large number of casualties generated by the war in Vietnam. By 1970 there were more than 1,000 fewer staff in VA hospitals than in 1965.

2376 **What we need is a program that will Vietnamize the peace rather than prolonging the war.**—*Clark Clifford, former Secretary of Defense, published views, 22 May 1970.*[474]

Clifford proposed unilateral withdrawal of U.S. forces from Indochina, leaving North and South Vietnam to negotiate the peace. He proposed all American forces be out of the country by the end of 1971, or sooner.

2377 **The indiscriminate firing of rifles into a crowd of students and the deaths that followed were unnecessary, unwarranted, and inexcusable.**—*An excerpt from the Scranton Commission Report, September 1970, pertaining to the Kent State shooting.*[887]

One of the students killed was actually involved in the demonstration that threatened the Guardsmen. The other three slain students were watching the demonstration or were simply moving through the area at the time.

2378 **It is time now to end our participation in the war. We must begin rapid, orderly, complete and scheduled withdrawal of United States forces from Indochina.**—*Clark Clifford, former Secretary of Defense, published views, 22 May 1970.*[474]

2379 **If I see an ounce of rice after this thing is over I think I'll scream.**—*PFC Robert A. Bear, 3/4 Cavalry, speaking to Army an reporter, May 1970.*[956]

Over several days of operations during the Cambodian incursion, the 3/4 Cavalry confiscated 400 tons of the enemy's rice supply. Bear was one of several men loading the rice onto APCs and helicopters for transport to Tay Ninh.

2380 **Violence is, essentially, a confession of ultimate inarticulateness.**—*Time magazine essay, 18 May 1970.*[938]

2381 **Although they don't shoot you with rice, they can't fight without food.**—*PFC Robert A. Bear, 3/4 Cavalry, speaking to an Army reporter, May 1970.*[956]

2382 **Not only is dialogue destroyed, but so is rationality, when protesters insist upon immediate capitulation to their "nonnegotiable demands." This is what infants demand—and totalitarians.**—*Time magazine essay, 18 May 1970.*[348]

The *Time* essay was discussing the debasement of language through repetitive use of certain phrases and words. Such words that when used sparingly would tend to excite or incite. Yet when used repeatedly in demonstrations and government rhetoric, lose their desired effect.

2383 **We must confront the President and force him to withdraw from Vietnam and leave the people there to determine their own fate.**—*Michael Tigar, UCLA Law professor, speaking at a Berkeley anti-war rally, May 1970.*[939]

2384 **Vietnam, Vietnam.... There are no sure answers.**—*Robert Shaplen, correspondent and author, 1970.*[344]

2385 **The national security of the United States is not involved in Vietnam, nor does our national interest in the area warrant our continued military presence there.**—*Clark Clifford, former Secretary of Defense, published views, 22 May 1970.*[474]

Clifford suggested that the original "Domino Theory" of Asian countries falling to communist control should South Vietnam fall, was not valid. He also raised the point that the countries of the "Domino Theory" (Singapore, Malaysia, Burma, Laos, Cambodia, Philippines, Indonesia, India, and Pakistan) have sent no combat troops to South Vietnam to stem the tide of communism. Only Thailand had sent combat troops, and the Philippines a token force (withdrawn in 1970).

2386 **I'm getting to feel like I'd actually enjoy going out and shooting some of these people. I'm just so goddamned mad. They're trying to destroy everything I've worked for—for myself, my wife and my children.**—*Unidentified man, comments to reporter, May 1970.*[939]

With the outbreak of increased anti-war demonstrations in the wake of the American incursion into Cambodia, many "middle of the road" Americans became impatient with the protest of American youth. This impatience and disgust polarized much of America into those who supported Nixon's policy in Vietnam and those who opposed it.

2387 **To hell with your movement. There are millions of people like me. We're fed up with your movement. You're forcing us into it. We'll have to kill you. All I can see is a lot of kids blowing a chance I never had.**—*Unidentified man confronting a group of student anti-war protesters at Northwestern University, May 1970.*[939]

With the outbreak of increased anti-war demonstrations in the wake of the American incursion into Cambodia, many "middle of the road" Americans became impatient with the protest of American youth.

2388 **I can not remain silent in the face of his [Nixon's] reckless decision to send troops to Cambodia, continuing a course of action which I believe to be dangerous to the welfare of our nation. It is my opinion that President Nixon is taking our**

nation down a road that is leading us more deeply into Vietnam rather than taking us out.—*Clark Clifford, former Secretary of Defense, published views, 22 May 1970.*[474]

Clifford was an adviser to Presidents Truman, Kennedy, and Johnson. He advocated American withdrawal from Vietnam.

2389 **The presidency as a positive force is a concept which has escaped Nixon. His Administration has an aura of negativism.**—*Hugh Sidey, Time magazine's Washington bureau chief, 1970.*[939]

2390 **They have 105 percent discipline. If someone does something wrong they just stand him up and beat the hell out of him.**—*Lt. Col. Donald Hiebert, liaison with the Korean 9th Infantry Division (ROK), November 1970.*[1028]

South Korea deployed combat troops in support of SVN in 1965. The ROK troops had a reputation for severe and effective control of their area of responsibility.

2391 **I consider it a delusion to suggest that the war in Vietnam is part of a worldwide program of Communist aggression.**—*Clark Clifford, former Secretary of Defense, published views, 22 May 1970.*[474]

Clifford was of the school that the war in Vietnam was a local phenomenon and not part of the worldwide communist conspiracy of "wars of liberation." The Soviets and Red Chinese both backed Hanoi in its quest to take over South Vietnam. Both these countries were glad to use North Vietnam as a thorn in the side of their common enemy in the west, the U.S.

2392 **There is about Nixon's presidency the feeling of theater. When the performance is over and the lights go out, there is an eerie nothingness — no heart, no feeling of movement or national momentum.**—*Hugh Sidey, Time magazine's Washington bureau chief, 1970.*[939]

2393 **[Campus troublemakers are] worse than Brown Shirts and Communist vigilantes — they're the worst type of people that we harbor in America.**—*James Rhodes, Governor of Ohio, comments on student unrest at Kent State University, May 1970.*[939]

Rhodes ordered National Guard troops to Kent, Ohio, to quell an outbreak of campus violence at Kent State University. Students set several fires and assaulted police, fireman and Guard troops with rocks.

2394 **I believe.... President Nixon continues to grossly exaggerate Vietnam's importance to our national security.**—*Clark Clifford, former Secretary of Defense, published views, 22 May 1970.*[474]

Clifford did not believe South Vietnam was a vital interest to the United States, and that our troops should be withdrawn.

2395 **The first duty of a revolutionist is not to get caught.**—*Abbie Hoffman, Yippee leader.*[939]

Hoffman was a 1960's American revolutionary. The media boiled his philosophy down to "the advocation of sex, drugs and rock 'n' roll, to counter society." Hoffman was called by some, "the last genuine American radical of the 20th century."

2396 **We should ... decide how to get out of Vietnam on a scheduled and orderly basis no later than the end of 1971. We should at the same time, make known our readiness to negotiate a much earlier withdrawal and we should move now to scale down the level of violence. Only in this way can we achieve the peace that all Americans want, and that American military might can never win.**—*Clark Clifford, former Secretary of Defense, published views, 22 May 1970.*[474]

2397 **Aviation is sometimes dangerous. The challenge lies not in the effort to cheat death, but rather in the effort to expand the envelope of life. It is deeply meaningful and profoundly spiritual for most pilots to fly. It is to some, what life is all about.**—*Lieutenant Daniel McDowell, U.S. Air Force, Weapons System Officer, 1970.*[496]

McDowell flew as an F-4 Phantom WSO with the 433d, 435th, and 497th Tactical Fighter Wings out of Ubon Royal Thai Air Force Base.

2398 **We cannot win a military victory in South Vietnam, and we must, therefore, cease trying to do so.**—*Clark Clifford, former Secretary of Defense, published views, 22 May 1970.*[474]

Due to restrictions placed on the military because of political considerations, victory in South Vietnam was unlikely. The source of support for the VC and NVA in the South was North Vietnam, and the military was not allowed to isolate the source.

2399 **Our problem in Vietnam is due not only to our inability to attain the military goals ... but to the fact that the struggle is basically a political one.**—*Clark Clifford, former Secretary of Defense, published views, 22 May 1970.*[474]

The military goal sought to destroy the enemy on the battlefield and eliminate his ability to continue to make war. The U.S. could kill the enemy within South Vietnam but, was unable to shut down the source of support of the insurgency in the South.

2400 **Any government that chooses to use these actions as a pretext for harming relations with the United States will be doing so on its own responsibility and on its own initiative, and we will draw the appropriate conclusions.**—*President Richard Nixon, in a nationally televised speech, 30 April 1970.*[937]

The speech notified the American public of Nixon's decision to send American troops into Cambodia with the mission of cleaning out enemy sanctuaries. Here, Nixon none too subtly warned communist countries against any retaliatory moves because of the U.S. move into Cambodia.

2401 **Mr. Nixon has the same right as all his predecessors in having a court jester. However, I am surprised at our being unable to laugh at what is obviously a political satire. Taking Nixon's vice president seriously is a sign of how uptight we have become.**—*Professor Roy G. Francis, from his commencement address, Hartford, Wisconsin, 3 June 1970.*[886]

Francis's intellectual condemnation of Vice President Spiro Agnew because of Agnew's hard-line stand against campus violence, dissent, and demonstrations.

2402 **We had to make it clear that our foreign policy was not made by street protests.**—*Henry Kissinger, as related by President Nixon, 1970.*[374]

According to Nixon, Kissinger took a hard line against anti-war protest.

2403 **[Dove attacks on American foreign policy were among] the most comprehensive, meticulously detailed, merciless and**

unremitting ever to be directed at a government of the United States in its conduct of foreign affairs.—*Robert Beisner, political scientist, in an article, June 1970.*[250]

2404 **Some glamorize the criminal misfits of society while our best men die in Asian rice paddies to preserve the freedom which most of those misfits abuse.**—*Vice President Spiro T. Agnew, speaking at West Point, 1970.*[378]

Agnew speaking out against the anti-war protesters and Vietnam Veterans opposing the war.

2405 **Yale, Harvard, and Princeton [Universities], have graduated two — repeat two young men in the whole course of the war, who were drafted and killed in action in Vietnam.**—*Stewart Alsop, correspondent, in a Newsweek article, 29 June 1970.*[1008]

During the same time frame, sixty graduates of Yale, Harvard, and Princeton Universities, volunteered for military service and were killed in Vietnam.

2406 **Nobody out there believes the body count. They couldn't possibly believe it. This is probably the most damning thing the Army has used recently.**—*Unidentified U.S. Army officer, from the results of a military study, 30 June 1970.*[89]

The incidents of inflated body counts grew steadily throughout the war, so much so that troops in the field discounted the high body counts announced by their higher headquarters. These high counts were well received at MACV and Washington as indication of progress in the war against the communists.

2407 **We have bought time for the South Vietnamese to strengthen themselves against the enemy.**—*President Richard Nixon, during a televised speech, 30 June 1970.*[886]

The speech detailed the results of the U.S./SVN incursion into Cambodia

2408 **The country is so polarized that campuses might again explode in a fresh cycle of violence and repression, which would jeopardize the very survival of the nation.**—*Excerpt from findings of a government commission, 1970.*[374]

The commission was appointed by Nixon to study the state of unrest in the nation's colleges and universities. The commission, headed by William Scranton, found the level of agitation extremely high.

2409 **The guerrilla fights the war of the flea, and his military enemy suffers the dog's disadvantages: too much to defend; too small, ubiquitous and agile an enemy to come to grips with.**—*Robert Taber, author, 1970.*[83]

Taber wrote several books on guerrilla warfare and internal revolutions.

2410 **There were 100,000 Vietnamese within 81mm mortar range of the Da Nang airfield. Anything that would instill a friendly attitude toward Marines among the civilian population would clearly help carry out the more conventional mission of the Marines.**—*General J.M. Platt, U.S. Marine Corps, Da Nang, 1970.*[714]

General Platt was noting the importance of winning the support of the civilian population. Maximum range of the Marine 81mm mortar was about 4,500 meters.

2411 **Fact is that every enlargement of U.S. military action has been a specific and measured response to escalation by the enemy.**—*General Lewis Walt, Commander III Marine Amphibious Force, Vietnam, 1970.*[972]

Through much of the war in South Vietnam the initiative was with the enemy. The U.S. launched many operations, but many of the large battles were initiated by the enemy.

2412 **This is in utter confidence & [sic] should not be committed to paper & I would want you not even to say a word of it to Dan [Berrigan] until we get a fuller grasp of it. I say it to you for two reasons. The first obviously is to get your thinking on it, the second to give you some confidence that people are thinking seriously of escalating resistance.**—*Sister Elizabeth McAlister, Catholic nun, in a letter to Father Philip Berrigan, August 1970.*[478]

Sister Elizabeth was briefing Father Philip Berrigan on a plan to kidnap Henry Kissinger and have him publicly answer questions about the administrations role in the Vietnam War. This, in an effort to make the government accountable to the people and listen to the demands of the people that the war be ended. The plan to kidnap Kissinger would have been an effort to escalate the visibility of the anti-war movement.

2413 **To kidnap — in our terminology make a citizens arrest of — someone like Henry Kissinger. Him because of his influence as policy maker yet sans cabinet status, he would therefore not be so much protected as one of the bigger wigs...**—*Sister Elizabeth McAlister, Catholic nun, in a letter to Father Philip Berrigan, August 1970.*[478]

Sister McAlister and five others were indicted for conspiracy in a plot to kidnap Henry Kissinger, January 1971. Their purpose was to make Kissinger publicly answer questions about the war and foreign policy in an effort to make the government accountable for its actions. They believed he was an easy target.

2414 **What we had thought was political progress was just so thin as to be illusory, [and the United States could go on winning battles but it would not make any difference because there was no way in which we could] bring about political progress in South Vietnam.**—*Paul Warnke, former Assistant Secretary of Defense, during an interview, 12 August 1970.*[240]

2415 **[I welcome] this opportunity to proclaim to the entire world the absolute, unequivocal and enthusiastic support and solidarity of black people in the U.S. for our Vietnamese comrades.**—*Eldridge Cleaver, minister of education, Black Panther Party, during a radio broadcast, August 1970.*[997]

Cleaver was just one of several black radicals and activists that made political broadcast for Hanoi over Radio Hanoi or South Vietnam Liberation Radio. The broadcasts were aimed at turning black troops against the war, emphasizing racial problems in the U.S. and the military, and black solidarity with the Vietnamese "struggle" against America in Southeast Asia. Cleaver made two broadcasts for Radio Hanoi in August 1970.

2416 **Somewhere in excess of 50 per cent of all the Viet Cong and North Vietnamese forces in Cambodia have been eliminated.**—*Spiro T. Agnew, Vice President, comments to correspondents, 1 September 1970.*[792]

At the end of the U.S. incursion into Cambodia, MACV

reported about 11,300 enemy KIA and 2,300 captured. Later estimates indicated that the total number of VC/NVA troops in the sanctuary areas along the border, prior to the incursion probably numbered in the 50,000-80,000 range.

2417 **[Vietnamization is a] bloody, hopeless, uncompelled, hence surely immoral prolongation of U.S. involvement in this war.**—*Daniel Ellsberg, Pentagon analyst, in a letter to the Carnegie Endowment for International Peace. September 1970.*[887]

2418 **You can be Black and Navy too.**—*Admiral Elmo R. Zumwalt, Jr., Chief of Naval Operations, 1970.*[998]

Zumwalt attempted to reform some of the Navy's discriminatory practices.

2419 **Vietnamese military science is obviously an invincible military science.... Our military science has defeated the military science of the U.S. imperialists—the craftiest and cruelest enemy of mankind.**—*General Vo Nguyen Giap, Minister of Defense, Democratic Republic of Vietnam, in a speech at a Hanoi military conference, September 1970.*[880]

2420 **Maybe we do have a little more corruption than you because we are not such a well organized society, and also remember we have been at war for twenty-four years. But corruption is only a question of degree. Do you really think you have any right to criticize Vietnamese corruption unless you are sure that you have none in your own country?**—*Nguyen Cao Ky, Prime Minister of South Vietnam, responding to demonstrators in Williamsburg, Virginia, 1970.*[629]

Ky encountered a group of anti-Vietnam protesters while on tour in the U.S. in 1970. Ky was questioned about the corruption in South Vietnam.

2421 **This war in Indochina has proved to be of one piece; it cannot be cured by treating only one of its areas of outbreak.**—*President Richard Nixon, from a televised broadcast, 7 October 1970.*[579]

Nixon called on the VC and North Vietnamese to join him in a cease-fire in-place. He also called for an international conference to put in place a cease-fire covering Laos and Cambodia. Nixon sought to include all of Indochina under a peace plan.

2422 **It's my life and I'd like to try and keep it.**—*PFC Duane Sedler, A Company, 8th Cavalry Regiment, October 1970.*[475]

Sedler refused to go on night ambush when ordered by his company commander. No disciplinary action was taken and the incident was dropped. Breaches in military discipline increased as the war wound down. Such behavior was virtually unheard of before 1969 as such refusals quickly resulted in courts-martial.

2423 **An unconventional war may require an unconventional truce; our side is ready to stand still and cease firing.**—*President Richard Nixon, during a televised broadcast, 7 October 1970.*[579]

2424 **They're all gooks ... not one of them is worth a damn.**—*Unidentified American Army Sergeant, Tay Ninh, October 1970.*[933]

In the early days of the war "Gook" was one of many derogatory names used to refer to the VC and the NVA. Later, it came to be commonly used to refer to any Vietnamese.

2425 **I have my life to preserve, but I have nothing against that little man out there. They're fighting for what they believe in, and you can't knock that.**—*PFC John Munn, A Company, 8th Cavalry Regiment, in an interview October 1970.*[475]

This was the attitude of many of the draftees filling the ranks of the Army after 1969. With the war winding down, no one wanted to be the last to die in Vietnam.

2426 **The object is to spend your year without getting shot at, or if you do, to get the fewest people hurt.**—*Joe Curry, Platoon Sergeant, A Company, 8th Cavalry Regiment, during an interview, October 1970.*[475]

The objective of most American soldiers who found themselves in Vietnam. Units initially deployed to Vietnam contained a high number of career soldiers. As the war drug on the ranks of the units were filled with draftees, many who not only did not want to be in Vietnam but did not want to be in the military.

2427 **I lie on my air mattress at night and I say what am I doing here? I can imagine a war back in the world that I'd fight and wouldn't mind dying in—to keep your people free.**—*PFC John Munn, A Company, 8th Cavalry Regiment, in an interview October 1970.*[475]

2428 **They [Martin Luther King and Stokley Carmichael] live in a free country, and somebody has to pay for it.**—*James H. Scott, U.S. Army, during an interview, 1970.*[1014]

Scott did not agree with the black civil right's movement protest against the Vietnam War.

2429 **The colonel told me every time we had contact, we would report at least two confirmed kills.**—*Captain Brian Utermahlen, Commander, A Company, 8th Cavalry Regiment, in an interview October 1970.*[475]

Higher headquarters continued its preoccupation with high enemy body count.

2430 **Two of them want to kill gooks, and the rest of us never want to see any again.**—*PFC Steve Wright, A Company, 8th Cavalry Regiment, during an interview, October 1970.*[475]

Company A consisted of 118 men at the time, 113 of them were draftees.

2431 **We don't try to frustrate the captain's attempts to kill gooks, but we don't put our hearts in it. If we did we could kill a lot more. Supposedly the mission comes first. I put the welfare of my men first.**—*Joe Curry, Platoon Sergeant, A Company, 8th Cavalry Regiment, during an interview, October 1970.*[475]

This reluctance to perform as ordered led to problems of command and control in some American units.

2432 **Dammit, it's nice to kill gooks.**—*Captain Brian Utermahlen, Commander, A Company, 8th Cavalry Regiment, in an interview October 1970.*[475]

2433 **We could kill a lot more of the enemy than we do, but we'd have to pay for it, and I won't sacrifice anybody. I won't let my companies charge into a bunker area. I'd rather take some criticism.**—*Lt.Col. Jack Galvin, Commander, 8th Cavalry Regiment, during an interview October 1970.*[475]

With the war winding down and troops being withdrawn, there were few instances of headlong attacks. U.S. forces operated primarily in a defense mode, typically conducting large operations only to facilitate that defense.

2434 **Charging up hills has gone right out of style.**—*Captain Brian Utermahlen, Commander, A Company, 8th Cavalry Regiment, in an interview October 1970.*[475]

The U.S. strategy switched to a defensive mode with a large reduction in the number of offensive operations conducted by American forces. Utermahlen was referring to the last major hill charge, which was the battle for Hamburger Hill in May 1969. Securing the hill cost America 442 wounded and killed.

2435 **A can of tear gas is like a first warning...**—*Unidentified soldier of, A Company, 8th Cavalry Regiment, as overheard by a reporter, October 1970.*[475]

Part of a conversation between two unidentified soldiers regarding a NCO fragging technique. If a NCO or other authority was perceived as causing grief a smoke grenade would be thrown into the NCO's quarters. If the NCO persisted in his perceived harassment, the next step could be a tear gas grenade to accent the warning—or a fragmentation grenade to end the dispute. Damages from the fragmentation grenade would remove the man form the area as either a wounded or dead NCO. Incidents of fragging increased sharply as the war wound down.

2436 **[Marijuana] has no place in the field where you rely on quick thought and reflexes.**—*Captain Brian Utermahlen, Commander, A Company, 8th Cavalry Regiment, in an interview October 1970.*[475]

Marijuana was readily available and used extensively by American troops in Vietnam. It was unusual, but not unheard of, for a man to smoke a joint while in the field. Smoking in the field was generally not tolerated by the grunts because it negatively impacted their security.

2437 **What they wear or look like out in the field is very low on my list of priorities. It's one of the compromises I make. As long as a man does his job, I don't care if he wears peace beads or symbols or if he shaves.**—*Captain Brian Utermahlen, Commander, A Company, 8th Cavalry Regiment, in an interview October 1970.*[475]

2438 **I'm still out to kill gooks; that is what I get paid for. The only thing you can do is force men into contact, but with their attitude now, I don't think we can go on like this for long.**—*First Sergeant, A Company, 8th Cavalry Regiment, during an interview October 1970.*[475]

The sergeant was a twenty-five year veteran of the Army, on his second tour in Vietnam. He did not adjust well to the "new army" of draftees, lax military courtesy, and deterioration of standard operating procedures.

2439 **Before everyone was gung ho and wanted to mix it with Charlie. Now it seems everyone's trying to avoid him.**—*First Sergeant, A Company, 8th Cavalry Regiment, during an interview October 1970.*[475]

The sergeant was a twenty-five year veteran of the Army, on his second tour in Vietnam. He did not adjust well to the "new army" of draftees, lax military courtesy, and deterioration of standard operating procedures. U.S. combat forces trained and initially deployed to Vietnam as whole units. In Vietnam the one year tour of duty meant personnel were constantly rotating through the unit, negatively impacting unit cohesion, effectiveness, and morale.

2440 **The strings attached to your aid program so often lead to more and more corruption in Vietnam.**—*Nguyen Cao Ky, Vice President of South Vietnam, speaking to Richard Nixon, at the White House, 1970.*[629]

2441 **If blacks can count for up to twenty-two percent of the dying they should at least have twenty-two percent of the juke box or the music on Armed Forces Radio.**—*Wallace Terry, journalist, from interviews with black soldiers in Vietnam, 1970.*[1014]

Early in the Vietnam War the casualty rate among blacks was 20-24 percent. Many blacks complained about the music available to them in the EM clubs and what they heard on AFVN, Armed Forces Radio Vietnam. It wasn't until after 1970 that the Department of Defense made moves to increase the cultural diversity available to members of the military. The predominant music in the juke boxes and AFVN was country and western, and rock.

2442 **I don't like to kill. I hate the thing they [communist] believe in, but not the people themselves. Our business is killing, but my heart's not in it.**—*PFC Wayne Johnson, A Company, 8th Cavalry, 1st Cavalry Division, in an interview October 1970.*[475]

2443 **[The air strikes will] show North Vietnam they can't use our unarmed planes for target practice.**—*Senator Peter H. Dominick of Colorado, 21 November 1970.*[580]

Dominick was commenting on a series of heavy air strikes against North Vietnamese targets in retaliation for North Vietnamese attacks against unarmed U.S. reconnaissance aircraft conducting missions over North Vietnam and the Ho Chi Minh Trail.

2444 **[I deplore the] renewed reliance on military pressure.**—*Senator Edmund Muskie of Maine, 21 November 1970.*[580]

Muskie was commenting on a series of heavy air strikes against North Vietnamese targets in retaliation for North Vietnamese attacks against unarmed U.S. reconnaissance aircraft conducting missions over North Vietnam and the Ho Chi Minh Trail.

2445 **I have noted erroneous reports from Hanoi that, in connection with our protective reaction strikes, we have bombed prisoner of war camps. Such reports are false...**—*Melvin R. Laird, Secretary of Defense, during a news conference, 23 November 1970.*[693]

During a series of air strikes against North Vietnam, Hanoi claimed the strikes had inflicted casualties on Americans held in a POW camp. The U.S. denied the claim and reminded Hanoi that they were responsible for the safety of any Americans they held in captivity.

2446 **Our policy has taken a new turn, with renewed reliance on military pressure to force a settlement on the other side ... the net effect is likely to be more fighting and killing, not less.**—*Senator Edmund Muskie of Maine, comments of protective reaction strikes, 23 November 1970.*[693]

Senator Edmund Muskie of Maine, commenting on "protective reaction strikes," 23 November 1970. The strikes were in retaliation for North Vietnamese fire directed against unarmed American reconnaissance aircraft. The White House termed the strikes, "protective reactive."

2447 **It would seem that the actual policy is to escalate the war and to seek a military victory.**—*Senator J. William Fulbright of Arkansas, comments to the press, 23 November 1970.*[581]

The Senate Foreign Relations Committee called on the Nixon Administration for an explanation for a series of heavy air strikes against North Vietnam on 21 November. Fulbright viewed the bombings as a new escalation of the war.

2448 **I want to state that we will continue to take protective reaction as necessary to protect the pilots of our unarmed reconnaissance planes.**—*Melvin R. Laird, Secretary of Defense, in a press release, 21 November 1970.*[580]

2449 **It is certainly a very provocative act to mount a physical invasion. It may lead to other things, who knows.**—*Senator J. William Fulbright of Arkansas, comments to the press, 23 November 1970.*[581]

Fulbright was commenting on the unsuccessful Son Tay raid conducted by a combined Army and Air Force group. The raid was carried out in secret and not disclosed until the group returned from the mission. The raid was an attempt to free American POWs held at the North Vietnamese prison camp at Son Tay, 23 miles west of Hanoi. The raiding party found the camp empty of POWs, the POWs having been moved several days before. The raiders killed 200 North Vietnamese in the process and suffered only one minor casualty from enemy fire.

2450 **[These are] limited duration protective reaction air strikes.**—*Melvin R. Laird, Secretary of Defense, during a news conference, 23 November 1970.*[693]

The Nixon Administration's name given to retaliatory air strikes directed against North Vietnam. Enemy missile and antiaircraft gun positions were targeted. The strikes were in retaliation for repeated North Vietnamese attacks on U.S. unarmed reconnaissance flights.

2451 **Vietnamization cannot be completed as far as I'm concerned until these prisoners are freed.**—*Senator Edmund Muskie of Maine, in testimony before the Senate Foreign Relations Committee, 13 December 1970.*[694]

The Secretary of Defense pledged U.S. troops would remain in Vietnam until American POWs held by Hanoi were released.

2452 **There is no black Navy, no white Navy—just one Navy—the United States Navy.**—*Admiral Elmo Zumwalt. Chief of Naval Operations, in Z-gram 66, 17 December 1970.*[500]

Z-gram was the nickname for Naval operations orders issued by Admiral Zumwalt, CNO. Z-gram 66 (Z-66), Equal Opportunity in the Navy, outlined a series of directives designed to eliminate official policies that discriminated against black naval personnel and their families.

2453 **If I had known you were planning this attack [on Son Tay] I would have gone along because I know the area like the back of my hand.**—*Nguyen Cao Ky, Prime Minister of South Vietnam, in conversation with President Richard Nixon, 1970.*[629]

Ky, referring to the U.S. raid on the POW camp near the town of Son Tay in North Vietnam. Ky was born and raised in Son Tay.

2454 **A man who murdered as a civilian is unacceptable to the Army, which trains men to kill. A convicted arsonist cannot be inducted for shipment to Vietnam, where American soldiers burn villages. In short, the citizens whose demonstrated talents indicate the greatest potential are summarily rejected by the military.**—*David Suttler, anti-draft authority, from his book, 1970.*[490]

Suttler counseled draft eligible males on avoiding military service by virtue of the deferment.

2455 **In 1967, it was practically impossible to avoid a battle. In 1970 you had to really search to find someone to fight.**—*Unidentified U.S. Army officer, 1970.*[713]

1971

The tragedy of war is that it uses man's best to do man's worst.
—Harry Emerson Fosdick

2456 **No systematic or serious examination of Vietnam's importance to the United States was ever undertaken within the government.**—*Leslie Gelb, former director of the Pentagon Papers Project, 1971.*[901]

2457 **I want to get out [of Vietnam] but I don't want to give up.**—*Unidentified American housewife, during an interview, 1971.*[326]

2458 **Use the sword as God intended.**—*Reverend Carl McIntire, from Bible Presbyterian Church, New Jersey, speaking during a support march in Washington, D.C., 10 May 1971.*[696]

Call from McIntire during a "win-the-war" rally in Washington, D.C., 10 May 1971. McIntire called on President Nixon to defeat communism and win the war in Vietnam.

2459 **If they can get the tail number out of the wreckage and glue a new chopper onto it, they'll never admit that the aircraft was loss.**—*Unidentified U.S. Air Force general, commenting on Army aircraft losses, 1971.*[913]

Air Force general's comment on the Army's reluctance to write a helicopter off as a loss. The Army was sensitive to complaints that the helicopter was vulnerable to enemy fire in Vietnam and high helicopter loss numbers would have confirmed this view. The Army went to great lengths to retrieve downed aircraft and return them (or the number) to operation.

2460 **The Army is fascist-oriented, but there's still hope for change.**—*Sgt. Fernando Gaxiola, Fort Carson Colorado, during an interview, January 1971.*[476]

2461 **The jungle is the safest place to be. No one knows where you're at, you can hear people coming a mile away, and it's very easy to protect yourself and hide.**—*PFC Thomas Kingsley, infantryman, 1st Cavalry Division, in a letter home, January 1971.*[865]

Private Kingsley died in Vietnam on 20 March 1971.

2462 **When you turn the military into a country club, discipline goes out the window.**—*F. Edward Hebert, Chairman of the House Armed Services Committee, January 1971.*[476]

Reaction to Army plans to liberalize rules and regulations in preparation for the all-volunteer army.

2463 **There's a bitter hatred between us and the South Viet Nam troops because they carry new weapons and we don't; and we do all the goddamn fighting while they sit on their asses all the time.**—*PFC Thomas Kingsley, infantryman, 1st Cavalry Division, in a letter home, January 1971.*[865]

During the rush to Vietnamize the war, large quantities of the new M-203 were issued to ARVN troops. A limited number were issued to American troops in Vietnam. The M-203 was a combination M-16 rifle with a 40mm grenade launcher fitted under the rifle barrel. Private Kingsley died in Vietnam on 20 March 1971 of friendly fire, when a booby trap accidentally detonated.

2464 **I don't mind soldiers' questions if they are honest but most of them simply question everything. There's not much time in combat to answer a private's questions.**—*SFC Ernest*

Sands, Fort Carson Colorado, during an interview, January 1971.[476]

Response by career NCO to the Army's proposed policy of liberalization of rules and regulations.

2465 **Shhh! I am trying to be invisible.**—*Lt. Daniel McDowell, WSO, U.S. Air Force 8th Tactical Fighter Wing, Ubon RTAFB, tour notes, 1 March 1971.*[497]

Comment from the WSO to the pilot (of an F-4), on the WSO's third combat mission where they took heavy ground fire over Route Pak 6. The WSO was responding to the pilot's query, "You are quiet. Is everything OK back there?"

2466 **This is not a retreat. Retreats have cohesion. Lam Son 719 has turned into a rout.**—*Lieutenant Earl Tilford, U.S. Air Force, intelligence briefing officer, March 1971.*[931]

Tilford was briefing the commanding general of the 7th/13th USAF, headquartered at Udorn RTAFB in Thailand on Operation Lam Son 719, the South Vietnamese incursion into Laos to cut the Ho Chi Minh Trail at Tchepone. Approximately 22,000 ARVN went into Laos and were forced out by four divisions of NVA.

2467 **I think when we judge whether this operation [Lam Son 719] is going to be labeled a success or a failure, we cannot judge it before it is concluded, and we cannot judge it even after it is concluded.**—*President Richard Nixon, during an interview, 22 March 1971.*[857]

Operation Lam Son 719 was the South Vietnamese incursion into Laos, intended to cut the Ho Chi Minh Trail at Tchepone. When the operation was over, Hanoi called the operation a failure, and many Americans questioned Vietnamization. South Vietnam's President Thieu called it South Vietnam's biggest victor, and President Nixon labeled the operation a sign of success of the Vietnamization program.

2468 **I have learned through some articles ... that the Vietnamese did not commit enough troops, that Vietnamese say that the United States had not provided enough support and that the redeployment of the Vietnamese troops from Laos is a defeat — disorder, disaster. I believe that this is not true and is completely wrong.**—*Nguyen Van Thieu, President, South Vietnam, during a news conference, 31 March 1971.*[584]

The ARVN committed 22,000 troops to the incursion into Laos, they were eventually countered by 36,000 NVA troops. The operation did not achieve its objective of holding the crossroads town of Tchepone for any significant length of time before the ARVNs were forced to withdraw across the border, back into South Vietnam. ARVN casualties were estimated at 3,800 killed, 5,200 wounded, 775 missing.

2469 **There is a feeling of togetherness in there, everyone is reasonably unhappy.**—*Representative Teno Roncalio of Wyoming, comments to the press, 31 March 1971.*[583]

Roncalio was commenting on the battle in the House Democratic Caucus to pass a resolution calling for a complete pullout of American troops from Vietnam by the end of 1971. Democratic doves did not think the resolution went far enough, and hawks complained the proposed resolution went too far.

2470 **The hamlet looked like a big ashtray.**—*Unidentified American pilot, commenting on the destruction of a South Vietnamese hamlet near Duc Duc, I Corps, April 1971.*[940]

After attacking the South Vietnamese Popular Force compound at Duc Duc, NVA sappers withdrew to a nearby civilian occupied hamlet. When the Popular Force troops pursued the enemy into the hamlet they were ambushed by enemy mortars. Enemy mortars and resulting fire destroyed two-thirds of the hamlet's 600 homes and killed or wounded 250 of its inhabitants.

2471 **Black people have a right to stand up and oppose the absurdity of sending our eighteen and nineteen year olds there to be killed. ... This country shackles black soldiers and sends them to Vietnam to fight and die.**—*Representative Ronald Dellums of California, speaking out against the war in Vietnam, April 1971.*[996]

Dellums, a former Marine, denounced the war in Vietnam and encouraged both black and white youths to resist the military. He was one of the more outspoken members of the Congressional Black Caucus.

2472 **[Operation Lam Son 719 was the] biggest victory ever for the armed forces of South Vietnam.**—*Nguyen Van Thieu, President, South Vietnam, during a news conference, 31 March 1971.*[584]

Thieu praised the South Vietnamese incursion into Laos to cut the Ho Chi Minh Trail and declared it a victory. He claimed the ARVN operation had sufficiently disrupted NVA supply lines, barring them from being able to launch any major offensives in the Northern provinces for the remainder of the year. Western sources disputed the effectiveness of the incursion and the conduct of the ARVN under fire.

2473 **My conscience will not let me vote to continue to conscript young Americans to fight a war which most Americans do not want and a war which the U.S. Government apparently lacks the courage to either win or stop.**—*John J. Flynt, Representative from Georgia, speaking to the House, April 1971.*[940]

Democrat Flynt had previously supported the Administrations policy in Vietnam. He change his position on the war and became an active opponent of that policy.

2474 **[Colorado is] the only place I know of where I can make a speech and hear the words come back exactly as I said them.**—*Spiro T. Agnew, Vice President, comments to Colorado legislators, 6 April 1971.*[695]

Agnew frequently complained to the media that their versions of his speeches seldom matched what he recalled saying. Agnew praised the echo qualities of the Colorado Rocky Mountains.

2475 **They tried to escape over the Mekong Delta.**—*Unidentified U.S. Army helicopter pilot to a MACV officer, repeated by Steve Noetzel as testimony before the Senate Foreign Relations Committee, 6 April 1971.*[376]

Noetzel served with the 5th Special Forces Group Augmentation, 1963-1964. He repeated the story of a group of sixteen VC prisoners en route to Saigon onboard two U.S. helicopters. Also onboard were South Vietnamese intelligence officers. By the time the helicopters arrived in Saigon there were only four prisoners left, the others were officially lost attempting to escape while flying over the Delta.

2476 **The rather abnormal fears and the conditions in a military operation are not subject to Monday-morning quarterback judgement by someone sitting comfortably in an office**

in Washington.—*Vice President Spiro T. Agnew, commenting on the conviction of Lt. William Calley, April 1971.*[940]

Calley was convicted, by military court-martial, of the premeditated murder of Vietnamese civilians at My Lai. His sentence was life at hard labor. All the jurors on the court had seen combat prior to the trial.

2477 **A lot of us spend 300 or 360 days a year in the jungle. We sleep in the rain, we eat out of cans, we stay wet ten or twelve days straight, until our bodies look like wrinkled prunes. The people back in the States think this war is over. It isn't.**—*SP/4 Schulte, C Company, 1st Battalion, 46th Regiment, Americal Division, to correspondents, April 1971.*[940]

Shulte was commenting on the plight of the American infantryman still in the field in Vietnam as the war wound down and the number of American combat troops dwindled.

2478 **The terrible thing we did to so many men in this country — and ultimately to the Vietnamese because of it — we sent them to fight a war without a reason to fight it. I don't know how many of you have experienced standing up in front of bullets, exposing your flesh to shrapnel, hand grenades, and so on. It's a fuck of a thing to do, to send somebody out and tell them to make their body a target, and never give them a fucking reason to do it.**—*Donald Duncan, former Master Sgt., U.S. Army 5th Special Forces, in testimony before the Senate Foreign Relations Committee, 7 April 1971.*[377]

Duncan spent 18 months with the Special Forces in Vietnam.

2479 **After a while, it gets to the point where you have to talk to somebody [about Vietnam] and when I tried to talk to somebody, even my parents, they didn't want to hear it. They didn't want to know. And that made me realize that no matter how painful it was for me I had to tell them. I mean, they had to know. The fact that they didn't want to know, told me they had to know.**—*Larry Rottmann, former Lieutenant, Public Information Officer, 25th Infantry Division, in testimony before the Senate Foreign Relations Committee, 7 April 1971.*[377]

Rottmann served in Vietnam, June 1967 to March 1968.

2480 **Tonight I can report that Vietnamization has succeeded.**—*President Richard Nixon, in a televised speech, 7 April 1971.*[585]

Nixon was referring to Operation Lam Son 719, the South Vietnamese incursion into Laos, an effort to cut the Ho Chi Minh Trail at Tchepone. Thieu claimed the operation a victory, yet the ARVN was routed by NVA counterattack and hastily retreated from Laos. Based on the claimed "victory" Nixon announced the withdrawal of 100,000 U.S. troops, leaving 184,000 American troops in Vietnam. Nixon used the announced, continued, troop reductions as proof that the Vietnamese were nearly ready to assume full responsibility for the war against the VC and the NVA.

2481 **Yesterday you stripped me of all my honor. Please, by your actions that you take here today, don't strip future soldiers of their honor.**—*Lt. William Calley Jr., speaking at his sentencing, April 1971.*[940]

2482 **Any member of this battalion who personally kills a Viet Cong will be presented a Sat Cong Badge for his gallant accomplishment. The Sat Cong Badge will only be given to those individuals who have accomplished the above mentioned feat. There will be no honorary presentations. Furthermore, only personnel who have killed a Viet Cong may wear the Sat Cong Badge. Company commanders will draw Sat Cong Badges from the Executive Officer, and will maintain all control.**—*Franklin Shepard, former SSgt., 5th Battalion, 60th Infantry, in testimony before the Senate Foreign Relations Committee, 7 April 1971.*[377]

Shepard read into the Congressional record from a copy of a Army Disposition Form establishing the battalion award for confirmation of the personal killing of an enemy soldier. Confirmation could be an eye witness account or by the bringing in of a part of the body of the dead enemy (ears were the easiest to transport). The VC/NVA had similar awards for the killing of Americans.

2483 **You did not strip him [Lt. William Calley] of his honor. What he did stripped him of his honor. It can never be honor to kill unarmed men, women and children.**—*Captain Aubrey M. Daniel III, court prosecutor, speaking to the jury during sentencing phase, April 1971.*[940]

The court-martial convicted Calley of the premeditated murder of Vietnamese civilians at My Lai in 1968. He was sentenced to life at hard labor, dismissal from the service and forfeit of all pay and allowances. Calley told the court their conviction of him had stripped him of his honor.

2484 **If I had a farm in Vietnam and a home in hell ... I'd sell my farm and go home.**—*Inscription from the Zippo lighter of an Army infantryman of the Americal Division, 1971.*[1026]

2485 **He [Calley] did not feel as if he were killing humans, but rather that they were animals with whom one could not speak or reason.**—*From the psychiatric review of Lt. William Calley, April 1971.*[940]

2486 **Vietnam is the wound in American life that will not heal...**—*Time magazine, 12 April 1971.*[940]

2487 **The court sentences you ... to be confined at hard labor for the length of your natural life.**—*Colonel Clifford H. Ford, Court-Martial President, reading the verdict against William Calley, 31 March 1971.*[582]

An Army court-martial found Lt. William Calley guilty of the murder of Vietnamese civilians at the village of My Lai (Song My) in 1968. Besides life at hard labor, he was to be dismissed from the Army and suffer the loss of all pay and allowances.

2488 **You can't apply the standards of World War I and World War II to the war in Southeast Asia. If you're going to try to convict an infantry lieutenant and an infantry captain, and you apply the same standards as Nuremberg, then we should take a look at the situation. The guilt will have to go all the way up.**—*Captain Ernest Medina, Commander, C Company, 11th Infantry Brigade, Americal Division, commenting on the conviction of William Calley, April 1971.*[940]

Medina was Calley's commander and reportedly issued orders prior to the start of the operation to kill everyone in the village of My Lai. He was tried and found not guilty of murder and conspiracy.

2489 **There was a crucifixion 2,000 years ago of a man named Jesus Christ. I don't think we need another crucifixion of a man named Rusty Calley.**—*Reverend Michael Lord, during a rally at Fort Benning, Georgia, April 1971.*[940]

The rally was one of several in support of Lt. William (Rusty) Calley, following his conviction of premeditated murder of Vietnamese civilians. He was sentenced to life at hard labor.

2490 **People back home in the world don't understand this war. We were sent here to kill dinks. How can they convict Calley for killing dinks? That's our job.**—*Unidentified soldier of the Americal Division, April 1971.*[940]

Calley was convicted, by a court-martial, of the premeditated murder of Vietnamese civilians at the village of My Lai.

2491 **I want to believe it didn't happen, that it was a hoax. I'll have to live with this verdict the rest of my life.**—*Major Harvey Brown, jury member, commenting on the verdict of Lt. William Calley, April 1971.*[940]

The court-martial convicted Calley of the premeditated murder of Vietnamese civilians at My Lai in 1968. He was sentenced to life at hard labor, dismissal from the service, and forfeit of all pay and allowances.

2492 **To carry out this trial publicly and in time of war does honor to the American nation. One has not yet heard of a trial of Viet Cong who filled the wells and craters of Hue with the corpses of men, women and children.**—*Editorial comment, France's Le Figaro, April 1971.*[940]

Regarding the court-martial and conviction of Lt. William Calley for the murder of Vietnamese civilians. During the VC occupation of Hue during the 1968 TET Offensive several thousand military and government personnel, and civilians were executed by the VC and buried in mass graves.

2493 **The guilt of My Lai runs up the chain of command to the White House.**—*Michael Brower of the Massachusetts Americans for Democratic Action, speaking of the conviction of Lt. William Calley, April 1971.*[940]

2494 **Our boys in Viet Nam have spoiled for me the feeling I've always had that Americans are nicer than other people—the good guys, who are in the right and win wars.**—*Roy McDonald, Atlanta, Georgia businessman, commenting to interviewer, April 1971.*[940]

The comments followed the conviction of Lt. William Calley on charges of murder in the deaths of Vietnamese civilians at the village of My Lai in March 1968.

2495 **We cannot consider ourselves America's best men when we are ashamed of and hated for what we were called on to do in Southeast Asia.**—*John Kerry, former U.S. Navy officer, in testimony before the Senate Foreign Relations Committee, 22 April 1971.*[378]

In a 1970 speech Vice President Agnew referred to the nation's "best men" fighting in Vietnam, compared to those demonstrating and protesting against the war on the streets of America. Kerry explained to the Senators why he took exception to what Agnew had said. Kerry was one of the outspoken leaders of the Vietnam Veterans Against the War.

2496 **It [the F-4 Phantom II] is the world's greatest fuel-to-noise converter ever engineered!**—*Lt. Daniel McDowell, WSO, U.S. Air Force 8th Tactical Fighter Wing, Ubon RTAFB, tour notes, April 1971.*[498]

McDowell was a Weapons System Operator, a back-seater in a F-4 Phantom II.

2497 **Each day to facilitate the process by which the United States washes her hands of Vietnam someone has to give up his life so that the United States doesn't have to admit something that the entire world already knows, so that we can't say that we have made a mistake. Someone has to die so that President Nixon won't be and these are his words, "the first President to lose a war."**—*John Kerry, former U.S. Navy officer, in testimony before the Senate Foreign Relations Committee, 22 April 1971.*[378]

Kerry was one of the outspoken leaders of the Vietnam Veterans Against the War, testifying against the war before the U.S. Senate.

2498 **We watched pride allow the most unimportant battles to be blown into extravaganzas, because we couldn't lose, and we couldn't retreat, and because it didn't matter how many American bodies were lost to prove that point, and so there were Hamburger Hills and Khesahns [*sic*] and Hill 81s and Fire Base 6s, and so many others.**—*John Kerry, former U.S. Navy officer, in testimony before the Senate Foreign Relations Committee, 22 April 1971.*[378]

Kerry was one of the outspoken leaders of the Vietnam Veterans Against the War, testifying against the war before the U.S. Senate.

2499 **[The all-volunteer military] ... it's probably going to come. I give it a better chance than young people do.**—*Curtis Tarr, Selective Service System Director, in an interview, 1971.*[477]

Tarr replaced General Lewis B. Hershey, December 1969. The Selective Service was to be phased out. The Nixon administration proposed a plan whereby the U.S. military force would consist of volunteers, replacing the draft. Even with the wind-down in the Vietnam War the draft system remained in place until December 1972.

2500 **[Lam Son 719]—The operation, conceived in doubt and assailed by skepticism, proceeded in confusion.**—*Henry Kissinger, National Security Adviser, commenting on the ARVN incursion into Laos, 1971.*[374]

Lam Son 719 represented the ARVN's first major force deployment under Vietnamization. The operation called for a thrust 20 miles into Laos to Tchepone, there to cut the Ho Chi Minh Trail. The 22,000-man force entering Laos was all South Vietnamese, accompanied by U.S. advisers only. U.S. combat troops and assets supported the operation, but did not take part in the ground operation. The operation failed its goal of cutting the Ho Chi Minh Trail and showed just how far the South Vietnamese military had not come to being an effective, cohesive combat force.

2501 **[The ARVN invasion of Laos had not ended in] defeat, disorder, disaster, but was in fact the biggest victory ever.**—*President Nguyen Van Thieu, comments to the press, at Dong Ha, April 1971.*[940]

More than 22,000 ARVN troops thrust into Laos to cut the Ho Chi Minh Trail at Tchepone. When they were finally driven out of Laos they had lost nearly 10,000 men in casualties, 54 tanks, 96 artillery pieces, and 298 other vehicles in their retreat. Questionable ARVN estimates of enemy dead were in excess of 13,000 men.

2502 **In 1970 we had about 250,000 true volunteers for the regular or reserve forces. Given the nation's confusion on our aims, you have to say something about the patriotism of young America when that many men step forward without being induced to do so by the draft.**—*Curtis Tarr, Selective Service System Director, in an interview, 1971.*[477]

Because of the U.S. troop withdrawals the chances of going to Vietnam diminished for young people entering the military. So it is not coincidental that enlistment would reach a high level. Had the enlistment levels been high during the active years of the war in Vietnam, the draft would not have been increased to fill the ranks of the military.

2503 **I don't believe we will become involved in any more military operations like Vietnam unless the nation is committed. And there's no question that Congress has become a greater check on the presidency. I think that's the lesson of Vietnam.**—*Curtis Tarr, Selective Service System Director, in an interview, 1971.*[477]

The military draft was phased out in 1972.

2504 **The Phantom was built by the lowest bidder, and in spite of that has proven itself to be a machine of devastating power and amazing capability.**—*Lt. Daniel McDowell, WSO, U.S. Air Force 8th Tactical Fighter Wing, Ubon RTAFB, tour notes, April 1971.*[498]

McDowell was a Weapons System Operator, a back-seater in a F-4 Phantom II.

2505 **I think a lot of people resented going [to Vietnam] because some got deferments. The big offender was the occupational deferment. The next big obstacle, which Congress may remove, is educational deferment. That has persuaded many young people to attend college for the wrong reasons. There's no question but that it worked to the advantage of brighter, wealthier young people.**—*Curtis Tarr, Selective Service System Director, in an interview, 1971.*[477]

Occupational deferments included such fields as law enforcement, Congressional aides, etc. The poor and poorly educated were initially more susceptible to the draft.

2506 **I have reservations about being able to attract a [all-volunteer] force as large as we have now. Some students I talked to in my office asked me what I thought about making men fight who don't believe in the war. I told them I'd rather live with that than with the consequences of our country doing nothing.**—*Curtis Tarr, Selective Service System Director, in an interview, 1971.*[477]

Going to an all-volunteer force was expected to result in a smaller military, which would mean U.S. commitments around the world would have to be carefully chosen.

2507 **It is insane! She writes all this in a letter to Philip Berrigan in prison and says, "Don't commit this to paper!"**—*Eqbal Ahmad, fellow at the Adlai Stevenson Institute of International Affairs, and peace activist, 1971.*[478]

Sister Elizabeth McAlister had written a letter to Philip Berrigan while he was in prison in which she eluded to a plan to kidnap Henry Kissinger. At a meeting on 16 August 1970, Ahmad, Sister Elizabeth, and four others met and discussed this plan. The group of six was later charged with conspiracy.

2508 **When a fellow says we can junk it all out [our military] and be better off, I say he's not being intellectually honest.**—*Curtis Tarr, Selective Service System Director, in an interview, 1971.*[477]

Some anti-war activists wanted to do away with the military and armaments completely. A country without a means of defending itself or its interest in the world is likely not to be an independent country for long.

2509 **The Army is the most racist pig organization you ever seen.... It's set up by dudes for dudes. Nothing for the brothers except trouble.**—*Unidentified U.S. Army GI, comments to the Pittsburgh Courier, 8 May 1971.*[980]

2510 **The Route 9–Southern Laos Victory ... the heaviest defeat ever for Nixon and Company.**—*Radio Hanoi, broadcast, 1971.*[913]

South Vietnam's President Thieu claimed the incursion (Operation Lam Son 719) into southern Laos to be South Vietnam's biggest victory ever. Nixon claimed the operation demonstrated the success of the Vietnamization program. Hanoi described the ARVN incursion as a total, expensive, failure. The ARVN were forced out of Laos by the NVA, in more rout than retreat, suffering nearly 50 percent casualties of the 22,000-man force committed to the operation.

2511 **Reverse your policy to give the world the leadership it needs in confronting and defeating communism.**—*Reverend Carl McIntire, from Bible Presbyterian Church, New Jersey, speaking during a support march in Washington, D.C., 10 May 1971.*[696]

This call was from McIntire during a "win-the-war" rally in Washington, D.C., 10 May 1971. McIntire called on President Nixon to defeat communism and win the war in Vietnam.

2512 **I want out of Vietnam, but I want out of Vietnam with a victory that will mean our boys have not died in vain.**—*Governor George Wallace of Alabama, during a telephone address, 10 May 1971.*[696]

Wallace, in Dallas, Texas, addressed a "win-the-war" rally in Washington, D.C., via telephone.

2513 **[A Cheeseburger] kills everything for a hundred yards, even the worms in the ground.**—*Air crewman, speaking of the Commando Vault, May 1971.*[482]

The Commando Vault was a 15,000 pound bomb used to make an instant LZ in a patch of dense jungle. The bomb, nicknamed Cheeseburger, was dropped from a C-130 and on impact cleared a circular area about 100 yards across. Almost all standing vegetation in the impact zone disappeared.

2514 **[I can] almost taste peace.**—*Henry Kissinger, National Security Adviser, comments to friends, June 1971.*[297]

After nearly two years of stalemate in the peace talks, Hanoi made a counter offer to Nixon's latest peace proposal. Their offer was unacceptable, but it was less rigid than previous offers, and Kissinger believed he and Hanoi's chief negotiator were reaching a point where a deal could be made.

2515 **While everyone has a right to protest peacefully, policy in this country is not made by protests.**—*President Richard Nixon, comments to the press, June 1971.*[374]

2516 **The dilemma of the U.S. involvement dating from the Kennedy era, was to use only limited means to achieve excessive ends.**—*From the Pentagon Papers, as quoted by Hedrick Smith in the New York Times, 1 July 1971.*[586]

John F. Kennedy opposed the introduction of U.S. combat troops to stabilize the military situation in Vietnam, but he did increase the number of advisers and military aid given to the Diem regime.

2517 **Our complicity in his overthrow [Diem] heightened our responsibilities and our commitment in Vietnam.**—*From the Pentagon Papers, as quoted by Hedrick Smith in the New York Times, 1 July 1971.*[586]

Secret information about U.S. policy in Vietnam was released with the leak of the Pentagon Papers in 1971.

2518 **The army's the most prejudiced place I've ever been in.**—*SP/4 William Gary, U.S. Army, during an interview, July 1971.*[860]

With the rise of black awareness, many young blacks did not accept the bigotry and double standards some of them experienced within the military. As the war dragged on black frustrations with the military system became more evident.

2519 **If you pulled all the blacks out of Vietnam, you'd have the biggest revolution you've ever seen in the United States ... when Nixon pulls us out there won't be no more United States. The blacks know demolition. The blacks know how to shoot. We're gonna use all that stuff "back in the world."**—*Unidentified black soldier, during an interview in Soul Alley, July 1971.*[860]

Many young blacks in the U.S. advocated armed revolution to change the way white America treated blacks. Many blacks looked upon their military experiences as training for "the revolution" some black militants called for.

2520 **I want to know who is behind this and I want the most complete investigation that can be conducted.... I don't want excuses. I want results. I want it done, whatever the costs.**—*President Richard Nixon, commands to his staff, 1971.*[374]

The Department of Defense study of the Vietnam War, called the Pentagon Papers, was leaked to *The New York Times* by Daniel Ellsberg. Nixon tried unsuccessfully to stop publication of the papers that disclosed the various failures of Government policy in the 1950s and 1960s.

2521 **Anyone who opposes us, we'll destroy. As a matter of fact, anyone who doesn't support us, we'll destroy.**—*Egil Krogh, White House assistant, 1971.*[374]

Krogh was reflecting the Nixon Administration's entrenchment against its enemies. The White House was under fire for the delay of the peace in Vietnam and the revelations brought about by the release of the previously secret Pentagon Papers. There were the ongoing private overtures to the Soviet Union and Red China, as well as the secret negotiations between Kissinger and Le Duc Tho in Paris, all of which needed to remain secret events until successful.

2522 **Far from giving security, there is every reason to suppose that the army, buttressed by the Civil Guard ... is regarded by the Southern peasant as a symbol of insecurity and repression.**—*Except from the Pentagon Papers, 1971.*[36]

The repressive nature of the ARVN alienated a large segment of the South Vietnamese population. Attempts by the Diem regime to wipe out the communist let to excesses in the countryside, eventually leading to more support from the peasantry for the communist. This information about Diem was derived from the Pentagon Papers. The secret Papers were leaked to the press by Daniel Ellsberg.

2523 **War is a profanity. It really is. It's terrifying. Nobody is more antiwar than an intelligent person who's been to war. Probably the most antiwar people I know are Army officers — but if we do have a war, I think it's going to be similar in nature to Vietnam and Korea. Limited in scope. And when they get ready to send me again, I'm going to have to stop and ask myself, "Is it worth it?" That's a very dangerous place for the nation to be when your own army is going to stop and question.**—*Lt.Col. Norman Schwarzkopf, U.S. Army battalion commander, during an interview, October 1971.*[854]

Schwarzkopf completed two tours of duty in Vietnam. He later went to war against Iraq in 1990.

2524 **The Americans are business men. They'll sell you out if you can no longer assure them a profit.**—*Hoang Duc Nha, aide and confidant to Nguyen Van Thieu, comments, 1971.*[374]

Hoang Duc Nha was a cousin of Thieu. He recently returned from obtaining an education in America.

2525 **I hate what Vietnam has done to our country! I hate what Vietnam has done to our Army!**—*Lt.Col. Norman Schwarzkopf, U.S. Army battalion commander, during an interview, October 1971.*[854]

Schwarzkopf completed two tours of duty in Vietnam.

2526 **We are ready to fight [the United States] for a century.**—*Hong Chuong, North Vietnamese newspaper editor, 1971.*[182]

2527 **We had all the assets to win this war. We had half a million troops, unlimited amounts of money and the backing of the administration. No doubt we could have won if we'd had commanders who knew how to use these assets, instead of these amateurs, these ticket punchers, who run in for six months, a year, and don't even know what the hell it's all about.**—*Colonel David Hackworth, former U.S. Army combat command officer, 1971.*[93]

In the sixties and seventies in the U.S. military, attaining higher levels of rank were dependent on an officer's accomplishments; completion of certain courses, combat command, staff work, etc. In order to accommodate the many officers in the Army it was determined that field officers would be assigned combat command for only six months, this allowed many officers to obtain the requisite command time for career advancement. This was referred to as ticket punching. It had a detrimental affect in the field since by the time an officer started to become proficient in Vietnam, his six months in the field were nearly up.

2528 **The ultimate aim [of American foreign policy in Vietnam] was neither power nor profit ... [nor] ... particular tangible interests, [but rather] image making.**—*Hannah Arendt, foreign affairs commentator, November 1971.*[902]

2529 **If we are winning while the enemy is being defeated, why have we encountered increasing difficulties.... Last year we could attack United States forces. This year we find it difficult to attack even puppet forces.... We failed to win the support of the people and keep them from moving back to enemy controlled areas.... At present, the enemy is weakened while we are exhausted.**—*Excerpt from a captured enemy document, 1971.*[713]

The document was a privately kept journal of a VC colonel. He indicates the trouble his units were having due to the successes of the U.S./GVN pacification program. The VC were successful as long as they had the support of the people, regardless of whether that support was voluntary or coerced. If they did not have access to the people they lost a major source of food, supplies, labor, taxes, and intelligence.

2530 **Many of the older pilots didn't like having another pure pilot in the back seat acting like a WSO (navigator). But when they finally got pure navs in the back seat, these same guys thought a pure nav was worthless ... until he had a MiG at his six and needed the extra pair of eyes to keep track of the bad guy while he (the pilot) got us the hell out of that fix.**—*Lt. Daniel McDowell, WSO, U.S. Air Force 8th Tactical Fighter Wing, Ubon RTAFB, tour notes, 21 November 1971.*[499]

McDowell was a Weapons System Operator, a back-seater in a F-4 Phantom II. A "pure nav" was a navigator who was not a qualified pilot.

2531 **It was ritualistic anti-communism and exaggerated power politics that got us into Vietnam.**—*Leslie Gelb, former director of the Pentagon Papers Project, 1971.*[904]

American administrations did not see Vietnam as strategically or vitally important to the security of the United States. Vietnam became important in the context of stopping the spread of communism in Southeast Asia. A communist Southeast Asia was seen to threaten Japan and Australia, and by extension America.

2532 **Jingle bells, mortar shells, VC in the grass.... Take your Merry Christmas cheer and shove it up your ass.**—*Anonymous, from a posted Christmas song, 1971.*[856]

From the chorus of a Christmas song, sung to the tune of "Jungle Bells." Posted in the style of a routine military bulletin board notice.

1972

Never interrupt your enemy when he is making a mistake.
—Napoleon Bonapart

2533 **If the enemy's answer to our peace offer is to step up their military attacks, I shall fully meet my responsibility as Commander-in-Chief of our Armed Forces to protect our remaining troops.**—*President Richard Nixon, during a nationwide address, January 1972.*[176]

At the end of 1971 the North Vietnamese broke off peace negotiations. Shortly thereafter they launched their 1972 Easter Offensive in the hopes of crushing South Vietnam's military before America could react. At the start of the offensive there were less than 7,000 U.S. combat troops on the ground in South Vietnam.

2534 **The solution in Vietnam is more bombs, more shells, more napalm ... till the other side cracks and gives up.**—*General William DePuy, Deputy ComUSMACV, 1972.*[262]

The U.S. used technology and firepower to counter enemy manpower.

2535 **[Vietnam is] a political jungle of warlords, sects, bandits, partisan troops and secret societies.**—*Frances Fitzgerald, description of the political climate of South Vietnam, 1972.*[275]

2536 **I always said we didn't have any business in that goddamned war anyhow. I wouldn't want to fight in a war without front lines.**—*Berwell "Stub" Duffey, in an interview, January 1972.*[480]

Berwell Duffey's son, Jerry, was the only American soldier killed in action during the last week in 1971. He was killed in a sapper attack on his outpost outside of Qui Nhon. The last week in December, 1971 had the lowest American death toll in Vietnam since early 1965.

2537 **If we're going to fight the war, let's fight. If not, let's go.**—*SP/4 Gordon Hass, U.S. Army, in an interview, January 1972.*[480]

Hass survived a VC sapper attack on his outpost 12 December 1971. Only one American was killed during the attack, Jerry Duffey. He was the only American reported killed in action for the last week of 1971.

2538 **In its very conception the [strategic hamlet] program was a study in misplaced analogy.**—*Frances Fitzgerald, historian, 1972.*[275]

The peasants were devoted to their land, it was the burial place of their ancestor and source of their existence. Relocation under the program deprived them of both.

2539 **In the final analysis we cannot expect the enemy to negotiate seriously with us until he is convinced nothing can be gained by continuing the war. This will require an all-out effort on our part during the coming dry season.**—*President Richard Nixon, during a NSC meeting, 2 February 1972.*[134]

Nixon saw the possibility of an enemy offensive in 1972. In preparation, he order a series of heavy strikes against enemy staging areas south of the 20th Parallel. He also gradually increased the number of air units in Southeast Asia in preparation for any enemy moves.

2540 **We will always have a remaining presence in Vietnam until the POW problem has been resolved.**—*Melvin R. Laird, Secretary of Defense, during a news conference, 15 January 1972.*[697]

He emphasized there would be a continued U.S. troop

commitment in Vietnam as long as Hanoi held American POWs, and that commitment would have the benefit of U.S. air support.

2541 **Good intentions and physical power are not enough.**—*Hans Morgenthau, Political scientist, comments to correspondent, February 1972.*[949]

Morgenthau was commenting on American policy towards Vietnam and the tools that were used in the U.S. attempts to conduct that policy.

2542 **The South Vietnamese lines may bend, [but] not break. If this proves to be the case, it will be the final proof that Vietnamization has succeeded.**—*President Richard Nixon, during a press conference, March 1972.*[944]

Nixon was referring to the invasion of South Vietnam, across the DMZ, by several NVA divisions supported by armor. The ARVN defensive line that faced the DMZ was rolled back, but did not break completely before the NVA advance slowed and turned.

2543 **The favorite time for blacks to [dap] was in line in the mess hall, and sometimes they would go into a five or ten minute dapping period, and the whites would not be real thrilled about waiting in line while a couple of the bro's went through their dapping procedures.**—*Captain Vernon Conner, U.S. Army, during an interview. 1972.*[1002]

The dap was an expressive handshake used by blacks in greeting each other. The series of taps, touches, finger grips and bumps, could last a few seconds or go on for several minutes. Many whites objected to the greeting, some officers viewed it as disrespectful, even though the greeting was only carried out between mutually agreeable dappers, and was not forced on anyone. The traditional military salute was given to officers, per military regulation.

2544 **The bombing proposals sent to me by the Pentagon could at best be described as mild.**—*President Richard Nixon, from his diary, April 1972.*[921]

Nixon, on the Linebacker I campaign planned to counter the North Vietnamese invasion of South Vietnam.

2545 **He has everything to lose except the honorable exit we are determined to enable him to make.**—*Pham Van Dong, Prime Minister, Democratic Republic of Vietnam, in a public statement, 1972.*[374]

One of the goals of the North Vietnamese Easter Offensive in 1972 was to show President Nixon the failure of his policy of Vietnamization. To show him the South Vietnamese military could not stop the North Vietnamese military. Dong believed once they had demonstrated this to Nixon he would see that his only way out of Vietnam was to concede to the North Vietnamese terms for peace.

2546 **The U.S. will not have a credible policy if we fail [in Vietnam], and I will have to assume responsibility for that development.**—*President Richard Nixon, diary entry, April 1972.*[162]

2547 **I want you to get down there [to Vietnam] and use whatever air you need to turn this thing around.**—*President Richard Nixon, to General John Vogt, Commander, U.S. 7th Air Force, 6 April 1972.*[913]

Operation Linebacker I was launched to counter the North Vietnamese invasion of South Vietnam. More than 550 U.S. Air Force combat aircraft were available to strike the invasion forces and North Vietnam.

2548 **Friendly troops may bug out at anytime. Request guidance. If friendlies bug out before guidance arrives, [I] will bug out with them.**—*Major Gary Hacker, U.S. Army adviser, in a radio message to his headquarters in Qui Nhon, April 1972.*[887]

Hacker was an acting adviser with the 40th ARVN Infantry Regiment during the communist Easter Offensive in 1972. The regiment was being pushed back by NVA troops near Hoi An.

2549 **I don't feel like I'm part of this war. I never see what we're shooting at, or whether it does any good.**—*Unidentified U.S. Navy gun crewman, aboard the USS Buchanan, to a correspondent, April 1972.*[943]

The *USS Buchanan* provided naval gunfire support, striking enemy targets around the DMZ. The Buchanan supported ARVN units defending against the North Vietnamese invasion of South Vietnam, during which three NVA divisions supported by 200 armored vehicles crossed the DMZ to attack South Vietnam.

2550 **You had the feeling you were really doing something significant.**—*Captain Donald E. Waddel, U.S. Air Force F-4 pilot, during an interview, April 1972.*[942]

Waddel was commenting on the wealth of targets available during the North Vietnamese invasion of South Vietnam. Three NVA divisions supported by 200 armored vehicles attack South Vietnam, crossing the DMZ. The area north and south of the DMZ became a target-rich environment for VNAF and U.S. aircraft.

2551 **Those who suggest that we can solve our public spending problem by peeling some easy billions off the defense budget are arguing not only with the Pentagon but with reality, and reality is a formidable opponent.**—*Defense Department report, 1972.*[699]

Defense was responding to Senator George McGovern's proposal to cut $30 billion from the $80+ billion annual Defense Department budget. McGovern, running as the Democratic candidate for president, campaigned that he would end U.S. involvement in Vietnam and drastically cut the defense budget, curtailing such entanglements in the future.

2552 **The real problem is that the enemy is willing to sacrifice in order to win, while the South Vietnamese simply aren't willing to pay that much of a price in order to avoid losing.**—*President Richard Nixon, writing in his personal diary, April 1972.*[374]

At the time, North Vietnam was in the process of pursuing its invasion of South Vietnam. In the early weeks of the communists offensive, ARVN units steadily lost ground. There were exceptions where ARVN units held firm against the enemy push, but withdrawal and retreat was the norm for ARVN units in the Central Highlands and in the northern provinces.

2553 **Claiming the nation is on a war footing when defense [spending] takes up only 4 per cent of the economy is "torturing the English language."**—*Defense Department report, 1972.*[699]

Defense was responding to Senator George McGovern's

proposal to cut $30 billion from the $80+ billion, annual Defense Department budget. McGovern, running as the Democratic candidate for president, campaigned that the $30 billion cut in Defense would move America from a war footing to a peace base. The Department of Defense pointed out the current U.S. economy was not on a war footing, there were no price controls, or special taxes levied to support the war in Vietnam.

2554 **The United States has embarked again on the old track of war escalation.**—*Chou En-lai, Premier, Communist China, in a public statement, 16 April 1972.*[587]

China and the Soviet Union complained of a renewed U.S. bombing campaign against North Vietnam. Heavy strikes hit targets in North Vietnam in response to the North Vietnamese Army invasion of South Vietnam.

2555 **We kept waiting for the northern end of the island to sink.**—*Unidentified U.S. 8th Air Force officer, April 1972.*[182]

The officer was commenting on the build up of B-52s at Andersen Air Force Base on Guam. In response to the enemy Easter Offensive, the normal allotment of approximately thirty B-52s at Guam was increased to more than 150. Such a large gathering of the big planes had never before cluttered the taxiways and parking lanes at the base.

2556 **We have been through so many springtimes of slaughter and folly and deception.... Now in the spring of 1972, it is happening again.**—*Senator Walter Mondale of Minnesota, speaking on the Senate floor, April 1972.*[945]

Mondale was referring to the March 1972 North Vietnamese invasion of South Vietnam. North Vietnam sent three divisions supported by armor across the DMZ into South Vietnam, rolling back many of the ARVN units in defensive positions along the DMZ. The U.S. responded with air strikes and naval gunfire in support of the ARVN.

2557 **It was like nothing we ever expected and nothing we ever saw [before].**—*SP/4 Michael Hill, U.S. Army, I Corps, during an interview, April 1972.*[944]

Hill was describing the North Vietnamese invasion of South Vietnam in April 1972. Three NVA infantry divisions supported by 200 armored vehicles cross the DMZ from North Vietnam, sweeping into I Corps.

2558 **There hasn't been anyone in the Viet Nam War who fought better.**—*Unidentified American adviser, to correspondent, Dong Ha, April 1972.*[944]

The adviser was referring to the ARVN 20th Armor Squadron, which was supported by two companies of South Vietnamese Marines. The ARVN units met a large NVA tank column on Highway 1, just north of the Cua Viet bridge. The ARVN stopped the progress of the enemy tanks, allowing the bridge to be destroyed. Destruction of the bridge ended the NVA drive south. The NVA attack was part of the North Vietnamese invasion of South Vietnam which saw three NVA divisions and 200 armored vehicles cross the DMZ.

2559 **If the war ended tomorrow, there would still be twenty years of surgery to do.**—*Thomas Miller, founder, Children's Medical Relief International, during a press interview, April 1972.*[941]

The CMRI was an international, private relief organization, which provided specialized medical services to wounded, maimed, and disfigured children in South Vietnam. The medical unit provided a wide variety of medical services including reconstructive surgery. In 1972 the hospital unit was conducting more than 150 operations a month. There were thousands of Vietnamese children, victims of the war, accidents, and birth defects that could have benefited from the CMRI services.

2560 **You could tell the old man [President Nixon] had made up his mind he won't be screwed.**—*Unidentified Nixon White House aide, commenting to a reporter, April 1972.*[945]

The aide was commenting on the deliberations Nixon made over which course of action to pursue in the wake of North Vietnam's invasion of South Vietnam. North Vietnam launched the invasion 31 March 1972, eventually committing more than 100,000 men and two armor regiments. In response to the invasion, Nixon ordered an intensive bombing campaign against North Vietnam's lines of communication, storage and fuel facilities.

2561 **We do not, in any way, want to impose a Communist regime in South Viet Nam.**—*Le Duc Tho, Chief North Vietnamese negotiator, to reporters on his arrival in Paris, April 1972.*[946]

2562 **[The South Vietnamese can contain the North Vietnamese invasion] if we continue to provide air and sea support.**—*General Creighton W. Abrams, ComUSMACV, 26 April 1972.*[588]

On 30 March 1972, 20,000 North Vietnam and 200 tanks invaded South Vietnam across the DMZ. The U.S. force in South Vietnam at the time consisted of 6,000 combat troops and 64-74,000 support troops. The full brunt of the North Vietnam invasion was borne by the ARVN. In support of the Vietnamese were round the clock air strikes and gun support from U.S. Navy ships in the Gulf of Tonkin and the South China Sea.

2563 **We are trying to compress the amount of time the North Vietnamese have to decide on whether the offensive is worth continuing and whether they have the means to continue it.**—*Unidentified Nixon administration official, speaking to the press, April 1972.*[945]

These comments regarding Nixon's decision to run an intensive bombing campaign against North Vietnamese supply and fuel facilities, and lines of communication between North Vietnam and Red China. The campaign was an effort to cut off supplies North Vietnam was using to support the invasion of South Vietnam.

2564 **We're not going to make any announcement about what we're not going to do. We think there has been altogether too much of that in this war.**—*William P. Rogers, Secretary of State, Congressional testimony, April 1972.*[945]

Rogers was referring to U.S. reaction to the North Vietnamese invasion of South Vietnam.

2565 **The only thing we have refused to do is to end the war by imposing a Communist government on South Vietnam.**—*Henry Kissinger, National Security Adviser, comments to reporters, May 1972.*[946]

2566 **[I don't really have anything against the North Vietnamese]. I just like to fly in combat situations.**—*Major Douglas Stockton, U.S. Air Force A-37 Pilot, speaking to a correspondent, April 1972.*[945]

Stockton flew missions against the North Vietnamese invasion force. He was based out of Bien Hoa.

2567 **You cannot refuel T-54 tanks with gasoline out of water bottles carried on bicycles.**—*Sir Robert Thompson, British authority on counterinsurgency, 1972.*[167]

When North Vietnam invaded South Vietnam in March 1972, they moved from guerrilla warfare to conventional warfare. They used massed infantry and armor in the invasion. Because of the use of armor large quantities of fuel and oil were required to keep the force moving. Replenishment of fuel and oil had to be done conventionally. The old tactics of supply by bicycle and truck were not sufficient. The new supply problems meant more NVA units were exposed to strikes by American aircraft.

2568 **The 40th Regiment has 25 per cent of its strength — 30 per cent were casualties and 40 per cent or so deserted. We lost Hoi An after that because the local militia troops were demoralized. They thought the regular army had let them down.**—*Unidentified South Vietnamese official, speaking to a correspondent, Qui Nhon, 1 May 1972.*[589]

North Vietnam invaded South Vietnam across the DMZ and pushed south. The ARVN regiment defending the area broke and was unable to stop the North Vietnamese Army. Many American observers considered the North Vietnamese invasion a test of Vietnamization, a test many ARVN units failed.

2569 **[South Vietnamese] Government troops of the Third Infantry Division ran from the fighting in one of the biggest retreats of the war. No one tried to stop them: their officers were running too.**—*Sydney H. Schanberg, correspondent, Hue, 2 May 1972.*[590]

On 30 March 1972, North Vietnam launched a major invasion of South Vietnam. 20,000 NVA troops supported by 200 tanks crossed the DMZ into South Vietnam while other NVA units attacked the Central Highlands. The invasion was seen as the first real test of Vietnamization.

2570 **Airpower can keep you from losing ground, but it can't get any back for you.**—*Anonymous.*[946]

U.S. and ARVN forces relied heavily on air support. American commanders favored the use of bombs and artillery shells in encounters with the enemy. ARVN troops were trained in U.S. combat techniques, thus, they too relied on air support.

2571 **Anyone still living in there is in such a state of shock that he couldn't pull a trigger for thirty minutes.**—*John Paul Vann, Director Second Regional Assistance Command, comments to reporters, May 1972.*[887]

At the time Vann, was hovering over a recently bombed area outside of Kontum, II Corps. The area had been bombed by a flight of B-52s and there were a few dazed NVA survivors in the area of the strike. The reporters accompanying Vann were worried about enemy fire.

2572 **We are trying desperately to dampen the panic, trying to get the local government to form an emergency committee to keep essential services going.... I've got my fingers in the dike, but I've got more holes than dike.**—*Unidentified American adviser, comments to correspondent, 3 May 1972.*[590]

As the North Vietnamese invasion force pushed south from the DMZ, the entire northern province of Quang Tri fell to the communist. Hue was the most northern city in South Vietnam still in South Vietnamese control. It was filled with civilian refugees as well as ARVN deserters and retreating troops.

2573 **Anytime the wind is blowing from the north where the B-52 strikes are turning the terrain into moonscape, you can tell from the battlefield stench that the strikes are effective.**—*John Paul Vann, Director Second Regional Assistance Command, comments to correspondent, May 1972.*[887]

During the North Vietnamese invasion of South Vietnam in 1972, the communists made a concerted effort to take over the Central Highlands by making a major drive on Kontum. Vann directed more than 300 B-52 tactical air strikes against enemy positions around Kontum. The strikes fell into enemy occupied positions where thousands of NVA were killed.

2574 **[ARVN deserters]—they ought to shoot them.**—*Unidentified American adviser, comments to correspondent, 3 May 1972.*[590]

ARVN troops deserted in large numbers as the North Vietnamese invasion force moved south from the DMZ, during the 1972 Easter Offensive.

2575 **If the U.S. had been running this operation, the whole province would have been secured a week ago.**—*Unidentified American adviser, commenting to a correspondent, April 1972.*[945]

The advisers complaint centered on the lack of progress by the 21st ARVN division to relieve the besieged town of An Loc in Binh Long Province. The ARVN commander, even with armor support, refused to press the relief force toward An Loc until the end of May. The siege began 13 April 1972. An Loc itself was nearly destroyed as over 78,000 NVA rockets and artillery, as well as bombs from U.S./South Vietnamese Air Force aircraft attacked NVA position within the city.

2576 **As Vietnamese we foresee the worst. We are ready to cope with any situation. Last year there was the biggest flooding [in] 55 years in North Vietnam — and we overcame it.**—*Unidentified North Vietnamese official, during comments to the press, Paris, France, 4 May 1972.*[591]

The U.S. broke off peace talks with North Vietnam in Paris, citing lack of any progress during the North Vietnamese Army's invasion of South Vietnam. Many Vietnamese believed the suspension of the talks signaled an increase in U.S. bombing of North Vietnam. Some, mistakenly, suspected the Red River dike system would be an American target. Destruction of the Red River Valley dikes would have caused widespread flooding and according to Hanoi, would have caused the deaths of thousands of North Vietnamese.

2577 **There has been so much fighting the people don't know which way to run.**—*Unidentified Government official in Saigon, comments to the press, 3 May 1972.*[700]

The NVA offensive in the northern provinces and Central Highlands of South Vietnam forced more than 350,000 people from their homes. The refugees swarmed away from heavy fighting, seeking shelter in Hue, Da Nang and Qui Nhon. With NVA attacks pushing the battle south and east, the refugees were concentrating in the coastal areas.

2578 **Goddamn! I'd go mad if I had to wear this brain bucket all the time.**—*Phil Stratford, U.S. Air Force, Flight Engineer aboard C-130, speaking to correspondent, May 1972.*[481]

Because of the hazardous nature of the mission, the crew of the C-130 wore flak jackets and steel helmets. They were making a night resupply drop to the ARVN in the besieged city of An Loc during the NVA Easter Offensive.

2579 **Generous in his bid for peace but firm in his determination that we will not surrender.**—*Representative Gerald R. Ford of Michigan, House Republican leader, comments on Nixon's Vietnam War policy, 8 May 1972.*[592]

Ford was commenting on Nixon's decision to mine North Vietnamese ports and isolate North Vietnam from the resupply of war materials. Nixon was responding to the North Vietnamese invasion of South Vietnam, which started 30 March 1972 when NVA troops and tanks crossed the DMZ into South Vietnam.

2580 **There are only two issues left for us in this war. First, in the face of a massive invasion do we stand by, jeopardize the lives of 60,000 Americans, and leave the South Vietnamese to a long night of terror? This will not happen. We shall do whatever is required to safeguard American lives and American honor. Second, in the face of complete intransigence at the conference table do we join with our enemy to install a Communist government in South Vietnam? This, too, will not happen. We will not cross the line from generosity to treachery.**—*President Richard Nixon, in a nationally televised speech, 8 May 1972.*[177]

Nixon initiated Linebacker I, in response to the North Vietnamese invasion of South Vietnam. The Linebacker I strikes were directed against North Vietnamese's ability to sustain its invasion force. Nixon was also responding to Hanoi's refusal to continue the peace negotiations they had walked out of in late-1971.

2581 **There are virtually no strings attached to the aid given to the North Vietnamese today.**—*Douglas Pike, American Vietnamologist, commenting on Le Duan's leadership, May 1972.*[948]

Under Ho Chi Minh and later, Le Duan, North Vietnam received huge amounts of aid from both the Soviet Union and Red China, but was not accountable to either. North Vietnam as an independent communist state, received the aid to carry on a proxy war against America in Vietnam, the common enemy of both Red China and the Soviets. At this time there was a decided antagonism between the two communist giants, which North Vietnam used to its advantage.

2582 **If U.S. air power had not been there to intervene, I think An Loc would have been a disaster.**—*Unidentified Senior U.S. Commander in Saigon, May 1972.*[481]

Two NVA divisions, supported by tanks, attempted to capture the city of An Loc, located in Binh Long Province. The NVA laid siege to the city in mid-April and tried for three months to rout the ARVN defenders. The NVA was unable to force the ARVN from An Loc. Much of the credit for An Loc's survival went to the USAF which not only attacked NVA troops and positions, but kept the ARVN and the civilians who were trapped in the city supplied with food, ammunition, and supplies. The ARVN stand at An Loc was one of the few times they held their own in combat against the enemy.

2583 **The moment the enemy agrees to the return of American prisoners of war and an internationally supervised cease-fire ... we will stop all acts of force throughout Indochina and proceed with the complete withdrawal of all forces within four months.**—*President Richard Nixon, from a televised speech, 8 May 1972.*[593]

Nixon announced the mining of North Vietnamese ports and the interdiction of rail lines between North Vietnam and China. Nixon was responding to the 30 March 1972 North Vietnamese invasion of South Vietnam. He also wanted to pressure Hanoi into fruitful negotiations, as the Paris negotiations had been at a standstill for quite a long time preceding the North Vietnamese invasion.

2584 **The President, by mining the port of Hai Phong and stepping up the air war, had taken the gravest step in the escalation of the war to date and thrown down an insolent challenge to the Vietnamese people, to the socialist countries, to all peace-loving nations, to the American people and to the peoples the world over.**—*Statement from the North Vietnamese delegation to the Paris peace talks, 9 May 1972.*[595]

On 8 May 1972 Nixon ordered the mining of North Vietnamese ports and air interdiction of rail lines between North Vietnam and Red China. The move was an effort to cut off war supplies from entering North Vietnam, thus reducing the supply of materials supporting the North Vietnamese invasion of South Vietnam. The move was also designed to pressure Hanoi to negotiate in good faith at the Paris peace talks.

2585 **We will take those steps that are necessary to prevent the delivery of supplies that can be used to help the North Vietnamese to carry out their military aggression in Southeast Asia.**—*Melvin R. Laird, Secretary of Defense, during a news conference, 10 May 1972.*[702]

Comments on the mining of North Vietnamese harbors and the interdiction of supply lines supporting the North Vietnamese war machine. Reporters at the conference attempted to pin Laird down as to just how far the U.S. was willing to go to block war supplies from entering North Vietnam.

2586 **I intend to stop at nothing to bring the enemy to his knees...**—*President Richard Nixon, to Henry Kissinger, as quoted in Nixon's memoirs, 10 May 1972.*[162]

Having notified the nation of America's intent to stand behind South Vietnam, Nixon was ready to punish Hanoi for the invasion of the South and their intransigence and foot-dragging at the negotiating table.

2587 **[The decision by President Nixon to seal off North Vietnam was] very painful and difficult, but had to be made because no honorable alternative was available.**—*Henry Kissinger, National Security Adviser, comments to the press, 9 May 1972.*[594]

Kissinger was referring to Nixon's decision to seal North Vietnam from the supply of war materials by mining North Vietnamese ports and interdicting rail supply lines between North Vietnam and Red China. The move was made in an effort to stop the ongoing North Vietnamese invasion of South Vietnam and to force the North Vietnamese to negotiate in good faith at the Paris peace talks.

2588 **As long as the Nixon Administration continues its aggression in Vietnam, continues its policy of Vietnamization of the war and escalation of the war, all the Vietnamese**

people, united as ever, will resolutely continue their resistance struggle until they reach their fundamental objectives, namely, independence, freedom and peace.—*Statement from the North Vietnamese delegation to the Paris peace talks, 9 May 1972.*[595]

On 8 May 1972 Nixon ordered the mining of North Vietnamese ports and air interdiction of rail lines between North Vietnam and Red China. The move was an effort to cut off war supplies from entering North Vietnam, thus reducing the supply of materials supporting the ongoing North Vietnamese invasion of South Vietnam. The move was also designed to pressure Hanoi to negotiate in good faith at the Paris peace talks. Thousands of NVA troops supported by tanks, who had invaded South Vietnam 30 March 1972, were conveniently ignored in the North Vietnamese statement.

2589 **They were ordered to go further but they flat refused and sat on their asses ... so that village does have friendly forces — not the most active friendly forces, but friendly.**—*Unidentified Air Force intelligence NCO, briefing an aircrew, May 1972.*[481]

The aircrew was preparing to make a night resupply drop to ARVN troops under siege in An Loc during the NVA Easter Offensive. The NCO was giving the crew a point of reference if they had to bailout in the area.

2590 **It was strong medicine but necessary.**—*Senator Robert P. Griffin of Michigan, comments to the press, 8 May 1972.*[592]

Griffin was commenting on President Nixon's decision to order the mining of North Vietnamese ports and the bombing of rail lines between North Vietnam and Red China. The move was an effort to cut off war supplies from reaching North Vietnam, supporting their invasion of South Vietnam.

2591 **The only way left to end the Vietnam war is to deprive the enemy of the supplies he needs to continue the invasion.**—*Representative Gerald R. Ford of Michigan, House Republican leader, comments on Nixon's Vietnam War policy, 8 May 1972.*[592]

Ford was commenting on Nixon's decision to mine North Vietnam's ports, and bomb North Vietnamese rail links with Red China in an attempt to isolate North Vietnam from the resupply of war materials. Nixon was responding to the North Vietnam invasion of South Vietnam, which started 30 March 1972 when NVA troops and tanks crossed the DMZ into South Vietnam.

2592 **You have handled a difficult situation uncommonly well.**—*Anatoly Dobrynin, Soviet Ambassador, speaking to Henry Kissinger, 10 May 1972.*[162]

Dobrynin was responding to the Nixon administration's restrained handling of the North Vietnamese invasion of South Vietnam. The North Vietnamese had also stopped any forward progress in the peace talks, perhaps hoping that the invasion would put them in a better position militarily to demand more concessions from the U.S. The Soviets did not let the situation between the U.S. and North Vietnam interfere with their quest for détente with America.

2593 **Countermeasures by the United States were, in the circumstances, inevitable.**—*Press statement from the British Foreign Office, 9 May 1972.*[596]

This was the British response to Nixon's decision to mine North Vietnamese ports and interdict rail supply lines between North Vietnam and Red China. The move was an effort to slow down the North Vietnamese invasion of South Vietnam, which started 30 March 1972. The move was also designed to apply pressure to Hanoi to negotiate in good faith at the Paris peace talks.

2594 **[American planes] deliberately struck at the dike system in Nam Ha Province [southeast of Hanoi].**—*Radio Hanoi, during broadcast on 9 May72.*[598]

Throughout the war Hanoi claimed U.S. strike aircraft hit the Red River Valley dike system surrounding Hanoi. The dike system held the Red River within its banks. Much of the flat land surrounding Hanoi was several feet below the level of the river. Destruction of the dikes would have caused massive flooding throughout the valley. The U.S. denied the dikes were targeted or struck.

2595 **Le Duan [laid] the foundations for the Viet Cong at the time of the [1954] Geneva agreement.**—*P.J. Honey, British Oriental specialist, comments on North Vietnamese leaders, May 1972.*[948]

Le Duan was first secretary of North Vietnam's Lao Dong (Workers) Party. In the late forties and early fifties he formed and led the communist Viet Minh forces in southern Vietnam. When the war against the French ended he moved to North Vietnam, but left behind the southern Viet Minh forces he had formed. These forces later became the Viet Cong of the second Indochina War. Duan became one of the members of the eleven-man Politburo, which ultimately ruled North Vietnam.

2596 **All distant critics like to see a scalp fall.**—*John Paul Vann, Senior American Adviser, II Corps (AID), comments to the press, 10 May 1972.*[701]

Vann was commenting on the sacking of General Ngo Dzu, South Vietnamese commander of the Central Highlands, for failing to stop the NVA offensive that swept eastward across the Central Highlands.

2597 **Finally we will be able to win the war.**—*Admiral Thomas Moorer, chairman of the JCS, comments, April 1972.*[1027]

Nixon authorized an extensive air campaign against NVA forces to counter their invasion of SVN. The JCS were given carte blanche to use air power to turn the invasion.

2598 **[The question is whether Giap] is merely Lawrence of Arabia, great in a special situation and with a peculiar set of national circumstances, or a Robert E. Lee, master of all military situations.**—*Unidentified U.S. general, comments to the press, May 1972.*[948]

The general was commenting on the pending battle between NVA forces and ARVN forces over the city of Hue. Giap was the engineer behind all of the major offenses conducted by the communist forces in Vietnam. His command experience went back to the Viet Minh and the defeat of the French. His latest offensive was the invasion of South Vietnam launched in March 1972. Giap's actions in the preceding years had won minor victories, but never accomplished the goal of defeating the U.S. military or forcing the total surrender of the South Vietnamese military.

2599 **Le Duan talks, thinks and acts like a Chinese.**—*Nikita Khrushchev, Premier of the Soviet Union (until 1964), comments.*[949]

Nikita Khrushchev, commenting on Le Duan's political ability to negotiate North Vietnam through the communist world of the Soviet Union and Red China, while at the same time not allowing North Vietnam to become the satellite of either communist power.

2600 **[The North Vietnamese are] more cohesive and more accustomed than the South Vietnamese to rigid government control and the austerity need for a protracted war.**—*Brian Jenkins, Rand Corporation analyst, during an interview, May 1972.*[948]

2601 **We don't have twelve years' experience in this country [Vietnam]. We have one year's experience twelve times.**—*John Paul Vann, Director Second Regional Assistance Command, comments to reporters, May 1972.*[886]

Vann's comment was in reference to the one-year tour (13 months for Marines) for Army, Air Force, and land based Navy personnel in Vietnam. The lessons learned during an individual's tour had to be relearned by the man who replaced him, and repeated again and again.

2602 **The willingness to sacrifice exhibited by the enemy exceeds anything in the past ... they are convinced that they're going to win.**—*Unidentified U.S. General, Saigon, comment to reporter, May 1972.*[948]

The general was speaking of the North Vietnamese invasion of South Vietnam and the push by more than 100,000 NVA troops supported by armor and artillery. In the first five weeks of the invasion a North Vietnamese force had seized control of South Vietnam's two northern most provinces, and was threatening to cut South Vietnam in half with a second force in the Central Highlands, as well as a large attacking force launched from Cambodia towards Saigon.

2603 **If we were to lose in Vietnam, there would have been no respect for the American President ... because we had the power and didn't use it.... We must be credible.**—*President Richard Nixon, comments, May 1972.*[319]

Nixon had maneuvered Russia to a point where there was chance for détente. A summit was scheduled between Nixon and the Soviet leader. Nixon was determined not to appear weak before the eyes of the Soviets.

2604 **Because of its ignominious defeats the United States does not dare re-escalate the war no matter how disastrous the consequences of this offensive and how great the danger of collapse will be for the puppet [South Vietnamese] army.... We will force the enemy to acknowledge his defeat and accept a political settlement on our terms.**—*Excerpt from a Communist Party journal, April 1972.*[127]

The North Vietnamese Politburo did not believe Nixon could respond to the North Vietnamese invasion of South Vietnam in such a way as to threaten NVN's plan to bring about the collapse of the GVN-Thieu regime. Their plan was to militarily put Saigon in such a weak position that the U.S. would have to accede to Hanoi's demands in order to save the remaining American forces in the country.

2605 **The bastards have never been bombed like they're going to be bombed this time.**—*President Richard Nixon, comments, May 1972.*[313]

In March, 1972 North Vietnam launched a full invasion of South Vietnam, 100,000 NVA troops supported by several armor and artillery regiments crossed the DMZ and struck the Central Highlands. During the fighting, Nixon made a secret offer to North Vietnam to allow their troops to remain in-place in South Vietnam if they would agree to the peace terms he sought. Their rejection of his offer angered him and he ordered a naval blockade of North Vietnam using mines and a resumption of the dormant air campaign against North Vietnam.

2606 **South Vietnam is not worth what it cost the United States in terms of U.S. values. In terms of South Vietnamese values these people are much further ahead today than they would have been either with peace and a non–Communist government or with peace and a Communist government. ... In 1962 the literacy rate was 15 percent. Today it's over 80 percent.**—*John Paul Vann, Director Second Regional Assistance Command, during a headquarters briefing, 7 June 1972.*[887]

2607 **If I had it to do over I would do the same thing, but I would check into the reporting procedure better.**—*General John D. Lavelle, former Commander, U.S. 7th Air Force, during Congressional hearings, 12 June 1972.*[703]

Lavelle testified before the House Armed Services Committee about his unauthorized air strikes against North Vietnamese gun and SAM sites. Lavelle authorized at least 28 strikes against North Vietnamese positions during the enemy build up before they launched their 1972 invasion of South Vietnam. Reports of the strikes made it to higher headquarters. When Lavelle could no longer cover-up the strikes he halted them. When the illegal strikes were discovered he was relieved of command of 7th Air Force.

2608 **Laser-guided bombs ... revolutionized tactical bombing.**—*General Eugene L. Hudson, U.S. 7th Air Force, Director of Intelligence, 1972.*[115]

During the Linebacker raids on North Vietnam, the U.S. made extensive use of smart bombs — laser and TV guided ordnance — to increase the effectiveness of the raids.

2609 **All the air power in the world, including strikes against Hanoi and Hai Phong, would not save South Vietnam if the South Vietnamese aren't able to hold on the ground.**—*President Richard Nixon, writing in his personal diary, April 1972.*[374]

Nixon applied massive amounts of American air power to blunt the North Vietnamese invasion of South Vietnam during the Easter Offensive of 1972. At the start of the offensive there were 6,000 American combat troops in Vietnam and 64-74,000 support troops. North Vietnam entered the era of the big unit war and its large, exposed, ground units were vulnerable to air attack.

2610 **So many of them come home with a stack of ribbons and their pride intact, but you seldom hear about them.**—*General Daniel "Chappie" James, Jr., U.S. Air Force, during an interview, July 1972.*[993]

James was speaking of black Vietnam War veterans returning home. Chappie was one of two blacks to attain the rank of general during the Vietnam War. He flew more than 75 combat missions over North Vietnam.

2611 **The fundamental purpose of a military force is to engage the enemy in combat, the premium is on manpower for combat arms. Failure to recognize or accept this premise**

created problems for many inductees.—*General William Westmoreland, U.S. Army Chief of Staff, in a report, 1972.*[1016]

Many recruits hoped to be sent for technical training after their basic combat course was complete. With a war going on, the need was for more combat troops.

2612 **The black or Spanish speaking enlisted man is often singled out for punishment by white authority figures where his white counterpart is not. There is enough evidence of intentional discrimination by individuals to convince the task force that selective punishment is in many cases racially motivated.**—*Excerpt from Department of Defense Task Force finding, 1972.*[994]

The Department of Defense was responding to allegations of discrimination and improper application of the rules of the Uniform Code of Military Justice throughout the U.S. military.

2613 **No military procedure has brought forth a greater number of complaints and evidences of racial discrimination than the administration of non-judicial punishment.**—*Finding of the Congressional Black Caucus, 1972.*[992]

Military offenses whose seriousness did not warrant a court-martial, could be dealt with by non-judicial punishment, which took the form of an Article-15 (Army, Air Force) or Captain's Mast (Navy/Marines). The punishment could be meted out for minor infractions and could consist of loss of rank, extra duty, loss of pay, restriction to barracks, or other punishments determined by the unit commander.

2614 **[The McGovern nomination] certainly helps the government of Hanoi and the Viet Cong, but not the attempts of Nixon who, above all, must disengage himself from Southeast Asia without the American prestige having to suffer too much.**—*Excerpt from the Vatican's newspaper, August 1972.*[713]

McGovern advocated an immediate withdrawal of all American troops from South Vietnam, virtually regardless of the condition of the Vietnamization program or the state of South Vietnam's military. U.S. troop strength in South Vietnam at the end of 1971 was 156,000 men.

2615 **You don't see many of the brothers out on the skeet range.**—*Unidentified black GI, from comments to the Congressional Black Caucus Study, 1972.*[990]

The comment addressed the limited recreational facilities designed with blacks or minorities in mind, on American military installations. The civil rights issues and visibility of racial disparity quickly became evident, even in the war zone of Vietnam.

2616 **We have reached the stage where the mere fact of private talks helps us very little—if at all.**—*Henry Kissinger, National Security Adviser, in a report to President Nixon, August 1972.*[134]

The Linebacker I bombing of North Vietnam started in mid-May 1972. By mid-July the North Vietnamese were ready to go back to the negotiating table. The talks made a little progress but bogged down again in mid-August. To pump some life into the talks Nixon ordered an increase in the Linebacker raids, by October 1972 there was significant progress in the peace talks, and the Linebacker I operation ended 23 October 1972.

2617 **Dapping has become a source of considerable friction both between the black serviceman and his white counterparts and between him and the military system. It seems to provoke a reaction of white anger out of proportion to its own importance.**—*Excerpted from a Department of Defense Task Force finding, 1972.*[994]

Excerpted from a Department of Defense Task Force finding, 1972. The dap was an expressive handshake used by blacks in greeting each other. Many whites objected to the greeting, some officers viewed it as disrespectful even though it was not forced on anyone. The traditional military salute was given to officers, per military regulation.

2618 **[The dap] was a very meaningful thing to young blacks. It meant a lot to them and sometimes, like in anything like that, what starts out to be meaningful sort of gets made into something sort of ridiculous.**—*Captain John Ellis, U.S. Army, during DoD interview, 1972.*[994]

The dap was an expressive handshake used primarily by blacks in greeting each other. The series of taps, touches, finger grips, and bumps could last a few seconds or go on for several minutes.

2619 **It is only fitting to discontinue showing Jane Fonda films.**—*C.M. Shearer, manager, Buena Vista Drive-in, Borger, Texas, 17 August 1972.*[704]

The discontinuation of screening Jane Fonda films was Shearer's way of protesting Fonda's trip to Hanoi in August 1972.

2620 **You reinforce success, you don't reinforce failure...**—*Unidentified Department of Defense analyst, comments to the press, 17 August 1972.*[704]

The Defense analyst's statement was regarding the North Vietnamese move to reinforce their troops just south of the DMZ in South Vietnam. The level of reinforcements was roughly equivalent to troops lost to combat during the North Vietnamese Easter Offensive, which started 30 March 1972. After deep advances into South Vietnam, NVA troops were pushed back to just south of the DMZ. Normal military doctrine dictates that you reinforce, then counterattack, or withdraw your force and rebuild. In this case Hanoi reinforced the retreat position and held.

2621 **[Chinese and Soviet détente with the United States is equivalent to] throwing a lifebuoy to a drowning pirate ... in order to serve one's narrow national interests.... This is a harmful compromise, advantageous to the enemy, and disadvantageous to the Revolution.**—*Nhan Dan editorial, 17 August 1972.*[149]

Nixon's policy of détente with both the Soviets and the Chinese had greatly reduced the threat of major intervention in Vietnam by either of the communists superpowers. This left Hanoi in the awkward position of no longer being able to successfully play China against the Russians for support against the Americans.

2622 **This is a war against Vietnam perhaps, but the tragedy is America's.**—*Jane Fonda, actress and anti-war activists, from a speech in Hanoi, 22 August 1972.*[351]

Fonda traveled to Hanoi, later condemning the American bombing of North Vietnam as criminal. She spoke of the crimes of America against the Vietnamese, but failed to mention the crimes of the Vietnamese against the Vietnamese. Her appeal for support of the communist way of life in North Vietnam was considered traitorous by U.S. troops in Vietnam.

2623 **[There is] evidence of blacks separating themselves from their non-black comrades in hostile ways, going beyond affirming their racial and cultural solidarity.**—*Excerpted from a Department of Defense Task Force finding, 1972.*[994]

As black militancy increased within the military some blacks formed protective groups to defend themselves against perceived white harassment. Racial clashes did not usually appear when blacks and whites were operating in the field, but surfaced when they returned to base camp or were standing down.

2624 **A very few men most of whom were below average in mental capacity ... and all of whom were black.**—*Representative Floyd Hicks of Washington, during a House investigation, 1972.*[1004]

Hick's description was of blacks involved in race riots onboard two U.S. Navy carriers in 1972. A House committee investigated the race riots onboard the *USS Kitty Hawk* (October 1972) and *Constellation* (November 1972). Even though whites and blacks were involved in the riots only the blacks were prosecuted. Representative Hick's view of the incidents were considered narrow, at best, by black activists seeking reforms in the Navy's discriminatory policies.

2625 **We have a saying we used in Vietnam, that we finally found out why there are two crew members in the F-4. One is to fly the airplane and one is to carry the briefcase full of the rules of engagement.**—*General John D. Lavelle, former Commander, U.S. 7th Air Force, 1972.*[886]

Lavelle took command of the 7th Air Force in August 1971. He was relieved in mid-1972 when it was discovered he had authorized several air strikes against unauthorized North Vietnamese targets. Under the Rules of Engagement American pilots could not attack North Vietnamese SAM sites unless they showed intent to do harm. Lavelle authorized strikes against several SAM sites which did not meet the requirement. He then altered the official records to cover-up some of the strikes.

2626 **Looking back on all these years — all of the blood and agony — I have to wonder what we accomplished.**—*General Paul D. Harkins, former ComUSMACV, during an interview, 1972.*[949]

In the early sixties Harkins was a strong supporter of the Diem regime and tried to build the South Vietnamese military into a force that could counter the communist insurgency of the Viet Cong.

2627 **I must complain that our Government has allowed us to enjoy too much democracy too soon.**—*Nguyen Van Thieu, President of South Vietnam, 10 September 1972.*[363]

Thieu voiced the opinion that there was a little too much freedom in South Vietnam and that it posed a security threat. The Thieu regime increased its pressure on dissidents and thousands of South Vietnamese were arrested. Thieu believed the dissidents posed a threat to his government. Those arrested included political rivals, student protesters, those linked to the VC/NLF, army deserters, and those resistant to the Thieu government.

2628 **I'd love to make a pass at you, but it would be like desecrating a national monument.**—*Unidentified man, speaking to POW/MIA activist Valerie Kushner.*[483]

Kushner was a staunch and very visible advocate for American POW/MIAs. She worked for McGovern's election in 1972 believing he was the best chance for a quick resolution to the war and the return of the POWs. Her husband, Captain Harold Kushner, was released from Hanoi in 1973.

2629 **For the first time in the Indochina wars the communist side was being compelled to negotiate in order to forestall the possibility of defeat.**—*Sir Robert Thompson, British authority on counterinsurgency, 1972.*[165]

After successes and territorial gains in the Central Highlands and I Corps, the North Vietnamese Easter Offensive began to falter. Massive U.S. air support bolstered the ARVN forces, who by August 1972 started to push NVA troops out of captured South Vietnamese territory. It was essential that Hanoi secure a cease-fire in-place before the gains of their offensive were lost. Nixon continued to strike North Vietnam and NVA troops in South Vietnam until October 1972.

2630 **If this fellow's testimony was right, more than one service was involved in preplanned bombing raids regardless of reaction.**—*Senator Stuart Symington of Missouri, during Senate hearings, September 1972.*[705]

During testimony before the Senate, a former Navy pilot identified illegal air strikes conducted against North Vietnam. Under the rules of engagement at the time combat aircraft were to escort reconnaissance aircraft and were not allowed to fire on North Vietnamese positions unless they [NV] fired first. Testimony from the ex-Navy pilot indicated that there were attacks against enemy gun and missile sites that had not initiated the combat, contrary to the rules of engagement as they existed at the time. The Senate proposed to investigate the allegations.

2631 **Because of the riches you brought us, we were forced to acknowledge our own poverty and to compete among ourselves to change as you wanted us to do. But now that you Americans are going home, we can again feel safe and comfortable with our illusions.**—*Unidentified Chinese merchant in Saigon, commenting to a CIA officer, October 1972.*[863]

2632 **My husband is no goddamn baby. He was a man when he went away and that's how he's coming home.**—*Unidentified POW wife lashing out at the press, October 1972.*[487]

The woman was reacting to "published implications" that some of the returning POWs may not be eager to resume their roles as husbands and fathers due to the strains of their captivity.

2633 **Part hero, part coward, part oddity, and part modern Rip Van Winkle.**—*Former POW, in an interview, 1972.*[487]

Characterization of how he felt as a POW returning home, after being held captive by Hanoi.

2634 **It wasn't no more than right that he do his duty. I really don't like the war, but I'm not the one to say who was right or wrong in this war.**—*Bettie Stanton, Massillion, Ohio, in an interview, November 1972.*[485]

This interview was taken after the announcement that a settlement of the war was close. Her brother, Ronald Stanton, was listed as missing in action in 1968 when his helicopter was downed over the DMZ.

2635 **Some chaplains are awful when they tell you that prayer will help. What's a praying wife or parent supposed to think when he doesn't come back then? That they didn't pray hard enough? That they didn't go to mass enough? Silence can be kinder than such advice.**—*Unidentified wife of a MIA soldier, in an interview, 1972.*[487]

2636 **Saigon is ... entitled to participate in the settlement of a war fought on its territory.... We will not be stampeded into an agreement until its provisions are right. We will not be deflected from an agreement when its provisions are right. And with this attitude, and with some cooperation from the other side, we believe that we can restore both peace and unity to America very soon.**—*Henry Kissinger, National Security Adviser, during a press conference, 26 October 1972.*[144]

Kissinger was informing South Vietnam that they could not stand in the way of the peace agreement. He also notified Hanoi that the U.S. would not be rushed into an agreement. Hanoi was anxious to have the cease-fire in-place take effect before they lost anymore of the South Vietnam's territory they had gained in the Easter Offensive.

2637 **I am confident we will succeed in achieving our objective—peace with honor—and not peace with surrender in Vietnam.**—*President Richard Nixon, during an airport rally, 26 October 1972.*[706]

By this date a cease-fire agreement had been nearly reached between the U.S. and NVN/PRG, but Saigon would not agree to the provisions. Saigon objected to the requirement for establishing a coalition government in Saigon which included the PRG (NLF/VC).

2638 **In other wars there was a togetherness in the country; if you had a boy fighting, everybody was worried. With this war, everybody is so busy that they don't have any time to let you put your head on their shoulder when you worry.**—*Irma Buckland, Massillion, Ohio, in an interview, November 1972.*[485]

This interview was taken after the announcement that a settlement of the war was close. Her son had completed two tours of duty in Vietnam.

2639 **[My critics fail] to understand the importance of great decisions and the necessity to stand by the President of the United States when he makes a terribly difficult, potentially unpopular decision.**—*President Richard Nixon, during a press conference, October 1972.*[950]

Nixon was speaking out against critics of his decision to mine North Vietnam's harbors, and strike rail links between North Vietnam and Red China.

2640 **This isn't our war! We're not going out in the bush. Why should we fight if nobody back home gives a damn about us?**—*Cries from members of a U.S. Army infantry company, collected by a New York Times correspondent, April 1972.*[1028]

The company was ordered out of Phu Bai on a security patrol, but a third of the 142-man company initially refused to go.

2641 **Concern over racial problems seemed more important than the question of good order and discipline.**—*Excerpt from findings of House Armed Services Committee on racial unrest aboard the USS Kitty Hawk and USS Constellation 1972.*[1003]

The House committee investigated the race riots onboard the U.S. Navy carriers the *Kitty Hawk* and the *Constellation*, laying the blame for the disturbances on poor discipline and permissiveness by Navy authorities. The House report played down the racial aspects that motivated some of the problems.

2642 **It is inevitable that in a war of such complexity that there should be occasional difficulties in reaching a final solution, but we believe that by far the largest part of the road has been traversed and what stands in the way of an agreement now are issues that are relatively less important than those that have already been settled.**—*Henry Kissinger, National Security Adviser, during a press conference, 26 October 1972.*[858]

Kissinger announce "peace was at hand," in the negotiations between the U.S. and Hanoi.

2643 **I hope we can walk out of it with an honorable cease-fire. I'd hate for these kids to have died in vain. My son thought we were there for a purpose.**—*Vivian McDonald, Massillion, Ohio, in an interview, November 1972.*[485]

This interview was taken after the announcement that a settlement of the war was close. Her son was killed in Vietnam before the cease-fire.

2644 **We believe peace is at hand. We believe that an agreement is within sight.**—*Henry Kissinger, President Nixon's National Security Adviser, comments to the press, 26 October 1972.*[347]

The U.S. and Hanoi reached a tentative agreement in October, but in order for the agreement to be complete the approval of South Vietnam's President Thieu was required. Thieu did not like the terms of the agreement and refused to cooperate. Kissinger hoped that his public statement would squeeze Thieu into agreement, and at the same time indicate to Hanoi that the U.S. was serious about the agreement.

2645 **To tell you to have hope is sometimes the cruelest thing people can do for you.**—*Unidentified wife of a MIA soldier, in an interview, 1972.*[487]

The wife of a man missing in Vietnam, as she waited to find out if he would be released when the prisoner exchange took place in 1973.

2646 **I would be ashamed if we had pulled out as McGovern suggested. I'm old-fashioned enough to think that national honor is important.**—*Tom Girdler interviewed in Massillion, Ohio, November 1972.*[485]

Girdler's son completed a tour of duty in Vietnam. This interview was taken after the announcement that a settlement of the war was close. During campaigning for the Democratic nomination for president, McGovern advocated unilateral withdrawal of American forces from South Vietnam.

2647 **[The negotiations are now at] a curious point ... we have an agreement that is 99 per cent completed ... the remaining 1 per cent requires a major decision by Hanoi.**—*Henry Kissinger, National Security Adviser, during a press conference, 16 December 1972.*[597]

Kissinger charged the North Vietnamese were delaying the

final agreement on the peace agreement by demanding last minute changes. At this point the negotiations broke off. To encourage Hanoi to consider bargaining in good faith Nixon launched the Operation Linebacker II raids against North Vietnam.

2648 **It is hard for most people to grasp, but it's the most continually draining thing that you can imagine.**—*Norma Mitchell, wife of a pilot missing in Vietnam, in an interview, 1972.*[487]

Her husband was listed as missing in 1968.

2649 **To be believed is (to some extent) to be trusted. Not to be believed — the present condition Washington often faces before the world and the American people — threatens the character of representative democracy.**—*Anthony Lake, former Foreign Service officer, 1972.*[949]

Lake resigned from government service in 1970 because of the government's conduct of the war in Vietnam.

2650 **We have to kill the Communists to the last man before we can have peace.**—*Nguyen Van Thieu, President, South Vietnam, comment reported up by the press, 1972.*[950]

2651 [GENERAL:] **Of course it looked bad. But the miracle of survival struck in the toughest places. It was terribly important that she make herself believe, until she knew otherwise, that her son could have survived. That hope must always be held. It would give her strength, and — who knows — it might even help her son.**

[MOTHER'S RESPONSE:] **Bullshit!**—*Exchange between Army casualty officer and the mother of a missing pilot, 1972.*[487]

The unidentified mother lost her son in a crash when his helicopter was shot down in spring 1969. By the end of 1972 she had given up hope of his return mostly because details of the crash indicated he probably did not survive.

2652 **To learn from Viet Nam the country would have to accept some very painful truths — most notably that it was wrong. The impossible truth for Americans is that we are capable of evil and have committed it on a large scale.**—*Robert Jay Lifton, Yale psychiatrist, comments to correspondent, 1972.*[949]

2653 **No one can claim that the United States won in Viet Nam. What the nation lost it is only beginning to measure.**—*Time magazine, The Shape of Peace, 6 November 1972.*[949]

2654 **[Vietnam] has been a disastrous undertaking from the beginning, and historians will give a bearish verdict to the whole operation. Many men of good will became obsessed with the need for success, but they lost sight of the country's larger interest.**—*George Ball, former Under Secretary of State, comments to correspondent, November 1972.*[949]

Ball, Under Secretary of State in the Johnson Administration, argued in 1965 against the sustained bombing of North Vietnam and the introduction of U.S. combat troops in the Vietnam War.

2655 **Nobody won this war, but I think you could call what Nixon has gotten a settlement within the bounds of honor.**—*Tom Girdler interviewed in Massillion, Ohio, November 1972.*[485]

This interview was taken after the announcement that a settlement of the war was close.

2656 **The methods we have used in fighting the war have scandalized and disgusted public opinion in almost all foreign countries. Not since we withdrew into comfortable isolation in 1920 has the prestige of the U.S. stood so low.**—*Hamilton Fish Armstrong, editor for Foreign Affairs magazine, 6 November 1972.*[949]

2657 **I admire your ability to change impossible demands to merely intolerable demands and call it progress.**—*Henry Kissinger, National Security Adviser, during peace negotiations with the North Vietnamese, 1972.*[486]

Kissinger was speaking to Le Duc Tho, North Vietnam's chief negotiator. According to Kissinger, Le Duc Tho had three "vitriolic epics" that he repeated, in lieu of honest, progressive negotiations. It wasn't until Sepember 1972 that the mood of the North Vietnamese changed and they started talking in earnest.

2658 **All we did was show our inability with 500,000 troops and vast technology to cope with a few hundred thousand guerrillas in black pajamas.**—*Arthur Schlesinger, Jr., historian, comments to correspondent, November 1972.*[949]

2659 **We misevaluated the situation. We thought the joint Soviet-Chinese efforts to Communize Southeast Asia would succeed. We were just dead wrong.**—*Clark Clifford, former Secretary of Defense, comments to correspondent, November 1972.*

Clifford was one of several former Johnson administration advisers to comment on the war when it appeared a peace agreement was nearly completed.

2660 **I never felt we should have gotten into Vietnam, but once in, we should have won it. We could have. We still could, but in terms of what it would do to this country, I don't think it is worth the price.**—*Tom Girdler interviewed in Massillion, Ohio, November 1972.*[485]

His son survived a tour of duty in Vietnam. This interview was taken after the announcement that a settlement of the war was close.

2661 **[The war in Vietnam is coming to a] fair and honorable conclusion. We do have victory because we've guaranteed their freedom. We accomplished our mission.**—*Theodore Cornelius Strong, former Army infantryman, during an interview, 1972.*[949]

Strong was commenting on the October 1972 Kissinger announcement that "peace was at hand," indicating that peace and a cease-fire agreement was nearly complete between the U.S. and Hanoi. In 1967 Strong lost his left leg and right arm in combat.

2662 **I am an American. As long as our men were there, I went.**—*Martha Raye, stage and screen performer and honorary Army Lieutenant Colonel, in an interview, November 1972.*[484]

Martha Raye toured, visiting with troops, in three wars (World War II, Korea and Vietnam).

2663 **It's sort of like planning to get married again, only I haven't seen the bridegroom in six years.**—*Lynda Gray, in an interview with Martha Faye, 1972.*[487]

Gray's husband, Air Force Captain David Gray, was shot down over North Vietnam 23 January 1967. She anticipated his release when the war in Vietnam finally ended.

2664 **I'm happy that it is finally about over. One reason it dragged on so long was that this country was divided by the protest. If I had been a Vietcong listening to Spock and Fulbright and McGovern, I would have kept on fighting and hoped one of them was elected.**—*Tom Girdler, interviewed in Massillion, Ohio, November 1972.*[485]

This interview was taken after the announcement that a settlement of the war was close.

2665 **I can't see why we kept on spilling American blood for a government that wasn't worth fighting for and people who won't fight for themselves. Eventually, they'll throw down their arms and the Communists will win.**—*Paul Coats, former Marine machine-gunner, during an interview, 1972.*[949]

Coats suffered nerve damage as a result of wounds received during an enemy rocket attack.

2666 **I feel bitter about the war. The American people were lied to for so long that I'm not sure they have any faith left in their government.**—*Bill Reynolds, interview, Massillion, Ohio, November 1972.*[485]

This interview was taken after the announcement that a settlement of the war was close.

2667 **You know some of these guys don't even know who Lee Trevino is.**—*Pentagon press officer, speaking to the media, 1972.*[487]

Speaking of the long interment of many of the prisoners of war held by the North Vietnamese, and the news that they missed during their imprisonment. In 1971 Trevino won three of golf's biggest competitions in succession — the U.S. Open, the Canadian Open, and the British Open.

2668 **Nobody has won this war, but maybe the biggest losers were the Americans.**—*Bill Reynolds, interviewed in Massillion, Ohio, November 1972.*[485]

This interview was taken after the announcement that a settlement of the war was close.

2669 **We may not be able to dictate peace to General Thieu, but he's not going to dictate war to us.**—*Senator George McGovern, of South Dakota, from a speech at Cleveland State University, February 1972.*[950]

McGovern speaking out on South Vietnam's President Nguyen Van Thieu's rejection of some of the conditions of the Paris peace accords.

2670 **[The U.S. experience in Vietnam is] the opposite of Korea. There we went in with a bad army and came out with a good one. In Vietnam we went in with a good army and came out with a bad one.**—*General Theodore Mataxis, Commander, Americal Division, 1972.*[103]

2671 **You have my absolute assurance that if Hanoi fails to abide by the terms of this agreement it is my intention to take swift and severe retaliatory action.**—*President Richard Nixon, to President Nguyen Van Thieu, November 1972.*[162]

The U.S. and Hanoi reached a tentative peace agreement in October 1972, but Nguyen Van Thieu rejected the terms of the agreement and wanted major modifications made before he would agree to sign. Nixon attempted to assure Thieu of U.S. support in the event Hanoi reneged on the agreement.

2672 **We shouldn't have been there in the first place.**—*Terry Tuersley, Vietnam War veteran during an interview, 1972.*[485]

Tuersley's opinion of American intervention in Vietnam. He is wheelchair bound after a battle accident in Vietnam.

2673 **[Search and destroy operations were] a natural response of American commanders deploying forces hugely superior in mobility and firepower against an elusive enemy who could not be brought to decisive battle. But his ability to control his own losses by evading contact and using sanctuaries frustrated our aims.**—*Robert Komer, former Special Assistant to President Johnson, in The Rand report, 1972.*[102]

2674 **Don't imagine we will have the same kind of fire power as we have now when the Americans leave.**—*Nguyen Cao Ky, Vice President, to Nguyen Van Thieu, 1972.*[629]

During the war, South Vietnam had the support of American artillery and aircraft. On the departure of the Americans, South Vietnam was to provide its own air and artillery support to its troops. Ky explained to Thieu that the level of South Vietnamese support would not be as high compared to support levels under the Americans.

2675 **There is nothing absolutely nothing, to describe what goes on inside a pilot's gut when he sees a SAM get airborne.**—*Commander Randy "Duke" Cunningham, U.S. Navy F-4 pilot, 1972.*

Cunningham and his RIO, Lt. William Driscoll, had five aerial victories against North Vietnamese MiGs during the Vietnam War.

2676 **It was just kind of amazing that we were actually going to do it ... I almost thought it was a joke at first.**—*Captain E.A. Petersen, U.S. Air Force, 307th Strategic Air Wing, U-Tapao Air Force Base, December 1972.*[180]

Peterson was reacting to confirmation that B-52s were going to be used against targets around Hanoi, for the first time in the war against targets in North Vietnam.

2677 **I don't want any more of this crap about the fact that we couldn't hit this target or that one. This is your chance to use military power effectively to win this war, and if you don't, I'll consider you personally responsible.**—*President Richard Nixon, to Admiral Thomas Moorer, December 1972.*[321]

The peace talks had almost reached agreement when they again stalled. In retaliation Nixon ordered a new round of intensified bombing of North Vietnam to force Hanoi back to the negotiating table to complete the agreement. On 18 December 1972 Operation Linebacker II was initiated. Moorer was the current Chairman of the JCS.

2678 **It is not possible to conclude a conflict successfully if those who direct it are convinced it cannot or should not be done.**—*Admiral Malcolm W. Cagle, former Deputy Chief of Naval Operations-Air, in a Naval Review article, 1972.*[961]

Cagle was referring to direction of the war from Washington, when those involved in its direction were not in unison as to the level at which the war should be pursued.

2679 **History will judge whether the decision not to blockade [North Vietnam] was a wise one, or whether it was a serious, perhaps the crucial, mistake of the whole Vietnam war.**—*Admiral Edward Wegener, Federal German Navy, in an article for Naval Review, 1972.*[959]

American military experts estimated that early in the war North Vietnam received more than 85 percent of its military equipment and supplies through the port of Hai Phong. By 1967 the Cambodian port of Sihanoukville was in full operation supplying the NVA/VC in the II, III, and IV Corps areas of South Vietnam, while supplies for upper II and I Corps moved south, down the Ho Chi Minh Trail from North Vietnam.

2680 **Just as [my] missile left the rail the MiG [-21] executed a maximum G, tight turning, starboard break turn. He couldn't have seen me. Either his wingman called a break or his tail warning radar was working. I had an instantaneous plan view of him and he was really hauling.... The missile couldn't handle it, exploding out of lethal range.**—*Commander Randy "Duke" Cunningham, U.S. Navy F-4 pilot, 1972.*

Cunningham and his RIO, Lt. William Driscoll, had five aerial victories against North Vietnamese MiGs during the Vietnam War.

2681 **The resumption of the bombings, while negotiations were proceeding, did not succeed in subjugating the Vietnamese people.**—*Nguyen Thanh Le, spokesman for the North Vietnamese delegation to the Paris peace talks, comments to the press, December 1972.*[84]

The Paris peace talks between Hanoi and the U.S. reached a stalemate in mid-December. In an effort to force Hanoi to resume talks and conclude the agreement, Nixon ordered intensified bombing of North Vietnam. After eleven days of heavy bombing Hanoi agreed to resume peace talks. Hanoi made several statements to the effect that the American bombing campaign was not a consideration in their decision to continue the negotiations.

2682 **I never went into the air thinking I would lose.**—*Commander Randy "Duke" Cunningham, U.S. Navy F-4 pilot, 1972.*

Cunningham and his RIO, Lt. William Driscoll, had five aerial victories against North Vietnamese MiGs during the Vietnam War.

2683 **I want the people of Hanoi to hear the bombs, but minimize damage to the civilian populace.**—*Admiral Thomas H. Moorer, chairman of the Joint Chiefs of Staff, instructions to General John C. Meyer, December 1972.*[117]

General Meyer was the Strategic Air Command, commander. SAC provided the B-52 bomber force used for air operations in Vietnam. Meyer was tasked with including B-52s in the Operation Linebacker II raids against Hanoi and Hai Phong.

2684 **A fighter pilot must be free to propose improvements (in tactics) or he will get himself killed.**—*Commander Randy "Duke" Cunningham, U.S. Navy F-4 pilot, 1972.*

Cunningham and his RIO, Lt. William Driscoll, had five aerial victories against North Vietnamese MiGs during the Vietnam War.

2685 **The President should explain successes. The staff explains failures.**—*John Erlichman, presidential adviser for domestic affairs, during discussion with Bob Haldeman, December 1972.*[188]

In October 1972 Kissinger publicly exclaimed that peace was at hand. Shortly after that Hanoi changed their cease-fire agreement offer, resulting in a collapse of the proposed agreement. Following Kissinger's announcement that "peace is at hand," Nixon informed the nation that the negotiations were near completion. The question discussed among the White House staff was whether or not Nixon should be the one to tell the nation that there were problems with the negotiations, and the agreement was not finalized.

2686 **Nothing is true in tactics.**—*Commander Randy "Duke" Cunningham, U.S. Navy F-4 pilot, 1972.*

Cunningham and his RIO, Lt. William Driscoll, had five aerial victories against North Vietnamese MiGs during the Vietnam War.

2687 **We simply have to take losses if we are going to accomplish our objectives.**—*President Richard Nixon, diary entry, December 1972.*[162]

Nixon's response to estimates from the military that aircraft loss among the B-52s of Linebacker II was estimated at 3 percent.

2688 **[They are the] victims of their own character deficiencies.**—*Charles Colson, special counsel to President Nixon, 1972.*[489]

Colson's characterization was of American military deserters of the Vietnam War.

2689 **I expect that we [Kissinger and Le Duc Tho] will meet again, but we will have to meet in an atmosphere that is worthy of the seriousness of our endeavor.**—*Henry Kissinger, National Security Adviser, during a press conference 16 December 1972.*[135]

At the news conference Kissinger announced that the peace talks were once again stalemated because of Hanoi's intransigence. A peace agreement had been close in October 1972, but changes demanded by South Vietnam's Thieu had blocked the agreement. Again in early December 1972 agreement was nearly reached when it was discovered that North Vietnamese negotiators had slipped un-agreed upon wording into the final working document.

2690 **[The North Vietnamese] were deliberately and frivolously delaying the [peace] talks.**—*President Richard Nixon, in a message to Hanoi, 17 December 1972.*[178]

Nixon proposed in the message to Hanoi that peace talks resume again any time after 26 December 1972. On 18 December 1972 Operation Linebacker II commenced, an effort to convince Hanoi to complete the negotiations.

2691 **We will not be blackmailed into an agreement. We will not be stampeded into an agreement ... and we will not be charmed into an agreement, until its conditions are right.**—*Henry Kissinger, National Security Adviser, during a press conference, 16 December 1972.*[975]

During this period the two negotiating sides, Hanoi and the U.S., were near an agreement. But there were charges and counter-charges by both sides of last minute changes in the agreement to which one side or the other objected. The result was a temporary stalemate in the negotiations.

2692 **General Haig's mission now represents my final effort to point out to you the necessity for joint action and convey my irrevocable intention to proceed, preferably with your cooperation, but, if necessary, alone ... work together in seeking a settlement along the lines I have approved or**

to go our separate ways.—*President Richard Nixon, in a letter to South Vietnam's President Nguyen Van Thieu, 18 December 1972.*[162]

Nixon sent General Alexander Haig to personally relay his message to Thieu.

2693 **They're just a bunch of shits. Tawdry, filthy shits.**—*Henry Kissinger, as relayed by Richard Nixon, 1972.*[374]

According to Nixon, Kissinger's attitude towards the communists was extremely bitter following their break-off of negotiations in December 1972. This followed Kissinger's public announcement that "peace was at hand."

2694 **[The Linebacker II] raids should outrage the conscience of all Americans.**—*Senator Edward Kennedy of Massachusetts, comments on raids against Hanoi, December 1972.*[182]

Kennedy's reaction to the Operation Linebacker II strikes carried out against North Vietnam, 18-29 December 1972.

2695 **War by tantrum.**—*Unspecified critics of the Nixon's Linebacker II raids against North Vietnam, December 1972.*[321]

Many of Nixon's critics called him a madman when he unleashed a new, intensive round of air strikes against North Vietnam. Nixon was angered by North Vietnam's refusal to complete the peace agreement that had been worked out. As an aside: he wanted to do as much damage as he could to North Vietnam before the end of the war to reduce their ability to threaten South Vietnam after the agreements were signed.

2696 **How did we get in a few short weeks from a prospect for peace that "you can bank on," to the most savage and senseless act of the war ever visited, over a scant ten days, by one sovereign people upon another?**—*Washington Post editorial, 28 December 1972.*[175]

The *Post* was reacting to the Linebacker II campaign against North Vietnam, 18-29 December 1972.

2697 **[Nixon has] taken leave of his senses.**—*Senator William Saxbe of Ohio, comments on the Linebacker II raids, December 1972.*[182]

Saxbe's reaction to the Operation Linebacker II strikes carried out against North Vietnam, 18-29 December 1972.

2698 **[The Linebacker II campaign is] not the conduct of a man who wants peace very badly.**—*London Times editorial, December 1972.*[145]

The *Times* was reacting to the Linebacker II campaign against North Vietnam, 18-29 December 1972.

2699 **Even without successful negotiations, we're preparing the way so that we can have an ally over there stand on his own without our help. Even if the bombs don't coerce the enemy into successful peace talks, they're destroying his will to fight.**—*Unidentified American officer, comments to correspondent, Washington, D.C., 30 December 1972.*[599]

The officer was speaking of the intensified, eleven-day bombing campaign against North Vietnam designed to pressure Hanoi into returning to the negotiating table and conclude a peace agreement.

2700 **Even allies must call this a crime against humanity.**—*Die Zeit, Hamburg, editorial, December 1972.*[132]

Die Zeit was reacting to the Linebacker II campaign against North Vietnam, 18-29 December 1972.

2701 **There is a business of coercion in there and that's the business of war.**—*Unidentified American officer, comments to correspondent, Washington, D.C., 30 December 1972.*[599]

The officer was speaking of the intensified, 11-day bombing campaign against North Vietnam designed to pressure Hanoi into returning to the negotiating table to conclude the peace agreement.

2702 **I want to meet their terms. I want to reach an agreement. I want to end this war before the election. It can be done, it will be done. What do you want us to do? Stay there forever?**—*Henry Kissinger during a meeting with NSC and State Department officers, October 1972.*[1027]

Kissinger was heatedly responding to accusations from the officers that he had caved into NVN's demands in order to secure a peace agreement in Paris.

1973

You can no more win a war than you can win an earthquake.
—Jeannette Rankin

2703 **I don't have a broom long enough to reach Taiwan, and you don't have a broom long enough to reach Saigon.**—*Mao Tse-tung, Chairman, People's Republic of China, speaking to Pham Van Dong, 1973.*[374]

Mao did not believe North Vietnam should push to unite South Vietnam, but should maintain the partition of the two countries while continuing to support the insurgent movement to undermine the Saigon regime.

2704 **I cannot understand why it is that people in this country are so quick to accuse their own country of taking these kinds of actions [obliteration bombing] when they are simply not true.**—*Admiral Thomas H. Moorer, chairman of the Joint Chiefs of Staff, comments following Linebacker II, January 1973.*[182]

Moorer was commenting on press reports of massive civilian casualties and damage in Hanoi. Hanoi claimed more than 1,800 civilians killed in and around the Hanoi-Hai Phong area during the eleven days of the Linebacker II campaign.

2705 **The best guarantee for the survival of South Vietnam is the unity of our two countries which would be gravely jeopardized if you persist in your present course.**—*President Richard Nixon, letter to President Nguyen Van Thieu, 5 January 1973.*[630]

Thieu refused to agree to a settlement worked out between the U.S. and Hanoi, allowing NVA troops to remain in South Vietnam and the formation of a coalition government including the VC (NLF/PRG).

2706 **I was sitting right here when we first started talking about B-52's. That was a concept. Boy that was going to be it. If we ever got B-52's, that would do it. There would be no problems from then on, and here this little backward, these "gooks" developed [sic], and they are knocking down your B-52's like clay pigeons, with all the sophisticated hardware which was beyond our own ken, being run by "gooks." This is some kind of lesson.**—*Congressman Daniel Flood of of Pennsylvania, speaking during House hearings, January 1973.*[125]

Of the 210 B-52s that participated in Operation Linebacker I & II, fifteen were shot down. These fifteen fell to the more than 1200 enemy SAMs launched during Linebacker II. Linebacker II exhausted the North Vietnam's supply of SAMs in the Hanoi-Hai Phong area.

2707 **I am convinced that your refusal to join us would be an invitation to disaster—to the loss of all that we together have fought for over the past decade. It would be inexcusable above all because we will have lost a just and honorable alternative.**—*President Richard Nixon, letter to President Nguyen Van Thieu, 5 January 1973.*[630]

Nixon's letter dated 5 January 1973, was personally delivered by General Alexander Haig to South Vietnam's President Nguyen Van Thieu. Thieu refused to agree to a settlement worked out between the U.S. and Hanoi in Paris, allowing NVA troops to remain in South Vietnam and the formation of a coalition government including the VC (NLF/PRG).

2708 **Because of the progress in negotiations between Dr. Kissinger and special adviser Le Duc Tho, President Nixon has directed that the bombing, shelling and any further mining of North Vietnam be suspended.**—*Ronald L. Ziegler, White House press secretary, in a press release, 15 January 1973.*[600]

Ziegler announced a tentative agreement on peace and cease-fire terms between North Vietnam and the U.S. had been reached.

2709 **You have my assurance of continued assistance in the post-settlement period and that we will respond with full force should the settlement be violated by North Vietnam.**—*President Richard Nixon, in a letter to South Vietnam's President Nguyen Van Thieu, 5 January 1973.*[162]

2710 **The unity of our country is no more a matter for negotiations than our independence.**—*Hanoi, 1973.*[276]

2711 **I have ... irrevocably decided to proceed to initial the Agreement on January 23, 1973 and to sign it on January 27, 1973 in Paris. I will do so, if necessary, alone. In that case I shall have to explain publicly that your Government obstructs peace. The result will be an inevitable and immediate termination of U.S. economic and military assistance which cannot be forestalled by a change in personnel in your government.**—*President Richard Nixon, in a letter to South Vietnam's President Nguyen Van Thieu, 14 January 1973.*[134]

The message was delivered by General Alexander Haig. Thieu relented in his stalling against the agreement and sent Foreign Minister Tram Van Lam to Paris to participate in the signing of the agreement on behalf of the South Vietnamese Government.

2712 **Our people have truly destroyed the Communist troops that have come from the North and North Vietnam now must respect the sovereignty and independence of South Vietnam.**—*Nguyen Van Thieu, President, South Vietnam, during a press conference, 24 January 1973.*[951]

Nguyen Van Thieu's views of the cease-fire reached in Paris between the U.S./SVN and NVN/PRG. At the time of the announced cease-fire more than 175,000 NVA troops controlled several areas of South Vietnam.

2713 **What's the point of reconstruction if the battle goes on?**—*Unidentified State Department official, comments to correspondent, January 1973.*[951]

The comment regarded a plan by President Nixon to pour $7.5 billon in reconstruction aid into Indochina. Very few military or political observers held out much hope that the cease-fire agreement would lead to a lasting peace in Vietnam.

2714 **It is clear there is no legal way by which North Vietnam can use military force against South Vietnam.**—*Henry Kissinger, National Security Adviser, during a news conference, 24 January 1973.*[133]

2715 **At 12:30 Paris time today, 23 January 1973, the agreement on ending the war and restoring peace in Vietnam was initialed by Dr. Henry Kissinger on behalf of the United States and Special Adviser Le Duc Tho on behalf of the Democratic Republic of Vietnam.**—*President Richard Nixon, during a televised announcement, 23 January 1973.*[604]

The announcement of the end of direct U.S. participation in the Vietnam War.

2716 **There has been a sharp decline in respect for authority in the United States as a result of the [Vietnam] war—a decline in respect not only for the civil authority of government but also for the moral authority of the schools, the universities, the press, the church and even the family.**—*James Reston, correspondent, Washington, D.C., 23 January 1973.*[602]

2717 **[The Vietnam War was] one of the most selfless enterprises in the history of nations.**—*President Richard Nixon, during a televised speech, 23 January 1973.*[951]

Nixon's description of the 2.7 million Americans who had served in Vietnam for more than twenty years.

2718 **The cease-fire will take effect at 2400 Greenwich Mean Time, January 27, 1973. The United States and the Democratic Republic of Vietnam express the hope that this agreement will insure stable peace in Vietnam and contribute to the preservation of lasting peace in Indochina and Southeast Asia.**—*President Richard Nixon, televised broadcast, 23 January 1973.*[630]

Nixon's announcement that a peace agreement had been reached in Paris between the U.S., North Vietnam, South Vietnam, and the PRG (VC/NLF).

2719 **In four days a decade of death and destruction will end.**—*Senator Edward W. Brooke of Massachusetts, comments to the press, 23 January 1973.*[601]

In reference to the official signing of the Paris Peace Accord between the U.S., NVN, SVN, and the PRG, 27 January 1973.

2720 **It is a moment of joy, a joy that is shared, the victory crowned a valiant combat conducted in unity by the army and the people of Vietnam on all fronts at the cost of innumerable sacrifices and privations.**—*Le Duc Tho, Chief North Vietnamese negotiator, during a press conference announcing cease-fire agreement, 24 January 1973.*[607]

2721 **[Peace in Vietnam] ... depends on the relative satisfaction and therefore on the relative dissatisfaction of all the parties concerned.**—*Henry Kissinger, President Nixon's National Security Adviser, press conference, 23 January 1973.*[951]

2722 **No one would have welcomed this peace more than he.**—*President Richard Nixon, during televised speech, 23 January 1973.*[951]

Nixon was referring to former President Lyndon Johnson, who died 22 January 1973, the day before Nixon announced that a cease-fire agreement had been reached between the U.S./SVN and NVN/PRG.

2723 **Of the [Paris] peace accord.... I consider it only as a cease-fire agreement. As to whether or not we will have real peace, we must wait and see.**—*Nguyen Van Thieu, President, South Vietnam, from a speech announcing the accord, 24 January 1973.*[603]

2724 **The people of South Vietnam have been guaranteed the right to determine their own future, without outside**

interference.—*President Richard Nixon, televised broadcast, 23 January 1973.*[630]

Under terms of the Paris settlement, a coalition government was to be formed between the GVN and PRG, with a vote at a later date to unify South Vietnam under one government. North Vietnamese troops in South Vietnam were not required to leave South Vietnamese territory.

2725 **[Erlichman]—How long do you figure the South Vietnamese can survive under this agreement?**

[Kissinger]—I think, that if they're lucky they can hold out for a year and a half.—*Exchange between Henry Kissinger and John Erlichman, at the White House, 24 January 1973.*[188]

Kissinger and Erlichman were discussing the cease-fire/peace agreement settlement between the U.S., NVN, SVN, and the PRG (NLF/VC).

2726 **We shall continue to aid South Vietnam within the terms of the agreement and we shall support efforts by the people of South Vietnam to settle their problems peacefully among themselves.**—*President Richard Nixon, televised broadcast, 23 January 1973.*[630]

Nixon announcing that a settlement had been reached in Paris between the U.S., NVN, GVN, and the PRG resulting in a cease-fire.

2727 **The agreement makes it clear that there is an entity called South Vietnam, and that any unification of North Vietnam and South Vietnam will be decided only by negotiations and not by military force...**—*Henry Kissinger, Chief U.S. negotiator at the Paris peace talks, during a press conference, 24 January 1973.*[605]

2728 **The important thing was not to talk about peace, but to get peace and to get the right kind of peace. This we have done.**—*President Richard Nixon, 23 January 1973.*[630]

Nixon announcing that a settlement had been reached in Paris between the U.S., NVN, GVN, and the PRG resulting in a cease-fire.

2729 **I only know four people who liked the war—Nixon, Johnson, Kennedy and Eisenhower.**—*Herbie Ehmann, patron at Wally's Bar, Queens, New York, 24 January 1973.*[606]

2730 **To the other major powers that have been involved even indirectly: Now is the time for mutual restraint so that the peace we have achieved can last.**—*President Richard Nixon, televised broadcast, 23 January 1973.*[630]

Nixon announcing that a settlement had been reached in Paris between the U.S., NVN, GVN, and the PRG, resulting in a cease-fire. Nixon aimed these words at China and the Soviet Union.

2731 **The United States had substantially achieved the negotiating goals it had set for an honorable agreement.**—*Henry Kissinger, Chief U.S. negotiator at the Paris peace talks, during a press conference, 24 January 1973.*[605]

2732 **To the people and Government of South Vietnam: By your courage, by your sacrifice, you have won the precious right to determine your own future and you have developed the strength to defend that right. We look forward to working with you in the future, friends in peace as we have been allies in war.**—*President Richard Nixon, televised broadcast, 23 January 1973.*[630]

Nixon announcing that a settlement had been reached in Paris between the U.S., NVN, GVN, and the PRG resulting in a cease-fire.

2733 **A triumph for the Vietnamese people ... a triumph over American imperialism.**—*Le Duc Tho, Chief North Vietnamese negotiator, during a press conference, 24 January 1973.*[951]

Tho's comments regarded the finalized Paris cease-fire agreement

2734 **The United States will continue to recognize the government of the Republic of Viet-Nam as the sole legitimate government of South Viet-Nam.**—*President Richard Nixon, January 1973.*[277]

The Paris Peace Accords allowed for the political recognition of the NLF/VC (reconstituted as the PRG-Provisional Revolutionary Government). The PRG and the GVN were to resolve their differences, supposedly without external interference.

2735 **Now that we have achieved an honorable agreement, let us be proud that America did not settle for a peace that would have betrayed our allies, that would have abandoned our prisoners of war, or that would have ended the war for us but would have continued the war for the 50 million people of Indochina.**—*President Richard Nixon, televised broadcast, 23 January 1973.*[630]

Nixon announcing that a settlement had been reached in Paris between the U.S., NVN, GVN, and the PRG resulting in a cease-fire.

2736 **There is no peace yet. This is only a standstill cease-fire. If the Communist commit small cease-fire violations, we will respond with small actions. If they commit big violations, we will respond with big actions.**—*Nguyen Van Thieu, President, South Vietnam, during a nationally broadcasted address, January 1973.*[951]

2737 **I thank God for those who stood, thank God for those who gave their lives, thank God for those who suffered. We're damned proud of them.**—*President Richard Nixon, speaking with Congressional leaders, January 1973.*[951]

2738 **It is only a piece of paper. Its value depends entirely on the future.**—*Unidentified South Vietnamese government minister, comments to correspondent, February 1973.*[951]

Comments on the announced cease-fire agreed upon in Paris by the U.S., South Vietnam, North Vietnam and the Vietcong. Many Vietnamese feared the collapse of Saigon in the vacuum that would follow the withdrawal of American forces and their military support.

2739 **[The war in Vietnam concludes] not with a cheer but a sigh.**—*Boston Globe, editorial.*[951]

2740 **This bomb is dedicated to the hope that all Marines here at Bien Hoa will soon be enjoying a good and everlasting "piece."**—*Anonymous inscription written on a 500-pound bomb, destined for its final mission in Vietnam, 26 January 1973.*[953]

Marine Air Group 12 was stationed at Bien Hoa air base and conducted the last air support mission by land-based American combat aircraft of the Vietnam War. The war officially ended for America, 27 January 1973.

2741 **The mark of Viet Nam is forever on me. My language is altered, my hair grayer, my eyes sadder. Hamburger Hill, My Lai, the Green Berets, assassinations, mistaken air strikes, refugees and kids with napalm burns. The U.S. may try to forget, but that will be hard.**—*Marsh Clark, Time correspondent, February 1973.*[952]

2742 **It's good to be a shooter, not a shootee. I hate to leave, it's really been fabulous.**—*Captain Steve Sunderman, A-4 Skyhawk pilot, U.S. Marine Air Group 12, Bien Hoa, 26 January 1973.*[953]

MAG-12 was the last operational American air combat unit in South Vietnam at the time of the cease-fire, 27 January 1973.

2743 **What kind of peace is it that gives the North Vietnamese the right to keep their troops here [in South Vietnam].**—*Nguyen Van Thieu, President, South Vietnam, during a nationally broadcasted address, January 1973.*[951]

At the time of the cease-fire, Hanoi had more than 175,000 troops in South Vietnam, a result of infiltration and the North Vietnamese invasion of South Vietnam in March 1972. Those troops were not required to leave South Vietnam as a condition of the cease-fire.

2744 **I don't think any of us enjoyed killing.**—*Captain Bill Peters, A-4 Skyhawk pilot, U.S. Marine Air Group 12, Bien Hoa, 26 January 1973.*[953]

MAG-12 was the last operational American air combat unit in South Vietnam at the time of the cease-fire, 27 January 1973.

2745 **We cannot rely too much on international treaties, for the Communist do not respect them. Nor can we rely too much on the International Control Commission. If a stranger enters your village, shoot him in the head.**—*Nguyen Van Thieu, President, South Vietnam, during a nationally broadcasted address, January 1973.*[951]

The International Commission for Control and Supervision was established under the Paris Peace Accords to monitor the cease-fire between the GVN the Viet Cong and the NVA troops in South Vietnam.

2746 **It should be clear by now that no one in the war has had a monopoly on anguish and that no one has a monopoly on insight.**—*Henry Kissinger, President Nixon's National Security Adviser, press comments, February 1973.*[951]

2747 **The high point of my time in Viet Nam will be going home.**—*Lieutenant David Mowrey, A-4 Skyhawk pilot, U.S. Marine Air Group 12, Bien Hoa, 26 January 1973.*[953]

MAG-12 was the last operational American air combat unit in South Vietnam at the time of the cease-fire, 27 January 1973.

2748 **Together with healing the wounds in Indochina, we can begin to heal the wounds in America.**—*Henry Kissinger, National Security Adviser, comments to the press, February 1973.*[951]

Kissinger's comments followed the annoncement that a cease-fire agreement had been reached in Paris.

2749 **My personal feelings are mixed on whether it was a success, whether it was worth it. But it's been a hell of an education.**—*Lieutenant David Mowrey, A-4 Skyhawk pilot, U.S. Marine Air Group 12, Bien Hoa, 26 January 1973.*[953]

MAG-12 was the last operational American air combat unit in South Vietnam at the time of the cease-fire, 27 January 1973.

2750 **We love to fly, but the sad thing is that in terms of quality and quantity, the best flying comes when you're in a war.**—*Lieutenant David Mowrey, A-4 Skyhawk pilot, U.S. Marine Air Group 12, Bien Hoa, 26 January 1973.*[953]

MAG-12 was the last operational American air combat unit in South Vietnam at the time of the cease-fire, 27 January 1973.

2751 **Your sacrifice has not been in vain.**—*President Richard Nixon in a conversation with Colonel Robinson Risner, 12 February 1973.*[707]

Nixon was speaking to Risner during a phone conversation with the recently released American POW. Risner called Nixon to thank him for his efforts in getting the American POWs released.

2752 **With the war out of the way the potential is there for creative tension instead of destructive disagreement.**—*Unidentified White House aide's comment to the press, February 1973.*[951]

The animosity between the White House and Congress steadily grew as the war in Vietnam dragged on. Both sides cautiously hoped with the devisiveness of the war out of the way, real progress could be made towards moving America forward.

2753 **We are 12,000 miles away. If we made a mistake in our assessment of the situation, it will be painful. If they [South Vietnam] made a mistake in the assessment, it can be fatal.**—*Henry Kissinger, National Security Adviser, press conference, 23 January 1973.*[951]

Kissinger was addressing complaints from the Saigon regime that NVA troops were not required to withdraw from South Vietnamese territory as a condition of the cease-fire agreement. At the time of the cease-fire there were more than 175,000 NVA troops in South Vietnam.

2754 **In war ... [nonchalance] ... was the only reaction one could afford.**—*Bill Marmon, Time magazine correspondent, February 1973.*[951]

Marmon's reference was to the seeming indifference of an American sailor recovering the body of a dead American Army soldier from a river following a combat operation in the area.

2755 **There was a deadlock which was described in the middle of December, and there was rapid movement when negotiations resumed. These facts have to be analyzed by each person for himself.**—*Henry Kissinger, National Security Adviser, press conference, 23 January 1973.*[951]

This was Kissinger's answer to press questions as to whether or not the "Christmas bombing" (Operation Linebacker II) of Hanoi had been instrumental in bringing Hanoi back to the negotiating table in Paris.

2756 **It is not easy to achieve through negotiations what has not been achieved on the battlefield.**—*Henry Kissinger,*

President Nixon's National Security Adviser, press conference, 23 January 1973.[951]

Kissinger was commenting on the fact that the Paris ceasefire agreement did not stipulate a requirement for North Vietnam's withdrawal of all its forces from South Vietnam. A point President Nguyen Van Thieu had insisted on during much of the negotiations.

2757 **Airpower, specifically strategic airpower, can be decisive when applied against strategic targets — industrial and military — in the heartland of the enemy regardless of the size of the nation.**—*Senator Barry Goldwater of Arizona, speaking in Congress, 26 February 1973.*[124]

Goldwater was speaking of the effectiveness of the Linebacker II bombing of North Vietnam in December 1972.

2758 **Last one out, please turn off the lights.**—*Anonymous notice, placed on the main bulletin board at MACV Headquarters, Saigon, 27 January 1973.*[951]

2759 **You can count on us.**—*President Richard Nixon, to President Thieu, San Clemente, California, March 1973.*[252]

Nixon assured President Thieu of full U.S. military and economic aid, and pledged to respond with force if Hanoi violated the Paris Peace agreements.

2760 **The only way we will keep North Vietnam under control is not to say we are out forever. We don't want to dissipate with them the reputation for fierceness that the President has earned.**—*Henry Kissinger, President Nixon's National Security Adviser, comments to the press, 1973.*[336]

Nixon and Kissinger saw the threat of force as the only deterrent Hanoi might recognize.

2761 **[The Communist will not respect the terms of the Paris Accords] because they have got the Americans out and that is the biggest victory the Communist have ever had. But it is not the first. They chased out the French and now, in a sense, they have chased out the Americans. That is an enormous step toward the total domination of Vietnam and there is no reason why they should stop now. The Communist in the North have always considered it a historical mission for them to achieve the unification of Vietnam.**—*Nguyen Cao Ky, former Vice President of South Vietnam, speaking to General Charles Timmes, 1973.*[629]

2762 **We ought to be sending all these advisers to North Vietnam — then, next time, they would lose.**—*Unidentified U.S.military officer, comments to reporter, 12 March 1973.*[363]

This comment was made as the officer watched a plane load of American, civilian advisers deplane at Tan Son Nhut in March 1973. As the final elements of American military forces withdrew from South Vietnam, civilian advisers were replacing them. These advisers were hired by private companies contracting with the Pentagon. The number of civilian advisers was expected to exceed 20,000.

2763 **[Colonel Summers] — You know you never defeated us on the battlefield.**

[NVA Colonel] — That may be so, but it is also irrelevant.—*Exchange between Colonel Harry G. Summers and unidentified North Vietnamese Colonel at war's end, 1973.*[374]

According to Summers the Americans won the major battles, but lost the war.

2764 **Fighting a war he could not believe in at a ten-hour-a-day desk job that took him three hours a day to do.**—*Jon Larsen, Time magazine correspondent, February 1973.*[951]

Larsen was interviewing an American GI "REMF" who was addicted to heroin.

2765 **Our mission has been accomplished. I depart with a strong feeling of pride in what we have achieved, and in what our achievement represents.**—*General Frederick C. Weyand, ComUSMACV, parting address to the South Vietnamese, 29 March 1973.*[610]

Weyand's farewell address to the South Vietnamese military and government officials.

2766 **There were many more casualties from the war [in Vietnam] than those expressed by the number of dead, wounded and missing.**—*Jon Larsen, Time magazine correspondent, February 1973.*[951]

Larsen was interviewing an American GI "REMF" who was addicted to heroin in 1971.

2767 **You can hold your heads up high for having been a part of this selfless effort.**—*General Frederick C. Weyand, ComUSMACV, in an address to his troops in Saigon, 29 March 1973.*[610]

Weyand spoke to the remaining American troops as MACV closed down operations and prepared for redeployment to the U.S.

2768 **Can you imagine someone putting you in a closet and closing the door and saying, "See you in six months?"**—*Colonel Robinson Risner, former U.S. POW, during a press conference, Andrews Air Force Base, Maryland, 29 March 1973.*[609]

Risner detailed for the press the torture and isolation techniques used against some American POWs by their North Vietnamese captors. Several such news conferences were held around the country by POWs, recently liberated from North Vietnam.

2769 **Peace with honor has been achieved.**—*General Frederick Weyand, ComUSMACV, 31 March 1973.*[709]

Weyand spoke to troops and dignitaries as the last of American combat forces departed South Vietnam.

2770 **[The American POW experience in North Vietnam] — severe torture, degradation, deprivation, humiliation, you name it.**—*Colonel Robinson Risner, former U.S. POW, during a press conference, Andrews Air Force Base, Maryland, 29 March 1973.*[609]

Risner detailed for the press the torture and isolation techniques used against some American POWs by their North Vietnamese captors. Several such news conferences were held around the country by POWs, recently liberated from North Vietnam.

2771 **Pictures and some press reports had given a visitor the impression Hanoi had suffered badly in the war — but in fact the city is hardly touched.**—*Tammy Arbuckle, correspondent for the Washington Star, in her article, 1 April 1973.*[166]

2772 **Living on hate...**—*Unidentified former American POW, comments to correspondent, 29 March 1973.*[609]

As related to the correspondent, many of the older Americans held by North Vietnam survived their captivity because of their hatred for their North Vietnamese captors and the communist system.

2773 **We shall insist that North Vietnam comply with the agreement. The leaders of North Vietnam should have no doubt as to the consequences if they fail to comply with the agreement.**—*President Richard Nixon, during a nationwide address, 29 March 1973.*[608]

2774 **What could be more joyous than to be delivered from your enemies and return to your friends.**—*Lt.Col. James W. O'Neill, returning American POW, comment to the press, 29 March 1973.*[708]

2775 **The commander of the Strategic Air Command and his staff ... were not told how to do the job; they were told what to do.**—*Admiral Thomas H. Moorer, chairman of the Joint Chiefs of Staff, comments following Linebacker II, April 1973.*[116]

During the Rolling Thunder Campaign against North Vietnam the air command was told by the White House how to do the job. This included the types of bomb loads to use, what targets could be struck, routes of ingress and egress, and a host of other operational details that should have been within the purview of commands in the field. Linebacker I & II control was different in that the White House described the desired results of the bombing and left it to the military to make it so.

2776 **As far as I'm concerned, I want to get the hell out [of Southeast Asia].**—*Representative Norris Cotton of New Hampshire, May 1973.*[327]

After the withdrawal of U.S. troops from Vietnam, air strikes continued in Cambodia in support of Lon Nol. Congress challenged the President on the bombing and in June 1973 passed an amendment cutting off all U.S. military action in and over Laos, Cambodia, and Vietnam. Nixon argued that the bombing support was essential to keep the communists from overrunning Cambodia — Congress did not agree.

2777 **We came to Vietnam to supervise a cease-fire but instead were observing a war.**—*Paraphrase of a comment made by the Canadian delegation to the ICCS, 29 May 1973.*[886]

The ICCS (International Commission of Control and Supervision) was established to monitor the terms of the 1973 Paris Peace Accords. The commission consisted of representatives from Canada, Indonesia, Poland, and Hungary. The aggression between the VC, NVA and ARVN was blatant with neither side really observing the cease-fire.

2778 **Never since 1954 had the Communists enjoyed such a strong political and military posture.**—*General Cao Van Vien, South Vietnamese Chief of Staff, 1973.*[881]

The General's comments of the final cease-fire settlement. When the Paris Peace Accords were signed more than 175,000 NVA troops were still in South Vietnam, the NLF was legitimized by the recognition of the PRG, and the PRG was granted equal political status to the GVN. In return, the U.S. was able to leave South Vietnam, retrieve its POWs from Hanoi, and leave the completion of the war to the South Vietnamese.

2779 **In order to preserve my emotional stability [I am going to reduce my involvement in the affairs of Indochina].**—*Henry Kissinger, National Security Adviser, comments to the press, 1973.*[347]

As the Watergate affair began to take center stage in the U.S., the security situation in South Vietnam was deteriorating. Kissinger had little leverage to force Hanoi to honor the Paris Accords.

2780 **The Paris Agreement of January 1973 served only the immediate purposes of the United States and North Vietnam. It enabled President Nixon to keep his promise to the American people. American prisoners of war were released and reunited with their families, and all U. S. troops left South Vietnam safely and honorably.**—*General Cao Van Vien, South Vietnamese Chief of Staff, 1973.*[881]

The peace agreement which resulted in the cease-fire in January 1973 was seen by many Vietnamese as the final American abandonment of South Vietnam. More than 175,000 NVA troops were still in South Vietnam when the last U.S. combat troops departed. There were also nearly 200,000 VC spread across the country.

2781 **I am not a draft evader, I'm a runaway slave. I left because I was not going to fight white America's war.**—*Unidentified black draft dodger, 1973.*[1013]

This particular draft dodger escaped to Canada rather than take the chance of serving in the U.S. military.

2782 **It would be idle to say that the authority of the executive has not been impaired.**—*Henry Kissinger, National Security Adviser, comments to the press, 1973.*[306]

Kissinger was commenting on an amendment passed by Congress to cut off U.S. military activity in Southeast Asia. The amendment rendered the President incapable of providing support to Vietnam or Cambodia that was not specifically approved by Congress.

2783 **We could see a definite change in the attitude of the Vietnamese. Before they had been defiant ... but it was a totally different situation with the B-52s.**—*General Robinson Risner, former U.S. Air Force pilot and Prisoner of War, 1973.*[922]

Risner's comments on the effectiveness of the eleven day Operation Linebacker II bombing campaign against North Vietnam in December 1972.

2784 **When we [Hanoi] are attacked, that is terrorism, when we do the attacking, that is a partisan freedom movement.**—*Alexander Solzhenitsyn, Nobel prize winner and Russian author, September 1973.*[626]

Solzhenitsyn relating the North Vietnamese outlook on terrorism, from a communist perspective.

2785 **It would be best for Vietnam and the rest of Indochina to relax for, say, five or ten years.**—*Chou En Lai, Chinese prime minister, to North Vietnam's prime minister, October 1973.*[374]

Pham Van Dong went to China to request additional military aid in October 1973. Hanoi requested the equipment to replace losses during the 1972 Easter Offensive and build-up for the eventual final offensive to take the rest of South Vietnam. The Chinese as well as the Soviets denied the request, forcing Hanoi to rely on its own stockpiles of equipment, which were considerable.

2786 **Airpower, given its day in court after a decade of frustration, confirmed its effectiveness as an instrument of**

national power — in just nine and a half flying days.—*Admiral Thomas H. Moorer, chairman of the Joint Chiefs of Staff, comments in Air Force magazine, November 1973.*[118]

Moorer attributed North Vietnam's eagerness to return to the negotiating table to the heavy bombing campaign of Operation Linebacker II, in December72.

2787 **In his life President [Lyndon B.] Johnson endured the vilification of those who sought to portray him as a man of war. But there was nothing he cared about more deeply than achieving a lasting peace in the world.**—*President Richard Nixon, televised broadcast, 23 January 1973.*[630]

Lyndon Johnson died the day before Nixon announced that a cease-fire agreement had been reached with North Vietnam.

1974–1975

In the End, we will remember not the words of our enemies, but the silence of our friends.
—Martin Luther King, Jr.

2788 **We have no victories to celebrate until we die; we did not win; our war, it is said, was not a just war. We are loners. Loners and losers.**—*Tim O'Brien, Vietnam War Veteran and author, writing in 1974.*[493]

O'Brien speaks of the difficulty of Vietnam War Veterans initially being accepted by veteran fraternities such as the Veterans of Foreign Wars and the American Legion.

2789 **[The Vietnam War:] It wasn't that it was finished, it was a loser.**—*Robert C. Seamans, Jr., Secretary of the Air Force, during an interview, March 1974.*[916]

2790 **The B-52 bombers, built as the ultimate weapon of their time to carry nuclear devastation to the homeland of an equally armed and powerful adversary, were used in Vietnam to destroy the barnyards, as well as the bridges, supply trucks and military emplacements of a small, largely agricultural and, until the war itself changed things, obscure state.**—*Alexander Kendrick, military historian, writing in 1974.*[90]

2791 **You will have to live with the unresolvable doubt that, but for your decision not to call, these children might still be alive.**—*Graham Martin, U.S. Ambassador to South Vietnam, in a letter to George Webber, 1974.*[629]

According to Nguyen Cao Ky, Martin sent Webber a package containing the photos of mutilated children with the above note. Webber had visited Saigon, and Martin requested he appeal to the Communist delegation in Saigon to stop terrorist attacks. Webber was an anti-war activist and president of the New York Theological Seminary. Webber departed Vietnam without having talked with the Communist delegation in Saigon.

2792 **The American people have come to accept the judgement that we made about the Vietnam War when we refused to fight in it. The only thing we were guilty of was premature morality.**—*Stanley J. Pietlock, self-exiled draft evader, comments to a correspondent, Toronto, Canada, 16 September 1974.*[612]

Pietlock was reacting on President Ford's amnesty program for military deserters and draft dodgers who were being allowed to re-enter American society provided they submitted to two years of public service work in order to earn their amnesty.

2793 **My sincere hope is that this [conditional amnesty for draft evaders and military deserters] is a constructive step towards calmer and cooler appreciation of our individual rights and responsibilities and our common purpose as a nation whose future is always more important than its past.**—*President Gerald R. Ford, during a news conference, 16 September 1974.*[611]

Ford announced a program of conditional amnesty for Vietnam War military deserters and draft evaders/resisters. Under the program, a clemency board would review those who were convicted for desertion or evasion. An individual petitioning for clemency was required to complete two years of public service to clear his record. The clemency board, determined the service.

2794 **A little corruption oils the machinery.**—*Graham Martin, U.S. Ambassador to South Vietnam, 1974.*[374]

Martin's response to field reports that morale in the South Vietnamese military was deteriorating rapidly due to low pay, high inflation, corruption, and a general lack of control by military authorities.

2795 **[American combat troops?] They won't come back even if we offered them candy.**—*Pham Van Dong, Prime Minister, Democratic Republic of Vietnam, during a meeting in Hanoi, January 1975.*[374]

During the meeting escalation of the timetable for the final offensive to take complete control of South Vietnam took place. In early January 1975, NVA forces captured the provincial capital of Phuoc Binh. There was no American response to the blatant violation of the cease-fire. The meeting focused on the possibility of American intervention if the offensive continued. The leaders in Hanoi resolved that there would be no American supportive reaction for South Vietnam.

2796 **If Americans have to go, I will take a million Vietnamese with me.**—*Graham Martin, U.S. Ambassador to South Vietnam, in a speech at the Embassy, 1975.*[629]

Martin promised a crowd of Vietnamese including embassy workers, that if evacuation became necessary they would not be left behind. The crowd represented Vietnamese working for the Americans in a variety of jobs. When the actual evacuation of the U.S. Embassy was complete, 6,000 Vietnamese had been extracted by helicopter.

2797 **I will be the last man to leave this embassy. You have my solemn word on that.**—*Graham Martin, U.S. Ambassador to South Vietnam, during a speech at the Embassy, 1975.*[629]

This was Martin's pledge to his Vietnamese staff and workers at the embassy. Martin was in the last group of American civilians to evacuate the Embassy. The very last Americans to leave the Embassy were the members of the U.S. Marine contingent deployed to provide additional security during the evacuation.

2798 **Thieu would never have remained [in power] without the backing of the Americans, who wanted stability above all else.**—*Nguyen Cao Ky, former Vice President of South Vietnam, speaking to a group of disgruntled officers, March 1975.*[629]

A group of Vietnamese Air Force officers wanted Ky's approval to bomb the presidential residence and kill President Nguyen Van Thieu. Ky talked them out of it on the grounds that the subsequent confusion in Saigon would make it easier for the NVA to move in and take over.

2799 **Vietnam has left a rancid aftertaste that clings to almost every mention of direct military intervention.**—*David Broder, journalist, March 1975.*[264]

2800 **Saigon must make the tough decision which province capitols can still be saved.**—*General George S. Brown, Chairman, Joint Chiefs of Staff, in a speech delivered to the Navy League, 19 March 1975.*[613]

Brown claimed that a lack of U.S. aid contributed to South Vietnam's difficulty in countering an all-out North Vietnamese attack in South Vietnam. Brown blamed Congressional cutbacks of military aid to Vietnam as a major reason for their [SVN's] lack of adequate ammunition and spare parts to keep their armor and aircraft operational.

2801 **How can we terminate our aid and leave these people helpless in the face of this Communist offensive? To cut off aid now would be viewed by much of the world as a fundamental lack of resolve on our part — or even worse, a suggestion that aggression pays.**—*General George S. Brown, Chairman, Joint Chiefs of Staff, in a speech delivered to the Navy League, 19 March 1975.*[613]

In early March 1975, North Vietnam started the final offensive against the Saigon regime and military. In less than sixty days South Vietnamese resistance to the communist ended and the country fell to the communist on 30 April 1975. Aid request presented to Congress by President Ford for South Vietnam were reduced and pledges to support South Vietnam against renewed communist aggression were not honored.

2802 **This [Saigon] is worth dying for. A battle the world will always remember.**—*Nguyen Cao Ky, former Vice President of South Vietnam, speaking to Father Thanh. March 1975.*[629]

Ky proposed that Thieu step down from power, handing power to a collective leadership headed by Ky. He also proposed that Saigon be fortified, with women and children evacuated to the Delta. He saw the defense of Saigon as a Vietnamese version of the battle of Stalingrad.

2803 **We will survive in Vietnam. Another million people may die perhaps, but we will survive and be proud.**—*Unidentified Vietnamese man, speaking to a correspondent, Saigon, 2 April 1975.*[614]

This man was saying his good-byes to an American friend departing South Vietnam. By 2 April 1975, more than two thirds of South Vietnam was under NVA control, and the rest of the country was quickly collapsing to communist control.

2804 **It is not in the interest of the United Nations to get involved...**—*Kurt Waldheim, Secretary General, United Nations, during an interview, 2 April 1975.*[615]

Waldheim declared the U.N. would not get involved with the rescue or support of Vietnamese refugees in the communist held areas of South Vietnam. Waldheim rejected the U.S. request that the U.N. intervene with the North Vietnamese. Waldheim cited the political realities of the war and the fact that the communist did not want to cooperate with the U.N. regarding the refugee issue.

2805 **If we refrain from giving aid in those cases in which we do not know the outcome, then we will, through a self-fulfilling prophecy, create the fall of many countries.**—*James R. Schlesinger, Secretary of Defense, during an interview, 6 April 1975.*[867]

Response to the question of whether or not U.S. aid to South Vietnam would "change the outcome significantly." North Vietnam had launched an all-out invasion against South Vietnam in March 1975. The Ford administration requested aid money to supply the South Vietnamese with necessary munitions, spare parts, and other supplies which would assist them in their defense against the renewed NVA attacks.

2806 **The American people as well as the American Congress must see now that they have got to do something for the people of South Vietnam...**—*Nguyen Van Thieu, President, South Vietnam, in a publicized plea, 4 April 1975.*[616]

Thieu pleaded for the U.S. to honor its commitments to South Vietnam, as NVA troops tightened their control around Saigon. At this point in time communist troops controlled more than two thirds of South Vietnam.

2807 **By day, interrogators and guards would inquire about our needs solicitously. The center of Hanoi was dead — even though like our prisons, thousands of yards from the drop zone. We knew the bombers knew where we were, and felt not only ecstatically happy, but confident. The North Vietnamese didn't.... They knew they lived through last night, but they also knew that if our forces moved their bomb line over a few thousand yards they wouldn't live through tonight.**—*Admiral James B. Stockdale, from an address to the Armed Forces Staff College, 9 April 1975.*[119]

Admiral Stockdale spent more than seven years as a prisoner of the North Vietnamese, he was released from the Hanoi Hilton in 1973.

2808 **I can't conceive of this Congress voting $722 million in military aid for South Vietnam.**—*Representative Thomas P. O'Neill, Jr. of Massachusetts, comments on aid request, 10 April 1975.*[617]

Democrats in Congress raised the most objections to funding additional military aid, even though South Vietnam was very near collapse under the ongoing NVA offensive.

2809 **It's dead. I oppose it. I don't know of any on the democratic side who will support it.**—*Senator Henry M. Jackson of Washington, comments on request for military aid for South Vietnam, 10 April 1975.*[617]

President Ford personally requested Congress to fund a $722 million emergency military aid package for South Vietnam. In light of the swiftly deteriorating military situation in South Vietnam, the aid was necessary if South Vietnam was to have any hope of stopping the communist advance.

2810 **I cannot, alas, leave in such a cowardly fashion. As for you, and in particular your great country, I never believed for a moment that you would have this sentiment of abandoning a people which has chosen liberty. You have refused us your protection, and we can do nothing about it.**—*General Sirik Matak, of the Cambodian Government, in a note to Ambassador Dean, 12 April 1975.*[867]

Matak was offered evacuation from Cambodia by U.S. Ambassador John Gunther Dean. Matak was on the Khmer Rouge's list of "traitors" to be executed. He was subsequently killed by the communists when the Cambodian government collapsed in 18 April 1975.

2811 **We always thought of the Saigon Embassy as the second Alamo.**—*SSgt. Colin Broussard, U.S. Marine Corps, April 1975.*[500]

Broussard served as bodyguard to Ambassador Martin in the final days of the official American presence in South Vietnam.

2812 **We cannot by our actions alone insure the survival of South Viet-Nam. But we can, alone, by our inaction assure its demise.**—*Henry Kissinger, Secretary of State, in a request to Congress, 15 April 1975.*[867]

Kissinger pleaded for Congress to help South Vietnam, as the NVA pressed their final assaults across South Vietnam.

2813 **We've sent, so to speak, battleship after battleship, and bomber after bomber, and 500,000 or more men, and billions and billions of dollars. If billions and billions didn't do at a time when we had all our men there, how can $722 million save the day?**—*Representative Millicent Fenwick of New Jersey, speaking during Congressional debate regarding military aid to South Vietnam, April 1975.*[871]

Congress was debating the Ford administration's request for military aid to Saigon. South Vietnam was near collapse as the North Vietnamese's Final Offensive overran South Vietnamese forces.

2814 **The failure of the United States to meet its commitments to Saigon had created this present tragic situation in South Vietnam.**—*President Gerald R. Ford, speaking at the convention of American Society of Newspaper Editors, 16 April 1975.*[618]

Ford blamed Congress for cutbacks and the ultimate cutoff of military aid funds for South Vietnam.

2815 **If the Americans do not want to support us any more, let them go, get out! No matter what we cannot accept, we are adults. We are going to continue to be insulted, because Americans will not help us. The Americans promised us — we trusted them. But you have not given us the aid you promised us. With that aid, I would not be afraid of the communists. Now my resignation will let the United States give you aid and open the way to negotiations.**—*Nguyen Van Thieu, President of South Vietnam, from his resignation speech, 21 April 1975.*[871]

The Thieu resignation speech took ninety minutes. Head of the government passed to Vice President Tran Van Huong.

2816 **Today, Americans can regain the sense of pride that existed before Vietnam. But it cannot be achieved by refighting a war that is finished.... These events, tragic as they are, portend neither the end of the world nor of America's leadership in the world.**—*President Gerald Ford, from a speech at Tulane University, 23 April 1975.*[374]

Ford was speaking as Saigon collapsed under North Vietnam's final offensive.

2817 **The United States has not respected its promises. It is unfair. It is inhumane. It is not trustworthy. It is irresponsible.**—*Nguyen Van Thieu, President of South Vietnam, from his resignation speech, 21 April 1975.*[871]

The Thieu resignation speech took ninety minutes. Head of the government passed to Vice President Tran Van Huong. Thieu departed Vietnam a few days later.

2818 **I resign but I do not desert.**—*Nguyen Van Thieu, President, South Vietnam, in a public resignation, 22 April 1975.*[619]

Thieu resigned after a one and a half hour speech. He bitterly denounced the United States for failing to honor its commitments to the Vietnamese people and labeled America as untrustworthy. He left a few days later for exile in Europe.

2819 **[Unite,] because we will die if we do otherwise. If we do not help ourselves, then our hope for the assistance of others is useless ... fight until the troops die or the country is lost...**—*Tran Van Huong, President of South Vietnam, from a speech, 21 April 1975.*[871]

Tran Van Huong became president when Nguyen Van

Thieu resigned. Huong called for the South Vietnamese people to fight the communists. Nine days later Saigon fell.

2820 **At the time of the peace agreement the United States agreed to replace equipment on a one-for-one basis. But the United States did not keep its word. Is America's word reliable these days?**—*President Nguyen Van Thieu, in his farewell address to South Vietnam, April 1975.*[629]

Appropriations for military aid for South Vietnam were cut from nearly $3 billion in 1973 to $300 million by 1975.

2821 **You ran away and left us to do the job that you could not do. We have nothing and you want us to achieve where you failed.**—*President Nguyen Van Thieu, in his farewell address to South Vietnam, April 1975.*[629]

Thieu was eventually forced out of office, blaming the U.S. for not supporting South Vietnam and failing its commitment of support.

2822 **An inhumane act by an inhumane ally.**—*Nguyen Cao Ky, former Prime Minister of South Vietnam, comments to the press, 25 April 1975.*[374]

Nguyen Cao Ky's characterization of the U.S. desertion of South Vietnam in 1975.

2823 **We are beaten. We accept humiliation; but it is better to be beaten by your brothers than by strangers. I hope the winners think of the South Vietnamese as their brothers.**—*Tran Van Lam, President of the South Vietnamese Senate, commenting to the press, 27 April 1975.*[867]

Spoken in the final days before the collapse of South Vietnam and complete conquest by North Vietnam.

2824 **The high hopes and wishful idealism with which the American nation had been born had not been destroyed, but they had been chastened by the failure of America to work its will in Indochina.**—*Newsweek, 28 April 1975.*[256]

Comments made regarding the fall of South Vietnam to the communists.

2825 **The Vietnam debate has run its course.**—*Henry Kissinger, Secretary of State, comments to the press, April 1975.*[312]

President Ford asked Congress for emergency military aid for South Vietnam to stem the tide of the North Vietnamese offensive. Congress rejected the aid measure, but did vote $300 million in humanitarian aid. Part of this money was to be used to evacuate American citizens from South Vietnam.

2826 **[The evacuation from Saigon] closes a chapter in the American experience.**—*President Gerald R. Ford, in a White House statement, 29 April 1975.*[621]

From President Ford's statement regarding the final fall of Saigon and South Vietnam.

2827 **Perhaps the United States could never have won the war. But even if one cannot achieve victory, the alternative is not necessarily the humiliation of abject surrender.**—*Nguyen Cao Ky, former Prime Minister of South Vietnam, April 1975.*[629]

Ky, in the final hours before the collapse of South Vietnam in 1975.

2828 **I ask all Americans to close ranks, to avoid recrimination about the past, to look ahead to the many goals we share and to work together on the great tasks that remain to be accomplished.**—*President Gerald R. Ford, in a White House statement, 29 April 1975.*[621]

From President Ford's statement regarding the final fall of Saigon and South Vietnam.

2829 **They just landed first and asked permission afterwards.**—*Unidentified Thai Foreign Office official, comments to the press, 29 April 1975.*[620]

In the final hours before the fall of Saigon seventy-four of South Vietnam's aircraft escaped from South Vietnam and made their way to the air force base at U-Taphao, Thailand. On board the planes were a combination of South Vietnamese refugees and aircraft crews. The South Vietnamese aircraft did not request clearance to land at the base, they simply landed. Thai government officials said the refugees would not be allowed to stay in Thailand.

2830 **All Vietnamese are victors and only the American imperialist have been vanquished.**—*Colonel Bui Tin, North Vietnamese Army officer, April 1975.*[374]

Tin was the NVA officer who accepted the initial surrender of Saigon, 30 April 1975.

2831 **The revolution has come. You have come.**—*General Duong Van Minh, President of South Vietnam, 30 April 1975.*[867]

Minh took over the presidency from Tran Van Huong, and surrendered the Saigon government to the first communist officer to enter the presidential palace.

2832 **[This is] a victory of historic significance for the South Vietnamese population.**—*Dinh Ba Thi, head of delegation, Provisional Revolutionary Government, Paris, 30 April 1975.*[622]

2833 **The Vietnam War is finished as far as the United States is concerned.**—*President Gerald Ford, April 1975.*[334]

2834 **Between Vietnamese, there are no victors and no vanquished. Only the Americans have been beaten. If you are patriots, consider this a moment of joy. The war for our country is over.**—*Colonel Bui Tin, deputy director of Quan Doi Nhan Dan, to General Duong Van Minh, 30 April 1975.*[374]

Bui Tin was covering the Final Offensive for the NVA newspaper. He was the first ranking office to meet with General "Big" Minh. Minh had been passed authority for the South Vietnamese government when Tran Van Huong resigned. Minh surrendered what was left of the Government to Bui Tin, the first NVA officer to enter the presidential palace.

2835 **Men, you have delivered these latest children of Israel. Now I want you to pray for Vietnam, and then I want you all to relax and have a little fun.**—*Chaplain aboard the USS Blue Ridge, announcement to all those onboard, April 1975.*[629]

According to Ky this was the chaplains message to the crew of the *Blue Ridge* and those involved in the evacuation of Saigon, April 1975.

2836 **Henceforth, South Vietnam is free and independent. The sacred testament of our beloved President Ho Chi Minh is realized.**—*Dinh Ba Thi, head of delegation, Provisional Revolutionary Government, Paris, 30 April 1975.*[622]

The NLF was reorganized and designated the PRG, and so recognized by the 1973 Paris accords. The PRG was treated as a fourth party to the negotiations. In Dinh Ba Thi's statement he makes reference to "his" President, Ho Chi Minh.

2837 **We all sacrificed everything in this war. We may have lost, but we are not the only losers — you Americans have lost, too.**—*Nguyen Cao Ky, former Vice President of South Vietnam, April 1975.*[629]

Ky had flown his helicopter out to the USS *Midway*, then transferred to the USS *Blue Ridge*. He was speaking to an unidentified American Colonel on the *Blue Ridge*.

2838 **[Remove your uniforms and dress in civilian clothes,] ... you have no army, no country any more.**—*Unidentified U.S. Navy officer, May 1975.*[863]

A group of South Vietnamese officers had escaped in the last evacuations before Saigon fell. They were temporarily taken to Guam and separated from the other evacuees. When they fled South Vietnam they were still in uniform. They were ordered to change into civilian clothes and abandon their uniforms and former rank.

2839 **Officially, we were separate [Hanoi and the NLF]. But in fact we were the same thing all the time; there was a single [communist] party; a single government; a single capital; a single country.**—*Huynh Tan Phat, General Secretary of the NLF, speaking to photojournalist, 1975.*[887]

For years the NLF claimed publicly that there was no political link between them and Hanoi. The U.S. insisted the communist rebellion in the south was supported and directed from Hanoi.

2840 **A poor man's war.**—*Van Tien Dung, North Vietnamese Chief of Staff, commenting on Saigon's predicament, 1975.*[334]

Dung was commenting on the severe problems the ARVN military were forced to deal with. Without American support the ARVN quickly disintegrated. The disintegration was completed when North Vietnam launched their final offensive against the South Vietnamese in early-1975.

2841 [INTERVIEWER:] **Why did the U.S. remain in Vietnam until 1972 if you believe the Cold War ended in the mid-Sixties.**

[HELLER:] **For no reason at all. That's the point! We often continue believing in things — and this is true of religions as well as ideologies — long after the circumstances that gave rise to the beliefs have disappeared. The belief in stopping communism wherever it threatens to advance simply carried over into another culture long after the reason for the belief disappeared. We weren't fighting communism in Vietnam. We were fighting culture lag.**—*Joseph Heller, author of Catch-22, during an interview, June 1975.*[905]

Heller believed the Vietnam War was an extension of the Cold War, started in the late-Forties with the panic over the spread of communism. He saw the Cold War ending in the mid-sixties as the perceived widespread threat of communism did not materialize. For Heller the threatened spread of communism, as proposed by the Domino Theory was not valid in the mid-sixties as it was used as a justification for the American intervention and escalation in Southeast Asia.

2842 **Although our aim was to fool the American press, the public, and Congress, we in intelligence succeeded best in fooling ourselves.**—*Samuel Adams, CIA anaylist in VC/NVA Order of Battle, September 1975.*[629]

According to Adams, MACV issued deliberately misleading enemy troop numbers to the White House and the press, indicating the enemy troop strength in South Vietnam to be 300,000 instead of the CIA intelligence estimate of 600,000.

2843 **Today it is almost as though the war had never happened. Americans have somehow blocked it out of their consciousness. They don't talk about it. They don't talk about its consequences.**—*Joseph C. Harsch, journalist, October 1975.*[293]

Aftermath of the fall of South Vietnam.

2844 **From my earliest associations with Vietnam (1951) I have been concerned about U.S. handling of information from that area .... This included deliberate and reflexive manipulation of information, restrictions on collection and censorship of reporting. The net result was that decision makers were denied the opportunity to get a complete form of information, determine its validity for themselves, and make decisions...**—*Lt.Col. Henry A. Shockley, formerly of the Defense Attaché Office, Saigon, in a memorandum to Congress, 29 November 1975.*[229]

Shockley's memorandum went to the House Select Committee on Intelligence.

1976–2000 Hindsight

All truth passes through three stages. First, it is ridiculed. Second, it is violently opposed. Third, it is accepted as being self-evident.

—Arthur Schopenhauer

2845 **The French saw the United States creating a new nation and threatening French interest, while the average Vietnamese found it difficult to understand why the Americans should give them roads, food, drugs to make life easier, and at the same time give the French guns and bombs to kill them.**—*Nguyen Cao Ky, former Prime Minister of South Vietnam, from his memoirs, 1976.*[629]

The U.S. poured money in to Vietnam in the form of military aid to the French and at the same time millions of dollars were given to the Bao Dai government for civic improvements. This was based on the principle that military might alone could not keep the communist out, but a prosperous healthy Vietnamese economy along with the French military efforts could.

2846 **The United States would be gravely concerned if any Indochina armistice agreed to by France would provide a road to a Communist takeover and further aggression.**—*John Foster Dulles, Secretary of State, during a nationwide radio address, 8 May 1954.*[655]

Dulles was warning France against giving away too much at the ongoing Geneva peace negotiations between France and the Viet Minh.

2847 **The provisions for free elections which would solve ultimately the problems of Viet-Nam was a device to hide the incompatibility of the Communist and Western positions, neither of which can admit the domination of all of Viet Nam by the other side.**—*Professor Hans Morgenthau, University of Chicago, as quoted by William P. Bundy, September 1967.*[82]

2848 **There is only one threat to world peace, the one that is presented by the international communist conspiracy.**—*Richard Nixon.*[83]

2849 **[The American solution to Vietnam was to] ... make everyone in South Vietnam happy, give everyone all the good things of life, and nobody would become a Communist.**—*Nguyen Cao Ky, former Prime Minister of South Vietnam, 1976.*[629]

2850 **I liked Diem, but I became convinced that he did not have the political knack, nor the strength of character, politically, to manage this bizarre collection of people in Vietnam.**—*General J. Lawton Collins, U.S. Envoy to South Vietnam.*[971]

Collins commanded the 25th Infantry division during World War II and served as U.S. Envoy to the State of Vietnam until 1955.

2851 **[Land Reform was] the single most important issue not only of the war in the south after 1960 but in the entire history of the Revolution.**—*Gabriel Kolko, political historian, 1985.*[21]

Vietnamese attachment to the land was very strong and central to their existence. Land reform programs that did not address the peasant farmers needs, but forced relocation, were major reasons for the GVN's loss of rural support. The communist promised land reform in their propaganda.

2852 **To those people in the huts and villages of half the globe struggling to break the bonds of mass misery, we pledge our best efforts to help them help themselves, for whatever period is required, not because the Communists may be doing it, not because we seek their votes, but because it is right. If a free society cannot help the many who are poor, it cannot save the few who are rich.**—*President John F. Kennedy.*[357]

2853 **Hanoi was willing to buy victory with blood; Saigon was not.**—*Dave Richard Palmer, historian and Vietnam War Veteran, 1978.*[713]

Palmer's evaluation of the Battle of Ap Bac, in which the ARVN 7th Infantry Division suffered a humiliating defeat, which was just one of many the ARVN were to experience throughout the war.

2854 **War will exist until that distant day when the conscientious objector enjoys the same reputation and prestige that the warrior does today.**—*President John F. Kennedy.*[83]

2855 **I didn't mind butchering the enemy, but we were butchering our own allies.**—*Unidentified CIA officer, comments to correspondent.*[374]

The officer was referring to secret operations financed and directed by the CIA in the early '60s. Teams of Vietnamese agents were infiltrated into North Vietnam on covert missions to gather intelligence and conduct sabotage. Because of the tightly controlled structure of North Vietnamese society, the outsiders were quickly recognized and killed or they were convinced to defect. Most of the teams inserted into North Vietnam never returned.

2856 **The President unquestionably felt that an American retreat in Asia might upset the whole world balance.**—*Arthur Schlesinger, Jr., White House aide and historian, in his peronsal history of his White House years, 1965.*[85]

Schlesinger states that by the end of 1961, Kennedy felt that America could not withdraw from Vietnam allowing it to be lost to the communists.

2857 **Nothing is further from [the] USG (U.S. Government) mind than [a] "neutral solution for Vietnam." We intend to win.**—*George Ball, Under Secretary of State, to Ambassador Henry Cabot Lodge, 16 December 1963.*[87]

2858 **The purposeless rule of the generals gave way to the buffoon antics of a man whose serious moments were rare.**—*Bui Diem, former South Vietnamese Ambassador to the United States, 1987.*[15]

Bui Diem was speaking about General Nguyen Khanh, who came to power in South Vietnam via a bloodless coup in 1964.

2859 **[The Kennedy Administration was confronted with] two undeclared wars, one with the Viet Cong, the other with the American press.**—*Chester L. Cooper, former NSC officer and author, from his book, 1970.*[194]

Cooper's characterization was of the problems faced by Kennedy in 1962 and 1963. Kennedy was receiving glowing reports of progress from MACV, GVN and some intelligence agencies, while at the same time he received pessimistic reports on the situation from other intelligence agencies and from news reports in the press.

2860 **[American advisers] were like the steel reinforcing rods in concrete.**—*General Earle Wheeler, former Chairman of JCS, 1978.*[713]

By the end of 1964 there were about 23,000 Americans in South Vietnam, many of them advisers down to the battalion level of the South Vietnamese Army. Wheeler credits the survival of South Vietnamese, at that time, to the presence of American advisers.

2861 **The war was not going well, the Vietnamese Army was not taking kindly to American advice, and Diem was not following through on his promises to liberalize his regime or increase its effectiveness.**—*Chester L. Cooper, former NSC officer and author, from his book, 1970.*[194]

2862 **A great many of us felt that the one-shot thing, after you did it a couple of times, conveyed to Hanoi the idea of weakness.**—*William Bundy, former Assistant Secretary of State, during an interview, 26 May 1969.*[179]

Bundy was speaking of the tit-for-tat retaliatory raids that had been carried out against North Vietnam prior to October 1964.

2863 **Presidential popularity is a major source of strength in gaining cooperation from Congress.**—*President Lyndon Johnson, in his memoirs, 1971.*[66]

By 1967 Johnson was losing support from hawks who wanted to move the war forward to completion and from social activists who wanted more progress in the Great Society programs.

2864 **You just couldn't start bombing North Vietnam de novo [to begin], what was required was a Communist act so atrocious that it would justify the new U.S. course; in the meantime, we would take our lumps until something very dramatic and very obscene happened.**—*Chester L. Cooper, former NSC officer, during an interview,August 1969.*[221]

The Johnson administration had decided that bombing North Vietnam might stop Hanoi's support and direction of the VC. It would also be a morale booster for the South Vietnamese. A plan for sustained air strikes was created but could not be activated without just cause. That cause came on 6 February 1965, when the VC attacked the U.S. installation at Pleiku, killing eight Americans and destroying five aircraft.

2865 **[The Generals] would have gone ahead even without American acquiescence. Their necks were stretched too far.**—*Lucien Conein, former U.S. CIA agent, during an interview, 1983.*[374]

Conein performed many functions for the CIA in Vietnam. During the preparations for the coup against Diem he operated as the liaison between the coup generals and the U.S. Embassy.

2866 **[The South Vietnamese Air Force] was a young and enthusiastic air force with more spunk than the army.**—*Joseph B. Treaster, New York Times.*[955]

2867 **I know that when things don't go well, they like to blame the president, and that is one of the things presidents are paid for.**—*President John F. Kennedy.*[355]

2868 **Once you're in a war, or you've made the decision to use military force to solve your problems, then you ought to use it.**—*General Curtis E. LeMay, former U.S. Air Force Chief of Staff, during an interview, 1986.*[141]

2869 **In the final analysis, I had the leverage to influence the South Vietnamese and they knew it, and both sides exercised a rare degree of tact.**—*General William Westmoreland, former ComUSMACV, from his memoirs, 1976.*[887]

This was Westmoreland's reasoning for not establishing a joint U.S.-Vietnamese, unified command. The joint command approach had been successfully used during the Korean War, where mixed units of Americans and South Koreans, lead by Americans, successful fought the communists. In Vietnam, the American and Vietnamese combat commands were separate.

2870 **America did eventually bomb [North Vietnam] with a view to bringing the North to the conference table. It would find that it was, instead of changing the North, sticking itself to a tar baby...**—*David Halberstam, correspondent-writer, from his book, 1972.*[206]

2871 **Quietly and without fanfare, he [President Johnson] launched what would become America's longest, must frustrating, and most divisive war, with only a dim perception of what lay ahead and no firm mandate from the nation.**—*George Herring, historian, 1979.*[347]

2872 **Everything I knew about history told me that if I got out of Vietnam and let Ho Chi Minh run through the streets of Saigon, then I'd be doing exactly what Chamberlain did in World War II. I'd be giving a big fat reward to aggression. And I knew that if we let Communist aggression succeed in taking over South Vietnam, there would follow in this country an endless national debate—a mean and destructive debate—that would shatter my Presidency, kill my administration, and damage our democracy. I knew that Harry Truman and Dean Acheson had lost their effectiveness from the day that the Communists took over in China. I believed that the loss of China had played a large role in the rise of Joe McCarthy. And I knew that all these problems, taken together, were chickenshit compared to what might happen if we lost Vietnam.**—*Lyndon Johnson, comments to his biographer.*[379]

2873 **If you let a bully come into your front yard one day, the next day he'll be up on your porch, and the day after that he'll rape your wife in your own bed.**—*Lyndon Johnson, to biographer Doris Kearns.*[372]

Johnson's analogy explaining why he felt he, and America, had to stand against communist aggression in Vietnam.

2874 **We had to win the war before we could indulge in the "luxury" of politics.**—*Attributed to Henry Cabot Lodge, U.S. Ambassador to South Vietnam, by Nguyen Cao Ky.*[629]

Saigon struggled politically since its formation. After the coup against Diem in 1963, South Vietnam was politically unstable, yet still involved in a war with the VC and NVA. Many were of the opinion that the war had to be completed before any lasting political stability could be brought to South Vietnam. Many others stressed political stability was required before meaningful reforms could be brought to the people of South Vietnam. Such change would make the struggle against the communists easier.

2875 **A crucial decision that never received the serious study and detached thought it deserved, a hasty and ill-advised message that constituted a green light to those who wanted Diem's downfall, and a serious blunder which launched a period of deep political confusion in Saigon that lasted almost two years.**—*Lyndon Johnson, in his memoirs, 1971.*[210]

Johnson's characterization of the State Department cable that was transmitted to the U.S. Embassy in Saigon in August 1963. This cable authorized Ambassador Lodge to give a group of South Vietnamese generals plotting a coup against Diem, America's tacit support for their effort to overthrow the Diem-Nhu regime.

2876 **Whatever his fears or his ultimate intentions, he bequeathed to his successor a problem eminently more dangerous than the one he had inherited from Eisenhower.**—*George C. Herring, 1979.*[347]

There is speculation as to what Kennedy's actual course would have been had he not been assassinated. Some believe he would have withdrawn from Vietnam, others that he would have increased the American commitment in Vietnam on a limited basis, perhaps seeking a negotiated settlement.

2877 **I saw our bombs as my political resources for negotiating a peace.**—*Lyndon Johnson, in his memoirs, 1976.*[912]

Johnson believed that bombing North Vietnam would apply sufficient pressure to cause them to abandon their support of the insurgency in South Vietnam. An insurgency that had been in progress since the end of World War II.

2878 **The time has come to stop beating our heads against stone walls under the illusion that we have been appointed policeman to the human race.**—*Walter Lippmann, political columnist.*[83]

Lippmann opposed the Johnson administration's policy in Southeast Asia and the introduction of American combat troops to Vietnam.

2879 **People are drifting towards Communism because they are poor. If you give the people everything they want—television sets, automobiles, and so on—none of them will go over to Communism.**—*Ellsworth Bunker, American Ambassador to South Vietnam, as related by Nguyen Cao Ky, 1976.*[629]

According to Ky, the Vietnamese people had no desire for the good things in life based on the American standard. America's efforts to raise the standard of living was not fully accepted or appreciated by the average Vietnamese.

2880 **Power, even if it does not always corrupt, often blinds people, changes their ideas, their hopes, and leads to frustration among their followers.**—*Nguyen Cao Ky, former Prime Minister of South Vietnam, from his memoirs, 1976.*[629]

Military and public leaders outside the Diem circle of power were growing discontented with the way the Diem regime was operating.

2881 **This war will have no end as long as it merely pits foreign troops against Communists. In the end, it is safety in the villages that is the object of the war.**—*McGeorge Bundy, former Special Assistant to the President for National Security Affairs, in a letter to the President.*[72]

Bundy was emphasizing the importance of the pacification program and the support of the South Vietnamese people.

2882 **[It was a] masterpiece of obliquity, and I was unhappy about it. To my mind the American people had a right to know forthrightly, within the actual limits of military security, what we were calling on their sons to do, and to presume that it could be concealed despite the open eyes of the press and television was folly.**—*General William Westmoreland, former ComUSMACV, 1983.*[374]

U.S. Marines were initially deployed to protect the American air base at Da Nang in March 1965. Shortly after their deployment they were released to conduct offensive operations against the VC. This fact was not made public until June 1965.

2883 **The Marines came in and just sat down and didn't do anything. They were involved in counterinsurgency of the deliberate, mild sort.**—*General William DePuy, operations officer, MACV, during an interview, 26 March 1979.*[382]

DePuy's characterization of the U.S. Marine Corps pacification program, the Combined Action Platoon.

2884 **The enemy will pass slowly from the offensive to the defensive. The blitzkrieg will transform itself into a war of long duration ... the enemy will be caught in a dilemma: He has to drag out the war in order to win it and he does not possess ... the psychological and political means to fight a long drawn-out war...**—*General Vo Nguyen Giap.*[501]

Giap, speaking during the early days of the Viet Minh war with the French. His statement ultimately also applied to the American involvement in Vietnam fifteen years later.

2885 **If I left the woman I really loved — the Great Society — in order to get involved with that bitch of a war on the other side of the world, then I would lose everything at home.**—*Lyndon Johnson, to biographer Doris Kearns.*[372]

Johnson felt trapped, if he concentrated on his domestic policy, he would lose the war against the communist in Vietnam and be tagged with having lost Southeast Asia and weakening the U.S. position throughout the world. If he focused on the war in Vietnam he would be hounded for ignoring the problems at home of hunger, illiteracy, race relations, and the poor.

2886 **Now we are committed to major combat in Vietnam. We had determined not to let that country fall under Communist rule as long as we could prevent it.**—*Lyndon Johnson, from his memoirs, 1971.*[68]

In July 1965 Johnson raised U.S. forces levels in Vietnam from 75,000 to 125,000.

2887 **We went to war because our country asked us to go, because our new President, Lyndon B. Johnson, ordered us to go, but more importantly because it was our duty to go.**—*General Harold G. Moore, 1992.*[501]

Moore commanded the 1st Battalion, 7th Cavalry Regiment at the battle of the Ia Drang, the first major battle between American troopers of the 1st Cavalry Division (Airmobile) and North Vietnamese regular soldiers.

2888 **The GI isn't tolerant. Never has been. His job is to kill. I've never seen the place where GIs could get along with the local populace.... To find this to have been the case in Vietnam and to say it was wrong is true, but irrelevant. It has always been that way.**—*Unidentified U.S. Army colonel, during a post war interview, released 1981.*[92]

2889 **The army, being the army, breeds a kind of man who instinctively hates the idea of being associated with an unsuccessful mission. I do not mean this in a disparaging way; it is merely an inbred army trait: you don't get promotion unless you succeed.**—*Nguyen Cao Ky, former Prime Minister of South Vietnam, from his memoirs, 1976.*[629]

In February 1965 the civilian Prime Minister resigned and a group of fifty military officers took on the task of selecting a new prime minister from their ranks. It took two days before one of them accepted the position, the recent failures of past governments firmly in all their minds. Ky was selected as the new Prime Minister.

2890 **As chief of state he [Thieu] did not have any real power. I had to make the decisions and this made him jealous. ... He wanted power and glory but he did not want to have to do the dirty work. That was the kind of man he was.**—*Nguyen Cao Ky, former Prime Minister of South Vietnam, from his memoirs, 1976.*[629]

According to Ky, Thieu turned down the position of Prime Minister and nominated Ky instead.

2891 **Kennedy's planners (now directing Johnson's war) increasingly inclined towards operations against the North as a way to overcome their inability to win the war in the South.**—*Noam Chomsky, political dissident and linguistics professor, writings, 1992.*[87]

2892 **We would go through a village before dawn ... the villagers were herded like cattle into a barbed wire compound ... [Several South Vietnamese police would start interrogations, some of the villagers would] ... be beaten pretty badly, maybe tortured. Or they might be hauled off to jail ... at the end of the day, the villagers were turned loose. Their homes had been wrecked, their chickens killed, their rice confiscated — and if they weren't pro — Vietcong before we got there, they sure as hell were by the time we left.**—*William Ehrhart, former U.S. Marine infantryman, during a post-war interview, 1981.*[374]

2893 **I had neither a real understanding of the nature of the war nor any clear idea as to how to win it.**—*General Lewis Walt, former Commander, III Marine Amphibious Force, 1986.*[13]

The Marines initially deployed to Vietnam to protect the American air base at Da Nang. Their exact mission at the time of deployment had still not been identified by the policy makers at the White House.

2894 **I still get shaky thinking of those first few nights.... It was nothing [previous experiences in combat] compared to that ville. That was the most scared I've ever been in my life.**—*Corporal William Beebe, U.S. Marine Corps, 1972.*[977]

Beebe commanded a squad of Marines who took up residence in the village of Binh Nghia, under the Combine Action Platoon program. The squad worked with the villagers and their local village defense force. Until the Marines moved in, the village belonged to the VC. The Marines and a small contingent of local militia held the village against the VC and earned the respect of the villagers. The CAP arrived in Binh Nghia in June 1966, departing the pacified village in October 1967.

2895 **It's tough.... I know your way is best, yet I feel that we have enough strength and I'm confident that in the end we'll win out.**—*General William Westmoreland, according to Nguyen Cao Ky, 1976.*[629]

According to Ky, Westmoreland agreed with him that the restrictions placed by Washington hampered the war effort. Westmoreland did not believe he had enough troops, because in 1967 he requested an additional 100,000 troops with an open future request for 100,000 more. He again requested 206,000 more troops in 1968.

2896 **Insisting that the hated President Diem should remain in power for so long and then discarding him so abruptly, the Americans created a political vacuum which only the Communist were able to exploit.**—*Nguyen Cao Ky, former Prime Minister of South Vietnam, in his memoirs, 1976.*[629]

Ky blamed the lack of effective leadership in Saigon on U.S. insistence that Diem remain in power. Yet no effective or popular Vietnamese leaders surfaced after Diem was deposed.

2897 **We tried to be sensible men.**—*General Earle Wheeler, former Chairman, Joint Chiefs of Staff, during an interview, 21 August 1969.*[157]

Wheeler was responding to the question why the JCS never proposed attacking the Red River dikes around Hanoi. The dikes protected the Red River valley from flooding, and allowed the area to be irrigated. The diked bank of the river was about twenty feet above the lowest land levels in Hanoi. Breaks in the dikes caused by bombing could have thoroughly flooded the valley area, put most of Hanoi under several feet of water and destroyed thousands of acres of cropland, without massive loss of civilian lives.

2898 **I did everything I could to drag them out and get them to fight.... They just wouldn't play. They just would not play. They don't know how to fight on land, particularly against guerrillas.**—*General Harry Kinnard, former Commander, 1st Cavalry Division, during an interview, 21 June 1982.*[382]

Kinnard was not very happy with the Marines' tactics, during the 1st Cavalry's time in I Corps.

2899 **Fighting spirit one must have. Even if a man lacks some of the other qualifications, he can often make up for it in fighting spirit.**—*General Robin Olds, former U.S. Air Force pilot and commander of the 8th Tactical Fighter Wing.*[189]

During Old's command of the 8th Tactical Fighter Wing he shot down four enemy MiGs.

2900 **The Poles had not only put the cart before the horse, when the time of reckoning came, they had no horse.**—*President Lyndon Johnson, comments on Marigold, 1971.*[146]

Johnson was commenting on the aborted peace attempt by the Polish diplomat Januscz Lewandoswski, code named Marigold. According to the Poles, Hanoi had agreed to meet with them regarding possible initiation of peace negotiations in December 1966. Hanoi did not show up at the appointed time or place. The Poles blamed American bombing near Hanoi for the North Vietnamese no show, Johnson believed the Pole-NVN peace talk to be a "phony."

2901 **There are pilots and there are pilots; with the good ones, it is inborn. You can't teach it. If you are a fighter pilot, you have to be willing to take risks.**—*General Robin Olds, former U.S. Air Force pilot and commander of the 8th Tactical Fighter Wing.*[189]

Olds took command of the 8th TFW in September 1966, based at Ubon Royal Thai Air Base. During his tour he shot down four enemy MiGs during missions against North Vietnam.

2902 **Our needs are simple because we are Asians; we are influenced by the sayings of Confucius. We are not interested in material gain like Westerners; commercial success does not attract us as it docs Americans, so we can be happy with little.**—*Nguyen Cao Ky, former Prime Minister of South Vietnam, 1976.*[629]

Ky's evaluation of his people stands in contrast to the wide spread corruption that covered South Vietnam.

2903 **I was always convinced that bombing was less important to a successful outcome in Vietnam than what was done militarily on the ground in the South.**—*Lyndon Johnson, from his memoirs, 1971.*[146]

2904 **The more you bomb them the more you stiffen their morale and the more troops they will send south.**—*Nguyen Cao Ky, former Prime Minister of South Vietnam, 1976.*[629]

Ky speaking to Dean Rusk. Ky did not believe bombing alone would stop the infiltration from North Vietnam.

2905 **The regulation specifies that nicknames must not: "express a degree of bellicosity inconsistent with traditional American ideals or current foreign policy"; "convey connotations offensive to good taste or derogatory to a particular group, sect, or creed"; "convey connotations offensive to [U.S.] allies or other Free World nations"; or employ "exotic words, trite expressions, or well-known commercial trademarks."**—*Department of Defense, Gregory C. Seiminski, in an article for Parameters, 1995.*[888]

Military regulation governing the limits of naming operations became an issue when President Johnson objected to the name selected for 1st Cavalry Operations on the Bong Son Plain. The original name of the operation was Masher, it was changed to White Wing.

2906 **It is my personal opinion that this discussion by the press contributed to the prolonged warning the North Vietnamese received during which they dispersed and protected their POL supplies.**—*Admiral Edwin B. Hooper, Commander Service Force Pacific, 1972.*[961]

When the air campaign began against North Vietnam, Washington put North Vietnamese POL facilities on the restricted target list. It was not until June 1966 that the first major U.S. air strikes went in against the enemy POL facilities. By this time, news reports in the U.S. press of the pending strikes gave North Vietnam sufficient time to redistribute the POL stocks and change the method of delivery from the supply nations of Russia and Red China.

2907 **The decision of Secretary of Defense McNamara in late 1966 to cut the requested number of self-propelled barracks ships by three eliminated berthing space for two of three infantry battalions ... the brigade was forced to operate without its third maneuver battalion.**—*General William B. Fulton, former Commander, 2d Brigade, 9th Infantry Division, report on riverine operations, 1973.*[963]

The 2d Brigade deployed as the Army part of Task Force 117, a combined Army-Navy riverine force, operating in the Delta region of IV Corps. The task force was originally designed to deploy a full brigade (3 battalions), but restrictions placed by McNamara limited the force to only two infantry battalions and the Navy component which provided transportation and support.

2908 **[It would be disruptive to Southeast Asia] to permit a Communist takeover in South Viet-Nam either through withdrawal or under cloak of a meaningless agreement.**—*William P. Bundy, Assistant Secretary for East Asian and Pacific Affairs, quoting President Johnson, College Park, Maryland, 15 August 1967.*[82]

2909 **The requirement of 1967 is for re-emphasis upon the role of the Vietnamese themselves, always with our advice and support.**—*McGeorge Bundy, former Special Assistant to the President for National Security Affairs, in a letter to the President.*[72]

Bundy was emphasizing the role of America as a shield to allow the South Vietnamese government to stabilize and win the support of its people.

2910 **The threat of Communist China is not so fanciful that it should not serve as a vivid assumption of policy.**—*William P. Bundy, Assistant Secretary for East Asian and Pacific Affairs, paraphrasing Adlai Stevenson, College Park, Maryland, 15 August 1967.*[82]

Bundy was sounding a word of caution that the threat of Chinese intervention in Vietnam and the rest of Indochina should be a consideration in any Administration policy towards Southeast Asia.

2911 **To have gone through with constructing the barrier, even in modified form that I proposed, would have been to invite enormous casualties.**—*General William Westmoreland, former ComUSMACV.*[851]

Westmoreland was speaking of the abandonment of "McNamara's Wall," the electronic and barbed wire barrier he proposed to be emplaced along the DMZ. The assignment was given to the USMC and Seabees started the project. The impracticality of the barrier soon surfaced and it was discontinued after great expense and loss of life.

2912 **Why should we fight? The Americans are doing the fighting for us. Let's relax.**—*Unidentified ARVN soldier as related by Ngyen Cao Ky, 1976.*[629]

According to Ky the perception of the ARVN was that America had taken over the war and the ARVN had become secondary in function. They felt Americans would fight and die to rid South Vietnam of the communists.

2913 **[We took Khe Sanh and held it] ... then they abandoned it. Those fuckers abandoned it. We took it, we won it, we died there, and then those fuckers abandoned it. That's what our lives meant to our government.**—*Unidentified U.S. Marine Corps veteran of Khe Sanh, during an interview, released in 1984.*[493]

The Marines suffered several hundred casualties in the taking of Khe Sanh and the hills overlooking the base. They suffered more casualties during the 77-day siege by the NVA. The siege was lifted in April, and the base abandoned in June 1968.

2914 **I should never have ceded power to someone so unworthy (Thieu). I must take the blame. It is the error I most regret in my entire military and political career.**—*Nguyen Cao Ky, former Prime Minister of South Vietnam, 1976.*[629]

Ky withdrew from any attempt to run for president against Thieu. According to Ky he did so to preserve military power and unity. He believes he was more popular than Thieu and that he would have won an election in which Thieu was his opponent.

2915 **[The My Lai massacre is] one of the most shameful chapters in the army's history.**—*General Michael Ackerman from an awards presentation speech, 6 March 1998.*[2]

Ackerman was presenting the Soldier's Medal to three Army helicopter crewman for their defense of a small group of Vietnamese during the My Lai massacre. My Lai took place 16 March 1968.

2916 **...for heroism above and beyond the call of duty while saving the lives of at least 10 Vietnamese civilians during the unlawful massacre of noncombatants by American forces at My Lai.**—*Citation wording for Soldier's Medal, awarded 6 March 1998.*[2]

This citation accompanied the Soldier's Medal awarded to Hugh Thomas. Thomas protected a small group of Vietnamese civilians during the My Lai massacre. There was no follow-up as to what was considered a "lawful massacre."

2917 **To Americans TET [1968] was only a victory in the sense that Dunkirk was a victory for the British in World War II.**—*Nguyen Cao Ky, former Prime Minister of South Vietnam, 1976.*[629]

American military claimed the communist TET Offensive a failure because it failed its goals of rallying the South Vietnamese to the side of the communist and overthrowing the Thieu-Ky regime. In addition, the VC suffered heavy casualties and was broken as a viable military force. After TET most of the enemy fighting, in South Vietnam was borne by NVA troops.

2918 **Anybody who doesn't have fear is an idiot. It's just that you must make the fear work for you. Hell when somebody shot at me, it made me madder than hell, and all I wanted to do was shoot back.**—*General Robin Olds, former U.S. Air Force pilot and commander of the 8th Tactical Fighter Wing.*[189]

2919 **I have seen men weep. I have seen men wet their pants. I have watched men shake or become paralyzed from fear. I have also seen men appear unaffected during these terrifying moments when death thunders and crashes all around. My reaction to overwhelming fear consisted of losing conscious control over my breathing.**—*Nick Boldrini, former U.S. Air Force radar technician, post war comments, 1996.*[906]

Boldrini was based at Tan Son Nhut and was there when the communists launched the TET Offensive of 1968. He speaks of the fear he experienced in the early hours of the offensive when several hundred VC attacked the air base at Tan Son Nhut.

2920 **Losing the Great Society was a terrible thought, but not so terrible as the thought of being responsible for America's losing a war to the Communists. Nothing could be worst than that.**—*Lyndon Johnson, to biographer Doris Kearns.*[372]

2921 **CIA nor MACV provided any warning at all of the magnitude or the targets of the enemy's TET Offensive; we were all completely surprised.**—*Robert Komer, former Special Assistant to the President, during an interview, 21 May 1990.*[209]

Komer was commenting on the lack of warning given by MACV's J-2 intelligence component and CIA analysts.

2922 **It did not occur to us that the enemy would undertake suicidal attacks in the face of our power.**—*General William Westmoreland, as related by Nguyen Cao Ky, 1976.*[629]

MACV believed there would be a major enemy offensive in 1968, but did not realize the scope, even though their gathered intelligence indicated such an event was in the offing. The 1968 TET Offensive exceeded MACV's expectations.

2923 **[Our objectives] were beyond our actual strength, founded in part on an illusion based on our subjective desires.**—*Tran Van Tra, former COSVN General, as published in a Vietnamese military history, 1982.*[374]

At TET 1968, the communist thought South Vietnamese resistance would crumble and large numbers of ARVN troops would rally to the communist side. They also expected the South Vietnamese civilians to welcome communist troops as liberators, resulting in a spontaneous uprising against the Saigon regime.

2924 **Savage, brilliantly executed, it caught all of us off guard.**—*Nguyen Cao Ky, former Prime Minister of South Vietnam, 1976.*[629]

Describing the communist offensive at TET, 1968.

2925 **[A] very great victory for the Vietnamese people, for the solidarity in combat of the three Indochinese people[s], for the socialist countries, the oppressed and all the peace-loving peoples of the world, including the American people who displayed their solidarity and gave devoted support to the just struggle of our people.**—*Le Duc Tho, Chief North Vietnamese negotiator, during a press conference announcing the cease-fire agreement, 24 January 1973.*[607]

The United States and North Vietnam made separate announcements that a final settlement had been reached in the peace negotiations. Washington claimed the peace had been won. Hanoi boasted that it had defeated America in Vietnam.

2926 **They were intelligent, experienced men. I had always regarded the majority of them as very steady and balanced. If they had been so deeply influenced by the reports of the TET offensive, what must the average citizen in the country be thinking?**—*President Lyndon Johnson, memoirs, 1971.*[53]

Johnson was speaking of his unofficial advisers, the "Wise Men." A majority advised him it was time for a change in Administration policy in Vietnam. They proposed an end to the bombing of North Vietnam, a ceiling to further troop increases, and the seeking of a political settlement to end the fighting.

2927 **To the Americans TET [1968] had all the horrors of another Pearl Harbor, and for the first time many Americans realized that they might not be able to win the war.**—*Nguyen Cao Ky, former Prime Minister of South Vietnam, 1976.*[629]

Ky may have over estimated the importance of the TET Offensive. Had it been the equivalent of another Pearl Harbor, America would have rallied and turned on the VC/NVA instead of deciding to back away from Vietnam.

2928 **Each ... [casualty] ... took a little piece of him.**—*Dean Rusk, former Secretary of State, 1987.*[52]

Rusk commenting on President Johnson's consuming concern over the siege at Khe Sanh. It is reported that he haunted the White House Situation Room at all hours of the night seeking the latest information on the situation at Khe Sanh and the casualties encountered.

2929 **[The resupply of the combat base at Khe Sanh was] the premier air logistical feat of the war.**—*General William Westmoreland, former ComUSMACV, 1976.*[872]

During the siege of Khe Sanh, the base was entirely supplied by air. More than 14,000 tons of supplies were delivered to Khe Sanh by direct air shipment or by parachute drop.

2930 **None of us was willing to assert that he could see "light at the end of the tunnel" or that American troops would be coming home by the end of the year.**—*Clark Clifford, former Secretary of Defense, in his reappraisal of the Vietnam War, July 1969.*[910]

Shortly after becoming Secretary of Defense, Clifford met with military leaders. The military could devise no plan to win the war in Vietnam based on the restrictions the military operated under. Those restrictions were the inability to close Hai Phong harbor, invade North Vietnam or pursue the enemy into Laos or Cambodia. Their only plan was to continue to kill the enemy (attrite) until the enemy had enough. In effect, no plan to end the war.

2931 **By holding out [against joining the initial peace negotiations] we deprived the Democrats of their election victory and Nixon became president instead.**—*Nguyen Cao Ky, former Prime Minister of South Vietnam, 1976.*[629]

The South Vietnamese government refused to send representatives to the initial peace conference in Paris in 1968. According to Ky, they were cautioned by Nixon supporters that they could get a better deal if they waited until after the U.S. election. Ky alleges that the Johnson administration attempted to blackmail the Saigon government into going, but they held out. Ky claims this holdout was the stroke that cost Humphrey an election victory, being unable to claim he was part of the Democratic administration that brought Saigon to the peace table with North Vietnam.

2932 **During TET of 1968 we did not correctly evaluate the specific balance of forces between ourselves and the enemy, did not fully realize that the enemy still had considerable capabilities and that our capabilities were limited, and set requirements that were beyond our actual strength.**—*General Tran Van Tra, former COSVN Commander, from his memoirs, 1982.*[42]

Tra was indicating that the TET 1968 offensive was not well

planned and was poorly executed. He still claimed it was a defeat for America and the "puppet government" of Saigon.

2933 **They were all enemy. They were all to be destroyed.**—*Lieutenant William Calley, Jr. commanded a platoon from the Americal Division.*[83]

Calley was convicted of the murder of civilians at the Vietnamese village of My Lai-4. Calley's platoon killed between 200 and 500 civilians in the ville in March 1968. The massacre was covered up by higher echelons of the division until the incident surfaced in the press in 1969. Calley was from C Company, 1st Battalion, 20th Infantry Regiment.

2934 **I remain convinced that the blow to morale was more of our own doing than anything the enemy had accomplished with its army. We were defeating ourselves.**—*President Lyndon Johnson, from his memoirs, 1971.*[374]

Johnson had a meeting with his advisers in March 1968 which indicated a lack of enthusiasm for continuing the war in Vietnam. A few months prior to the meeting the same group had recommended escalation of the war effort. But the events of TET 1968, and the increase in America's disaffection for the war gave Johnson pause to consider other alternatives for Vietnam.

2935 **The TET offensive was probably unique in that the side that lost completely in the tactical sense came away with an overwhelming psychological and hence political victory.**—*Bernard Brodie, political science writer, 1976.*[267]

The Communist TET Offensive resulted in tens of thousands of enemy casualties and no long-term terrain gain. But the timing and scope of the attack negated the Johnson administration's claims of progress in Vietnam and overall reduction in enemy capabilities.

2936 **No single endeavor caused more grief and frustration [for me].**—*Lt.Col. Stuart Herrington, U.S. District adviser for the Phoenix Program, 1981.*[374]

Herrington's comments regard the abuses, corruption and inefficiency of the Phoenix Program in Vietnam.

2937 **We never feared a division of troops, but the infiltration of a couple of guys into our ranks created tremendous difficulties for us.**—*Nguyen Thi Dinh, former Vietcong leader, during an interview, 1981.*[374]

Nguyen Thi Dinh was referring to the Phoenix Program and its attack of the VC infrastructure. According to William Colby, the program eliminated more than 60,000 Viet Cong (or suspected Vietcong) agents during its four years of operation under American control.

2938 **[The Phoenix Program was] a devious and cruel operation that cost the loss of thousands of our cadres.**—*Colonel Bui Tin, senior North Vietnamese officer, comments to correspondent, 1981.*[374]

Bui Tin was referring to the CIA-organized Phoenix Program, which attacked the VC infrastructure. According to William Colby, the program eliminated more than 60,000 Viet Cong (and suspected Viet Cong) agents during its four years of operation under American control.

2939 **By the ... TET offensive in January 1968, [in] the air war in the North [the U.S.] had scored a major victory over the North Vietnamese Air Force. It was essentially a defeated air force and was withdrawn from battle.**—*General William Momyer, former Commander, U.S. 7th Air Force, in publication, 1978.*[914]

The U.S. maintained air superiority over Vietnam for the length of the war. But the air campaign was unable to stop the flow of men and materials from North Vietnam to South Vietnam. Air power was instrumental in supporting friendly units on the ground in South Vietnam, but unable to force a political change in Hanoi.

2940 **We didn't achieve our main objective, which was to spur uprisings throughout the south. Still, we inflicted heavy casualties on the Americans and their puppets, and that was a big gain for us. As for making an impact in the United States, it had not been our intention — but it turned out to be a fortunate result.**—*General Tran Do, former Deputy Commander, Communist Forces in South Vietnam, during an interview, 1981.*[374]

An estimated 67,000 VC/NVA took part in the TET Offensive. The DoD reported casualty figures for February and March 1968 were 3,895 Americans killed, 4,954 ARVN killed, and 58,000 VC/NVA killed. The majority of communist forces involved in the TET attacks were VC units, with NVA units providing support and blocking forces.

2941 **The Vietnamese people had bent like bamboo in the wind, but they did not break in any direction. The stoicism and caution of the people had rejected the Communist political commanders just as it rejected the American efforts to rouse the country behind the Siagon government.**—*Don Oberdorfer, journalist and author, 1971.*[653]

During the TET Offensive Hanoi expected the population of South Vietnam to rise up in a general uprising and join communist forces in expelling the Americans and the Saigon regime. The VC entered the cities with an expectation that such an uprising of the people would take place. The VC were unable to hold the cities long enough to convince the people to join them.

2942 **In savvy Washington circles it was said that there were two CIAs: a George Carver CIA, which was the CIA at the top, generally optimistic in its reporting to Rostow; and the rest of the CIA, which was far more pessimistic.**—*David Halberstam, journalist, from his book, 1972.*[206]

George Carver, CIA Special Assistant for Vietnamese Affairs, was generally upbeat about the American war effort in Vietnam, but in mid-March 1968, there was a shift in his position. He became pessimistic of the war effort and began to reflect the views of many of his CIA staff.

2943 **There is no profit at this time in hashing over the might-have-beens of the past, nor is there any value in finger-pointing.**—*Senator Mike Mansfield of Montana, commenting on the fall of South Vietnam,August 1976.*[294]

With the fall of South Vietnam the expected hue and cry and "finger-pointing" did not occur. The few voices that did cry out were largely ignored by the American public, shunned by the media, and avoided by the politicians.

2944 **There are always three choices — war, surrender, and present policy.**—*Henry Kissinger, National Security Adviser.*[83]

2945 **No government can function without a minimum of trust. This was being dissipated under the harshness of our alternatives and the increasing rage of domestic controversy.**—*Henry Kissinger, former Secretary of State, in his memoirs, 1979.*[23]

The credibility gap which blossomed during the Johnson administration continued to grow through the Nixon administration in 1969. Nixon came into office on a pledge of soon ending the war in Vietnam. But American casualties continued to mount and there was no progress at the Paris peace negotiations.

2946 **Whatever our original war aims, by 1969 our credibility abroad, the reliability of our commitments, and our domestic cohesion were alike jeopardized by a struggle in a country as far away from the North American continent as our globe permits.... The comity by which a democratic society must live had broken down.**—*Henry Kissinger, former Secretary of State, in his memoirs, 1979.*[23]

2947 **Ten guys who cared for each other were a lot safer than twenty guys who didn't.**—*Unidentified, former 25th Infantry Division infantryman, 1991.*[42]

After 1968 there was a notable diminishing of the quality of some American troops and their attitude towards winning the war. This was mainly influenced by the new direction of the war and partly by the rise in drug use, racial conflict, and the lowering of draft standards for intelligence and social adaptability. Combat battalions tended to field smaller units, which were not bloated with men bearing drug and psychological handicaps, or those mentally challanged.

2948 **The problem with Thieu is that he agrees to everything, but does nothing.**—*Ellsworth Bunker, U.S. Ambassador to South Vietnam, as related by Nguyen Cao Ky, 1976.*[629]

Nguyen Van Thieu was repeatedly accused of not being able to take a stand or commit, yes or no, to a given question or proposal.

2949 **We could have flattened everything in and around Hanoi. That doesn't mean it would stop the war, but it would certainly have made it extremely difficult to continue effectively.**—*General Maxwell Taylor, former U.S. Ambassador to South Vietnam, from an interview, 10 February 1969.*[158]

2950 **A seizure of power unprecedented in modern American foreign policy.**—*Roger Morris, National Security Adviser, 1988.*[374]

When Nixon became president he made Henry Kissinger his National Security Adviser. Kissinger's first duty was to "revitalize" the National Security Council. The restructured council screened out much interference from the departments of State, Defense, and the CIA, giving Kissinger more direct control over recommendations that were given to the president.

2951 **Kent State, 1970 means we no longer have our daughter, but it also means something to all Americans.... Our court battles establish without a doubt one thing. There is no constitution. There is no Bill of Rights.**—*Arthur Krause, Father of slain Kent State student, comments to the press, 1979.*[380]

2952 **If it takes a blood bath to deal with campus demonstrations let's get it over with.**—*Ronald Reagan, Governor of California, April 1970.*[576]

2953 **A month of an unprovoked North Vietnamese offensive, over a thousand Americans dead, elicited after weeks of anguished discussion exactly one American retaliatory raid within three miles of the Cambodian border in an area occupied by North Vietnamese for over four years. And this would enter the folklore as example of wanton "illegality."**—*Henry Kissinger, former Secretary of State, in his memoirs, 1979.*[23]

The 1969 North Vietnamese offensive saw widespread enemy attacks against American and South Vietnamese positions. In retaliation Nixon ordered air strikes against one of the NVA base areas, along the South Vietnamese border, inside Cambodia. The raid was considered a success. Nixon then authorized a continuous bombing campaign against NVA sanctuaries inside the Cambodian border. These strikes against the NVA bases became the secret "Menu" operations.

2954 **They always point out that my daughter had gravel in her pockets ... that this was the rationale for killing her.... Why didn't they throw gravel at her?**—*Arthur Krause, father of slain Kent State student, comments to the press, 1979.*[381]

Krause was referring to some of the hate mail he received after his daughter's death and the subsequent investigation of the shooting at Kent State. Allison Krause was the only student killed who had actually participated in the demonstration which the National Guard attempted to break up. The Guardsmen had been attacked with rocks as they tried to disperse the crowd. Rocks were found in Allison Krause's pockets during the investigation.

2955 **The longer deterrence succeeds, the more difficult it is to demonstrate what made it work.**—*Henry Kissinger, President Nixon's National Security Adviser.*[83]

2956 **The political talk, "peace with honor" and such things, had very little meaning in South Vietnam because everyone knew that, with each step we took to withdraw, the North Vietnamese and the VC were doubling their efforts to take over the country. We knew that when we left, the country would be overwhelmed by the VC and the North Vietnamese.**—*Jim Ross, former member of the 25th Infantry Division, 1991.*[42]

The 25th Infantry Division officially departed Vietnam on December 19, 1970. The division's 2d Brigade was designated a separate command and remained in Vietnam until April 1971. Battalions of the brigade operated from Xuan Loc and Long Binh.

2957 **In the disciplined force of American troops that had first arrived in South Vietnam, the problem [of heroin] might have been restricted to a few, but by the early seventies U.S. Command estimated that 10 percent of the troops in Vietnam were taking heroin and 5 percent were addicts.**—*Nguyen Cao Ky, former Prime Minister of South Vietnam, from his memoirs, 1976.*[629]

Heroin was cheap and of high quality in Vietnam. It was readily available and very potent compared to what was available on the streets in the U.S. and Europe.

2958 **Lam Son 719 was indeed a costly operation to the South Vietnamese and U.S. helicopter forces. Costly because of weak**

planning that produced inadequate tactical air support.—*General William W. Momyer, Commander, U.S. 7th Air Force.*[914]

American helicopter crews supported the bulk of the ARVN forces during the operation. During the two months of the operation 107 U.S. helicopters were shot down, with crew losses totaling 55 killed and 34 missing.

2959 **[Reporter]—As a door gunner, often under fire, do you find it hard to shoot women and children?**

[Doorgunner]—Nah, you just don't lead them as much.—*Exchange, related by Vietnam War Veteran, 1976.*[1020]

An exchange that supposedly took place between a correspondent and a Army helicopter door gunner at Pleiku in 1971.

2960 **Vietnam was unique, and the United States should not set as the central objective the redesign of our foreign and defense policy so as to avoid another Viet-Nam.**—*McGeorge Bundy, former National Security Adviser, 1976.*[295]

2961 **It was my firm conviction that we must not be responsible — or be portrayed as being responsible — for the breakdown of the talks.**—*Richard Nixon, from his memoirs, 1978.*[162]

After near agreement in the peace talks there was a breakdown and stalemate in November 1972. Nguyen Van Thieu insisted on changes to the agreement reached in private negotiations between the U.S. and Hanoi. Hanoi balked at Thieu's changes. The U.S. put pressure on Thieu to accept the bulk of the peace plan.

2962 **We will not put up with our ally's intransigence any more than we will do so with our enemy.**—*Henry Kissinger, former National Security Adviser, 1979.*[134]

Kissinger recommended pressure be brought to bear on South Vietnam's Nguyen Van Thieu to accept the peace proposal arrived at in Paris. Some of Thieu's changes had been incorporated, but he was still reluctant to be a willing participant. Nixon considered excluding South Vietnam from the cease-fire agreement, establishing a final agreement just between the U.S. and Hanoi, should Thieu continue to block the peace agreement.

2963 **The Christmas bombings of 1972 should have taken place in 1965.**—*T.R. Milton, former U.S. Air Force General, during a magazine interview, March 1983.*[908]

Operation Linebacker II, also referred to as the Christmas bombing, covered the eleven days of heavy bombing of the Hanoi-Hai Phong area, 18-29 December 1972.

2964 **As the summer wore on, our losses had become prodigious, and we began to see that many of the territorial advances could not be sustained.**—*Truong Nhu Tang, former Minister of Justice, PRG, 1985.*[170]

Speaking of the North Vietnamese Easter Offensive, launched 31 March 1972. The offensive initially made large gains in the Central Highlands and south of the DMZ. But by August 1972, the South Vietnamese army, with the help of massive U.S. air support, began to roll the NVA back from captured areas of South Vietnam.

2965 **Vietnamese FACs are at the bottom of the military and social totem pole ... the ALCs (air liaison officers) that are assigned to direct FAC operations are often selected because of previous shortcomings.**—*Colonel Howard B. Fisher, U.S. Air Force, comment on the Easter Offensive, 1985.*[920]

In 1972 South Vietnamese FACs directed air strikes by South Vietnamese and U.S. Air Force aircraft against the NVA invasion force. Because the FACs were required to be bi- or trilingual they were looked down upon in South Vietnamese society. This was a carryover from French colonial days when bilingual middle-men were used to pass on the orders of the French to the Vietnamese. During the Vietnam War some of the upper-crust Vietnamese officers (on the ground and in the air) were uncomfortable conversing with the "lower class" FACs. The result was poor air to ground coordination of air support during the initial weeks of the North Vietnam invasion of South Vietnam.

2966 **When President Nixon decided to use our available military power in a manner that truly hurt North Vietnam, negotiations began to move in a substantive way.**—*General William Westmoreland, former ComUSMACV, 1977.*[181]

Westmoreland was speaking of the intensified bombing of North Vietnam carried out under Operation Linebacker I. This was Nixon's response to the North Vietnamese invasion of South Vietnam in 1972 and Hanoi's intransigence at the negotiating table.

2967 **After Linebacker I, the enemy was suing for peace. They were hurt real bad. Most of the major targets had been obliterated in the North ... and they were ready to conclude an agreement.**—*General John W. Vogt, Jr., former Commander, U.S. 7th Air Force, during an interview, August 1978.*[172]

Operation Linebacker I was President Nixon's response to the North Vietnamese invasion of South Vietnam in 1972 and Hanoi's intransigence at the negotiating table. Linebacker I consisted of heavy bombing of North Vietnam, NVA positions in South Vietnam, and the mining of North Vietnam's ports.

2968 **I simply did not have enough numbers to put a squad of Americans in every village and hamlet; that would have been fragmenting resources and exposing them to defeat in detail.**—*General William Westmoreland, former ComUSMACV, from his book, 1976.*[1019]

Westmoreland's reasoning behind not instituting a program of pacification similar to that used by the U.S. Marine Corps, the Combined Action Platoon. Under the CAP program a squad of Marines lived in a village and helped the inhabitants protect themselves from the VC. The CAP also furnished rudimentary medical care and assisted with civic improvements. There were approximately 11,000 villages in South Vietnam, at 15 men per village, 165,000 men would have been required. At one time there were more than 500,000 American servicemen in Vietnam.

2969 **Look, we screwed up in 1973. We screw up all the time. My job is to see that we don't screw up again. Certainly you are not suggesting that we pay for them [American POWs in Vietnam]. What do you want, another hostage crisis?**—*William Casey, Director, CIA, as related by Congressman Robert K. Dornan during a conversation in 1986.*[488]

According to Dornan (Representative from California), Casey told him that Reagan opposed paying ransom for the release of Americans held as POWs by the Vietnamese. Other recent hostage incidents included: 52 Americans held in Iran in 1979-81, and 3 Americans held in Lebanon, 1985-86.

2970 **It was a measure of the extremity in which Hanoi found itself that it felt it could not wait for the almost certain aid cutoff and proceeded with the negotiations.**—*Henry Kissinger, former National Security Adviser, 1979.*[134]

The "cutoff" Kissinger spoke of was an expected move by Congress to cut off all funding for Southeast Asian military operations. Kissinger and Nixon believed Hanoi was holding out for that "cutoff." If it happened it would have required the U.S. to withdraw without a real peace agreement, leaving South Vietnam without adequate guarantees of aid and protection. Such a cut in funding would have made it difficult for Nixon to back up his promises of quick, retaliatory support for South Vietnam if the need arose.

2971 **We can anticipate no lasting peace in the wake of a consummated agreement.... We will probably have little chance of maintaining the agreement without evident hair-trigger readiness ... to enforce its provisions.**—*Henry Kissinger, former National Security Adviser, reflecting on the Paris Peace Agreement, 1979.*[134]

Kissinger's views of the near final peace plan, as it stood in early December 1972.

2972 **Our cadres and men were fatigued, we had not had time to make up for our losses, all units were in disarray, there was a lack of manpower, and there were shortages of food and ammunition.... The troops were no longer capable of fighting.**—*General Tran Van Tra, former Commander, Communist Forces, Southern Vietnam, during an interview, 1985.*[119]

The results of the American Linebacker I & II operations and the mining of North Vietnamese ports negatively impacted Hanoi's ability to supply its troops in South Vietnam and along the DMZ. The air strikes sealed off much of the border between North Vietnam and China, greatly restricting the flow of supplies overland. The closure of the ports through mining rendered them unusable for resupply. Many of the supplies stored within the country had been damaged or destroyed by the intensive bombing.

2973 **There was no intractable, substantive issue separating the two sides, but rather an apparent North Vietnamese determination not to allow an agreement to be completed.**—*Henry Kissinger, former National Security Adviser, writing in his book, 1979.*[915]

Kissinger believed the North Vietnamese were stalling at completing the peace agreement in hopes that there would be a split between Washington and Saigon over the terms of the cease-fire. They also hoped when Congress reconvened in early 1973 they would legislate an end to U.S. involvement in Vietnam. If either took place North Vietnam would win and the U.S. would withdraw.

2974 **There wasn't a whole lot of time devoted during the briefing to the intelligence aspect as to what your target was. All you knew was that you were going "Downtown," and that you might not be coming home.**—*Major John R. Allen, U.S. Air Force, formerly of the 307th Strategic Wing, during an interview regarding Linebacker II, 22 September 1981.*[138]

Operation Linebacker II was the first use of B-52s against targets in Hanoi and Hai Phong. The operation was initiated on Nixon's order to punish Hanoi's intransigence and delay during the peace negotiations, and was designed to show how serious Nixon was in obtaining an agreement.

2975 **We had now reached the point where only the strongest action would have any effect in convincing Hanoi that negotiating a fair settlement with us was a better option for them than continuing the war.**—*Richard Nixon, from his memoirs, 1978.*[162]

In mid-December 1972 the peace negotiations broke down completely when it was discovered that the near final peace document agreed on in Paris had been secretly changed by the North Vietnamese. The draft of the final agreement included more than a dozen changes that were slipped into the document by the communist which were not jointly agreed upon during the negotiations. The changes were detected when U.S. linguistic experts reviewed the document.

2976 **They [the military briefers] didn't belabor the point of what the targets were because it didn't make any difference—you were committed and you were going.**—*Major John R. Allen, U.S. Air Force, formerly of the 307th Strategic Wing, during an interview regarding Linebacker II, 22 September 1981.*[138]

Operation Linebacker II was the first use of B-52s against targets in Hanoi and Hai Phong. The operation was initiated on Nixon's order to punish Hanoi's intransigence and delay during the peace negotiations, and was designed to show how serious Nixon was in obtaining an agreement.

2977 **One look at any [North] Vietnamese officer's face told the whole story. It telegraphed accommodation, hopelessness, remorse, fear. The shock was there; our enemy's will was broken.**—*Admiral James B. Stockdale, former U.S. Navy pilot and prisoner of war, 1981.*[919]

Reflecting on his perception of the effectiveness of the eleven day Linebacker II bombing campaign against North Vietnam in December 1972. Commander Stockdale was shot down over North Vietnam in September 1965, and held until April 1973.

2978 **By the tenth day [of Operation Linebacker II], there were no missiles, there were no MiGs, there was no AAA [antiaircraft artillery]—there was no threat. It was easy pickings.**—*Major John R. Allen, U.S. Air Force, formerly of the 307th Strategic Wing, during an interview regarding Linebacker II, 22 September 1981.*[138]

Linebacker II started 18 December, ending 29 December after 1,216 sorties against North Vietnam, including 729 B-52 sorties. Many of the sorties struck in and around Hanoi and Hai Phong. By the end of Linebacker II, North Vietnam had expended most of its SAM missiles in defense of the Hanoi-Hai Phong area.

2979 **[I was] totally alienated from the policy, but helpless as to how to change it.**—*James Thompson, National Security Council staff member, in an article about the direction of the war, 1974.*[288]

Thompson, along with several other White House staff members resigned. They repeatedly pointed out the lack of progress in the war effort and the fact that the bombing campaign was not forcing Hanoi to negotiate nor was it stopping the flow of men and material into the South.

2980 **Thieu had so consolidated his position that a really free election was impossible. He had made laws that rendered**

it difficult for any opponent to run, let alone win.—*Nguyen Cao Ky, former Vice President of South Vietnam, 1976.*[629]

Ky, referring to the 1971 presidential election in South Vietnam. President Nguyen Van Thieu instituted political measures against the Vietnamese press and his political opponents to insure a victory in the October 1971 elections.

2981 **They behaved as if they had conquered us.**—*Dr. Duong Quynh Hoa, South Vietnamese physician and Communist Party member, during an interview with a correspondent, 1981.*[374]

Depletion of the VC ranks because of heavy losses during TET 1968, forced large numbers of NVA troops to bolster the ranks of VC units and cells in the South, the NVA typically taking leadership roles. After the fall of South Vietnam many of these same North Vietnamese became local leaders in the united Vietnam, looking down on the southern communist who had survived the war.

2982 **Airpower should be used sparingly, though overwhelmingly when necessary.**—*Nguyen Cao Ky, former Prime Minister of South Vietnam, 1976.*[629]

Ky sites the lack of South Vietnamese air resources as the reason for his philosophy. American air power was typically not hindered by a lack of resources so it was used extensively.

2983 **Strong ropes inching gradually, day by day, around the neck, arms, and legs of a demon, awaiting the order to jerk tight and bring the creature's life to an end.**—*General Van Tien Dung, Commanded North Vietnamese Army force in South Vietnam, 1981.*[374]

Van Tien Dung's description of the preparations of the NVA for the final assault on South Vietnam.

2984 **The collapse of South Vietnam just fifty-five days after the onset of the North Vietnamese offensive was symptomatic of the malaise which had afflicted the nation since its birth.**—*George C. Herring, historian, 1979.*[347]

2985 **Showing the suffering and savage combat was the price we paid for a free press.**—*Lyndon Johnson, related by Nguyen Cao Ky, 1976.*[629]

Ky, relating part of a conversation he had with the former president following Johnson's retirement.

2986 **The inability to foresee what form the war would take was the first great failure of our military involvement in Vietnam.**—*Dave Richard Palmer, historian and Vietnam War Veteran, 1978.*[713]

2987 **Short of being physically destroyed, collapse, surrender, or disintergration was ... simply not within their capabilities.**—*Konrad Kellen, Rand Corporation analyst's comment about North Vietnam.*[374]

Characterization of the Hanoi's attitude in seeking the reunification of Vietnam under Hanoi's communist control.

2988 **If you were black and spoke up, you were a trouble maker, an instigator, whatever. If you were white, you were considered an innovator.**—*Allen Thomas Jr., U.S. Army.*[1018]

The late-sixties, early-seventies military was not always open to hear the complaints and concerns of its members.

2989 **The 3d Brigade of the 25th Division would suffer more casualties in Duc Hue in one day than all of the RF/PF did in one year. It was an insult.**—*Colonel Jack Weissinger, Hau Nghia Province Senior Adviser, postwar comments, 1991.*[42]

Weissinger was commenting on the ineffectiveness of most of the RF/PF units and operations in Hau Nghia Province. The province was located just northwest of Saigon and was an important area to the VC as the western boundary of the province bordering Cambodia.

2990 **The war in Vietnam was bad for America because it was a bad war, as all wars are bad if they consist of rich boys fighting poor boys when the rich boys have an advantage in the weapons.**—*Norman Mailer, Pulitzer Prize-winning author.*[83]

2991 **Countries, like human beings, make mistakes. We made an honest mistake. I feel no sense of shame. Nor should the country feel any sense of shame. We felt that we were doing what was necessary. It proved to be unsound.**—*Clark Clifford, former Secretary of Defense.*[374]

Referring to American intervention in Vietnam.

2992 **If I left that war [in Vietnam] and let the Communists take over South Vietnam, then I would be seen as a coward and my nation would be seen as an appeaser and we would both find it impossible to accomplish anything for anybody anywhere on the entire globe.**—*Lyndon Johnson, to biographer Doris Kearns.*[128]

Johnson was torn between his Great Society programs and winning the war in Vietnam. Much of the money he needed for his domestic programs was being drained to support the ever-expanding war effort in Vietnam.

2993 **If I had been in complete command of the war with half a million Americans under my orders I would have fought for a quick victory, and for that there is only one way—an all-out war with no holds barred. If we had fought that way we would have won.**—*Nguyen Cao Ky, former Prime Minister of South Vietnam, 1976.*[629]

Ky wanted to take the ground war to North Vietnam. It should be noted that Ky never mentioned the more than 600,000 men South Vietnam had under arms at the time.

2994 **The PSDF was a farce in Hau Nghia ... it was one big lie. Some weapons were never issued out, and everyone who was supposed to be protected stayed inside the barbed wire. We had member after member of the PSDF open the gate so attackers could come in. It was a miserable failure.**—*Colonel Jack Weissinger, Hau Nghia Province Senior Adviser, postwar comments, 1991.*[42]

The PSDF (People's Self Defense Force, also known as the PF—Popular Forces) were the GVN's village and hamlet security forces. Their main function was to protect the villagers and weed out the VC in their area. Most PF units, with very few exceptions, were rated as poor.

2995 **By God, we've kicked the Vietnam syndrome once and for all.**—*President George Bush, from a speech, 1991.*[1]

The Vietnam syndrome was the tendency within the U.S. after the Vietnam War, to compare all communist led wars of national liberation to the Vietnam War and its origins. U.S. involvement in such conflicts was highly suspect by those who wanted to avoid another "Vietnam" type entanglement and not become involved in the internal affairs of another country.

2996 **[During a road clearing sweep] it was like a circus. Walking with us were girls and kids selling soda, beer, cigarettes, lighters, jackets, etc. ... It looked like a parade. ... As soon as they wouldn't go any further, we got uneasy real fast.**—*Dan Vandenberg, former rifleman with the 25th Infantry Division, 1991.*[42]

The Vietnamese in an area invariably knew what areas to avoid, where the mines and traps were hidden, or where the ambush would take place. The unspoken rule was that they did not share this information with passing American troops, nor reveal it under interrogation, or remain visible in the aftermath.

2997 **We could have flattened every war-making facility in North Vietnam. But the hand-wringers had center stage.... The most powerful country in the world did not have the willpower needed to meet the situation.**—*Admiral Ulysses S. Grant Sharp, U.S. Navy, Commander in Chief, Pacific.*[67]

2998 **Small nations must be wary of the Americans, since U.S. policies shift quickly as domestic politics and public opinion change.**—*Bui Diem, former South Vietnamese Ambassador to the U.S.*[374]

2999 **If President Johnson was determined to succeed in Vietnam ... I saw no solution, while waiting results from the bombing and expanded ARVN forces, other than to put our own finger in the dike.**—*General William Westmoreland, former ComUSMACV, 1976.*[22]

3000 **Politicians avoided all the institutions that had prior responsibility ... making decisions about the morality of the war and even about the wisdom of it fell to a large extent upon people who had no political power.**—*Eugene J. McCarthy, former Minnesota Senator, speaking at a symposium in Arlington, Virginia, May 1998.*[6]

3001 **There should be another Vietnam monument to those who opposed the war ... a monument for everybody else that did anything about it ... especially to young people who opposed the war because it was the most significant historically of any development that accompanied the war in Vietnam.**—*Eugene J. McCarthy, former Minnesota Senator, speaking at a symposium in Arlington, Virginia, May 1998.*[6]

McCarthy, on the proposal for a memorial to the anti-war movement during the Vietnam War.

3002 **I believe that if Westmoreland had come into the category of people like MacArthur, I would be writing this book in Saigon and it would have a different story to tell.**—*Nguyen Cao Ky, former Prime Minister of South Vietnam, 1976.*[629]

Ky did not believe Westmoreland's personality was sufficiently dynamic to sway public opinion in the United States to support the war in Vietnam as Ky wanted it waged.

3003 **If you see two arms, two legs, and one head lying on the ground, you've got five bodies.**—*Unidentified combat veteran, comments on the "body count," 1991.*[42]

The body counts of enemy dead called into higher headquarters were frequently inflated. There was pressure throughout the war to statistically show progress against the enemy. One of the main statistics used was the enemy kill ratio, which was confirmed by a count of the enemy dead on the field after an engagement.

3004 **In pitched battles we gained experience surviving. The guys got much closer and would sort of hook together. We would try to watch over and protect some of the weaker guys. We developed an arrogance: We weren't going to die, the enemy was.**—*Michael Willis, former infantryman with the 25th Infantry Division, comments on his tour, 1991.*[42]

Willis was part of the 2d Battalion, 14th Infantry Regiment, operating in III Corps.

3005 **The nation knows they're there. Everybody knows they're there, but there's no ground swell of support for getting them out.**—*William Casey, Director, CIA, as related by William Hendon, 1986.*[488]

Casey was speaking about American POWs still believed held in North Vietnam and/or Laos. William Hendon, a former North Carolina Congressman, was relaying Casey's comments on the POW/MIA issue.

3006 **I thought that McNamara didn't know what the hell he was talking about because they were claiming that the bombing wasn't effective.**—*Admiral Thomas Moorer, U.S. Navy, Chairman of the Joint Chiefs of Staff.*[69]

Moorer was chairman of the Joint Chiefs of Staff from 1970 to 1974. Many in the military believed the bombing of North Vietnam and the Ho Chi Minh Trail was effective. DoD studies indicated otherwise.

3007 **The men's commitment to each other—and to self-preservation—was sufficient to make most units in the 25th Division generally fearsome in battle. A massed attack on an element of the Tropic Lightning Division, with its skill and firepower, was a virtual death sentence for any opponent.**—*Eric M. Bergerud, historian, 1991.*[42]

3008 **Morale was high and most people believed they were doing the right thing. But soon, everyone was counting the days. The subtle objective was to go home.**—*Unidentified combat veteran of the 25th Infantry Division, 1991.*[42]

3009 **You fight like you train.**—*Motto, U.S. Navy Fighter Weapons School (TOPGUN).*

3010 **It's amazing how fear can keep you awake all night and keep you going the next day, but it reaches a point where you have to try to get your buddy to stay awake for you because you're saying, "I have to sleep. I don't care if they come up and slit my throat or shoot me in the head, I just can't take it any more."**—*C.W. Bowman, former infantryman with the 25th Infantry Division, 1991.*[42]

For troops in the field, a day often consisted of patrol, from just after sun up, until just before dark. Just before dark the unit would stop and dig in for the night. After a full day of moving through jungle, paddies, or hilly terrain, the men still had to maintain a guard. For those assigned ambush duty, there was even less sleep. With the rise of the sun the next day the routine began again.

3011 **[The National Liberation Front was] ... the most sinister enemy we had to fight in Vietnam, for it was a shadowy opponent within our country, a ghostly army that lived underground, emerging to fight only at night, but impossi-**

ble to bring to battle like regular troops. It was also a political force that fought us for the minds of the people.—*Nguyen Cao Ky, former Prime Minister of South Vietnam, 1976.*[629]

Hanoi announced the formation of the NLF in December 1960. Prior to this, former Viet Minh members conducted terrorist activities against the Diem government. Diem labeled the insurgents Viet Cong.

3012 **They were pathetic farmers caught in the middle of a tragic conflict that they did not understand and who really wanted to be left alone to follow their ancestral ways.**—*Thomas A. Giltner, former Platoon Leader, 27th Infantry Regiment, 1991.*[42]

3013 **I never had a chance really to say goodbye to the friends of mine who died there, I never had any chance to mourn, I never collectively had a chance to catch my breath and say a prayer or think about them.**—*Dennis Mannion, former U.S. Marine.*[350]

Mannion survived the North Vietnamese siege of Khe Sanh and the "Hill Fights" of 1968.

3014 **Thirteen years after the fall of Saigon, the time has come for increased efforts to resolve the legacies of the Vietnam War.**—*Senator John McCain of Arizona, in a speech on the Senate floor, April 1988.*[72]

McCain introduced legislation to create a dialogue between America and Hanoi in an effort to facilitate the resolution of the American POW/MIA issue of Vietnam.

3015 **Fight to fly, fly to fight, fight to win.**—*Motto, U.S. Navy Fighter Weapons School (TOPGUN).*

3016 **Year after year — in power and out — I watched as the wishful thinking [about the ARVN] grew into a cloud of hopeless exaggeration, if not downright lies, until finally it hung, like the mushroom of an A-bomb, across the land.**—*Nguyen Cao Ky, former Prime Minister of South Vietnam, from his memoirs, 1976.*[629]

Ky was commenting on the lack of truthfulness in information presented to American Presidents on the true condition, motivation, and abilities of the ARVN.

3017 **I found a dead VC medic who had tied himself to a bamboo clump, with a morphine syringe stuck in his arm, as he was bleeding to death. He had an RPG at the ready with the safety off.**—*Jerry Liuci, former infantryman with the 27th Infantry Regiment, 1991.*[42]

A demonstration of the determination and tenacity of the enemy.

3018 **[It is] one of the most savage pieces of terrain in the world.**—*General William Westmoreland, former ComUSMACV, from his book, 1976.*[962]

Westmoreland was referring to the Rung Sat Special Zone, also called the Forest of Assassins. The Rung Sat was a large, dense mangrove swamp area between Saigon and the South China Sea. It was a long-time VC base area and home of the 9th VC Division.

3019 **I would follow Bull Simons to hell and back for the sheer joy of being with him on the visit.**—*Unidentified U.S. Army officer, 1976.*[852]

The officer was on Colonel Bull Simons's White Star team which enter Laos in 1960 to train Lao forces in counterinsurgency tactics. The team trained several battalions of Meo tribesmen during their six-month tour in Laos.

3020 **The only reason to go to war is to overthrow a government you don't like.**—*Admiral Thomas H. Moorer, former chairman, Joint Chiefs of Staff.*[374]

Moorer was Chief of Naval Operations, 1967-70 and went on to become Chairman of the JCS, 1970-74.

3021 **We should have fought in the north, where everyone was the enemy, where you didn't have to worry whether or not you were shooting friendly civilians.**—*Admiral Thomas H. Moorer, former chairman, Joint Chiefs of Staff.*[374]

3022 **The Communist told me they would never release me as a prisoner. Therefore, when I returned to the United States, I would be tried as a deserter and a traitor.**—*Robert Garwood, former Marine held in North Vietnam until 1979, during an interview, 1987.*[488]

Garwood claims he was held prisoner by North Vietnam until released in 1979. A Marine court-martial convicted him of collaboration with the enemy and he was dishonorably discharged. He claimed that at the time of his release there were other Americans still held by the Vietnamese.

3023 **There isn't a day or night I don't think about the men I know were still there [in Vietnam] when I got out in 1979.**—*Robert Garwood, former Marine private held in North Vietnam until 1979, in an interview, 1987.*[488]

Garwood has always claimed that he was not the only American still held by Hanoi after the publicized release of 587 American POWs in March 1973.

3024 **Friendly civilians were seen as no such thing. To us, there were no friendly civilians, only ones who posed no immediate threat. But because they were perceived as (at best) harmless for the moment, they we treated with ambivalence.**—*Jay Lazarin, former infantryman with the 27th Infantry Regiment, 25th Infantry Division, 1991.*[42]

The Vietnamese who were encountered in the field rarely volunteered any helpful information to American troops moving through the area. And more importantly, they did not warn American soldiers of booby-traps and mines, so even a village that was not openly hostile was still regarded with suspicion by U.S. troops.

3025 **Charlie was really good. Everyone at least respected his abilities. The NVA were damned good, and they wouldn't chicken out. They had to take more than we did. We didn't have to go through bombing and artillery. What they took was incredible.**—*Dan Vandenberg, former infantryman of the 25th Infantry Division, reminiscing, 1991.*[42]

3026 **Here is a country that has broken every goddamn provision in the agreement...**—*Henry Kissinger, former National Security Adviser, during an interview for Life magazine, 1987.*[488]

Kissinger, responding to questions about the POW/MIA issue and the resolution that was supposed to be forthcoming following the withdrawal of U.S. forces. Nixon had promised $3.4 billion to North Vietnam in reconstruction aid, but withheld it when Hanoi did not honor its agreement to remove its troops from Cambodia and continued to press South Vietnam militarily. In retaliation Hanoi refused further cooperation on U.S. POWs as secretly agreed upon. According to Kissinger the U.S. was under no obligation to pay reparations to North Vietnam.

3027 **We have met the enemy and he was us.**—*General William Westmoreland, former ComUSMACV.*[83]

3028 **Probably the greatest single error made by America in its history.**—*George Ball, former Under Secretary of State.*[374]

Ball's opinion of the Vietnam War.

3029 **[The Government of South Vietnam] with all its faults it was preferable to Communism.**—*Unidentified, former member of the South Vietnamese Parliament, Ho Chi Minh City, 1981.*[374]

Before the collapse in 1975, this former member of the South Vietnamese Parliament was a dissident, opposing the Saigon regime.

3030 **Until we know the enemy and know our allies and know ourselves, we'd better keep out of this dirty kind of business. It's very dangerous.**—*General Maxwell Taylor, former Ambassador to South Vietnam.*[374]

Taylor was commenting on the Vietnam War, the U.S. underestimation of the North Vietnamese, and the damage they were willing to suffer, the South Vietnamese philosophy of life and their weaknesses, and the lack of preparedness of U.S. forces to fight a major land battle in Asia.

3031 **Killing the enemy was not the problem; it was identifying him. Killing him was easy once you found him and identified him. In fact, sometimes it was much easier to do the killing first and the identifying afterwards.**—*Michael Clodfelter, former infantryman with the 502d Airborne, 101st Airborne, 1984.*[869]

Clodfelter served in Vietnam with the 2d/502d Airborne, 101st Airborne Division in 1965.

3032 **The guy who wins [a dogfight] is the guy who makes the fewer gross mistakes.**—*Lieutenant Jim "Huck" Harris, U.S. Navy instructor pilot, U.S. Navy Fighter Weapons School.*

3033 **It was a mistake to intervene in Vietnam.**—*Cyrus R. Vance, former Deputy Secretary of Defense, during Senate confirmation hearings, 11 January 1977.*[623]

Vance was undergoing questioning during confirmation hearings on his appointment as Secretary of State in the Carter administration.

3034 **We deeply regret and strongly protest the President's action. Mr. Carter's decision would be more divisive than healing.**—*William J. Rogers, National Commander, American Legion, in a press release, 22 January 1977.*[624]

On 21 January 1977, President Carter pronounced a blanket pardon for nearly all of America's Vietnam War draft evaders.

3035 **It is a sad day in the history of our nation. The President has shown a lack of concern for the 30 million living veterans who have served our nation in time of war.**—*Cooper Holt, executive director, Washington office of the Veterans of Foreign Wars, comments to the press, 22 January 1977.*[624]

On 21 January 1977, President Carter pronounced a blanket pardon for nearly all of America's Vietnam War draft evaders. The pardon of draft dodgers was one of Carter's first official acts as president.

3036 **A contribution to healing the wounds of war and to reconstruct the country was an American obligation that must be linked to establishment of relations.**—*Socialist Republic of Vietnam position statement, 1977.*[625]

Reportedly President Nixon promised Hanoi billions of dollars in aid for their cooperation in completing the Paris Peace Accords. They repeatedly clamored over the years for the establishment of formal relations between the U.S. and Vietnam, but made such relations dependent on reparations. The U.S. refused both reparations and recognition as long as Vietnam was not forthcoming on providing information on American MIAs in Vietnam. It became obvious that reparations would go the same way as Nixon's promises of support to the South Vietnamese government following the cease-fire in 1973.

3037 **The North Vietnamese were beginning to grasp the immensity of the economic problems confronting them. A property survey, undertaken at the Soviets' behest, revealed that waste, inefficiency, and even corruption were far more widespread than the leadership had ever imagined.**—*Frank Snepp, CIA agent, observations, 1977.*[863]

After the January 1973 cease-fire Hanoi requested military arms and equipment from China and the Soviet Union. The request was meant to replace arms and equipment lost during the invasion of South Vietnam in 1972. The Soviets and Chinese increased economic aid to Hanoi, but did not replace the lost military equipment.

3038 **[Operation Linebacker II] was something that had been long overdue, because in an eleven day period we brought [North Vietnam's] civilization ... to a grinding, screeching halt.**—*Colonel Robert D. Clark, former U.S. Air Force B-52 pilot, during an interview, 3 January 1983.*[136]

Clark's characterization of the Linebacker II bombing of North Vietnam in December 1972.

3039 **[Operation Linebacker II was] the single, most important action in the Vietnam campaign which convinced the North Vietnamese that they should negotiate.**—*Colonel Clyde E. Bodenheimer, U.S. 8th Air Force officer, during an interview, 7 January 1983.*[137]

Bodenheimer's characterization of the Linebacker II bombing of North Vietnam in December 1972.

3040 **[When] we marched into the rice paddies on that damp March afternoon, we carried, along with our packs and rifles, the implicit conviction that the Viet Cong would be quickly beaten.**—*Philip Caputo, Lieutenant, U.S. Marine Corps, 1977.*[318]

The first combat Marines deployed to Vietnam in March 1965.

3041 **When all the final accounting is made it may well be concluded that the single most important branch in Vietnam was not the infantry or the artillery or the air force, but the grimy builders of roads and ports and bridges and airfields—the Corps of Engineers.**—*Dave Richard Palmer, historian and Vietnam War Veteran, 1978.*[713]

Military engineering units and private contractors constructed roads, bases, dock facilities, logistic complexes, etc., throughout South Vietnam.

3042 **We were going to continue fighting until the Communists agreed to negotiate a fair and honorable peace or until the South Vietnamese were able to defend themselves on their own — whichever came first.**—*Richard Nixon, from his memoirs, 1978.*[162]

3043 **There was an obfuscation and a confusion and a lack of understanding, a lack of clarity, and a lack of declaration right from the President on down that really created difficulties and set the stage for not only our mistakes but also our eventual defeat.**—*General Glen W. Martin, Deputy Chief of Staff, U.S. Air Force, during an interview, February 1978.*[140]

Martin was deputy under Air Force Chief of Staff, John P. McConnell. Martin spoke of the restrictions placed on targeting and the aircrews who conducted the strikes against North Vietnam.

3044 **One of the lessons of the Vietnamese conflict is that rather than simply counter your opponent's thrusts, it is necessary to go for the heart of the opponent's power; destroy his military forces rather than simply being involved endlessly in ancillary military operations.**—*James Schlesinger, former Nixon Secretary of Defense, 1978.*[272]

Reflecting the perception that the American public would not tolerate long, drawn-out conflicts in the future.

3045 **The handling of the Vietnam affair was a shameful national blunder.**—*General William Westmoreland, speaking at the U.S. Army Command and General Staff College, Fort Leavenworth, Kansas, 11 April 1978.*[113]

3046 **I was prepared to step up the bombing after the election, but there was no way of knowing whether that would make [the North Vietnamese] adopt a more reasonable position before the American public's patience ran out, before the bombing began to create serious problems with the Chinese and the Soviets or before Congress just voted us out of the war.**—*Richard Nixon, from his memoirs, 1978.*[162]

3047 **It is lamentable that so many did all possible to erode support for a policy associated with six presidents and endorsed by nine Congresses.**—*General William Westmoreland, speaking at the U.S. Army Command and General Staff College, Fort Leavenworth, Kansas, 11 April 1978.*[113]

A retired General Westmoreland, speaking to students at Command and General Staff College.

3048 **The United States cannot and should not be the world's policeman, but it has a moral obligation to support nations in their endeavor to remain independent when we, and we alone, possess the means to do so.**—*Guenter Lewy, political scientist, 1978.*[280]

3049 **In a nutshell you should tell them that they have violated all understandings, they [have] stepped up the war, they have refused to negotiate seriously. As a result, the President has had enough and now you have only one message to give them — Settle or else!**—*President Richard Nixon, instructing Henry Kissinger, from Nixon's memoirs, 1978.*[162]

Hanoi broke off the Paris peace talks just before they launched the invasion of South Vietnam. Nixon stepped up air attacks against North Vietnam, and promised even heavier bombing if Hanoi did not return to the negotiating table. At a meeting in Paris, 2 May 1972, Kissinger tried to impress upon the North Vietnamese the seriousness of the President's attitude. The North Vietnamese ignored Kissinger. In response Nixon ordered the commencement of Operation Linebacker I.

3050 **It's hard to explain what happens once you start seeing people die. We might have seen it on TV or in the movies, but that's all. We very seldom hold a guy and watch him die like soldiers do in Vietnam. You think, Oh my God look at 'em, what is this, I could be next.**—*Unidentified, former U.S. Marine Corps captain, during an interview, released 1984.*[493]

3051 **The pouring of more and more men [Americans] into the country without some clearly defined plan for military victory was a useless endeavor.**—*General Tran Van Don, former senior ARVN officer, post war comments, 1978.*[713]

Tran Van Don was a senior military officer under Diem and later participated in the coup which deposed him [Diem] in November 1963.

3052 **Terror has been aptly defined as the propaganda of the dead.**—*Dave Richard Palmer, historian and Vietnam War Veteran, 1978.*[713]

3053 **The Vietnam war was more than a mistake, it was fundamentally wrong and immoral.**—*John E. Rielly, correspondent, December 1978.*[288]

Rielly was announcing the results of a poll that indicated 72 percent of the American public thought as above.

3054 **The continued desperate flight of refugees from Vietnam added but another tragic chapter to an epic that seemed to have no end.**—*George C. Herring, historian, 1979.*[347]

Since the collapse of South Vietnam more than 280,000 Vietnamese have escaped Vietnam, many other thousands died in the attempt.

3055 **Militarily we were successful ... we didn't lose a single battle above company level.**—*General William Westmoreland, former ComUSMACV, during an interview, 30 April 1978.*[113]

3056 **I love the smell of napalm in the morning. ... It smells like victory.**—*Robert Duvall as Lieutenant Colonel Kilgore, in Apocalypse Now, 1979.*[83]

3057 **If we wanted to force a diplomatic solution, we had to create an impression of implacable determination to prevail; only this would bring about either active Soviet assistance in settling the war or else Soviet acquiescence in our mounting military pressures, on which we were determined should diplomacy fail.**—*Henry Kissinger, former National Security Adviser, 1979.*[134]

In response to the North Vietnamese offensive in April 1972, Nixon ordered B-52s to strike targets around Hanoi and Hai Phong. This was an indication to Hanoi that Nixon was serious about completing the peace negotiations and that he was not going to abandon South Vietnam.

3058 **By intervening in what was essentially a local struggle, it [the United States] placed itself at the mercy of local forces, a weak client, and a determined adversary.**—*George C. Herring, historian, 1979.*[347]

3059 **They could booby-trap everything. A cigarette package — anything — and leave it around. There was unbelievable terror of everything booby-trapped.**—*Tom Hagel, Vietnam War Veteran, during an interview, released 1984.*[493]

The VC became experts in the art of booby-traps and mines. They started out against the Japanese during World War II, continued their education against the French, moved through South Vietnamese forces and finally graduated with the Americans.

3060 **After four years of implacable insistence that we dismantle the political structure of our ally and replace it with a coalition government, Hanoi had now essentially given up its political demands.**—*Henry Kissinger, former National Security Adviser, in his book, 1979.*[134]

A breakthrough in the peace negotiations took place 8 October 1972 when Hanoi dropped its requirement for the dissolution of the Saigon government. For over three years they had demanded the Nguyen Van Thieu be ousted from the Saigon government and the NLF be recognized as the true government of South Vietnam.

3061 **In Vietnam you learn to love each other, intimately; I was closer to men over there than I ever was to my family.**—*Hubert Brucker, former U.S. Army Lieutenant, during an interview, released 1984.*[493]

Brucker was an infantry platoon leader with the 4th Infantry Division, 1967-68.

3062 **We had not heard such a polite tone from the North Vietnamese since the middle of October.**—*Henry Kissinger, former National Security Adviser, 1979.*[134]

The attitude of the North Vietnamese members of the peace conference was indignant, superior, and abrasive following the U.S. October 1972 attempt to include agreement changes favorable to the GVN. There was a distinct change in their attitude when they returned to the negotiations following the Linebacker II raids against Hanoi and Hai Phong.

3063 **Kissinger, that SOB! He can burn in hell, as far as I'm concerned. He knew the consequences of his actions, could reflect on them, and still said, "To hell with the human issues."**—*Jack Smith, psychologist and former Marine, during an interview, released 1984.*[493]

3064 **Vietnam veterans have special problems, but I don't know that we can spend money running programs to provide centers and rap sessions and so forth. I just think that's a dispensable expenditure.**—*David Stockman, budget director, Office of Management and Budget, during a press conference, 1981.*[493]

When Stockman became Reagan's OMB director he proposed drastic cutbacks in Federal spending in an attempt to balance the budget. One area of cuts he identified was funding for the Veterans Administration, specifically, some of the outreach programs supporting Vietnam Veterans.

3065 **Maybe if he'd had the balls to go, he'd have the compassion to understand some of the problems of veterans.**—*James Webb, USMC Vietnam War Veteran and author, comments on proposed VA budget cuts, 1981.*[493]

Webb was speaking of Ronald Reagan's director of the Office of Management and Budget who proposed cuts to VA programs supporting Vietnam Veterans. David Stockman had avoided the draft, the military, and the Vietnam War by attending Michigan State University and Harvard Divinity School. After Divinity School he went into politics.

3066 **The atrocities of war are caused when there is no recourse. When there is no recourse, Americans are just as brutal as any person.**—*Peter Krutschewski, former U.S. Army gunship pilot, during an interview, 1981.*[493]

Krutschewski was one of the most highly decorated Army pilots of the Vietnam War. He completed two tours of duty in Vietnam.

3067 **The pain and the loneliness were shallow complaints compared to finding yourself stripped of all entitlement to reputation, love, or honor at home.**—*Admiral James B. Stockdale, former U.S. Navy pilot and prisoner of war, 1981.*[374]

Commander Stockdale was shot down over North Vietnam in September 1965, and held until his release in April 1973. Reflecting on the torture and abuse some American POWs suffered at the hands of their North Vietnamese captors, and the treatment some Vietnam veterans received when they returned to America.

3068 **After a few months [in the field], it began to seem crazy ... maybe we Americans weren't the guys in white hats, riding white horses. Maybe we shouldn't be in Vietnam.... Still it never occurred to me to lay down my rifle and quit. Instead, you develop a survival mentality. You stop thinking about what you're doing, and you count days.**—*William Ehrhart, former U.S. Marine infantryman, during a post-war interview, 1981.*[374]

3069 **I have the highest esteem for what I did in Vietnam. I didn't like many of the things I saw in Vietnam, but the bottom line is we were there because our government sent us. A soldier does not pass judgement on his country's decisions.**—*Peter Krutschewski, former U.S. Army gunship pilot, during an interview, 1981.*[493]

Krutschewski was one of the most highly decorated Army pilots of the Vietnam War. He completed two tours of duty in Vietnam, his last was served as a high profile, short-life expectancy, Cobra gunship pilot.

3070 **When you make contact with the enemy, you went from the most horrible boredom to the most intense excitement I've ever known in my life. You couldn't remain detached. Someone was trying to kill you and you were trying to kill someone, and it was like every thrill hitting you all at once.**—*Mark Smith, former member of the 1st Cavalry Division, to a correspondent, 1981.*[374]

3071 **[Mao] was always ready to fight to the last Vietnamese.**—*Pham Van Dong, Prime Minister, Socialist Republic of Vietnam, commenting to a writer, 1981.*[374]

Mao Tse-tung was eager for North Vietnam to engage the U.S. in battle, draining both the North Vietnamese and American armies.

3072 **Neither our military actions nor political or psychological warfare efforts seem to have made an appreciable dent on the enemy's overall motivation or morale.**—*Konrad Kellen, of the Rand Corporation, 1981.*[374]

Kellen interrogated NVA/VC prisoners of war. In his

opinion the bombing of North Vietnam did not reduce the NVA's will to fight in South Vietnam, but rather it increased their resolve and made them more determined to expel the Americans from Vietnam.

3073 **For us ... there is no such thing as a single strategy. Ours is always a synthesis, simultaneously military, political and diplomatic...**—*General Vo Nguyen Giap, defense minister of North Vietnam, during an interview, Hanoi, 1981.*[374]

Giap was the principal planner of the 1968 TET Offensive, whose results failed militarily, did not inspire the South Vietnamese to rise in support of the communist, but had a deep impact on the America people's sense of the war.

3074 **No matter how cautious a man might try to be, artillery is not a pinpoint effective weapon. Rounds fall short, or coordinates are off. Sooner or later you drop rounds where they're not suppose to fall and civilians die.**—*Unidentified former U.S. Army artillery officer, during an interview, released 1981.*[92]

3075 **The thought of compromise in the current struggle, even in return for concessions, seems alien to these men. They see the war entirely as one of defense of their country against the invading Americans, who, in turn, are seen merely as successors to the French.**—*Konrad Kellen, of the Rand Corporation, 1981.*[374]

Kellen interrogated NVA/VC prisoners of war. In his opinion the bombing of North Vietnam did not reduce the NVA's will to fight in South Vietnam, but rather it increased their resolve and made them more determined to expel the Americans from Vietnam. The communist and nationalistic propaganda fed to NVA troops before their trip south was very effective for many years of the war.

3076 **The horrible smell [of death]. You tasted it as you ate your rations, as if you were eating death...**—*Myron Harrington, former Company Commander, U.S. Marine Corps, comments to author, 1981.*[374]

Harrington's company fought to clear Hue and the Citadel of the VC/NVA during the TET Offensive in February 1968.

3077 **I don't look back on our meetings with any great joy, yet he was a person of substance and discipline who defended the position he represented with dedication.**—*Henry Kissinger, former Secretary of State, during an interview with a correspondent, 1981.*[374]

Kissinger made this comment about Le Duc Tho, Hanoi's chief peace negotiator in Paris. Kissinger and Tho carried on secret peace negotiations for over two years before the shape of a settlement was finally reached.

3078 **I felt intimidated by the subtle, incomprehensible villages — whole societies right in front of us, yet impenetrable even after we had entered them, never understanding anything or seeing anything understandable, the people staring at us as if we were from Mars.**—*Mark Smith, former member of the 1st Cavalary Division, to a correspondent, 1981.*[374]

Smith was describing the difficulty of Americans identifying with, and being accepted by the rural Vietnamese, and to be thought of as the saviors and protectors the not yet disillusioned Americans, believed themselves to be.

3079 **The point man almost has to have second vision. If he gets hit, we all get hit.**—*Ronald Benoit, former U.S. Marine Reconnaissance Commander, 1981.*[493]

The point man in a patrol served as the eyes and the ears of the patrol. He was typically the first man the enemy saw as the patrol moved forward.

3080 **[Paul Warnke was] a persistent rebel whose spell transformed Clifford into a dove and a defeatist.**—*General William Westmoreland, Former ComUSMACV, 1981.*[374]

Westmoreland's opinion of Warnke, Assistant Secretary of Defense. Warnke believed the war was stalemated in 1968, and that further escalation would only lead to a higher level of stalemate.

3081 **Vietnam was a fungus, slowly spreading its suffocating crust over the great plans of the president, both here and overseas. No matter what we turned our hands and minds to, there was Vietnam, its contagion infecting everything that it touched, and it seemed to touch everything.**—*Jack Valenti, Special Assistant to the President, 1981.*[374]

3082 **We all realized that the country had been invaded, and that to get home sooner, we had to fight the war. As long as the war continued ... we could not put our own happiness above our duty.**—*Unidentified North Vietnamese soldier, to a correspondent, after the war, 1981.*[374]

NVA troops were repeatedly told that the reason for the war was to expel the Americans from Vietnam, remove the "puppet" government of South Vietnam, and reunite all of Vietnam as one free, independent country under Ho Chi Minh and his communist party in Hanoi.

3083 **If America wants its Vietnam veterans to be cleansed, it must give them genuine compassion, dignity, and respect: compassion for having been misused, dignity for having answered the call to arms and doing their duty as they saw it, respect for having had the courage and tenacity to survive.**—*Philip Caputo, U.S. Marine Corp Vietnam War Veteran and author, during an interview, January 1982.*[492]

Caputo served a tour as a Marine officer in Vietnam. After his war he authored several books.

3084 **Vietnam is still with us. It has created doubts about American judgement, about American credibility, about American Power — not only at home, but throughout the world. It has poisoned our domestic debate. So we paid an exorbitant price for the decisions that were made in good faith and for good purpose.**—*Henry Kissinger, former Secretary of State.*[374]

3085 **Young men should never be sent into battles unless the country is going to support them.**—*General William Westmoreland, former ComUSMACV, during an interview, 1982.*[374]

3086 **A lot of mothers that raised kids until they were eighteen don't have no kids anymore. They only got flags. That's all they got left of their kids.**—*Unidentified, U.S. Marine Vietnam War Veteran, during an interview, released 1984.*[493]

Traditionally the caskets of American servicemen are draped with an American flag until the burial. The flag is folded and presented to the next of kin as the body is laid to rest.

3087 **John F. Kennedy authorized the sending in of a division of marines, that was the first move toward combat moves in Vietnam...**—*President Ronald Reagan, during news conference, April 1982.*[886]

President Reagan's revisionist history of the Vietnam War. Two Marine utility helicopter units deployed to South Vietnam in 1962 to support ARVN operations. Two battalions of combat Marines deployed to South Vietnam in March 1965. The Marine battalions were later followed by the 1st Marine Division.

3088 **The country didn't give a shit about the guys coming back [from Vietnam], or what they'd gone through. The feeling towards them was, "Stay away—don't contaminate us with whatever you've brought back from Vietnam."**—*John Kerry, former Lieutenant Governor of Massachusetts and Vietnam War Veteran, during an interview, 1982.*[374]

3089 **I envy those guys for having gone—so they never have to apologize for it. I apologize every day of my life to them.**—*Unidentified draft dodger, during an interview, released 1984.*[493]

3090 **I have seen the realities of Communism. It is failure—mismanagement, corruption, privilege, repression.**—*Dr. Duong Quynh Hoa, an ardent communist and former member of the Provisional Revolutionary Government, speaking to a correspondent.*[374]

Hoa was a former ardent Communist.

3091 **It's easy to be omniscient when you're sitting 1,500 feet up in the air. I wonder how those bastards with their free advice would have fared had they been down there with me!**—*Unidentified former U.S. Army infantry officer, during an interview, released 1981.*[92]

A company commander, in contact on the ground, could find himself talking to his battalion commander hovering above him in a command and control helicopter, and above him would be the brigade commander, and possibly above him the division commander. All these commanders requesting updates on the action on the ground, all on different radio frequencies, and regrettably, all of them advising or ordering the ground commander what action to take, all resulting in over-supervision, based on no direct knowledge of the conditions on the ground.

3092 **It has always been a disaster for Vietnam to rely on one large friend.**—*Pham Van Dong, Prime Minister, Socialist Republic of Vietnam.*[374]

Referring to France, America, China, and the Soviet Union over several hundred years of Vietnamese history.

3093 **It must be Vietnamese morality and communist morality, which combine to form the virtue of Ho Chi Minh.** —*General Tran Van Tra, former COSVN Commander, after the war, 1982.*[39]

Tra's definition of revolutionary virtue.

3094 **When the army is committed the American people are committed; when the American people lose their commitment it is futile to try to keep the army committed.**—*General Frederick Weyand, former ComUSMACV.*[374]

Weyand was the last MACV commander of U.S. troops in Vietnam.

3095 **We killed. We died. We died for less than nothing.**—*Cry from an unidentified protester at a dedication ceremony in Washington, D.C., November 1982.*[386]

Several groups protested the dedication of the Vietnam Veterans Memorial in 1982.

3096 **I always thought those college kids in the marches were a bunch of assholes. They didn't even know what they were protesting. We did.**—*Unidentified Vietnam War Veteran, during an interview for MacPherson's book, released 1984.*[493]

As the war progressed more and more military veterans, returned from the war in Vietnam, began to march and demonstrate against the war. These veterans had first hand knowledge of the war and its cost.

3097 **Mr. McNamara came from American business and he was very statistically oriented. He was very anxious to fight this war as efficiently as possible. I have heard him say that he wanted to end the war without having great stockpiles of materials as we had in World War II.**—*General William Westmoreland, former ComUSMACV, Vietnam, during trial deposition, 1983.*[71]

Westmoreland was commenting on McNamara's direction of the Department of Defense. Before becoming DoD Secretary McNamara, a Harvard graduate, was president of Ford Motor Company.

3098 **The only reality about death in Vietnam was its regularity, not its cause.**—*Stanley Karnow, author, 1983.*[374]

3099 **So many [Vietnam Veterans] of them say it was so terrible, the way they went from the field of battle to home within hours ... but I don't know anybody, including me, who was willing to come home by troop ship rather than by jet.**—*Jeff Barber, Vietnam War Veteran, during an interview, released 1984.*[493]

An American soldier in the field in Vietnam on Monday could be standing outside the main gate of Oakland Army Base on Tuesday. That was how swiftly the transition from soldier in Vietnam, to soldier on a U.S. street could be made. For many GIs the transition was a day or two longer depending on whether they were getting out of the military on their return to the U.S. or simply passing through on leave before arrival at their next duty station.

3100 **We defeated the United States. But now we are plagued by problems. We do not have enough to eat. We are a poor, underdevelpoed nation. Waging a war is simple, but running a country is very difficult.**—*Pham Van Dong, Prime Minister, Socialist Republic of Vietnam, 1983.*[374]

3101 **[For a newcomer] the war soon lost a lot of glory because of the deaths and carnage and because there seemed no purpose to it.**—*Hubert Brucker, former U.S. Army Lieutenant, during an interview, released 1984.*[493]

Brucker, an infantry platoon leader, was with the 4th Infantry Division, 1967-68.

3102 **We write no last chapters. We close no books. We put away no final memories. An end to American involvement in Vietnam cannot come before we've achieved the fullest possible accounting of those missing in action.**—*President Ronald Reagan, 1984.*[710]

3103 **We realized collectively we had nothing to fight for, that nobody cared about us, and we didn't give a shit about them. Our sense of motivation was a buddy system: "we are in this and nobody cares, but at least we care about each other."**—*Phil Bidler, former infantryman, during an interview, released 1984.*[493]

This was the attitude which took hold of an increasing number of American combat troops after 1967, as it became apparent that there was no winning strategy for a successful conclusion of the war. For troops in the field the point was to survive the tour of duty and go home.

3104 **In an ambush, the Army used to turn around and dig in. And get their ass whipped. The Marines went straight at the gun. We'd lose a third. But it's better than everybody.**—*Unidentified, U.S. Marine Vietnam War Veteran, during an interview for a book, released 1984.*[493]

3105 **The military is a reward system for violence. They reward you for that — with promotions, medals, prestige, peer admiration — and that's what keeps the military together.**—*Michael Jones, Vietnam War Veteran, during an interview, released 1984.*[493]

Jones was in Marine Reconnaissance, 1965-66.

3106 **The best thing all of us could have done was simply to go home. With faulty leadership at the top there was no way we could ever accomplish our mission.**—*Unidentified U.S. Army Colonel, during an interview, released 1981.*[92]

The officer said he would have refused another tour of duty in Vietnam.

3107 **[Estimating guerrilla forces was tantamount] to trying to estimate roaches in your kitchen.**—*General William Westmoreland, during the Westmoreland vs. CBS libel trial, 1984.*[72]

3108 **It seemed a laughable country and a laughable war — until we started running into the explosive evidence of the enemy's existence, until we started seeing and becoming a part of the red results of their cunning and courage. And then, slowly, as fear mounted frustration and rode down a crippled confidence, as callousness started taking over from condescension in our attitude toward the Vietnamese, our vision blurred, clouded over, and refocused. Where before we had found it difficult to see the enemy anywhere, now we saw him everywhere. It was simple now; the Vietnamese were the Viet Cong, the Viet Cong were the Vietnamese. The killing became so much easier now.**—*Michael Clodfelter, former artilleryman/infantryman with the 101st Airborne, 1984.*[869]

3109 **How could anyone feel guilty about not going to that [Vietnam] war? Vietnam was a mess. Besides it didn't fit into my career plans.**—*Unidentified congressman's son, during an interview for MacPherson's book, released 1984.*[493]

3110 **[I have encountered] a great deal of evidence that live Americans are being held in Southeast Asia.**—*General Eugene Tighe, DIA Chief, 1977-81, in testimony before a Congressional panel in 1985.*[488]

Tighe believed that 50-60 Americans were being held in Vietnam, but he was unable to get his agency to verify the documented sightings. The Defense Intelligence Agency (DIA), had overall responsibility for POW/MIA issues after the collapse of South Vietnam.

3111 **The Party tried to kill any (government [GVN]) official who enjoyed the people's sympathy and left the bad officials unharmed in order to wage propaganda and sow hatred against the government.**—*Ronald H. Spector, historian, 1985.*[34]

The "Party" refered to the NLF, the Viet Cong, the communist party apparatus. This policy was very effective in the early years of the insurgency when sabotage and terror were the primary weapons of the Viet Cong.

3112 **Cu Chi was a springboard for attacking Saigon, the enemy brain center. It was like a thorn stabbing in the eye.**—*Le Duc Tho, Foreign Minister, Socialist Republic of Vietnam, during an interview, 1985.*[28]

Cu Chi was located in the province of Hau Nghia, northwest of Saigon. This province also bordered Cambodia, making it an excellent enemy base and staging area for attacks against Saigon.

3113 **It was adequate to ensure the survival of South Vietnam — as long as the United States stood ready to enforce its terms.**—*Richard Nixon, from his memoirs, 1985.*[163]

Nixon indicated he knew the Paris Peace Agreement was flawed, but he believed overall it was workable, provide the U.S. remained a guarantor and continued to support Saigon against the communist.

3114 **The most power I ever had and probably ever will again. I got to play God for a year. I had the ultimate power. I could look down on the ground and see a man and could say, "I'm gonna kill him or let him live."**—*Tim Noyes, former U.S. Army helicopter pilot, during an interview, released 1984.*[493]

Noyes was a gunship pilot in Vietnam in 1968.

3115 **[Black soldiers] had pride in their individual service, but they're also dealing in a lot of guilt. Many feel they have two strikes — being black and a Vietnam veteran.**—*Forest Farley, former Marine, during an interview released 1984.*[493]

Farley worked extensively with Vietnam Veterans after the war.

3116 **I thought the North Vietnamese would reach a point, like the Chinese and North Koreans in Korea, and Stalin during the Berlin airlift, when they would finally give in.**—*Dean Rusk, former Secretary of State, during an interview, 15 July 1985.*[182]

Rusk was indicating that his underestimation of the North Vietnamese was one of his greatest errors of the Vietnam War.

3117 **You know, it's funny. People feel that a person's handicap affects the mind in some way. ... If they see a guy rolling down the street in a wheelchair — it has an effect on his mind, they figure. They shout at you, as if losing a leg affects your hearing.**—*Jeff Barber, Vietnam War Veteran, during an interview, released 1984.*[493]

Barber lost a leg in Vietnam.

3118 **The first few times I experienced a B-52 attack it seemed, as I strained to press myself into the bunker floor, that I had been caught in the Apocalypse. The terror was complete. One lost control of bodily functions as the mind**

screamed incomprehensible orders to get out.—*Truong Nhu Tang, former Minister of Justice, PRG, 1985.*[170]

The B-52s typically bombed from a minimum of 30,000-feet. At that altitude their approach could not be heard or seen from the ground.

3119 **We never thought we could suffocate North Vietnamese supplies by bombing. We could cause some effect; perhaps with Rolling Thunder it took two months instead of two weeks for a given amount of supplies to arrive in the South.**—*Dean Rusk, former Secretary of State, interview, 15 July 1985.*[182]

3120 **Neither the Longest War nor the Longest Wait are over—not until the last life has been accounted for.**—*Stars and Stripes, 1986.*[710]

3121 **I think a lot who raised so much hell of not wanting to go maybe were trying to justify their fear of going, justifying a reason to get out of it.**—*Dale Wilson, Vietnam War Veteran, during an interview, released 1984.*[493]

Wilson was a Marine Corps infantryman. He served in Vietnam, April 1969 to February 1970, ending his tour when he lost both legs and an arm to an enemy mine.

3122 **It was search and destroy and "Get the last little bastard." ... And that absolutely superfluous adjective—favorable body counts! Somehow these deaths are justifiable because we managed to kill more that day than last.... When both strategy and tactics are flawed, you have no winnable war.**—*Colonel William Corson, U.S. Marine Corps (Retired), during an interview, released 1984.*[493]

American strategy in Southeast Asia: containment of communism. Westmoreland's tactic to achieve containment was through attrition of the enemy.

3123 **Many times they've said there are no live POWs in Vietnam. But I think there's a loophole. As far as I know, they've never said that there are no live POWs in Laos or Cambodia, which are totally under the domination of Hanoi.**—*William Westmoreland, former ComUSMACV, during an interview, 1987.*[488]

Westmoreland believed Hanoi was playing word games. According to the *Life* article several hundred servicemen were held in Laos at the war's end-none of whom were returned.

3124 **If such a sum [$4 billion] had been put on the table by the Vietnamese, Ronald Reagan would have said, "Let's try 'em at $1.8." No one would have passed up that kind of opportunity.**—*Richard Allen, President Reagan's national security advisor, during an interview, 1987.*[488]

Allen denied rumors that the SRV had demanded $4 billion from the Reagan administration for the release of American Vietnam War POWs it supposedly held.

3125 **I thought it [the Vietnam War] was fucking madness. The object was to outstay the enemy. That's too costly. If it cost ten Americans to kill one VC, then, goddamn it, you won't win.**—*Colonel William Corson, U.S. Marine Corps (Retired), during an interview released 1984.*[493]

Corson, on the American strategy of containment of communism and attrition of the enemy.

3126 **There is almost universal allegiance to a draft among yesteryear's [draft] dodgers—a fair draft—for a younger generation.... There is seldom a moment of chagrin at their asking another generation to do what they were unwilling to do.**—*Myra MacPherson, political journalist, from her book, 1984.*[493]

The draft dodgers and evaders of the Vietnam War era, today, champion a call today for a reinstatement of the draft and obligatory public service.

3127 **I don't think they are interested in executing those allied personnel held by them, but in securing from the allied countries something in exchange for their freedom.**—*Rhee Dai Yong, South Korean diplomat to South Vietnam and former DRV/SRV captive, during an interview, October 1987.*[488]

Rhee was captured when Saigon fell to the communist in 1975. The communist denied holding Rhee, yet in 1980 he was released by the SRV after South Korea bartered for his freedom.

3128 **War is fear cloaked in courage.**—*General William Westmoreland, former ComUSMACV.*[83]

3129 **A prostitution of intelligence; [the CIA] had sacrificed its integrity on the altar of public relations and political expediency.**—*George Allen, former CIA Analyst, during trial, 1988.*[233]

Allen's characterization of the CIA's decision not to publicly dispute the enemy Order of Battle issued by MACV. In 1967 there was a discrepancy between MACV's count of the enemy and the numbers calculated by the CIA. MACV's numbers indicated progress in the war, reflecting a reduction in enemy strength. The CIA numbers indicated VC/NVA strength was continuing to grow despite Westmoreland's war of attrition against the enemy.

3130 **The first missions were the scariest. One was worried about making a mistake and thereby getting oneself killed or captured.**—*Robert B. Piper, former U.S. Air Force F-105 pilot, 1988.*[84]

3131 **To be a Marine pilot is to be the chosen of the chosen.**—*Jon Boulle, former U.S. Marine Corps helicopter pilot, 1988.*[84]

3132 **Who can doubt that the cause for which our men fought was just? It was—however imperfectly pursued—the cause of freedom.**—*President Ronald Reagan, from a speech at the Vietnam Veterans Memorial, 1988.*[386]

3133 **Military commanders recognized that Vietnam would be a long war. Hanoi could accept the conditions of stalemate longer than the United States. Stalemate was tantamount to victory for Hanoi.**—*Larry Berman, author, 1989.*[72]

Stalemate involved hundreds of thousands of U.S. troops in Vietnam, suffering casualties daily, with no end in sight. This condition would soon weaken the resolve on the American home front. Hanoi could continue to send troops South in numbers above those being eliminated, maintaining the stalemate. Once America tired of the conflict and backed out, Hanoi would be in place.

3134 **[Vietnam,] that war cleaves us still. But, friends, that war began in earnest a quarter of a century ago; and surely the statute of limitations has been reached. This is a fact: The final lesson of Vietnam is that no great nation can long afford to be sundered by a memory. A new breeze is blowing, and the old bipartisanship must be made new again.**—*President George Bush, Inaugural Address, 20 January 1989.*[367]

3135 **Enemy losses rose and fell with their choice of whether or not to fight.... Hanoi could prolong the war indefinitely by strategically controlling the rate of their losses.**—*Larry Berman, author, 1989.*[72]

Most of the combat in Vietnam was initiated by the VC/NVA. When they chose not to fight, they were difficult to bring under fire. With the sanctuaries along the border the enemy was able to often avoid combat unless it was on his terms. Infiltration South could be slowed but not stopped and it took so little supply to maintain the enemy forces that the small amounts of supply that trickled in was sufficient to maintain enemy troops in the South.

3136 **Among the [Vietnamese] peasantry, the Front was often supported, usually respected, and always feared.**—*Eric M. Bergerud, historian, 1991.*[42]

The "Front" referred to the National Liberation Front, the political arm of the Viet Cong. The NLF was later named the PRG (People's Revolutionary Government). The Front was supported and directed from Hanoi.

3137 **The majority of the [ARVN] armed forces could have more easily been termed armed farces! They were very poor fighters, with the exception of the Rangers, and were much more eager to avoid combat than to engage in it.**—*Unidentified ARVN Lieutenant, as related by John Pancrazio, reminiscing, 1991.*[42]

Pancrazio was an adviser to a unit of the 25th ARVN Infantry Division. The ARVN Rangers, Marines and the 1st ARVN Infantry Division were the notable exceptions to the rule the American GI came to learn about his ARVN counterpart.

3138 **The most troubling aspect was always the knowledge that as soon as we left, they would be back, and, most likely, so would we...**—*Jay Lazarin, former infantryman with the 27th Infantry Regiment, 25th Infantry Division, 1991.*[42]

American strategy early in the war sought the destruction of the enemy, not the holding of terrain. At the end of an operation to clear the enemy from an area, the units conducting the operation moved on to another area. Usually no force, ARVN or allied, was left to secure the area. The result was the enemy quickly returned. Some weeks or months later another operation would be mounted to clear the same area again.

3139 **Charlie made a big deal about moving his dead, and he was smart. It was demoralizing because you'd rarely actually see any results. You began to doubt if you could shoot straight.**—*Dan Vandenberg, former infantryman of the 25th Infantry Division, reminiscing, 1991.*[42]

The enemy went to great lengths to police the battlefield when they retreated after an engagement.

3140 **They were losers. They didn't have any initiative whatsoever. I guess it would have been hard knowing you might shoot up your brother or uncle.**—*Michael Willis, former infantryman of the 25th Infantry Division, reminiscing, 1991.*[42]

Under the Vietnamization program the U.S. 25th Infantry Division worked with the 25th ARVN Infantry Division. The 25th ARVN was perhaps the lowest rated division in the South Vietnamese Army.

3141 **We had absolutely no respect for ARVN. They wouldn't do a thing when we were around.... Hell, if ARVN could have fought, we wouldn't have been there.**—*Phil Boardman, former infantryman of the 25th Infantry Division, reminiscing, 1991.*[42]

3142 **Each time we took casualties, they became our priorities.... I am not saying that this was bad.... It just didn't seem aggressive enough then or certainly now. I'm not now sorry for it; this kind of tactic probably kept most of us alive.**—*Jay Lazarin, former infantryman with the 27th Infantry Regiment, 25th Infantry Division, 1991.*[42]

The enemy tactic in battle was to press an attack, with much less concern for the wounded. When the battle was over or during the retreat, the enemy would collect their wounded they could conveniently reach. The enemy went to great lengths to remove their dead. The dead were a definite indication of how the battle had progressed, and with the American fixation on body count, the enemy did his best to cloud the issue.

3143 **[ARVN was] a joke. I despised the whole lot of them. They were all cowards. In the morning, their uniforms were spotless and weapons clean. They'd look the same at the end of the day. We did all their work. We looked like tramps.... We would rather go it alone: At least you only had to fight one enemy.**—*Dan Vandenberg, former infantryman of the 25th Infantry Division, reminiscing, 1991.*[42]

3144 **The majority of the enemy were dedicated fighting men and women. They truly believed in their cause and many of them, especially the NVA, were good and fierce fighters.**—*John Pancrazio, former adviser to the 25th ARVN Infantry Division, comments on the enemy, 1991.*[42]

Most American combat troops had more respect for the enemy they fought, than for the ARVN they were in Vietnam to assist. There were some good ARVN units, but they were the exception to the rule.

3145 **There was a real difference between [ARVN] officers and men. The officers were urban, spoke French, and were often Catholic. The soldiers were rural Buddhists.... The officers treated their troops and NCOs like dirt. We believed that some of the officers were VC, VC sympathizers or fence sitters.**—*Sgt. Richard O'Hare, former U.S. adviser with the Duc Hue advisory team, 1991.*[42]

3146 **The fact is that three months before the [TET] offensive both Westmoreland and Ellsworth Bunker ... loudly proclaimed that enemy strength was decreasing.... [Their] telegrams contained not one word of warning about the possibility of large-scale, coordinated attacks in the future. On the contrary, they ... must rank among the most erroneous assessments ever sent by field commanders.**—*Clark Clifford, former Secretary of Defense, as written in the New Yorker, May 1991.*[198]

3147 **One area we failed to investigate during those early years of the American buildup was the growing gap between the optimistic reports of progress that were coming in through the official chain of command and the increasingly skeptical reporting by some of the journalists covering the war.**—*Clark Clifford, former Secretary of Defense, in an article, May 1991.*[234]

3148 **A lot of us didn't try to understand the people or make friends: Everybody was a zip, gook, or animal. New guys**

would give candy to the kids: Vets would throw it at them and try to hit them. Some of the guys hated them. ... A lot of us wanted to be friends with the civilians, but we knew we couldn't trust them. There were a lot of VC sympathizers.—*C. W. Bowman, former infantryman with the 25th Infantry Division, 1991.*[42]

3149 **They [U.S. soldiers] used to destroy in a few minutes time all that I could possibly conjure up with all the civic action programs and begging and pleading and whatever else you could think of. They could counteract what I could do in a month in three or four minutes.**—*Donald Pearce, former U.S. Army Major, Cu Chi District Adviser, 1991.*[42]

Pearce complained of the retaliatory measures taken by some troops of the 25th Infantry Division. Notably their quickness to respond with massive fires when fired upon. Such fires were often brought to bear on villages and tree lines harboring hamlets in the area. Later, the 25th Division's rules of engagement were changed, reducing such fires, but during TET 1968 and for several months thereafter, the use of heavy retaliatory fire was the norm.

3150 **In the jungle, you don't think in terms of black and white ... it doesn't matter, it can't matter.... Out in the jungle thirty, forty days at a time, we just thought of each other, together.**—*James Hawkins, Jr., former U.S. Army infantryman, during an interview, 9 July 1991.*[999]

3151 **Boo Coo V.C. there. My Dai-Uy [captain] will kill me if I go down there.**—*Unidentified ARVN Lieutenant, as related by John Pancrazio, reminiscing, 1991.*[42]

Pancrazio was an adviser to a unit of the 25th ARVN Infantry Division. The unit was tasked to conduct an ambush, but the ARVN officer refused to move into the preplanned ambush position. Pancrazio drew his weapon on the ARVN officer and gave him the option of dying where he stood or taking his chances with his Dai-Uy later. The ARVN continued into the ambush position. ARVN commanders of the 25th ARVN Division were extremely reluctant to put themselves in harms way.

3152 **The ARVN 25th [Infantry Division] was known to be a particularly poor unit in a not very illustrious army.**—*Eric M. Bergerud, historian, 1991.*[42]

The 25th ARVN suffered from leadership bankruptcy and was militarily ineffective. It primarily was deployed in the III Corps area.

3153 **Often, command-detonated mines were blown off before we'd enter a village. We'd sweep it and find only mamasan. We'd go into a hooch and find fifty pair of chopsticks and other small things. You knew the village was VC...**—*C. W. Bowman, former infantryman with the 25th Infantry Division, 1991.*[42]

Unlike an automatic mine, a command-detonated mine required manual detonation. The enemy, secreted in a spider hole, behind a berm, or hidden in a treeline, would touch two wires together, pull a string, or press a plunger to trigger the detonation of the mine. The enemy would then slip away while those attacked spread out in a defensive formation and treated the wounded and wrapped the dead.

3154 **The armed forces sent to Vietnam were by far the best ever sent to war by the United States.**—*Eric M. Bergerud, historian, 1991.*[42]

3155 **If there was a national strategy, it never filtered down to the regular soldier. Everyone knew that the South Vietnamese governments, no matter who they had in there, were all corrupt. We all wondered: Why do we want those guys in there? Are they any better than the guys we are fighting?**—*Jerry Headley, former platoon leader, 3d Squadron, 4th Cavalry Regiment, 1991.*[42]

The "3/4 Cav" was the 25th Infantry Division's reconnaissance squadron.

3156 **When friends started to die from booby-traps and you don't see the enemy, men became embittered and grew hardhearted. You had to be to survive.**—*C. W. Bowman, former infantryman with the 25th Infantry Division, 1991.*[42]

3157 **If the VC perceived our reluctance to fire on a certain area, they would exploit it to the hilt. They would hit us from a village or hamlet they thought we were reluctant to fire upon. Or else they would fire outside a village and retreat into the hamlet thinking we would fire back...**—*Thomas A. Giltner, former Platoon Leader, 27th Infantry Regiment, 1991.*[42]

This tactic could have multiple advantages for the VC. Their initial fire could generate a few casualties among the American patrol approaching the ville. If the Americans took the bait and fired on the ville, called in artillery or an air strike, it fortified the communist propaganda that framed the Americans as invaders who had no regard for the people of the ville. With the ville between the VC and the advancing American patrol, the enemy could easily slip away.

3158 **Many of our countrymen came to hate the war we fought. Those who hated it most — the professionally sensitive — were not, in the end, sensitive enough to differentiate between the war and the soldiers who had been ordered to fight it. They hated us as well, and we went to ground in the crossfire, as we had learned in the jungles.**—*General Harold G. Moore, 1992.*[501]

3159 **The Kennedy assassination, had no large-scale effect on policy, and not even any great effect on tactics, when account is taken of the objective situation and how it was perceived.**—*Noam Chomsky, political dissident and linguistics professor, writings, 1992.*[87]

Chomsky was addressing speculation that Kennedy was killed because of the course he may have taken for America in Vietnam.

3160 **All they [the officer and NCOs] saw was body counts.... A lifer is a lifer.... They were unfair to everybody, regardless of race.**—*SP/4 James Edward Hawkins, Jr., former U.S. Army infantryman, during an interview, 1997.*[1018]

3161 **No event in American history is more misunderstood than the Vietnam War. It was misreported then, and it is misremembered now. Rarely have so many people been so wrong about so much. Never have the consequences of their misunderstanding been so tragic.**—*Richard Nixon, from his memoirs, 1985.*[632]

The Long View

It is well that war is so terrible, or we would get too fond of it.
— Robert E. Lee

3162 **We had the power ... [but] in the final analysis ... [we] didn't have the will.**—*General William Westmoreland, former ComUSMACV, during an interview, 30 April 1978.*[113]

3163 **Intelligence is not written for history; it's written for an audience—[meaning that it's useless if the audience for whom it's written refuses to read it].**—*George Carver, Special Assistant for Vietnamese Affairs, CIA, 1979.*[207]

Carver speaking of the many CIA intelligence estimates that were available to the White House and the Pentagon, many of which were dismissed, ignored, or rebuked.

3164 **"Uncommon valor" was indeed a common occurrence if it involved saving a comrade's life or moving forward to help a trapped American unit.**—*Eric M. Bergerud, historian, 1991.*[42]

3165 **Now it is not good for the Christian's health to hustle the Asian brown / ... For the Christian riles and the Asian smiles and he weareth the Christian down / ... And the end of the fight is a tombstone white with the name of the late deceased / ... And the epitaph drear: "A fool lies here who tried to hustle the East."**—*Rudyard Kipling, from Naulahka, late-1800s.*[424]

Kipling's poem was about the white man's troubles in the Eastern part of the world, completely appropriate to the troubles in Vietnam. This poem is often repeated in works about the Vietnam Wars.

3166 **Grab 'em by the balls, and their hearts and minds will follow.**—*Anonymous.*[374]

A standing joke among many Americans in Vietnam about the official MACV program known as WHAM (winning the hearts and minds of the Vietnamese people). Many of the military actions seeking to destroy or dislodge the enemy inevitably destroyed or turned the very people the military was seeking to help and protect, into refugees and the focus of funeral processions.

3167 **Any danger spot is tenable if—brave men—will make it so.**—*John F. Kennedy.*[501]

3168 **Television brought the brutality of war into the comfort of the living room. Vietnam was lost in the living rooms of America—not on the battlefields of Vietnam.**—*Herbert Marshall McLuhan.*[83]

McLuhan, a literary and communications media scholar, wrote extensively of the effects of media on current culture. Born 1911, died 1980, he was best known for the phrase "the medium is the message."

3169 **Communist guerrillas hide among the people. If you win the people over to your side, the Communist guerrillas have no place to hide. With no place to hide, you can find them. Then, as military men, fix them ... finish them!**—*Colonel Edward Lansdale, Special Assistant to Ambassador Lodge, during a counterinsurgency lecture.*[374]

Lansdale was CIA station chief for the newly created Saigon Military Mission, June 1954. He directed covert CIA operations throughout Vietnam for several years.

3170 **Victory has a thousand fathers, but defeat is an orphan.**—*President John F. Kennedy.*[83]

3171 **One of the facts of life about Vietnam was that it was never difficult to decide what should be done, but it was almost impossible to get it done.**—*General Maxwell Taylor, former Ambassador to South Vietnam.*[374]

Taylor was referring to the difficulty in getting the South Vietnamese political and military situations to a state where they could command the respect of the people and successfully prosecute the war against the communist insurgents.

3172 **The point where logic touches ego.**—*Douglas Pike, historian.*[713]

Pike's characterization of Hanoi's belief, throughout the Vietnam War that they could militarily defeat the United States.

3173 **I didn't come home; I just came back. Home had changed so much that I didn't recognize it. And no one recognized me, either.**—*Unidentified GI, on his return from Vietnam.*[886]

3174 **What can they do to me: send me to Vietnam?**—*Anonymous and universal.*[475]

Typical attitude of the American grunt in Vietnam regarding any disciplinary action the military might threaten him with.

3175 **It's not much of a war, but it's the only war we've got.**—*Anonymous.*[931]

This phrase was popularly used in the Pentagon, in reference to the low-key nature of the conflict in Vietnam in the early sixties when Americans were lightly and quietly engaged in combat with the Viet Cong.

3176 **What you do is, you load all the Friendlies onto ships and take them out to the South China Sea. Then you bomb the country flat. Then you sink the ships.**—*Anonymous, ultimate solution to the war in Vietnam.*[309]

3177 **Diplomacy has rarely been able to gain at the conference table what cannot be gained or held on the battlefield.**—*General Walter Bedell Smith, Under Secretary of State.*[347]

Also phrased as "You don't win at the conference table what you've lost on the battlefield." This was stated about the proposed peace talks between the French and the Viet Minh in 1953.

3178 **In Vietnam, the only measure of victory was one of the most hideous, morally corrupting ideas ever conceived by the military mind — the body count.**—*Philip Caputo, former Lieutenant, U.S. Marine Corps, during a magazine interview.*[186]

3179 **The unwilling, led by the unqualified, doing the unnecessary for the ungrateful.**—*Anonymous.*[100]

The "unwilling" were the thousands of draftees and short-term enlisted men who did not want to be in Vietnam. The "unqualified" were those running the war, and at the lower levels, officers fighting an unconventional war with conventional tactics. The "unnecessary" were the tactics of the war, large unit actions, where small unit stealth would have been more effective. The "ungrateful" refers to the Vietnamese and the American public. Also referred to as "UUUU."

3180 **When they're not red, they're yellow.**—*Anonymous.*[494]

Popular derogatory description of the Vietnamese flag. The flag featured a yellow background with three horizontal red stripes. GI tradition held that the yellow background represented the lack of courage of the South Vietnamese military — and the red stripes represented the communist VC; when the Vietnamese weren't yellow, they were communists.

3181 **I believe in compulsory cannibalism. If people were forced to eat what they killed there would be no more war.**—*Abbie Hoffman, Yippie leader and radical activist.*[83]

3182 **"Peace" is when nobody's shooting. A just "peace" is when our side gets what it wants.**—*Bill Mauldin, cartoonist and journalist.*[83]

3183 **[We] fought over the same ground again and again, month after month, [our] only object to kill more of them than they did of [us]. When we did, the official logic went, that week at least we had won the war — even if the contested area was still controlled by the enemy, even if we hadn't won any "hearts or minds" in the countryside. Commanders liked good body counts, even when they were fudged, which was not uncommon. They liked high kill ratios — it meant they were doing something right.**—*Philip Caputo, former Lieutenant, U.S. Marine Corps, during a magazine interview.*[186]

3184 **Anyone who runs is a Viet Cong, any one who stands still is a "well disciplined" Viet Cong.**—*Anonymous, GI philosophy.*[114]

3185 **The Americans are walking in the same footsteps as the French although dreaming different dreams.**—*Bernard Fall, as relayed by David Halberstam.*[873]

3186 **The trouble with our policy in Vietnam has been that we guessed wrong with respect to what the North Vietnamese reaction would be. We anticipated that they would respond like reasonable people.**—*Paul Warnke, Assistant Secretary of Defense.*[374]

Many within the Johnson administration believed that when North Vietnam was confronted with the overwhelming power of American military might and economic power they would cease and desist from further support of the VC insurgents in South Vietnam.

3187 **Statistics ... [are] no substitute for strategy.**—*Earl H. Tilford, author and historian, 1993.*[931]

3188 **The majority of the Vietnamese, still hungering for independence, had no side to join. They were opposed to both the Communist Viet Minh and the French. As the war raged around their families and homes, they gave lip service to whichever side was locally dominant, in order to stay alive.**—*Colonel Edward Lansdale, U.S. Air Force, special adviser to President Diem, from his writings, 1972.*[861]

In the mid-fifties Lansdale advised Diem, helping him to consolidate his power in South Vietnam. Diem, under the influence of his brother Nhu, began to slip away from the American idealism Lansdale was attempting to instill in the Diem regime. With Diem's fall from power, Lansdale departed Vietnam, returning in 1966 as special assistant to Ambassadors Henry Cabot Lodge and Ellsworth Bunker.

3189 **Nothing is more precious than freedom and independence.**—*Ho Chi Minh, President, Democratic Republic of Vietnam.*[501]

3190 **The application of military, war-making power is an ugly thing — stark, harsh, and demanding — and it cannot be made nicer by pussy-footing around with it.**—*Admiral U.S. Grant Sharp, former Commander-in-Chief, Pacific Command, from his book, 1978.*[120]

Sharp was a long time advocate of the heavy use of U.S. air power against North Vietnam, in an attempt to quickly resolve the war.

3191 **A hush came over the cabin of the plane. All of the joking, singing, and cajoling stopped. You could have heard a pin drop. The stewardess was crying, and some of the men were, too.**—*Gerald Kolb, U.S. Army replacement, comments on his arrival in Vietnam, 1991.*[42]

Most American replacements to Vietnam arrived by chartered airline, having departed the U.S. from Travis Air Force Base.

3192 **In the rear with the beer.**—*Anonymous.*[4]

Reference to troops in the "rear" at the major bases and in the towns where the availability of creature comforts was extremely high.

3193 **It was the hallmark of the war, you could never tell who was the enemy and who was not. Therefore, you treated everybody with suspicion and distrust. The enemy was everywhere and everybody at all times, and we were the foreigners in their country.**—*Thomas A. Giltner, former Platoon Leader, 27th Infantry Regiment, 1991.*[42]

3194 **Soldiers are trained to fight and kill. If you put them in a war, they're going to fight and kill — and when they come home you can't tell them it was wrong.**—*Al Wilder, Vietnam War Veteran, during an interview, released 1984.*[493]

Wilder was a platoon leader in 1966, his tour cut short when he was wounded in an ambush.

3195 **Judgements of history are too subtle and too complex to be resolved with the simplicity of a jury's verdict. It may be for the best that the verdict will be left to history.**—*Judge Pierre Leval, in closing Westmoreland vs CBS slander trial, 1984.*[72]

The CBS show aired 23 January 1982, accusing Westmoreland and MACV of concealing from the White House information on enemy troop strength. Westmoreland denied the charges and sued CBS. The suit was settled out of court.

3196 **I'd rather kill a nigger instead of a gook.**—*Anonymous graffito.*[1018]

Racial slurs could be found scrawled on the walls of latrines in rear areas at American bases in Vietnam. Such graffiti was more often than not ignored by command responsible for the troops.

3197 **The military don't start wars. The politicians start wars.**—*General William Westmoreland, ComUSMACV.*[83]

3198 **Failure never comes easily, but it comes especially hard when success is anticipated at little cost.**—*George Herring, historian, 1979.*[347]

Initially the Johnson administration and the U.S. military believed American military power and technology would be sufficient to put down the insurgency in South Vietnam and convince Hanoi to cease supporting the Viet Cong.

3199 **Americans searched for enemy troops until those soldiers allowed themselves to be found.**—*Military historian writing under the pen name Cincinnatus, 1981.*[113]

The nature of U.S. search and destroy operations seldom surprised the enemy. Fly-overs by command helicopters, preparatory air strikes, or artillery fire on the LZ, and the clatter of helicopters gave away the American force's location. At that point the enemy could chose to stay in the area or retreat, thus he often had the initiative as to when battle would take place.

3200 **The left hated us for killing, and the right hated us for not killing enough.**—*Unidentified Vietnam War Veteran, during an interview for MacPherson's book, released in 1984.*[493]

3201 **American boys should not be seen dying on the nightly news. Wars should be over in three days or less, or before Congress invokes the War Powers Resolution. Victory must be assured in advance. And the American people must be all for it from the onset.**—*Evan Thomas, Newsweek Magazine.*[83]

3202 **Our air power did not fail us; it was the decision makers...**—*Admiral U.S. Grant Sharp, former Commander-in-Chief, Pacific Command, from his book, 1978.*[120]

Sharp contends that had the military been allowed to conduct the military aspect of the war, the air campaign (Rolling Thunder) would have resolved itself very differently.

3203 **Give Nixon Time With His Withdrawal Program — Withdrawal is something Nixon's father should have done 58 years ago**—*Anonymous graffito.*[886]

Two lines, from two different hands, posted on a latrine wall in South Vietnam.

3204 **Despite all the highfalutin gadgets, intelligence, for the most part, was extremely poor. We did not know who we were looking for or where to look, in most cases.**—*Carl Quickmire, former Armored Cavalry Troop Commander, 25th Infantry Division, 1991.*[42]

3205 **The bombs in Vietnam explode at home; they destroy hopes and possibilities for a decent America.**—*Dr. Martin Luther King, Jr., religious leader and civil rights activist.*[83]

3206 **You've got to be worried. If you're not, you don't know the situation.**—*General John H. Cushman, comments made while in Vietnam.*[93]

3207 **It's practically impossible — to tell civilians — from the Vietcong;— after a while,— you quit trying.**—*W.D. Ehrhart, former Vietnam GI and poet, from his poem, "Guerrilla War."*[883]

3208 **Artillery lends dignity to what would otherwise be a vulgar brawl.**—*Anonymous.*[501]

Artillerist have long considered themselves the Kings of Battle. While the infantry are known as the Queen of Battle.

3209 **An all-encompassing strategy of revolutionary war which caused the enemy troops to suffocate, to worry apprehensively day and night, and think that all places had to be defended and they could be safe only with large forces.**—*General Tran Van Tra, former COSVN Commander, after the war, 1982.*[39]

For the allies the enemy was perceived to be everywhere. This necessitated that units be constantly on guard, not knowing where or when the VC/NVA might strike again.

3210 **The test of character is not "hanging in" when you expect light at the end of the tunnel, but performance of duty and persistence of example when you know no light is coming.**—*Admiral James B. Stockdale, former U.S. Navy pilot and Prisoner of War.*[361]

Admiral Stockdale was shot down in April 1965, and was released from North Vietnamese captivity in 1973.

3211 **Why can't you guys conduct your pacification as well as the marines with their Civic Action Program?**—*Question asked by a reporter during a Congressional junket, 1967.*[4]

MACV was often asked this question by reporters or visiting Congressional members who had reviewed the Marines' pacification program in I Corps. The Marine CAP program was successful, but was not universally applied throughout South Vietnam. The program was limited in its scope and contrary to the MACV design of pacification. Prior to 1968 pacification was a low priority in MACV's war plan.

3212 **The brother is here, and he's raising hell. We're proving ourselves.**—*Unidentified U.S. Marine Corps private, South Vietnam.*[1018]

3213 **The Establishment center ... has led us into the stupidest and cruelest war in all history. That war is a moral and political disaster—a terrible cancer eating away at the soul of our nation.**—*Senator George McGovern, of South Dakota.*

3214 **The only good gook is a dead gook.**—*Anonymous.*[359]

3215 **When your country says go, it is not up to us to decide whether it's right or wrong.**—*Dale Wilson, Vietnam War Veteran, during an interview, released 1984.*[493]

Wilson was a Marine Corps infantryman. He served in Vietnam, April 1969 to February 1970, ending his tour when he lost both legs and an arm to an enemy mine.

3216 **When you are trying to survive there is no such thing as too much firepower. We were not military tacticians or logistics people; we were infantryman trying to kill them before they killed us.**—*Jay Lazarin, former infantryman with the 27th Infantry Regiment, 25th Infantry Division, 1991.*[42]

3217 **In all the insurgencies of the past twenty-five years, since the Second World War, none has been sustained, let alone successful, without substantial outside support.**—*Sir Robert Thompson, British counterinsurgency specialist.*[713]

Thompson was speaking of the sanctuary of VC/NVA bases along the Cambodian and Laotian borders. These bases were off limits to American attack, as designated by the Johnson administration. The protected bases allowed the enemy to attack across the border then return to the sanctuary to rearm and refit depleted units. Enemy units decimated in South Vietnam regrouped in Cambodia then returned at a later date to attack again.

3218 **No one starts a war—or rather, no one in his senses ought to do so—without first being clear in his mind what he intends to achieve by that war and how he intends to conduct it.**—*Lt.Col. Harold G. Moore, former Commander, 1st Battalion, 7th Cavalry Regiment, writing in 1992.*[501]

3219 **Non Gratum Anus Rodentum.**—*Slogan adopted by Tunnel Rats of several American units.*[494]

Tunnel Rats were volunteer soldiers who searched and explored VC tunnels. It was extremely dangerous work. As the Tunnel Rats became more specialized, one of their number designed a special patch (unauthorized) of distinction, bearing their motto "Non Gratum Anus Rodentum," dog-latin for "Not Worth A Rat's Ass." Many Army Tunnel Rats of different units wore the patch.

3220 **We have not enough information. We act with ruthlessness, like a steamroller.**—*General Harold K. Johnson, U.S. Army Chief of Staff, 1983.*[374]

3221 **We Vietnamese had trouble understanding why this vast and highly competent force did not come in and really get to the business of winning the war. It seemed to serve as more of an instrument of intimidation and reinforcement of policy than as a genuine war machine.**—*General Tran Van Don, former senior ARVN officer, post war comments, 1978.*[713]

3222 **Justly the returned prisoners became public heroes. Unjustly, until many years later they were the only veterans of the Vietnam War who were recognized publicly as heroes.**—*Frank Uhlig, naval historian, 1986.*[960]

3223 **The Americans thought that the more bombs they dropped, the quicker we would fall to our knees and surrender. But the bombs heightened rather than dampened our spirit.**—*Dr. Ton That Tung, North Vietnamese scientist, 1981.*[374]

Tung was a medical doctor and scientist, later studying the lasting effects of defoliants used in Vietnam.

3224 **Why the hell don't they [ARVN] stand and fight the VC instead of running away?**—*Question often raised by American soldiers in the field.*[4]

To the average GI, the ARVN's failures and retreats were more evident than those occasions when the ARVN held their ground or actively sought out the enemy.

3225 **Within the soul of each Vietnam Veteran there is probably something that says, "bad war, good soldier."**—*Max Cleland, Vietnam War Veteran and former director of the Veterans Administration.*[83]

In April 1968 Cleland was a U.S. Army captain in Vietnam when he lost both legs and his right arm to a grenade explosion.

3226 **The night belongs to Charlie.**—*Anonymous proverb of the war.*[249]

The nights were when most enemy movement took place. During the day enemy movement was more easily detected, making them the targets of air strikes, artillery barrages, or combat assaults.

3227 **War is never anything but ugly and brutal.**—*William P. Bundy, Assistant Secretary for East Asian and Pacific Affairs, during a public address in College Park, Maryland, 15 August 1967.*[82]

3228 **Vietnam is a military problem. Vietnam is a political problem; and as the war goes on it has become more clearly a moral problem.**—*Senator Eugene J. McCarthy from Minnesota.*[83]

3229 **Of all the United States forces [in Vietnam] the Marine Corps alone made a serious attempt to achieve permanent**

and lasting results in their tactical area of responsibility by seeking to protect the rural population.—*Sir Robert Thompson, British counterinsurgency expert, 1986.*[382]

Thompson speaking of the Marine's efforts at pacification in the rural villages and hamlets of South Vietnam, under their Combined Action Companies (CAC) and Combined Action Platoons (CAP).

3230 **The brother does all right here.... You see it's just about the first time in his life that he finds he can compete with whites on an equal—or very close to equal basis.**—*Unidentified U.S. Army officer, an adviser to the South Vietnamese Army.*[931]

3231 **One of the greatest casualties of the war in Vietnam is the Great Society ... shot down on the battlefield of Vietnam.**—*Dr. Martin Luther King, Jr., religious leader and civil rights activist.*[38]

3232 **The conventional army loses if it does not win. The guerrilla wins if he does not lose.**—*Henry Kissinger, President Nixon's National Security Adviser.*[83]

3233 **[The helicopter in Vietnam] exaggerated the two greatest weaknesses of the American character—impatience and aggressiveness.**—*Observation of an unidentified Englishman.*[713]

The helicopter allowed American units unprecedented mobility, this advantage was tempered by the enemy's use of terrain and the vulnerability of the helicopter.

3234 **Vietnam and our generation changed "wine, women and song" to "drugs, sex, and rock 'n' roll."**—*Unidentified, former military helicopter pilot, during an interview, released 1984.*[493]

3235 **Despite six years of war and scores of major engagements, American ground forces did not lose a single battle in Vietnam.**—*Eric M. Bergerud, historian, 1991.*[42]

This statement should be qualified as battles of battalion size or larger. There were several instances where an American company was rendered combat ineffective due to casualties suffered, but not completely wiped out to the last man, as was the case with the French.

3236 **Burn yourselves, not your draft cards...**—*Anonymous, 1965.*[114]

This chant by counter anti-war demonstrators came into vogue in late-1965 after two American anti-war protesters, in separate incidents, put themselves to the torch in protest of the war in Vietnam. Anti-war and anti-draft rallies often attracted crowds of counter-demonstrators.

3237 **Ninety-nine percent of the time as I dropped bombs, someone was shooting at me.**—*Unidentified American fighter-bomber pilot, 1981.*[374]

The pilot's testimony was regarding North Vietnam's antiaircraft defenses. North Vietnam boasted some of the densest antiaircraft defenses in the world. Most of the ground base air defense systems were supplied by the Soviet Union. More than 8,000 antiaircraft guns and 200 Surface to Air missile batteries, and tens of thousands of small arms were used for the air defense of North Vietnam.

3238 **You can tell a fighter pilot, but you can't tell him much.**—*Proverb, that made the journey from World War II through the Korean War to American pilots during the Vietnam War.*[249]

3239 **For most [Vietnamese] people, the only ideology that counts is a full stomach.**—*Unidentified Communist Cadre, comment to correspondent, Ho Chi Minh City.*[374]

Cadre comments on the ideology many of the Vietnamese were following after several years of communist control of Vietnam.

3240 **Although it [the Vietnam War] was the best documented and the most reported in our history, it was paradoxically the least comprehended.**—*Dave Richard Palmer, historian and Vietnam War Veteran, 1978.*[713]

3241 **Americans were good soldiers but they fought the wrong war.**—*General Tran Van Tra, of the PRG delegation in 1973.*[83]

3242 **[Problems facing African Americans stem from inequities in American society and these are problems] which the draft can't cure and for which it should not be blamed.**—*Hanson Baldwin, correspondent for The New York Times.*[1018]

3243 **I do not believe that the men who served in uniform in Vietnam have been given the credit they deserve. It was a difficult war against an unorthodox enemy.**—*General William Westmoreland, former ComUSMACV.*

3244 **A revolution is interesting insofar as it avoids like the plague the plague it promised to heal.**—*Daniel Berrigan, Catholic priest and social activist.*[83]

Berrigan became an anti-war activist, demonstrating against the Vietnam War.

3245 **When the door of the plane opened, we were hit with a musty, rank, urine-like odor. It was very hot. We passed a bunch of guys whooping and hollering: They were going home. My God, what a low, low feeling.**—*Gerald Kolb, U.S. Army replacement, comments on his arrival in Vietnam, 1991.*[42]

Most American replacements to Vietnam arrived by chartered airline, having departed the U.S. from Travis Air Force Base. Replacements filed off the plane, past troops waiting to board the same plane for their return trip to the U.S.

3246 **When lives are at stake it takes a very tough commander, as required in this type of war, who is prepared to risk increased casualties to achieve the right effect rather than hold down casualties (by using massive fire-power) to get a statistical result but the wrong effect. That the fewer casualties may have been entirely wasted does not occur to the many.**—*Sir Robert Thompson, British counterinsurgency specialist.*[711]

American field commanders in Vietnam relied heavily on artillery and air strike firepower to destroy the enemy. Maneuvering to close with the enemy was used less frequently than the tactic of making contact with the enemy, then falling back to call in artillery or air strikes on the enemy position. This tactic saved American lives, but allowed the enemy more avenues of escape.

3247 **[It was] a war of no frontlines but many sidelines.**—*General William Westmoreland, former ComUSMACV, postwar comments, 1978.*[713]

Commenting on the many aspects of the war in Vietnam.

3248 **It was hard to explain to them [the Americans] that a villager who suddenly became rich was not so much respected as pointed at in shame.**—*Nguyen Cao Ky, former Prime Minister of South Vietnam, 1976.*[629]

For the Vietnamese peasant, rich was living on his own land, worshipping his ancestors and taking care of his family. To be uprooted from his land, placed in a refugee camp or village and given a high paying job was not considered by the Vietnamese as being successful.

3249 **I am not acting when I say that I am obliged to cry ... at the suffering and the losses.**—*Pham Van Dong, Prime Minister, Democratic Republic of Vietnam.*[374]

Reflecting on Hanoi's estimates of 100,000 civilians killed during the course of U.S. bombing of North Vietnam.

3250 **Most Americans sent to Vietnam were relatively safe, the men who were in harm's way fought one of the bloodiest wars in American history.**—*Eric M. Bergerud, historian, 1991.*[42]

The ratio of combat soldier to support soldiers varied during the war from 6-10:1; for every combat soldier in the field there were 6-10 soldiers providing some kind of support duty. In World War II the ratio was about 4-5:1.

3251 **Violence is as American as cherry pie.**—*H. Rap Brown.*[936]

3252 **We were far from home, and we felt forgotten by the country that had sent us. And we were scared — of death, certainly, but also of being abandoned. It was considered bad luck to talk about the fear of death, so it tended to be absorbed into the other fear, into worrying about the women we had left behind. Each mail call, like the trails we walked down, could be booby-trapped; a Dear John letter was as feared as a mine.**—*William Broyles, Jr., Vietnam War Veteran, 1985.*[187]

3253 **You know when I am out in the bush carrying a grenade launcher, no white man is going to call me nigger.**—*Unidentified U.S. Army infantryman of the 9th Infantry Division.*[992]

3254 **What the United States wants for South Vietnam is not the important thing. What North Vietnam wants for South Vietnam is not the important thing. What is important is what the people of South Vietnam want for South Vietnam.**—*Richard Nixon.*[83]

3255 **When you drink out of the same canteen and eat off the same spoon, you get real tight together.**—*Unidentified paratrooper of the U.S. Army 173d Airborne Brigade.*[1017]

For combat units in the field their were few instances of racial problems. The problems were most prevalent when the unit returned to base camp for a break or on standdown. The dependency on each other, under combat, was a great racial equalizer.

3256 **If your aircraft designation doesn't start with an "A," then you're just there to support those that do.**—*Steve "Krusty" Morris, U.S. Navy All-Weather attack pilot.*

In the U.S. Navy, aircraft with an "A" designation were attack aircraft, such as the A-6 Intruder, A-7 Corsair II, and A-8 Crusader.

3257 **Where a guerrilla force enjoys support from the people, whether willing or forced, it can never be defeated by military means, however much it is harassed and attacked, shelled, mortared, and bombed by superior forces of infantry and artillery, air and sea power.**—*Sir Robert Thompson, British authority on counterinsurgency.*[106]

3258 **All wars are popular for the first thirty days.**—*Arthur Schlesinger, Jr., historian and former White House aide.*[83]

3259 **In revolutionary war, you lose if you do not win.**—*Sir Robert Thompson, guerrilla war expert and adviser to the South Vietnamese Army.*[374]

Under the Thompson doctrine, if a smaller guerrilla force, could continually stage hit and run attacks on a large more power enemy force, and maintain these small scale attacks, the larger enemy force would eventually wear itself out attempting to be everywhere, all the time. The larger enemy force would be required to feed more men and materials into the war just to maintain a stalemate. Eventually those supporting the enemy force would tire of the loss in men and treasure and seek some way out of the war. If the large force can quickly engage and eliminate the guerrilla force, it wins, but to draw the war out is equivalent to loss.

3260 **Success or failure depends on whether our cadres are good or bad.**—*Ho Chi Minh.*[374]

The cadres were an integral part of the NVA and the Viet Cong. They functioned as the political arm of the units in the field, maintaining control and direction. They worked closely with the military commander of the unit, and were considered leaders and motivators.

3261 **An American would be lost without a future to conquer, a Vietnamese is lost without the refuge of the past.** —*Nguyen Cao Ky, former Prime Minister of South Vietnam, 1976.*[629]

Vietnamese culture has intense ties to the land and their ancestors.

3262 **It's silly talking about how many years we will have to spend in the jungles of Vietnam when we could pave the whole country and put parking stripes on it and still be home by Christmas.**—*Ronald Reagan, then Governor of California.*[83]

3263 **More might have been won, and won long ago, if only there had not been such political inhibition.**—*T.R. Milton, former U.S. Air Force General, during a magazine interview, June 1975.*[909]

Milton was one of many military professionals who blamed the loss of South Vietnam on the civilian administration in Washington.

3264 **A wingman is only allowed to say three things: "Roger One," "Bingo," and "Lead, you're on Fire."**—*Anonymous Lead pilot.*

"Roger One" was the wingman's acknowledgement to instructions from the lead. "Bingo" was radio code for declaring the aircraft was low on fuel.

3265 **I am convinced that the best service a retired general can perform is to turn in his tongue along with his suit and to mothball his opinion.**—*General Omar Bradley, former World War II Army commander and Chairman of the JCS.*[83]

His opinions on the war in Vietnam were sought by President Johnson. He advocated an enclave policy in Vietnam.

3266 **A potential major victory turned into a disastrous retreat through mistaken estimates, loss of nerve, bad advice, failure in leadership and a tidal wave of defeatism.**—*S.L.A. Marshall, author and military historian.*[713]

Marshall's characterization of the results of the communist TET Offensive, in which a military defeat of the enemy on the battlefield, was negated by political upheaval in Washington, D.C.

3267 **Vietnam was the first war ever fought without any censorship. Without censorship, things can get terribly confused in the public mind.**—*General William Westmoreland, former ComUSMACV.*[83]

3268 **However clever Front [Viet Cong] forces had been in confusing allied intelligence, the actual fighting showed they had neither the command control to wage a multidivisional battle nor the staying power required to prevail in sustained combat.**—*Eric M. Bergerud, historian, 1991.*[42]

As a follow-up to the initial TET Offensive the enemy launched a second series of attacks against Saigon in May 1968. During the May offensive the enemy deployed a larger force, but they were unable to reach Saigon, suffering heavy casualties in the attempt.

3269 **If you are to wage a limited war, then you must fight it according to rules that will allow you to win.**—*Nguyen Cao Ky, former Prime Minister of South Vietnam, 1976.*[629]

3270 **The strategist in Hanoi indirectly manipulated our open society, and hence our political system.**—*General William Westmoreland, former ComUSMACV, comments after the war.*[374]

Many in the military believed the media shared a great responsibility in the forming of American public opinion about the war. Going so far as to accuse the media of aiding and abetting the enemy through news coverage and editorials.

3271 **Without any Russians or Chinese killing Americans, the two power blocks fought each other, using pawns in Vietnam, and the United States was defeated.**—*Nguyen Cao Ky, former Prime Minister of South Vietnam, 1976.*[629]

The Soviet Union and China provided arms and supplies enabling North Vietnam to carry on the fight against South Vietnam and the American troops sent to assist the ARVN.

3272 **If it's dead and Vietnamese, its VC.**—*GI Proverb.*[318]

Due to the difficulty in distinguishing the difference between a VC and a civilian noncombatant, many American GI's adopted the above rule. Because of the U.S. dependency on statistics to measure progress in the war, any dead Vietnamese often qualified as an enemy body count.

3273 **A young man who does not have what it takes to perform military service is not likely to have what it takes to make a living.**—*President John F. Kennedy.*[358]

3274 **A silent majority and government by the people is incompatible.**—*Tom Hayden, student radical leader.*[353]

Hayden was a co-founder of the SDS which initially agitated for free speech on campus and reforms in the American universities. The SDS later embraced the anti-war movement. Nixon spoke of the "silent majority" of Americans that backed his presidency and his policies in Vietnam, as opposed to the noisy minority who were protesting against the war and Nixon.

3275 **Any pilot who does not privately consider himself the best in the game is in the wrong game.**—*Anonymous pilot.*

3276 **The first advice I am going to give my successor is to watch the generals and to avoid feeling that just because they were military men their opinions on military matters were worth a damn.**—*President John F. Kennedy.*[83]

3277 **[The Vietnam War is a] war of presidential imperial vanity [designed to feed the greedy] military-industrial complex, [a brutal extension of America's] evil empire.**—*Gore Vidal, critic-novelist-dramatist.*[386]

3278 **[American search and destroy operations] permitted Hanoi to hold the strategic initiative by accepting the casualties in order to achieve her political aim.**—*Sir Robert Thompson, British authority on counterinsurgency.*[105]

Search and destroy operations were a policy of attrition, but the enemy held the initiative, allowing him to decide when a major battle would take place. American troops would sweep through an area and then leave. The enemy would flow out of the area as the U.S. troops came in, and flow back after they left.

3279 **If everyone has to go, senators' sons and bank presidents' sons, maybe the country will be slower to move into another involvement.**—*Myra MacPherson, political journalist, 1984.*[493]

Of the 27 million men that were of draft age during the Vietnam War, nearly 2.8-million of them served in Vietnam.

3280 **I'll do anything except swallow my honor and betray my country to get peace.**—*President Lyndon Johnson.*[954]

3281 **We can never win the war this way, when we are not allowed to fight as we should.**—*Nguyen Cao Ky, former Prime Minister of South Vietnam, 1976.*[629]

Ky complaining about combat restrictions imposed by Washington. He wanted to invade North Vietnam.

3282 **[Creating a coalition government including the Viet Cong would be like] putting the fox in a chicken coop.**—*Hubert H. Humphrey, during a press conference.*[285]

As part of negotiations, the North Vietnamese insisted that the NLF/VC was the rightful representative of the South Vietnamese people. The Saigon government wanted no part of a coalition government including the Viet Cong.

3283 **Extremism in defense of liberty is no vice.**—*Senator Barry Goldwater, of Arizona, during his nomination acceptance speech, July 1964.*[374]

3284 **There are not enough jails, not enough policemen, not enough courts to enforce a law not supported by the people.**—*Hubert H. Humphrey, then Vice President of the United States.*[353]

3285 **Restriction of free thought and free speech is the most dangerous of all subversions. It is the one un-American act that could most easily defeat us.**—*William O. Douglas, U.S. Supreme Court Justice.*[353]

Douglas was appointed to the Supreme Court in 1939, remaining on the bench until 1975. He was an advocate of free speech rights in America.

3286 **Every F-4 takes off with two in flight emergencies: (1) It's on fire. (2) It's low on fuel.**—*Anonymous, U.S. Navy F-4 Pilot.*

3287 **If it's natural to kill why do men have to go into training to learn.**—*Joan Baez, folk singer.*[83]

3288 **You can't separate peace from freedom because no one can be at peace unless he has his freedom.**—*Malcom X, Muslim Black Nationalist.*[83]

3289 **[Peace with Honor—]there was no way we could do that. The fact that we retreated nullifies the words.**—*Colonel Robert D. Clark, former U.S. Air Force B-52 pilot, during an interview, 3 January 1983.*[136]

Clark was a B-52 pilot during Operation Linebacker II, attacking North Vietnam several times during the course of the eleven day operation.

3290 **If it is true that power corrupts, it is also true that power deludes.**—*Nguyen Cao Ky, former Prime Minister of South Vietnam, from his memoirs, 1976.*[629]

Ky was referring to General Nguyen Khanh, who became South Vietnam's Prime Minister in 1964 and again in 1965. Khanh became dictatorial in his wielding of power and was eventually displaced by a coup.

3291 **When the enemy advances, withdraw; when he defends, harass; when he tires, attack; when he withdraws, pursue.**—*North Vietnamese adaptation of Mao Tse-Tung's rules of guerrilla warfare.*[889]

Mao is considered by many military historians to be the father of modern guerrilla warfare in Asia. North Vietnamese leaders studied Mao's tactics, adapting them to their own particular situations. The withdraw-harass-attack-pursue tactics were used to great effect against Allied troops during the Vietnam War.

3292 **Duplicity became so automatic that lower headquarters began to believe the things they were forwarding to higher headquarters. It was on paper, therefore, no matter what might have actually occurred, the paper graphs and charts became the ultimate reality.**—*Major William I. Lowry, writing in a paper for USACGSC, 1976.*[98]

There was often pressure from higher headquarters upon field units to show more positive results of operations in the field. The statistics of enemy killed and weapons captured were two of the main indicators the commanders used to judge progress in the war. If such numbers remained low they did not indicate success. The powers in MACV and Washington based many of their conclusions about progress in the war on these statistical indicators.

3293 **The bayonet is the best weapon for counterinsurgency.**—*Military maxim.*[42]

Close in work among the people was the most successful method of dealing with insurgents. The bayonet was precise, bombs and artillery cast a wide net, and could be widely indiscriminate.

3294 **You cannot use a steamroller against a shadow.**—*Nguyen Cao Ky, former Prime Minister of South Vietnam, 1976.*[629]

The NLF infrastructure was referred to as the shadow government of the VC. The NLF functioned in secret and was difficult to root out using conventional military methods. In the above phrase the steamrollers were the U.S. tactics of surrounding villes and trying to capture NLF members. What was needed was a quiet, stealthy approach equal to that of the NLF in order to catch them at their own game. Such an organization (Phoenix), was not successfully organized until 1967, but by then it was too late to accomplish its mission of control and elimination of the NLF.

3295 **We couldn't protect it, and they couldn't hold it.**—*Duong Van Khang, speaking to an interviewer, at the village of Phung Thuong, 1981.*[374]

The village was defended by a local Viet Minh force. It was attacked several times by the French. The Viet Minh defending the village were too weak to hold it against the French. The French in turn were not able to permanently hold the village, retreating after their attacks, only to attack it again at a later date.

3296 **Only by revolutionary violence can the masses defeat aggressive imperialism and its lackeys, and overthrow the reactionary administration to take power.**—*Vo Nguyen Giap, Commander North Vietnamese Military Forces.*[374]

3297 **The struggle for us was a matter of life or death ... for the Americans, it was merely an unhappy chapter in their history...**—*Bui Diem, former South Vietnamese Ambassador to the U.S.*[374]

Bui Diem remained in America during and after the collapse of South Vietnam in 1975.

3298 **Negotiation in the classic diplomatic sense assumes parties more anxious to agree than to disagree.**—*Dean Acheson, former Secretary of State and adviser to President Johnson.*[83]

3299 **The average Vietnamese wouldn't know the definitions of democracy, communism, or socialism; wouldn't know who Thieu was; wouldn't know who Johnson was. These guys were just trying to exist and their life is being threatened by the Viet Cong and North Vietnamese. ... "And just to show you we mean business, we'll rape your sister and cut the head off your mother." That [kind of] terrorism makes a believer out of you.**—*Michael Jones, Vietnam War Veteran, during an interview, released in 1984.*[493]

Jones was in Marine Reconnaissance, 1965-66.

3300 **Yea though I fly through the valley of the shadow of death.... I fear no evil ... for I fly the biggest, baddest, meanest, fastest motherfucker in the whole damn valley.**—*Anonymous*[189]

Popular phrase repeated in several variations during the Vietnam War years.

3301 **The struggle was in the rice paddies ... in and among the people, not passing through, but living among them, night and day ... and joining with them in steps toward a better life long overdue.**—*General Lewis Walt, U.S. Marine Corps (Retired).*

3302 **Aggressive conduct, if allowed to go unchecked and unchallenged, ultimately leads to war.**—*President John F. Kennedy.*[360]

3303 **[Marine tactics were insufficiently aggressive, they] left the enemy free to come and go as he pleased throughout**

the bulk of the region and, when and where he chose, to attack the periphery of the [Marine] beachheads.—*General William Westmoreland, former ComUSMACV, from his book, 1976.*[1019]

3304 **Attrition is not a strategy. It is, in fact, irrefutable proof of the absence of any strategy. A commander who resorts to attrition admits his failure to conceive of an alternative. He rejects warfare as an art and accepts it on the most non-professional terms imaginable. He uses blood in lieu of brains.**—*Dave Richard Palmer, historian and Vietnam War Veteran, 1978.*[713]

3305 **C-130 Takeoff Instructions for Passengers: In the event of a power failure on takeoff, bend over at the waist; grasp your ankles firmly with your hands, tuck your head between your knees and kiss your ass good-bye.**—*Anonymous, latrine philosophy.*[114]

These words of preparation were inscribed on the wall of the enlisted men's latrine located along the landing strip at Pleiku.

3306 **The war didn't end in March 1968, and neither did the opposition to the war. What ended was the American commitment to fight and win the war.**—*Thomas Powers, author, 1973.*[850]

In March 1968 Johnson announced the replacement of Westmoreland with Abrams, signaling a shift in the direction of the war. He also announced he would not seek another term as President, thus indicating a strategic change in the orchestration of war policy in Vietnam. The communists' 1968 TET Offensive changed America's perception of the winability and need for the war, yet militarily TET served to seriously deplete the ranks of the VC, requiring Hanoi to refill those ranks with NVA soldiers.

3307 **He should own the land who rubs it between his hands each season.**—*Vietnamese proverb.*[20]

Vietnamese attachment to the land was very strong and central to their existence. Land reform programs that did not address the peasant farmers' needs and forced them to relocation were major reasons for the GVN's loss of rural support. The communist propaganda promised land reform.

3308 **Re-gas, bypass, haul-ass...**—*Anonymous.*[42]

Armor maxim, practiced when American armor units rushed to the aid and reinforcement of friendly units under fire.

3309 **If Americans had offered their skills, weapons, and know-how as discreetly as the Russians did, the conscience of America would never have been tortured.**—*Nguyen Cao Ky, former Prime Minister of South Vietnam, 1976.*[629]

Many American military leaders were not sufficiently impressed with South Vietnam's military skills, its leaders or many of its troops to hope the ARVN could "pull it together" in time to stop the collapse of South Vietnam to the communists.

3310 **[Vietnam will trap you in] a bottomless military and political swamp.**—*Charles de Gaulle, President, France, advice to President John Kennedy.*[374]

3311 **No country can act wisely simultaneously in every part of the globe at every moment of time.**—*Henry Kissinger, National Security Adviser.*[83]

3312 **There are only two types of aircraft—fighters and targets.**—*Doyle "Wahoo" Nicholson, U.S. Marine Corps pilot.*[189]

3313 **I know I'm goin' to heaven, 'cause I done spent my time in hell.**—*Anonymous.*[890]

This phrase was elevated to permanent stature from its start as a helmet cover pronouncement. It could be found etched on cigarette lighters and shell-casing ashtrays, and stitched on the backs of camo tour jackets and party coats.

3314 **They did an awful lot with an awful little...**—*Thomas A. Giltner, former Platoon Leader, 27th Infantry Regiment, 1991.*[42]

Early in the war the local VC took on ARVN and American units armed with outdated or homemade weapons. Many of their mines and booby-traps were made from captured or unexploded ordinance. Later in the war VC units received new weapons and war materiel.

3315 **You're not suppose to be so blind with patriotism that you can't face reality. Wrong is wrong no matter who does it or who says it.**—*Malcom X, Muslim Black Nationalist.*[83]

Malcom X broke with the Nation of Islam (Black Muslims) and formed his own Muslim group, the Organization of Afro-American Unity. He advocated racial separation which excluded black men fighting in white America's wars.

3316 **The guys who went and those who avoided all feel cheated. We missed a chance to be heroes ... to be with your comrades. We missed a chance to fight in a "good war"...**—*Unidentified U.S. Army deserter, during an interview in Toronto, Canada.*[493]

This particular deserter was inducted into the Army, but fled to Canada rather than complete his military obligation.

3317 **We held the day ... In the palm ... Of our hand ... They ruled the night ... And the night ... Seemed to last as long as six weeks ... On Parris Island ... We held the coastline... They held the highlands.**—*Billy Joel, composer and performer, words from "Goodnight Saigon," 1981.*[364]

3318 **Inactivity and incompetence were rewarded with safety, and military skill and anti-Communist enthusiasm brought the risk of death.**—*Eric M. Bergerud, historian, 1991.*[42]

As American troops withdrew from Vietnam, village security was almost exclusively handled by RF/PF forces. Many hamlet PF forces came to an arrangement with the local VC forces, whereby, the VC would not bother the PF as long as the PF restricted or eliminated its operations against the VC. Those few RF/PF units that did not meet the accommodation were the subject of enemy attack.

3319 **[Ho] was totally intractable. I doubt that there was ever any way in which Ho could be dealt with. He had only one dream, and that was the freedom of Vietnam.**—*Unidentified American who knew Ho Chi Minh in the 1940s.*[451]

3320 **As ignorance is not the same thing as stupidity, the failure of Rolling Thunder is not an indictment of the efficacy of air power. It is ... an example of the misapplication of air power under aegis of an inappropriately advised strategy.**—*Earl H. Tilford, author and historian, 1993.*[931]

Rolling Thunder was intended to eliminate or reduce the flow of NVA troops and material bolstering the communist insurgency in South Vietnam. It was also intended to apply pressure to the Hanoi regime, encouraging them to seek or agree to negotiations. Rolling Thunder damaged North Vietnam, but was not able to block the flow of men and material south, nor was it able to coerce Hanoi to the negotiating table.

3321 **War is an obscene blot on the face of the human race.**—*Dean Rusk, Secretary of State in the Kennedy and Johnson administrations.*[83]

3322 **It doesn't require any particular bravery to stand on the floor of the Senate and urge our boys in Vietnam to fight harder, and if this war mushrooms into a major conflict and a hundred thousand young Americans are killed, it won't be U. S. Senators who die. It will be American soldiers who are too young to qualify for the Senate.**—*Senator George McGovern, of South Dakota.*

3323 **What the hell's the difference between Vietnam and Korea anyway?**—*Unidentified American advisor, overheard by Nguyen Cao Ky, Prime Minister of South Vietnam.*[629]

The advisor commenting on the similarities between Vietnam and Korea in an attempt to understand the differences and why the Vietnamese reacted so differently to war than the Koreans.

3324 **Kill them all and you know for damn sure you're killing the enemy. If they're not all VC now, they could fuckin' well become VC. Solve the problem before it starts.**—*Michael Clodfelter, former artilleryman/infantryman with the 101st Airborne, 1984.*[869]

Clodfelter was voicing an attitude familiar to many American GIs. It was often impossible to tell the difference between a part-time VC guerrilla and a full time civilian.

3325 **Yea though I walk through the valley of the shadow of death I will fear no evil for I am the meanest motherfucker in the valley.**—*Anonymous, ubiquitous.*[886]

GI's version of the 23d Psalm. The phrase could be found engraved on cigarette lighters, written on helmet covers, stitched on the back of party/tour jackets, or etched on commemorative unit plaques. There were variants; aircrews could "fly through the valley," or PBRs could "negotiate the river in the valley;" "Baddest" or "ugliest," could replace "meanest;" And in the valley itself besides a "motherfucker," you could be a "sonofabitch."

3326 **There's a consensus out there that it's OK to kill when your government decides who to kill. If you kill inside the country you might get in trouble. If you kill outside the country, right time, right reason, latest enemy, you get a medal.**—*Joan Baez, folk singer and song writer.*[83]

During the Vietnam War she was an anti-war activist and social/political protester. She made a trip to Hanoi in December 1972.

3327 **Less than victory is unthinkable.**—*Francis Cardinal Spellman, Archbishop of New York, speaking while on tour with American troops in Vietnam, December 1966.*[421]

Spellman was making his 21st annual Christmas tour, visiting American troops overseas. During his recent Christmas message, the Pope had called for peace talks putting himself at odds with Spellman.

3328 **Black soldiers do not fight us, we're people of color too.**—*North Vietnamese propaganda phrase.*[493]

Throughout the war North Vietnam used the racial tensions between black and white Americans to try to further divide the American combat force arrayed against them. The phrase was heard over radio broadcast (Hanoi Hannah) and printed on propaganda leaflets left in areas where American troops operated.

3329 **The American Century floundered on the shores of Vietnam.**—*Daniel Bell, author and sociologist.*[374]

The "American Century" was a vision of Henry Luce in which America would lead the world in the 20th Century.

3330 **One Slow — Four Quick.**—*A North Vietnamese battle tactic, as endorsed by General Vo Nguyen Giap.*[114]

The One Slow — Four Quick rule was preached by North Vietnamese command. One Slow — slowly prepare each operation.... Four Quick — advance quickly on the battlefield ... quickly exploit success and pursue the enemy ... quickly clear the battlefield of weapons, ammo, the dead and wounded ... quickly withdraw. These five rules were followed in Vietnam by the VC and the NVA, with good results.

3331 **I was awakened by a rocket attack that seemed like it lasted seconds or hours. I was thrilled and at the same time scared: this was the face of war! Organized mayhem, orchestrated to the epitome of destruction by its participants.**—*Jon Boulle, former U.S. Marine Corps helicopter pilot, 1988.*[84]

Lieutenant Boulle deployed to Vietnam in April 1969 Marine Squadron HMM-161 out of Quang Tri, as a CH-46 helicopter pilot.

3332 **We will always live with what we killed in Vietnam.**—*Unidentified Vietnam War Veteran.*[72]

3333 **Let no one doubt for a moment that we have the resources and the will to follow this course as long as it may take. No one should think for a moment that we will be worn down, nor will we be driven out, and we will not be provoked into rashness.**—*President Lyndon Johnson.*[374]

3334 **The bombing [of North Vietnam] was not so much unsuccessful as it was irrelevant to the war in the South.**—*Paraphrase of Earl H. Tilford, author and historian, 1993.*[931]

Infiltration into South Vietnam from the North continued to increase throughout the bombing — supplies continue to get through. The bombing did reduce the flow, but not sufficiently to impact the war in the South. Communist supplies were also delivered through the Cambodian port of Sihanoukville and distributed along the South Vietnamese-Cambodian border. The supply route was not part of the U.S. interdiction campaign until 1970.

3335 **Slowly the hamlets were eaten away by small VC initiated incidents and massive U.S. retaliation.**—*Ollie Davidson, former civilian adviser to the Hau Nghia Province advisory team, 1991.*[42]

Thousands of homes scattered across the hamlets of Hau Nghia Province were lost to combat, creating a high number of refugees. The VC fired on U.S. units from the hamlets. American units responded with air strikes and/or artillery. The resulting damage to the homes of the targeted hamlet made them uninhabitable, generating more refugees and Vietnamese hateful of the Americans and their firepower.

3336 **I never felt the war was wrong. ... I think the way we fought it was wrong.**—*Edison McGhee, former infantryman with the 173d Airborne Brigade, during an interview, released 1984.*[493]

McGhee served with the Airborne 1967-68.

3337 **What is the use of physicians like myself trying to help parents to bring up children healthy and happy, to have them killed in such numbers for a cause that is ignoble?**—*Dr. Benjamin Spock, noted pediatrician and anti-war activist.*

3338 **We can endure the hardships of a lengthy war, but they are unable to endure the hardships of such a war because they are well-to-do people. A poor man can subsist by spending one piaster a day, but a man who is accustomed to living in comfort is uncomfortable though he spends ten piasters a day.**—*General Tran Do, Deputy Commander, Communist Forces in South Vietnam, speaking to troops.*[653]

3339 **I saw a rain and sweat drenched man in green, laden like a pack mule, aged 21 going on 50, cutting his way through jungle by day to find and attack the enemy, then laying all night in paddy fields or on trails in ambush.**—*Brigadier Colin Kahn DSO, Royal Australian Army officer, speaking of the Australian soldier in Vietnam, 1987.*[356]

Australian soldiers spent nearly eleven years in South Vietnam before their final departure in June 1973.

3340 **He who controls the Central Highlands controls South Vietnam.**—*Vietnamese military maxim.*[501]

Control of the Highlands literally cut South Vietnam in two, allowing defeat in detail of a defending army.

3341 **I would like to offer a salute to that skinny little Viet Cong somewhere out there in the jungle shivering in the monsoon rains. ... He is one hell of a fighting man.**—*General Edwin H. Simmons, U.S. Marine Corps, Anthology of Marines in Vietnam, 1954-1973.*[893]

All Marine ground and air combat operations of the III Marine Amphibious Force ended April 1972. A mixed brigade of air and ground units remained until May, when they too departed Vietnam.

3342 **For those who have fought, life has a flavor the protected will never know.**—*Attributed to a Vietnam War Veteran.*

Phrase often found engraved on Zippo lighters owned by American troops in Vietnam.

3343 **[It] was time for Jane to go back to the people who love her ... the North Vietnamese.**—*Jay Leno, from his monologue, repeated on NBC, January 2000.*[387]

Jay Leno announced that Jane Fonda and Ted Turner were getting divorced. He said the relationship had been a long one but it was at an end. Fonda was previously married to antiwar activist Tom Hayden. She is remembered, without fondness, by many Vietnam War Veterans for her trip to Hanoi in 1972 where she publicly supported Hanoi's position against America in the Vietnam War.

3344 **As I slide down the banister of life I'll always remember Vietnam as a splinter in my ass.**—*Anonymous GI graffito, Saigon.*[886]

Source Notes

1. ABC News article, "Rewind," 15 June 1999.
2. ABC News, Reuters, 1998.
3. Adams.
4. Anderson.
5. Associated Press, Mike Feinsibler, 22 December 1997.
6. *Baltimore Sun*, Germond and Witcover.
7. "Hau Nghia Province Report," April 1968, in Bergerud.
8. "Hau Nghia Province Report," August 1967, in Bergerud.
9. "III Corps CTZ Overview," May 1969, in Bergerud.
10. Interview with Vietnam war participant, January 1967, in Bergerud.
11. "Studies of the National Liberation Front of South Vietnam," RAND Corporation, in Bergerud.
12. "Trang Bang," *Army*, January 1967, in Bergerud.
13. A. J. Bacevich, *The Pentomic Era* (1986), in Bergerud.
14. Bernard Fall, *The Two Vietnams* (1967), in Bergerud.
15. Bui Diem, *In the Jaws of History* (1987), in Bergerud.
16. Captured Cu Chi district report, in Bergerud.
17. Cook and Pabst, Reports and Evaluation Division (CORDS), 29 May 1968, in Bergerud.
18. CORDS cable, 1 January 1968, in Bergerud.
19. Department of the Army, "A Program for the Pacification and Long Term Development of South Vietnam," 1966, in Bergerud.
20. Douglas Pike, *Viet Cong* (1967), in Bergerud.
21. Gabriel Kolko, *Anatomy of a War* (1985), in Bergerud.
22. General William C. Westmoreland, *A Soldier Reports* (1976), in Bergerud.
23. Henry Kissinger, *White House Years* (1979), in Bergerud.
24. Jeffrey Race, *War Comes to Long An* (1972), in Bergerud.
25. John Paul Vann, "Harnessing the Revolution in South Vietnam," 10 September 1965, in Bergerud.
26. Lt. General Bernard Rogers, *Cedar Falls, Junction City* (1974), in Bergerud.
27. Luce and Sommer, *Vietnam: The Unheard Voices* (1969), in Bergerud.
28. Mangold and Penycate, *The Tunnels of Cu Chi* (1985), in Bergerud.
29. Peter Braestrup, *Big Story* (1978), in Bergerud.
30. Prisoner speech, May 1968, in Bergerud.
31. RAND Corporation, "Interview with Vietnam War Participant," February 1966, in Bergerud.
32. RAND Corporation, "Studies of the National Liberation Front of South Vietnam," in Bergerud.
33. RAND Corporation, "Studies of the National Liberation Front of South Vietnam," in Bergerud.
34. Ronald H. Spector, *Advice and Support* (1985), in Bergerud.
35. Simulantics Corporation, "Interview with Vietnam War Participant," February 1966, in Bergerud.
36. *The Pentagon Papers* (Senator Mike Gravel edition, 1971), in Bergerud.
37. *The Pentagon Papers* Senator Mike Gravel edition, 1971), in Bergerud.
38. William Robert Miller, *Martin Luther King* (New York: Weybright and Talley, 1968) in Powers.
39. Tran Van Tra, *Vietnam: History of the Bulwark B2 Theatre* (Hanoi, 1982), in Bergerud.
40. William R. Corson, *The Betrayal* (1968), in Bergerud.

41. Daniel Ellsberg, *Papers on the War* (1972), in Bergerud.

42. Bergerud.

43. Berman.

44. "Actions Recommended for Vietnam," in Berman.

45. As recorded, in notes of the meeting, in Berman.

46. Clark M. Clifford, "A Viet Nam Reappraisal," *Foreign Affairs*, July 1969, in Berman.

47. Congressional record, in Berman.

48. From notes of the meeting, in Berman.

49. George Ball, *The Past Has Another Pattern*, (1982), in Berman.

50. Herbert Shandler, *Lyndon Johnson and Vietnam* (1977), in Berman.

51. Stanley Karnow, *Vietnam: A History* (1983), in Berman.

52. Kenneth Thompson, *The Johnson Presidency* (Lanham, 1987), in Berman.

53. Lyndon Johnson, *The Vantage Point* (1971), in Berman.

54. Meeting notes, 25 July 1967, in Berman.

55. Meeting notes, 25 July 1967, in Berman.

56. *New York Times*, 4/6 September 1967, in Berman.

57. *New York Times*, December 1967, in Berman.

58. *Newsweek*, 2 February 1968, in Berman.

59. Notes Manuscript, 27 April 1967, in Berman.

60. *Pentagon Papers*, 1971, in Berman.

61. R.W. Apple, *New York Times*, 24 December 1967, in Berman.

62. Tom Johnson's meeting notes, 1968, in Berman.

63. Transcript of the meeting, 23 December 1967, in Berman.

64. "Vietnam Prognosis for 1967-68," in Berman.

65. Walt Rostow, *The Diffusion of Power* (1972), in Berman.

66. Lyndon Johnson, *The Vantage Point* (1971), in Berman.

67. Admiral U.S. Sharp, *Strategy for Defeat* (1978), in Berman.

68. Lyndon Johnson, *The Vantage Point* (1971), in Berman.

69. Oral history transcript, 1968, in Berman.

70. *Time*, 18 February 1966, in Berman.

71. *Time*, 18 February 1983, in Berman.

72. Berman.

73. Bowman.

74. Glenn Munson, *Letters from Vietnam* (1966), in Brown, Heschel and Novak.

75. *New York Times* magazine, 9 October 1966, in Brown, Heschel and Novak.

76. *New York Times*, 15 January 1967, in Brown, Heschel and Novak.

77. *Newsweek*, 12 September 1966, in Brown, Heschel and Novak.

78. U.S. Government Printing Office, *Vietnam: The Struggle for Freedom* (1964), in Brown, Heschel and Novak.

79. Brown, Heschel and Novak.

80. Roger Hilsman, *To Move a Nation* (1967), in Bundy.

81. Theodore C. Sorensen (1965) in Bundy.

82. Bundy.

83. Charlton.

84. Chinnery.

85. Arthur M. Schlesinger, *A Thousand Days* (1965), in Noam Chomsky, "Vane Hopes, False Dreams," *Z Magazine*, September 1992.

86. General Earle Wheeler, oral history, July 1964 in Noam Chomsky, "Vane Hopes, False Dreams," *Z Magazine*, September 1992.

87. "Vane Hopes, False Dreams," *Z Magazine*, September 1992, in Noam Chomsky, "Vane Hopes, False Dreams," *Z Magazine*, September 1992.

88. "Vane Hopes, False Dreams," *Z Magazine*, September 1992, *New York Times*, October 1962 in Noam Chomsky, "Vane Hopes, False Dreams," *Z Magazine*, September 1992.

89. "Study on Military Professionalism," USAWC, 30 June 1970, in Cincinnatus.

90. Alexander Kendrick, *The Wound Within* (1974), in Cincinnatus.

91. Gabriel Kolko, *The Roots of American Foreign Policy* (1969), in Cincinnatus.

92. Interview, in Cincinnatus.

93. Johnson and Wilson, *Army in Anguish* (1972), in Cincinnatus.

94. *Life* magazine, 5 April 1968, in Cincinnatus.

95. Lt. Col. Carl F. Bernard, "The War, in Vietnam," USACGSC student paper, 1969, in Cincinnatus.

96. Lt. Col. William D. Barnes, "The Vietnam Barrier," USAWC, 27 October 1967, in Cincinnatus.

97. Lt. Col. Y. Y. Philipps, *The ROAD Battalion, in Vietnam, Army*, September 1966, in Cincinnatus.

98. Major William I. Lowry, "Strategic Assessment of the War, in Vietnam," USACGSC, 1976, in Cincinnatus.

99. *New York Times* magazine, 9 June 1968, in Cincinnatus.

100. *New York Times*, 6 December 1962, in Cincinnatus.

101. Norman Hannah, "Vietnam: Now We Know," *National Review*, 11 June 1976, in Cincinnatus.

102. R.W. Komer, *Bureaucracy Does Its Thing* (1972), in Cincinnatus.

103. Richard Boyle, "Flower of the Dragon," 1972, in Cincinnatus.

104. Robert Taber, *The War of the Flea* (1965), in Cincinnatus.

105. Robert Thompson, *No Exit from Vietnam* (1970), in Cincinnatus.

106. Roger Hilsman, *To Move A Nation* (1967), in Cincinnatus.

107. *The New Yorker*, 2 March 1968, in Cincinnatus.

108. *Time* magazine, 28 September 1963, in Cincinnatus.
109. Alexander Kendrick, *The Wound Within* (1974), in Cincinnatus.
110. Edward G. Lansdale, "Viet Nam: Do We Understand Revolution?" *Foreign Affairs*, October 1964, in Cincinnatus.
111. Robert Taber, *The War of the Flea* (1965), in Cincinnatus.
112. *Time*, 15 September 1967, in Cincinnatus.
113. Cincinnatus.
114. Clark.
115. "Headquarters, 7th Air Force, History," 1972, in Clodfelter.
116. "Linebacker II USAF Bombing Survey," April 1973, in Clodfelter.
117. "Linebacker II USAF Bombing Survey," April 1973, in Clodfelter.
118. "What Admiral Moorer Really Said about Airpower's Effectiveness, in SEA," *Air Force*, November 1973, in Clodfelter.
119. Address to the Armed Forces Staff College, 9 April 1975, in Clodfelter.
120. Admiral U.S. Grant Sharp, *Strategy for Defeat* (1978), in Clodfelter.
121. Cabinet meeting notes, 22 July 1965, in Clodfelter.
122. CINCPAC files, in Clodfelter.
123. CINCPAC files, in Clodfelter.
124. Congressional Record, 26 February 1973, in Clodfelter.
125. Congressional Record, in Clodfelter.
126. Curtis E. LeMay, *Mission with LeMay* (1965), in Clodfelter.
127. Don Tate, "Nixon Seeks to Pound Sense into N. Vietnam," *Columbus Citizen-Journal*, 30 December 1972, in Clodfelter.
128. Doris Kearns, *Lyndon Johnson and the American Dream* (1976), in Clodfelter.
129. General Vo Nguyen Giap, *Big Victory, Great Task* (1968), in Clodfelter.
130. George Ball, "How Valid are the Assumptions Underlying Our Viet Nam Policies?" *Atlantic Monthly*, July 1972, in Clodfelter.
131. Halberstam, David, *The Best and the Brightest* (1969), in Clodfelter.
132. Hamburg, "*Die Zeit*," December 1972, in Clodfelter.
133. Henry A. Kissinger, news conference regarding the agreement on ending the war, 24 January 1973, in Clodfelter.
134. Henry A. Kissinger, *The White House Years* (1979), in Clodfelter.
135. Henry Kissinger, news conference, 16 December 1972, in Clodfelter.
136. Interview, 3 January 1983, in Clodfelter.
137. Interview, 7 January 1983, in Clodfelter.
138. Interview, 22 September 1981, in Clodfelter.
139. Interview, 29 May 1969, in Clodfelter.
140. Interview, February 1978, in Clodfelter.
141. Interview, 1986, in Clodfelter.
142. Jack Broughton, *Thud Ridge* (1969), in Clodfelter.
143. John Morrocco, *Thunder from Above* (1984), in Clodfelter.
144. Kissinger news conference, 26 October 1972, in Clodfelter.
145. *London Times*, December 1972, in Clodfelter.
146. Lyndon Baines Johnson, *The Vantage Point* (1971), in Clodfelter.
147. Meeting notes, McGeorge Bundy, September 196, in Clodfelter.
148. Merskey and Polmar, *The Naval Air War in Vietnam* (Annapolis, 1981), in Clodfelter.
149. *Nhan Dan*, 17 August 1972, in Clodfelter.
150. NSAM 273, in Clodfelter.
151. NSC History, 2 April 1965, in Clodfelter.
152. NSC History, 7 February 1965, in Clodfelter.
153. NSC History, July 1965, in Clodfelter.
154. NSC History, meeting notes, in Clodfelter.
155. NSC History, in Clodfelter.
156. Oliver Todd, "The Americans Are Not Invincible," *New Left Review*, January–February 1968, in Clodfelter.
157. Interview, 21 August 1969, in Clodfelter.
158. Interview by Dorothy Pierce, Washington, D.C., 10 February 1969, in Clodfelter.
159. *Pentagon Papers* (1971), in Clodfelter.
160. Personal papers of General McConnell, 1969, in Clodfelter.
161. RAND Corporation Memorandum, 1966, in Clodfelter.
162. Richard M. Nixon, *RN: The Memoirs of Richard Nixon* (1978), in Clodfelter.
163. Richard Nixon, *No More Vietnams* (1985), in Clodfelter.
164. Senate Committee proceedings, 27 and 29 August 1967, in Clodfelter.
165. Sir Robert Thompson, *Peace Is Not at Hand* (1974), in Clodfelter.
166. Tammy Arbuckle, "Bombing Was Pinpointed," *Washington Star*, 1 April 1973, in Clodfelter.
167. Thompson and Frizzell, *The Lessons of the Vietnam War* (1977), in Clodfelter.
168. Tom Johnson's notes of meetings, Johnson Library, in Clodfelter.
169. Townsend Hoopes, *The Limits of Intervention* (1969), in Clodfelter.
170. Truong Nhu Tang, *A Viet Cong Memoir* (1985), in Clodfelter.
171. U.S. Senate, 90th Congress, 22 and 25 August 1967, in Clodfelter.

172. USAF oral history interview, 8–9 August 1978, in Clodfelter.
173. Van Tien Dung, *Some Great Experiences* (1969), in Clodfelter.
174. Walt W. Rostow, *The Diffusion of Power* (1972), in Clodfelter.
175. *Washington Post*, 28 December 1972, in Clodfelter.
176. Weekly compilation of presidential documents, 31 January 1972, in Clodfelter.
177. Weekly compilation of presidential documents, 15 May 1972, in Clodfelter.
178. Weekly compilation of presidential documents, 18 December 1972, in Clodfelter.
179. William Bundy interview, 26 May 1969, in Clodfelter.
180. Headquarters 307th Strategic Air Wing, history, July 1973, in Clodfelter.
181. Thompson and Frizzell, *The Lessons of the Vietnam War* (1977), in Clodfelter.
182. Clodfelter.
183. Committee on Foreign Relations, U.S. Senate, *Background Information relating to Southeast Asia and Vietnam*, 3d rev. ed. (1967).
184. Dodds, Paisley, Associated Press, 24 Nov. 1998.
185. Drendel.
186. *Playboy* magazine interview, in Edelman.
187. Edelman.
188. Ehrlichman.
189. English.
190. "Conflict in Indo-China," *Herald Tribune*, 28 January 1952, in *Far East Spotlight*.
191. "Conflict in Indo-China," *Herald Tribune*, 28 January 1952, in *Far East Spotlight*.
192. Arthur Schlesinger, *A Thousand Days* (1965), in Ford.
193. Carver memorandum, March 1967, CIA files, in Ford.
194. Chester Cooper, *The Lost Crusade* (1970), in Ford.
195. CIA files, in Ford.
196. CIA/DCI files, in Ford.
197. CIA/DDI files, in Ford.
198. Clark M. Clifford, *The New Yorker*, 3 May 1991, in Ford.
199. Clark M. Clifford, "A Viet Nam Reappraisal," *Foreign Affairs*, July 1969, in Ford.
200. Cooper oral history, John Kennedy Library, June 1966, in Ford.
201. Department of Defense, United States-Vietnam Relations, 1945–1967 (*The Pentagon Papers*), in Ford.
202. Dr. William Conrad Gibbons, *The U.S. Government and the Vietnam War*, 98th Congress, 2d Session, 1984, in Ford.
203. Harold P. Ford, memorandum, 8 April 1965, in Ford.
204. George Allen, *The Indochina Wars*, in Ford.
205. George Allen, *The Indochina Wars*, in Ford.
206. Halberstam, David, *The Best and the Brightest* (1972), in Ford.
207. Helms and Powers, *The Man Who Kept the Secrets* (1979), in Ford.
208. Helms memorandum for the record, in Ford.
209. Interview, 21 May 1990, in Ford.
210. Lyndon Johnson, *The Vantage Point* (1971), in Ford.
211. McCone memorandum, CIA Files, 10 May 1962, in Ford.
212. McCone memorandum, CIA Files, 10 September 1962, in Ford.
213. McNamara memorandum, CIA files, in Ford.
214. Meeting memorandum, 25 November 1963, in Ford.
215. Mendenhall memorandum, 16 May 1962, in Ford.
216. *New York Times*, 3 February 1968, in Ford.
217. *New York Times*, 7 May 1963, in Ford.
218. *New York Times*, 15 January 1963, in Ford.
219. *New York Times*, 21 November 1967, in Ford.
220. O'Neill memorandum, CIA files, in Ford.
221. Oral History, University of Texas, August 1969, in Ford.
222. Dave Richard Palmer, *Summons of the Trumpet* (1978), in Ford.
223. *Pentagon Papers* (DoD edition), in Ford.
224. *Pentagon Papers* (Gravel edition), in Ford.
225. *Pentagon Papers* (*New York Times* edition), in Ford.
226. Raborn memorandum, 6 May 1965, in Ford.
227. Richard M. Nixon, "Needed on Vietnam: The Will to Win," *Reader's Digest*, August 1964, in Ford.
228. Robert H. Ferrell, *The Eisenhower Diaries* (1981), in Ford.
229. Shockley memorandum, CIA files, 29 November 1975, in Ford.
230. State Department files, 1964, in Ford.
231. State Department files, in Ford.
232. State Department files/CIA files, in Ford.
233. T. L. Cubbage II, Westmoreland vs. CBS., July 1988, in Ford.
234. *The New Yorker*, 6 May 1991, in Ford.
235. *Washington Post*, 6 February 1968, in Ford.
236. Wheeler memorandum, CIA files, 27 March 1963, in Ford.
237. Willard Matthias, "How Three Estimates Went Wrong," *Studies in Intelligence*, Winter 1968, in Ford.
238. William E. Colby memorandum of meeting, 3 March 1967, in Ford.
239. Halberstam, David, *The Best and the Brightest* (1972), in Ford.
240. Interview, 12 August 1970, in Ford.
241. Ford.

242. W. W. Rostow, *View from the Seventh Floor* (1964), in Galbraith.
243. Galbraith.
244. Robert W. Komer, "Bureaucracy Does Its Thing," (1972), RAND Corporation, in Gibson.
245. Grafitti written on the wall of a three-holer, in Cu Chi, 1970.
246. *Hair* (Broadway musical), 1968.
247. Halberstam.
248. State Department archives, 1961–1963, in Ford.
249. Harvey.
250. "1889 and 1968: The Anti-Imperialists and the Doves," *Political Science Quarterly*, June 1970, in Herring.
251. "France Holds on to the Indo-China Tiger," *New York Times* magazine, 8 June 1952, in Herring.
252. "RAND Report on the Fall of South Vietnam," 7 January 1979, in Herring.
253. "Special Report," 7 March 1960, in Herring.
254. A.J. Langguth, "General Abrams Listens to a Different Drummer," *New York Times* magazine, 5 May 1968, in Herring.
255. Alexander Kendrick, *The Wound Within: America in Vietnam, 1945–1974* (1974), in Herring.
256. "An Irony of History," *Newsweek*, 28 April 1975, in Herring.
257. Anthony Austin, *The President's War* (Philadelphia, 1971), in Herring.
258. Anthony Lake, *The Vietnam Legacy* (1976), in Herring.
259. Benjamin Read memorandum, 23 July 1965, in Herring.
260. Bernard Fall, *The Two Vietnams* (1967), in Herring.
261. C. L. Sulzberger, *Seven Continents and Forty Years* (New York, 1977), in Herring.
262. Daniel Ellsberg, *Papers on the War* (1972), in Herring.
263. Dave Richard Palmer, *Summons of the Trumpet* (1978), in Herring.
264. David Broder, "Isolationist Sentiment Not Blind to Reality," *Washington Post*, 22 March 1975, in Herring.
265. David Halberstam, "Return to Vietnam," *Harpers*, December 1967, in Herring.
266. David Halberstam, *The Making of a Quagmire* (1964), in Herring.
267. *Decisive Battles of the Twentieth Century* (1976), in Herring.
268. Don Oberdorfer, *TET!* (1971), in Herring.
269. Doris Kearns, *Lyndon Johnson and the American Dream* (1976), in Herring.
270. Dwight D. Eisenhower papers, 1954, in Herring.
271. Dwight D. Eisenhower papers, 1955, in Herring.
272. Earl C. Ravenal, *Never Again* (1978), in Herring.
273. Edward G. Lansdale, *In the Midst of Wars* (1972), in Herring.
274. Ernest K. Lindley, "An Ally Worth Having," *Newsweek*, 29 June 1959, in Herring.
275. Frances Fitzgerald, *Fire in the Lake* (1972), in Herring.
276. Gareth Porter, *A Peace Denied: The United States, Vietnam and the Paris Agreements* (1975), in Herring.
277. Gareth Porter, *Peace Denied* (1975), in Herring.
278. George W. Ball, "Top Secret," *The Atlantic*, July 1972, in Herring.
279. Gordon Gray memorandum, Eisenhower papers, September 1959, in Herring.
280. Guenter Lewy, *America, in Vietnam* (1978), in Herring.
281. H.R. Haldeman, *The Ends of Power* (1978), in Herring.
282. Henry A. Kissinger, "The Vietnam Negotiations," *Foreign Affairs*, January 1969, in Herring.
283. Henry Brandon, *The Retreat of American Power* (1974), in Herring.
284. Henry Cabot Lodge, Jr., *As It Was* (1976), in Herring.
285. Henry Graff, *The Tuesday Cabinet* (1970), in Herring.
286. Henry Trewhitt, *McNamara* (1971), in Herring.
287. Herbert L. Schandler, *Lyndon Johnson and Vietnam* (1977), in Herring.
288. James C. Thompson, "Getting Out and Speaking Out," *Foreign Policy*, Winter 1973–1974, in Herring.
289. Johnson papers, 1964, in Herring.
290. Johnson papers, National Security file, in Herring.
291. Johnson papers, in Herring.
292. Jonathan Schell, *The Village of Ben Suc* (1967), in Herring.
293. Joseph C. Harsch, "Do You Recall Vietnam," *Louisville Courier-Journal*, 2 October 1975, in Herring.
294. Joseph Siracusa, "Lessons of Vietnam and the Future of American Foreign Policy," *Australian Outlook*, August 1976, in Herring.
295. Joseph Siracusa, *Australian Outlook*, August 1976, in Herring.
296. Judson J. Conner, *Army Information Digest*, November, 1960, in Herring.
297. Kalb, *Kissinger* (1974), in Herring.
298. Kennedy papers, 1962, in Herring.
299. Kennedy papers, March 1961, in Herring.
300. Kennedy papers, November 1961, in Herring.
301. Kennedy, John F., "America's Stake, in Vietnam," 1956, in Herring.
302. Lawrence J. Korb, *The Joint Chiefs of Staff* (1976), in Herring.
303. Lyndon Baines Johnson, *The Vantage Point* (1971), in Herring.
304. Lyndon Johnson, *The Vantage Point* (1971), in Herring.

305. Malcolm W. Browne, *The New Face of War* (1968), in Herring.

306. Marvin and Bernard Kalb, *Kissinger* (1974), in Herring.

307. Maxwell D. Taylor, *Swords and Ploughshares* (1972), in Herring.

308. Memorandum of the conversation, State Department, in Herring.

309. Michael Herr, *Dispatches* (1978), in Herring.

310. Milton C. Taylor, *Pacific Affairs*, 1961, in Herring.

311. Minutes of NSC meeting, 4 May 1950, in Herring.

312. *New York Times*, 18 April 1975, in Herring.

313. Nixon transcript, *New York Times*, 29 June 1972, in Herring.

314. Notes from meeting of Johnson and the Wise Men, 26 March 1968, in Herring.

315. NSC report, 5 August 1953, USVN, Book 9, in Herring.

316. O'Donnell and Powers, *Johnny, We Hardly Knew Ye* (1973), in Herring.

317. Pentagon papers, 1971, in Herring.

318. Philip Caputo, *A Rumor of War* (1977), in Herring.

319. Raymond Price, *With Nixon* (1977), in Herring.

320. Richard M. Nixon, "Asia After Vietnam," *Foreign Affairs*, October 1967, in Herring.

321. Richard M. Nixon, *RN: The Memoirs of Richard Nixon* (1978), in Herring.

322. Robert H. Whitlow, *The United States Military*, in *South Vietnam, 1954–1960*, University of Kentucky, 1972, in Herring.

323. Robert Shaplen, *The Road from War: Vietnam, 1965–1970* (1970), in Herring.

324. Roger Hilsman, *To Move A Nation* (1967), in Herring.

325. Roger Morris, *Uncertain Greatness* (1977), in Herring.

326. Samuel Lubell, *The Hidden Crisis in American Politics* (1971), in Herring.

327. Senate diary, in Herring.

328. State Department papers, April 1955, in Herring.

329. Tad Szulc, *The Illusion of Peace* (1978), in Herring.

330. Thomas G. Paterson, *Virginia Quarterly Review*, Spring 1978, in Herring.

331. *Time* magazine, 30 April 1965, in Herring.

332. Townsend Hoopes, *The Limits of Intervention* (1970), in Herring.

333. Tregaskis, *Vietnam Diary*, in Herring.

334. Van Tien Dung, *Our Great Spring Victory* (1977), in Herring.

335. Westmoreland, William C., *A Soldier Reports* (Garden City, 1976), in Herring.

336. William Safire, *Before the Fall* (1975), in Herring.

337. Edward R. Stettinius, Jr., papers, University of Virginia, in Herring.

338. Henry A. Kissinger, "The Vietnam Negotiations," *Foreign Affairs*, January 1969, in Herring.

339. Jean Lacouture, *Ho Chi Minh: A Political Biography* (1968), in Herring.

340. Kennedy papers, May 1961, in Herring.

341. NSC 48/1, U.S. Congress, Committee on Armed Services, 23 December 1949, in Herring.

342. Office of Strategic Services paper, Harry S. Truman Library, Independence, Mo., in Herring.

343. Philip Caputo, *A Rumor of War* (1977), in Herring.

344. Robert Shaplen, *The Road from War: Vietnam, 1965-1970* (1970), in Herring.

345. Roger Hilsman, *To Move a Nation* (1967), in Herring.

346. U.S. Senate, Committee on Foreign Relations, 1947, in Herring.

347. Herring.

348. *Time* magazine, 18 May 1970.

349. Holmberg, Major William, "Civic Action," *Marine Corps Gazette*, June 1966.

350. http://abcnews.go.com/century/timecapsule/war_peace/vietnam_war/TET_frame.html

351. http://chss.montclair.edu. Speech Transcript, as collected by Congress, 1972

352. http://more.abcnews.go.com/sections/us/jfk_vietnam1222/index.html-22 December 1997.

353. http://pacific.discover.net/~dansyr/quotes5.html

354. http://vassun.vassar.edu/~robrigha/—Copy of speech document

355. http://www.ahlan.com/qq.htm

356. http://www.ausvets.powerup.com.au/vietnam/vietnam.htm

357. http://www.cyber-nation.com/victory/quotations

358. http://www.cyber-nation.com/victory/quotations/subjects/quotes_draft.html

359. http://www.dickshovel.com/ind.html#Note61

360. http://www.salsa.net/peace/quotes.html

361. http://www.texaseagle.org/quotes/quotes.htm

362. http://www.washingtonpost.com/wp, srv/national/longterm/vietnam/chronology.htm

363. *Indochina Bulletin*, April 1973.

364. Joel.

365. Johnson, Lyndon B., library, speech text.

366. Johnson, Lyndon B., speech to the nation, 31 March 1968.

367. Johnson, Lyndon B., inaugural speech text.

368. Johnson, Lyndon B., message to Congress, Joint Resolution of Congress, H.J. RES 1145, August 1964.

369. Johnson.

370. Joint Resolution of Congress, H.J. RES 1145, 7 August 1964, Department of State bulletin, 24 August 1964.

371. Jury.

372. Doris Kearns, *Lyndon Johnson and the American Dream* (1976), in Karnow.

373. *Washington Post*, 29 December 1967, in Karnow.
374. Karnow.
375. John F. Kennedy, speech text, John F. Kennedy Library.
376. Congressional Record, 6 April 1971, in Kerry.
377. Congressional Record, 7 April 1971, in Kerry.
378. Kerry.
379. Kimball.
380. Krause family interview, at www.Emerson.edu/acadepts/cs/comm/allison.html
381. Krause family interview, at www.Emerson.edu/acadepts/cs/comm/allison.html
382. Krepinevich.
383. LCpl. Paul W. Reneau, "Dateline: Vietnam," in *Leatherneck* magazine, November 1967.
384. SSgt. Bruce Martin, "Kilo's Killers," in *Leatherneck* magazine, November 1967.
385. SSgt. Bruce Martin, "The Bridge," in *Leatherneck* magazine, November 1967.
386. "Uses of the Past: Vietnam as a Metaphor," December 1997, in Lefever.
387. Jay Leno, "The Tonight Show," NBC, January 2000.
388. "The Climax, in Vietnam," in *Life* magazine, 11 October 1963.
389. "G.O.P. Victor from South Vietnam," in *Life* magazine, 20 March 1964.
390. Marc Crawford, "Newsfront," in *Life* magazine, 20 March 1964.
391. Hugh Sidey, "The Presidency," in *Life* magazine, October 1964.
392. Akihiko Okamura, "The Ugly War in Asia," in *Life* magazine, 12 June 1964.
393. Bill Maudlin, "Critical Turn in Vietnam," in *Life* magazine, 19 February 1965.
394. "Editorial," in *Life* magazine, 19 February 1965.
395. "Editorial," in *Life* magazine, 12 March 1965.
396. "Letters to the Editor," in *Life* magazine, 12 March 1965.
397. "Washington Report," in *Life* magazine, 12 March 1965.
398. Akihiko Okamura, "Back from a Vietcong Prison," in *Life* magazine, 2 July 1965.
399. "Editorial," in *Life* magazine, 6 August 1965.
400. Richard B. Stolley, "Newsfronts," in *Life* magazine, 6 August 1965.
401. John Frook, "Doubling Up the Draft," in *Life* magazine, 20 August 1965.
402. Michael Mok, "Reality of Vietnam," in *Life* magazine, 26 November 1965.
403. Hugh Sidey, "Measure of the Man," in *Life* magazine, 3 December 1965.
404. *Life* magazine, 3 December 1965.
405. "A Whirlybird Academy," in *Life* magazine, 14 January 1966.
406. "Editorial," in *Life* magazine, 14 January 1966.
407. Sylvia Wright, "Norman Thomas: Dean of Protest," in *Life* Magazine, 14 January 1966.
408. "Peace Proposals for Ho Chi Minh," Richard B. Stolley, by *Life* magazine, 14 January 1966.
409. "Letters to the Editor," in *Life* magazine, 11 February 1966.
410. "Operation Masher: The War Goes On," in *Life* magazine, 11 February 1966.
411. Hedley Donovan, "Editorial," in *Life* magazine, 25 February 1966.
412. "Key Elements of the War," in *Life* magazine, 25 February 1966.
413. Sam Angeloff, "Saigon," in *Life* magazine, 25 February 1966.
414. David Nevin, "The Dissent," in *Life* magazine, 25 February 1966.
415. "Marines Blunt the Invasion from the North," in *Life* magazine, 28 October 1966.
416. Hugh Sidey, "The Presidency," in *Life* magazine, 28 October 1966.
417. Keith Wheeler, "Election with a Difference," in *Life* magazine, 4 November 1966.
418. Hugh Sidey, "The Presidency," in *Life* magazine, 4 November 1966.
419. Richard B. Stolley, "The President's Mission to Asia," in *Life* magazine, 4 November 1966.
420. Donald Jackson, "Ducking the Draft — Who and How," in *Life* magazine, 9 December 1966.
421. "Newsfronts," in *Life* magazine, 6 January 1967.
422. "New Front in a Widening War," in *Life* magazine, 13 January 1967.
423. "Editorial," in *Life* magazine, 20 January 1967.
424. Robert Sherrod, "Notes on a Monstrous war," in *Life* magazine, 27 January 1967.
425. Don Moser, "Battle Jump," in *Life* magazine, 10 March 1967.
426. "Letters to the Editor," in *Life* magazine, 10 March 1967.
427. "Newsfront," in *Life* magazine, 31 March 1967.
428. "Editorial," in *Life* magazine, 31 March 1967.
429. "Newsfronts," in *Life* magazine, 9 June 1967.
430. "Mr. & Mrs. Ambassador," in *Life* magazine, 9 June 1967.
431. Colin Leinster, "The Two Wars of General Walt," in *Life* magazine, 26 June 1967
432. "Guest Column," Bayard Hooper, in *Life* magazine, 7 July 1967.
433. "Editorial," in *Life* magazine, 7 July 1967.
434. "Editorial," in *Life* magazine, 25 August 1967.
435. Don Moser, "Their Mission: Defend, Befriend," in *Life* magazine, 25 August 1967.
436. "Editorial," in *Life* magazine, 20 October 1967.
437. Margery Byers, "U.S. Prisoners, in North Vietnam," in *Life* magazine, 20 October 1967.

438. David Douglas Duncan, "Con Thien," in *Life* magazine, 27 October 1967.

439. "Editors' Note," in *Life* magazine, 27 October 1967.

440. William A. McWhirter, "National Guard: Awake or Asleep?" in *Life* magazine, 27 October 1967.

441. Hugh Sidey, "The Presidency," in *Life* magazine, 27 October 1967.

442. "A Rare Private Interview with Aleksei Kosygin," in *Life* magazine, 2 February 1968.

443. "Editorials," in *Life* magazine, 9 February 1968.

444. Hugh Sidey, "The Presidency," in *Life* magazine, 9 February 1968.

445. *Life* magazine, 9 February 1968.

446. Hal Wingo, "Close-Up," in *Life* magazine, 16 February 1968.

447. George P. Hunt, "Editors' Note," in *Life* magazine, 16 February 1968.

448. "Letters to the Editors," in *Life* magazine, 23 February 1968.

449. Hugh Sidey, "The Presidency," in *Life* magazine, 23 February 1968.

450. Janos Radvanyi, "A Bizarre Adventure in Make-believe Diplomacy," in *Life* magazine, 22 March 1968.

451. "A Study in Intransigence," in *Life* magazine, 22 March 1968.

452. "Peace Feelers," in *Life* magazine, 22 March 1968.

453. "Close-up," in *Life* magazine, 12 April 1968.

454. "Letters to the Editor," in *Life* magazine, 12 April 1968.

455. Don Moser, "The Edge of Peace," in *Life* magazine, 8 November 1968.

456. George P. Hunt, "Editor's Note," in *Life* magazine, 8 November 1968.

457. *Life* Magazine, 14 March 1969.

458. Stanley Hoffman, "Policy for the 70s," in *Life* magazine, 21 March 1969.

459. *Life* magazine, 21 March 1969.

460. *Life* magazine, 28 March 1969.

461. Colin Leinster, "Close-Up," in *Life* magazine, 25 April 1969.

462. "Editor's Note," in *Life* magazine, 25 April 1969.

463. Frank McCulloch, "Dilemma of Military Dissent," in *Life* Magazine, 23 May 1969.

464. Hugh Sidey, "The Presidency," in *Life* magazine, 23 May 1969.

465. "The American Dead in Vietnam," in *Life* magazine, 27 June 1969.

466. Frank McCulloch, "A Lovely War for Profiteers," in *Life* magazine, 1 August 1969.

467. "Editorial," in *Life* magazine, 24 October 1969.

468. Hugh Sidey, "The Presidency," in *Life* magazine, 24 October 1969.

469. Hal Wingo, "Under A Sign of Peace," in *Life* magazine, 24 October 1969.

470. Frank McCulloch, "Colonel Robert Rheault, ex-Green Beret," in *Life* magazine, 14 November 1969.

471. "Editorial," in *Life* magazine, 14 November 1969.

472. Hugh Sidey, "Crisis for Nixon," in *Life* magazine, 15 May 1970.

473. Charles Childs, "Assignment to Neglect," in *Life* magazine, 22 May 1970.

474. "Clark Clifford on the War," in *Life* magazine, 22 May 1970.

475. John Saar, "You Can't Just Hand Out Orders," in *Life* magazine, 23 October 1970.

476. *Life* magazine, 5 February 1971.

477. Margery Byers, "Close-up: Curtis Tarr, Draft Director," in *Life* magazine, 21 May 1971.

478. Lee Lockwood, "The Drama Inside the Berrigan Circle," in *Life* magazine, 21 May 1971.

479. Harold Wilson, "When the War Might Have Ended," in *Life* magazine, 21 May 1971.

480. Dale Wittner, "The One Boy Who Died," in *Life* magazine, 21 January 1972.

481. John Saar, "Shock of War," in *Life* magazine, 12 May 1972.

482. *Life* magazine, 21 May 1971.

483. Karen Thorsen, "A POW Wife Turns Political," in *Life* magazine, 29 September 1972.

484. "Parting Shots," in *Life* magazine, 10 November 1972.

485. "Some Paid the Price of War...," in *Life* magazine, 10 November 1972.

486. Hugh Sidey, "The Presidency," in *Life* magazine, 10 November 1972.

487. Loudon Wainwright, "When Johnny Comes Marching Home," in *Life* magazine, 10 November 1972.

488. "Missing," in *Life* magazine, November 1987.

489. Baskir and Strauss, *Chance and Circumstance* (1978), in MacPherson.

490. David Suttler, *IV-F-A Guide to Draft Exemptions* (1970), in MacPherson.

491. *Life* magazine, 10 October 1969, in MacPherson.

492. *Playboy*, January 1982, in MacPherson.

493. MacPherson.

494. Mangold and Penycate.

495. "On Protracted War," May 1938, in Mao Tse-tung.

496. Daniel Q. McDowell, from deployment notes, 1970.

497. Daniel Q. McDowell, tour notes, 1 March 1971.

498. Daniel Q. McDowell, tour notes, April 1971.

499. Daniel Q. McDowell, tour notes, 21 November 1971.

500. *Military Times*, "The American Century," 1999.

501. Moore and Galloway.

502. Dean Brelis, "*The Face of South Vietnam*," (1968), in Moore and Galloway.

503. Luther A. Huston, in *New York Times*, 5 February 1950.

504. *New York Times*, 5 February 1950.
505. William S. White, in *New York Times*, 7 May 1954.
506. William S. White, in *New York Times*, 8 May 1954.
507. Harold Callender, in *New York Times*, 30 April 1955.
508. Associated Press, in *New York Times*, 12 May 1961.
509. Jack Langguth, in *New York Times*, 2 November 1963.
510. Hedrick Smith, in *New York Times*, 23 May 1964.
511. Peter Grose, in *New York Times*, 23 May 1964.
512. Associated Press, in *New York Times*, 3 August 1964.
513. Arnold H. Lubasch, in *New York Times*, 5 August 1964.
514. *New York Times*, 5 August 1964.
515. Joseph A. Loftus, in *New York Times*, 6 August 1964.
516. Thomas J. Hamilton, in *New York Times*, 6 August 1964.
517. *New York Times*, 6 August 1964.
518. E.W. Kenworthy, in *New York Times*, 8 August 1964.
519. Peter Grose, in *New York Times*, 8 August 1964.
520. John W. Finney, in *New York Times*, 23 December 1964.
521. Tom Wicker, in *New York Times*, 8 February 1965.
522. *New York Times*, 8 February 1965.
523. *New York Times*, 12 February 1965.
524. Thomas J. Hamilton, in *New York Times*, 25 February 1965.
525. Charles Mohr, in *New York Times*, 26 February 1965.
526. David Halberstam, in *New York Times*, 8 April 1965.
527. Clyde H. Farnsworth, in *New York Times*, 18 June 1965.
528. John D. Pomfret, in *New York Times*, 28 July 1965.
529. Tom Wicker, in *New York Times*, 29 July 1965.
530. Max Frankel, in *New York Times*, 2 February 1966.
531. Seymour Topping, in *New York Times*, 2 February 1966.
532. E.W. Kenworthy, in *New York Times*, 8 February 1966.
533. Max Frankel, in *New York Times*, 22 May 1966.
534. E.W. Kenworthy, in *New York Times*, 30 June 1966.
535. Max Frankel, in *New York Times*, 27 October 1966.
536. *New York Times*, 9 January 1966.
537. Anthony Lewis, in *New York Times*, 14 February 1967.
538. John W. Finney, in *New York Times*, 14 February 1967.
539. Neil Sheehan, in *New York Times*, 7 March 1967.
540. Raymond H. Anderson, in *New York Times*, 7 March 1967.
541. Roy Reed, in *New York Times*, 16 March 1967.
542. Max Frankel, in *New York Times*, 21 March 1967.
543. R.W. Apple, in *New York Times*, 21 April 1967.
544. Peter Kihss, in *New York Times*, 25 April 1967.
545. R.W. Apple, in *New York Times*, 4 August 1967.
546. Raymond H. Anderson, in *New York Times*, 22 October 1967.
547. Agence *France-Presse*, in *New York Times*, 29 December 1967.
548. E.W. Kenworthy, in *New York Times*, 29 December 1967.
549. John Leo, in *New York Times*, 2 February 1968.
550. Max Frankel, in *New York Times*, 2 February 1968.
551. *New York Times*, 2 February 1968.
552. Max Frankel, in *New York Times*, 3 February 1968.
553. *New York Times*, 10 February 1968.
554. Henry Tanner, in *New York Times*, 25 February 1968.
555. John W. Finney, in *New York Times*, 25 February 1968.
556. Robert B. Semple, Jr., in *New York Times*, 6 March 1968.
557. Max Frankel, in *New York Times*, 1 April 1968.
558. *New York Times*, 3 April 1968.
559. James Reston, in *New York Times*, 4 April 1968.
560. John L. Hess, in *New York Times*, 4 April 1968.
561. *New York Times*, 4 April 1968
562. Neil Sheehan, in *New York Times*, 31 October 1968.
563. Gene Roberts, in *New York Times*, 1 November 1968.
564. Edward C. Burks, in *New York Times*, 2 November 1968.
565. Gene Roberts, in *New York Times*, 2 November 1968.
566. Hedrick Smith, in *New York Times*, 2 November 1968.
567. Robert B. Semple, Jr., in *New York Times*, 5 March 1969.
568. Terence Smith, in *New York Times*, 9 June 1969.
569. Tillman Durdin, in *New York Times*, 4 September 1969.
570. Max Frankel, in *New York Times*, 3 November 1969.
571. *New York Times*, 5 April 1970.
572. John W. Finney, in *New York Times*, 30 April 1970.
573. John W. Finney, in *New York Times*, 1 May 1970.
574. Robert B. Semple, Jr., in *New York Times*, 1 May 1970.
575. John Kifner, in *New York Times*, 4 May 1970.
576. Bernard Gwertzman, in *New York Times*, 5 May 1970.
577. John W. Finney, in *New York Times*, 5 May 1970.
578. Robert D. McFadden, in *New York Times*, 5 May 1970.

579. Robert B. Semple, Jr., in *New York Times*, 8 October 1970.

580. William Beecher, in *New York Times*, 22 November 1970.

581. Tad Szulc, in *New York Times*, 23 November 1970.

582. Homer Bigart, in *New York Times*, 31 March 1971.

583. Majorie Hunter, in *New York Times*, 1 April 1971.

584. *New York Times*, 1 April 1971.

585. Max Frankel, in *New York Times*, 8 April 1971.

586. Hedrick Smith, in *New York Times*, 1 July 1971.

587. Hedrick Smith, in *New York Times*, 17 April 1972.

588. Robert B. Semple, Jr., in *New York Times*, 27 April 1972.

589. Craig R. Whitney, in *New York Times*, 2 May 1972.

590. Sydney H. Schanberg, in *New York Times*, 3 May 1972.

591. John L. Hess, in *New York Times*, 5 May 1972.

592. John W. Finney, in *New York Times*, 9 May 1972.

593. Robert B. Semple, Jr., in *New York Times*, 9 May 1972.

594. Bernard Gwertzman, in *New York Times*, 10 May 1972.

595. John L. Hess, in *New York Times*, 10 May 1972.

596. *New York Times*, 10 May 1972.

597. Bernard Gwertzman, in *New York Times*, 17 December 1972.

598. Henry Giniger, in *New York Times*, 31 December 1972.

599. Seymour M. Hersh, in *New York Times*, 31 December 1972.

600. John Herbers, in *New York Times*, 16 January 1973.

601. James M. Naughton, in *New York Times*, 24 January 1973.

602. James Reston, in *New York Times*, 24 January 1973.

603. Sylvan Fox, in *New York Times*, 24 January 1973.

604. *New York Times*, 24 January 1973.

605. Bernard Gwertzman, in *New York Times*, 25 January 1973.

606. George Vecsey, in *New York Times*, 25 January 1973.

607. *New York Times*, 25 January 1973.

608. John Herbers, in *New York Times*, 30 March 1973.

609. Steven V. Roberts, in *New York Times*, 30 March 1973.

610. Treaster, Joseph B., in *New York Times*, 30 March 1973.

611. Majorie Hunter, in *New York Times*, 17 September 1974.

612. William Borders, in *New York Times*, 17 September 1974.

613. John W. Finney, in *New York Times*, 20 March 1975.

614. Bernard Weinraub, in *New York Times*, 3 April 1975.

615. Paul Hofmann, in *New York Times*, 3 April 1975.

616. *New York Times*, 5 April 1975.

617. Richard L. Madden, in *New York Times*, 11 April 1975.

618. Philip Shabecoff, in *New York Times*, 17 April 1975.

619. Malcolm W. Browne, in *New York Times*, 21 April 1975.

620. David A. Andelman, in *New York Times*, 30 April 1975.

621. John W. Finney, in *New York Times*, 30 April 1975.

622. Flora Lewis, in *New York Times*, 1 May 1975.

623. Bernard Gwertzman, in *New York Times*, 12 January 1977.

624. Robert D. McFadden, in *New York Times*, 22 January 1977.

625. Flora Lewis, in *New York Times*, 5 May 1977.

626. Alexander Solzhenitsyn, *Peace and Violence* (1973), in Nguyen.

627. In reference to Robert Thompson, *Peace Is Not at Hand, in* Nguyen.

628. Robert Shaplen, *The Road from War* (1966), in Nguyen.

629. Nguyen.

630. Richard M. Nixon, text from Presidential Documents, Vol. 9 (1973).

631. Richard M. Nixon, presidential address text, 30 April 1970.

632. Nixon.

633. Frank McGee Sunday Report, 10 March 1968, in Oberdorfer.

634. NBC News special, "Vietnam," December 1965, in Oberdorfer.

635. Bernard Fall, *Vietnam Witness* (1966), in Oberdorfer.

636. Joseph Cabanes Bernard, *Agence France-Presse*, 25 December 1967, in Oberdorfer.

637. Captured document, 25 April 1968, in Oberdorfer.

638. Congressional Record, 20 February 1970, in Oberdorfer.

639. Congressional Record, 30 January 1968, in Oberdorfer.

640. Congressional Record, in Oberdorfer.

641. Department of Commerce Joint Publications Research Service, 26 March 1968, in Oberdorfer.

642. "House to House," *Leatherneck*, May 1968, in Oberdorfer.

643. Matthew B. Ridgeway interview, 20 April 1970, in Oberdorfer.

644. *New York Times*, 4 February 1968, in Oberdorfer.

645. *New York Times*, 6 February 1968, in Oberdorfer.

646. *Newsweek*, 18 March 1968, in Oberdorfer.

647. Oriana Fallaci, *Washington Post*, 6 April 1969, in Oberdorfer.

648. Theodore H. White, *The Making of the President 1968* (1969), in Oberdorfer.

649. Tran Ngoc Chau, *Forty-Five Days, in the Capitals of USA, France, England, and Italy* (1968), in Oberdorfer.

650. Vanden Heuvel and Gwirtzman, *On His Own* (1970), in Oberdorfer.

651. *Wall Street Journal*, 23 February 1968, in Oberdorfer.

652. Walter Cronkite, CBS News, "Special Report: Vietnam Perspective," (1965), in Oberdorfer.

653. Oberdorfer.

654. John Ricks, in Olson.

655. *Pacific Stars and Stripes*, 8 May 1954.

656. *Pacific Stars and Stripes*, 8 May 1954.

657. *Pacific Stars and Stripes*, 21 July 1954.

658. *Pacific Stars and Stripes*, 10 March 1962.

659. *Pacific Stars and Stripes*, 22 March 1962.

660. *Pacific Stars and Stripes*, 20 May 1962.

661. *Pacific Stars and Stripes*, 25 July 1962.

662. Forest Kimler, in *Pacific Stars and Stripes*, 4 September 1962.

663. SSgt. Steve Stibbens, in *Pacific Stars and Stripes*, 1 November 1963.

664. *Pacific Stars and Stripes*, 1 November 1963.

665. *Pacific Stars and Stripes*, 3 November 1963.

666. *Pacific Stars and Stripes*, 4 November 1963.

667. *Pacific Stars and Stripes*, 27 January 1964.

668. *Pacific Stars and Stripes*, 7 August 1964.

669. *Pacific Stars and Stripes*, 25 November 1964.

670. *Pacific Stars and Stripes*, 25 December 1964.

671. *Pacific Stars and Stripes*, 13 February 1965.

672. *Pacific Stars and Stripes*, 8 March 1965.

673. *Pacific Stars and Stripes*, 9 April 1965.

674. *Pacific Stars and Stripes*, 29 May 1965.

675. *Pacific Stars and Stripes*, 27 June 1965.

676. *Pacific Stars and Stripes*, 28 July 1966.

677. *Pacific Stars and Stripes*, 30 July 1965.

678. *Pacific Stars and Stripes*, 1 December 1965.

679. *Pacific Stars and Stripes*, 26 December 1965.

680. *Pacific Stars and Stripes*, 15 September 1966.

681. Tom Dreiling, in *Pacific Stars and Stripes*, 21 May 1967.

682. *Pacific Stars and Stripes*, 9 September 1967.

683. *Pacific Stars and Stripes*, 2 April 1968.

684. *Pacific Stars and Stripes*, 2 October 1968.

685. *Pacific Stars and Stripes*, 3 November 1968.

686. *Pacific Stars and Stripes*, 21 November 1968.

687. *Pacific Stars and Stripes*, 10 July 1969.

688. *Pacific Stars and Stripes*, 1 August 1969.

689. *Pacific Stars and Stripes*, 25 October 1969.

690. *Pacific Stars and Stripes*, 22 April 1970.

691. *Pacific Stars and Stripes*, 3 May 1970.

692. *Pacific Stars and Stripes*, 1 September 1970.

693. *Pacific Stars and Stripes*, 23 November 1970.

694. *Pacific Stars and Stripes*, 13 December 1970.

695. *Pacific Stars and Stripes*, 9 April 1971.

696. *Pacific Stars and Stripes*, 10 May 1971.

697. *Pacific Stars and Stripes*, 15 January 1972.

698. *Pacific Stars and Stripes*, 29 January 1973.

699. *Pacific Stars and Stripes*, 12 April 1972.

700. *Pacific Stars and Stripes*, 3 May 1972.

701. *Pacific Stars and Stripes*, 10 May 1972.

702. *Pacific Stars and Stripes*, 12 May 1972.

703. *Pacific Stars and Stripes*, 14 June 1972.

704. *Pacific Stars and Stripes*, 17 August 1972.

705. *Pacific Stars and Stripes*, 30 September 1972.

706. *Pacific Stars and Stripes*, 28 October 1972.

707. *Pacific Stars and Stripes*, 14 February 1973.

708. Lou Truckenmiller, in *Pacific Stars and Stripes*, 31 March 1973, SP/5.

709. *Pacific Stars and Stripes*, 31 March 1973.

710. *Pacific Stars and Stripes*, 1986.

711. Robert Thompson, *No Exit from Vietnam* (1970), in Palmer.

712. Russell F. Weigley, *History of the United States Army* (1967), in Palmer.

713. Palmer.

714. General J. M. Platt, "Military Civic Action," *Marine Corps Gazette*, September 1970.

715. "Pull Out, All Out, or Stand Fast, in Vietnam?" *Look* magazine, 5 April 1966, in Powers.

716. Alice Lynd, *We Won't Go* (Boston: Beacon Press, 1968), in Powers.

717. Arthur Herzog, *McCarthy for President* (1969), in Powers.

718. Arthur M. Schlesinger, Jr., *The Crisis of Confidence* (1969), in Powers.

719. *Berkeley Barb*, 15 September 1967, in Powers.

720. *Berkeley Barb*, 20 October 1967, in Powers.

721. Bruce Ladd, *Crisis in Credibility* (1968), in Powers.

722. Chester L. Cooper, *The Lost Crusade* (1970), in Powers.

723. Cohen and Hale, *The New Student Left* (1967), in Powers.

724. D. Lyle, "Dr. Spock Misbehaves," *Esquire*, February 1969, in Powers.

725. David Halberstam, *The Making of a Quagmire* (1965), in Powers.

726. Department of State Bulletin, 10 April 1967, in Powers.

727. Eichel, Jost, Luskin and Neustadt, *The Harvard Strike* (1970), in Powers.

728. Eric F. Goldman, *The Tragedy of Lyndon Johnson* (1969), in Powers.

729. Evans and Novak, *Johnson, Lyndon B.: The Exercise of Power* (1966), in Powers.

730. Ferber and Lynd, *The Resistance* (1971), in Powers.

731. Goulden, *Truth is the First Casualty* (Chicago: 1969), in Powers.

732. *Harper's*, February 1966, in Powers.

733. Hugh Sidney, *A Very Personal Presidency* (1968), in Powers.

734. Jack Newfield, *A Prophetic Minority* (1966), in Powers.

735. Jane Kramer, *Allen Ginsberg in America* (1969), in Powers.

736. Jessica Mitford, *The Trial of Dr. Spock* (1969), in Powers.

737. Johnson and Gwertzman, *Fulbright the Dissenter* (1968), in Powers.

738. Jon Neary, *Julian Bond* (1971), in Powers.

739. Joseph C. Goulden, *Truth is the First Casualty* (1969), in Powers.

740. *Liberation*, April 1967, in Powers.

741. *Liberation*, May 1965, in Powers.

742. *Liberation*, June, July 1965, in Powers.

743. *Liberation*, July 1967, in Powers.

744. *Liberation*, November 1967, in Powers.

745. Lipset and Wolin, *The Berkeley Student Revolt* (1965), in Powers.

746. Margaret Long, "The Movement," *New South*, Winter 1966, in Powers.

747. Marquis Childs, *Washington Post*, 21 February 1966, in Powers.

748. Menashe and Radosh, *Teach-ins: USA.* (1967), in Powers.

749. *New Republic*, 27 January 1968, in Powers.

750. *New York Post*, 17 January 1969, in Powers.

751. *New York Times*, 9 February 1965, in Powers.

752. *New York Times*, 10 August 1965, in Powers.

753. *New York Times*, 1 April 1968, in Powers.

754. *New York Times*, 1 December 1967, in Powers.

755. *New York Times*, 1 February 1966, in Powers.

756. *New York Times*, 1 July 1966, in Powers.

757. *New York Times*, 1 November 1966, in Powers.

758. *New York Times*, 2 November 1965, in Powers.

759. *New York Times*, 3 December 1967, in Powers.

760. *New York Times*, 3 February 1967, in Powers.

761. *New York Times*, 3 January 1968, in Powers.

762. *New York Times*, 3 March 1967, in Powers.

763. *New York Times*, 3 March 1967, in Powers.

764. *New York Times*, 4 August 1964, in Powers.

765. *New York Times*, 4 May 1967, in Powers.

766. *New York Times*, 4 November 1966, in Powers.

767. *New York Times*, 5 April 1967, in Powers.

768. *New York Times*, 5 January 1965, in Powers.

769. *New York Times*, 5 November 1966, in Powers.

770. *New York Times*, 5 September 1967, in Powers.

771. *New York Times*, 7 April 1967, in Powers.

772. *New York Times*, 7 December 1967, in Powers.

773. *New York Times*, 7 March 1968, in Powers.

774. *New York Times*, 8 April 1967, in Powers.

775. *New York Times*, 8 February 1965, in Powers.

776. *New York Times*, 8 January 1968, in Powers.

777. *New York Times*, 8 May 1967, in Powers.

778. *New York Times*, 9 January 1964, in Powers.

779. *New York Times*, 10 February 1967, in Powers.

780. *New York Times*, 10 November 1966, in Powers.

781. *New York Times*, 11 March 1968, in Powers.

782. *New York Times*, 12 July 1967, in Powers.

783. *New York Times*, 12 March 1968, in Powers.

784. *New York Times*, 13 January 1966, in Powers.

785. *New York Times*, 13 October 1967, in Powers.

786. *New York Times*, 14 July 1965, in Powers.

787. *New York Times*, 15 May 1964, in Powers.

788. *New York Times*, 16 November 1965, in Powers.

789. *New York Times*, 16 October 1965, in Powers.

790. *New York Times*, 17 August 1967, in Powers.

791. *New York Times*, 17 February 1968, in Powers.

792. *New York Times*, 17 July 1964, in Powers.

793. *New York Times*, 18 August 1967, in Powers.

794. *New York Times*, 18 May 1966, in Powers.

795. *New York Times*, 19 March 1968, in Powers.

796. *New York Times*, 19 November 196, in Powers.

797. *New York Times*, 19 November 1968, in Powers.

798. *New York Times*, 20 November 1967, in Powers.

799. *New York Times*, 22 April 1966, in Powers.

800. *New York Times*, 22 February 1964, in Powers.

801. *New York Times*, 22 March 1968, in Powers.

802. *New York Times*, 22 May 1966, in Powers.

803. *New York Times*, 23 March 1968, in Powers.

804. *New York Times*, 23 May 1964, in Powers.

805. *New York Times*, 23 November 1966, in Powers.

806. *New York Times*, 24 April 1967, in Powers.

807. *New York Times*, 25 April 1967, in Powers.

808. *New York Times*, 25 February 1965, in Powers.

809. *New York Times*, 27 February 1966, in Powers.

810. *New York Times*, 27 January 1965, in Powers.

811. *New York Times*, 27 January 1966, in Powers.

812. *New York Times*, 28 May 1967, in Powers.

813. *New York Times*, 28 November 1965, in Powers.

814. *New York Times*, 29 April 1966, in Powers.

815. *New York Times*, 29 October 1965, in Powers.

816. *New York Times*, 30 December 1966, in Powers.

817. *New York Times*, 30 September 1967, in Powers.

818. *New York Times*, 31 January 1968, in Powers.

819. *Newsweek*, 26 September 1966, in Powers.

820. Paul Good, "On the March Again, New York," *The Nation*, 1 May 1967, in Powers.

821. Paul Good, "The Meredith March," *New South*, Summer 1966, in Powers.

822. Richard T. Stout, *People*, 1970, in Powers.

823. Robert G. Sherrill, "Democratic Rebels in Congress," *The Nation*, 10 October 1966, in Powers.

824. Robert Sherrill, "Bubble of Unreality," *The Nation*, 20 June 1966, in Powers.

825. Sally Belfrage, *Freedom Summer* (1965), in Powers.

826. Steven Kelman, *Push Comes to Shove* (1970), in Powers.

827. *The Guardian*, 25 November 1967, in Powers.

828. *The Nation*, 18 March 1968, in Powers.

829. Vietnam hearings (1966), in Powers.

830. Theodore H. White, *The Making of the President* (1965), in Powers.
831. Tom Wolfe, *The Electric Kool-Aid Acid Test* (1968), in Powers.
832. Townsend Hoopes, *The Limits of Intervention*, New York, 1969, in Powers.
833. *U.S. News and World Report*, 9 October 1967, in Powers.
834. Vietnam hearings (1966), in Powers.
835. *Village Voice*, 25 January 1968, in Powers.
836. *Washington Post*, 1 December 1967, in Powers.
837. *Washington Post*, 1 February 1966, in Powers.
838. *Washington Post*, 7 February 1966, in Powers.
839. *Washington Post*, 8 February 1966, in Powers.
840. *Washington Post*, 12 February 1966, in Powers.
841. *Washington Post*, 13 March 1968, in Powers.
842. *Washington Post*, 17 February 1966, in Powers.
843. *Washington Post*, 25 January 1966, in Powers.
844. William Robert Miller, *Martin Luther King* (1968), in Powers.
845. *WIN* magazine, 7 April 1967, in Powers.
846. *WIN* magazine, 16 June 1967, in Powers.
847. Andrew Kopkind, *New Republic*, 4 June 1966, in Powers.
848. Joanne Grant, *Black Protest* (1968), in Powers.
849. Richard J. Walton, *The Remnants of Power* (1968), in Powers.
850. Powers.
851. Prados and Stubbe.
852. Benjamin F. Schemmer, *The Raid* (1976), in Pratt.
853. Bill Adler, *Letters from Vietnam* (1967), in Pratt.
854. C.D.B. Bryan, *Friendly Fire* (1976), in Pratt.
855. Congressional Record, in Pratt.
856. Courtesy of John Sutten, in Pratt.
857. Department of State Bulletin, 11 December 1967, in Pratt.
858. Department of State Bulletin, 13 November 1972, in Pratt.
859. Department of State Bulletin, 15 April 1968, in Pratt.
860. Donald Kirk, *Tell It to the Dead* (Chicago, 1975), in Pratt.
861. Edward Geary Lansdale, in *the Midst of* Wars (1972), in Pratt.
862. Elaine Shepard, *The Doom Pussy* (1967), in Pratt.
863. Frank Snepp, *Decent Interval* (1977), in Pratt.
864. Gareth Porter, *Vietnam: The Definitive Documentation of Human Decisions* (1979), in Pratt.
865. *Harpers*, June 1974, in Pratt.
866. Henry Kissinger, *White House Years* (1979), in Pratt.
867. HQ PACAF, *The Fall and Evacuation of South Vietnam* (1978), in Pratt.
868. Lao Dong Party Central Committee Activity, "Viet Nam Documents and Research Notes," Saigon, March 1970, in Pratt.
869. Michael Clodfelter, untitled manuscript, 1984, in Pratt.
870. Michael Herr, *Dispatches* (1977), in Pratt.
871. Morita, USSAG/7AF, in Pratt.
872. Office of Marine Corps History (Washington, D.C.), in Pratt.
873. *Parade*, 2 May 1982, in Pratt.
874. Paul Hoffman, *Moratorium* (1970), in Pratt.
875. *Pentagon Papers* (Government edition), in Pratt.
876. *Pentagon Papers* (Gravel edition), in Pratt.
877. *Personal Diary*, 1962, in Pratt.
878. Richard B. Sexton diary, in Pratt.
879. Robert Payne, *Red Storm Over Asia* (1951), in Pratt.
880. "Vietnam Documents and Research," Saigon, December 1970, in Pratt.
881. U.S. Army Center of Military History, *Reflections on the Vietnam War* (1980), in Pratt.
882. Viet Nam Documents, 1971, in Pratt.
883. W.D. Ehrhart, *The Awkward Silence* (1980), in Pratt.
884. Department of State Bulletin, 26 April 1965, in Pratt.
885. Henry Kissinger, *The White House Years* (1979), in Pratt.
886. Pratt.
887. "Scranton Commission Report on Campus Unrest," 27 September 1970.
888. Sieminski, Gregory C., "The Art of Naming Operations," *Parameters*, Autumn 1965
889. Starry.
890. Terry.
891. C. J. Merdinger, "Civil Engineers, Seabees, and Bases, in Vietnam," May 1970, in *The Marines*, in *Vietnam 1954-1973*, Department of the Navy, Headquarters United States Marine Corps, January 1974.
892. *Quang Doi Nhan Dan*, September 1967, in Department of the Navy.
893. Department of the Navy.
894. *The Old Reliable*, Ninth Infantry Division, Vol. 2, No. 10, 13 March 1968.
895. PFC Michael Smith, in *The Old Reliable*, Vol. 2, No. 8, 28 February 1968.
896. *The Old Reliable*, Vol. 2, No. 8, 28 February 1968.
897. SP/4 Tom Farley, in *The Old Reliable*, Vol. 2, No. 10, 13 March 1968.
898. *The Old Reliable*, Vol. 2, No. 10, 13 March 1968.
899. *The Pentagon Papers* (Gravel edition: 1971).
900. Chester L. Cooper, *The Lost Crusade* (1970), in "*The Pentagon Papers* and U.S. Imperialism in South East Asia," Noam Chomsky, *The Spokesman*, Winter 1972/3.

901. *Foreign Policy*, "Vietnam: The System Worked," Summer 1971, in Noam Chomsky, "*The Pentagon Papers* and "U.S. Imperialism in South East Asia," *The Spokesman*, Winter 1972/3.

902. Noam Chomsky, "*The Pentagon Papers* and U.S. Imperialism in South East Asia," 18 November 1971, in *The Spokesman*, Winter 1972/3.

903. Noam Chomsky, "*The Pentagon Papers* and U.S. Imperialism in South East Asia," in *The Spokesman*, Winter 1972/3.

904. Noam Chomsky, "*The Pentagon Papers* and U.S. Imperialism in South East Asia," *New York Review*, 2 December 1971, in *The Spokesman*, Winter 1972/3.

905. Joseph Heller interview, *Playboy* magazine, June 1975, in *The Vietnam Generation Big Book*, Vol. 5 No. 1–4, March 1994.

906. Nick Boldrini, "Attack," in *The Vietnam Generation Big Book*, Vol. 5 No. 1–4, March 1964.

907. "Air Power Can Do More in Vietnam," *Air Force and Space Digest*, May 1966, in Tilford.

908. "The Lessons of Vietnam," *Air Force* magazine, March 1983, in Tilford.

909. "USAF and the Vietnam Experience," *Air Force* magazine, June 1965, in Tilford.

910. Clark M. Clifford, "A Viet Nam Reappraisal," *Foreign Affairs*, July 1969, in Tilford.

911. Department of State bulletin, 22 June 1964, in Tilford.

912. Doris Kearns, *Lyndon Johnson and the American Dream* (1976), in Tilford.

913. Fulghum and Maitland, *South Vietnam on Trial* (1984), in Tilford.

914. General William W. Momyer, *Air Power in Three Wars* (1978), in Tilford.

915. Henry Kissinger, *White House Years* (1979), in Tilford.

916. Interview, U.S. Air Force Oral History Program, March 1974, in Tilford.

917. J. S. Butz, Jr., "Those Bombings, in the North," *Air Force and Space Digest*, April 1966, in Tilford.

918. James Clay Thompson, *Rolling Thunder* (1980), in Tilford.

919. Jim and Sybil Stockdale, in *Love and War* (1984), in Tilford.

920. Major A. J. C. Lavalle, *Airpower and the Spring 1972 Invasion* (1985), in Tilford.

921. Richard M. Nixon, *The Memoirs of Richard M. Nixon* (1978), in Tilford.

922. Robinson Risner, *The Passing of the Night* (1973), in Tilford.

923. Sharp, "Report on Air and Naval Campaigns Against North Vietnam," 1966, in Tilford.

924. The *Pentagon Papers* (*New York Times* edition, 1971), in Tilford.

925. The *Pentagon Papers* (Senator Mike Gravel edition, 1971), in Tilford.

926. Thomas Coffey, *Iron Eagle* (1986), in Tilford.

927. William Appleman Williams, *America in Vietnam: A Documentary History* (1985), in Tilford.

928. General John P. McConnell, "USAF's Score, in Limited War: Impressive," *Air Force and Space Digest*, September 1966, in Tilford.

929. Henry A. Kissinger, *Nuclear Weapons and Foreign Policy* (1957), in Tilford.

930. Message JCS to CINCPAC, 26 December 1962, Kennedy Library, in Tilford.

931. Tilford.

932. "The Nation," in *Time* magazine, 20 June 1969.

933. "The Nation," in *Time* magazine, 24 October 1969.

934. "The Nation," in *Time* magazine, 5 December 1969.

935. A letter from the publisher, Henry Luce, in *Time* magazine, 5 December 1969.

936. *Time* Essay, in *Time* magazine, 5 December 1969.

937. "The Nation," in *Time* magazine, 11 May 1970.

938. "Essay," in *Time* magazine, 18 May 1970.

939. "The Nation," in *Time* magazine, 18 May 1970.

940. "The Nation," in *Time* magazine, 12 April 1971.

941. "Medicine," in *Time* magazine, 17 April 1972.

942. David DeVoss, "The World — The Air War," in *Time* magazine, 17 April 1972.

943. Stanley Cloud, "The World — The Sea War," in *Time* magazine, 17 April 1972.

944. "The World," in *Time* magazine, 17 April 1972.

945. "The Nation," in *Time* magazine, 1 May 1972.

946. "The Nation," in *Time* magazine, 15 May 1972.

947. "The World," *Quan Doi Nhan Dan*, 1969, in *Time* magazine, 15 May 1972.

948. "The World," in *Time* magazine, 15 May 1972.

949. "Special Section," in *Time* magazine, 6 November 1972.

950. "The Nation," in *Time* magazine, 6 November 1972.

951. "Cease-Fire," in *Time* magazine, 5 February 1973.

952. "Editorial," Ralph P. Davidson, in *Time* magazine, 5 February 1973.

953. Gavin Scott, "The Last Bombing Show," in *Time* magazine, 5 February 1973.

954. "The Nation," in *Time* magazine, 5 February 1973.

955. Nguyen Cao Ky, *How We Lost the Vietnam War* (1976), in Joseph B. Treaster, *New York Times*.

956. SP/4 Tom Bozzuto, "Rice Times," in *Tropic Lightning News*, 1 June 1970.

957. Brig. Gen. Edwin H. Simmons, *Naval Review*, 1968, in Uhlig.

958. Captain Charles J. Merdinger, "CEC, U.S. Navy," *Naval Review*, 1970, in Uhlig.

959. Edward Wegener, "Theory of Naval Strategy, in the Nuclear Age," *Naval Review* 1972, in Uhlig.

960. John D. Hayes, "Sea Power," July 1966, in Uhlig.
961. Vice Admiral Malcolm W. Cagle, in Uhlig.
962. William C. Westmoreland, *A Soldier Reports* (1976), in Uhlig.
963. William B. Fulton, *Riverine Operations 1966–1969* (Washington, D.C., 1973), in Uhlig.
964. Uhlig.
965. "Landmarks Since 1960, in the PLAF March Towards Complete Victory," in *Vietnam Courier*, 16 December 1968.
966. "NLF Role Decisive...," in *Vietnam Courier*, 16 December 1968.
967. "Revolutionary Power Strengthened, in South Viet Nam, in *Vietnam Courier*, 16 December 1968.
968. "The NLF Prodigious Architect and Leader..., in *Vietnam Courier*, 16 December 1968.
969. "Viet Nam and the World at Large," in *Vietnam Courier*, 16 December 1968.
970. *Vietnam Courier*, 16 December 1968.
971. *Vietnam: A Television History, America's Mandarin, 1954-1963* (1983).
972. Walt.
973. Walter Pincus, in *Washington Post*, 12 October 1966.
974. Watt.
975. *Life* magazine, 4 November 1966, in *We Remember, 2d Battalion, 1st Marines* (1993).
976. *We Remember, 2d Battalion, 1st Marines* (1993).
977. West.
978. "An Undying Love," *Black Panther*, 16 March 1968, in Westheider.
979. "GI's Body, in Cemetery He Selected," *Baltimore Afro-American*, 10 January 1970, in Westheider.
980. "GIs Complain About Bias, in Armed Services," *Pittsburgh Courier*, 8 May 1971, in Westheider.
981. "How Negro Americans Perform, in Vietnam," *U.S. News and World Report*, 15 August 1966, in Westheider.
982. "Long Live Ho Chi Minh," *Black Panther*, May 1969, in Westheider.
983. "No Room, in the Cemetery," *Baltimore Afro-American*, 4 June 1966, in Westheider.
984. "Poor Communication Seen as Cause of Marine Trouble," *Baltimore Afro-American*, 10 January 1970, in Westheider.
985. "Veteran Says Vietnamese Support Black Struggle," *Baltimore Afro-American*, 17 January 1970, in Westheider.
986. "Viet Hero Sees Racial Bias, in Big Lie," *Baltimore Afro-American*, 26 February 1966, in Westheider.
987. "Viet Rebuke Stirs Storm," *Baltimore Afro-American*, 22 January 1966, in Westheider.
988. *Baltimore Afro-American*, 2 April 1966, in Westheider.
989. Bernard Weinraub, "Rioting Disquiets GI., in Vietnam," *New York Times*, 8 April 1968, in Westheider.
990. Black Congressional Caucus Report, 1972, in Westheider.
991. Bobby Seale, "Letter from Chairman Bobby No. 3," *Black Panther* September 1969, in Westheider.
992. Congressional Black Caucus Report, 1972, in Westheider.
993. Daniel "Chappie" James, Jr., "Rapping with Chappie," *Air University Review*, July 1972, in Westheider.
994. Department of Defense, Office of the Deputy Assistant of Defense for Equal Opportunity and Safety Policy, Task Force, 1972, in Westheider.
995. Diane Nash Bevel, "Black Woman Views Genocidal War, in Vietnam," *Black Liberator*, May 1969, in Westheider.
996. Erwin Knoll, "Representative Ron Dellums: Black, Radical, and Hopeful," *The Progressive*, June 1971, in Westheider.
997. House Committee on Internal Security, in Westheider.
998. Jack D. Foner, *Blacks and the Military*, in *American History* (1974), in Westheider.
999. James Hawkins, Jr., interview, Cincinnati, Ohio, 9 July 1991, in Westheider.
1000. Johnny Woods, "Draft Resistance,"*Black Liberator*, September 1969, in Westheider.
1001. L. Deckle McLean, "The Black Man and the Draft," *Ebony*, August 1968, in Westheider.
1002. Lt. Col. Vernon L. Conner interview, Senior Officer Oral History Project, Command Series, 1972, in Westheider.
1003. Phillip S. Foner, *Blacks and the Military in American History* (1974), in Westheider.
1004. Robert D. Heinl, Jr., "The Collapse of the Armed Forces," *Armed Forces Journal*, 7 June 1971, in Westheider.
1005. Robert W. Mullen, *Blacks*, in *American Wars* (1973), in Westheider.
1006. Sol Stern, "When the Black GI Comes Back from Vietnam," *New York Times* magazine, 24 March 1968, in Westheider.
1007. Steven Morris, "How Blacks Upset the Marine Corps," *Ebony*, December 1969, in Westheider.
1008. Stewart Alsop, "The American Class System," *Newsweek*, 29 June 1970, in Westheider.
1009. Thomas Johnson, "Negro Expatriates," *New York Times*, 30 April 1969, in Westheider.
1010. Thomas Johnson, "Negro, in Vietnam Uneasy about U.S.," *New York Times*, 1 May 1969, in Westheider.
1011. Thomas Johnson, "Negroes, in Nam," *Ebony*, August 1968, in Westheider.
1012. Thomas Johnson, "The U.S. Negro, in Vietnam," *New York Times*, 29 April 1969, in Westheider.
1013. Vietnam Veterans Against the War, "Position Paper on Amnesty," New Mexico, 19–23 April 1973, in Westheider.

1014. Wallace Terry, "Bringing the War Home," *Black Scholar*, November 1970, in Westheider.

1015. Whitney Young, Jr., Baltimore Afro-American, 1966, in Westheider.

1016. William Westmoreland, "Report of the Chief of Staff of the United States Army, 1 July 1968 to June 30 1972," in Westheider.

1017. Zalin B. Grant, "Whites Against Blacks, in Vietnam," *New Republic*, 18 January 1969, in Westheider.

1018. Westheider.

1019. Westmoreland.

1020. Gene Wilson, interview, December 1976.

1021. Esper.

1022. Sidney Lens, *Liberation*, February 1966, in Greene.

1023. Walter Lippmann, San Francisco *Chronicle*, 2 January 1966.

1024. James Reston, *New York Times*, 18 May 1966.

1025. Esper.

1026. Fiorella.

1027. Olson and Roberts.

1028. Bishop.

References

Books

Adams, Sam. *War of Numbers: An Intelligence Memoir*. Vermont: Steerforth Press, 1994.

Anderson, Charles R . *Vietnam: The Other War*. New York: Warner. November, 1990.

Bergerud, Eric M. *The Dynamics of Defeat: The Vietnam War in Hau Nghia Province*. Boulder: Westview Press, 1993.

Berman, Larry. *Lyndon Johnson's War, The Road to Stalemate in Vietnam*. New York: Norton, 1989.

Bishop, Chris. *Vietnam War Diary*. New York: Military Press, 1990.

Boettcher, Thomas D. *Vietnam the Valor and the Sorrow*. Boston: Little, Brown and Co., 1985.

Bowman, John S. General Editor: *The World Almanac of the Vietnam War*. New York: World Almanac, 1986.

Brown, Robert McAfee, Abraham Herschel, and Michael Novak. *Vietnam: Crisis of Conscience*. Association Press: New York, 1967

Charlton, James. *The Military Quotation Book*. New York: St. Martin's Press, 1990.

Chinnery, Philip D. *Full Throttle*. St. Martin's Press, 1988.

Cincinnatus. *Self-Destruction*. New York: W. W. Norton, 1981.

Clark, Gregory R. *Words of the Vietnam War*. Jefferson, North Carolina: McFarland & Company, 1990.

Clodfelter, Mark. *The Limits of Air Power*. New York: Free Press, 1989

Department of the Navy. *The Marines in Vietnam 1954-1973*. Headquarters United States Marine Corps, January 1974.

Drendel, Lou. *Air War Over Southeast Asia*. Carrollton: Squadron/Signal Publication, 1982.

Edelman, Bernard. *Dear America: Letters from Vietnam*. New York: W. W. Norton & Co., 1985.

Ehrlichman, John. *Witness to Power: The Nixon Years*. New York: Simon and Schuster, 1982.

Emerson, Gloria. *Winners and Losers*. New York: Harcourt Brace Jovanovich, 1976.

English, Dave. *Slipping the Surly Bonds*. New York, McGraw-Hill, 1998.

Esper, George. *The Eyewitness History of the Vietnam War*. New York: Villard Press, 1983.

Fiorella, Jim. *The Vietnam Zippo*. Atglen: Schiffer, 1998.

Galbraith, John Kenneth. *How to Get Out of Vietnam*. New York: Signet, 1967.

Gibson, James William. *The Perfect War: Technowar in Vietnam*. Boston: The Atlantic Monthly Press, 1986.

Gravel, Mike. *The Pentagon Papers*. Boston. Beacon Press, 1982.

Greene, Felix. *Vietnam! Vietnam!* Palo Alto: Fulton Publishing, 1966.

Halberstam, David. *The Best and the Brightest*. New York, Random House, 1969

Harvey, Frank. *Air War Vietnam*. New York: Bantam Book, 1967.

Herring, George C. *America's Longest War*. McGraw Hill, 1986.

Johnson, Lyndon Baines. *Quotations from Chairman LBJ*. New York, 1968.

Jury, Mark. *The Vietnam Photo Book*. New York: Grossman, 1971

Karnow, Stanley. *Vietnam: A History*. New York, Viking, 1972.

Kerry, John. *The New Soldier*. New York: Macmillian Company, 1971.

Kimball, Jeffrey P. *To Reason Why*. New York: McGraw-Hill, 1990.

Krepinevich, Andrew F., Jr. *The Army and Vietnam.* John Hopkins University Press 1986.
MacPherson, Myra. *Long Time Passing.* Garden City: Doubleday, 1984
Mangold, Tom & Penycate, John. *The Tunnels of Cu Chi.* New York: Random House 1985.
Mao Tse-tung. *Quotations from Chairman Mao Tse-tung.* Peking, 1972.
Moore, Harold & Galloway, Joseph L. *We Were Soldiers Once....* New York: Random House, 1992.
Nguyen Cao, Ky. *How We Lost the Vietnam War.* New York Scarborough books 1978
Nixon, Richard. *No More Vietnams.* New York Arbor House, 1985.
Oberdorfer, Don. *TET!* Garden City: Doubleday, 1971.
Olsen, James. *Where the Domino Fell.* New York: St. Martins Press, 1991.
Olson, James. *Dictionary of the Vietnam War.* New York: Greenwood Press, 1988.
Palmer, Dave Richard. *Summons of the Trumpet.* San Rafeal: Presido Press, 1978.
Powers, Thomas. *Vietnam: The War at Home.* Boston: G. K. Hall & Co., 1984.
Prados, John & Stubbe, Ray W. *Valley of Decision: The Siege of Khe Sanh.* Boston, MA: Houghton Mifflin Co., 1991.
Pratt, John Clark. *Vietnam Voices.* New York, Penguin Books, 1984.
Sheehan, Neil. *A Bright Shining Lie.* New York: Random House, 1988.
Starry, Donn A. *Armoured Combat in Vietnam.* United Kingdom: Blandford Press, 1981.
Terry, Wallace. *Bloods.* New York: Random House, 1984
Tilford, Earl H. *Crosswinds: The Air Force's Setup In Vietnam.* College Station: Texas A & M Press, 1993.
Uhlig, Frank. *Vietnam the Naval Story.* Annapolis, Maryland: Naval Institute Press, 1987.
Walt, Lewis W. *Strange War, Strange Strategy.* New York: Funk & Wagnalls, 1970.
Watt, Allan. *Vietnam: An Australian Analysis.* Melbourne F. W. Cheshire 1968
We Remember. 2d Battalion, 1st Marines, Virginia, 1993.
West, F. J., Jr. *The Village.* Harper & Row, New York., 1972.
Westheider, James E. *Fighting on Two Fronts.* New York: University Press, 1997.
Westmoreland, William C. *A Soldier Reports.* Garden City: Doubleday & Co., 1976.

Government Reports and Documents

Bundy, William P. *The Path to Viet-Nam: A Lesson in Involvement.* Speech transcript, September 1967.
Committee on Foreign Relations. *U.S. Senate, Background Information Relating to Southeast Asia and Vietnam,* 3d rev. ed. (Washington, US GPO 1967).
Joint Resolution of Congress. H. J. RES 1145, 7 August 1964, Department of State Bulletin, 24 August 1964.
Presidential documents, John F. Kennedy.
Presidential documents, Lyndon B. Johnson.
Presidential documents, Richard M. Nixon.
Scranton Commission Report on Campus Unrest, 27 September 1970.
U.S. Government and the Vietnam War, 98th Congress, 2d Session, 1984.

Periodicals and Pamphlets

Baltimore Sun, newspaper.
Far East Spotlight, periodical, 1952.
Indochina Bulletin, periodical.
Leatherneck magazine, periodical.
Liberation, periodical.
Life magazine, periodical.
Marine Corps Gazette, periodical.
Military Times, The American Century, 1999.
New York Times, periodical.
Old Reliable, 9th Infantry Division newspaper.
Pacific Stars and Stripes, newspaper.
Parameters, Autumn 1995, periodical.
San Francisco Chronicle, periodical.
The Spokesman, Winter 1972/3, periodical.
Time magazine, periodical.
Tropic Lightning News, periodical.
Vietnam Courier, periodical.
Vietnam Generation, periodical.
Washington Post, periodical.
Z magazine, September 1992, periodical.

Interviews, Miscellaneous

ABC News.
Associated Press.
Hair (Broadway musical), 1968.
Ford, Harold P., *CIA and the Vietnam Policymakers.* CIA, Center for the Study of Intelligence, 1998.
Graffiti written on the wall of a three-holer in Cu Chi, 1970.
Joel, Billy, "The Nylon Curtain," CBS, 1981.
Lefever, Ernest W., *Uses of the Past Vietnam as a Metaphor.* December 1997.
McDowell, Daniel, tour notes, 1 March 1971.
The Tonight Show, hosted by Jay Leno, aird on NBC, January 2000.
Wilson, Gene, interview, December 1976.

Internet

http: //abcnews.go.com/century/timecapsule/war_peace/vietnam_war/TET_frame.html
http: //chss.montclair.edu.-Speech Transcript, as collected by Congress, 1972.
http: //more.abcnews.go.com/sections/us/jfk_vietnam1222/index.html-22 December 1997.
http: //pacific.discover.net/~dansyr/quotes5.html
http: //vassun.vassar.edu/~robrigha/— copy of speech document
http: //www.ahlan.com/qq.htm
http: //www.ausvets.powerup.com.au/vietnam/vietnam.htm
http: //www.cyber-nation.com/victory/quotations
http: //www.dickshovel. com/ind.html#Note61
http: //www.emerson.edu/acadepts/cs/comm/allison.html Krause family interview
http: //www.salsa.net/peace/quotes.html
http: //www.texaseagle.org/quotes/quotes.htm
http: //www.washingtonpost.com/wp-srv/national/longterm/vietnam/chronology.htm

Index

References are to entry numbers